COMPLETE

Technology in Action

7th Edition

Alan Evans • Kendall Martin
Mary Anne Poatsy

Prentice Hall

Boston Columbus Indianapolis New York San Francisco Upper Saddle River
Amsterdam Cape Town Dubai London Madrid Milan Munich Paris Montréal Toronto
Delhi Mexico City São Paulo Sydney Hong Kong Seoul Singapore Taipei Tokyo

Editor in Chief: Michael Payne
Associate VP/Executive Acquisitions Editor, Print: Stephanie Wall
Managing Editor, Editorial: Eileen Bien Calabro
Editorial Project Manager: Laura Burgess
Development Editors: Jennifer Lynn, Linda Harrison
Editorial Assistant: Nicole Sam
Director of Marketing: Kate Valentine
Marketing Manager: Tori Olson Alves
Marketing Coordinator: Susan Osterlitz
Marketing Assistant: Darshika Vyas
Senior Managing Editor: Cynthia Zonneveld
Associate Managing Editor: Camille Trentacoste
Production Project Manager: Mike Lackey
Operations Director: Alexis Heydt
Senior Operations Specialist: Natacha Moore
Senior Art Director: Jonathan Boylan
Text and Cover Designer: Jonathan Boylan
Cover Photo: David Wall\Alamy Images
Manager, Visual Research: Beth Brenzel

Photo Researcher: David Tietz
Manager, Rights and Permissions: Zina Arabia
Image Permission Coordinator: Richard Rodrigues
Manager, Cover Visual Research & Permissions: Karen Sanatar
Rights and Permissions Manager: Shannon Barbe
Text Permission Researcher: Michele Pridmore
AVP/Director of Online Programs, Media: Richard Keaveny
AVP/Director of Product Development, Media: Lisa Strite
Product Development Manager, Media: Cathi Profitko
Media Project Manager, Editorial: Alana Coles
Media Project Manager, Production: John Cassar
Full-Service Project Management: MPS Content Services
Composition: MPS Limited, A Macmillan Company
Printer/Binder: Quebecor World Color/Versailles
Cover Printer: Lehigh-Phoenix Color/Hagerstown
Text Font: 10/12 Palatino

Credits and acknowledgments borrowed from other sources and reproduced, with permission, in this textbook appear on appropriate page within text (or on pages 679–684).

Microsoft® and Windows® are registered trademarks of the Microsoft Corporation in the U.S.A. and other countries. Screen shots and icons reprinted with permission from the Microsoft Corporation. This book is not sponsored or endorsed by or affiliated with the Microsoft Corporation.

Many of the designations by manufacturers and seller to distinguish their products are claimed as trademarks. Where those designations appear in this book, and the publisher was aware of a trademark claim, the designations have been printed in initial caps or all caps.

CIP Data on File

Prentice Hall
is an imprint of

www.pearsonhighered.com

10 9 8 7 6 5 4 3 2 1

ISBN 10: 0-13-509669-3
ISBN 13: 978-0-13-509669-7

Contents at a Glance

seventh **7** EDITION

Contents

Chapter 1

TECHNOLOGY IN FOCUS

Chapter 2

Chapter 3

Using the Internet:
Making the Most of the Web's Resources 94

seventh
EDITION
7

Chapter 4

Application Software: Programs That Let You Work and Play

Chapter 5

Using System Software: The Operating System, Utility Programs, and File Management

Chapter 7

Networking Connecting
Computing Devices

TECHNOLOGY IN FOCUS

Under the Hood

Chapter 8

Chapter 9

TECHNOLOGY IN FOCUS

Chapter 10

Chapter 11

Behind the Scenes: Databases and Information Systems

Chapter 12

Behind the Scenes: Networking and Security in the Business World

Chapter 13

Behind the Scenes: The Internet: How It Works

Dedication

For my wife Patricia, whose patience, understanding, and support continue to

make this work possible … especially when I stay up past midnight writing!

And to my parents, Jackie and Dean, who taught me the best way to achieve

your goals is to constantly strive to improve yourself through education.

Alan Evans

For all the teachers, mentors, and gurus who have popped

in and out of my life.

Kendall Martin

For my husband Ted, who unselfishly continues to take on more than his fair

share to support me throughout this process; and for my children, Laura,

Carolyn, and Teddy, whose encouragement and love have been inspiring.

Mary Anne Poatsy

What's New
Technology in Action, Seventh Edition

Thank you for your continued use of *Technology in Action*. To ease your transition, here are highlights of changes for the 7th edition.

The following list includes comprehensive changes for the 7th edition:

- Microsoft Windows 7 Coverage
  All chapters and Student CD content have been updated to cover the Windows 7 operating system.

- New "How cool is this?" Opener Feature
  Each chapter now begins with a section that discusses new and interesting developments in technology that relate directly to the real world.

- New and Updated "Active Helpdesks"
  All Active Helpdesks have been updated to cover current software and technologies. Several Active Helpdesks are new to this edition: "Evaluating Computer System Components," "Doing Business Online," "Keeping Your Data on Hand," and "Using Portable Media Players."

The following list includes changes specific to each chapter for the 7th edition:

Chapter 1: Why Computers Matter to You: Becoming Computer Literate
- Updates to career statistics and bridging the digital divide
- New section on facial expression training software

Chapter 2: Looking at Computers: Understanding the Parts
- New coverage of portable mice and screen sizes
- Updates to printer, processor, and ports coverage
- New section on Organic Light Emitting Diode (OLED) displays

Chapter 3: Using the Internet: Making the Most of the Web's Resources
- New coverage of Web 2.0 technologies, Twitter, Web gaming, PayPal, Google Chrome, and the semantic Web
- Updates to information on e-mail privacy, instant messaging, VoIP, wikis, and social bookmarking and tags
- New Trends in IT: Computers in Society—Online Storage and Secure Backup for Your Valuable Digital Assets

Chapter 4: Application Software: Programs That Let You Work and Play
- New sections on Google applications, brain training software, mapping software, and Microsoft Office for mobile apps
- New coverage of on-demand software deployment and software license agreements
- New information on the MP4 video format

Chapter 5: Using System Software: The Operating System, Utility Programs, and File Management
- All system software content updated
- Updates to coverage of RAM
- Updates to the Disk Cleanup, Error-checking, and System Restore utilities
- New content on logging in during the boot process

Chapter 6: Understanding and Assessing Hardware: Evaluating Your System
- Updates to all hardware statistics, including processors
- New Bits and Bytes: HDTV on Your Notebook
- New Ethics in IT: Optical Technology: A Free Lunch—Or at Least a Free Copy
- New coverage of HDMI and eSata ports

Chapter 7: Networking: Connecting Computing Devices
- New information on home area networks, home network servers, and digital media receivers
- New sections on how to verify network adapters and testing Internet connection speeds
- New Bits and Bytes: Wireless Hot Spots—How to Find One on the Go?
- New Ethics in IT feature: Sharing Your Internet Connection with Your Neighbors: Legal? Ethical? Safe?"

Chapter 8: Digital Lifestyle: Managing Digital Data and Devices
- New coverage of digital telephony, input/output devices for smartphones, connection speeds, data transfer, and privacy
- New information on digital television and connectivity
- New Ethics in IT: Digital Photo Rights
- New Trends in IT: Managing Your Copyrights

Chapter 9: Digital Lifestyle: Protecting Digital Data and Devices
- New section on testing password strength
- New coverage of hoaxes and urban legends
- New Ethics in IT feature: Big Brother Is Watching… But Should He Be Allowed to Do So?

Chapter 10: Behind the Scenes: Building Applications
- New coverage of PHP and AJAX
- New samples of code for programming languages

Chapter 11: Behind the Scenes: Databases and Information Systems
- New section on data staging
- Updates to Microsoft Access coverage
- New Trends in IT: Emerging Technologies—Can Your Business Partner Deliver the Goods? Enhanced Databases Can Help You Decide!

Chapter 12: Behind the Scenes: Networking and Security in the Business World
- New coverage of Vi-Fi and the 802.11n standard
- New coverage of using PC adapters to access wireless networks
- New information on data theft, data destruction, and protecting networks

Chapter 13: Behind the Scenes: The Internet: How It Works
- New section on cloud computing
- New coverage of AJAX
- Updates to emerging technologies

About the Authors

Alan Evans, MS, CPA

aevans@mc3.edu

Alan is currently a faculty member at Manor College and Montgomery County Community College teaching a variety of computer science and business courses. He holds a B.S. in accounting from Rider University and an M.S. in information systems from Drexel University, and he is a certified public accountant. After a successful career in business, Alan finally realized his true calling was education. He has been teaching at the college level since 2000. Alan enjoys giving presentations at technical conferences and meets regularly with computer science faculty and administrators from other colleges to discuss curriculum development and new methods of engaging students.

Kendall Martin, PhD

kmartin@mc3.edu

Kendall has been teaching since 1988 at a number of institutions, including Villanova University, DeSales University, Arcadia University, Ursinus College, County College of Morris, and Montgomery County Community College, at both the undergraduate and graduate level.

Kendall's education includes a B.S. in electrical engineering from the University of Rochester and an M.S. and a Ph.D. in engineering from the University of Pennsylvania. She has industrial experience in research and development environments (AT&T Bell Laboratories) as well as experience with several start-up technology firms.

At Ursinus College, Kendall developed a successful faculty training program for distance education instructors. She makes conference presentations throughout the year.

Mary Anne Poatsy, MBA, CFP

mpoatsy@mc3.edu

Mary Anne is a senior faculty member at Montgomery County Community College, teaching various computer application and concepts courses in face-to-face and online environments. She enjoys speaking at various professional conferences about innovative classroom strategies. She holds a B.A. in psychology and education from Mount Holyoke College and an MBA in finance from Northwestern University's Kellogg Graduate School of Management.

Mary Anne has more than 12 years of educational experience, ranging from elementary and secondary education to Montgomery County Community College, Muhlenberg College, and Bucks County Community College, as well as training in the professional environment. Before teaching, she was a vice president at Shearson Lehman Hutton in the Municipal Bond Investment Banking Department.

Acknowledgments

First, we would like to thank our students. We constantly learn from them while teaching, and they are a continual source of inspiration and new ideas.

We could not have written this book without the loving support of our families. Our spouses and children made sacrifices (mostly in time not spent with us) to permit us to make this dream into a reality.

Although working with the entire team at Prentice Hall has been a truly enjoyable experience, a few individuals deserve special mention. The constant support and encouragement we receive from Stephanie Wall, Associate Vice President/Executive Editor, continually makes this book grow and change. Our heartfelt thanks go to Jennifer Lynn and Linda Harrison, our developmental editors. Jennifer and Linda have had a positive impact on the book, and we have benefited greatly from their creative ideas and efficient time management skills. In addition, Laura Burgess, our project manager, has done a fantastic job of coordinating all details of the project and always keeping the entire project on track. As Media Development Manager, Alana Coles works tirelessly to ensure that the media accompanying the text is produced professionally and is delivered in a timely fashion. Despite the inevitable problems that crop up when producing multimedia, she handles all challenges with a smile. And we can't forget Natalie Anderson, former VP/Editorial Director. Natalie has a wonderful sense of humor, which helps smooth over the inevitable bumps in the road encountered on a project of this magnitude. We also would like to extend our appreciation to Mike Lackey, our Production Project Manager, who works tirelessly to ensure that our book is published on time and looks fabulous. The timelines are always short, the art is complex, and there are many people with whom he has to coordinate tasks.

There are many people whom we do not meet in person at Prentice Hall and elsewhere who make significant contributions by designing the book, illustrating, composing the pages, producing multimedia, and securing permissions. We thank them all. We would also like to thank the supplement authors for this edition: Linda Arnold, Sharon Behrens, Lynn Bowen, Julie Boyles, Diane Coyle, Penny Cypert, Dennis Faix, Trina Maurer, Tony Nowakowski, LaDonna Rankin, Bill Tucker, Bonita Volker, Sandy Weber, and Dawn Wood.

And finally, we would like to thank the reviewers and the many others who contribute their time, ideas, and talents to this project. We appreciate their time and energy, as their comments help us turn out a better product each edition.

Reviewers

Prentice Hall and the authors would like to thank the following people for their help and time in making this book what it is. We couldn't publish this book without their contributions.

Nazih Abdallah	University of Central Florida
Allen Alexander	Delaware Technical & Community College
Joan Alexander	Valencia Community College—West
Beverly Amer	Northern Arizona University
Wilma Andrews	Virginia Commonwealth University
Gregg W. Asher, Ph.D.	Minnesota State University—Mankato
LaDonna Bachand	Santa Rosa Junior College
Wendy Barron	Lehigh Carbon Community College
LeeAnn Bates	
Elise J. Bell, MA, Educ.	City College of San Francisco
Linda Belton	Springfield Technical Community College
David Billings	Guilford Technical Community College
Kim Binstead, Ph.D	University of Hawaii at Manoa
Susan Birtwell	Kwantlen University College
Henry Bojack	Farmingdale State University of New York
Julie Boyles	
Brenda K. Britt	Fayetteville Technical Community College
Cathy J. Brotherton	Riverside Community College
Gerald U. Brown Jr.	Tarrant County College
Jeff Burton	Daytona Beach Community College
Kristen Callahan	Mercer County Community College
Judy Cameron	Spokane Community College
Jill Canine	Ivy Tech Community College of Indiana
Heather Cannon	Blinn College
Judy Cestaro	California State University—San Bernardino
Deborah Chapman	University of Southern Alabama
Gerianne Chapman	Johnson & Wales University
John P. Cicero, Ph.D	Shasta College—Redding, CA
Dan Combellick	Scottsdale Community College
Joann Cook	College of DuPage
Mark Connell	SUNY Cortland
Gail Cope	Sinclair Community College
Françoise Corey	California State University, Long Beach
John Coverdale	Riverside Community College
Thad Crews	Western Kentucky University
Doug Cross	Clackamas Community College
Geoffrey Crosslin	Kalamazoo Valley Community College
Becky Cunningham	Arkansas Tech University
John Cusaac	Fullerton College
James Bac Dang	Tarrant County College
Marvin Daugherty	Ivy Tech
Ronald G. Deardorff	Shasta Community College
Joseph DeLibero	Arizona State University
K. Kay Delk	Seminole Community College
Charles DeSassure	Tarrant County College
Gretchen V. Douglas	State University of New York at Cortland
Susan N. Dozier	Tidewater Community College
Annette Duvall	Albuquerque Technical Vocational Institute

Laurie Eakins	East Carolina University
Roland Eichelberger	Baylor University
James Fabrey	West Chester University
Catherine L. Ferguson	University of Oklahoma
Marj Feroe	Delaware County Community College
Judy Firmin	Tarrant County College
Beverly Fite	Amarillo College
Howard Flomberg	The Metropolitan State College of Denver
Richard A. Flores	Citrus College
Alicen Flosi	Lamar University
Linda Foster-Turpen	Central New Mexico Community College
Susan Fry	Boise State University
Yvonne Galusha	University of Iowa
Barbara A. Garrell	Delaware County Community College
Ernest Gines	Tarrant County College
Tim Gottleber	North Lake College
Sherry Green	Purdue University—Calumet Campus
Debra Gross	The Ohio State University
Vivian Haddad	Nova Southeastern University
Don A. Halcomb	Bluegrass Community and Technical College
Lewis Hall	Riverside City College
Rachelle Hall	Glendale Community College
Eric Hamilton	Community College of Denver
Bill Hammerschlag	Brookhaven College
Terry Hanks	San Jacinto College—South Campus
Susan Hanson	Albuquerque Technical Vocational Institute
Marie Hartlein	Montgomery County Community College
Ronda D. Hayes	North Lake College
Susan E. Hoggard	Tulsa Community College
Jim Hendricks	Pierce College
Catherine Hines	Albuquerque Technical Vocational Institute
Norm Hollingsworth	Georgia Perimeter College
Bill Holmes	Chandler-Gilbert Community College
Mary Carole Hollingsworth	Georgia Perimeter College
Sherry Hopkins	Anne Arundel Community College
Christie Jahn Hovey	Lincoln Land Community College
Jeffrey Howard	Finger Lakes Community College
John L. Howard	East Carolina University
Judy Irvine	Seneca College
Glen Johansson	Spokane Community College
Kay Johnson	Community College of Rhode Island
Stephanie Jones	South Plains College
Steve St. John	Tulsa Community College
Kathy Johnson	DeVry Chicago
Richard B. Kalman	Atlantic Cape Community College
Dr. K. Kamel	TSU
Darrel Karbginsky	Chemkeketa Community College
Linda Kavanaugh	Robert Morris University
Robert R. Kendi	Lehigh University
Annette Kerwin	College of DuPage
David Kight	Brewton-Parker College
Kai S. Koong	University of Texas Pan American
Frank Kuehn	Pikes Peak Community College

Jackie Lamoureux	Albuquerque Technical Vocational Institute
David K. Lange	Grand Valley State University
Joanne Lazirko	University of Wisconsin—Milwaukee
Michael R. Lehrfeld	Brevard Community College
Yvonne Leonard	Coastal Carolina University
Judith Limkilde	Seneca College—King Campus
Richard Linge	Arizona Western College
Christy Lopez	East Carolina University
Joelene Mack	Golden West College
Lisa Macon	Valencia Community College
Donna Madsen	Kirkwood Community College
Daniela Marghitu	Auburn University
Norma Marler	Catawba Valley Community College
Carol Prewitt Martin	Louisiana State University at Alexandria
Toni Marucco	Lincoln Land Community College
Evelynn McCain	Boise State University
Dana McCann	Central Michigan University
Lee McClain	West Washington University
Sandra M. McCormack	Monroe Community College
Sue McCrory	Missouri State University
Phil McCue	Lone Star College—Montgomery
Helen McFadyen	Mass Bay Community College—Framingham
Charles J. McNerney Ph.D.	Bergen Community College
Dr. Dori McPherson	Schoolcraft College
Laura Melella	Fullerton College
Josephine Mendoza	California State University, San Bernardino
Mike Michaelson	Palomar College
Gina Bowers Miller	Harrisburg Area Community College
Johnette Moody	Arkansas Tech University
Dona Mularkey	Southern Methodist University
Rebecca A. Mundy	University of Southern California
Linda Mushet	Golden West College
Lisa Nademlynsky	Johnson & Wales University
Maguerite Nedreberg	Youngstown State University
Brad Nicolajsen	Carteret Community College
Omar Nooraldeen	Cape Fear Community College
Judy Ogden	Johnson County Community College
Connie O'Neill	Sinclair Community College
Claudia Orr	Northern Michigan University
James R. Orr	East Carolina University
Sung Park	Pasadena City College
Brenda Parker	Middle Tennessee State University
Patricia Partyka	Schoolcraft College
Woody Pekoske	North Carolina State University
Judy Perhamus Perry	Riverside Community College—Norco Campus
Carolyn Poe	Lone Star College—Montgomery
Mike Puopolo	Bunker Hill Community College
Paul Quan	Albuquerque Technical Vocational Institute
Ram Raghuraman	Joliet Junior College
Patricia Rahmlow	Montgomery County Community College
Shirley Reid	Indian Hills Community College
Ruth Robbins	University of Houston—Downtown
Teresa Roberts	Wilson Community College

Catherine J. Rogers — Laramie County Community College
Russell Sabadosa — Manchester Community College
Peg Saragina — Santa Rosa Junior College
Judith Scheeren — Westmoreland County Community College
Samuel Scott — Pierce College
Vicky Seehusen — The Metropolitan State College of Denver
Ralph Shafer — Truckee Meadows Community College—Reno
Mirella Shannon — Columbia College
Laurie Evin Shteir — Temple University
Sheila Smart Sicilia — Onondaga Community College
Greg A. Simpson — Phoenix College—Phoenix, AZ
Robert G. Sindt — Johnson County Community College
Gary R. Smith — Paradise Valley Community College
Steven Singer — Kapi'olani Community College
Robert Smolenski — Delaware County Community College
Diane Stark — Phoenix College
James Stark — Milwaukee Area Technical College
Suzanne Mello Stark — Community College of Rhode Island
Kriss Stauber — El Camino College
Neal Stenlund — Northern Virginia Community College
Linda Stoudemayer — Lamar Institute of Technology
Catherine Stoughton — Laramie County Community College
Lynne Stuhr — Trident Technical College
Song Su — East Los Angeles College
John Taylor — Hillsborough Community College—Brandon Campus
Dennie Templeton — Radford University
Joyce Thompson — Lehigh Carbon Community College
Lou Thompson — University of Texas at Dallas
Janine Tiffany — Reading Area Community College
Janet Towle — New Hampshire Community Technical College—Nashua
Goran Trajkovski — Towson University
Deborah Tyler — Tarrant County College
Pamella M. Uhlenkamp — Iowa Central Community College—Fort Dodge, Iowa
Erhan Uskup — Houston Community College—Northwest
Emily Vandalovsky — Bergen Community College
Bill VanderClock — Bentley Business University
Glenna Vanderhoof — Missouri State University
Michelle Vlaich-Lee — Greenville Technical College
Karen Weil-Yates — Hagerstown Community College
Catherine Werst — Cuesta College
Janice L. Williams — Seward County Community College
Melanie Williamson — Bluegrass Community and Technical College
Steven H. White — Anne Arundel Community College
Barbara Yancy — Community College of Baltimore County—Essex Camp
Thomas Yip — Passaic County Community College
Mary Zajac — Montgomery County Community College
Mary T. Zegarski — Northampton Community College
Mary Ann Zlotow — College of DuPage

Letter from the Authors

Why We Wrote This Book

Our combined 40 years of teaching computer concepts have coincided with sweeping innovations in computing technology that have affected every facet of society. From iPhones to Web 2.0, computers are more than ever a fixture of our daily lives—and the lives of our students. But although today's students have a greater comfort level with their digital environment than previous generations, their knowledge of the machines they use every day is still limited.

We wrote *Technology in Action* to focus on what matters most to today's student. Instead of a history lesson on the microchip, we focus on what tasks students can accomplish with their PCs and what skills they can apply immediately in the workplace, the classroom, and at home. We strive to be as current as the publishing timelines will allow us, constantly looking for the next technology trend or gadget. The result is a book that sparks student interest by focusing on the material they want to learn (such as how to set up a home network) while teaching the material they need to learn (such as how networks work). The sequence of topics is carefully set up to mirror the typical student learning experience.

As they read through this text, your students will progress through stages of increasing difficulty:

1. Examining why it's important to be computer fluent and how computers impact our society

2. Examining the basic components of the computer

3. Connecting to the Internet

4. Exploring software

5. Learning the operating system and personalizing the computer

6. Evaluating and upgrading the PC

7. Exploring home networking and keeping the computer safe from hackers

8. Going mobile with PDA/smartphones, Tablet PCs, and laptops

9. Going behind the scenes, looking at technology in more detail

We have written the book in a "spiraling" manner, intentionally introducing on a basic level in the earlier chapters those concepts that students have trouble with and then later expanding on those concepts in more detail when students have become more comfortable with them. Thus, the focus of the early chapters is on practical uses for the computer, with real-world examples to help the students place computing in a familiar context. For example, we introduce basic hardware components in Chapter 2, and then we go into increasingly greater detail on some hardware components in Chapters 6, 8, and 9.

The Behind the Scenes chapters venture deeper into the realm of computing through in-depth explanations of how elements of the system unit (CPU, motherboard, RAM) work. They are specifically designed to keep more experienced students engaged and to challenge them with interesting research assignments.

We have also developed a comprehensive multimedia program to reinforce the material taught in the text and to support both classroom lectures and distance learning. The Helpdesk training content, created specifically for *Technology in Action*, enables students to take on the role of a helpdesk operator and work through common questions asked by computer users. Exciting Sound Byte multimedia—fully integrated with the text—accelerates student mastery of complex topics.

Now that the computer has become a ubiquitous tool in our lives, a new approach to computer concepts is warranted. This book is designed to reach the students of the twenty-first century and prepare them for the challenges they will face in the new global economy.

Visual Walk-Through

TOPIC SEQUENCE

Concepts are covered in a spiraling manner between chapters to mirror the typical student learning experience.

Hardware First Introduced
Chapter 2 is the first time students read about introductory hardware. It is covered at the beginning level because this is their experience level at this point of the book.

Hardware Taught in More Depth in Additional Chapters
In later chapters, students are taught hardware in greater depth because they are more experienced and comfortable working with their computer.

NEW

How Cool is This?
Highlights the latest and greatest websites, gadgets, and multimedia.

Multimedia Cues
Visual integration of multimedia.

Student Textbook

seventh EDITION **7**

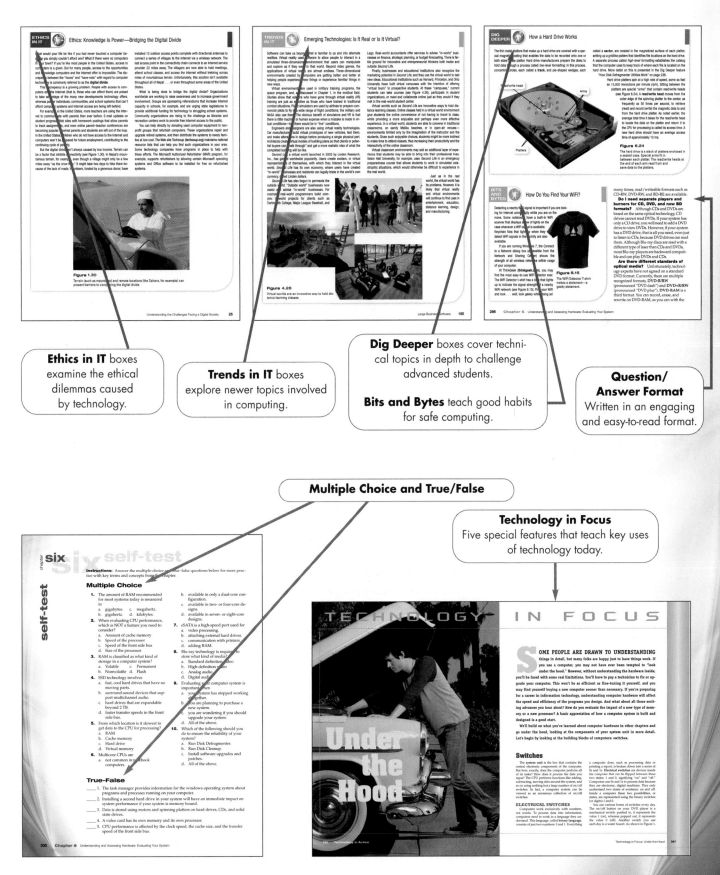

Ethics in IT boxes examine the ethical dilemmas caused by technology.

Trends in IT boxes explore newer topics involved in computing.

Dig Deeper boxes cover technical topics in depth to challenge advanced students.

Bits and Bytes teach good habits for safe computing.

Question/Answer Format Written in an engaging and easy-to-read format.

Multiple Choice and True/False

Technology in Focus Five special features that teach key uses of technology today.

The Multimedia

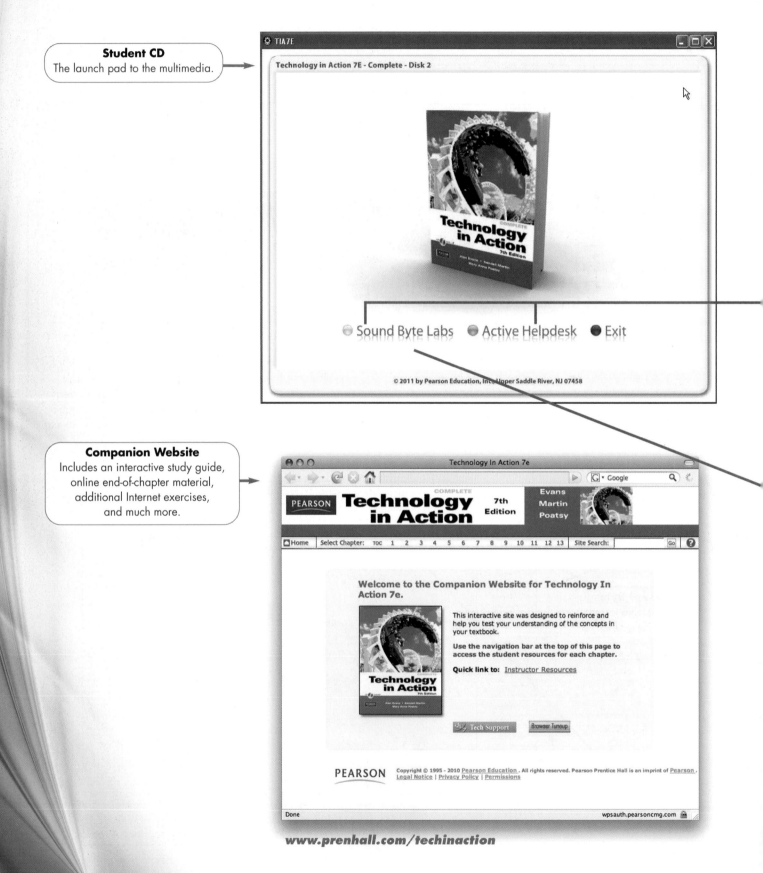

Student CD
The launch pad to the multimedia.

Companion Website
Includes an interactive study guide,
online end-of-chapter material,
additional Internet exercises,
and much more.

www.prenhall.com/techinaction

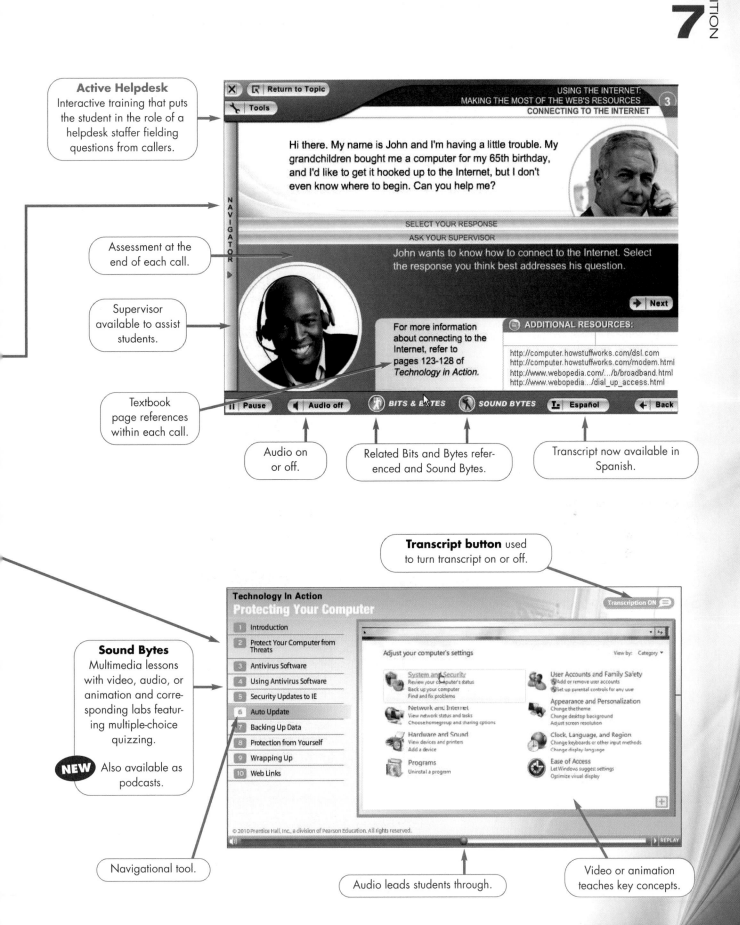

Active Helpdesk
Interactive training that puts the student in the role of a helpdesk staffer fielding questions from callers.

Assessment at the end of each call.

Supervisor available to assist students.

Textbook page references within each call.

Audio on or off.

Related Bits and Bytes referenced and Sound Bytes.

Transcript now available in Spanish.

Transcript button used to turn transcript on or off.

Sound Bytes
Multimedia lessons with video, audio, or animation and corresponding labs featuring multiple-choice quizzing.

NEW Also available as podcasts.

Navigational tool.

Audio leads students through.

Video or animation teaches key concepts.

seventh
EDITION **7**

Annotated Instructor Edition

Provided with each chapter are two divider pages like the ones outlined below.

FRONT OF CHAPTER TAB

On the front side of each chapter tab, you will find the following categories:

IN THE CLASSROOM: Activities you can use in a classroom or in online classes, including:

- PowerPoint Presentations
- Discussion Exercises
- Active Helpdesk Calls
- Sound Bytes

HOMEWORK: Activities used out of class for assessment or preparation for the next chapter, including:

- Web Resource Projects
- Active Helpdesk Calls
- Sound Byte Labs
- Online Study Guides

ASSESSMENT:

- Blackboard
- WebCT
- TestGen
- myitlab

The back side of each chapter tab includes the relevant Sound Bytes for that chapter.

FRONT OF ETHICS TAB

On the front of the Ethics tab, you will find the following:

OPPOSING VIEWPOINTS TABLE: Outlines debatable ethics topics that you can use in the classroom.

KEYWORDS: Provides you with additional words to search the Internet for more information related to the ethics topic.

For a list of the resources available for every chapter and where they are located, see the back of this tab.

Instructor Resource CD

GREATLY ENHANCED

Instructor Resource CD
- **NEW! Interactive Course Builder** to help you integrate all the instructor resources.
- **NEW! Recommended chapter lectures** written by the authors that you can customize.
- All resources included with the *Technology in Action* Instructional System.

Contact your local Prentice Hall sales rep to learn more about the
Technology in Action instructional system.

Technology in Action

7th Edition

one

why computers matter to you:

becoming computer literate

objectives

After reading this chapter, you should be able to answer the following questions:

1. What does it mean to be "computer literate"? *(p. 4)*

2. How does being computer literate make you a savvy computer user and consumer? *(pp. 4–6)*

3. How can becoming computer literate help you in a career? *(pp. 6–20)*

4. How can becoming computer literate help you understand and take advantage of newly emerging careers? *(pp. 20–22)*

5. How does becoming computer literate help you deal with the challenges associated with technology? *(p. 23)*

resources

Active Helpdesk

This chapter has no Active Helpdesks.

Sound Bytes

- Questions to Ask Before You Buy a Computer **(p. 6)**
- The History of the Personal Computer **(p. 22)**

Companion Website

The Companion Website includes a variety of additional materials to help you review and learn more about the topics in this chapter. Go to: ***pearsonhighered.com/techinaction***

how cool is *this?*

Whether you want a handmade piece of jewelry, a vintage handbag, or a **hand-blown glass** vase, Etsy (**etsy.com**) is the site for you. This person-to-person e-commerce site is **beautifully** designed and allows low-tech crafty people to take full advantage of technology and connect with customers around the globe.

If you are thinking of opening a storefront for your own handmade goods, Etsy provides an extremely easy entry into e-commerce. It costs just 20 cents to list an item, and **Etsy** provides workshops, marketing support, and forums for storeowners to exchange ideas.

In the full spirit of the modern Web, Etsy enthusiasts have created a variety of ways to connect and collaborate. These include blogs about Etsy (**www.etsy.com/storque**) and a **wiki** with info for Etsy buyers and sellers (**etsywiki.com**). You'll also find a MySpace page for Etsy, mentions of Etsy on **Flickr** photography sites, and an interview with Etsy's founder, Rob Kalin, on YouTube.

Now the **craftiest** among us can easily use technology to expand our world.

Why Should You Become Computer Literate?

It's safe to say that computers are nearly everywhere in our society. You find them in schools, cars, airports, shopping centers, toys, medical devices, and homes, and in many people's pockets. You interact with computers almost every day, sometimes without even knowing it. Whenever you buy something with a credit card, you interact with a computer. And, of course, most of us can't imagine our lives without e-mail. Even if you don't yet have a computer and don't feel comfortable using one, you still feel the impact of technology: Countless ads for computers, cell phones, digital cameras, and an assortment of Web sites surround us each day. We're constantly reminded of the ways in which computers, the Internet, and technology are integral parts of our lives.

So, just by being a member of our society, you already know quite a bit about computers. But why is it important to learn more about computers, becoming what is called *computer literate?* Being **computer literate** means being familiar enough with computers that you understand their capabilities and limitations (see Figure 1.1), and you know how to use them. Being computer literate means more than just knowing about the parts of your computer. The following are some other benefits:

- As a computer literate individual, you can use your computer more

wisely and be a more knowledgeable consumer.
- Computer literate employees are sought after in almost every vocation.
- Becoming computer literate will help you better understand and take advantage of future technologies.

In addition, understanding computers and their ethical, legal, and societal implications will make you a more active and aware participant in society.

Anyone can become computer literate—no matter what your degree of technical expertise. Being computer literate doesn't mean you need to know enough to program a computer or build one yourself. With a car for example, you should know enough about it to take care of it and to use it effectively, but that doesn't mean you have to know how to build one. You should try to achieve the same familiarity with computers.

Becoming a Savvy Computer User and Consumer

One of the benefits of becoming computer literate is being a savvy computer user and consumer. What does this mean? The following are just a few examples of what it may mean to you:

- **Avoiding hackers and viruses.** Do you know what hackers and viruses are? Both can threaten a computer's security.

Figure 1.1

Do you know what all the words in a computer ad mean? Can you tell whether the ad includes all the information necessary to make a purchasing decision?

Processor:	Intel i7-965 Extreme, Factory O'Cd to 3.73 GHz
RAM:	12 GB Tri Channel Corsair DDR3 (1066 MHz)
Video:	ATI Radeon HD 4870 X2 with 2048 MB
Audio:	Creative Labs X-Fi Elite Pro; HDA 7.1 surround channel sound
Network:	Native Gigabit Ethernet
Optical Drive:	Blu-ray burner
Storage Drive:	1 TB Serial ATA hard drive with support for up to 3 additional drives with RAID options
Ports:	10 USB 2 DVI and 1 S-Video 2 IEEE 1394 1 S/PDIF out
Physics Accelerator:	Ageia PhysX Card
Cooling:	Two-stage liquid cooling system
Portable Storage:	Bluetooth wireless 19-in 1-media hub with VoIP stereo headset
Operating System:	Windows 7 Ultimate 64-bit

Being aware of how hackers and viruses operate and knowing the damage they can do to your computer can help you avoid falling prey to them.

- **Protecting your privacy.** You've probably heard of identity theft—you see and hear news stories all the time about people whose "identities" are stolen and whose credit ratings are ruined by "identity thieves." But do you know how to protect yourself from identity theft when you're online?

- **Understanding the real risks.** Part of being computer literate means being able to separate the real privacy and security risks from things you don't have to worry about. For example, do you know what a *cookie* is? Do you know whether it poses a privacy risk for you when you're on the Internet? What about a *firewall*? Do you know what one is? Do you really need one to protect your computer?

www.CartoonStock.com

"Wow! I've got one from someone I know!"

Figure 1.2

Understanding how to use e-mail effectively is just one example of what it means to be computer literate.

- **Using the Internet and the Web wisely.** Anyone who has ever searched the Web can attest that finding information and finding good information are two different things. People who are computer literate make the Internet a powerful tool and know how to find the information they want effectively. How familiar with the Web are you, and how effective are your searches?

- **Avoiding online annoyances.** If you have an e-mail account, chances are you've received electronic junk mail, or **spam** (see Figure 1.2). How can you avoid being overwhelmed by spam? What about *adware* and *spyware*—do you know what they are? Do you know what **software** (programs or instructions that tell the computer what to do) you should install on your computer to avoid online annoyances?

- **Being able to maintain, upgrade, and troubleshoot your computer.** Learning how to care for and maintain your computer and knowing how to diagnose and fix certain problems can save you a lot of time and hassle. Do you know how to upgrade your computer if you want more memory, for example? Do you know which software and computer settings can help you keep your computer in top shape?

- **Making good purchasing decisions.** Everywhere you go, you see ads like the one in Figure 1.1 for computers and other devices: notebooks (laptops), printers, monitors, cell phones, digital cameras, and GPS (global positioning system) devices. Do you know what all the words in the ads mean? What is *RAM*? What is a *CPU*? What are *MB*, *GB*, *GHz*, and *cache*? How fast do you need your computer to be, and how much memory should it have? Understanding computer buzzwords and keeping current with technology will help you better determine which computers and devices match your needs.

- **Knowing how to integrate the latest technology with your equipment.** Finally, becoming computer literate means knowing which technologies are on the horizon and how to integrate them into your home setup when possible (see Figure 1.3). Can you connect your notebook to a wireless network? What is *Bluetooth*, and does your computer "have" it? Can a device with a USB 2.0 connector be plugged into an old USB 1.0 port? (For that matter, what *is* a USB port?) How much memory should your cell phone have? Knowing the answers to these and other questions will help you make better purchasing decisions.

The benefits of being computer literate will help you in your career and in running your

Figure 1.3

Can you identify all of these devices? Do you know how to get them all to work well together?

National Research Council concludes that by the year 2030 computers will displace humans in 60 percent of the current occupations. It will be more critical than ever for employees to have advanced skills. For more information about computers and the workplace, see the Technology in Focus section, "Careers in IT."

Becoming truly computer literate—understanding the capabilities and limitations of computers and what you can do with them—will undoubtedly help you perform your job more effectively. It also will make you more desirable as an employee and more likely to earn more and advance your career. So, let's begin with a look at how computer systems are used in a wide range of careers. Whether you become an employee in one of these industries or a user of its services, you will have a great advantage if you understand computer systems.

personal life. You'll be able to save money, time, and endless frustration by having a strong background in the basics of how computers and computer systems operate.

Being Prepared for Your Career

Computer careers are on the rise. Regardless of which profession you pursue, if computers are not already in use in that career, they most likely will be soon. **Information technology (IT)** is the set of techniques used in information handling and automatic retrieval of information. Information technology includes computers, telecommunications, and software deployment. IT careers are on the rise, and the seven fastest growing occupations are computer related. The changes technology is forcing on the workplace demand new skill levels from employees. A study from the

Computers in Today's Careers

We all are used to seeing computers at the checkout counter in stores, at the check-in area at an airport, and so on, but there are many ways that computers are being used that you probably weren't aware of. Before we begin looking at a computer's parts and how it operates, let's take a look at a whole range of industries and examine how computers are a part of getting work done. Whether you plan on a career in one of these fields or will just be a user of their products and services, your life will be affected by the use of computers in areas including

- Business
- Arts
- Education
- Law
- Agriculture
- Sciences

Retail: Working in a Data Mine

Businesses accumulate a lot of data, but how do they manage to make sense of all of it? How do they separate the anomalies from the trends? They use a technique known as **data mining**, the process of searching huge amounts of data with the hope of finding a pattern. For example, large retailers often study the data gathered from register terminals to determine which products are selling on a given day and in a specific location. This helps managers figure out how much merchandise they need to order to replace stock that is sold. Managers also use mined data to determine that for a certain product to sell well, they must lower its price—especially if they cut the price at one store and see sales increase, for example. Data mining thus allows retailers to respond to consumer buying patterns.

Did you ever wonder how Amazon or Netflix can suggest items that fit your taste? Or how such Web sites automatically display lists of items people bought after they ordered the camera you just picked out? Data mining can keep track of the purchases customers are making, along with their geographic data, past buying history, and lists of items they examined but did not purchase. This can be translated into extremely specific marketing, immediate and customized to your shopping experience. This is the motivation behind all of the "discount cards" that grocery stores and drugstores offer. In exchange for tracking your personal buying habits, they offer you some kind of special pricing. How much is your private information worth?

Business: Data on the Go

Did you know that United Parcel Service (UPS) handles more than 3.9 billion packages and letters a year? Just how does the "brown" company ensure that all its customers' packages get from points A to B without ending up forever at point C? The company uses a sophisticated database and a highly efficient package tracking system that follows the packages as they move around the world.

For UPS, package tracking starts when the sender drops off a package and the company creates a "smart label" for the package (see Figure 1.4a). In addition to the standard postal bar code and a bar code showing UPS customer numbers, this smart label contains something called a *MaxiCode*. The MaxiCode is a specially designed, scannable sticker that resembles an inkblot and contains all the important information about the package (class of service, destination, etc.). When the package is handled in processing centers, UPS workers scan the Maxi-Code using portable handheld devices (see Figure 1.4b). These devices use **Bluetooth technology** (a type of wireless communication) to transmit the scanned data through radio waves to a terminal. This terminal then sends the data across a wireless network, where it is recorded in the UPS database.

To track package delivery, UPS carriers use delivery acquisition devices (see Figure 1.4c) that feature wireless networking capability, infrared scanners (to scan the smart labels and transmit the information back to the UPS database),

Figure 1.4

(a) Package tracking starts when the package is sent with the generation of a smart label, which includes the UPS MaxiCode. (b) Portable handheld devices allow UPS personnel to scan packages for accurate transfer of information. (c) Devices with built-in GPS systems are used to find directions to customers, capture customer signatures, and transfer information.

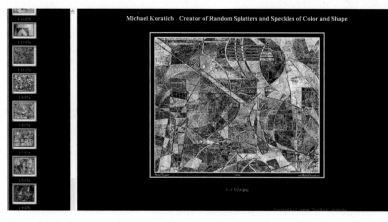

Figure 1.5

Artists like Michael Koratich display and sell their creations by using custom Web galleries such as this one (michaelkoratich.com).

and an electronic pad to capture customer signatures. By capturing all of this data and making it available on its Internet database, UPS enables its customers to track their packages. UPS is also able to make informed decisions about staffing and deploying equipment (trucks, airplanes, etc.) based on the volume and type of packages in the system at any given time.

Arts: Shall We Dance?

Some art students think that because they're studying art, there is no reason for them to study computers. However, unless you plan to be a "starving artist," you'll probably want to sell your work. To do so, you'll need to advertise to the public and contact art galleries to convince them to purchase or display your work. Wouldn't it be

Figure 1.6

A dancer is wired with light electronic sensors so that her movements can be digitized for computer analysis.

helpful if you knew how to create a Web site like the one shown in Figure 1.5?

Using computers in the arts and entertainment fields goes far beyond using the Internet. Dance and music programs like the ones at the Atlanta Ballet and the Julliard School of Music use computers to create new performances for audiences. As shown in Figure 1.6, a live dancer can be wired with sensors that are connected to a computer that captures the dancer's movements. Based on the data it collects, the computer generates a virtual dancer on a screen. The computer operator can easily manipulate this virtual dancer, as well as change the dancer's costume, with the click of a mouse. This allows artists to create new experiences for the audience.

Of course, not all artwork is created using traditional materials such as paint and canvas. Many artists today work exclusively with computers. Mastery of software programs such as Adobe Illustrator, Adobe Photoshop, and Adobe Flash is essential to creating digital art.

Other artists are pushing the envelope of creating art with computers even further. For example, through her series *External Measures*, artist Camille Utterback uses a computer to create a work of art that reacts to the presence—and the absence—of movement of the viewers in the gallery (see Figure 1.7). When no one is near the art piece, the image paints a small series of dots. However, as onlookers in the gallery move closer to the work, a camera mounted on the ceiling of the art gallery captures the onlookers' movements and dimensions. A computer with specialized software then uses this captured data to create smears of color and patterns of lines that reflect their movements. Because the image itself is created from the current and past movements and sizes of the gallery patrons, the work looks different each time it is viewed.

Video Game Development: A Long Way from Pac-Man

Revenues from video game sales in the United States are now larger than the movie industry's box office. Computer gaming topped $21 billion in 2008 and is projected to continue its rapid growth over the next decade. If you're a gamer, you know games must be creative to grab their audience. Large-scale games are impossible

Figure 1.7

Computers even figure directly into the development of artwork. Artist Camille Utterback develops interactive art that changes with the presence and movement of viewers in the gallery.

to create on your own—you must be part of a team. The good news is that because computer games are best developed for a local market by people native to that market, game development will most likely stay in the United States instead of being **offshored** (sent to other countries), as many other types of programming jobs have been.

You'll need an in-depth knowledge of computers to pursue a career in game programming or as a gaming artist. Mastering software animation tools, such as 3ds Max, will enable you to create compelling new worlds and new characters like those in the story-driven adventure game Metal Gear Solid 4 (see Figure 1.8).

Education: Teaching and Learning

Today's teachers need to be at least as computer savvy as their students. Computers are part of most schools, even preschools. In fact, at many colleges, students are required to have their own computers. Courses are designed around course management software such as Blackboard or Moodle so that students can communicate outside of class, take quizzes online, and find their class materials easily. Teachers must therefore have a working knowledge of computers to integrate computer technology into the classroom effectively.

The Internet has obvious advantages in the classroom as a research tool for students, and effective use of the Internet allows teachers to expose students to places students otherwise could not access. There are simulations and instructional software on the Web that are incredible learning

tools. Teachers can employ these to give students a taste of running a global business (see Figure 1.9) or provide the experience of dissecting a virtual human cadaver.

Many museums have virtual tours on their Web sites that allow students to examine objects in the museum collections. Often, these virtual tours include three-dimensional photos that can be viewed from all angles. So, even if you teach in Topeka, Kansas, you can take your students on a virtual tour of the Smithsonian Institution in Washington, D.C.

But what about when you want to take your students to visit museums in person? Today, technology is often used to enhance visitors' experiences at museums. New York's Museum of Modern Art, for example, offers PDA tours that provide visitors with additional information about the art they're viewing. By using a **personal digital**

Figure 1.8

Using powerful software, game developers can create complex worlds and characters to satisfy even the most demanding gamer.

Figure 1.9

Internet applications have become sophisticated learning resources. IndustryMasters.com allows students to compete online for domination of a global market while giving instructors the chance to introduce many business concepts.

assistant (PDA), a small device that enables users to carry digital information, you can listen to music that the artist listened to when he or she was creating a particular work or look at other works that reflect similar techniques or themes to those of the one you're viewing (see Figure 1.10). While looking at works by more modern artists, you can watch interviews with the artist explaining his or her motivation for the work. You can even use the PDA to contact other members of your group and direct them to specific works you want them to see. Knowing how to use a PDA effectively may

help make a museum tour even more memorable.

Computers in the classroom will become more prevalent as prices continue to fall and parents demand that their children be taught the computer skills they will need to be successful in the workplace. Therefore, as an educator, being computer literate will help you integrate computers constructively into lesson plans for your students and use technology to interact with them.

Law Enforcement: Put Down that Mouse—You're Under Arrest!

Today, wearing out shoe leather to solve crimes is far from the only method available to investigators trying to catch criminals. Computers are being used in police cars and crime labs to solve an increasing number of crimes. For example, facial reconstruction systems like the one shown in Figure 1.11 can turn a skull into a finished digital image of a face, allowing investigators to proceed far more quickly with identification.

One technique used by modern detectives to solve crimes employs computers to search the vast number of databases on the Internet. Proprietary law enforcement databases such as the National Center for the Analysis of Violent Crime database

Figure 1.10

Multimedia tours using PDAs and wireless technology are commonplace in museums and galleries.

enable detectives to analyze a wealth of information about similarities between crimes, trying to detect patterns that may reveal serial crimes. Where the law permits, detectives can also use their knowledge of wireless networking to intercept and read a criminal suspect's e-mail messages and chat sessions when he or she is online, all from the comfort of a car parked outside the suspect's home.

Figure 1.11

(a) The FastScan wand lets forensics teams quickly grab three-dimensional images of skulls. (b) Tissue rendering programs then add layers of muscles, fat, and skin to create faces that can be used to identify victims.

As detective work goes more high tech, so, too, does crime. To fight modern crime, a law enforcement specialty called **computer forensics** is growing. This specialty employs computer systems and techniques to gather potential legal evidence. The ability to recover and read deleted or damaged files from a criminal's computer is already providing evidence for trials.

Every day, businesses across the world use complicated forecasting models to make predictions about their sales and inventory levels. Thanks to recent technological advancements, law enforcement officials might soon have access to specialized software that can forecast criminal activity, helping police officers take preventive measures to stop crime.

Don't believe it? Criminologists Jacqueline Cohen and Wilpen Gorr and computer scientist Andreas Olligschlaeger received funding from the U.S. Department of Justice to study police reports from Rochester, New York, and Pittsburgh, Pennsylvania. After entering data about criminal offenses, precinct staffing, and patrol routes, the researchers used trend spotting programs to analyze the data.

As a result, the program was able to predict criminal activity before it happened an astounding 80 percent of the time. The key to the analysis was identifying and studying leading indicators that trigger crime sprees. Whereas consumer researchers may look at consumer spending patterns and levels of disposable income, criminologists study soft crime statistics such as disorderly conduct and trespassing. Increases in these types of crimes indicate that serious crimes may soon be on the rise. When a trend is identified, patrols in the area can be stepped up to try to head off crimes before they occur. Building, analyzing, and fine-tuning such models will keep law enforcement officials busy for years.

Computers are also used in training law enforcement officers to be more effective. For example, the Federal Bureau of Investigation (FBI) and the Transportation Security Administration (TSA) use computer-based training to teach officers to recognize lies and evasive behavior. Dr. Paul Ekman has spent a career studying *microexpressions*, brief (1/25th of a second) flashes of emotion. When a person is being deceptive, microexpressions, which cannot be controlled, reveal true emotions in their body language. The Microexpression Training Tool software system (**paulekman.com**), a program developed by Dr. Ekman's company, trains users to recognize emotions like fear, disgust, contempt, and anger in these flashes of microexpressions (see Figure 1.12). You can try the online demo to see if you are a "natural," one of the rare people who can recognize and read emotion with no training.

Figure 1.12

The Microexpression Training Tool software trains law enforcement officials to distinguish true emotion from deception.

You're probably already using your computer in many different ways to fit your lifestyle. Perhaps you're ripping your CD collection to MP3 files so that you can transfer them from your computer to your iPod. Maybe you're burning a CD of all your favorite songs for a party you're having. But wouldn't it be great if you could manage the music for your party straight from your computer, using the iTunes software? And what about that video of your friend's birthday party you shot last week? You've already imported it to your computer, edited it, and added a music track. But when your friends come over for the party this weekend, wouldn't it be fun to be able to show them the video on the TV in the living room instead of having them crowd around your computer monitor?

When in the future will you be able to do all this? Right now if you set up a digital home. Setting up a **digital home** means having an appropri-ate computer and digital devices that are all connected to a home network. Let's discuss the key components you need to get started with a digital living room, some of which are shown in Figure 1.13.

1. **A media computer:** A computer is the nerve center of any digital home, allowing you to interface with all the different digital devices you have connected to the network. For a Windows-based computer (see Figure 1.14), you should opt for a computer running the current version of Microsoft Windows 7 or Windows Vista as its operating system. (We'll discuss operating systems in more detail in Chapter 5.) A typical media PC includes the following components:

   a. **A TV tuner:** A TV tuner allows your computer to receive televi-sion channels from a cable connection and display them on

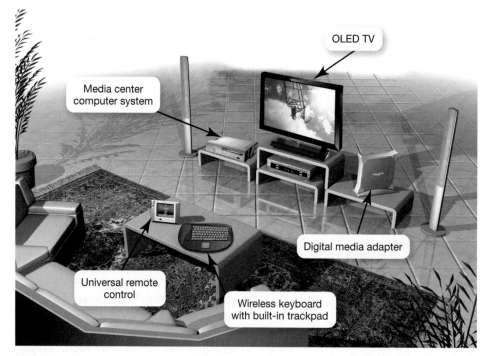

Figure 1.13

You can create a digital living room with only a few devices.

Legal System: Welcome to the Virtual Courtroom

In courtrooms today, videos of crimes in progress (often captured by cameras at convenience stores or gas stations) are sometimes shown to juries to help them understand how crimes unfolded. But what happens if no surveillance camera recorded a crime? Paper diagrams, models, and still photos of a crime scene used to be the only choice for attorneys seeking to illustrate their cases. Now there is a much more exciting and lively alternative: computer forensics animations.

Computer forensics animations are extremely detailed and often lifelike re-creations that computers generate based on forensic evidence, depositions of witnesses, and the opinions of experts. Using sophisticated animation programs, similar to the ones used to create movies such *Up* and

Figure 1.14

Media Center in Microsoft Windows 7 allows you to manage all your media entertainment from your computer.

your computer monitor. In fact, you can install more than one TV tuner on your computer, allowing you to receive multiple television channels at the same time.

b. **A radio tuner:** A radio tuner allows you to tune into Internet radio stations and record their broadcasts as digital files on your computer.

c. **Media software:** In addition to a computer and tuners, you'll also need software. Windows 7 includes software called Media Center, which functions as a digital video recorder (DVR), a video player, and a music player. You can use Media Center to view and organize the digital audio and video files on your computer. In combination with a TV tuner, digital video recorder software that is included as part of Windows Media Center allows you to turn your computer into a DVR similar to TiVo. Digital video recorders record TV programs like VCRs do, but they use your computer's hard drive to store the video. If you have multiple TV tuners installed in your computer, you can record several programs onto your computer's hard drive at the same time.

d. **Blu-ray, DVD, and CD players and recorders:** To make it easy to transfer your audio or video files from one device to another, high-definition recorders and DVD and CD players and recorders allow you to record files onto high-definition media (such as Blu-ray discs) or onto standard-resolution DVDs and CDs instead of your hard drive.

e. **A network adapter:** A network adapter is a special device that is installed in your computer and allows it to communicate with other devices on a network. (You'll learn more about network

adapters in Chapter 7.) For digital devices to communicate with each other, they need to be connected to a network.

2. **A network:** Unless you're going to view digital and audio files only on your computer, you will need a network to transfer files easily to other devices (such as televisions) in your home. A wireless network has an advantage over a wired network because it is easier to relocate devices on a wireless network. For example, suppose you rearrange your living room and need to move your TV to the opposite end of the room. If your TV was connected to a wired network, you might have to run a new cable or relocate the existing one. With a wireless network, you'd just move the TV and be done with it. (You'll learn all about wired and wireless networks in Chapter 7.)

3. **A digital television:** Newer plasma and organic light emitting diode (OLED) televisions (see Figure 1.13) or high-definition TVs (HDTVs) are an important part of any digital home because they are the best way to show off all your digital entertainment (digital photos and so on). Note that even if you don't have a plasma or OLED television, as long as you bought your TV within the last five years or so, you can probably use it to display digital content. However, televisions are not usually ready to be integrated into a network right out of the box. For this, you need a digital media adapter.

4. **A digital media adapter:** A digital media adapter (see Figure 1.13) allows you to transfer media such as videos, digital photos, or MP3s from your computer to your other media devices, such as your plasma TV. Digital media adapters are also known as *media center extenders*. A digital media adapter allows you to integrate your TV into your home network. This device connects to your computer network (either wired or wirelessly) and then to your TV through specially designed audiovisual connectors.

5. **A universal remote:** A universal remote is a single remote control that works with any infrared controlled device (such as your computer, digital media adapters, amplifiers, or receivers) and allows you to access media such as MP3 files no matter where in the house it is stored. Universal remotes such as the Pronto from Philips (see Figure 1.13) come with software that allows you to program your own custom interface for the remote. You can even program macros that perform multiple commands with the press of a button.

With these devices installed, you can get the maximum benefit from your computer and all your digital entertainment devices. When you're in your living room, you can play digital music files stored on your computer (in the den) for the party you're throwing. You can also display the video of your friend's birthday party (downloaded to your computer) on the TV for your friends to see. And when you're in your room, you can watch the latest episode of *CSI*, which you recorded on your computer's hard drive, while your sister is listening to MP3 files stored on your computer on the TV in the living room.

Bolt, forensic animators can depict one side's version of how events occurred, allowing the jury to watch it unfold.

Of course, being able to display sophisticated multimedia, televise trials, or record witness testimony for archiving requires modern courtrooms to be wired. Those such as Florida's Ninth Judicial Circuit Court (see Figure 1.15) are on the cutting edge, complete with robot-controlled video cameras that pivot to record whoever is

speaking on the microphone at the time. Video images can be streamed directly to a Web site for immediate viewing or stored for archival purposes. Meanwhile, the judge uses a touch-screen terminal to control the action in the courtroom, including turning on real-time closed captioning by linking in the court reporter's transcription terminal. Lawyers have access to wireless touch-screen handheld devices that allow them to access and display evidence they have stored on the

Figure 1.15

Courtrooms such as Florida's Ninth Judicial Circuit Court are on the cutting edge.

courtroom's multimedia systems. Attorneys can also connect their own notebook computers to the system, and audio recordings of all proceedings are captured and available for immediate playback.

Outside the courtroom, lawyers and other legal professionals use vast online legal libraries and databases, such as LexisNexis, to research cases and prepare for court.

Agriculture: High-Tech Down on the Farm

You might think that ranching and farming are low-tech operations that have little use for computers and software. The growing season can't be changed by any computer program! Even so, new technologies are changing life on farms and ranches in many ways.

Ranchers face many challenges in modern meat production. For example, they must watch for and prevent diseases such as hoof and mouth, mad cow, and *E. coli* outbreaks. The meat you purchase can be introduced to these dangers at many different places in the processing chain, from the ranch to the supermarket.

Fortunately, outbreaks can be managed and minimized with the use of **radio frequency identification tags (RFID tags)**. These RFID tags are small versions of the roadway electronic toll systems used in many states to collect tolls automatically as you pass through the toll station. Each tag looks like a tiny button and is attached to a cow's ear. It contains a microchip that holds a unique sequence of numbers used to identify that animal. When the cow walks past a panel reader, its location is automatically recorded and tracked in a database.

If a cow is identified as having a disease, all of its recorded movements can be checked in the database that stores the RFID information. It is then simple to identify exactly which food lots that and other animals ate at.

Using RFID tags, potential crises can be averted or at least better controlled.

In cranberry bogs, computer technology is being used in some interesting ways. For example, cranberry crops easily can be destroyed by frost. In the past, growers had to race to protect the bogs of berries on cold nights by turning on water pumps to surround the berries with water and keep them from freezing. Today, growers use a Web-based system that can automatically control the pumps. It analyzes information about the time, the temperature measured near the berries, watering schedules, rainfall, and wind conditions, and then automatically turns the pumps around the bog fields on and off as needed.

Automotive Technology: Sensors and CPUs

An automotive technician is required to have knowledge of a range of tools—impact hammers, wrenches, pneumatic tools, lathes, and welding and flame cutting equipment. Individuals considering a career in automotive repair today require a sophisticated level of computer literacy as well (see Figure 1.16). Environmental trends and governmental regulation are driving auto manufacturers to develop vehicles that produce lower emissions as the push for more efficient cars and higher gas mileage continues.

These changes have increased the number of sensors and computer CPU (central processing unit) systems needed in a typical vehicle. The fuel injection and engine management systems possible today go far beyond what a simple carburetor can do. Several sensors measure everything from air pressure to air temperature, engine temperature, and throttle position, for example. The data from these sensors is then used to compute the precise amount of fuel to spray into the cylinders, resulting in less fuel waste and reduced pollution. The braking, transmission, and steering systems also are primarily controlled by computers and electronic components.

As consumers come to expect digital music systems, airbags, voice-controlled phones, and GPS navigation screens in their cars, the number of computer subsystems will continue to grow. In addition to these driver-friendly features,

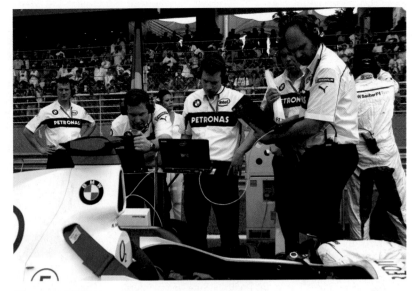

Figure 1.16

These automotive technicians for BMW Sauber gather around their car before the start of the Malaysian Grand Prix. They need computer skills to run all of the electronic checks of automotive subsystems.

the computers in today's cars even alert drivers when it's time to take the car in for maintenance or repair.

As a result, automotive technicians must be able to update documentation through the Internet, use computer databases to learn about common problems and solutions, and use computer systems to interface with and run diagnostics on all the different automotive computer systems. The days of working on a car in the driveway with some screwdrivers and a socket wrench are fading quickly.

Medicine: Fact or Fiction?

In some movies set in the distant future, humans interface with computers just by thinking and looking at a screen or monitor. Until recently, such scenes took place only in movies. But since 2006, companies such as Cyberkinetics have been working to understand the human neural interface system. In testing the company's software, known as BrainGate, a man suffering from amyotrophic lateral sclerosis (ALS, which is also known as Lou Gehrig's disease), who no longer had any control of muscle movement, was able to control the movement of a robotic arm.

The BrainGate software translates his thoughts into commands to the robotic limb. The patient has had a tiny array of microelectrodes implanted in his brain

Figure 1.17

(a) The BrainGate Neural Interface is implanted in the patient's brain. (b) A signal converter recognizes patterns and then translates them into commands to a robotic arm.

(see Figure 1.17a). The computer equipment receiving data from his neural activity (see Figure 1.17b) identifies the impulses that the brain associates with physical movement (of his arm, for example) and then translates the instructions into commands to the robot. Patient Stephen Heywood explained, "After being paralyzed for so long, it is almost impossible to describe the magical feeling of imagining a motion and having it occur."

In addition to being an integral part of many medical research projects, computers are helping doctors and nurses learn their trades. Training for physicians and nurses can be difficult at the best of times. Often, the best way for medical students to learn is to experience a real emergency situation. The problem is that students are then confined to watching as the emergency unfolds and trained personnel care for patients. Students rarely get to train in real-life situations; when they do, a certain level of risk is involved.

Medical students now have access to better training opportunities thanks to a computer technology called a **patient simulator** (see Figure 1.18). Patient simulators are life-sized, computer-controlled mannequins that can speak, breathe, and blink (their eyes respond to external stimuli). They have a pulse and a heartbeat, and they respond just like humans to procedures such as the administration of intravenous drugs.

Medical students can train on patient simulators and experience firsthand how a human would react to their treatments. The best thing about these "patients" is that if they "die," students can restart the computer simulation and try again. Even the U.S. military is using patient simulators to train medics to respond to terrorist attacks that employ chemical and biological agents.

Even more exciting than patient simulators is the work being done on modeling complete human biological systems. The Physiome Project began as the brainchild of the Bioengineering Institute in Auckland, New Zealand. It now is a global **public domain** effort (not

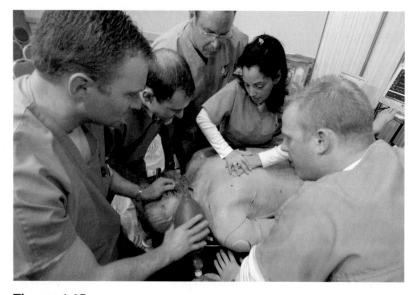

Figure 1.18

Patient simulators allow health care students to practice medical procedures without risk of injury or death to real patients.

covered by copyright) in which bioengineers are creating realistic computer simulations of all systems and features of the human anatomy. (An example is shown in Figure 1.19.)

Although the Physiome Project's current system models a theoretical human's lungs, researchers hope to one day use computers to simulate a specific person's anatomical systems. With such a system, imaging scans (CTs, MRIs, etc.) of your body and a sample of your DNA would be fed into a computer, which would create an exact computer model of your body. This would allow doctors to experiment with different therapies to see how you would react to specific treatments. A great deal of work is still to be done before this refinement becomes a reality, and computer-literate medical professionals will be needed to make it happen.

Figure 1.19

The Physiome Project has an ambitious goal of creating a complete digital model of a human being. This goal will require the joint efforts of collaborators from all over the world.

Surgeons are even using computer-guided robots to perform surgery. Surgeons are often limited by their manual dexterity and can have trouble making small, precise incisions. Robots can help. Robotic surgery devices can exercise much finer control when making delicate incisions than can a human guiding a scalpel. To use the robots, doctors look into a surgery control device where they manipulate controls that move robotic devices hovering over the patient (see Figure 1.20). One robot control arm contains a slender imaging rod that allows the doctor to see inside the patient when the rod is inserted into the patient. Doctors can now perform a coronary bypass by making two small incisions in the patient and inserting the imaging rod in one incision and another robotic device with a scalpel into the other. The ability to make small incisions instead of the large ones required by conventional surgery means less trauma and blood loss

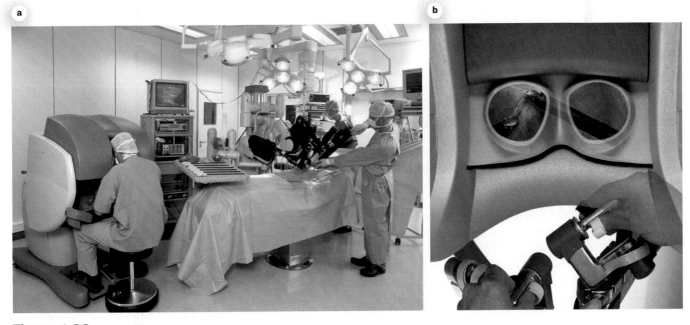

Figure 1.20

(a) A doctor manipulates controls that move the robotic instrument tips inside the patient. (b) This shows what surgeons might see as they operate on the patient.

for the patient. Theoretically, surgeons do not even have to be in the same room as the patient. They could be thousands of miles away, controlling the movements of the robotic devices from a control station.

Medicine: The Chip Within

When you mention implanting technology into the human body, some people conjure up images of the Terminator, a futuristic cybernetic life form from the movie of the same name that looks human but is mostly machine. The goal of modern biomedical chip research is to provide technological solutions to physical problems and to provide a means for positively identifying individuals. Figure 1.21 shows a nerve cell on a silicon chip. The cell was cultured on the chip until it formed a network with nearby cells. The chip contains a transistor that stimulates the cell above it, which in turn passes the signal to neighboring neurons.

One potential application of biomedical chip implants is to provide sight to the blind. Macular degeneration and retinitis pigmentosa are two diseases that account for the majority of blindness in developing nations. Both diseases result in damage to the photoreceptors contained in the retina of the eye. (Photoreceptors convert light energy into electrical energy that is transmitted to the brain, allowing us to see.) Researchers are experimenting with chips containing microscopic solar cells that are implanted in the damaged retina of a patient. The idea is to have the chip take over for the damaged photoreceptors and transmit electrical images to the

Figure 1.21

Researchers are experimenting with implantable chips such as this one to repair nerve damage and restore movement or sensation to parts of the body.

brain. Although these chips have been tested in patients, they have not yet restored anyone's sight. But biomedical chips such as these exemplify the types of medical devices you may "see" in the future.

One type of chip is already being implanted in humans as a means of verifying a person's identity. Called the VeriChip, this "personal ID chip" is about the size of a grain of rice and is implanted under the skin. When exposed to radio waves from a scanning device, the chip emits a signal that transmits its unique serial number to the scanner. The scanner then connects to a database that contains the name, address, and medical conditions of the person in whom the chip has been implanted.

Hitachi has a similar device, called the μ-chip (mu-chip), which is smaller than the period at the end of this sentence (see Figure 1.22). The μ-chip could be easily attached to, or ingested by, a person without his or her knowledge.

The creators of the VeriChip envision it speeding up airport security and being used together with other devices (such as electronic ID cards) to provide tamperproof security measures. If someone stole your credit card, that person couldn't use it if a salesclerk had to verify your identity by scanning a chip in your arm before authorizing a transaction.

Currently, nonimplant versions of identity chips are used in hospitals. When chips are attached with bands to newborn infants, the hospital staff can monitor the location of any baby instantly. Elevators and doors are designed to allow only certain people to enter with a specific baby, even if the hospital power is interrupted. Although the use of these tags is becoming more

Figure 1.22

No bigger than the period at the end of this sentence, the Hitachi μ-chip can hold digital information, which can then be read when it passes a detector.

commonplace, it remains to be seen whether the general public will decide that the advantages of having personal identity and medical data quickly available justifies having chips implanted into their bodies.

Science: Simulating Reality

Thanks to a partnership between the National Severe Storms Lab and the National Center for Supercomputing Applications,

tornado forecasting may be getting more accurate. Scientists have been able to create a model so detailed that it takes nine days for a supercomputer to generate it, even though the computer is executing four trillion operations each second. Simulations also can model the structure of solar magnetic flares, which can interfere with broadcasts on Earth (see Figure 1.23). By studying the data produced by these simulations, forecasters hope to improve their predictions about weather phenomena.

Other technological applications in the sciences are being used on some of the oldest sites on Earth. The ancient site of Pompeii has been under the intense scrutiny of tourists and archaeologists for decades. Sadly, all the foot traffic and exposure to the elements is eroding portions of the ruins. Today scientists are using three-dimensional scanners and imaging software to capture a detailed record of the current condition of the ruins (see Figure 1.24). The virtual re-creation of the ruins is so lifelike that archaeologists can study the ruins on screen instead of at the actual site. Using the scans as well as satellite imagery, aerial photography, and other data, scientists will eventually be able to re-create missing portions of the ruins in a virtual model. And scientists won't stop at Pompeii. This method will soon be used to make records of other decaying sites.

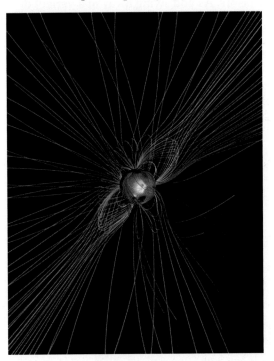

Figure 1.23

A simulation from the University of Michigan shows the structure of the magnetic fields around the sun and how they change in time.

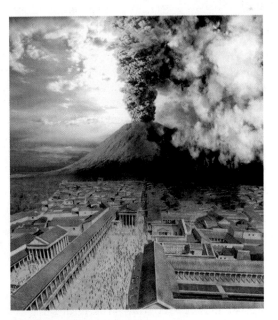

Figure 1.24

A digital re-creation of the ruins of Pompeii allows archaeologists to study the ruins without even being there, as well as re-create Pompeii as it looked before the devastation.

Sports Science: Compute Your Way to a Better Game

Want to be a world-class swimmer or baseball player? Getting an Olympic-caliber coach and training for hours every day are no longer enough. To get that competitive edge, you really need to use a computer.

That's right, computers are now being used to help athletes analyze their performance and improve their game. How does this work? First, video recordings are made of the athlete in action. The video is then transferred into special motion analysis software on a computer. This software measures the exact angles of the athlete's body parts as they progress through ranges of motion, such as the angle of a baseball player's left arm relative to his body as he swings the bat. Minor adjustments can be made on the computer regarding positioning of body parts and the force used in performing various movements. This

helps baseball players, for example, enhance their performance by determining what adjustments they should make to hit the ball harder and farther.

The U.S. Olympic Training Center in Colorado makes extensive use of computers in training athletes such as swimmers. The major objective in training swimmers to swim faster is to reduce drag from the water and minimize turbulence, which also can slow down a swimmer. Software has been developed that simulates the way water flows around the parts of a swimmer's body when in motion. Coaches can use the software to experiment with small changes in the position of a swimmer's arms or legs and determine whether turbulence and drag are reduced. The coaches can then train the swimmers to use the new techniques to improve their strokes and speed.

Aren't planning on competing in the next Olympics or playing in the major leagues? How about improving your weekend golf game? Employees in golf shops are now using sophisticated motion-capture equipment to improve golfers' swings. To have your golf swing analyzed, golf shop personnel hook you up into shoulder, leg, and hip harnesses containing motion sensors. As you swing away at a variety of shots (drives, chips, and so on), computers capture information about the motion of your swing, comparing it to a database of the ideal positions of pro golfers (see Figure 1.25). Trainers then suggest adjustments you can make so that your

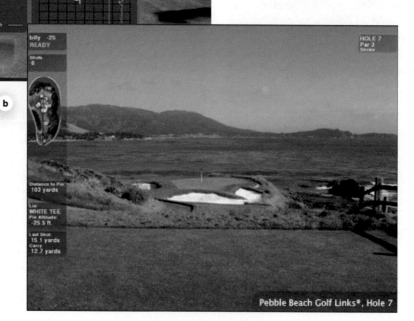

Figure 1.25

(a) High Definition Golf does a complete analysis on your swing and projects the flight path the ball would have taken. (b) It can also simulate many popular golf courses, like Pebble Beach.

swing more closely emulates that of successful golfers. Even weekend warriors can benefit from high-tech analysis.

Athletic equipment is also getting a technology boost. Even in a sport such as soccer, where not much equipment is involved, technology is making an impact. Adidas is developing a new soccer ball that contains an integrated circuit chip. When the company's Smartball crosses the goal line, it sends a radio signal to the referee's watch. The ball is not yet approved for World Cup play, but you can expect to see Smartballs showing up in professional soccer matches soon.

Nanotechnology: Careers Yet to Come

Have you ever heard of nanoscience? Developments in computing based on the principles of nanoscience are being touted as the next big wave in computing. Ironically, this realm of science focuses on incredibly small objects. **Nanoscience** involves the study of molecules and structures (called *nanostructures*) that range in size from 1 to 100 nanometers. It will provide numerous career paths and high-tech positions over the next several decades.

The prefix *nano* stands for one billionth. Therefore, a nanometer is one billionth of a meter. To put this in perspective, a human hair is approximately fifty thousand nanometers wide. Put side by side, 10 hydrogen atoms (the simplest atom) would measure approximately one nanometer. Anything smaller than a nanometer is just a stray atom or particle floating around in space. Therefore, nanostructures represent the smallest human-made structures that can be built.

Nanotechnology is the science of using nanostructures to build devices on an extremely small scale. Right now, nanoscience is limited to improving existing products, such as enhancing fibers used in clothing with coatings so that they repel stains, resist odors, or stop wrinkles. However, someday scientists hope to use nanostructures to build computing devices that will be too small to be seen by the naked eye. Nanowires (see Figure 1.26), which are extremely small conductors, could be used to create extremely small pathways in computer chips. Developments

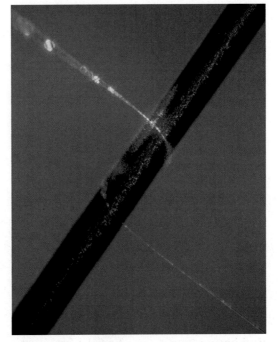

Figure 1.26

Nanowires hold promise for use in constructing even smaller computing devices.

such as this could lead to computers the size of a pencil eraser that will be far more powerful than today's desktop computers.

If you've ever watched *Star Trek*, then you know that *nanoprobes* (tiny machines that can be injected into the bloodstream) have already been envisioned. Nanotechnology researchers are now beginning to use carbon nanotubes to create devices that deliver medicine and information. We are still a long way from developing nanoscale machines, and some scientists don't think this will ever be possible. However, researchers are investigating the use of nanostructures to deliver precise doses of drugs on a

NASA Wants You . . . to Learn

As you read this chapter, hundreds of satellites are orbiting the globe and taking wonderfully detailed pictures of Earth. Until recently, these photos weren't available to the general public. However, thanks to NASA (and U.S. taxpayer dollars) and some savvy software developers, an application called World Wind is now making some 10 trillion bytes of imagery available to you. Do you need a picture of Mount Fuji for your science project or an aerial picture of your house for your PowerPoint presentation? Just download the software from **learn.arc.nasa.gov**, and you're ready to go. You'll find several terrific learning applications here as well. "Virtual Lab" lets you pretend you have your own scanning electron microscope, and "What's the Difference" takes you on a tour of the planets, complete with information about their composition and atmosphere and fly-throughs. With a few clicks, you can have interactive learning resources that open the world to you.

molecule-by-molecule basis within the human bloodstream. Universities and government laboratories are investing billions of dollars in nanotechnology research every year. If you have the background and interest in computing technology and science, this is the time to pursue an education in nanoscience.

Psychology: You Should Smile. . . Now

Science fiction shows and movies such as *Star Wars* have always been populated with robots that emulate humans, seemingly effortlessly. So, when will we have C-3PO, R2-D2, or the Terminator laughing at our jokes or bringing us our favorite snack when they recognize we're sad? It is a question that pushes us to explore the nature of being human and the nature of machines.

Psychologists and computer scientists are jointly conducting research to develop computer systems that respond to human affect and emotional expression, and to enable computer systems to develop social and emotional skills. **Affective computing** is computing that relates to emotion or deliberately tries to influence emotion. Most computers with which you are familiar can perform calculations and the tasks for which they are programmed much faster than humans can, but they fail miserably in telling a good joke or modifying their behavior based on your frustration. This wide gap in the computing abilities of computers versus their emotional abilities is the target of research in affective computing.

One project to emerge is the emotional social prosthesis (ESP) device, developed by a group at the Massachusetts Institute of Technology (MIT) Media Lab. The ESP system is

Figure 1.27

Robots with articulated joints that mimic human limbs can balance, stand, walk and even hug.

targeted at helping people who have autism. Autistic individuals can have extremely high intelligence but do not easily sense nonverbal cues such as facial expressions and tone of voice. ESP is a wearable system that isolates the movements and facial expressions of people, interprets what their mood and intention probably are, and communicates this information back to the user.

Another project at the Media Lab will help people who have difficulty maintaining focus on a specific task. This project centers on the creation of computer systems that can analyze a person's movements, watch their use of the mouse, and interpret the pressure patterns on the chair in which the person is seated. That data is then used to determine the individual's level of attention. The computer could then interrupt an individual who is beginning to lose concentration and refocus him or her on a certain task.

While engineers work to create computers that can understand us emotionally, psychologists and computer scientists are also working to evolve systems toward a more human appearance (see Figure 1.27). Teams at the University of Michigan, Ohio State University, and the French Institute of Computer Science Research are working on robots that move in a more human fashion. Their biped (two-legged) robot, named Rabbit, is able to walk, run, and climb stairs. It may lead to industrial robots that can tackle new tasks for us.

SOUND BYTE

The History of the Personal Computer

In this Sound Byte, you will explore the history of the personal computer, including the events that led to the development of today's computers and the people who made them possible.

Understanding the Challenges Facing a Digital Society

Part of becoming computer literate is being able to understand and form knowledgeable opinions on the challenges that face a digital society. Although computers offer us a world of opportunities, they also pose ethical, legal, and moral challenges and questions. For example, how do you feel about the following?

- Since the tragic events of September 11, 2001, various nationwide surveillance programs have been proposed. Some programs include installing surveillance cameras in public places that could be considered attractive areas in which to stage terrorist activities. These cameras would be monitored via the Internet, possibly by volunteers. Should the government be allowed to monitor your activities in public places, à la George Orwell's famous book *1984*, to help keep the country secure?

- Advances in surveillance device technology (see Figure 1.28) are allowing these devices to become smaller and less noticeable. In certain jurisdictions, courts have upheld the rights of employers to install surveillance devices in the workplace (sometimes without needing to notify employees) to cut down on theft and prevent industrial espionage. Do you know if your employer is watching you? Do you think your employer should have this right?

- Many employees don't know that employers have the right to monitor e-mail and network traffic on the systems they use at work, because those systems are provided at the employer's expense for the sole purpose of allowing employees to do their jobs. Have you

Figure 1.28

With cameras becoming smaller, you could unknowingly be under surveillance at any time. Should the government be allowed to install such cameras or should your privacy be respected?

visited Web sites that you don't want your employer to know about (such as employment sites as part of a new job search)? Have you sent personal e-mail through your company e-mail system? Does your employer know about these activities? Should employers have the right to know?

These are just a few examples of the kind of questions active participants in today's digital society need to be able to think about, discuss, and, at times, take action on. Being computer literate enables you to form educated opinions on these issues and to take stands based on accurate information rather than media hype and misinformation. Here are a few other questions that you, as a member of our digital society, may be expected to think about and discuss:

- What privacy risks do biomedical chips such as the VeriChip pose? Do the privacy risks of such chips outweigh the potential benefits?

- Should companies be allowed to collect personal data from visitors to their Web sites without their permission?

- Should spam be illegal? If so, what penalties should be levied on people who send spam?

- Is it ethical to download music off the Web without paying for it (see Figure 1.29)? What about copying a friend's software onto your computer?

- What are the risks involved in humans attempting to create computers that can learn and become more human?

- Should we rely solely on computers to provide security for sensitive areas such as nuclear power plants?

As a computer user, you must consider these and other questions to define the boundaries of the digital society in which you live.

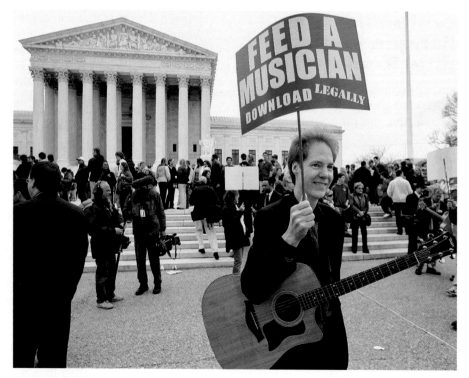

Figure 1.29

Does downloading music without paying for it hurt anyone? Or is it merely a cost absorbed by huge record companies? How will your choices create the music market you will experience in the future?

Ethics: Knowledge Is Power—Bridging the Digital Divide

What would your life be like if you had never touched a computer because you simply couldn't afford one? What if there were no computers in your town? If you're like most people in the United States, access to computers is a given. But for many people, access to the opportunities and knowledge computers and the Internet offer is impossible. The discrepancy between the "haves" and "have-nots" with regard to computer technology is commonly referred to as the **digital divide**.

This discrepancy is a growing problem. People with access to computers and the Internet (that is, those who can afford them) are poised to take advantage of the many new developments technology offers, whereas poorer individuals, communities, and school systems that can't afford computer systems and Internet access are being left behind.

For example, in the United States, more teachers are using the Internet to communicate with parents than ever before. E-mail updates on student progress, Web sites with homework postings that allow parents to track assignments, and even online parent–teacher conferences are becoming popular. Unwired parents and students are left out of the loop. In the United States, children who do not have access to the Internet and computers won't be prepared for future employment, contributing to the continuing cycle of poverty.

But the digital divide isn't always caused by low income. Terrain can be a factor that inhibits connectivity (see Figure 1.30). In Nepal's mountainous terrain, for example, even though a village might only be a few miles away "as the crow flies," it might take two days to hike there because of the lack of roads. Volunteers, funded by a generous donor, have installed 12 outdoor access points complete with directional antennas to connect a series of villages to the Internet via a wireless network. The last access point in the connectivity chain connects to an Internet service provider 22 miles away. The villagers are now able to hold meetings, attend school classes, and access the Internet without trekking across miles of mountainous terrain. Unfortunately, this solution isn't available throughout all of Nepal . . . or even throughout some areas of the United States.

What is being done to bridge the digital divide? Organizations worldwide are working to raise awareness and to increase government involvement. Groups are sponsoring referendums that increase Internet capacity in schools, for example, and are urging state legislatures to provide additional funding for technology to struggling school systems. Community organizations are rising to the challenge as libraries and recreation centers work to provide free Internet access to the public.

You can help directly by donating used computer equipment to nonprofit groups that refurbish computers. These organizations repair and upgrade retired systems, and then distribute the systems to needy families at low cost. The Web site Techsoup (**techsoup.org**) maintains national resource lists that can help you find such organizations in your area. Some technology companies have programs in place to help with these efforts. The Microsoft Authorized Refurbisher (MAR) program, for example, supports refurbishers by allowing certain Microsoft operating systems and Office software to be installed for free on refurbished systems.

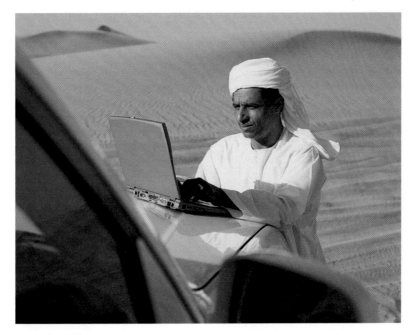

Figure 1.30

Terrain (such as mountains) and remote locations (the Sahara, for example) can present barriers to conquering the digital divide.

one summary

1. What does it mean to be "computer literate"?

Computer literacy goes beyond knowing how to use a mouse and send e-mail. If you are computer literate, you understand the capabilities and limitations of computers and know how to use them wisely. Being computer literate also enables you to make informed purchasing decisions, use computers in your career, and understand the many ethical, legal, and societal implications of technology today. Anyone can become computer literate.

2. How does being computer literate make you a savvy computer user and consumer?

By understanding how a computer is constructed and how its various parts function, you'll be able to get the most out of your computer. Among other things, you'll be able to avoid hackers, viruses, and Internet headaches; protect your privacy; and separate the real risks of privacy and security from those you don't have to worry about. You'll also be better able to maintain, upgrade, and troubleshoot your computer; make good purchasing decisions; and incorporate the latest technologies into your existing equipment.

3. How can becoming computer literate help you in a career?

As computers become more a part of our daily lives, it is difficult to imagine any career that does not use computers in some fashion. Understanding how to use computers effectively will help you be a more productive and valuable employee, no matter which profession you choose.

4. How can becoming computer literate help you understand and take advantage of newly emerging careers?

In today's world many changes are a result of new computer technologies. Understanding how today's computers function should help you utilize technology effectively now. And by understanding computers and how they work today, you can contribute to the technologies of tomorrow, like nanoscience and new medical technologies.

5. How does becoming computer literate help you deal with the challenges associated with technology?

Although computers offer us great opportunities, they also pose ethical, legal, and moral challenges and questions. Being computer literate enables you to form educated opinions on these issues and to take stands based on accurate information rather than media hype and misinformation.

Word Bank

- affective computing
- Bluetooth technology
- computer forensics
- computer literate
- data mining
- digital divide
- digital home
- information technology (IT)
- nanotechnology
- offshoring
- patient simulator
- personal digital assistant (PDA)
- public domain
- radio frequency identification tags (RFID tags)
- spam

Instructions: Fill in the blanks using the words from the Word Bank above.

As technology advances continue, many fields of study are available now that were unheard of a few years ago. (1) _____, the study of incredibly small computing devices built at the molecular level, is providing major advances in the miniaturization of computing. (2) _____ is taking criminologists beyond what they could accomplish with conventional investigation techniques. And as the science of (3) _____ advances, computers will perform more and more like human beings in emotion and social cueing.

There are many reasons to become (4) _____, or to understand more about the capabilities and limitations of computers. Doing so can help you manage computer annoyances like unwanted e-mails, called (5) _____. You will also know how to upgrade your system to the latest standards, like the wireless (6) _____.

More and more aspects of how our homes are run are being coordinated through computers, giving rise to the term (7) _____. You may even find you enjoy computers so much you want to explore careers in (8) _____.

People who fail to keep up with the knowledge of how to use and maintain computer systems will fall to one side of the gap known as the (9) _____. When an entire country begins to fall behind in computer expertise, jobs are relocated to other, more tech-savvy countries. This shift of work is known as (10) _____.

becoming computer literate

Using the key terms and ideas you learned in this chapter, write a one- or two-paragraph summary for your school advisor so that he or she can use it to explain to students the importance of being computer literate in today's job market. Using the Internet, find additional examples of careers most people would not expect to require computer knowledge and show how computer literacy is still critical to success in those careers. Add these examples to your document to support your advice further.

Instructions: Answer the multiple-choice and true–false questions below for more practice with key terms and concepts from this chapter.

Multiple Choice

1. Which of the following is NOT a current use of computers in the legal environment?
   a. Creating animations that simulate a crime for use in the courtroom
   b. Tracking criminal behavior patterns
   c. Predicting criminal behavior patterns
   d. Conducting interviews with suspects

2. Art interfaces with technology by
   a. using a computer to generate images that respond to the environment.
   b. having computers suggest appropriate solutions to a dispute.
   c. using software that completes the plot of a story.
   d. having Web sites search for prospective clients for artists.

3. Affective computing is the science of relating computers and
   a. effective organizational skills.
   b. results-oriented outcomes.
   c. emotional and social skills.
   d. the calculation of interest rates.

4. Computer systems CANNOT be trained to understand
   a. the U.S. tax code.
   b. human emotion.
   c. a good joke.
   d. the perfect golf swing.

5. Automotive technology requires an understanding of computers to
   a. properly bill customers.
   b. control computerized pneumatic tools.
   c. keep carburetor settings at optimal positions.
   d. run sensors and CPU diagnostics for a vehicle's many computerized subsystems.

6. A device that tracks movement is
   a. a PSS.
   b. an RFID tag.
   c. a PDA.
   d. a patient simulator.

7. Criminologists use computer technology to
   a. reconstruct faces from bare skulls.
   b. create software programs that predict criminal activity.
   c. reconstruct deleted files from criminals' computers.
   d. All of the above.

8. IT careers
   a. are only about programming and software development.
   b. are many of the fastest-growing occupations.
   c. are on the decline.
   d. have largely been outsourced to India.

9. Computer forensics
   a. uses computer technology to gather potential legal evidence.
   b. helps identify the remains of bodies.
   c. investigates a suspect's home computer for evidence.
   d. All of the above.

10. Robotic surgery devices help physicians because
   a. they make incisions that are more accurate.
   b. the doctor does not have to be involved in the surgery.
   c. they monitor and make suggestions to the surgeon during the procedure.
   d. if the operation runs into complications, they can suggest creative alternatives.

True-False

_____ 1. Computer simulations are used for gaming purposes, but they are not yet accurate enough for criminal investigations.

_____ 2. Affective computing is the science that attempts to produce machines that make people comfortable because they look human in form.

_____ 3. Artists use computers for the business side of their work—for example, advertising or record keeping—but not for creative artistic work.

_____ 4. Ranchers tag their cattle and use computer systems to track and record their movements.

_____ 5. In many hospitals, infants are "chipped," or injected with a small, computerized tracking device, so that nurses can monitor their location and keep them safe.

making the
transition to...
next semester

one chapter

making the
transition to...
next semester

1. Computer Literacy

In your college career, you'll be spending time understanding the requirements of the degree program you choose. At many schools, computer literacy requirements exist either as incoming requirements (skills students must have before they are admitted) or outgoing requirements (skills students must prove they have before graduating). Does your program require specific computer skills? Which skills are these? Should they be required? How can students efficiently prove that they have these skills? How often does the set of skills need to be reviewed and updated?

2. Computing and Education

Think about the schedule of courses you will be taking next semester. How many courses will require you to produce papers in electronic format? How many will require you to use course management software, such as Blackboard or Moodle? Will any course require you to use some specialty software product such as a nutrition monitoring program or a statistics training application? Do any require specialized hardware such as a scanner for your computer? How many require the use of collaborative meeting software?

3. Old Technologies Holding On

What courses and careers have not felt the impact of computer technology? Think of three courses that are taught effectively with no use of technology. Think of three careers that do not use computers in a significant way. Research and find the average salary and the rate of growth in these careers.

4. Using Biomedical Implants

If having such a chip implanted meant you would never need to carry cash or a credit card because your financial information was encoded on the chip, would you want one? If the chip could help instructors take attendance automatically in your class by reading your personal information, would that be an acceptable use? Would you consider using such a chip if it could be disabled whenever you wanted it to be or if only individuals you authorized had access to the information? Would you agree to have your chip communicate your financial information directly to the Internal Revenue Service (IRS)?

5. Campus Policing

In this chapter, the use of trend spotting programs to predict criminal activity was discussed. If existing criminal statistics are used to help identify trouble spots (such as wild parties) on your campus and the potential for serious criminal activity, is this the same as profiling? Does your campus police force have the right to take proactive steps to prevent crime based solely on developing trends? Should someone be held accountable if such information is not acted upon and a crime occurs?

making the
transition to...
the workplace

1. Computer-Free Workplaces?

In this chapter, we listed several careers that require computer skills. How are computers used in the profession you are in or plan to enter? Can you think of any careers in which people do not use computers? Can you imagine computers being used in these careers in the future? If so, how? Are there benefits to having a "computer-free" zone in some aspects of some careers? How do computers affect creativity?

2. Medical Computing Applications

In their training and work, doctors and nurses rely on computers. What about patients? Does having access to a computer and computer skills help a patient find better health care options? Does having access to a computer help when filing an insurance claim? Does it help with finding the best doctor or hospital for a specific procedure? Explain your answers by giving specific examples.

3. Preparing for a Job

An office is looking for help and needs an employee able to manipulate data on Excel spreadsheets, coordinate the computer file management for the office, and conduct backups of critical data. How could you prove to the interviewer that you have the skills to handle the job? How could you prove you have the ability to learn the job?

4. Career Outlook

Which career fields are growing most rapidly? (Suggestion: Try searching at **ask.com**.) Which fields are growing fastest in the state where you live? What computer skills and knowledge do the top 10 career paths demand? What kinds of continuing training in technology can you imagine would be required as you progress in these careers?

5. IT Careers

Information technology (IT) careers are suited to a wide range of people at different points in their lives. The Technology in Focus piece "Careers in IT" on page 450 gives more detail about IT careers. Review that section and then answer the following questions:

a. Would an IT career have advantages for a single parent? How?
b. How might an IT career be able to help someone pursue a later career in a nontechnical field?
c. How might an IT career assist someone in completing a college degree?
d. Would an IT career be a good choice if you wanted geographic independence (i.e., the ability to live in a location different from your work)?

6. Job Skills Assessment

Frequently, job seekers are asked about their computer literacy when applying for a job.

a. How do you think computer skill levels are determined by employers? How should they be determined?
b. If your interpretation of "expert" doesn't match your prospective employer's definition, does that make you wrong?

Instructions: Albert Einstein used *Gedankenexperiments*, or critical thinking questions, to develop his theory of relativity. Some ideas are best understood by experimenting with them in our own minds. The following critical thinking questions are designed to demand your full attention but require only a comfortable chair—no technology.

1. Rating Your Computer Literacy

This chapter lists many ways in which knowing about computers (or becoming computer literate) will help you. How much do you know about computers? What else would you like to know? How do you think learning more about computers will help you in the future? How would you suggest measuring computer literacy?

2. Data Mining

This chapter briefly discusses data mining, a technique companies use to study sales data and gather information from it. Have you heard of data mining before? How might companies like Wal-Mart or Target use data mining to better run their business? Can you think of any privacy risks data mining might pose?

3. Nanotechnology

As you learned in the chapter, nanotechnology is the science of using nanostructures to build devices on an extremely small scale. What applications of tiny computers can you think of? How might nanotechnology affect your life?

4. Biomedical Chips

This chapter discusses various uses of biomedical chips. Many biomedical chip implants that will be developed in the future will most likely be aimed at correcting vision loss, hearing loss, or other physical impediments. But chips could also be developed to improve physical or mental capabilities of healthy individuals. For example, chips could be implanted in athletes to make their muscles work better together, thereby allowing them to run faster. Or your memory could be enhanced by providing additional storage capacity for your brain.

a. Should biomedical implant devices that increase athletic performance be permitted in the Olympics?
b. What about devices that repair a problem (such as blindness in one eye) but then increase the level of visual acuity in the affected eye so that it is better than normal vision?
c. Would you be willing to have a chip implanted in your brain to improve your memory?
d. Would you be willing to have a VeriChip implanted under your skin?

5. Affective Computing

Affective computing is the science that attempts to produce machines that understand and can respond to human emotions and social mores. Do you think humans will ever create a machine that cannot be distinguished from a human being? In your opinion, what are the ethical and moral implications associated with that development?

6. The World Stage

How might access to (or denial of) electronic information improve the education of a country's citizens? Could that affect who the world's next technology power will be? Could it eliminate third world status?

Promoting Future Technologies

Problem

People are often overwhelmed by the relentless march of technology. Accessibility of information is changing the way we work, play, and interact with our friends, family, and co-workers. In this Team Time, we consider the future and reflect on how the advent of new technologies will affect our daily lives 10 years in the future.

Task

Your group has just returned from a trip in a time machine 10 years into the future. Amazing changes have taken place in just a short time. To a large extent, consumer acceptance of technology makes or breaks a new technology. Your mission is to develop a creative marketing strategy to promote the technological changes you observed in the future and accelerate their acceptance.

Process

Divide the class into three or more teams.

1. With the other members of your team, use the Internet to research up-and-coming technologies (**howstuffworks.com** is a good starting point). Prepare a list of innovations that you believe will occur in the next 10 years. Determine how they will be integrated into society and the effect they will have on our culture.
2. Present your group's findings to the class for debate and discussion. Note specifically how the rest of the class reacts to your reports on the innovations. Are they excited? Skeptical? Incredulous? Do they laugh off your ideas, or do they become wildly enthusiastic?
3. Write a marketing strategy paper that details how you would promote the technological changes that you envision for the future. Note some barriers to acceptance the technology may have to overcome, as well as any legal or ethical challenges or questions you see the new technology posing.

Conclusion

The future path of technology is determined by dreamers. If not for innovators such as Thomas Edison, Alexander Graham Bell, and Albert Einstein, we would not be as advanced a society as we are today. Innovators come from all walks of life, and we must exercise our creative energies to keep them in shape. Don't be afraid to suggest technological advancements that seem outrageous today. In 1966, when the original *Star Trek* series was on television, handheld communicators seemed astounding and beyond our reach. Yet the dreamers who created those communication devices for a science fiction series helped to inspire a multibillion-dollar cell phone industry in the 21st century. The next technological wave may start in your imagination!

In addition to the review materials presented here, you'll find additional materials in the book's multimedia, including the *Technology in Action* Student Resource CD and the Companion Website (**pearsonhighered.com/techinaction**), which will help reinforce your understanding of the chapter content. These materials include the following:

Active Helpdesk

In Active Helpdesk calls, you'll assume the role of helpdesk operator, taking calls about the concepts you've learned in this chapter. You'll apply what you've learned and receive feedback from a supervisor to review and reinforce those concepts. The Active Helpdesk calls for this chapter are listed below and can be found on your Student Resource CD:

- This chapter has no Active Helpdesks.

Sound Bytes

Sound Bytes are dynamic multimedia tutorials that help demystify even the most complex topics. You'll view video clips and animations that illustrate computer concepts and then apply what you've learned by working through the Sound Byte Labs, which include quizzes and activities specifically tailored to each Sound Byte. The Sound Bytes for this chapter are listed below and can be found on your Student Resource CD.

- Questions to Ask Before You Buy a Computer
- The History of the Personal Computer

Companion Website

The *Technology in Action* Companion Website includes a variety of additional materials to help you review and learn more about the topics in this chapter. The resources available at **pearsonhighered.com/techinaction** include:

- **Online Study Guide.** Each chapter features an online true–false and multiple-choice quiz. You can take these quizzes, automatically check the results, and e-mail the results to your instructor.
- **Web Research Projects.** Each chapter features several Web research projects that ask you to search the Web for information on computer-related careers, milestones in computer history, important people and companies, emerging technologies, and the applications and implications of different technologies.

The History of the PC

D o you ever wonder how big the first personal computer was, or how much the first portable computer weighed? Computers are such an integral part of our lives that we don't often stop to think about how far they've come or where they got their start. In just 35 years, computers have evolved from expensive, huge machines that only corporations owned to small, powerful devices found in millions of homes. In this Technology in Focus feature, we look at the history of the computer. Along the way, we will discuss some developments that helped make the computer powerful and portable, as well as some people who contributed to its development. However, we will start with the story of the personal computer and how it grew to be as integral to our lives as the automobile is.

The First Personal Computer: The Altair

Our journey through the history of the personal computer starts in 1975. At that time, most people were unfamiliar with the mainframes and supercomputers that large corporations and the government owned. With price tags exceeding the cost of buildings, and with few if any practical home uses, these monster machines were not appealing or attainable to the vast majority of Americans. That began to change when the January 1975 cover of *Popular Electronics* announced the debut of the **Altair 8800**, touted as the first personal computer (see Figure 1). For just $395 for a do-it-yourself kit or $498 for a fully assembled unit (about $2,000 in today's dollars), the price was reasonable enough that computer fanatics could finally own their own computers.

The Altair was a very primitive computer, with just 256 bytes (not *kilo* bytes, just bytes) of memory. It didn't come with a keyboard, nor did it include a monitor or printer. Switches on the front of the machine were used to enter data in machine code (strings of 1s and 0s). Flashing lights on the front indicated the results of a program. User-friendly it was not—at least by today's standards.

Despite its limitations, computer "hackers" (as computer enthusiasts were called then) flocked to the machine. Many people who bought the Altair had been taught to program, but until that point, they had access only to big, clumsy computers. These people were often hired by corporations to program routine financial, statistical, or engineering programs in a workplace environment. The Altair offered these enthusiasts the opportunity to create their own programs. Within three months, Micro Instrumentation and Telemetry Systems (MITS), the company behind the Altair, received more than 4,000 orders for the machine.

The release of the Altair marked the start of the personal computer (PC) boom. In fact, two men who would play large roles in the development of the PC were among the first Altair owners. Recent high school graduates Bill Gates and Paul Allen were so enamored by this "minicomputer," as these personal computers were called at the time, that they wrote a compiling program

Why Was It Called the "Altair"?

For lack of a better name, the Altair's developers originally called the computer the PE-8, short for Popular Electronics 8-bit. However, Les Soloman, the *Popular Electronics* writer who introduced the Altair, wanted the machine to have a catchier name. The author's daughter, who was watching *Star Trek* at the time, suggested the name Altair. (That's where the *Star Trek* crew was traveling that week.) The first star of the PC industry was born.

Figure 1

In 1975, the Altair was touted as the "world's first minicomputer" in the January issue of Popular Electronics.

(a program that translates user commands into commands that the computer can understand) for the Altair. The two friends later convinced the Altair's developer, Ed Roberts, to buy their program. This marked the start of a small company called Microsoft. We'll get to that story later. First, let's see what their future archrivals were up to.

The Apple I and II

Around the time the Altair was released, **Steve Wozniak**, an employee at Hewlett-Packard, was becoming fascinated with the burgeoning personal computer industry and was dabbling with his own computer design. He would bring his computer prototypes to meetings of the Homebrew Computing Club, a group of young

Figure 2 *Steve Jobs (a) and Steve Wozniak (b) were two computer hobbyists who worked together to form the Apple Computer Company.*

Figure 3 *The first Apple computer, the Apple I, looked like a typewriter in a box. It was one of the first computers to incorporate a keyboard.*

computer fans in Palo Alto, California who met to discuss computer ideas. **Steve Jobs**, who was working for computer game manufacturer Atari at the time, liked Wozniak's prototypes and made a few suggestions. Together, the two built a personal computer, later known as the **Apple I**, in Wozniak's garage (see Figures 2 and 3). In that same year, on April 1, 1976, Jobs and Wozniak officially formed the **Apple Computer Company**.

No sooner had the Apple I hit the market than Wozniak began working to improve it. A year later, in 1977, the **Apple II** was born (see Figure 4). The Apple II included a color monitor, sound, and game paddles. Priced around $1,300 (almost $4,700 in today's dollars), it included 4 kilobytes (KB) of random access memory (RAM) as well as an optional floppy disk drive that enabled users to run additional programs. Most of these programs were games. However, for many users, there was a special appeal to the Apple II: The program that made the computer function when the power was first turned on (the operating system) was stored in read-only memory (ROM).

Figure 4 *The Apple II came with a monitor and an external floppy disk drive.*

Previously, the operating system had to be rewritten every time the computer was turned on The friendly features of the operating system on the Apple II, such as automatic loading, encouraged less technically oriented computer enthusiasts to try writing their own software programs.

An instant success, the Apple II would be the most successful product in the company's early line, outshining even its successor, the **Apple III**, which was released in 1980. Eventually, the Apple II would include a spreadsheet program, a word processor, and desktop publishing software. These programs gave personal computers like the Apple functions beyond gaming and special programming, and led to their increased popularity. We will talk more about these advances later. For now, we will look at which other players were entering the market.

Enter the Competition

Around the time that Apple was experiencing success with its computers, a number of competitors entered the market. The largest among them were Commodore, RadioShack, and IBM. As Figure 5 shows, just a few years after the introduction of the Altair, the market was filled with personal computers from a variety of manufacturers.

The Commodore PET and TRS-80

Among Apple's strongest competitors were the **Commodore PET 2001**, shown in Figure 6, and Tandy RadioShack's **TRS-80**, shown in Figure 7. Commodore introduced the PET in January 1977. It was featured on the cover of *Popular Science* in October 1977 as the "new $595 home computer." Tandy RadioShack's home computer also garnered immediate popularity. Just one month after its release in 1977, the TRS-80 Model 1 had sold approximately 10,000 units. Priced at $594.95, the easy-to-use machine included a monochrome display and 4 KB of memory. Many other manufacturers followed suit over the next decade, launching new desktop computers, but none were as successful as the TRS-80 and the Commodore.

The Osborne

The Osborne Company introduced the industry's first portable computer, the **Osborne**, in April 1981 (see Figure 8). Although portable, the computer weighed 24.5 pounds, and its screen was just five inches wide. In addition to its hefty weight, it came with a hefty price tag of $1,795. Still, the Osborne included 64 KB of memory, two floppy disk drives, and preinstalled programs such as word processing and spreadsheet software. The Osborne was an overnight success, and its sales quickly reached 10,000 units per month. Despite the Osborne's popularity, the

Why Is It Called "Apple"?

Steve Jobs wanted Apple Computer to be the "perfect" computer company. Having recently worked at an apple orchard, Jobs thought of the apple as the "perfect" fruit because it was high in nutrients, came in a nice package, and was not easily damaged. Thus, he and Wozniak decided to name their new computer company Apple.

Figure 5

Personal Computer Development

YEAR	APPLE	IBM	OTHER
1975			MITS Altair
1976	Apple I		
1977	Apple II		Tandy RadioShack's TRS-80 Commodore PET
1980	Apple III		
1981		IBM PC	Osborne
1983	Lisa		
1984	Macintosh	286-AT	IBM PC clones

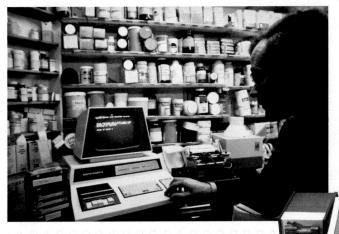

Figure 7 *The TRS-80 hid its circuitry under the keyboard. The computer was nicknamed "trash-80," which was more a play on its initials than a reflection of its capabilities.*

Figure 6 *The Commodore PET was well received because of its all-in-one design.*

Photo Courtesy of The Computer History Museum

release of a successor machine, called the **Executive**, reduced sales of the Osborne significantly, and the Osborne Company eventually closed. Compaq bought the Osborne design and in 1983 produced its first portable computer.

IBM PCs

By 1980, IBM recognized that it needed to get its feet wet in the personal computer market. Up until that point, the company had been a player in the computer industry, but primarily made mainframe computers, which it sold only to large corporations. It had not taken the smaller personal computer seriously. In August 1981, however, IBM released its first personal computer, appropriately named the **IBM PC**. Because many companies were already familiar with IBM mainframes, they readily adopted the IBM PC. The term *PC* soon became

Photo Courtesy of The Computer History Museum

Figure 8 *The Osborne was introduced as the first portable personal computer. It weighed a whopping 24.5 pounds and contained just 64 KB of memory.*

the term used to describe all personal computers.

The IBM PC came with 64 KB of memory, expandable to 256 KB, and prices started at $1,565. IBM marketed its PC through retail outlets such as Sears and Computerland in order to reach the home market, and it quickly dominated the playing field. In January 1983, *Time* magazine, playing on its annual "man of the year" issue, named the computer "1982 machine of the year" (see Figure 9).

Other Important Advancements

It was not just the **hardware** of the personal computer that was developing during the 1970s and 1980s. At the same time, advances in programming languages and operating systems and the influx of application software were leading to more useful and powerful machines.

Figure 9 *The IBM PC was the first (and only) nonhuman object chosen as "man of the year" (actually, "machine of the year") by* Time *magazine. This designation, in* Time's *January 1983 issue, indicated the impact the PC was having on the general public.*

The Importance of BASIC

The software industry began in the 1950s with the development of programming languages such as FORTRAN, ALGOL, and COBOL. These languages were used mainly by businesses to create financial, statistical, and engineering programs for corporate enterprises. However, the 1964 introduction of **Beginners All-Purpose Symbolic Instruction Code (BASIC)** revolutionized the software industry. BASIC was a programming language that the beginning programming student could easily learn. It thus became enormously popular—and the key language of the PC. In fact, **Bill Gates** and **Paul Allen** (see Figure 10) used BASIC to write their program for the Altair. As we noted earlier, this program led to the creation of **Microsoft**, a company that produced software for the microcomputer.

Figure 10 *Bill Gates and Paul Allen are the founders of Microsoft.*

The Advent of Operating Systems

Because data on the earliest personal computers was stored on audiocassettes (not floppy disks), many programs were not saved or reused. Rather, programs were rewritten as needed. Eventually Steve Wozniak developed a floppy disk drive called the **Disk II**, which he introduced in July 1978. With the introduction of the floppy drive, programs could be saved with more efficiency, and operating systems (OSs) developed.

Operating systems were (and still are) written to coordinate with the specific processor chip that controlled the computer. Apples ran exclusively on a Motorola chip, while PCs (IBMs and so on) ran exclusively on an Intel chip. **Disk Operating System (DOS)**, developed by Wozniak and introduced in December 1977, was the OS that controlled the first Apple computers. The **Control Program for Microcomputers (CP/M)**, developed by Gary Kildall, was the first OS designed for the Intel 8080 chip (the processor for PCs). Intel hired Kildall to write a compiling program for the 8080 chip, but Kildall quickly saw the need for a program that could store computer operating instructions on a floppy disk rather than on a cassette. Intel wasn't interested in buying the CP/M program, but Kildall saw a future for the program and thus founded his own company, Digital Research.

In 1980, when IBM was considering entering the personal computer market, it approached Bill Gates at Microsoft to write an OS program for the IBM PC. Although Gates had written versions of BASIC for different computer systems, he had never written an OS. He therefore recommended that IBM investigate the CP/M OS, but no one from Digital Research returned IBM's call. Microsoft reconsidered the opportunity and developed **MS-DOS** for IBM computers. (This was one phone call that Digital Research certainly regretted not returning!)

MS-DOS was based on an OS called **Quick and Dirty Operating System (QDOS)** that was developed by Seattle Computer Products. Microsoft bought the nonexclusive rights to QDOS and distributed it to IBM. Eventually, virtually all personal computers running on the Intel chip used MS-DOS as their OS. Microsoft's reign as one of the dominant players in the PC landscape had begun. Meanwhile, many other programs were being developed, taking personal computers to the next level of user acceptance.

The Software Application Explosion: VisiCalc and Beyond

Inclusion of floppy disk drives in personal computers not only facilitated the storage of operating systems, but also set off an application software explosion, because the floppy disk was a convenient way to distribute software. Around that same time, in 1978, Harvard Business School student Dan Bricklin recognized the potential for a spreadsheet program that could be used on PCs. He and his friend Bob Frankston (see Figure 11) created the program **VisiCalc**. VisiCalc not only became an instant success, but was also one of the main reasons for the rapid increase in PC sales. Finally, ordinary home users could see how owning a personal computer could benefit their lives. More than 100,000 copies of VisiCalc were sold in its first year.

Figure 11 *Dan Bricklin and Bob Frankston created VisiCalc, the first business application developed for the personal computer.*

After VisiCalc, other electronic spreadsheet programs entered the market. **Lotus 1-2-3** came on the market in 1982, and **Microsoft Excel** entered the scene in 1985. These two products became so popular that they eventually put VisiCalc out of business.

Meanwhile, word processing software was gaining a foothold in the PC industry. Up to this point, there were separate, dedicated word processing machines, and the thought hadn't occurred to anyone to enable the personal computer to do word processing. Personal computers, it was believed, were for computation and data management. However, once **WordStar**, the first word processing application, came out in disk form in 1979 and became available for personal computers, word processing became another important use for the PC. In fact, word processing is now one of the most common PC applications. Competitors such as **Word for MS-DOS** (the precursor to Microsoft Word) and **WordPerfect** soon entered the market. Figure 12 lists some of the important dates in application software development.

The Graphical User Interface

Another important advancement in personal computers was the introduction of the **graphical user interface (GUI)**, which allowed users to interact with the computer more easily. Until that time, users had to use complicated command- or menu-driven interfaces to interact with the computer. Apple was the first company to take full commercial advantage of the GUI, but competitors were fast on its heels, and soon the GUI became synonymous with personal computers. Who developed the idea of the GUI?

You'll probably be surprised to learn that a company known for its photocopiers was the real innovator.

Xerox

In 1972, a few years before Apple launched its first PC, photocopier manufacturer **Xerox** was hard at work in its Palo Alto Research Center (PARC) designing a personal computer of its own. Named the **Alto** (shown in Figure 13), the computer included a word processor, based on the What You See Is What You Get (WYSIWYG) principle, that incorporated a file management system with directories and folders. It also had a mouse and could connect to a network. None of the other personal computers of the time had any of these features. For a variety of reasons, Xerox never sold the Alto commercially. Several years later, it developed the Star Office System, which was based on the Alto. Despite its convenient features, the Star never became popular, because no one was willing to pay the $17,000 asking price.

The Lisa and the Macintosh

Xerox's ideas were ahead of its time, but many of the ideas of the Alto and Star would soon catch on. In 1983, Apple introduced the **Lisa**,

Figure 12	*Application Software Development*
YEAR	**APPLICATION**
1978	**VisiCalc:** First electronic spreadsheet application. **WordStar:** First word processing application.
1980	**WordPerfect:** Thought even now to be the best word processing software for the PC, WordPerfect was eventually sold to Novell, and was later acquired by Corel.
1982	**Lotus 1-2-3:** Added integrated charting, plotting, and database capabilities to spreadsheet software.
1983	**Word for MS-DOS:** Introduced in the pages of *PC World* magazine on the first magazine-inserted demo disk.
1985	**Excel:** One of the first spreadsheets to use a graphical user interface. **PageMaker:** The first desktop publishing software.

Figure 13 *The Alto was the first computer to use a graphical user interface, and it provided the basis for the GUI that Apple used. However, because of marketing problems, the Alto never was sold.*

figure 14 *The Lisa was the first computer to introduce a GUI to the market. Priced too high, it never gained the popularity it deserved.*

shown in Figure 14. Named after Apple founder Steve Jobs's daughter, the Lisa was the first successful PC brought to market that used a GUI. Legend has it that Jobs had seen the Alto during a visit to PARC in 1979 and was influenced by its GUI. He therefore incorporated a similar user interface into the Lisa, providing features such as windows, drop-down menus, icons, a hierarchical file system with folders and files, and a point-and-click device called a mouse. The only problem with the Lisa was its price. At $9,995 ($21,530 in today's dollars), few buyers were willing to take the plunge.

A year later, in 1984, Apple introduced the **Macintosh**, shown in Figure 15. The Macintosh was everything the Lisa was and then some, and at about a third of the cost. The Macintosh was also the first personal computer to utilize 3.5-inch floppy disks with a hard cover, which were smaller and sturdier than the previous 5.25-inch floppies.

The Internet Boom

The GUI made it easier for users to work on the computer. The Internet provided another reason for consumers to buy computers. Now they could conduct research and communicate with each other in a new and convenient way. In 1993, the Web browser **Mosaic** was introduced. This browser allowed users to view multimedia on the Web, causing Internet traffic to increase by nearly 350 percent.

Meanwhile, companies discovered the Internet as a means to do business, and computer sales took off. IBM-compatible PCs became the personal computer system of choice when, in 1995, Microsoft (the predominant software provider to PCs) introduced Internet Explorer, a Web browser that integrated Web functionality into Microsoft Office applications, and **Windows 95**, the first Microsoft OS designed to be principally a GUI OS, although it still was based on the DOS kernel.

About a year earlier, in mid-1994, Jim Clark, founder of the computer company Silicon

Figure 15 *The Macintosh became one of Apple's best-selling computers, incorporating a graphical user interface along with other innovations such as the 3.5-inch floppy disk drive.*

Graphics Inc., Marc Andreessen, and others from the Mosaic development team developed the Netscape commercial Web browser. Netscape's popularity grew quickly, and it soon became a predominant player in browser software. However, pressures from Microsoft became too strong. In the beginning of 1998, Netscape announced it was moving to the open source market, would no longer charge for the product, and would make the code available to the public.

Making the PC Possible: Early Computers

Since the first Altair was introduced in the 1970s, more than a billion personal computers have been distributed around the globe. Because of the declining prices of computers and the growth of the Internet, it's estimated that a billion more computers will be sold within the next decade. What made all of this possible? The computer is a compilation of parts, each of which is the result of individual inventions. From the earliest days

Figure 16 *The Jacquard Loom used holes punched in stiff cards to make complex designs. This technique would later be used in punch cards that controlled the input and output of data in computers.*

of humankind, we have been looking for a more systematic way to count and calculate. Thus, the evolution of counting machines led to the development of the computer we know today.

The Pascalene Calculator and the Jacquard Loom

The **Pascalene** was the first accurate mechanical calculator. This machine, created by the French mathematician **Blaise Pascal** in 1642, used revolutions of gears, like odometers in cars do, to count by tens. The Pascalene could be used to add, subtract, multiply, and divide. The basic design of the Pascalene was so sound that it lived on in mechanical calculators for more than 300 years.

Nearly 200 years later, **Joseph Jacquard** revolutionized the fabric industry by creating a machine that automated the weaving of complex patterns. Although not a counting or calculating machine, the **Jacquard loom** (shown in Figure 16) was significant because it relied on stiff cards with punched holes to automate the weaving process. Much later, this punch-card process would be adopted as a means for computers to record and read data.

Babbage's Engines

Decades later, in 1834, **Charles Babbage** designed the first automatic calculator, called the **Analytical Engine** (see Figure 17). The machine was actually based on another machine called the **Difference Engine**, which was a huge steam-powered mechanical calculator that Babbage designed to print astronomical tables. Babbage stopped working on the Difference Engine to build the Analytical Engine. Although it was never developed, Babbage's detailed drawings and descriptions of the Analytical Engine include components similar to those found in today's computers, including the store (akin to RAM) and the mill (a central processing unit), as well as input and output devices. This invention gave Charles Babbage the title of "father of computing."

Meanwhile, Ada Lovelace, who was the daughter of poet Lord Byron and was a student of mathematics (which was unusual for women of that time), was fascinated with Babbage's Engines. She translated an Italian paper on Babbage's machine, and at the request of Babbage added her own extensive notes. Her efforts are thought to be the best description of Babbage's Engines.

The Hollerith Tabulating Machine

In 1890, **Herman Hollerith**, while working for the U.S. Census Bureau, was the first to take Jacquard's punch-card concept and apply it to computing. Hollerith developed a machine called the **Hollerith Tabulating Machine** that used punch cards to tabulate census data. Up until that time, census data had been tabulated manually in a long, laborious process. Hollerith's tabulating machine automatically read data that had been punched onto small punch cards, speeding up the tabulation process. Hollerith's machine became so successful that he left the Census Bureau in 1896 to start the Tabulating Machine Company. His company later changed its name to International Business Machines, or IBM.

The Z1 and the Atanasoff–Berry Computer

German inventor **Konrad Zuse** is credited with a number of computing inventions. His first, in 1936, was a mechanical calculator called the **Z1**. The Z1 is thought to be the first computer to include certain features that are integral to today's systems, such as a control unit and separate memory functions. These were important breakthroughs for future computer design.

In late 1939, John Atanasoff, a professor at Iowa State University, and his student Clifford Berry built the first electrically powered digital computer, called the **Atanasoff–Berry Computer (ABC)**, shown in Figure 18. The computer was the first to use vacuum tubes, instead of the mechanical switches used in older computers, to store data. Although revolutionary at its time, the machine weighed 700 pounds, contained a mile of wire, and took about 15 seconds for each calculation. (In comparison, today's personal computers can perform billions and billions of calculations in

Figure 17 *The Analytical Engine, designed by Charles Babbage, was never fully developed, but included components similar to those found in today's computers.*

Photo Courtesy of The Computer History Museum

15 seconds.) Most importantly, the ABC was the first computer to use the binary system. It was also the first computer to have memory that repowered itself upon booting. The design of the ABC would end up being central to that of future computers.

The Harvard Mark I

From the late 1930s to the early 1950s, **Howard Aiken** and **Grace Hopper** designed the Mark series of computers at Harvard University. The U.S. Navy used these computers for ballistic and gunnery calculations. Aiken, an electrical engineer and physicist, designed the computer, while Hopper did the programming. The **Harvard Mark I**, finished in 1944, could perform all four arithmetic operations (addition, subtraction, multiplication, and division).

However, many believe Hopper's greatest contribution to computing was the invention of the **compiler**, a program that translates

Figure 18 *The Atanasoff–Berry Computer laid the design groundwork for many computers to come.*

English-language instructions into computer language. The team was also responsible for a common computer-related expression. Hopper was the first to "debug" a computer when she removed a moth that had flown into the Harvard Mark I and caused the computer to break down (see Figure 19). After that, problems that caused a computer not to run were called "bugs."

The Turing Machine

Meanwhile, in 1936, the British mathematician **Alan Turing** created an abstract computer model that could perform logical operations. The **Turing Machine** was not a real machine, but rather was a hypothetical model that mathematically defined a mechanical procedure (or algorithm). Additionally, Turing's concept described a process by which the machine could read, write, or erase symbols written on squares of an infinite paper tape. This concept of an infinite tape that could be read, written to, and erased was the precursor to today's RAM.

The ENIAC

The **Electronic Numerical Integrator and Computer (ENIAC)**, shown in Figure 20, was another U.S. government-sponsored machine developed to calculate the settings used for weapons.

Created by **John W. Mauchly** and **J. Presper Eckert** at the University of Pennsylvania, it was placed in operation in June 1944. Although the ENIAC is generally thought of as the first successful high-speed electronic digital computer, it was big and clumsy. The ENIAC used nearly 18,000 vacuum tubes and filled approximately 1,800 square feet of floor space. Although inconvenient, the ENIAC served its purpose and remained in use until 1955.

The UNIVAC

The **Universal Automatic Computer**, or **UNIVAC**, was the first commercially successful electronic digital computer. Completed in June 1951 and manufactured by the company Remington Rand, the UNIVAC operated on magnetic tape. This set it apart from its competitors, which ran on punch cards. The UNIVAC gained notoriety when, in a 1951 publicity stunt, it was used to predict the outcome of the Stevenson–Eisenhower presidential race. After analyzing only 5 percent of the popular vote, the UNIVAC correctly identified Dwight D. Eisenhower as the victor. After that, UNIVAC soon became a household word. The UNIVAC and computers like it were considered **first-generation computers** and were the last to use vacuum tubes to store data.

Figure 19 *Grace Hopper coined the term* computer bug *when a moth flew into the Harvard Mark I, causing it to break down.*

Actual moth pasted into notebook

Transistors and Beyond

Only a year after the ENIAC was completed, scientists at the Bell Telephone Laboratories in New Jersey invented the **transistor**, which was another means to store data. The transistor replaced the bulky vacuum tubes of earlier computers and was smaller and more powerful than tubes were. It was used in almost everything, from radios to phones. Computers that used transistors were referred to as **second-generation computers**. Still, transistors were limited as to how small they could be made.

A few years later, in 1958, **Jack Kilby**, while working at Texas Instruments, invented the world's first **integrated circuit**, a small chip capable of containing thousands of transistors. This consolidation in design enabled computers to become smaller and lighter. The computers in this early integrated-circuit generation were considered **third-generation computers**.

Other innovations in the computer industry further refined the computer's speed, accuracy, and efficiency. However, none were as significant as the 1971 introduction by the Intel Corporation of the **microprocessor chip**, a small chip containing millions of transistors. The microprocessor functions as the central processing unit (CPU), or brains, of the computer. Computers that used a microprocessor chip were called **fourth-generation computers**. Over time, Intel and Motorola became the leading manufacturers of microprocessors. Today, the Intel Itanium 2 chip, shown in Figure 21, is one of Intel's most powerful processors.

As you can see, personal computers have come a long way since the Altair, and have a number of inventions and people to thank for their amazing popularity. What will the future bring? If current trends continue, computers will be smaller, lighter, and more powerful. The advancement of wireless technology will also play a big role in the development of the personal computer.

Photo Courtesy of The Computer History Museum

Figure 20 *The ENIAC took up an entire room and required several people to manipulate it.*

Figure 21 *The Intel Itanium 2 is one of Intel's most powerful processors.*

two
looking at
computers:
understanding the parts

objectives

After reading this chapter, you should be able to answer the following questions:

1. What exactly is a computer, and what are its four main functions? *(p. 50)*
2. What is the difference between data and information? *(p. 50)*
3. What are bits and bytes, and how are they measured? *(pp. 50–51)*
4. What devices do I use to get data into the computer? *(pp. 53–61)*
5. What devices do I use to get information out of the computer? *(pp. 61–67)*
6. What's on the motherboard? *(p. 69–70)*
7. Where are information and programs stored? *(pp. 71–73)*
8. How are devices connected to the computer? *(pp. 74–77)*
9. How do I set up my computer to avoid strain and injury? *(pp. 78–81)*

resources

Active Helpdeskk

- Understanding Bits and Bytes **(p. 51)**
- Using Input Devices **(p. 58)**
- Using Output Devices **(p. 64)**
- Exploring Storage Devices and Ports **(p. 74)**

Sound Bytes

- Binary Numbers Interactive **(p. 50)**
- Tablet and Notebook Tour **(p. 59)**
- Virtual Computer Tour **(p. 70)**
- Port Tour: How Do I Hook It Up? **(p. 75)**
- Healthy Computing **(p. 80)**

Companion Website

The Companion Website includes a variety of additional materials to help you review and learn more about the topics in this chapter. Go to: *pearsonhighered.com/techinaction*

how cool is *this?* If you have ever thought

about **customizing** the layout of your **keyboard**, this Luxeed Dynamic Pixel LED Keyboard is the one for you. If you're a gamer, you can program specific keys to control your game and to **glow** with different colors that indicate each key **action**. If you're not a gamer but just would like to add a bit of fun to your otherwise dull keyboard, you can **animate** colored scenarios to "play" on the keys, or create an **illuminated** pattern or design. With 430 LEDs, the Luxeed is capable of individually lighting each key in your choice of color.

The keyboard comes in either black or white. The keys of the white keyboard light up more brightly and have a semi-transparent look. The keys of the black keyboard can be set so just the letters light up.

Understanding Your Computer

After reading Chapter 1, you can see why becoming computer literate is so important. But where do you start? You've no doubt gleaned some knowledge about computers just from being a member of society. However, although you certainly know what a computer is, do you really understand how it works, what all its parts are, and what these parts do? In this section, we discuss what a computer does and how its functions make it such a useful machine.

Computers Are Data Processing Devices

Strictly defined, a **computer** is a data processing device that performs four major functions:

1. It *gathers* data, or allows users to input data.
2. It *processes* that data into information.
3. It *outputs* data and information.
4. It *stores* data and information.

What is the difference between data and information? People often use the terms *data* and *information* interchangeably. Although they may mean the same thing in a simple conversation, the actual distinction between data and information is an important one.

In computer terms, **data** is a representation of a fact, figure, or idea. Data can be a number, a word, a picture, or even a recording of sound. For example, the number 6125553297 and the names Derek and Washington are pieces of data. Alone, these pieces of data probably mean little to you.

Information is data that has been organized or presented in a meaningful fashion. When your computer provides you with a contact listing that indicates Derek Washington can be reached by phone at (612) 555-3297, then the previous data suddenly becomes useful—that is, it becomes information.

How do computers interact with data and information? Computers are excellent at **processing** (manipulating or organizing) data into information. When you first arrived on campus, you probably were directed to a place where you could get an ID card. You most likely provided a clerk with personal data (such as your name and address) that was entered into a computer. The clerk then took your picture with a digital camera (collecting more data). This information was then processed appropriately so that it could be printed on your ID card (see Figure 2.1). This organized output of data on your ID card is useful information. Finally, the information was probably stored as digital data on the computer for later use.

Bits and Bytes: The Language of Computers

How do computers process data into information? Unlike humans, computers work exclusively with numbers (not words). To process data into information, computers need to work in a language they understand.

SOUND BYTE   Binary Numbers Interactive

This Sound Byte helps remove the mystery surrounding binary numbers. You'll learn about base conversion between decimal, binary, and hexadecimal interactively using colors, sounds, and images.

Figure 2.1

Computers process data into information.

This language, called **binary language**, consists of just two digits: 0 and 1. Everything a computer does, such as processing data or printing a report, is broken down into a series of 0s and 1s. Each 0 and 1 is a **binary digit**, or **bit** for short. Eight binary digits (or bits) combine to create one **byte**. In computers, each letter of the alphabet, each number, and each special character (such as the @ sign) consists of a unique combination of eight bits, or a string of eight 0s and 1s. So, for example, in binary (computer) language, the letter K is represented as 01001011. This equals eight bits, or one byte. (We discuss binary language in more detail in the Under the Hood TIF.)

What else can bits and bytes be used for? You've probably heard the terms *kilobyte (KB)*, *megabyte (MB)*, and *gigabyte (GB)*. Bits and bytes not only are used as the language that tells the computer what to do, but also are what the computer uses to represent the data and information that it inputs and outputs. Word processing files, digital pictures, and even software are represented inside a computer as a series of bits and bytes. These files and applications can be quite large, containing thousands or millions of bytes.

To make it easier to measure the size of these files, we need units of measure larger than a byte. Kilobytes, megabytes, and

ACTIVE HELP-DESK | **Understanding Bits and Bytes**

In this Active Helpdesk call, you'll play the role of a helpdesk staffer, fielding calls about the difference between data and information, what bits and bytes are, and how they are measured.

gigabytes are therefore simply amounts of bytes. As shown in Figure 2.2, a **kilobyte (KB)** is approximately 1,000 bytes, a **megabyte (MB)** is about 1 million bytes, and a **gigabyte (GB)** is around 1 billion bytes. As our information-processing needs have grown, so too have our storage needs. Today, many business computers can store up to a petabyte of data, and the Google search engine processes more than 20 petabytes of data per day—that's a lot of bytes!

How does your computer process bits and bytes? Your computer uses a combination of hardware and software to process data into information and enable you to complete tasks such as writing a letter or playing a game. An anonymous person once said that hardware is any part of a computer that you can kick when it doesn't work properly. A more formal definition of **hardware** is "any part of the computer you can physically touch."

Figure 2.2 | HOW MUCH IS A BYTE?

Name	Abbreviation	Number of Bytes	Relative Size
Byte	B	1 byte	Can hold one character of data.
Kilobyte	KB	1,024 bytes (2^{10} bytes)	Can hold 1,024 characters or about half of a double-spaced typewritten page.
Megabyte	MB	1,048,576 bytes (2^{20} bytes)	Can hold approximately 768 pages of typed text.
Gigabyte	GB	1,073,741,824 bytes (2^{30} bytes)	Approximately 786,432 pages of text; 500 sheets of paper is approximately 2 inches, so this represents a stack of paper 262 feet high.
Terabyte	TB	1,099,511,627,776 bytes (2^{40} bytes)	This represents a stack of typewritten pages almost 51 miles high.
Petabyte	PB	1,125,899,906,842,62 bytes (2^{50} bytes)	The stack of pages is now 52,000 miles high, or approximately one-fourth the distance from the Earth to the moon.
Exabyte	EB	1,152,921,504,606,846,976 bytes (2^{60} bytes)	The stack of pages is now 52 million miles high, or just about twice the distance between the Earth and Venus.
Zettabyte	ZB	1,180,591,620,717,411,303,424 bytes (2^{70} bytes)	The stack of pages is now 52 billion miles high. That's some 20 times the distance between the Earth and Pluto.

However, a computer needs more than just hardware to work: It also needs some form of software (computer programs). Think of a book without words or a CD without music. Without words or music, these two common items are just shells that hold nothing.

Similarly, a computer without software is a shell full of hardware components that can't do anything. *Software* is the set of computer programs that enables the hardware to perform different tasks. There are two broad categories of software: application software and system software.

When you think of software, you are most likely thinking of application software. **Application software** is the set of programs you use on a computer to help you carry out tasks such as writing a research paper. If you've ever typed a document, created a spreadsheet, or edited a digital photo, for example, then you've used a form of application software.

System software is the set of programs that enables your computer's hardware devices and application software to work together. The most common type of system software is the **operating system (OS)**—the program that controls the way in which your computer system functions. It manages the hardware of the computer system, such as the monitor and the printer. The operating system also provides a means by which users can interact with the computer. We'll cover software in greater depth in Chapters 4 and 5. For the rest of this chapter, we'll explore hardware.

Your Computer's Hardware

Are all computers the same?

Considering the amount of amazing things computers can do, they are really quite simple machines. You learned in the previous section that a basic computer system is made up of software and hardware. There are two basic designs of computers. A **notebook computer** (or laptop computer) is a portable computer that is powered by batteries (or a handy electrical outlet) and has

Figure 2.3

The Apple iMac is an example of an all-in-one computer.

keyboards, monitors, and other devices integrated into a single compact case. A **desktop computer** is intended for use at a single location. Desktop computers consist of a separate case that houses the main components of the computer plus peripheral devices. A **peripheral device** is a component, such as a monitor or keyboard, which is connected to the computer. An **all-in-one computer** such as the Apple iMac (see Figure 2.3), the Dell XPS One, or the Gateway One houses not just the computer's processor and memory but also its monitor.

Are there other types of computers besides desktop and notebook computers? Desktop and notebook computers are the computers that you will most likely encounter. Although you may never come into direct contact with the following types of computers, they are still important to our society:

- A **mainframe** is a large, expensive computer that supports hundreds of users simultaneously. Mainframes are often used in insurance companies, for example, where many people are working on similar operations (such as claims processing) all at once. Your college also may use mainframe computers to handle the multitude of processing needs throughout the campus. Mainframes excel at executing many different computer programs at the same time.

- A **supercomputer** is a specially designed computer that can perform complex calculations extremely rapidly. Supercomputers are used in situations in which complex models requiring intensive mathematical calculations are needed (such as weather forecasting or atomic energy research). The main difference between a supercomputer and a mainframe is that supercomputers are designed to execute a few programs as quickly as possible, while mainframes

Data

Input

Processing

Storage

Output

Information

Figure 2.4

Each part of the computer serves a special function.

are designed to handle many programs running at the same time but at a slower pace.

• An **embedded computer** is a specially designed computer chip that resides inside another device, such as your car or the electronic thermostat in your home. Embedded computers are self-contained computer devices that have their own programming and typically neither receive input from you nor interact with other systems.

In the following sections, we look more closely at your computer's hardware (the parts you can actually touch). Each part has a specific purpose that coordinates with one of the functions of the computer—input, processing, output, or storage (see Figure 2.4).

Additional devices, such as modems and routers, help a computer communicate with the Internet and other computers to facilitate the sharing of documents and other resources. We begin our exploration of hardware by looking at your computer's input devices.

used to enter typed data and commands, and a **mouse** is used to enter user responses and commands.

There are other input devices as well. Microphones input sounds, and scanners and digital cameras input nondigital text and digital images, respectively. A **stylus** is an input device that looks like a skinny pen but has no ink. Electronic pens are also becoming quite popular and are often used in conjunction with graphics tablets that can translate a user's handwriting into digital input.

Keyboards

Aren't all keyboards the same? Most desktop and notebook computers come with a standard **QWERTY keyboard** (see Figure 2.5). This keyboard layout gets its name from the first six letters in the top-left row of alphabetic keys on the keyboard and is the standard English-language keyboard layout. Over the years, there has been some debate over what is the best keyboard layout. The QWERTY layout was originally designed for typewriters and was meant to slow typists down and prevent typewriter keys from jamming. Although the QWERTY layout is considered inefficient because it slows typing speeds, efforts to change to more efficient layouts,

Input Devices

An **input device** enables you to enter data (text, images, and sounds) and instructions (user responses and commands) into the computer. The most common input devices are the keyboard and the mouse. A **keyboard** is

Figure 2.5

Most notebook and desktop keyboards share the same QWERTY keyboard layout.

such as that of the Dvorak keyboard, have not been met with much public interest. The Dvorak keyboard is an alternative keyboard layout that puts the most commonly used letters in the English language on "home keys," which are the keys in the middle row of the keyboard The Dvorak keyboard's design reduces the distance your fingers travel for most keystrokes, increasing typing speed.

How do notebook keyboards differ? To save space and weight, some of the smaller notebook keyboards (14" and under) are more compact than standard desktop keyboards and, therefore, have fewer keys. To retain the same functionality as a standard keyboard, many of the notebook keys have alternate functions. For example, many notebook keyboards do not have a separate numeric keypad. Instead, some letter keys function as number keys when they are pressed in combination with another key such as the function (Fn) key. The keys you use as numeric keys on notebooks have number notations on them so you can tell which keys to use (see Figure 2.6).

What if the standard keyboard doesn't work for me? Because users are demanding more portability from their computing devices, recent development efforts have focused on reducing the size and weight of keyboards. Flexible keyboards are terrific if you want a full-sized keyboard for your notebook. You can roll one up and fit it in your backpack. The virtual laser keyboard (see Figure 2.7) is about the size of a cellular phone. It projects the image of a keyboard on any surface, and sensors detect the motion of your fingers as you "type" on a desk or other flat surface. Data is transmitted via **Bluetooth** technology, which is a wireless transmission standard that facilitates the connection of electronic computing devices such as cell phones, smartphones, and computers to peripheral devices such as keyboards and headsets. We'll discuss Bluetooth in further detail in Chapter 8.

Gamers love keyboards such as the DX1 from Ergodex (see Figure 2.7). These keyboards allow placement of the keys in any position on the keyboard pad. The keys can be programmed to execute individual keystrokes or macros (a series of tasks) to perform specific tasks. This makes it easy for gamers to configure a keyboard in the most desirable way for each game they play.

How can I use my keyboard most efficiently? All keyboards have the standard set of alphabetic and numeric keys that you regularly use when typing. As shown in Figure 2.8, many keyboards for notebook and desktop computers have additional keys that perform special functions. Knowing how to use these special keys will help you improve your efficiency.

- The numeric keypad allows you to enter numbers quickly.
- Function keys act as shortcut keys you press to perform special tasks. They are sometimes referred to as the "F" keys because they start with the letter F followed by a number. Each software application has its own set of tasks assigned to various function keys. For example, the F2 key moves text or graphics in Microsoft Word but allows editing of the active cell in Microsoft Excel. Many keys are universal: the F1 key is the Help key in most applications.
- The Control (Ctrl) key is used in combination with other keys to perform shortcuts and special tasks. For example, holding down the Control (Ctrl) key while pressing the B key adds bold formatting to selected text. The Alt key works with other keys to execute additional shortcuts and special tasks. (On Macs, the Control function is the Apple key or Command key, and the Alt function is the Option key.)
- The Windows key is specific to the Windows operating system. Used alone, it opens the Start menu, although you use it most often in combination with other keys to perform shortcuts. For example, in

Figure 2.6

On many notebooks, certain letter keys can function as number keys.

a

b

Windows 7 and Vista, pressing the Windows key plus the M key minimizes all windows.

What are some other features on keyboards? Some keyboards (such as the one shown in Figure 2.8) also include multimedia and Internet keys or buttons that enable you to open a Web browser, view e-mail, access Help features, or control your CD/DVD player. These buttons are not always in the same position on every keyboard, but the symbols on top of the buttons generally help you determine their function. Some desktop keyboards include USB ports to facilitate attaching other devices, such as mice.

Another set of controls on standard keyboards are the cursor control keys that move your *cursor* (the flashing *I* symbol on the monitor that indicates where the next character will be inserted). A cursor control key is also known as an *arrow key* because each one is represented by an arrow on standard keyboards. The arrow keys move the cursor one space at a time in a document, either up, down, left, or right.

Above the arrow keys, you'll usually find keys that move the cursor up or down one full page or even to the document's beginning (Home), or to the end of a line of text or

Figure 2.8

Keyboards have a variety of keys that help you work more efficiently.

Keystroke Shortcuts

Did you know that you can combine certain keystrokes to take shortcuts within an application, such as Microsoft Word, or within the operating system itself? The following are a few of the most helpful Windows shortcuts. Use them to make more efficient use of your time. For more shortcuts for Windows-based PCs, visit **support.microsoft.com**. For a list of shortcuts for Macs, see **apple.com/support**.

Text Formatting	File Management	Cut/Copy/ Paste	Windows Controls
CTRL+B Applies (or removes) **bold** formatting to selected text	**CTRL+O** Opens the Open dialog box	**CTRL+X** Cuts (removes) selected text from document	**Alt+F4** Closes the current window
CTRL+I Applies (or removes) *italic* formatting to selected text	**CTRL+N** Opens a new document	**CTRL+C** Copies selected text	**Ctrl+Esc** Opens the Start menu
CTRL+U Applies (or removes) underlining to selected text	**CTRL+S** Saves a document	**CTRL+V** Pastes selected text (previously cut or copied)	**Windows Key + F1** Opens Windows Help
	CTRL+P Opens the Print dialog box		**Windows Key + F** Opens the Search (Find Files) dialog box

Insert key inserts new text within a line of existing text. When toggled off, the Insert key replaces (or overwrites) existing characters with new characters as you type. Other toggle keys that switch between an on state and an off state include the Num Lock key and the Caps Lock key.

Are all conventional keyboards connected to the computer via wires? Although most desktop PCs ship with wired keyboards, wireless keyboards are available. Wireless keyboards are powered by batteries. They send data to the computer using a form of wireless technology that uses radio frequency (RF). A radio transmitter in the keyboard sends out radio wave signals that are received in two ways. In one, a small receiving device sits on your desk and is plugged into the back of the computer where the keyboard would normally plug in. In the case of Bluetooth-compatible computers, a receiving device is contained in the system unit. RF keyboards used on home computers can be placed as far as 6 feet to 30 feet from the computer, depending on their quality. RF keyboards that are used in business conference rooms or auditoriums can be placed as far as 100 feet away from the computer, but they are far more expensive than traditional wired keyboards.

document (End). The Delete (Del) key allows you to delete characters, and the Insert key allows you to insert or overwrite characters within a document. The Insert key is a *toggle key* because its function changes between one of two options each time you press it: When toggled on, the

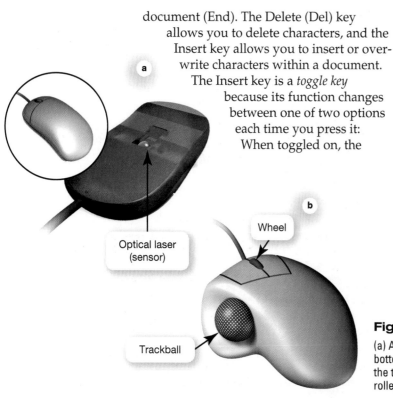

Optical laser (sensor)

Wheel

Trackball

Mice and Other Pointing Devices

What kinds of mice are there? The mouse type you're probably most familiar with is the **optical mouse** (see Figure 2.9). An optical mouse uses an internal sensor or laser to detect the mouse's movement. The sensor sends signals to the computer, telling it where to move the pointer on the screen. Optical mice are often preferable to other types of mice because they have few moving parts, which lessens the chances that dirt will interfere with the mechanisms or that parts will break down. Optical mice also do not require a mouse pad, though you can still use one to protect your work surface from being scratched. Optical mice are most common now, but you may still find a mouse at

Figure 2.9

(a) An optical mouse has an optical laser (or sensor) on the bottom that detects its movement. (b) A trackball mouse turns the traditional mouse on its back, allowing you to control the rollerball with your fingers.

home or in school that has a rollerball on the bottom, which moves when you drag the mouse across a mouse pad. The movement of the rollerball controls the movement of the cursor that appears on the screen.

A **trackball mouse** (see Figure 2.9) is basically a traditional mouse that has been turned on its back. The rollerball sits on top or on the side of the mouse, and you move the ball with your fingers, allowing the mouse to remain stationary. A trackball mouse doesn't demand much wrist motion, so it's considered better for the wrist than an optical mouse. Mice also have two or three buttons that enable you to execute commands and open shortcut menus. (Mice for Macs sometimes have only one button.) Many mice have additional programmable buttons and wheels that let you quickly scroll through documents or Web pages.

Do notebook computers include a mouse? Most notebooks do not come with a mouse. Instead, they have an integrated pointing device such as a **touchpad**, a small, touch-sensitive area at the base of the keyboard (see Figure 2.10). To use the touchpad, you simply move your finger across the pad. Some touchpads are sensitive to taps, interpreting them as mouse clicks, while others have buttons beneath the pads to record mouse clicks. Other notebooks incorporate a **trackpoint device**, a small, joystick-like nub that allows you to move the cursor with the tip of your finger.

Are there wireless mice? Just as there are wireless keyboards, there are wireless mice, both optical and trackball. Wireless mice are similar to wireless keyboards in that they use batteries and send data to the computer by radio frequency or Bluetooth technologies. If you have an RF wireless keyboard, then your RF wireless mouse and keyboard usually can share the same RF receiver. Wireless mice for notebooks have their own receivers that

Figure 2.10

Touchpads and trackpoint devices take the place of a mouse on notebook computers.

often clip into the bottom of the mouse for easy storage when not in use.

Small, compact devices like the MoGo Mouse (see Figure 2.11) are designed for portability. The MoGo Mouse fits into a peripheral slot on the side of a notebook; this slot serves to store the mouse, protect it, and charge its batteries all at the same time. The MoGo Mouse is wireless and uses Bluetooth technology to transmit data to the notebook.

What else can I do with my mouse? Manufacturers of mice are constantly releasing new models that allow you to perform useful tasks with a few clicks of the mouse. On some mouse models, Microsoft and Logitech now provide features such as the following:

- **Magnifier:** Pulls up a magnification box that you can drag around the screen to enhance viewing of hard-to-read images (see Figure 2.12). This feature is often used by people with visual disabilities.

- **Customizable buttons:** Provide extra buttons on the mouse that you can program to perform the functions that you use most often to help you speed through tasks.

- **Web search:** Allows you to quickly highlight a word or phrase and then press the search button on the mouse to start a Web search.

- **File storage:** Includes a wireless USB receiver that contains flash memory

Figure 2.11

The MoGo Mouse is a portable mouse that stores and charges in a PC Card slot.

Figure 2.12

The magnifier is a mouse feature that provides instant magnification of images or text.

to store or back up your files (for example, a USB thumb drive).

What other input devices are used with games? Game controllers such as joysticks, game pads, and steering wheels are also considered input devices because they send data to the computer. Game controllers, which are similar to the devices used on gaming consoles, such as the Xbox 360 and the PlayStation, are also available for use with computers. They have buttons and miniature pointing devices that provide input to the computer. Force-feedback joysticks and steering wheels deliver data in both directions. They translate your movements to the computer and translate its responses into forces on your hands, creating a richer simulated experience. Most game controls, such as those for Rock Band and the Wii system, are wireless to provide extra mobility.

Touchscreens

How else can I input data and commands? You've seen and used touch-sensitive screens in fast food restaurants, airport check-in kiosks, and ATM machines for quite some time. A **touchscreen** is a display screen that responds to commands initiated by a touch with a finger or a stylus. Touchscreens are becoming increasingly popular on many computing devices including desktops, notebooks, smartphones, and portable media players. A **tablet PC** is similar to a notebook PC but features a touch-sensitive screen that can

Figure 2.13

Tablet PCs use the finger or a stylus to input data and commands on a touchscreen display that twists and folds flat.

swivel and fold flat (see Figure 2.13). Users input data and commands on a tablet PC via a stylus or with their fingers. Although all tablet PCs have built-in keyboards that allow you to type text just as you would with a normal keyboard, the touchscreen functionality often makes it a better choice when inputting with a keyboard is impractical or unwieldy. Portable gaming devices such as the Nintendo DS also feature touch-sensitive screens that use a stylus (or finger) for input. Dell and Hewlett Packard have released all-in-one desktop PCs with touchscreen displays.

Tablet PCs, which were developed primarily because many people find it easier to write than to type input into a computer, are expensive compared to conventional notebooks. An alternative is a digital pen like the EPOS Digital Pen (see Figure 2.14). This pen works in conjunction with a flash drive (a portable electronic storage device that connects to a USB port on a computer). You can write with the pen on any conventional paper. The pen captures your writing and then wirelessly transmits and stores it in the flash drive. When the flash drive is connected to a computer, you can use software to translate your writing into digital text.

Figure 2.14

The EPOS Digital Pen captures writing and stores it in a flash drive for later transfer to a computer. No typing is required!

Image Input

How can I input digital images into my computer? Digital cameras,

ACTIVE HELP-DESK

Using Input Devices

In this Active Helpdesk call, you'll play the role of a helpdesk staffer, fielding calls about different input devices, such as the different mice and keyboards on the market, what wireless input options are available, and how to best use these devices.

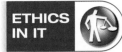

ETHICS IN IT

Ethics: What Is Ethical Computing?

If you were asked to cite an example of unethical behavior while using a computer, you could easily provide an answer. You've probably heard news stories about people using computers to commit such crimes as unleashing viruses or committing identity theft. You may also have read about students who were prosecuted for illegally sharing copyrighted material such as videos. All of these are examples of unethical behavior while using a computer. However, if you were asked what constitutes *ethical* behavior while using a computer, could you provide an answer just as quickly?

Loosely defined, *ethics* is a system of moral principles, rules, and accepted standards of conduct. So what are the accepted standards of conduct when using computers (see Figure 2.15)? The Computer Ethics Institute developed the Ten Commandments of Computer Ethics, which is widely cited as a benchmark for companies that are developing computer usage and compliance policies for employees. The ethical computing guidelines listed below are based on the Computer Ethics Institute's work.

Ethical Computing Guidelines

1. Avoid causing harm to others when using computers.
2. Do not interfere with other people's efforts at accomplishing work with computers.
3. Resist the temptation to snoop in other people's computer files.
4. Do not use computers to commit theft.
5. Agree not to use computers to promote lies.
6. Do not use software (or make illegal copies for others) without paying the creator for it.

7. Avoid using other people's computer resources without appropriate authorization or proper compensation.
8. Do not claim other people's intellectual output as your own.
9. Consider the social consequences of the products of your computer labor.

Figure 2.15

Make sure the work you claim as your intellectual output is the product of your intellect alone.

10. Only use computers in ways that show consideration and respect for others.

The United States has enacted laws that support some of these guidelines, such as Guideline 6, the breaking of which would violate copyright laws, and Guideline 4, which is enforceable under numerous federal and state larceny laws. Other guidelines, however, require more subtle interpretation as to what behavior is unethical because there are no laws designed to enforce them.

Consider Guideline 7, which covers unauthorized use of resources. The college you attend probably provides computer resources for you to use for coursework. But if the college gives you access to computers and the Internet, is it ethical for you to use those resources to run a business on eBay in between classes or on the weekends? Although it might not be technically illegal, you are tying up computer resources that could be used by other students for their intended purpose: learning and completing coursework. (This behavior also violates Guidelines 2 and 10.)

Throughout the chapters in this book, we touch on many topics related to these guidelines. So keep them in mind as you study, and think about how they relate to the actions you take as you use computers in your life.

---

camcorders, and cell phones are common devices for capturing pictures and video, and all of them are considered input devices. Digital cameras and camcorders are usually used in remote settings (away from a computer) to capture images for later downloading to the computer. These devices either connect to a computer with a data cable or

SOUND BYTE

Tablet and Notebook Tour

In this Sound Byte, you'll take a tour of a Tablet PC and a notebook computer, learning about the unique features and ports available on each.

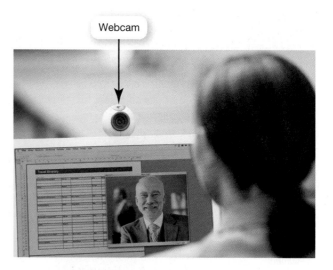

Figure 2.16

A webcam is either built into a notebook monitor or placed on top of a monitor.

transmit data wirelessly. Windows automatically recognizes these devices when they are connected to a computer and makes the input of the digital data to the computer simple and easy.

How do I capture live video from my computer? A webcam (see Figure 2.16) is a small camera that sits on top of a computer monitor (connected to the computer by a cable) or is built into a notebook computer. Although some webcams are able to capture still images, they are used mostly for transferring live video directly to a computer. Webcams make it possible to transmit live video over the Web. They are often used to facilitate videoconferencing or calls made with video phones. Videoconferencing technology allows a person sitting at a computer equipped with a webcam and a microphone to transmit video and audio across the Internet.

Sound Input

Why would I want to input sound to my computer? Equipping your computer to accept sound input opens up a variety of possibilities. You can conduct audio conferences with work colleagues, chat with friends or family over the Internet instead of using a phone, record podcasts,

Figure 2.17

Professional-quality microphones such as the Snowball are essential for producing quality podcasts.

and more. Inputting sound to your computer requires equipping it with a **microphone** or **mic**, a device that allows you to capture sound waves (such as your voice) and transfer them to digital format on your computer. Many notebook computers come with built-in microphones, and some desktop computers come with inexpensive microphones. If you don't have a microphone or you aren't getting the quality you need from your existing microphone, then you probably need to shop for one.

What types of microphones are available? There are several different types of microphones available for a variety of needs. Desktop microphones, which have an attached base that allows them to sit on a flat surface (see Figure 2.17), are convenient for recording podcasts or in other situations in which you might need your hands to be free. Unidirectional microphones pick up sound from only one direction. These are best used for recording podcasts with a single voice or making phone calls over the Internet with only one person on the sender's end of the call. Omnidirectional microphones pick up sounds from all directions at once. These mics are best for recording more than one voice, such as during a conference call when you need to pick up the voices of multiple speakers.

Clip-on microphones (also called *lavaliere microphones*) are useful in environments, such as presentations, where you need to keep your hands free for other activities (such as writing on a white board) or move around the room. Many of these microphones are wireless.

Close-talk microphones, which are usually attached to a headset, facilitate using speech-recognition software, video-conferencing, or making telephone calls. With a microphone attached to a headset, your hands are free to perform other tasks while you speak (such as making notes or referring to paper documents), and the headset allows you to listen as well (such as when making Internet phone calls).

What input devices are available for people with disabilities? Many people who have physical challenges use computers often, but they sometimes need special input devices to access them. For visually impaired users, voice recognition is an obvious option. For those users whose visual limitations are less severe, keyboards with larger keys are available. Keyboards that display on a touchscreen can make input easier for some individuals. These keyboards are displayed as graphics on the computer monitor. The user presses the keys with a pointing device or simply presses on the touchscreen monitor.

People with motor control issues may have difficulty with pointing devices. To aid such users, special trackballs are available that can easily be manipulated with one finger and can be attached to almost any surface, including a wheelchair. When arm motion is severely restrained, head-mounted pointing devices can be used. Generally, these involve a camera mounted on the computer monitor and a device attached to the head (often installed in a hat). When the user moves his or her head, the camera detects the movement, which controls the cursor on the screen. In this case, mouse clicks are controlled by a switch that can be manipulated by the user's hands or feet or even by using an instrument that fits into the mouth and senses the user blowing into it.

Output Devices

An **output device** enables you to send processed data out of your computer in the form of text, pictures (graphics), sounds

(audio), or video. One common output device is a **monitor** (sometimes referred to as a **display screen**), which displays text, graphics, and video as soft copies (copies you can see only on screen). Another common output device is the **printer**, which creates hard copies (copies you can touch) of text and graphics. Speakers and earphones (or earbuds) are the output devices for sound.

Monitors

What are the different types of monitors?
There are two basic types of monitors: CRTs and LCDs. If your monitor is big and boxy, then it has a picture-tube device called a **cathode ray tube (CRT)** such as the one shown in Figure 2.18. If your monitor is flat, it's using **liquid crystal display (LCD)** technology (see Figure 2.18). An LCD monitor, also called a **flat-panel monitor**, is lighter and more energy efficient than a CRT monitor, making it perfect for portable computers such as notebooks. The sleek style of LCD monitors also makes them a favorite for users with small workspaces, and now they have become the standard type of display monitor, replacing the CRT. Today CRT monitors are difficult to find or buy because they are fast becoming **legacy technology**, or computing devices or peripherals that use techniques, parts, and methods from an earlier time that are no longer popular. Although legacy technology may still be functional, it is quickly being replaced by newer technological advances. This doesn't mean that if you have a CRT monitor that is functioning well you should replace it with an LCD monitor. However, when your CRT

Figure 2.18

(a) CRT monitors are big and bulky. (b) LCDs (flat-panel monitors) save precious desktop space and weigh considerably less than CRT monitors.

Rear glass

Colored light

Polarizer

Front glass

Unpolarized
white light
from backlight

Polarizer

Liquid crystals

Color filters

Figure 2.19

A magnification of a single
pixel in an LCD monitor.

monitor fails, you will most likely only be
able to replace it with an LCD monitor.

**Why have LCD monitors replaced
CRT monitors?** LCD monitors are much
smaller than CRT monitors are and therefore
take up far less space on a work surface.
They are also generally brighter than CRT
monitors are and use different refresh methods for the tiny dots of color, which causes
less eyestrain. Another advantage is that
LCD monitors use significantly less energy
and emit less electromagnetic radiation,
making them more environmentally
friendly. Finally, LCD monitors weigh less
than CRT monitors, making them the obvious choice for mobile devices.

How do monitors work? Monitor
screens are grids made up of millions of tiny
dots, each of which is called a **pixel**. Illuminated pixels create the images you see on
your monitor. Each pixel is actually comprised of three subpixels of the colors red,
blue, and green. LCD monitors are made of
two or more sheets of material filled with a
liquid crystal solution (see Figure 2.19). A
fluorescent panel at the back of the LCD
monitor generates light waves. When electric current passes through the liquid crystal
solution, the crystals move around and
either block the fluorescent light or let the
light shine through. This blocking or passing
of light by the crystals causes images to form
on the screen. The various combinations of
red, blue, and green make up the components of color we see on our monitors.

**What factors affect the quality of
an LCD monitor?** The most important
factor to consider when choosing an LCD
monitor is its **resolution**: the clearness or
sharpness of the image. Resolution is controlled by the number of pixels displayed on the screen. The higher the
resolution, the sharper and clearer the
image will be. Monitor resolution is
listed as a number of pixels. A high-
end monitor may have a native (or
maximum) resolution of 1,600 × 1,200,
meaning it contains 1,600 vertical
columns with 1,200 pixels in each column. Note that you can adjust a monitor's resolution either to make the image
displayed on the screen larger (reducing the
resolution) or to fit more on your screen
(increasing the resolution). You cannot
increase the resolution of an LCD monitor
beyond its native (maximum) resolution.
Generally, you should select a monitor with
the highest resolution available for the
screen size (measured in inches).

Other factors to consider when judging
the quality of an LCD monitor include the
following:

- **Viewing angle:** An LCD's viewing angle,
  which is measured in degrees, tells how
  far you can move to the side of (or above
  or below) the monitor before the image
  quality degrades to unacceptable levels.
  For monitors that measure 17 inches or
  more, a viewing angle of at least 150 degrees is usually recommended.

- **Contrast ratio:** This is a measure of the
  difference in light intensity between the
  brightest white and the darkest black
  that the monitor can produce. If the contrast ratio is too low, colors tend to fade
  when you adjust the brightness to a
  high or low setting. A contrast ratio
  between 400:1 and 600:1 is preferable.

- **Brightness:** Measured as candelas per
  square meter (cd/m2) or *nits*, brightness
  is a measure of the greatest amount of
  light showing when the monitor is displaying pure white. A brightness level of
  250cd/m2 or greater is recommended.

- **Response time:** This is the measurement
  (in milliseconds) of the time it takes for
  a pixel to change color. A lower response
  time means faster transitions; therefore,
  moving images will appear less jerky on
  the monitor. A response time lower than
  15 milliseconds is important when using

a monitor to play a game or display full-motion video such as movies or television.

Is a bigger screen size always better? The bigger the monitor, the more you can display, and depending on what you want to display, size may matter. In general, the larger the panel, the larger number of pixels it can display. For example, a 21-inch monitor will typically be able to display 1680 × 1050 pixels, while a 19-inch monitor may only be able to display 1440 × 900 or 1280 × 1024. If you watch many high-definition movies on your monitor, you will need a monitor with at least the 1920 × 1080 resolution required to display HD-DVDs and Blu-Ray movies. Larger screens can also allow you to view multiple documents or Web pages at the same time, creating the effect of using two separate monitors side by side. Again, be mindful of cost. Buying two smaller monitors might be cheaper than buying one large monitor. For either option—a big screen or two screens—you should check that your computer has a video card to support these devices.

Another size issue is whether you should get a wide screen or a standard 4:3 ratio screen. Wide-screen monitors are helpful if you work with multiple windows, use the sidebar gadgets included with the Windows 7 or Vista operating system, or watch movies often. The standard 4:3 ratio means that the monitor is 4 units wide and 3 units tall (in other words, the height is ¾ of the width). The monitor with a standard ratio is fine for basic computing needs.

What other features should I look for in an LCD monitor? Some monitors, especially those on notebook computers, come with convenient built-in features such as speakers, webcams, and microphones. A built-in multiformat card reader is convenient to display images directly on the monitor or to download pictures quickly from a camera memory card to the PC. Another nice feature to look for in a desktop LCD monitor is a built-in USB hub. This will enable you to connect extra peripherals easily without reaching around the back of the PC.

If these features are important to you, you should look for a monitor that has them, but be careful that the price of buying a monitor with these additional features isn't more than what it would cost you to buy the monitor and extra peripherals separately.

Cleaning Your Monitor

Have you ever noticed how quickly your monitor attracts dust? It's important to keep your monitor clean because dust buildup can act like insulation, keeping heat in and causing the electronic components to wear out much faster. To clean your LCD monitor, follow these steps:

1. Turn off the monitor (or your notebook computer) and make sure it is unplugged from the electrical power outlet.
2. Use a 50/50 solution of rubbing alcohol and water on a soft cloth and wipe the screen surface gently. Never spray anything directly onto the monitor. (Check your monitor's user manual to see if there are cleaning products you should avoid using.)
3. In addition to wiping the screen, wipe away the dust from around the case.

Also, don't place anything on top of the monitor or pack anything closely around it. This may block air from cooling it. Finally, avoid placing magnets (including your speaker system's subwoofer) anywhere near the monitor because they can interfere with the mechanisms inside the monitor.

Figure 2.20

Inexpensive projectors are showing up more frequently in business and the home to provide large images for movie viewing and gaming.

How do I show output to a large group of people? Crowding large groups of people around your computer isn't practical. However, it is possible to use a **projector**, a device that can project images from your computer onto a wall or viewing screen (see Figure 2.20). Projectors are commonly used in business and education settings such as conference rooms and classrooms. These projectors are small and lightweight, and some, like the 3M MPro 110, are small enough to fit into the palm of your hand! These portable projectors are ideal for businesspeople that have to make presentations at client locations. *Entertainment projectors,* such as the Wonderwall, include stereo speakers and an array of multimedia connectors, making them a good option for use in the home to display TV programs, DVDs, digital images, or video games in a large format.

Printers

What are the different types of printers? There are two primary categories of printers: impact and nonimpact. An **impact printer** has tiny hammer-like keys that strike the paper through an inked ribbon, making marks on the paper. The most common impact printer is the dot-matrix printer. In contrast, a **nonimpact printer** sprays ink or uses laser beams to transfer marks onto the paper. The most common nonimpact printers are inkjet printers and laser printers. Today, nonimpact printers have replaced impact printers almost entirely. They tend to be less expensive, quieter, and faster, and they offer better print quality. The only place you may see a dot-matrix printer is at a company that still uses them to print multipart forms. For most users, dot-matrix printers are truly legacy technology.

What are the advantages of inkjet printers? An **inkjet printer** (see Figure 2.21) is the standard type of printer found in most homes. Inkjet printers are popular because they are affordable and produce high-quality color printouts quickly and quietly. Inkjet printers work by spraying tiny drops of ink onto paper and are great for printing black-and-white text as well as color images. In fact, when loaded with the right paper,

Figure 2.21

Inkjet printers are popular among home users, especially with the rise of digital photography. Many inkjet printers are optimized for printing photos from digital cameras.

higher-end inkjet printers can print images that look like professional-quality photos. One thing to consider when buying an inkjet printer is the type and cost of the ink cartridges the printer needs. Some printers use two cartridges: black and color. Other printers use four or more cartridges, typically black, magenta, cyan, and yellow. Often the cost of buying replacement cartridges is more than that of a brand-new printer! Depending on how frequently you print, you might want to consider a laser printer.

Why would I want a laser printer? Laser printers (see Figure 2.22) are most often used in office or classroom settings because they have a faster printing speed than inkjet printers and produce higher-quality printouts. A **laser printer** uses laser beams and static electricity to deliver toner (similar to ink) onto the correct areas of the page. Heat is used to fuse the toner to the page, making the image permanent. In the past, laser printers generally were not found in the home because of their high purchase price and because they did not produce great color images. Recently, however, the price and quality of color laser printers have fallen dramatically, making them highly price competitive with high-end inkjet printers. When you include the price of ink or toner in the overall cost, laser printers can be more economical than inkjets.

What kind of printer can I take with me? Although some inkjet printers

Figure 2.22

Laser printers print quickly and offer high-quality printouts.

are small enough to carry with you, you may want to consider a printer designed for portability for added mobility and flexibility (see Figure 2.23). Portable printers are often compact enough to fit in a briefcase, are lightweight, and sometimes run on battery power instead of AC current.

Are there wireless printers? One of the reasons you may have bought a notebook was to be able to use a computer without the restriction of wires. Wireless printing

Figure 2.23

Modern portable printers feature Bluetooth connectivity, allowing them to be used with mobile devices.

offers you the same freedom. In addition, wireless printers allow several people to print to the same printer from different places. There are two different types of wireless printers: Wi-Fi and Bluetooth. Both Wi-Fi and Bluetooth printers have a range of up to approximately 300 feet. Wi-Fi, however, sends data more quickly than Bluetooth. If your printer is not Bluetooth enabled, you can add Bluetooth by plugging a Bluetooth adapter into a USB port. This lets you take advantage of a great printing solution for photos stored on your cell phone or any other Bluetooth-enabled portable device.

Are there any other types of specialty printers? An **all-in-one printer** is a device that combines the functions of a printer, scanner, copier, and fax into one machine. Popular for their space-saving convenience, all-in-one printers can use either inkjet or laser technology. A **plotter** is another type of printer. Plotters produce oversize pictures that require the drawing of precise and continuous lines, such as maps, detailed images (see Figure 2.24), and architectural plans. Plotters use a computer-controlled pen that provides a greater level of precision than the series of dots that laser or inkjet printers are capable of making.

A **thermal printer**, such as the one shown in Figure 2.25, is another kind of specialty printer. These printers work either by melting wax-based ink onto ordinary paper (a process called *thermal wax transfer printing*), or by burning dots onto specially coated paper (a process called *direct thermal printing*). They are used in stores to print receipts and in airports for electronic ticketing, among other places. Thermal printers are also emerging as a popular technology for mobile and portable printing in conjunction with smartphones and similar devices. Many models, such as the printers that car rental agencies use to give you an instant receipt when you drop off your rental car, feature

Figure 2.24

Plotters are large printers used to print oversize images, maps, and architectural plans.

Figure 2.25

Thermal printers are used in many restaurants to print receipts.

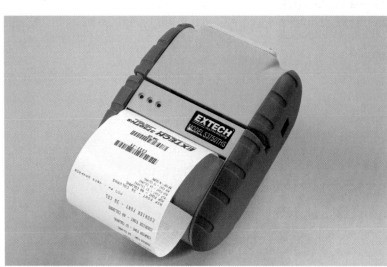

wireless infrared technology for complete portability.

How do I select the best printer?
There is a printer for every printing need. First, you need to decide whether you want just a printer or a device that prints and scans, copies, or faxes (an all-in-one). In addition, you should decide whether you want an inkjet or laser printer. As we discussed previously, that decision is typically determined by price and by the type of printing you do. Once you have narrowed down the type of printer you want, the following criteria will help you determine the best model to meet your needs.

- **Speed:** A printer's speed determines how many pages it can print per minute. Print speed is expressed as *pages per minute* or *ppm*. The speed of inkjet printers has improved over the years, and many inkjet printers now print as fast as laser printers. Printing speeds vary by model and range from 8 ppm to 38 ppm for both laser and inkjet printers. Text documents printed in black and white print faster than documents printed in color.

- **Resolution:** A printer's resolution (printed image clarity) is measured in dots per inch (dpi), which is the number of dots of ink in a one-inch line. The higher the dpi, the greater the level of detail and quality of the image. You'll sometimes see dpi represented as a horizontal number multiplied by a vertical number, such as 600 × 600, but you may also see the same resolution simply stated as 600 dpi. For general-purpose printing, 300 dpi is sufficient. For printing photos, 1,200 dpi is better. The dpi for professional photo-quality printers is twice that.

- **Color output:** If you're using an inkjet printer to print color images, buy a four-color printer (cyan, magenta, yellow, and black) or a six-color one (four-color plus light cyan and light magenta) for the highest-quality output. While some printers come with a single ink cartridge for all colors and others have two ink cartridges (one for black and one for color), the best setup is to have an individual ink cartridge for each color so you can replace only the specific color cartridge that is empty. Color laser printers have four separate toner cartridges (black, cyan, magenta, and yellow), and the toner is blended in various quantities to produce the entire color spectrum.

- **Memory:** Printers need memory to print. Inkjet printers run slowly if they don't have enough memory. If you plan to print small text-only documents on an inkjet printer, then 1 to 2 MB of memory should be enough. You need approximately 4 MB of memory if you expect to print large text-only documents and 8 MB if you print graphics-heavy files. Unlike inkjet printers, laser printers won't print at all without sufficient memory. To ensure your laser printer meets your printing needs, buy one with at least 16 MB of memory. Some printers allow you to add more memory later.

- **Use and cost of the printer:** If you will be printing mostly black-and-white, text-based documents or will be sharing your printer with others, then a black-and-white laser printer is best because of its printing speed and overall economy for volume printing. If you're planning to print color photos and graphics, then an inkjet printer or color laser printer is a must, even though the cost per page will be higher.

- **Cost of consumables:** You should carefully investigate the cost of consumables (such as printer cartridges and paper) for any printer you are considering purchasing because the cost of inkjet cartridges often can exceed the cost of the actual printer when purchased on sale. Reviews in consumer magazines such as *PC World* and *Consumer Reports* can help you evaluate the overall cost of producing documents with a particular printer.

Sound Output

What are the output devices for sound? Most computers include inexpensive speakers. A **speaker** is an output device for sound. These speakers are sufficient to play the standard audio clips you find on the Web and usually enable you to participate in videoconferencing or phone calls made over the Internet. However, if you plan to digitally edit audio files or are particular about how your music sounds, you may want to upgrade to a more sophisticated speaker system, such as one that includes subwoofers (special speakers that produce only low bass sounds) and surround-sound speakers. A **surround-sound speaker** is part of a speaker system whose design makes the user feel surrounded by sound. Wireless speaker systems are available now to help you avoid cluttering up your rooms with speaker wire. We discuss surround sound in more detail in Chapter 6.

If you work in close proximity to other employees or travel with a notebook, you may need to use headphones or earbuds for your sound output to avoid distracting other people. Both devices will plug into the same jack on the computer that speakers connect to, so using them with a computer is easy. Studies of users of portable media players have shown that hearing might be damaged by excessive volume,

Does It Matter What Paper I Print On?

The quality of your printer is only part of what controls the quality of a printed image. The paper you use and the printer settings that control the amount of ink used are equally important. If you're printing text-only documents for personal use, then using low-cost paper is fine. You also may want to consider selecting draft mode in your printer settings to conserve ink. However, if you're printing more formal documents such as résumés, you may want to choose a higher-quality paper (determined by the paper's weight, whiteness, and brightness) and adjust your print setting to "normal" or "best."

The weight of paper is measured in pounds, with 20 pounds being standard. A heavier paper may be best for projects such as brochures, but be sure to check that your printer can handle the added thickness. The degree of paper whiteness is a matter of personal preference. Generally, the whiter the paper, the brighter colors appear. However, for more formal documents, such as résumés, you may want to use a creamier color. The brightness of paper usually varies from 85 to 94. The higher the number, the brighter the paper, and the easier it is to read printed text. Opacity is especially important if you're printing on both sides of the paper because it determines the amount of ink that shows through from the opposite side of the paper.

If you're printing photos, then paper quality can have a big impact on the results. Photo paper is more expensive than regular paper and comes in a variety of textures ranging from matte to high gloss. For a photo-lab look, high-gloss paper is the best choice. Semigloss (often referred to as *satin*) is good for portraits, while a matte surface is often used for black-and-white printing.

especially when using earbuds, because they fit into the ear canals. Therefore, you should exercise caution when using these devices.

Processing and Memory on the Motherboard

We just looked at the components of your computer that you use to input and output data. But where does the processing take place, and where is the data stored? The **motherboard** is the main circuit board that contains the central electronic components of the computer, including the computer's processor (its brain), its memory, and the many circuit boards that help the computer function. On a desktop, the motherboard is located inside the **system unit**, the metal or plastic case that also houses the power source and all the storage devices (CD/DVD drive and hard drive). With a notebook computer, the system unit is combined with the monitor and the keyboard into a single package.

Ever wonder how a printer knows what to print and how it puts ink in just the right places? Most inkjet printers use drop-on-demand technology, in which the ink is "demanded" and then "dropped" onto the paper. Two different processes use drop-on-demand technology: Thermal bubble is used by Hewlett-Packard and Canon, and piezoelectric is used by Epson. The difference between the two processes is how the ink is heated within the print cartridge reservoir (the chamber inside the printer that holds the ink).

In the thermal bubble process, the ink is heated in such a way that it expands (like a bubble) and leaves the cartridge reservoir through a small opening, or nozzle. Figure 2.26 shows the general process for thermal bubble.

In the piezoelectric process, each ink nozzle contains a crystal at the back of the ink reservoir that receives an electrical charge, causing the ink to vibrate and drop out of the nozzle.

Laser printers use a completely different process. Inside a laser printer is a big metal cylinder (also called a drum) that is charged with static electricity. When asked to print something, the printer sends signals to the laser in the laser printer, telling it to "uncharge" selected spots on the charged cylinder. These spots correspond to characters and images in the document you wish to print. Toner, a fine powder that is used in place of liquid ink, is only attracted to those areas on the drum that are not charged (the areas where the desired characters and images are to be printed). The toner is transferred to the paper as it feeds through the printer. Finally, the toner is melted onto the paper. All unused toner is swept back to the toner hopper before the next job starts the process all over again.

Inkjet Printer

Print cartridges

Print head

Nozzles

Inverted print cartridge

The print cartridge is positioned inside your inkjet printer so that the print head faces down toward the paper. The print head has 50 to several hundred nozzles, or small holes, through which ink droplets fall. These nozzles are narrower than a human hair. Inside the print head of color inkjet printers, there are three ink reservoirs that hold magenta (red), cyan (blue), and yellow ink. Depending on your printer, a fourth ink reservoir may be required to hold black ink, as well. (In non-color inkjet printers, there is only one ink reservoir for the black ink.)

(1) Ink, Resistor, Firing chamber, Nozzle

(2) Bubble forming, Ink forced out of the nozzle

(3) Ink drop

(4) Ink dot

STEP 1: Once the printer receives the command to print, electrical pulses flow through thin resistors in the print head to heat the ink.

STEP 2: The heated ink forms a bubble. The bubble continues to expand until it is forced out of the nozzle.

STEP 3: The ink drops onto the paper.

STEP 4: As the ink leaves the cartridge, the chamber begins to cool and contract, creating a vacuum to draw in the ink for the process to begin again.

Figure 2.26
How a thermal bubble inkjet printer works.

What's on the motherboard? The motherboard contains the set of chips that powers the system, including the central processing unit (CPU). The motherboard also houses the chips that provide the short-term memory for the computer and a set of slots for expansion cards (see Figure 2.27). The various circuit boards have specific functions that augment the computer's basic functions. A circuit board that provides additional functionality is usually referred to as an **expansion card** (or **adapter card**). Typical expansion cards found in the system unit are the sound and video cards. A **sound card** provides a connection for the speakers and microphone, whereas a **video card** provides a connection for the monitor. Many low-end computer models have video and sound capabilities integrated into their motherboards. High-end models still use expansion cards to provide video and sound capabilities. Other expansion cards provide a means for network and Internet connections. These include the **modem card**, which provides the computer with a connection to the Internet via a traditional phone line, and a **network interface card (NIC)**, which enables your computer to connect with other computers or to a cable modem to facilitate a high-speed Internet connection. Lastly, some expansion cards provide additional USB and FireWire ports.

Memory

What exactly is RAM? Random access memory (RAM) is the place in a computer where the programs and data the computer is currently using are stored. Sometimes RAM is referred to as *primary storage*, but it should not be confused with other types of permanent storage devices such as the hard drive. RAM is much faster to read from and write to than the hard drive and other forms of storage. The

BITS AND BYTES — Maintaining Your Printer

In general, printers require minimal maintenance. Occasionally, it's a good idea to wipe the case of the printer with a damp cloth to free it from accumulated dust. However, do not wipe away any ink residue that has accumulated inside the printer. If you are experiencing streaking or blank areas on your printed paper, then your print head nozzles may be clogged. To fix this, run the printer's cleaning cycle. (Check your printer's manual for instructions, because every printer is different.) If this doesn't work, you may want to use a cleaning sheet to brush the print head clean. These sheets often come with printers or with reams of photo paper. If you still have a problem, try a cleaning cartridge. Cleaning cartridges contain a special fluid that scrubs the print head. These cartridges can be found where most ink cartridges are sold. As with ink cartridges, make sure you buy one that is compatible with your printer.

processor can request the RAM's contents, which can be located, opened, and delivered to the CPU for processing in a few nanoseconds (billionths of a second). If you look at a motherboard, you'll see RAM as a series of small cards (called *memory cards* or *memory modules*) plugged into slots on the motherboard.

Because the entire contents of RAM are erased when you turn off the computer, RAM is a temporary or **volatile storage** location. To save data permanently, you need to save it to the hard drive or to another permanent storage device such as a

Figure 2.27

A motherboard contains the CPU, the memory (RAM) modules, and slots for expansion cards.

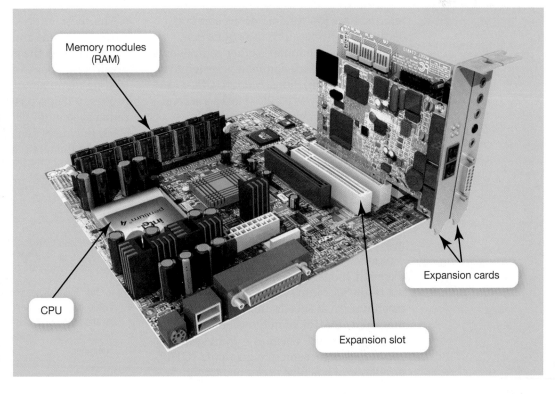

Memory modules (RAM)

CPU

Expansion cards

Expansion slot

Single path vs. dual path processors for data

Path 1

Path 2

Single execution core

Single core processor

Path 1

Path 2

Dual execution cores

Dual core processor

Figure 2.28

Two are faster than one! With their dual core processors, Intel CPUs can work in parallel, processing two separate programs at the same time instead of switching back and forth between them.

CD or flash drive. You can think of RAM as the computer's short-term memory, and the hard drive as long-term memory.

Does the motherboard contain any other kinds of memory besides RAM? In addition to RAM, the motherboard also contains a form of memory called **read-only memory (ROM)**. ROM holds all the instructions the computer needs to start up when the computer is powered on. Unlike data stored in RAM, which is volatile storage, the instructions stored in ROM are permanent, making ROM a nonvolatile storage location. This means the data is not erased when the power is turned off.

Processing

What is the CPU? The **central processing unit** (**CPU**, or **processor**) is sometimes referred to as the "brains" of the computer because it controls all the functions performed by the computer's other components and processes all the commands issued to it by software instructions. Modern CPUs can perform as many as 6 billion tasks a second without error, making them extremely powerful components.

How is processor speed measured? Processor speed is measured in units of hertz (Hz). Hertz means "machine cycles per second." A machine cycle is the process of the CPU getting the data or instructions from RAM and decoding the instructions into something the computer can understand. Once the CPU has decoded the instructions, it executes them and stores the result back into system memory. Older machines ran at speeds measured in **megahertz (MHz)**, or millions of machine cycles per second, whereas current systems run at speeds measured in **gigahertz (GHz)**, or billions of machine cycles per second.

Therefore, a 3.8 GHz processor performs work at a rate of 3.8 billion machine cycles per second. It's important to realize, however, that CPU clock speed alone doesn't determine the performance of the CPU.

Is speed the only measure of processor performance? While speed is an important consideration when determining processor performance, CPU performance also is affected by other factors. One factor is the number of *cores*, or processing paths, a processor has. Until just a few years ago, processors only could handle one instruction at a time. Now, processors have been designed so that they can have two, four, and even eight different paths, allowing them to process more than one instruction at a time (see Figure 2.28). Applications such as virus protection software and the operating system, which are always running behind the scenes, can have their own processors, freeing up the other processor to run other applications such as a Web browser, Word, or iTunes more efficiently.

Besides the number of cores, are there other factors that determine processing power? In addition to the number of cores in a processor, other factors such as additional memory and how fast data is exchanged between the CPU and RAM should be considered. These factors will be discussed in greater detail in Chapter 6. The "best" processor will depend on your particular needs and is not always the processor with the highest GHz and the greatest number of cores. Intel, one of the leading manufacturers of computer processor chips, has created a pictorial rating system for CPU chips. Instead of stars, Intel uses one to five brains to illustrate the relative computing power of each type of CPU within the Intel line of processors. It also provides an overall

SOUND BYTE

Virtual Computer Tour

In this Sound Byte, you'll take a video tour of the inside of a system unit. From opening the cover to locating the power supply, CPU, and memory, you'll become more familiar with what's inside your computer.

Figure 2.29

Intel uses a five-brain rating system to illustrate the power of its processors.

ranking of "smart," "smarter," and "genius" and an overview of each processor's key benefits (see Figure 2.29).

Storing Data and Information

Earlier we characterized RAM as temporary or volatile memory because the entire contents of RAM are erased when you turn off the computer. Thus, if you want to save the files you're working on permanently, as well as your music, digital images, and any software applications you use, you need to store them in a different location than RAM. To save data permanently, you need to save it to the hard drive or to another permanent storage device such as a CD, DVD, or flash drive. Each of these permanent storage devices is located in your desktop or notebook computer in a space called a **drive bay** (see Figure 2.30). There are two

kinds of drive bays—internal and external—as described below:

- Internal drive bays cannot be seen or accessed from outside the system unit. Generally, internal drive bays are reserved for internal hard drives. An **internal hard drive** usually holds all permanently stored programs and data.

- External drive bays can be seen and accessed from outside the system unit. External drive bays house CD and DVD drives, for example. On desktop computers, sometimes there are empty external drive bays that can be used to install additional drives. These extra spaces are covered by a faceplate on the front panel. Notebook computers generally do not give you the ability to add additional drives. Such expansion is done by attaching an external drive to the computer through a USB port.

You may occasionally see a PC that still has a bay for a *floppy disk drive*, which reads and writes to easily transportable floppy disks that hold a limited amount of data (1.44 MB). Some computers also feature what's called a *Zip disk drive*, which resembles a floppy disk drive but has a slightly wider opening. Zip disks work just like standard floppy disks but can carry much more data (up to 750 MB). These storage devices are fast becoming legacy technologies and are not found on new computers.

Figure 2.30

Storage devices in desktop and notebook computers.

CD/DVD drive

Empty drive bay

Hard drive

Photo courtesy of Iomega Corporation

Figure 2.31

(a) Internal hard drives hold the data and instructions that the computer needs and are inaccessible from outside the system unit. (b) High-capacity external hard drives are often used to back up data on internal hard drives. (c) Smaller external hard drives enable you to take a significant amount of data and programs on the road with you.

Figure 2.32

Flash drives are a convenient means of portable storage, and come in many different shapes and sizes.

Hard Drives

Which storage device holds the most data?
The **hard drive** (see Figure 2.31) is your computer's primary device for permanent storage of software and documents. The hard drive is a **nonvolatile storage** device, meaning it holds the data and instructions your computer needs permanently, even after the computer is turned off. Today's internal hard drives, with capacities of as much as 2 **terabyte (TB)**, can hold more data than would fit in the books in a school's library.

Are all hard drives located inside the system?
Because the hard drive stores all of the computer's data and programs, special measures are taken to protect the hard drive from any possible damage. Unlike other storage devices on the computer, the hard drive is enclosed in a case and is not accessible from the outside of the

system unit. If you need a more portable solution, external hard drives are readily available. An **external hard drive** (see Figure 2.31) is essentially like an internal hard drive. However, it has been made portable by making it small and lightweight and enclosing it in a protective case. Some external hard drives, which are small enough to fit into your pocket, have storage capacities of 1 or 2 TB (or larger). An external hard drive is often used to back up (make a copy of) data that is contained on an internal hard drive in case a problem develops with the internal hard drive and data needs to be recovered. Other external hard drives have more limited storage capacity (up to 500 GB). These are even smaller and are designed for the ultimate portability of files between computers (see Figure 2.31).

Optical Storage

What other kinds of storage devices are available?
Internal hard drives are used to store your data, files, and installed software programs. Hard drives store their data on magnetized platters. Also included on most desktop and notebook computers is at least one **optical drive** that can read from and maybe even write to CDs, DVDs, or Blu-ray discs. Data is saved to a **compact disc (CD)**, **digital video disc (DVD)**,

or **Blu-ray disc (BD)** as tiny pits that are burned into the disc by a high-speed laser. CDs were initially created to store audio files. DVDs are the same size and shape as CDs but can hold more than 25 times as much data. If you're looking for more storage capacity than CDs or DVDs, a double-layer DVD is the next step. These discs have up to 8.5 GB of storage. What if you want even more storage capacity? Blu-ray is the latest incarnation of optical storage to hit the market. Although a dual-layered DVD can store approximately 8.5 GB of information, this isn't enough to hold movies in the high-definition (HD) digital format that has become so popular. Blu-ray discs, which are similar in size and shape to CDs and DVDs, can hold as much as 50 GB of data. This is enough to hold approximately 4.5 hours of high-definition video. Many systems are now available with BD-ROM drives and even Blu-ray burners. External BD drives are another inexpensive way to add HD storage capacity to your system.

Flash Storage

A **flash drive**, sometimes referred to as a **jump drive**, **USB drive**, or **thumb drive**, is a newer way of storing portable data. Flash drives plug into USB ports. These devices originally were more or less the size of a thumb, but now they vary in size, and are often combined with other devices such as pens or pocketknives (see Figure 2.32). Despite their diminutive size, flash drives have significant storage capacity—currently as much as 64 GB.

Several manufacturers now also include slots on the front of the system unit in which you can insert a portable **flash memory card** such as a Memory Stick or CompactFlash card. Many notebooks also include slots for flash memory cards in the sides. Flash memory cards let you transfer digital data between your computer and devices such as digital cameras, PDAs, smartphones, video cameras, and printers. Although incredibly small—some are just the size of a postage stamp—these memory cards have capacities that exceed the capacity of a DVD. We discuss flash memory in more detail in Chapter 8.

Figure 2.33 shows the storage capacities of the various portable storage media used in your computer's drive bays.

Figure 2.33 | STORAGE MEDIA CAPACITIES

MEDIUM	IMAGE	CAPACITY
Hard drive		External: as much as 2 TB Internal: as much as 750 GB
Portable hard drive		Up to 500 GB
Flash drive		64 GB or more
Blu-ray (dual layer)		50 GB
Flash memory card		Up to 32 GB
Blu-ray (BD)		25 GB
DVD DL (dual layer)		9.4 GB
DVD		4.7 GB
CD		700 MB

Connecting Peripherals to the Computer

Throughout this chapter, we have discussed peripheral devices that input, store, and output data and information. A **port** is a place through which a peripheral device attaches to the computer so that data can be exchanged between it and the operating system. Many ports are located on the back of a notebook computer (see Figure 2.34) and the system unit of a desktop computer (see Figure 2.34). However, some commonly used ports are placed on the front and sides of many desktop and notebook computers for easier access when connecting devices such as flash drives or digital and video cameras.

High Speed and Data Transfer Ports

What is the most common way to connect devices to a computer? A **universal serial bus (USB) port** is now the most common port type used to connect input and output devices to the computer. This is mainly because of a USB port's ability to transfer data quickly. USB 2.0 ports (see Figure 2.35) are the current standard, and transfer data at 480 megabits per second (Mbps), approximately 40 times faster than the original USB ports did. USB ports can connect a wide variety of peripherals to the computer, including keyboards, printers, mice, smartphones, external hard drives, flash drives, and digital cameras.

A traditional **serial port** sends data one bit (piece of data) at a time. Serial ports were often used to connect modems (devices used to transmit data over telecommunications lines) to the computer. Sending data one bit at a time was a slow way to communicate. A **parallel port** could send data between devices in groups of bits at speeds of 500 Kbps and was much faster than traditional serial ports. Parallel ports were often used to connect printers to computers. The speed advantage offered by USB ports is quickly making serial and parallel ports legacy technology.

What are the fastest ports available? Interfaces such as **FireWire 400** (or **IEEE 1394**) and **FireWire 800** are the fastest ports available. The FireWire 400 interface moves data at 400 Mbps, while the newer FireWire 800 doubles the rate to 800 Mbps. Devices such as external hard drives, digital video cameras, portable music players, and digital media players all benefit from the speedy data transfer capabilities of FireWire. The USB 3.0 standard is currently under development. When this standard is ratified, it should

ACTIVE HELP-DESK

Exploring Storage Devices and Ports

In this Active Helpdesk call, you'll play the role of a helpdesk staffer, fielding calls about the computer's main storage devices and how to connect various peripheral devices to the computer.

Figure 2.34

The same ports are on the back of many (a) notebook and (b) desktop computers.

USB ports

Serial ports

Parallel port

S-video

Ethernet port

Audio ports

Video ports

Modem port

FireWire ports

a

b

Figure 2.35
A USB port and a USB connector.

provide transfer speeds of 4.8 Gbps, which is 10 times the speed of USB 2.0. USB 3.0 should quickly become the unofficial port of choice. FireWire 400 ports and connectors have two different configurations, as shown in Figure 2.36. FireWire 400 ports on computers generally have six pins, while FireWire ports on digital cameras have four pins. To transfer data between the two devices, a special cable that has an appropriate connector at each end is needed. The faster

Figure 2.36
FireWire ports come in different configurations, some of which are illustrated here.

FireWire 800 requires a nine-pin connection and is found on storage devices such as external and portable hard drives.

Connectivity and Multimedia Ports

Which ports help me connect with other computers and the Internet? Another set of ports on your computer helps you communicate with other computers. A **connectivity port** can give you access to networks and the Internet or enables your computer to function as a fax machine. To find a connectivity port, look for a port that resembles a standard phone jack but is slightly larger. This port is called an **Ethernet port** (see Figure 2.37). Ethernet ports transfer data at speeds up to 1,000 Mbps. You can use an Ethernet port to connect your computer to a digital subscriber line (DSL) or cable modem, or a network. Many computers still feature a second connectivity port that will accept a standard phone line connector. This jack is the **modem port**. It uses a traditional telephone signal to connect to the Internet over a phone line.

How do I connect monitors and multimedia devices? Other ports on the back of the computer include the audio and video ports (see Figure 2.38). Video ports are necessary to hook up monitors. Whether you are attaching a monitor to a desktop computer, or adding a second, larger display to a notebook computer, you will use video ports. The **video graphics array (VGA)** port is the port to which CRT monitors connect. Many older LCD monitors also connect with a VGA port. The newer LCD monitors, as well as other multimedia devices such as televisions,

SOUND BYTE Port Tour: How Do I Hook It Up?

In this Sound Byte, you'll take a tour of both a desktop system and a notebook system to compare the number and variety of available ports. You'll also learn about the different types of ports and compare their speed and expandability.

Figure 2.37

An Ethernet port and an
Ethernet connector

Figure 2.39

HDMI is the latest digital connector type for
HD home theatre equipment.

DVD players, and projectors, connect to
digital video interface (DVI) and **S-video
(super video)** ports. Audio ports are where
you connect headphones, microphones, and
speakers to the computer.

**How can I connect my computer to
TVs and gaming consoles?** The latest
digital connector designed for use in high-
definition home theatre environments is
HDMI. An all-digital connector, it carries

both high-definition video and uncompressed digital audio on one cable. (DVI can
only carry video signals.) Because HDMI
can only transmit uncompressed audio
and video, there is no need to convert the
signal, which could ultimately reduce the
quality of the sound or picture. Most devices
such as DVD players, TVs, and game consoles have at least one HDMI port (see
Figure 2.39).

Adding Ports: Expansion Cards and Hubs

**What if I don't have all the ports I
need?** New port standards are developed
every few years, and special expansion
cards are usually the only way to add the
newest ports to an older computer or to
expand the number of ports on your
computer. For example, your computer may
have only USB 1.0 ports, but you may have
several devices that would run better with
USB 2.0 ports. You can install expansion
cards in your system unit to provide additional ports (such as USB 2.0 and FireWire).
Like other expansion cards, these cards
clip into an open expansion slot on the motherboard. Figure 2.40 shows an example of
such an expansion card.

**What if there are no open slots on
the motherboard where I can insert
an expansion card?** If there are no
open slots on the motherboard and you still
need extra ports, you can add an expansion
hub (shown in Figure 2.41). An expansion
hub is a device that connects to one port,
such as a USB port, to provide four or eight
new ports. It works like the multiplug extension cords used with electrical appliances.
Because almost everything connects to your
computer using USB ports, your machine
should have at least six USB ports and you

VGA port for CRTs
and analog LCDs

S-video port for
connecting your
PC to your TV

DVI port for
digital LCDs

Figure 2.38

DVI, VGA, and S-video ports connect your monitors and multimedia devices to the
computer.

should have an expansion hub handy to cover any additional needs.

You also can add ports to an empty drive bay, giving you easy-to-reach new ports. The Koutech 10-in-1, shown in Figure 2.42, fits into a regular drive bay and adds front-panel access to two USB 2.0 ports, two FireWire ports, three audio jacks, and a six-in-one digital media card reader.

USB

FireWire

Figure 2.40

This expansion card provides your computer with additional ports.

Power Controls

What's the best way to turn my computer on and off? The **power supply**, which is housed inside the system unit, transforms the wall voltage to the voltages required by computer chips. A desktop system typically has a power-on button on the front panel of the system unit, though you may also find power-on buttons on some keyboards. On notebooks, the power-on button is generally located near the top of the keyboard. Powering on your computer from a completely turned off state, such as when you start your computer in the morning, is called a **cold boot**. Although you use the power-on button to turn on your system, you don't want to use it to turn off (power off) your system. Modern operating systems want control over the shutdown procedure, so you turn off the power from the Start menu, not by pushing the main power button. In fact, for many operating systems, pushing the power button might just put the computer into hibernation or sleep mode.

If you do shut off the power using the main power button without shutting down your operating system first, nothing on your system will be permanently damaged. However, some files and applications may not close properly, so the operating system may need to do extra work the next time you start your computer.

Should I turn off my computer every time I'm done using it? Some people say you should leave your computer

Figure 2.41

If you don't have enough USB ports to support your USB devices, consider getting an expansion hub, which can add four or eight USB ports to your system.

on at all times. They argue that turning your computer on and off throughout the day subjects its components to stress because the heating and cooling process forces the components to expand and contract repeatedly. Other people say you should shut down your computer when you're not using it. They claim that it's not as environmentally friendly, and you'll end up wasting money on electricity to keep the computer running all the time. Modern operating systems include power management settings that allow the most power-hungry components of the system (the hard drive and monitor) to shut down after a short idle period. With the power management options of Windows 7, for

Figure 2.42

You can use an empty drive bay to add additional ports and even a flash card reader to the front panel of the system unit.

example, you really need to shut down your computer completely only when you need to repair or install hardware in the system unit or move the system unit to another location.

If you use the computer sporadically throughout the day, it may be best to keep it on if you're apt to use it soon and power it down only when you're sure you won't be using it for a long time. However, if you use your computer only for a little while each day, it would be best to power it off completely after each daily use.

Can I "rest" my computer without turning it off completely? As mentioned earlier, your computer has power management settings that help it conserve energy. In Windows 7, the two main methods of power management are Sleep and Hibernate. When your computer enters **Sleep mode**, all of the documents, applications, and data you were using remain in RAM (memory), where they are quickly accessible when you restart your computer. (In Windows XP this mode is called Standby.)

Hibernate is another power-saving mode that stores your data in memory and saves it to your computer's hard drive.

Figure 2.43

The Sleep and Hibernate settings are good for the environment and for your wallet.

> To open the Power Options dialog box, click the **Start** button, click **Control Panel**, click **System and Security**, and then click **Power Options**.

In either Sleep or Hibernate mode, the computer enters a state of greatly reduced power consumption, which saves energy. The big advantage to using Hibernate is that if there is a power failure while your computer is conserving power, your information is protected from loss, because it is saved on the hard drive. To put your computer into Sleep or Hibernate, open the Start menu, and select the appropriate Sleep or Hibernate option. To wake up your computer, tap a key on the keyboard or move the mouse. In a few seconds, the computer will resume with exactly the same programs running and documents displayed as when you put it to sleep.

In Windows 7, you can change what happens when you press the power button on the Start menu. By accessing the Power Options screen (see Figure 2.43), you can decide if you want your computer to sleep or hibernate when you click the power button.

What's the restart option in Windows for? If you're using Windows 7, you have the option to restart the computer when you click the right arrow button next to the lock button on the Start menu (see Figure 2.44). Restarting the system while it's powered on is called a **warm boot**. You might need to perform a warm boot if the operating system or other software application stops responding or if you have installed new programs. It takes less time to perform a warm boot than to power down completely and then restart all of your hardware.

Setting It All Up

It's important that you understand not only your computer's components and how they work together, but also how to set up these components safely. *Merriam-Webster's Dictionary* defines **ergonomics** as "an applied science concerned with designing and arranging things people use so that the people and things interact most efficiently and safely." In terms of computing, ergonomics refers to how you set up your computer and other equipment to minimize your risk of injury or discomfort.

Why is ergonomics important? Workplace injuries related to musculoskeletal disorders occur frequently in the United States. More than 336,000 workers experienced such disorders in 2007 (the latest year for which data is available), and these disorders required an average of seven days off from work, as reported by the U.S. Department of Labor's Bureau of Labor Statistics (**bls.gov/news.release/osh2.nr0.htm**). Although the rate of injury declined from the previous year, workplace injuries are still significant. Affected businesses incurred billions of dollars of direct costs (sick pay and medical bills) and even more in indirect costs (lost productivity, overtime, value of employee time involved in the accident, cost of record keeping and investigation, etc.). Avoiding workplace injuries is not only good for employees, but also financially beneficial for businesses.

How can I avoid injuries when I'm working at my computer? As Figure 2.45 illustrates, it is important to arrange your monitor, chair, body, and keyboard in ways that will help you avoid injury, discomfort, and eyestrain as you work on your computer. The following additional guidelines can help keep you comfortable and productive:

- **Position your monitor correctly.** Studies suggest it's best to place your monitor at

Figure 2.44

The Start menu in Windows 7 presents several power options. For a warm boot, choose **Restart**. To power down the computer completely, choose **Shut Down**. To put your computer into a lower power mode, select **Sleep** or **Hibernate**.

>To select a particular power option, click the **Start** menu button in the taskbar and then click the right arrow button.

Right arrow button

Figure 2.45

Using proper equipment that is adjusted correctly helps prevent repetitive strain injuries while working at a computer.

least 25 inches from your eyes. You may need to decrease the screen resolution to make text and images more readable at that distance. Experts recommend that the monitor be positioned either at eye level or so that it is at an angle 15 to 20 degrees below your line of sight.

- **Purchase an adjustable chair.** Adjust the height of your chair so that your feet touch the floor. (You may need to use a footrest to get the right position.) The back support needs to be adjustable so that you can position it to support your lumbar (lower back) region. You should also be able to move the seat or adjust the back so that you can sit without exerting pressure on your knees. If your chair doesn't adjust, placing a pillow behind your back can provide the same support.

Figure 2.46

Ergonomic keyboards that curve and contain built-in wrist rests help maintain proper hand position and minimize wrist strain.

- **Assume a proper position while typing.** A repetitive strain injury (RSI) is a painful condition caused by repetitive or awkward movements of a part of the body. Improperly positioned keyboards are one of the leading causes of RSIs in computer users. Your wrists should be flat (unbent) with respect to the keyboard, and your forearms should be parallel to the floor. Additionally, your wrists should not be resting on the keyboard while typing. You can either adjust the height of your chair or install a height-adjustable keyboard tray to ensure a proper position. Specially designed ergonomic keyboards such as the one shown in Figure 2.46 can help you achieve the proper wrist position.

- **Take breaks from computer tasks.** Remaining in the same position for long periods of time increases stress on your body. Shift your position in your chair and stretch your hands and fingers periodically. Likewise, staring at the screen for long periods of time can lead to eyestrain, so rest your eyes by periodically taking them off the screen and focusing them on an object at least 20 feet away.

- **Ensure the lighting is adequate.** Ensuring that you have proper lighting in your work area is a good way to minimize eyestrain. To do so, eliminate any sources of direct glare (light shining directly into your eyes) or reflected glare (light shining off the computer screen) and ensure there is enough light to read comfortably. If you still can't eliminate glare from your computer screen, you can purchase an antiglare screen to place over your monitor. Look for ones that are polarized or have a purplish optical coating. These will provide the greatest relief.

Is ergonomics important when using mobile devices? Working with mobile computing devices presents interesting challenges when it comes to injury prevention. For example, many users work with notebooks resting on their laps, placing the monitor outside of the optimal line of sight and thereby increasing neck strain. The table in Figure 2.47 provides guidelines on preventing injuries when computing on the go.

So whether you're computing at your desk or on the road, consider the ergonomics of your work environment. Doing so will help you avoid injury and discomfort.

Figure 2.47 | PREVENTING INJURIES WHILE ON THE GO

	PDA/Smartphone RSIs	PMP Hearing Damage	Small-Screen Vision Issues	Lap Injuries	Back, Neck, and Shoulder Injuries
Malady	Repetitive strain injuries (such as DeQuervain's tendonitis) from constant typing of instant messages.	Hearing loss from high decibel sound levels in earbuds or headphones.	Blurriness and dryness caused by squinting to view tiny screens on mobile devices.	Burns on legs from heat generated by notebook.	Pain caused from carrying notebook (messenger) bag hung over your shoulder.
Preventative measures	Restrict length and frequency of messages, take breaks often, and perform other motions with your thumbs and fingers during breaks to relieve tension.	Turn down volume (you should be able to hear external noises such as people talking), use software programs that limit sound levels (not over 60 decibels), and use external, over-ear style headphones instead of earbuds.	Blink frequently or use eye drops to maintain moisture level in eyes, after 10 minutes take a break and focus your eyes on something at least 8 feet away for 5 minutes, use an adequate amount of light, increase the size of fonts.	Place a book, magazine, or notebook cooling pad between your legs and your notebook.	Use a conventional backpack with two shoulder straps, lighten the load by only carrying essential equipment, and consider buying a lightweight notebook.

Emerging Technologies: Displays That You Can Take With You

Today, LCD monitors dominate the desktop PC and notebook markets. Lighter and less bulky than previous monitors, they can be easily moved and take up less space on a desk. LCD technology has improved significantly over the past several years, and now monitors are sporting increased viewing angles, higher resolutions, and faster pixel response time, which makes full-motion video (critical for gamers) appear extremely smooth.

LCD technology has also infiltrated the television market and, along with plasma technology, will make the boxy TV as obsolete as the CRT monitor. However, as good as LCD technology is, some technology that is beginning to hit the market is even better.

OLED Displays

Organic Light Emitting Diode (OLED) displays use organic compounds that produce light when exposed to an electric current. Unlike LCDs, OLEDs do not require a backlight to function, and therefore draw less power and have a much thinner display, sometimes as thin as 3mm. They are also brighter, cheaper to manufacture, and more environmentally friendly than plasma displays or LCDs. Because of their lower power needs, OLED displays run longer on a single battery charge than do LEDs, which is why OLED technology is currently being used in small screens of mobile devices such as cell phones, portable media players, and digital cameras.

More recently, OLED technology has been incorporated in some high-end televisions. The benefits of OLED technology may make LCD flat-panel displays quickly obsolete (see Figure 2.48). The pixels in OLED screens illuminate quickly, like light bulbs, and produce brighter images than does LCD technology. Because of the quick on–off illumination capacity of OLED pixels, the faster refresh rate enables these screens to display full-motion videos with life-like motion. Sony and Toshiba have already produced OLED televisions. Eventually, you might not even need a separate display device; it could very well be built into the walls of your house!

Flexible Screens

An offshoot of OLED technology is flexible OLEDs (FOLEDs). Unlike LCDs, which use rigid surfaces such as glass, FOLED screens use lightweight,

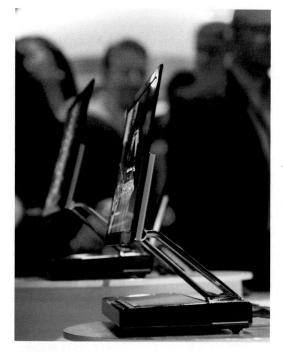

Figure 2.48

Because they do not need a backlight, OLED displays are much thinner than LEDs, making LCD screens seem bulky!

inexpensive, flexible material such as transparent plastics or metal foils. As shown in Figure 2.49, these flexible screens can play a full-motion video while being completely bent.

This 2.5-inch screen is playing a full-motion video while being bent into a semicircle.

Figure 2.49

FOLEDs would allow advertising to progress to a new dimension. Screens could be hung where posters hang now (such as on billboards). Wireless transmission of data to these screens would allow advertisers to display easily updatable full-motion images. Combining transparency and flexibility, these displays can be mounted on windshields and eyeglasses.

Wearable Screens

Who needs a computer screen when you can just wear one? With the rise of the iPod and other portable devices that play digital video, users are demanding larger viewing areas. Although a larger screen is often incompatible with the main design features of portable devices (light weight and long battery life), wearable virtual displays offer a solution. Personal media viewer displays such as the **myvu**, shown in Figure 2.50, are available now (**myvu.com**). Eventually, when the technology advances sufficiently, you might be able to purchase conventional eyeglasses with displays built right in. Wearable displays might eventually replace heavier screens on notebooks, desktops, and even PDAs.

"Bistable" Screens

Your computer screen constantly changes its images when you are surfing the Internet or playing a game. Because PDA and cell phone screens don't

Figure 2.50

Personal media viewers allow you to have a big-screen experience with your mobile devices. The display is projected in front of your eyes, giving you an "in the action" experience.

necessarily change that often, something called a "bistable" display, which is currently used in retail stores for pricing signs and in Amazon's Kindle (a wireless reading device), may one day be used in these devices. A bistable display has the ability to retain its image even when the power is turned off. In addition, bistable displays are lighter than LCD displays and reduce overall power consumption, resulting in longer battery life—perhaps as much as 600 times longer, according to Motorola. Because the market for portable devices such as smartphones continues to explode, you can expect to see bistable technologies emerging in mobile computer screens.

1. What exactly is a computer, and what are its four main functions?

Computers are devices that process data. They help organize, sort, and categorize data to turn it into information. The computer's four major functions are (1) to gather data (or allow users to input data), (2) to process that data (perform calculations or some other manipulation of the data), (3) to output data or information (display information in a form suitable for the user), and (4) to store data and information for later use.

2. What is the difference between data and information?

Data is a representation of a fact or idea. The number 3 and the words *televisions* and *Sony* are pieces of data. Information is data that has been organized or presented in a meaningful fashion. An inventory list that indicates that "three Sony televisions" are in stock is processed information. It allows a retail clerk to answer a customer query about the availability of merchandise. Information is more powerful than raw data.

3. What are bits and bytes, and how are they measured?

To process data into information, computers need to work in a language they understand. This language, called binary language, consists of two numbers: 0 and 1. Each 0, and each 1, is a binary digit, or bit. Eight bits create one byte. In computers, each letter of the alphabet, each number, and each special character consists of a unique combination of eight bits (one byte)—a string of eight 0s and 1s. For describing large amounts of storage capacity, the terms *megabyte* (approximately 1 million bytes), *gigabyte* (approximately 1 billion bytes), and *terabyte* (approximately 1 trillion bytes) are used.

4. What devices do I use to get data into the computer?

An input device enables you to enter data (text, images, and sounds) and instructions (user responses and commands) into a computer. You use keyboards to enter typed data and commands, whereas you use the mouse to enter user responses and commands. Keyboards are distinguished by the layout of the keys as well as the special keys found on the keyboard. The most common

keyboard is the QWERTY keyboard. Notebook keyboards are more compact, and generally have fewer keys, than standard keyboards. Consequently, many notebook keys have alternate functions so that you can get the same capabilities from their limited number of keys as you do from the special keys on standard keyboards.

Most desktop computers come with wired optical mice. Other options include trackball mice and wireless mice. An optical mouse uses an internal sensor or laser to control the mouse's movement. Wireless mice use batteries and send data to the computer via radio frequency or Bluetooth technology. Notebooks incorporate the mouse into the keyboard area. Notebook pointing devices include trackpoints and touchpads.

Touchscreens are display screens that respond to commands initiated by a touch with a finger or a stylus. Tablet PCs feature a touchscreen display that swivels and folds flat. Other devices that feature touchscreens are portable media players, cell phones, smartphones, and portable gaming devices.

Images are input into the computer with digital cameras, camcorders, and cell phones. Live video is captured with webcams and digital video recorders. Microphones capture sounds. There are many different types of microphones, including desktop, headset, and clip-on models.

5. What devices do I use to get information out of the computer?

Output devices enable you to send processed data out of your computer. It can take the form of text, pictures, sounds, or video. Monitors display soft copies of text, graphics, and video, while printers create hard copies of text and graphics. LCDs are the most popular type of monitor. Also called *flat-panel monitors*, they take up less space and are lighter and more energy efficient than older CRT monitors (which are big and boxy), making LCDs perfect for portable computers. Today's LCD monitors support high screen resolutions, have wide viewing angles, and feature fast pixel response times so that full-motion video appears smooth.

There are two primary categories of printers: impact and nonimpact. Impact printers have hammerlike keys that strike the paper through an inked ribbon. Nonimpact printers spray ink or use laser beams to transfer marks to the paper. The most common nonimpact printers are inkjet printers and laser printers. Specialty printers are also available. These include all-in-one printers, plotters, and thermal printers. When choosing a printer, you should be aware of factors such as speed, resolution, color output, memory, and cost.

Speakers are the output devices for sound. Most computers include speakers. However, you may want to upgrade to a more sophisticated speaker system, such as one that includes subwoofers and surround sound.

6. What's on the motherboard?

The motherboard, the main circuit board of the system, contains a computer's central processing unit (CPU), which coordinates the functions of all other devices on the computer. The performance of a CPU is affected by the speed of the processor (measured in gigahertz), the amount of cache memory, the speed of the front side bus (FSB), and the number of processing cores. RAM, the computer's volatile memory, is also located on the motherboard. RAM is where all the data and instructions are held while the computer is running. ROM, a permanent type of memory, is responsible for housing instructions to help start up a computer. The motherboard also houses a set of slots for expansion cards. The various circuit boards have specific functions that augment the computer's basic functions. They are usually referred to as expansion cards or adapter cards. Typical expansion cards found in the system unit are the sound and video cards.

7. Where are information and programs

To save programs and information permanently, you need to save them to the hard drive or to another permanent storage device such as a CD, DVD, or flash drive. The hard drive is your computer's primary device for permanent storage of software and files. The hard drive is a nonvolatile storage device, meaning it holds the data and instructions your computer needs permanently, even after the computer is turned off. External hard drives are essentially internal hard drives that have been made portable by enclosing them in a protective case and making them small and lightweight. Optical drives that can read from, and maybe even write to,

CD, DVD, or Blu-ray discs are another means of permanent, portable storage. Data is saved to compact discs (CDs), digital video discs (DVDs), and Blu-ray discs (BDs) as tiny pits that are burned into the disc by a high-speed laser. Flash drives are another portable means of storing data. These devices can hold 64 GB or more of data. Flash drives plug into USB ports. Flash memory cards let you transfer digital data between your computer and devices such as digital cameras, smartphones, video cameras, and printers.

8. How are devices connected to the computer?

There are a wide variety of ports that allow you to hook up peripheral devices (such as your monitor and keyboard) to your system. The most common type of port used to connect devices to a computer is the USB port. It has replaced serial ports and parallel ports, which are now considered legacy technology. FireWire ports provide even faster data transfer.

Connectivity ports give you access to networks and the Internet and enable your computer to function as a fax machine. Connectivity ports include Ethernet ports and modem ports. Multimedia ports include VGA, DVI, and S-video ports. They connect the computer to monitors and other multimedia devices. Audio ports are where you connect headphones, microphones, and speakers to the computer. HDMI ports connect monitors, TVs, and gaming consoles to the computer and work with both audio and video content.

9. How do I set up my computer to avoid strain and injury?

Ergonomics refers to how you arrange your computer and equipment to minimize your risk of injury or discomfort. This includes positioning your monitor correctly, buying an adjustable chair that ensures you have good posture while using the computer, assuming a proper position while typing, making sure the lighting is adequate, and not looking at the screen for long periods of time. Other good practices include taking frequent breaks and using other specially designed equipment such as ergonomic keyboards. Ergonomics is also important to consider when using mobile devices.

key terms

Word Bank

- CPU
- CRT
- DVI
- ergonomics
- external hard drive
- FireWire
- inkjet printer
- laser printer
- LCD
- microphone
- monitor
- mouse
- notebook
- optical mouse
- QWERTY
- RAM
- ROM
- speakers
- system unit
- USB
- webcam

Instructions: Fill in the blanks using the words from the Word Bank above.

Austin had been getting a sore back and stiff arms when he sat at his desk, so he redesigned the (1) _____ of his notebook setup. He placed the notebook in a stand so the (2) _____ was elevated to eye level and was 25 inches from his eyes. He decided to improve his equipment in other ways. His (3) _____ was old, so he replaced it with a(n) (4) _____ that didn't need a mouse pad. To plug in the mouse, he used a(n) (5) _____ port on the side of his (6) _____. He considered buying a larger (7) _____ keyboard with a number pad because it's not convenient to input numeric data with his current keyboard. Because he often printed flyers for his band, Austin decided to buy a printer that could print text-based pages quickly. Although he decided to keep his (8) _____ to print photos, he decided to buy a new (9) _____ to print his flyers faster. While looking at printers, Austin also noticed widescreen (10) _____ monitors that would provide a larger display than that on his notebook so he bought one on sale. He hooked up the monitor to the (11) _____ port on the back of the notebook. He also bought a(n) (12) _____ headset and a(n) (13) _____ so he could talk to his friends over the Internet. Austin also knew he had to buy a(n) (14) _____ to back up all his files. Finally, knowing his system could use more memory, Austin checked out prices for additional (15) _____.

becoming computer literate

Your parents live a day's drive from your school and have just called asking you for help in setting up their new computer.

Instructions: Because you can't help them in person, prepare a setup guide for your parents. Format it as either a Word document or a PowerPoint presentation. Your setup guide should illustrate and define all the components of a computer system. In addition, you should describe with illustrations and words the types of ports your parents will need to use to attach various peripheral devices to the system unit. You may use the Internet for information, device pictures, and illustrations, but remember to credit all sources at the end of your guide.

self-test

Instructions: Answer the multiple-choice and true–false questions below for more practice with key terms and concepts from this chapter.

Multiple Choice

1. Which of the following devices are considered input devices?
a. Keyboard and mouse
b. Monitor and inkjet printer
c. Hard drive and speakers
d. Laser printer and CD-ROM drive

2. Which of the following handles the processing for a computer?
a. RAM   c. ROM
b. CPU   d. USB

3. Which of the following is an output device?
a. Mouse   c. Hard drive
b. Monitor   d. Microphone

4. The resolution of a monitor is governed by the
a. size of the screen.
b. cost of the monitor.
c. number of pixels on the screen.
d. contrast of the pixels on the screen.

5. All of the following are important to consider when buying an LCD monitor EXCEPT
a. brightness.
b. pixel swap rate.
c. viewing angle.
d. resolution.

6. Restarting the system while the computer is running is called
a. a warm boot.   c. hibernation.
b. a standby start. d. a cold boot.

7. An Ethernet port is used for connecting your computer to a
a. network.   c. monitor.
b. printer.   d. digital camera.

8. Which of the following devices is considered volatile storage?
a. ROM   c. RAM
b. Optical disc d. Flash drive

9. Which of the following statements about hard drives is false?
a. Hard drives are not always installed inside the system unit of a computer.
b. Hard drives are considered volatile storage devices.
c. External hard drives are often used for backups.
d. Hard drives are considered nonvolatile storage devices.

10. Which of the following is not a reason to have an ergonomically correct setup for your computer?
a. It reduces eyestrain.
b. It prevents repetitive strain injuries.
c. It complies with federal laws.
d. It saves businesses money.

True–False

_____ 1. Data is information that has been organized or presented in a meaningful fashion.

_____ 2. ROM is volatile storage that is located on the motherboard.

_____ 3. Bluetooth devices have a shorter range of functionality than Wi-Fi devices.

_____ 4. USB ports are the most common type of port used for connecting peripherals to a computer.

_____ 5. A computer needs a cold boot when it resumes activity after hibernation.

1. Choosing the Best Keyboard

Once you become more familiar with software products such as Microsoft Office, you may want to migrate to a customized keyboard design. Although keyboards have similar setups, some keyboards provide special keys and buttons to support different users. For example, some keyboards are designed specifically for multimedia use, Internet use, and gaming use. Which one is best for you?

a. Examine the various keyboard setups at the Microsoft Web site (**microsoft.com/hardware/mouseandkeyboard/default.mspx**). Which keyboard would best suit your needs and why? What features would be most useful to you? How would you evaluate the additional costs versus the benefits?

b. When would you need a keyboard for a portable computing device, such as a smartphone? What is the current price for a portable folding keyboard? Would the virtual keyboard described in the chapter be a better choice for you? Explain your answers.

2. Watching Device Demos

YouTube is a great resource for product demonstrations. Open your browser, navigate to the YouTube Web site (**youtube.com**), search on any type of computer peripheral discussed in this chapter, and see if you can find a demonstration of a cool product. How helpful are these demonstrations? Try making a demonstration and uploading it to YouTube.

3. Communicating with the Computer

You want to start using Voice over Internet Protocol (VoIP) to chat over the Internet with your family and friends who live far away. You know you and your family members need speakers, a microphone, and a webcam. On the Web, investigate the following:

a. How much does a good pair of headphones cost? Would having separate speakers and a microphone be just as effective? Why or why not?

b. How much does a webcam cost? Which kind would you most likely purchase? Would you get the same kind for your parents? Why or why not?

4. Exploring Scanners

Scanners are one type of input device that we did not discuss in the text. Conduct the following research on the Web to find out about scanners:

a. What are the different kinds of scanners on the market?

b. What qualities do good scanners have?

c. How much do scanners cost?

Create a table comparing the qualities, features, and costs of several different scanners. Highlight the scanner you would be most interested in purchasing.

5. Green Computing

Reducing energy consumption and promoting the recycling of computer components are key aspects of businesses' "green" (environmentally friendly) initiatives. Using the Web, research the following:

a. What are the key attributes of the Energy Star and EPEAT Gold green PC certifications? Does your PC have these certifications?

b. What toxic components are contained in computers and monitors? Where can you recycle computers and monitors in your area?

c. Check out **goodcleantech.com** and find out which companies are currently working toward better green technology. If your school had to replace computers in a lab, which environmentally friendly company would you recommend? Why?

making the transition to... the Workplace

1. Desktop versus Notebook

There are two main types of computers in the workplace: desktop computers with separate system units and monitors, and notebook computers that are portable and have the monitor, keyboard, and the system unit within a single case. If you were being interviewed for a job, what types of questions would you need to ask your prospective boss about the job to determine whether you would be using a desktop or a notebook computer?

2. What System Will You Use?

When you arrive at a new position for a company, you'll most likely be provided with a computer. Based on the career you are in now or are planning to pursue, answer the following questions:

a. What kind of computer system would you most like to use—desktop, notebook, tablet PC, or something else?

b. If you were required to use a type of computer you had never used before (such as a Mac instead of a PC), how would you go about learning to use the new computer?

c. What kind of keyboard, mouse, monitor, and printer would you like to have?

d. Would you need any additional input or output devices to perform your job?

3. Going Wireless

Investigate the wireless options for mice, keyboards, printers, and monitors. What are the costs associated with these wireless devices? Are they more expensive than their wired counterparts are? What are the benefits of having wireless technology? What are the factors to take into consideration when buying and using wireless devices? Which devices would work best for you?

4. Choosing the Best Printer

You are looking for a new printer for your home business. You have always had an inkjet printer, but now that the costs for color laser printers are dropping, you're considering buying a color laser printer.

a. Using the Web, investigate the merits of different inkjet and color laser printers. Focus on one printer in each category and note the initial cost of each.

b. Research the cost of ink or toner for each printer. Calculate the cost of ink or toner supplies for each printer, assuming you will print 5,000 color pages per year. How much will printing cost per page, not including the initial cost of the printer itself?

c. Investigate all-in-one printers that have faxing, scanning, and copying capabilities. How much more expensive are they than traditional inkjet or laser printers? Are there any drawbacks to these multipurpose machines? Do they perform each function as well as their stand-alone counterparts do? Can you print in color on these machines?

d. Based on your research, which printer would be the most economical?

5. Office Ergonomics

Your boss has designated you as the "ergonomics coordinator" for the department. She has asked you to design a flyer to be posted around the office to inform your co-workers of the proper computer setup as well as the potential risks if such precautions are ignored. Create an ergonomics flyer, making sure it fits on an 8.5 × 11-inch piece of paper.

Instructions: Albert Einstein used *Gedankenexperiments*, or critical thinking questions, to develop his theory of relativity. Some ideas are best understood by experimenting with them in our own minds. The following critical thinking questions are designed to demand your full attention but require only a comfortable chair—no technology.

1. **Keyboard of the Future**

   What do you think the keyboard of the future will look like? What capabilities will it have that keyboards currently don't have? Will it have ports, cables, or special communication capabilities?

2. **Touchscreen Technology**

   Touchscreen technology is quickly becoming part of digital devices. Examples include the iPhone, Blackberry Storm, iPod touch, and HP Touchsmart PC. How do you think touchscreen technology could improve other devices, such as cars or home appliances?

3. **Storage Devices of the Future**

   How do you think storage devices will change in the future? Will increased storage capacity and decreased size affect the ways in which we use computers? Will we need storage devices in the future, or will we access all of our data via the Internet?

4. **Computers Decreasing Productivity?**

   Can you think of any situations in which computers actually decrease productivity? Why? Should we always expect computers to increase our productivity? What do you think the impact of using computers would be:

   a. in a third-grade classroom?
   b. in a manager's office for a large chain supermarket?
   c. for a retired couple who just purchased their first computer?

5. **"Smart" Homes**

   The Smart Medical Home project of the University of Rochester's Center for Future Health is researching how to use technology to monitor many aspects of your health. The Smart Medical Home is the creation of a cross-disciplinary group of scientists and engineers from the college, the medical center, and the university's Center for Future Health. This particular "smart home" includes a sophisticated computer system that helps keep track of items such as eyeglasses or keys, and a kitchen equipped with a new kind of packaging to signal the presence of dangerous bacteria in food. Spaces between ordinary walls are stuffed with gadgetry, including banks of powerful computers.

   a. What abilities should a smart home have to safeguard and improve the quality of your life?
   b. Could a smart home have potential hazards?

6. **Toy or Computer?**

   When do you think a toy becomes a computer? The Microsoft Xbox 360 has a hard drive, a processor with three cores, internal RAM, and wireless capability. Apple iPods also have hard drives (or flash memory and a processor). Are these devices computers or toys? What capabilities do you think next-generation gaming consoles and iPods should have?

Notebook versus Desktop: Which Is Best?

Problem

You have joined a small business that is beginning to evaluate its technology setup. Because of the addition of several new sales representatives and other administrative employees, many new computers need to be purchased. You are trying to decide which would be better to purchase: notebook computers or desktops.

Task

Split your class into small groups, divide each group into two teams, and assign the following tasks:

> Team A explores the benefits and downfalls of desktop computers.
>
> Team B explores the benefits and downfalls of notebook computers.

Process

1. Form the groups and teams. Think about what the technology goals are for the company and what information and resources you need to tackle this project.
2. Research and then discuss the components of each system you are recommending. Are any components better suited for the particular needs of the various employees (sales representatives versus administrative staff)? Consider all the input, output, processing, and storage devices. Are any special devices or peripherals required?
3. Write a summary position paper. Support your system recommendation for

   Team A—purchase desktop computers

   Team B—purchase notebook computers

Conclusion

Desktop and notebook computers have their own merits as computing systems. Beyond portability, there are other things to think about. Being aware of the options in the marketplace and knowing how to analyze the trade-offs of different designs allows you to become a better consumer as well as a better computer user.

In addition to the review materials presented here, you'll find additional materials featured with the book's multimedia, including the *Technology in Action* Student Resource CD and the Companion Website (**pearsonhighered.com/techinaction**), which will help reinforce your understanding of the chapter content. These materials include the following:

Active Helpdesk

In Active Helpdesk calls, you'll assume the role of helpdesk operator, taking calls about the concepts you've learned in this chapter. You'll apply what you've learned and receive feedback from a supervisor to review and reinforce those concepts. The Active Helpdesk calls for this chapter are listed below and can be found on your Student Resource CD:

- Understanding Bits and Bytes
- Using Input Devices
- Using Output Devices
- Exploring Storage Devices and Ports

Sound Bytes

Sound Bytes are dynamic multimedia tutorials that help demystify even the most complex topics. You'll view video clips and animations that illustrate computer concepts and then apply what you've learned by reviewing with the Sound Byte Labs, which include quizzes and activities specifically tailored to each Sound Byte. The Sound Bytes for this chapter are listed below and can be found on your Student Resource CD:

- Binary Numbers Interactive
- Tablet and Notebook Tour
- Virtual Computer Tour?
- Port Tour: How Do I Hook It Up
- Healthy Computing

Companion Website

The *Technology in Action* Companion Website includes a variety of additional materials to help you review and learn more about the topics in this chapter. The resources available at **pearsonhighered.com/techinaction** include:

- **Online Study Guide.** Each chapter features an online true–false and multiple-choice quiz. You can take these quizzes, automatically check the results, and e-mail the results to your instructor.
- **Web Research Projects.** Each chapter features several Web research projects that ask you to search the Web for information on computer-related careers, milestones in computer history, important people and companies, emerging technologies, and the applications and implications of different technologies.

three
using the Internet:
making the most of the Web's resources

resources

Active Helpdesk

- Doing Business Online **(p. 111)**
- Getting Around the Web **(p. 118)**
- Using Subject Directories and Search Engines **(p. 121)**
- Connecting to the Internet **(p. 124)**

Sound Bytes

- Creating a Web-Based E-mail Account **(p. 98)**
- Blogging **(p. 103)**
- Welcome to the Web **(p. 116)**
- Finding Information on the Web **(p. 120)**
- Connecting to the Internet **(p. 123)**

Companion Website

The Companion Website includes a variety of additional materials to help you review and learn more about the topics in this chapter. Go to: *pearsonhighered.com/techinaction*

how cool is *this?* Want to find out about the
newest sites on the Web? Check out **Looqe.com!**

With so many **new applications** popping up on the Web daily, it's
practically impossible to keep up with what's new and current. Looqe.com is a type of
directory that lets you quickly preview all these new **Web apps**. When
you click a category from the tag cloud, a group of thumbnail screenshots displays so
you can easily see what each site looks like. Hover your mouse over a thumbnail for a
brief description, or click on the thumbnail to be taken directly to the site.

The Looqe **tag cloud** has topics such as "Am bored" and "Have a few minutes to kill" that help you fill some empty minutes in your day. "Travel," "Hotels," and
"Trips" help you plan your next vacation. Additionally, there are helpful educational topics such as "Questions and Answers," "Knowledge," and "Learning" in which you'll
find great how-to, reference, and other **useful** Web sites.

Check out Looqe.com to discover how cool it really is.

The Internet

It's hard to imagine life without the Internet. We use it to shop, to communicate, to research, to find places and get directions, and to entertain ourselves (see Figure 3.1). It's accessible from our computers, smartphones, and portable music players (PMPs), and we can get to it while at home, at work, at school—even at Starbucks. But what exactly is the Internet, and how did it begin?

Why was the Internet created?

The **Internet**, or "Net" as it is sometimes called, is the largest computer network in the world—actually, a network of networks—that connects billions of computer users. The concept of the Internet was developed while the United States was in the midst of the Cold War with the Soviet Union. At that time, the U.S. armed forces were becoming increasingly dependent on computers to coordinate and plan their activities. They needed a computer system that would operate efficiently and that was located in various parts of the country so that it could not be disrupted easily in the event of an attack.

At the same time, researchers hoped the Internet would address the problems involved with getting different computers to communicate with each other. Although computers had been networked since the early 1960s, there was no reliable way to connect computers from different manufacturers because they used different proprietary designs and methods of communication. What was lacking was a common communications method that all computers could use. The Internet was created to respond to these two concerns: establishing a secure form of military communications and creating a means by which all computers could communicate.

Who invented the Internet?

The modern Internet evolved from an early U.S. government–funded "internetworking" project called the Advanced Research Projects Agency Network (ARPANET). ARPANET began as a four-node network involving UCLA, Stanford Research Institute, the University of California at Santa Barbara, and the University of Utah in Salt Lake City. The first real communication occurred in late 1969 between the computer at Stanford and the computer at UCLA. Although the system crashed after the third letter was transmitted, it was the beginning of a revolution. Many people participated in the creation of the ARPANET, but two men who worked on the project, Vinton Cerf and Robert Kahn, are generally acknowledged as the "fathers" of the Internet. They earned this honor because in the 1970s they were primarily responsible for developing the communications protocols (standards) that are still in use on the Internet today.

So are the Web and the Internet the same thing?

Because the **World Wide Web** (**WWW** or the **Web**) is what we use the most, we sometimes think of the

Figure 3.1

From buying guitars on eBay to getting directions on your cell phone to checking e-mail or the latest snow stats, the Internet makes it all possible.

"Net" and the "Web" as being interchangeable. However, the Web is the means we use to access information over the Internet. What distinguishes the Web from the rest of the Internet is its use of

- common communication protocols that enable different computers to talk to each other and display information in compatible formats
- special links (called *hyperlinks*) that enable users to jump from one place to another on the Web.

Did the same people who invented the Internet invent the Web? The Web was invented many years after the original Internet. In 1989, Tim Berners-Lee, a physicist at the European Organization for Nuclear Research (CERN), wanted a method for linking his research documents so that other researchers could access them. In conjunction with Robert Cailliau, Berners-Lee developed the basic architecture of the Web and created the first Web browser (a software application that enables a user to display and interact with text and other media on the Web). The original browser could handle only text and was usable only on computers running the NeXT operating system, a commercially unsuccessful operating system (OS), which limited its usage. So Berners-Lee put out a call to the Internet community to assist with development of browsers for other platforms.

In 1993, the National Center for Supercomputing Applications released its Mosaic browser for use on the Macintosh and Windows operating systems. Mosaic could display graphics as well as text. The once-popular Netscape Navigator browser evolved from Mosaic and heralded the beginning of the Web's monumental growth.

How much has the Internet grown? The Internet experienced explosive growth in the early to mid-1990s. By 1997, nearly everyone in the world had access to an Internet connection.

Because of such global Internet availability and access, as well as the increasing capabilities of hardware and software, the number of Web sites (locations on the Internet) grew exponentially, as shown in Figure 3.2. In December 1990, the first Web site appeared on the Web. Four years later, approximately 10,000 sites were online; by June 1996, a whopping 252,000 Web sites were created.

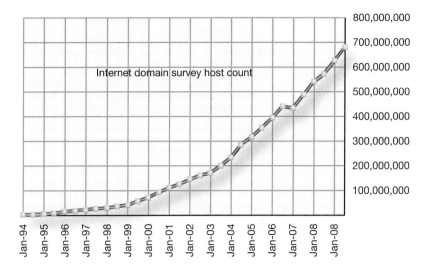

The Web experienced its greatest amount of growth in the year 2000—more than 160 percent in a single year. The growth of the Web has since begun to slow down, but is by no means complete. In January 2009, almost 700 million Web sites were online. The Web's growth is expected to continue, with more than 200 million Web sites anticipated by 2010.

Figure 3.2

The growth of the number of Web sites on the Internet has been explosive since the first Web site was hosted in 1990.

Source: **carolina-advertising. com/free-advertising/ internet-growth.gif/**

Communicating Through the Internet: E-Mail and Other Technologies

E-mail is fast becoming the main form of communication in the 21st century, and it is the primary use of the Web. However, e-mail is not the only type of Internet-based communication. You can use instant messaging, blogs, podcasts, social networks, chat rooms, newsgroups, and more for communicating via the Internet. (You can even talk over the phone through the Internet with Voice over Internet Protocol (VoIP) which will be discussed in Chapter 8.) Like any other means of communication, you need to know how to use these tools efficiently to get the most out of them.

E-Mail

Why did e-mail catch on so quickly?
E-mail (short for **electronic mail**) is a written message that is sent and received over the Internet. The messages can be formatted and enhanced with graphics and may also include other files as attachments. E-mail

Creating a Web-Based E-mail Account

In this Sound Byte, you'll see a step-by-step demonstration that explains how to create a free Yahoo! Web-based e-mail account. You'll also learn the options available with such accounts.

controversial content in an e-mail. It could come back to haunt you. Finally, remember that even after you've deleted a message, it doesn't really vanish. Many Internet service providers and company e-mail servers archive e-mail, which can then be accessed or subpoenaed in the event of a lawsuit or investigation.

What do I need to send and receive e-mail? All you need to send and receive e-mail is a computer, an Internet connection, and an e-mail account. Each component, however, entails additional considerations. Although it's most common to send and receive e-mail from your computer, today many e-mail messages are exchanged wirelessly among smartphones and other portable devices.

has become the primary method of electronic communication because it's fast and convenient and reduces the costs of postage and long-distance phone calls. In addition, with e-mail, the sender and receiver don't have to be available at the same time in order to communicate. Because

Figure 3.3

You can organize your e-mail and assign messages to topic-specific folders.

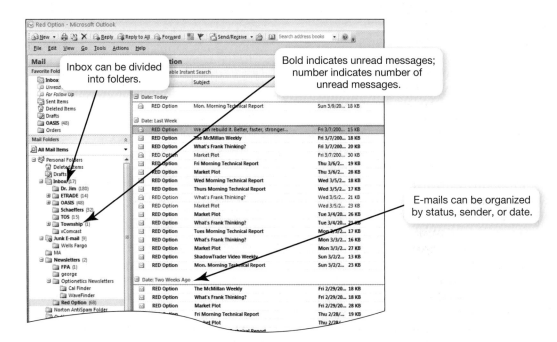

of these and other reasons, approximately 92 percent of Americans who access the Internet claim that their main online activity is sending and receiving e-mail.

Is e-mail private? E-mails are not private. In fact, the information in e-mail is no more private than a postcard. E-mails can be easily viewed by others, either by being printed out or forwarded, so you never know who eventually could read your e-mail. Also, because it is not encrypted, you shouldn't use e-mail to send personal or sensitive information such as bank account numbers or Social Security numbers, which could lead to identity theft. Employers have access to e-mail sent from the workplace, so use caution when putting negative or

Are there different types of e-mail accounts? To read, send, and organize your e-mail, you can use an e-mail client. **E-mail clients** such as Microsoft Outlook are software programs running on your computer that access your Internet service provider's (ISP's) server. However, with these e-mail clients, you are able to view your e-mail only from a computer on which the client program is installed, which can be less than convenient if you travel or want to view your e-mail when you're away from that computer.

Today, most broadband providers and ISPs offer the services of a Web-based e-mail client so that users can look at their e-mail directly from the Web. Web-based e-mail uses the Internet as the client; therefore, you can access a Web-based e-mail account from any computer that has access to the Web. No special client software is needed. Free e-mail accounts such as Yahoo! Mail, Hotmail, or Gmail are Web-based e-mail clients. Some e-mail providers—AOL, for example—offer both client-based and Web-based access to e-mail.

What are the advantages of a Web-based e-mail account? Unlike client-based e-mail, which is accessible only from a computer on which the client is installed, Web-based e-mail accounts make your e-mail accessible from any computer as long as you can access the Internet. Even if you use a client-based account, having a secondary Web-based e-mail account also provides you with a more permanent e-mail address. Your other e-mail accounts and addresses may change when you switch ISPs or change employers, so having a permanent e-mail address is important.

Why would I need a client-based e-mail program? Many people have more than one e-mail account. You may have a personal account, a work account, and an account you use when filling out forms on the Internet. One of the benefits of using a client-based e-mail program such as Microsoft Outlook is that you can download your e-mail from many different e-mail accounts so that it all can be accessed in one location. In addition, client e-mail programs offer several features to help you manage and organize your e-mail and coordinate e-mail with your calendar, tasks, and contact lists. As you can see in Figure 3.3, you can organize your e-mail by task, sender, or priority, or you can distribute your messages to designated folders within your inbox. Some Web-based e-mail systems such as Yahoo! feature many

of the same organizational tools, but client-based programs are generally more fully featured.

Instant Messaging

How does instant messaging work?
Instant messaging (IM) services are programs that enable you to communicate in real time with others who are online (see Figure 3.4). Although IM is most often used for casual conversations between friends, many businesses use IM as a means of quick and instant communication between co-workers.

AOL's AIM is one of the most popular instant messaging services. ICQ, Yahoo!, Google, and Windows Live Messenger also host popular instant messaging services. These services are proprietary, meaning you can chat only with those who share the same IM service. But there are universal chat clients such as Trillian, Pidgin, and Zango Messenger that allow users of all the popular IMs to chat with each other regardless of the service they use. Meebo is a new Web-based universal chat service (no installation required) that lets you communicate with users on a variety of IM services from any computer anywhere. No software download is required.

How do I keep track of my IM contacts?
When you use IM, you set up a list of contacts, often called a buddy list. To communicate (or chat) with someone from your buddy list, that person must be online at the same time as you are. When someone wants to chat with you, a window pops open with his or her message. If it's not convenient to chat at that time, you can close or ignore the message. Some programs such as Yahoo! and AOL's AIM offer stealth

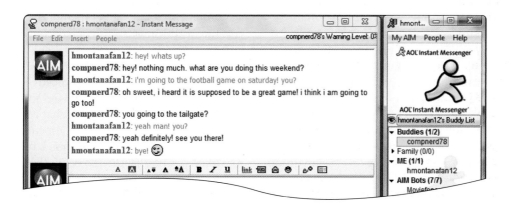

Figure 3.4

Instant messaging services such as AOL Instant Messenger enable you to have real-time online conversations with friends and family.

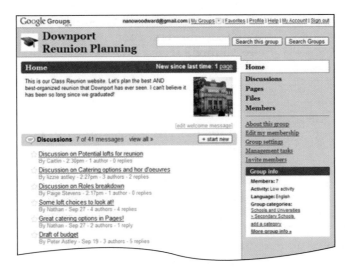

Figure 3.5

Google Groups is a convenient means to join a group or to create your own.

settings so that you can appear offline to certain buddies.

If you want to chat with more than one person, you can hold simultaneous individual conversations, or if you all want to chat together, you can create custom IM chat rooms. Many IM services such as AIM and Live Messenger offer chat services so you can speak with your buddies if you have a microphone and speakers. A webcam allows you to see them as you chat.

Group Communication

What kinds of online group communication exist?   You can interact with a wide variety of people online in many ways. Some forms are in real time, or synchronous; others are asynchronous. Some of the ways in which you can communicate and interact with a group of people online are through chat rooms, newsgroups, and listservs.

A **chat room**, such as those found at **icq.com/icqchat**, is a form of synchronous communication in which online conversations occur in real time and are visible to everyone in the chat room. Usually, chat rooms are organized around a specific theme or topic. Wireclub (**wireclub.com**) has a variety of chat rooms to suit every interest. A **newsgroup** is similar to a discussion group or forum in which people create threads (conversations). In a thread, a newsgroup

member posts messages and reads and replies to messages from other members of the newsgroup. Google Groups is a great source for various newsgroups. Google Groups (see Figure 3.5) allows you to join a group or create your own. A **listserv** is an electronic mailing list of e-mail addresses of people who are interested in a certain topic or an area of interest. Information and updates on shared topics of interest are exchanged between members through e-mail. Tile.net (**tile.net**) is a good source of discussion lists.

Social networking is another popular means of communicating with many people, which we will discuss in the Web 2.0 section later in this chapter.

Do dangers exist in group communications?   When you use group communications, you generally need to register and sign in with a username and password. It's best not to disclose your identity but rather to "hide" behind a username, thus protecting your privacy. On the other hand, the people you are chatting with are also hiding their identities. Some chatters use this veil of privacy to cover dishonest intentions. You have probably heard of individuals, especially young teenagers, who were deceived (and sometimes harmed) by someone they met in a chat room. Several Web sites such as **chatdanger.com** try to protect vulnerable people, especially children, from malicious online users (see Figure 3.6).

Are there special ways to behave with group communication?   General rules of etiquette, often referred to as **netiquette**, exist across chat rooms and other online forums, including obvious standards of behavior such as introducing yourself when you enter the room and specifically addressing the person to whom you are talking. Chat room users also are expected to refrain from swearing, name-calling, and using explicit or prejudiced language, and they are not allowed to harass other participants. In addition, chat room users cannot post the same text repeatedly with the intent to disrupt the chat, a behavior called *flooding*. Similarly, users shouldn't type in all capital letters, because this is interpreted as shouting.

Figure 3.6

Childnet International works to make the Internet safe. The site **chatdanger.com** provides a lot of good safety advice for using chat rooms, mobile phones, e-mail, instant messaging programs, and games.

Web 2.0 Technologies: Collaborating and Communicating Through the Internet

Over time our use of the Internet has evolved from passively reading and using Web content created for us to actively creating, sharing, and collaborating on our own Web content. **Web 2.0** describes a new trend of Web interactions between people, software, and data. It can be classified as the social Web, in which the user is also a participant. Additionally, Web 2.0 describes a trend of new applications to combine the functionality of multiple applications. Hundreds of companies now exist to help us share, recommend, collaborate, create, and socialize (see Figure 3.7). The following

discussions focus more on the social, collaborative, and communicative nature of Web 2.0 applications. Other Web-based productivity applications will be discussed in Chapter 4.

Weblogs (Blogs) and Video Logs (Vlogs)

What is a blog? A **weblog**, or **blog**, is a personal log or journal posted on the Web. The beauty of blogs is that they are simple to create, manage, and read. Anyone can create a blog, and there are millions of blogs available to read, follow, and comment on.

Several key characteristics define a blog. Blogs are generally written by a single author and are arranged as a listing of entries on a single page, with the most recent blog (entry) appearing at the top of the list. In addition, blogs are public. Blogs have searchable and organized content, making them user friendly. They are accessible from anywhere using a Web browser.

Are blogs just text? The traditional form of a blog is primarily text-based but may also include images and audio. A **video log** (**vlog** or **video blog**) is a personal journal that uses video as the primary content. It can also contain text, images, and audio. Vlogs quickly are becoming a highly popular means of personal expression, and many can

Figure 3.7

Hundreds of companies and Web sites make up the Web 2.0 landscape, which helps us share, recommend, collaborate, create, and socialize.

Figure 3.8

Video logs use video in addition to text, images, and audio. Blinkx is a video search engine that helps you sift through the increasing number of vlogs.

be found by searching the most popular video-sharing site today, YouTube (**youtube.com**). Software such as Vlog It! makes adding video content to your blog easy, although you can easily upload unedited video straight from your computer, video camera, or cell phone. Blinkx (**blinkx.com**) is a video search engine that helps you sift through all the video posted on the Web (see Figure 3.8). For a true video conversation, try Seesmic (**seesmic.com**), in which people post and reply to posts with videos.

What do people write in blogs?
Many people use blogs as a sort of personal

scrapbook. Whenever the urge strikes, they just write a stream-of-consciousness flow of thoughts or a report of their daily activities. Many blogs, however, focus on a particular topic. For example, **themovieblog.com** is a blog that contains reviews and opinions about movies, and **engadget.com** (see Figure 3.9) is a blog that devotes itself to discussing techno-gadgets. Blogcatalog (**blogcatalog.com**) and Bloghub (**bloghub.com**) are two of many blog directories that can help you find blogs that best fit your interests.

How do I create a blog? It is easy to write and maintain a blog, and many Web sites provide the necessary tools for you to create your own. Two sites that offer free blog hosting are **blogger.com** and **livejournal.com**. You can add other features to your blog such as pictures or subpages. Another alternative is to host your blog yourself. Hosting your own blog requires that you have your own Web site and a URL so that people can access it.

Are there problems with blogs?
The popularity of blogs has brought about a new problem: spam blogs (splogs), which are artificially created blog sites filled with fake articles or stolen text (a tactic known as *blog scraping*). Spam blogs, which contain links to other sites associated with the splog's creator, have the intention of either increasing traffic to, or increasing search engine rankings for, these usually

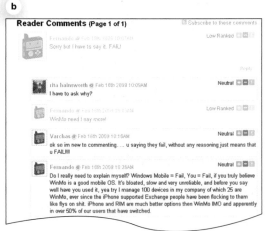

Figure 3.9

(a) Some blogs, like this one from **engadget.com**, are set up as online reviews organized by category. (b) Alternatively, they can appear as personal journals that record a blogger's thoughts, viewpoints, and feelings in reverse chronological order.

disreputable or useless Web sites. Although not terribly bad, splogs are another unwanted form of content that continues to grow like weeds on the Web.

Wikis

What are wikis?   Unlike traditional Web content, which the viewer of the site cannot change, a **wiki** is a type of Web site that allows users to change its content by adding, removing, or editing the content (see Figure 3.10). Wikis add the extra benefit of tracking revisions so that past versions can be easily accessed at any time by any reader. The popular collaborative online encyclopedia Wikipedia (**wikipedia.org**) uses wiki technology so that the content can be updated continually. Some Web-based document products, such as Google Docs (**docs.google.com**), have wiki-like features to promote online collaboration.

How accurate is Web content that anyone can change?   The idea behind publicly managed and edited content, such as that found in wikis, is that the public will keep the content valid. Those challenging the validity of publicly editable wikis argue that the content cannot be trusted because wikis are easily tampered with, whereas supporters argue that the community of users can quickly catch erroneous content and correct it.

In late 2005, Wikipedia content was measured for accuracy in its scientific content and was found to be as accurate as the *Encyclopedia Britannica*. Nonetheless, free and easy access to edit pages also can lead to improper manipulation, which results in tighter access controls. To thwart malicious editing of the wiki content, for example, users who want editing privileges are required to register. Citizendium (**citizendium.org**), another

Elijah provides initial text (in black)

Jordan includes additional text (in green)

Stephanie inserts extra detail (in blue)

Mackenzie-Jordan Law Associates has a significant number of celebrity clients. One of the most important aspects of our legal counsel to these individuals is to help protect the use of their images and likenesses.
Sometimes this is referred to as the right of publicity. This right is a valuable asset because there are endless licensing opportunities that can be quite lucrative. Some states have a publicity law that protects a celebrity's image and likeness for 100 years, but as yet that law has not been enacted in the state of Texas.
The merchandising of celebrity images has become a huge source of income for many celebrities as well as others.
In recent years, legal disputes have resulted from artists and illustrators manipulating celebrity images.
In the past, courts have typically protected the First Amendment rights of artists in these cases. But recently there have been a few cases where celebrities have been allowed to sue creators of fictional works for the violation of the right of publicity.
The right of publicity is intended to prevent others from capitalizing on a celebrity's fame. Many people in the entertainment industry are fearful that unauthorized biographies, docudramas, and celebrity spoofs and satires will no longer be protected. Many entertainment lawyers say a celebrity's right to publicity is intended solely for ads and merchandise, not for literary works.

Figure 3.10

Rather than collaborating by exchanging e-mails and attachments—and potentially losing track of the most recent version of a document—different users can collaborate on a wiki page.

open wiki encyclopedia, requires contributors to provide real names and sign an ethics pledge, and all postings are monitored.

Are wikis used for anything other than encyclopedias and manuals? Wikis provide an excellent source for collaborative writing, both in and out of the classroom. Wiki technology is currently incorporated in Blackboard, a popular online course-management application, to encourage collaborative learning in online courses. Wikis are also becoming popular tools for business collaboration. Rather than passing documents back and forth via e-mail and losing track of which updated version is the most recent, wikis allow all who have access to the page to post their ideas and modify the content of just one document. A history of all changes is kept, so users can revert to earlier versions if desired.

These same collaborative efforts also extend to user manuals. One site, wikiHow (**wikihow.org**), is an online project that uses both wikis and the collaborative process to build a large, online how-to manual. Blender (**blender.org**), an open source software application for 3D modeling, uses MediaWiki, a more feature-rich wiki implementation product, to provide users with documentation, help with game development and 3D modeling, and tutorials for Blender software.

Like blogs, wikis also can be used to express thoughts and opinions about certain topics. Unlike blogs, wikis can be edited and therefore can present an emergent "common" opinion, rather than the individual opinion of the initial writer.

Podcasts and Webcasts

What is a podcast? A podcast is a clip of audio or video content that is broadcast over the Internet using compressed audio and video files such as MP3s and MP4s. This content might include radio shows, audiobooks, magazines, and even educational programs. The word "podcast" is a combination of "broadcasting" and "iPod"—not because you have to use an iPod but because iPods are the most popular form of portable media player

(PMP) and because people download audio files to listen to on their iPods. However, you don't have to listen to podcasts on a portable media player. You can listen to podcasts on your computer or even on a smartphone as long as the device can play the content. To listen to a podcast on your computer, you'll need a media player such as iTunes, RealPlayer, or Windows Media Player. If you want to enjoy a video podcast on your PMP, you need to make sure your mobile device can play video as well as audio files.

So what makes podcasting different from just listening to an audio file on the computer or a PMP player? The difference is that podcasts are files that come to you through syndication so you do not have to search for them. Perhaps you are used to getting your news from a certain Web site, but the only way you can determine that new content has been added is to go to the site and look for the newly added information. In contrast, if you subscribe to podcasts, when the content changes, it is brought to you. What's more, if you have several favorite Web sites, rather than individually checking the content, you can collect all the site updates in one place. Podcasts are possible because of RSS technology, which makes it more efficient for you to gather updates to your favorite content.

What is RSS? Really Simple Syndication (RSS) is an XML-based format that facilitates the delivery of frequent content updates on Web pages. Using RSS, Web content can be formatted in such a way that **aggregators** can find it and download only the new content to your computer. Aggregators are software programs that go out and grab the latest updates of Web material according to your specifications. They are

Figure 3.11

Podcasts are available in a wide variety of topics and content. Web sites such as **podcast.com** allow you to add your own podcast to their directories.

available for all major operating systems as well as some mobile devices such as smartphones. Some aggregators work with Atom, another specification, to distribute new Web content.

Where can I find podcasts?
Podcasts can be found all over the Web. Most newspapers, TV news organizations, and radio sites offer podcasts of their programs. Although many podcasts are news related, many podcasts offer more entertaining and informative content. The television network ABC, for example, offers podcasts of some of its most popular TV shows, such as *Grey's Anatomy* and *Lost.* Sites such as Yoga Today offer extensive yoga classes. Many schools are beginning to recognize this format as a way to supply students with course content updates, and instructors create podcasts of their lectures.

iTunes (**itunes.com**), Podcast Alley (**podcastalley.com**), and Podcast.com (**podcast.com**) are aggregators as well as great directories of podcasts, organized by genre, to help you easily locate podcasts of most interest to you (see Figure 3.11). If there is a particular topic for which you'd like to hear a podcast, Podscope (**podscope.com**) is a podcast-specific search engine that searches podcasts for specific words or phrases and then displays the results with audio clips. YouTube is also becoming a popular source of RSS feeds for video content.

Can I create my own podcast? It is simple to create audio content that can be delivered to the Web and then listened to by people all over the world. In fact, you could become a radio broadcaster overnight. Although high-end equipment always will produce a more sophisticated output, you really need only the most basic equipment to make your own podcast.

To record the content, at the minimum you need a computer with a microphone. If you want to make a video podcast, you also need a Web camera (webcam) or video camera. Additional software may be needed to edit the digital audio and video content. After the podcast content has been recorded and edited, it needs to be exported to MP3 format. Sound editing software, such as the freeware program Audacity, can be used to record and edit audio files and then export them to MP3 format. The last steps involve creating an RSS feed and then uploading the content to the Web.

What's a webcast? A **webcast** is the broadcast of audio or video content over the Internet. Unlike podcasts that are prerecorded and made available for download, most webcasts are live or are a one-time event. Webcasts are not updated automatically, but some, such as Microsoft's On-Demand Webcasts, are RSS feeds. Webcasts use a special kind of media technology that continuously feeds the multimedia content, which facilitates the viewing and downloading process of large audio and video files. Webcasts can include noninteractive content such as simulcasts of radio or TV broadcasts. More recent webcasts invite interactive responses from the viewing or listening audience. For example, **ORLive.com** provides surgical webcasts that demonstrate the latest surgical innovations and techniques (see Figure 3.12). Many of these webcasts present live procedures and then allow time afterward for a panel of physicians to answer viewers' questions. Webcasts also are used in the corporate world to broadcast annual meetings and in the educational arena to transmit seminars.

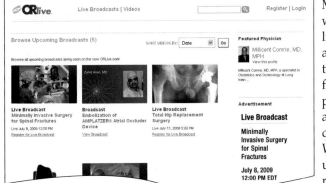

Figure 3.12

ORLive provides webcasts that demonstrate the latest surgical techniques.

Social Networking

What is social networking? Social **networking** is a means by which people use the Internet to communicate and share information among their immediate friends, and meet and connect with others through common interests, experiences, and friends

Computers in Society: Online Storage and Secure Backup for Your Valuable Digital Assets

The hard drive on most notebook or desktop computers sold today can hold more than 500 GB of data. Chances are you have a lot of important school files, personal and financial documents, e-mails, digital photos and videos of your friends and family, music files, and more. Although it's convenient to have all your information readily available, your precious data is extremely vulnerable.

Hard drive crashes, virus attacks, and physical damage (especially to dropped notebooks) can render the data stored on your hard drive useless. For this reason, many people choose to buy external hard drives as a simple, cost-effective alternative to store and back up

their digital assets, keeping them from being lost or damaged if their computer is harmed or stolen. However, even external hard drives are not immune to data loss. Your computer or external device could be destroyed by a fire, flood, or hurricane, or it could be stolen. If that happens, all those digital photographs, your music collection, and everything else will be lost. One alternative that helps avoid this problem is online storage or backup. Most likely you need both.

In essence, You can think of online storage as using the Internet as an alternative to a portable storage device such as a flash drive or external hard drive (see Figure 3.13). The beauty of online storage is that your data is available anywhere you are; you do not need to be at your computer or lug around your external hard drive to access the information. More importantly, because the information is stored online, it is in a secure, remote location, so data is much less vulnerable to all the potential disasters that could harm data stored in physical devices such as your desktop or notebook computer or external hard drive. Some services also offer sharing capabilities that allow you to share your photos and videos more easily with others. Several easy-to-use services offer free storage for a

Notebook

INTERNET

Online storage and backup

Home Computer

Figure 3.13

Online storage and backup uses the Internet as an alternative to external hard drives.

(see Figure 3.14). Social networking services such as Facebook (**facebook.com**) and MySpace (**myspace.com**) have become amazingly popular because they provide ways for members to communicate with their friends by voice, chat, instant message, videoconference, and blogs so that members don't need separate communication accounts. These services were first accepted broadly among the younger, nonprofessional population, but now many adults create their own social networking profiles on Facebook and MySpace. Ning (**ning.com**) is a social networking site that allows you to create your own network around your own common topic or join a social networking group that has already been formed.

Is social networking just for fun?

Networking has long been a means of creating links between you and your friends—and their friends and acquaintances. Traditionally, networking has been helpful in

the business community for the purposes of finding and filling open job positions. The Internet, with its speedy connections and instantaneous means of communicating, facilitates such business networking as well as promoting more socially based networks. In addition to the more social networks of Facebook and MySpace, the professional, business-oriented online networks such as LinkedIn (**linkedin.com**) are helpful for members seeking to find potential clients, business opportunities, jobs, or job candidates. Like a true business network, LinkedIn helps you meet other professionals through the people you know.

Are there precautions I should take with my social networking content?

When social networking sites first became popular, there was huge concern over privacy issues, especially for young teenagers who put personal information on their pages without considering the possibility of that information being misused by a stalker limited amount of data. If you are taking advantage of one of these free on-line storage services, selectivity is the key. Although you might have hundreds of gigabytes of data sitting on your computer, perhaps you only need to store several gigabytes online so that they are always available.

Online storage may be a good solution for housing files that need "always available" access. But if you want to make a complete copy of your hard drive that will protect all your digital assets in case of a complete failure, you might also consider online backup. Plenty of services are available for these larger and more secure backup needs.

For the most protection, you should initially choose to image your hard drive, a process that copies all the files on your computer. In addition to your data files, *imaging* captures all the operating system files (such as Windows or OS X files) and application files (such as Microsoft Office). The idea of imaging is to make an exact copy of the setup of your computer so that in the event of a total hard drive failure, you could copy the image to a new hard drive and have your computer configured exactly the way it was before the crash.

Even with modest use, your files change. Therefore, it is important to back up the system periodically to capture the changes. You can do either an incremental or a total backup.

Incremental backups involve backing up only files that have changed or been created since the last backup was performed. Incremental back-ups won't make full copies of the stored data every time. Many of the key documents that you want to protect change only periodically: monthly banking statements, yearly tax returns, weekly employee payment records, or daily work documents. You should choose an online service that allows incremental backups. It will save a tremendous amount of time because backing up files that haven't changed is redundant.

A *total backup* means that all system, application, and data files are backed up, not just the files that have changed. While incremental backups are most efficient, you should still perform a total backup of your computer at least monthly to capture changes to application files, such as automatic software updates, that an incremental backup might not capture.

Another issue to consider when choosing online storage and backup services is security. Security might not be an issue if you're just using online storage for your family pictures. However, it is important to consider if you are backing up sensitive or essential files. Some services encrypt your data or scatter it among several servers. For the utmost in security, some services even offer you the option of being the only person to hold the decryption key. However, be forewarned that if you choose this option, there is no way you can restore your data should you forget your password!

All of these services are great, but only if you can retrieve your data should the original source become unavailable. That is the reason you go through a backup process, after all. Different services offer different features depending on whether you just want to restore the data on the original machine or whether you need to restore your data to a new computer (because the original computer was completely destroyed or stolen). Make sure your service can easily restore data to a different computer. Some popular online services include Carbonite Online PCBackup, HP Upline, IDrive, and MozyHome Online Backup.

Protecting our most important data is an often-forgotten step in our daily computing lives. Local backup or imaging to a DVD, external hard drive, or other local network storage device is still a viable option, especially with the cost of these local storage devices continuing to drop. However, if you really care about preserving and protecting your irreplaceable digital photos, documents, and other files, or want anytime-and-anywhere access, look into taking advantage of one of these online storage and backup services.

Figure 3.14

Social networking sites are popular places for people to keep up with friends and learn more about the people they meet.

What's Everyone Twittering About?

Twitter is a social networking and micro-blogging service that enables you to exchange short text messages with your friends or "followers" (see Figure 3.15). It also lets you specify which Twitter users you want to follow so you can read their messages in one place. All you need is a device (such as your computer or mobile device) connected to the Internet.

Twitter messages, called *tweets*, are limited to 140 characters, so comments exchanged in Twitter are short and simple. While Twitter works well among close-knit groups for messages such as "Joe and I are going to Murphy's Café. See you there," it can also be used to gain a sense of the "pulse" of what the general public is talking about within a broader community. Twitter received a lot of attention during the 2008 presidential campaigns when the masses were "twittering" their opinions about the various presidential candidates and positions. Your Twitter account tracks the number of "followers," or people who are paying attention to your tweets, and the number of "friends," or people you are following. So, "twitter" away to stay connected.

Figure 3.15

Twitter is a social networking and micro-blogging service for staying connected to "followers" in real time.

or identity thief. While those concerns still exist, many of the most popular social networking sites have improved their privacy policies, thereby reducing, but not eliminating, such concerns. Still, users must be cautious about the type of content they post on these sites. For example, think before you add information like "your mother's maiden name" or "your first pet's name" because these are often security questions that businesses use to verify your identity.

Social networking sites are a great way to exchange photos, but again, use caution when posting images. Although privacy settings may offer some comfort, some images may be available for view through search engines and may not require site registration to be viewed. Online images may become public property and subject to reproduction, and there might be some images that you don't want distributed. Additionally, many employers use social networks as another means of gaining information about a potential job candidate before granting an

interview or extending a job offer. The responsibility for your content rests with you. Make sure your profile, images, and site content project an image that accurately represents you.

Web Entertainment: Multimedia and Beyond

Internet radio, MP3 music files, streaming video, and interactive gaming are all part of a growing entertainment world available over the Internet. What makes the Web appealing to many people is its rich multimedia content. **Multimedia** is anything that involves one or more forms of media in addition to text.

Many types of multimedia are used on the Web. Graphics (drawings, charts, and photos) are the most basic form of multimedia. Audio files are what give sound to the Web—the clips of music you hear when you visit certain Web sites, MP3 files that you download, or live broadcasts you can listen to through Internet radio. Video files on the Web range from the simple (such as short video clips) to the complex (such as hour-long live concerts). In addition to movies, you can watch live or prerecorded television broadcasts, movie trailers, and sporting events. **Hulu.com** is a great Web site where you can find popular TV shows and movies for free.

What are streaming audio and video? Because of the large file sizes of media content, watching video files such as movies or TV shows, listening to live audio broadcasting, and playing online games is possible because of streaming media. **Streaming audio** continuously feeds an audio file to your browser so you avoid having to wait for the entire file to download completely before listening to it. Likewise, **streaming video** continuously feeds a video file to your browser so that you can watch large files as they download instead of first having to download the files completely.

What kinds of games are played on the Web? Streaming audio and video helped to bring popularity to online user interactivity and online gaming. Many game Web sites, such as AddictingGames (**addictinggames.com**), offer thousands of free online games in arcade, puzzle, sports, shooting, word, and strategy categories. Simple multiplayer games such as backgammon, chess, and checkers became popular and offered users the chance to play the game with others from around the world.

In addition, there are many **multiplayer online games**, in which play occurs among hundreds or thousands of other players over the Internet in a persistent (or always-on) game environment. In these games, you can interact with other players around the world in a meaningful context by trading, chatting, or playing cooperative or combative mini-games. There are several types of massive multiplayer online games. Role-playing games such as World of Warcraft (**worldofwarcraft.com**) and Guild Wars (**guildwars.com**) are the best-known type of massive multiplayer games. Other types include first-person shooter (**battlegroundeurope.com**), sports (**footballsuperstars.com**), and racing (**needforspeed.com**). Second Life (**secondlife.com**) can also be considered a massive multiplayer online social game, but with its own well-established, in-world virtual economy, it has transcended into a much bigger concept and function.

Do I need anything besides a browser to view or hear multimedia on the Web? Without any additional software, most graphics on the Web will appear in your browser. However, to view and hear some multimedia files—for example, podcasts, videos on YouTube, and MP3 files—you might need a special software program called a **plug-in** (or **player**). Figure 3.16 lists the most popular plug-ins.

If you purchased your computer within the past several years, many plug-ins probably came preinstalled with your browser. If a Web site requires a plug-in you don't have, it usually displays a message on the screen that includes links to a site where you can download the plug-in free of charge. For example, to use streaming audio on a Web site, your browser might send you to adobe.com, where you can download Shockwave Player.

Do I need to update players and plug-ins? As with most technological resources, improvements and upgrades are available for players and plug-ins, and most will alert you to check for and download upgrades when they are available. It is best to keep the players and plug-ins as current as possible so that you get the full effects of the multimedia running with these players.

Figure 3.16 | POPULAR PLUG-INS AND PLAYERS AND THEIR USES

	Plug-In or Player Name	Where You Can Get It	What It Does
	Adobe Reader	**adobe.com**	Views and prints portable document format (PDF) files
	Authorware Web Player	**adobe.com**	Helps to deliver engaging e-learning applications
	Flash Player	**adobe.com**	Plays animation and other graphics files
	QuickTime Player	**apple.com**	Plays MP3 animation, music, musical instrument digital interface (MIDI), audio, and video files
	RealPlayer	**real.com**	Plays streaming audio, video, animations, and multimedia presentations
	Shockwave Player	**adobe.com**	Plays interactive games, multimedia, graphics, and streaming audio and video on the Web
	Windows Media Player	**microsoft.com**	Plays MP3 and WAV files, music files and live audio, and views movies and live video broadcasts on the Web

Are there any risks with using plug-ins? When a browser requires a plug-in to display particular Web content, it usually automatically accesses the plug-in. Sometimes, depending on your settings, this access happens without asking you for consent to start the plug-in. Such automatic access can present security risks. To minimize such risks, update your plug-ins and browser software frequently so that you will have the most up-to-date remedies against identified security flaws.

Is there any way to get multimedia Web content to load faster? When you're on the Internet, your browser keeps track of the Web sites you've visited so that it can load them faster the next time you visit them. This *cache* (temporary storage place) of the text pages, images, and video files from recently visited Web sites can make your Internet surfing more efficient, but it also can congest your hard drive. To keep your system running efficiently, delete your temporary Internet cache periodically. All popular Web browsers have an option to clear the Internet cache manually, and most have a setting to allow you to clear the cache automatically every time you exit the browser.

BITS AND BYTES

Using PayPal for Safe Online Payments

Many people were not initially comfortable buying online from sites such as eBay because the sites required them to exchange personal financial information such as credit card numbers or banking information with complete strangers. PayPal (**paypal.com**) resolved that issue and is now a standard means of online payment exchanges. PayPal also offers buyer protection and dispute resolution services.

Here's how PayPal works (see Figure 3.17):

1. You provide your financial information to PayPal, which stores it on PayPal servers.
2. You provide only your PayPal e-mail address to the merchant.
3. The merchant receives payment from PayPal without seeing your financial information.

PayPal acts as a payment intermediary and allows anyone to pay with credit cards, bank accounts, or buyer credit without sharing financial information. PayPal is now owned by eBay, the online auction site.

PayPal is not without controversy, however. Many criticisms of the company focus on its poor customer service and freezing of accounts without explanation. So, diligence and care are still as important as they are with anyone who has access to your personal financial information.

| Provide your information to PayPal | PayPal securely stores your information | Merchant receives payment from PayPal |

Figure 3.17
PayPal is an online payment intermediary, allowing anyone to shop without sharing financial information with the seller.

Conducting Business over the Internet: E-Commerce

E-commerce, or **electronic commerce**, is the process of conducting business online, such as through advertising and selling products. A good example of an e-commerce business (also called an *e-business*) is Amazon.com. The company's online presence offers customers a convenient way to shop for almost anything. Its success is the result of creative marketing, an expanding product line, and reliable customer service and product delivery—all hallmarks of traditional businesses as well.

Are there different types of e-commerce businesses? Traditional stores with an online presence are referred to as *click-and-brick* businesses. These stores, such as Best Buy (**bestbuy.com**) and Target (**target.com**), provide a variety of services on their Web sites. Customers can visit their sites to check the availability of items or to get store locations and directions. Some click-and-bricks allow online purchases and in-store pickup and returns.

A significant portion of e-commerce consists of **business-to-consumer (B2C)** transactions—exchanges that take place between businesses and consumers—such as the purchases that consumers make at online stores. There is also a **business-to-business (B2B)** portion of e-commerce; this consists of businesses buying and selling goods and services to other businesses. An example is Omaha Paper Company (**omahapaper.com**), which distributes paper products to other companies. Finally, the **consumer-to-consumer (C2C)** portion of e-commerce consists of consumers selling to each other through online auction and exchange sites such as eBay (**ebay.com**) and Craigslist (**craigslist.com**).

What are the most popular e-commerce activities?
Approximately $100 billion each year is spent on goods purchased over the Internet, accounting for approximately 25 percent of all retail sales. So what is everyone buying online? Consumers buy books, music and videos, movie and event tickets, and toys and games more often online than in retail stores. Travel items such as plane tickets, hotel reservations, and rental car reservations are also frequently made online. With the advent of more lenient return policies, online retail sales of clothing and shoes also have increased. Sites such as eBay and Craigslist, together with payment exchange services such as PayPal and Google Checkout, are becoming the online equivalent of the weekend yard sale and have dramatically increased in popularity.

But e-commerce encompasses more than just shopping opportunities. Today, anything you can do inside your bank you can do online, and more than 50 percent of U.S. households do some form of online banking. Many people use online services to check their account balances, and checking stock and mutual fund performances is also popular. Credit card companies allow you to view, schedule, and pay your credit card bill; brokerage houses allow you to conduct investment activities online; and banks allow you to pay you bills online.

E-Commerce Safeguards

Just how safe are online transactions? When you buy something online, you most likely use a credit card; therefore, the exchange of money is done directly between you and a bank. Because online shopping eliminates a salesclerk or other human intermediary from the transaction, it can actually be safer than traditional retail shopping. Still, because users are told to be wary of online transactions and because the integrity of online transactions is the backbone of e-commerce, businesses must have some

ACTIVE HELP-DESK Doing Business Online

In this Active Helpdesk call, you'll learn about e-commerce and what e-commerce safeguards protect you when you're.

"Just how safe are online transactions?"

form of security certification to give their customers a level of comfort. Businesses hire security companies such as VeriSign to certify that their online transactions are secure. Thus, if the Web site displays the VeriSign seal (see Figure 3.18), you can usually trust that the information you submit to the site is protected.

Another indication that a Web site is secure is the appearance of a small icon of a closed padlock (in both Microsoft's Internet Explorer and Mozilla's Firefox), as shown in Figure 3.18. In addition, the beginning of the URL of the site changes from "http://" to "https://"—with the "s" standing for *secure socket layer* (see Figure 3.18).

How else can I shop safely online?
To ensure that your online shopping experience is a safe one, follow these guidelines:

- **Shop at well-known, reputable sites.** If you aren't familiar with a site, then investigate it with the Better Business Bureau (**bbb.org**) or at **bizrate.com** or **webassured.com**. When you place an order, print a copy of the order and make sure you receive a confirmation number. Make sure the company has a phone number and street address in addition to a Web site.

- **Pay by credit card, not debit card.** Federal consumer credit laws protect credit card users, but debit card users do not have the same level of protection. If possible, reserve one credit card for Internet purchases only; even better, use a prepaid credit card that has a small credit limit.

- **Check the return policy.** Print a copy and save it. If the site disappears overnight, this information may help you in filing a dispute or reporting a problem to a site such as the Better Business Bureau.

Figure 3.18

The VeriSign seal, a
closed padlock icon, and
"https" in the URL are
indications that the site
is secure.

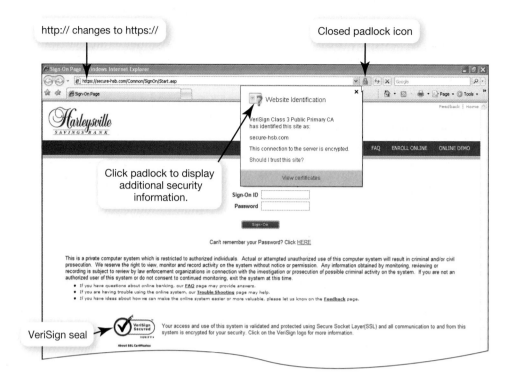

Accessing the Web: Web Browsers

None of the activities for which we use the Web could happen without an important software application: a Web browser. A **Web browser**, or **browser**, is software installed on your computer system that allows you to locate, view, and navigate the Web. Most browsers in use today are graphical browsers, meaning they can display pictures (graphics) in addition to text and other forms of multimedia such as sound and video.

What are some common Web browsers? Internet Explorer (IE) is the main browser from Microsoft and is included in the Windows operating system. It has been the most widely used browser since 1999, and still enjoys predominant market share, although its popularity has slipped over the years. Other browsers, discussed below, have become popular alternatives to Internet Explorer.

- **Firefox** is a popular open source browser from Mozilla (**mozilla.org**). Firefox continues to enjoy increasing popularity, capturing approximately 21.5 percent of the U.S. browser market. Add-ons are available to customize and increase the functionality of Firefox. Examples include the Video Download Helper that converts Web videos, like those found on YouTube, to savable files and a Facebook toolbar that integrates Facebook functionality into your browser. Other handy features found in Firefox are spell checking for e-mail, blogs, and other Web postings, as well as Session Restore, which brings back all your active Web pages if the system shuts down unexpectedly.

- **Safari** is a browser developed by Apple (**apple.com**). Although it was created as the default browser for Macintosh computers and is included with the Mac

BITS AND BYTES
Why Should You Run the Latest Version of Browser Software?

When new file formats are developed for the Web, browsers need new plug-ins to display content properly. Constantly downloading and installing plug-ins can be a tedious process. Although many Web sites provide links to sites that enable you to download plug-ins, not all do, resulting in frustration when you can't display the content you want. When new versions of browsers are released, they normally include the latest versions of popular plug-ins. Corrections of security breaches are typically included in these versions of browser software as well. Therefore, upgrading to the latest version of your browser software provides for safer, more convenient Web surfing. Fortunately, most updates are free, and you can set most of the popular Web browsers to notify you when updates are available or to download the updates automatically.

OS, a Windows-based version is also available. Safari has quickly gained public acceptance, and it now has approximately an 8 percent share of the U.S. browser market.

- **Google Chrome** is the newest browser on the market, distributed by Google (**google.com**) (see Figure 3.19). The unique features offered by Chrome include thumbnail access to your most recently visited sites from the home page and shortcuts to Google applications.

What features do browsers offer?

Most browsers' toolbars provide convenient navigation and Web page management tools. The most recent features include tabbed browsing and quick tabs (see Figure 3.20). Quick tabs, in Internet Explorer 7 and higher, shows thumbnail images of all open Web pages in open tabs, and Google Chrome offers thumbnail images of most recently visited sites on the home page. Most of the popular Web browsers have tabbed browsing in which Web pages are loaded in "tabs" within the same browser window. Rather than having to switch among Web pages in several open windows, you can flip between the tabs in one window. You can even open several of your favorite Web sites from one folder and choose to display them as tabs. You may also save a group of tabs as a Favorites group, if there are several tabs you often open at the same time.

Most browsers also include a built-in search box in which you can designate your preferred default search engine and tools for printing, page formatting, and security settings.

Getting Around the Web: URLs, Hyperlinks, and Other Tools

You gain initial access to a particular **Web site**, or location on the Web, by typing its unique address, or **Uniform Resource Locator** (**URL**), pronounced "you-are-ell"),

Figure 3.19

Google Chrome includes thumbnails of most recently visited Web sites for easy access.

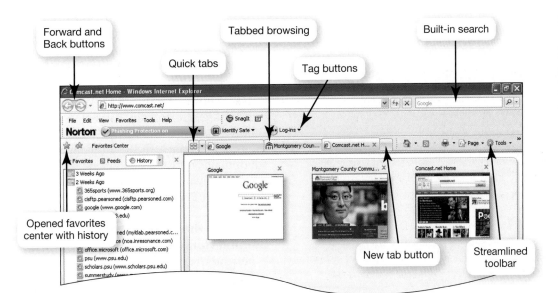

Forward and Back buttons

Quick tabs

Tabbed browsing

Tag buttons

Built-in search

Opened favorites center with history

New tab button

Streamlined toolbar

Figure 3.20

Internet Explorer 7 (IE7) includes tabbed browsing and quick tabs. IE7 has also reduced the display of navigation tools to a simple toolbar and built a Google search engine right into the browser.

Figure 3.21

The parts of a URL.

in your browser. For example, the URL of the Web site for *Popular Science* magazine is popsci.com. By typing this URL for *Popular Science* magazine, you connect to the **home page**, or main page, of the Web site. Once you are in the home page, you can move all around the site by clicking specially formatted pieces of text called *hyperlinks*. Let's look at these and other navigation tools in more detail.

URLs

What do all the parts of the URL mean? As noted above, a URL is a Web site's address. Like a regular street address, a URL is composed of several parts that help identify the Web document for which it stands (see Figure 3.21). The first part of the URL indicates the *protocol* (set of rules) used to retrieve the specified document. The protocol is generally followed by a colon,

two forward slashes, *www* (indicating *World Wide Web*), and the **domain name**. (Sometimes the domain name is also thought to include the *www*.) The domain name is also referred to as the *host name*.

What's the protocol? Most URLs begin with *http*, which is short for **hypertext transfer protocol (HTTP)**. HTTP is the protocol (or set of rules) that allows files to be transferred from a computer that hosts the Web site you are requesting (known as a *Web server*) so that you can see the Web site on your computer by using a browser.

Another common protocol used to transfer files over the Internet is **file transfer protocol (FTP)**. It is used to upload and download files from one computer to another. FTP files use an FTP file server, whereas HTTP files use a Web server. To connect to most FTP servers, you need a user ID and a password. FTP addresses, like e-mail addresses or URLs, identify one location on the Web. They can have several formats, such as ftp://ftp.microsoft.com or ftp://wuarchive.wustl.edu. To upload and download files from FTP sites, you can use a Web browser or file transfer software such as WS_FTP, Fetch, or CuteFTP.

What's in a domain name? The domain name identifies the site's **host**. For example, **berkeley.edu** is the domain name for the University of California at Berkeley. Although using *www* is conventional, it is not necessary.

The suffix in the domain name after the dot (such as .com or .edu) is called the **top-level domain**. This suffix indicates the kind of organization to which the host belongs. Figure 3.22 lists the most frequently used top-level domains.

Each country has its own top-level domain. These are two-letter designations such as .za for South Africa and .us for the United States. A sampling of country codes is shown in Figure 3.23. Within a country-specific domain, further subdivisions can be made for regions or states. For instance, the .us domain contains subdomains for each state, using the two-letter abbreviation of the state. For example, the URL for Pennsylvania's Web site is **state.pa.us**.

What's the information after the domain name that I sometimes see? When the URL is only the domain name (such as nytimes.com), you are requesting a site's home page. However, sometimes a

Figure 3.22

COMMON TOP-LEVEL DOMAINS AND THEIR AUTHORIZED USERS

Domain Name	Who Can Use It
.biz	Businesses
.com	Originally for commercial sites, but now can be used by anyone
.edu	Degree-granting institutions
.gov	United States government
.info	Information service providers
.int	Limited to organizations, offices, and programs that are sanctioned by a treaty between two or more nations
.mil	United States military
.name	Individuals
.net	Originally for networking organizations, but no longer restricted
.org	Organizations (often nonprofits)

Figure 3.23 | EXAMPLES OF COUNTRY CODES

Country Code	Country
.au	Australia
.ca	Canada
.uk	United Kingdom
.us	United States
.mx	Mexico

Note: For a full listing of country codes, refer to **norid.no/domenenavnbaser/domreg.html**.

forward slash and additional text follow the domain name, such as in nytimes.com/pages/cartoons. The information after the slash indicates a particular file or **path** (or **subdirectory**) within the Web site. In this example, you would connect to the cartoon pages on the *New York Times* site.

Hyperlinks and Beyond

What's the best way to get around in a Web site? Unlike text in a book or a Microsoft Word document, which is linear (meaning you read it from top to bottom, left to right, one page after another), the Web is anything but linear. As its name implies, the Web is a series of connected paths, or links, that connect you to different Web sites. You can jump from one location, or Web page, to another within the same Web site or navigate to another Web site altogether by clicking on a specially coded element called a **hyperlink**, as shown in Figure 3.24. Generally, text that operates as a hyperlink appears in a different color (often blue) and is underlined. Sometimes images also act as hyperlinks. When you pass your cursor over a hyperlinked image, for example, a cursor may change to a hand with a finger pointing upward. To access the hyperlink, you simply click the image.

How do I return to a Web page I've already visited? To retrace your steps, some sites also provide a **breadcrumb list**—a list of pages within a Web site you've visited. It usually appears at the top of a page. Figure 3.24 shows an example of a breadcrumb list. "Breadcrumbs" get their name from the fairy tale "Hansel and Gretel," in which the characters drop

breadcrumbs on the trail to find their way out of a forest. By clicking on earlier links in a breadcrumb list, you can retrace your steps back to the page on which you started.

To get back to your original location or visit a Web page you viewed previously, you use the browser's Back and Forward buttons (see Figure 3.24). To back up more than one page, click the down arrow next to the Back button to access a list of most recently visited Web sites. By selecting any one of these sites in the list, you can return directly to that page without having to navigate through other Web sites and Web pages you've visited.

The History list (see Figure 3.24) on your browser's toolbar is also a handy feature. The History list shows all the Web sites and pages that you've visited over a certain period of time. These Web sites are organized according to date and can go back as far as three weeks. To access the history list on IE7, click the down arrow next to the navigation arrows. On the Firefox toolbar, the history button is the alarm clock icon.

Favorites, Live Bookmarks, and Tagging

What's the best way to mark a site so I can return to it later? If you want an easy way to return to a specific Web page

Figure 3.24

When you click on a hyperlink, you jump from one location in a Web site to another. When you click on the links in a breadcrumb list, you can navigate your way back through a Web site.

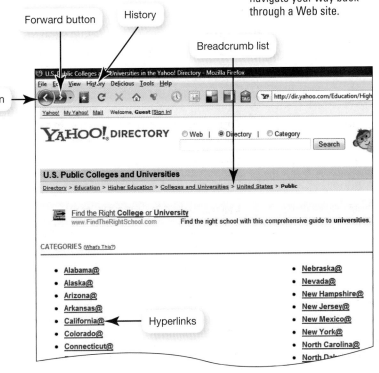

without having to remember to type in the address, you can use your browser's **Favorites** or **Bookmarks** feature. Internet Explorer and Safari call this feature Favorites; Firefox and Google Chrome call the same feature a Bookmark. This feature places a marker of the site's URL in an easily retrievable list in your browser's toolbar. To organize the sites into categories, most browsers offer tools to create folders. Most browsers also provide features to export the list of bookmarks to another computer or another browser.

Favorites and Bookmarks are great for quickly locating those sites you use the most, but they are accessible to you only when you are on your own computer. One way to access your Bookmarks and Favorites from any computer is to use MyBookmarks (**mybookmarks.com**), a free Internet service that stores your Bookmarks and Favorites online.

What are live bookmarks? The **live bookmark** feature of the Firefox browser adds the technology of RSS feeds to bookmarking. Because the Web is constantly changing, the site you bookmarked last week may subsequently change and add new content. Traditionally, you would notice the change only the next time you visited the site. With live bookmarks, the content comes to you. Instead of constantly checking your favorite Web pages for new content, a live bookmark delivers updates to you as soon as they become available. Live bookmarks are useful if you are interested in the most up-to-date news stories, sports scores, or stock prices.

What is social bookmarking? Social bookmarking, also known as *tagging*, lets you store, organize, and manage bookmarks (or tags) of Web pages. A **social bookmark** or **tag** is a keyword or term that is assigned to a piece of information such as a Web page, digital image, or video. A tag describes the item so that it can be found again by browsing or searching. Tags were

popularized by Web 2.0 Web sites such as YouTube and Flickr.

The social bookmarking Web site Delicious (**delicious.com**) gives you the ability to add tags as bookmarks to your favorite Web sites (see Figure 3.25). Digg (**digg.com**) and Newsvine (**newsvine.com**) offer similar systems for organizing news content. The tag can be something meaningful to you, or you can select one from a list of suggested tags. Later, you can go back to Delicious, conduct a search using your tag, and find bookmarks tagged with the same word from everyone in your network. You can also see how many other Web users tagged the same site.

Delicious offers convenient toolbars for your browsers, and many Web sites incorporate bookmarking icons for ease of use. Figure 3.26 lists several popular social bookmarking tag tools. StumbleUpon (**stumbleupon.com**) recommends Web sites based on your personal preferences, and the recommendations of people you know or the general surfing public.

Searching the Web Effectively

With its billions of Web pages, the Internet offers visitors access to masses of information on virtually any topic. To narrow down the quantity of Web information to something more useful, we use a search engine and a keyword query. A **search engine** is a set of programs that searches the Web for **keywords**—specific words you wish to look for (*query*)—and then returns a

Figure 3.25

Icons of some popular social bookmarking Web sites.

list of the Web sites on which those keywords are found. Popular search engines include Google, Yahoo!, and Ask.com.

For some searches you also can search the Web using a **subject directory**, which is a structured outline of Web sites organized by topics and subtopics. Librarians' Internet Index (**lii.org**) is a subject directory and some popular search engines such as Yahoo! also feature directories. If you can't decide which search engine is best, you may want to try a **metasearch engine**. Metasearch engines search other search engines rather than individual Web sites. Figure 3.27 lists search engines and subject directories that are alternatives to Google, Yahoo!, and Ask.com.

Search Engines

How do search engines work? Search engines have three parts. The first part is a program called a **spider**. The spider constantly collects data on the Web, following links in Web sites and reading Web pages. Spiders get their name because they crawl over the Web using multiple "legs" to visit many sites simultaneously. As the spider collects data, the second part of the search engine, an indexer program, organizes the data into a large database. When you use a search engine, you interact with the third part: the search engine software. This software searches the indexed

Figure 3.26

Tagging tools are incorporated into Web browsers and in some Web pages for easy access.

Figure 3.27 | POPULAR SEARCH ENGINES AND SUBJECT DIRECTORIES

Search Tools on the Internet		
AltaVista	**altavista.com**	Keyword search engine
Bing	**bing.com**	New search engine from Microsoft
Clusty	**clusty.com**	Keyword search engine that groups similar results into clusters
ChaCha	**chacha.com**	Don't like your search results? This site lets you chat with a real live professional guide who helps you search, and it's free of charge.
Complete-Planet	**completeplanet.com**	Deep Web directory that searches databases not normally searched by typical search engines
Dogpile	**dogpile.com**	Metasearch engine that searches Google, Yahoo!, MSN Search, and Ask
Excite	**excite.com**	Portal with keyword search capabilities
InfoMine	**infomine.com**	Subject directory of academic resources with keyword search engine capabilities
Rollyo	**rollyo.com**	Short for Roll Your Own Search Engine. Basically, this site lets you create your own search engine (searchroll) that searches just the sites you want it to search.
Open Directory Project	**dmoz.org**	Subject directory with keyword search capabilities
Stumbleupon	**stumbleupon.com**	Lets you rate pages "thumbs up" or "thumbs down." As it learns your preferences, your search results improve.
Technorati	**technorati.com**	A great search engine for blog content

Note: For a complete list of search engines, go to **searchengineguide.com**.

data, pulling out relevant information according to your search. The resulting list appears in your Web browser as a list of hits (sites that match your search).

Why don't I get the same results from all search engines? Each search engine uses a unique formula, or *algorithm*, to formulate the search and create the resulting index of related sites. In addition, search engines differ in how they rank the search results. Most search engines rank their results based on the frequency of the appearance of your queried keywords in Web sites as well as the location of those words in the sites. Thus, sites that include the keywords in their URL or site name most likely appear at the top of the hit list. After that, results vary because of differences in each engine's proprietary formula.

In addition, search engines differ as to which sites they search. For instance, Google and Ask.com search nearly the entire Web, whereas specialty search engines search only sites that are relevant to a particular subject. Specialty search engines exist for almost every industry or interest. For example, **dailystocks.com** is a search engine used primarily by investors that searches for corporate information to help them make educated decisions. Search Engine Watch (**searchenginewatch.com**) has a list of

many specialty search engines organized by industry.

Can I use a search engine to search for images and videos? With the increasing popularity of multimedia, search engines such as Google, Ask.com, and Yahoo! have capabilities to search the Web for digital images and audio and video files. YouTube (**youtube.com**) is one of many sites that has gained recent popularity because of its wealth of video content. In addition to the amusing videos that are captured in popular news, YouTube contains instructional and informational videos.

How can I refine my searches for better results? When you conduct a Web search, you may receive a list of hits that includes thousands—even millions—of Web pages that have no relevance to the topic you're trying to search. Initially Boolean operators were needed to help refine a search. **Boolean operators** are words such as AND, NOT, and OR that describe the relationships between keywords in a search.

Today, most search engines offer an advanced search page that provides the same types of strategies in a well-organized form (see Figure 3.28). Using the advanced search form can make your Internet research a lot more efficient. With the simple addition of a few words or constraints, you can narrow your search results to a more manageable and more meaningful list.

Are there other helpful search strategies? Instead of using the advanced search form, you can use other strategies to help refine your searches when entering your search phrases.

- **Search for a phrase.** To search for an exact phrase, place quotation marks around your keywords. The search engine will look for only those Web sites that contain the words in that exact order. For example, if you want information on the movie *Lord of the*

Google **Advanced Search**

Advanced Search Tips | Abo

Use the form below and your advanced search will appear here

Find web pages that have...

all these words:

this exact wording or phrase: · · · · · tip

one or more of these words: · · · OR · · · OR · · · tip

But don't show pages that have...

any of these unwanted words: · · · · · tip

Need more tools?

Results per page: 10 results

Language: any language

File type: any format

Search within a site or domain: ·

(e.g. youtube.com, .edu)

⊞ Date, usage rights, numeric range, and more

Advanced Search

Figure 3.28

Most search engines have an advanced search form to help you refine your searches.

Rings and you type these words without quotation marks, your search results will contain pages that include either of the words *Lord* and *Rings,* although not necessarily in that order. Typing *"Lord of the Rings"* in quotes guarantees that search results will include this exact phrase.

- **Search within a specific Web site.** To search just a specific Web site, you can use the search keyword, then *site:* followed by the Web site's URL. For example, searching with *processor site:wired.com* returns results about processors from the Wired.com Web site. The same works for entire classes of sites in a given top-level domain or country code.

- **Use a wildcard.** The asterisk "*" is a wildcard, or placeholder, feature that is helpful when you need to search with unknown terms. For example, searching with *Congress voted *on the* bill* returns sites that mention how Congress voted on various bills.

How else can I customize my searches? A lot of other specialty search strategies and services are available. Clicking on the "more" hyperlink in the Google search engine, for example, takes you to all the various search products Google offers. Google Scholar searches scholarly literature such as

peer-reviewed papers, theses, and publications from academic organizations. Each search result contains bibliographic information as well. Google Custom Search enables you to create a customized search engine to search only a selected set of sites tailored to your specific needs. This specialized search engine can be added to a Web site or blog, or designed for a specific organization. Google Book Search enables you to search through the full-text content of millions of books. Google News searches through thousands of news stories from around the world. Google News can be further customized to search stories within specific categories such as Business or Entertainment, and a News Archives Timeline shows selected results from relevant time periods (see Figure 3.29).

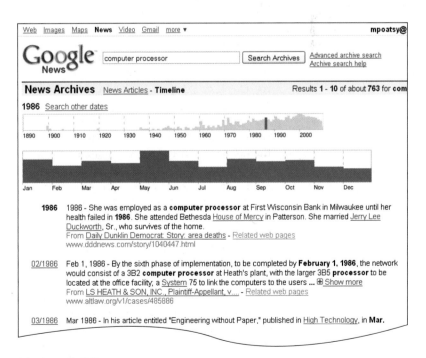

Figure 3.29

The Google News Archives Timeline enables you to zero in on search results from a specific period.

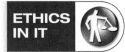
Ethics: What Can You Borrow from the Internet?

You've no doubt heard of plagiarism—claiming another person's words as your own. And you've probably heard the term *copyright violation*, especially if you've been following the music industry's battle to keep "free" music off the Web. But what constitutes plagiarism, and what constitutes copyright violation? And what can you borrow from the Web? Consider these scenarios:

1. You find a political cartoon that would be terrific in a PowerPoint presentation you're creating for your civics class. You copy it into your presentation.

2. Your hobby is cooking. You design a Web site that includes videos of you preparing recipes, as well as the recipes themselves. Some of these recipes you take from your favorite cookbooks; others you get from friends. You don't cite your sources, nor do you obtain permission from the originators of the recipes you post to your Web site.

3. You're pressed for time and need to do research for a paper due tomorrow. You find information on an obscure Web site and copy it into your paper without documenting the source.

4. You download a song from the Internet and incorporate it into a PowerPoint presentation for a school project. Because you figure everyone knows the song, you don't credit it in your sources.

Which of the preceding scenarios represent copyright violations? Which represent plagiarism? The distinctions between these scenarios are narrow in some cases, but it's important to understand the differences.

As noted earlier, plagiarism occurs when you use someone else's ideas or words and represent them as your own. In today's computer society, it's easy to copy information from the Internet and paste it into a Word document, change a few words, and call it your own. To avoid plagiarism, use quotation marks around all words you borrow directly, and credit your sources for any ideas you paraphrase or borrow. Avoiding plagiarism means properly crediting all information you obtain from the Internet, including words, ideas, graphics, data, and audio and video clips.

Web sites such as **turnitin.com** help teachers, students, and other interested parties check for plagiarism violations. Turnitin.com will scan a document and, within a few minutes, determine the percentage of the document that has exact wording from Web sites, highlight those areas of the document that have exactly the same wording as a Web site, and provide you with the Web site in question. Although some common phrasing may be truly coincidental, plagiarism that is more purposeful is reasonably easy to identify. Students can use Turnitin.com before submitting an assignment to ensure their paper will not be confused with plagiarized work.

Copyright violation is more serious because it, unlike simple plagiarism, is punishable by law. Copyright law assumes that *all* original work—including text, graphics, software, multimedia, audio and video clips, and other intellectual property—is copyrighted even if the work does not display the copyright symbol (©). Copyright violation occurs when you use another person's material for your own personal economic benefit, or when you take away from the economic benefit of the originator. Don't assume that by citing a source you're abiding by copyright laws. In most cases, you need to seek and receive written permission from the copyright holder.

There are exceptions to this rule. For example, there is no copyright on government documents, so you can download and reproduce material from NASA, for example, without violating copyright laws. The British Broadcasting Corporation (BBC) is also beginning to digitize and make available its archives of material to the public without copyright restrictions.

Teachers and students receive special consideration regarding copyright violations. This special consideration falls under a provision called *academic fair use*. As long as the material is being used for educational purposes only, *limited* copying and distribution is allowed. One standard applied to academic fair use is the effect the use has on the potential market. For example, an instructor could make copies of a book chapter and distribute it to her class one time, but could not do it on a regular basis or over different semesters because that might affect the potential market or sales of the book. Similarly, a student can include a cartoon in a PowerPoint presentation without seeking permission from the artist. However, to avoid plagiarism in these situations, you still must credit your sources of information.

So, do you now know which of the four scenarios above are plagiarism or copyright violations? Let's review them.

1. You are not in violation because the use of the cartoon is for educational purposes and falls under the academic fair use provision. You must still credit the source, however.

2. If you maintain your Web site for your economic benefit, you would be in violation of copyright laws because no credit was given for the recipes, and you are presenting them as your own.

3. You are guilty of plagiarism because you copied content from another source and implied it was your own work.

4. Again, because your copying is for a school project, you are not in violation because of the academic fair use provision. However, it's always important to document your sources.

SOUND BYTE

Finding Information on the Web

In this Sound Byte, you'll learn how and when to use search engines and subject directories. Through guided tours, you'll learn effective search techniques, including how to use Boolean operators and metasearch engines.

Evaluating Web Sites

How can I make sure a Web site is appropriate to use for research?

When you're using the Internet for research, you shouldn't assume that everything you find is accurate and appropriate to use. Before you use an Internet resource, consider the following.

1. **Authority:** Who is the author of the article or the sponsor of the site? If the author is well known or the site is published by a reputable news source (such as the *New York Times*), then you can feel more confident using it as a source than if you are unable to locate such information. *Note:* Some sites include a page with information about the author or the site's sponsor.

2. **Bias:** Is the site biased? The purpose of many Web sites is to sell products or services or to persuade rather than inform. These sites, though useful in some situations, present a biased point of view. Look for sites that offer several sets of facts, or consider opinions from several sources.

3. **Relevance:** Is the information in the site current? Material can last a long time on the Web. Some research projects (such as historical accounts) depend on older records. However, if you're writing about cutting-edge technologies, you need to look for the most recent sources. Therefore, look for a date on information to make sure it is current.

4. **Audience:** For what audience is the site intended? Ensure that the content, tone, and style of the site match your needs. You probably wouldn't want to use information from a site geared toward teens if you were writing for adults, nor would you use a site that has a casual style and tone for serious research.

5. **Links:** Are the links available and appropriate? Check out the links provided on the site to determine whether they are still working and appropriate for your needs. Don't assume that the links provided are the only additional sources of information. Investigate other sites on your topic as well.

The answers to these questions will help you decide whether you should consider a Web site to be a good source of information.

The Internet and How It Works

The Internet is such an integral part of our lives that it's hard to imagine life without it. Looking forward, our ability to use and interact with the Internet and the World Wide Web will converge even more with our daily lives. Therefore, it's important to understand how the Internet works and the choices available for connecting to it.

The Internet's Clients and Servers

How does the Internet work?
Computers connected to the Internet communicate with (or "talk" to) each other in turns, just as we do when we ask a question and get an answer. Thus, a computer connected to the Internet acts in one of two ways: it is either a **client**, a

BITS AND BYTES

Citing Web Site Sources

After you've evaluated a Web site and determined it to be a credible source of information that you will use in a research paper, you will need to list the source in the Works Cited section of your paper. There are formal guidelines as to how to cite Web content. Unlike those for citing books and periodicals, however, these standards are still being developed. At a minimum, the following components should be included in the citation: author, title of document or publication, date of publication or last revision, complete URL, and date accessed. The following are examples of Web citations in both Modern Language Association (MLA) and American Psychological Association (APA) style for an article found in *BusinessWeek* online:

Example of MLA style
MacMillian, Douglas. "Facebook Moves onto Twitter's Turf." *BusinessWeek.* 16 March 2009. 17 March 2009. http://www.businessweek.com/technology/content/mar2009/tc20090316_227152.htm?chan=technology_technology+index+page_top+stories

Example of APA Style
MacMillian, D. (March 16, 2009). Facebook Moves onto Twitter's Turf. *BusinessWeek.* Retrieved March 17, 2009, from http://www.businessweek.com/technology/content/mar2009/tc20090316_227152.htm?chan=technology_technology+index+page_top+stories

For further assistance, go to **citationmachine.net**, which is an interactive tool designed to output citations in proper MLA or APA format, using information you provide in an online form. Microsoft Word 2007 also includes citation and bibliography formatting for most of the standard formats.

computer that asks for data, or it is a **server**, a computer that receives the request and returns the data to the client. Because the Internet uses clients and servers, it is referred to as a **client/server network**. (We'll discuss such networks in more detail in Chapter 7.)

How do computers talk to each other? Suppose you want to access the Web to check out snow conditions at your favorite ski area. As Figure 3.30 illustrates, the following events take place:

1. When you type the Web site address of the ski area in your Web browser, your computer acts as a client computer because you are asking for data from the ski area's Web site.

2. Your browser's request for this data travels along several pathways that can be likened to interstate highways. The largest and fastest pathway is the main artery of the Internet, called the **Internet backbone.** All intermediary pathways connect to this backbone.

3. Your data flows along the backbone and then on to smaller pathways until it reaches its destination, which is the server computer for the ski area's Web site.

4. The server computer returns the requested data to your computer using the most expedient pathway system (which may be different from the pathway the request took).

5. Your Web browser interprets the data and displays it on your monitor.

How does the data get sent to the correct computer? Each time you connect to the Internet, your computer is

Figure 3.30

How the Internet's Client/ Server Network Works.

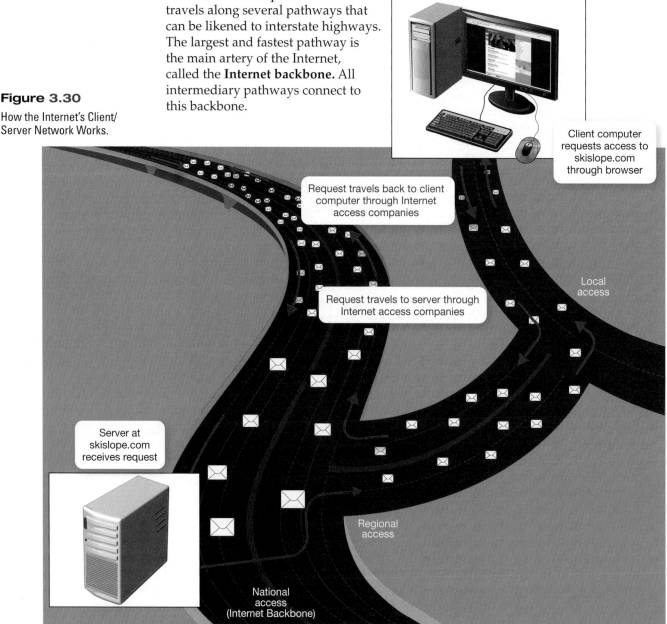

Client computer requests access to skislope.com through browser

Request travels back to client computer through Internet access companies

Request travels to server through Internet access companies

Local access

Server at skislope.com receives request

Regional access

National access (Internet Backbone)

assigned a unique identification number. This number, called an **Internet Protocol address** (or **IP address**), is a set of four numbers separated by periods and is commonly referred to as a *dotted quad* or *dotted decimal*, such as 123.45.245.91. IP addresses are the means by which all computers connected to the Internet identify each other. Similarly, each Web site is assigned an IP address that uniquely identifies it. However, because the long strings of numbers that make up IP addresses are difficult for people to remember, Web sites are given text versions of their IP addresses. So the ski area's Web site mentioned earlier may have an IP address of 66.117.154.119 and a text name of skislope.com. When you type "skislope.com" into your browser window, your computer (with its own unique IP address) looks for the ski area's IP address (66.117.154.119). Data is exchanged between the ski area's server computer and your computer using these unique IP addresses.

> **"What types of broadband are available?"**

Connecting to the Internet

To take advantage of the resources the Internet offers, you need a means to connect your computer to it. Home users nowadays have several connection options available. Originally, the only means to connect to the Internet was with a **dial-up connection**. With dial-up connections, you connect to the Internet using a standard telephone line. However, dial-up connections are becoming legacy technology because other, faster connection options exist. In many parts of the world, these faster connections are quickly becoming the preferred method of connecting to the Internet.

Broadband Connections

What is broadband?   Broadband, often referred to as "high-speed Internet," refers to a type of connection that offers a faster means to connect to the Internet. Broadband usually has a maximum data transmission rate of 256 Kbps (kilobits per second) or greater. This high rate of access is in contrast to dial-up Internet access, which has a maximum transmission speed of 56 Kbps.

What types of broadband are available?   The standard broadband technologies in most areas are **digital subscriber line (DSL)**, which uses a standard phone line to connect your computer to the Internet, and **cable**, which uses your television's cable service provider to connect to the Internet. **Fiber-optic service (FiOS)**, which uses plastic or glass cables to transfer data at the speed of light, has just recently become available as a broadband service to the home. Satellite broadband is mostly used in rural or mountain areas that cannot get DSL, cable, or fiber-optic service.

Why would I choose a broadband connection?   The reason you would choose broadband over dial-up is simple: speed. Cable and DSL are much faster than dial-up, and fiber-optic is the fastest of all. No matter which type of broadband technology you use, the quality of your Web experience will be greatly enhanced because the capabilities of the Web are designed with the assumption that the majority of Internet users are accessing the Internet via some form of broadband connection. A faster connection means that Web pages and multimedia content such as videos and games load more quickly and run more smoothly. You can also upload data and download files faster with a broadband connection.

How does cable work?   A cable Internet connection uses the same coaxial cable used by cable TV; however, cable TV and cable Internet are separate services. Cable TV is a one-way service in which the cable company feeds programming signals to your television. To bring two-way Internet connections to homes, cable companies must upgrade their networks with two-way data transmission capabilities.

How does DSL work?   Similar to a dial-up connection, DSL uses telephone lines

SOUND BYTE   Connecting to the Internet

In this Sound Byte, you'll learn the basics of connecting to the Internet from home, including useful information on the various types of Internet connections and selecting the right ISP.

to connect to the Internet. However, unlike dial-up, DSL allows phone and data transmission to share the same line, thus eliminating the need for an additional phone line. Phone lines are made of three twisted copper wires known as *twisted-pair wiring*. Think of this twisted copper wiring as a three-lane highway on which only one lane is used to carry voice data. DSL uses the remaining two lanes to send and receive data separately at much higher frequencies. Thus, although it uses a standard phone line, a DSL connection is much faster than a dial-up connection.

Can anyone with a phone line have DSL? Having a traditional phone line in your house doesn't mean that you have access to DSL service. Your local phone company must have special DSL technology to offer you the service. Although more phone companies are acquiring DSL technology, many areas in the United States, especially rural ones, still do not have DSL service available.

How does fiber-optic service work? Fiber-optic service (FiOS) uses fiber-optic lines, which are strands of optically pure glass or plastic that are as thin as a human hair. They are arranged in bundles called *optical cables* and transmit data via light signals over long distances. Because light travels so quickly, this technology can bring an enormous amount of data to your home at superfast speeds. When the data reaches your house, it's converted to electrical pulses that transmit digital signals your computer can "read."

What special equipment do I need to hook up to broadband? A broadband Internet connection requires a **modem**. Depending on the type of broadband service you have, you will have either a cable modem or DSL modem. The modem works to translate the broadband signal into digital data and back again. With both cable and DSL services, the modem allows the data to travel on the unused capacity of the transmission medium.

Cable runs to network interface card

Figure 3.31

You need a special DSL modem to connect to the Internet using DSL.

For example, a DSL modem (see Figure 3.31) separates voice signals from data signals so that they can travel in the right "lane" on the twisted-pair wiring. Voice data is sent at the lower speed, while digital data is sent at data transfer rates ranging from 500 Kbps to 6 megabits per second (Mbps), which is 6,000 Kbps. Sometimes a DSL filter is required in DSL installations. Filters are necessary to reduce interference caused when the DSL equipment shares the same lines as the standard phone line. If a filter is required, the phone line fits into the filter, and the filter plugs into the phone wall jack.

Generally, the modem is located somewhere near your computer and is connected to an expansion (or adapter) card called a **network interface card (NIC)**, which is located inside your computer. If you want to share your Internet connection with more than one computer, you will also need a router.

What options exist when cable and DSL are not available? Satellite Internet is another way to connect to the Internet. Most people choose satellite Internet when other high-speed options are unavailable. To take advantage of satellite Internet, you need a satellite dish, which is placed outside your home and connected to your computer with coaxial cable, the same type of cable used for cable TV. Data from your computer is transmitted between your personal satellite dish and the satellite company's receiving satellite dish by a satellite that sits in a geosynchronous orbit thousands of miles above the Earth.

ACTIVE HELP-DESK

Connecting to the Internet

In this Active Helpdesk call, you'll play the role of a helpdesk staffer. You will field calls about various options for connecting to the Internet and how to choose an Internet service provider.

Wireless

Why is wireless Internet access necessary? In our ever-more-mobile lifestyles, accessing the Internet wirelessly can make our lives more productive, and perhaps a bit more fun, while we are away from our desk. Students can send instant messages to each other across campus, and business travelers can quickly grab their e-mail between flights. At home, wireless networks allow us to share an Internet connection and print from our notebooks from any room without having to attach and detach wires. In some communities, organizations are now installing wireless or Wi-Fi networks; and in some cities and towns, local governments are installing municipal Wi-Fi networks. The newest wireless access technology to be deployed for mobile and stationary broadband access is WiMAX. WiMAX is designed to extend local Wi-Fi networks across greater distances, such as across a campus. Mobile WiMAX is an alternative to cellular transmission of voice and high-speed data.

How does one access the Internet wirelessly? To access the Internet wirelessly, you need to be in a wireless fidelity (Wi-Fi) hot spot and have the right equipment on your mobile device. Most notebooks, smartphones, game systems, and PMPs sold in the past several years come equipped with a network interface card, but if your notebook does not have wireless capability built in, several wireless adapters are available that can fit into the PC card slot or a USB port.

It's simple to set up a wireless network at home (see Chapter 7 for details), and many businesses and schools, as well as public places such as airports, libraries, bookstores, and restaurants, offer Wi-Fi. Some public places offer free access to Wi-Fi, but many others require you to buy wireless access through a wireless access service plan. For example, McDonald's provides Wi-Fi access through AT&T, and Barnes & Noble provides Wi-Fi through T-Mobile. To access these Wi-Fi services, you can pay for a single session or a monthly membership, or you can sign up for a longer-term subscription in which you receive monthly bills. Wi-Fi Free Spot (**wififreespot.com**) will help you locate a free hot spot wherever you are planning to go, and **Wi-FiHotSpotList.com** provides a means to find any hot spot.

Figure 3.32

Aircards like the ones pictured here fit into the USB port or PC card slot on your notebook to allow you to surf the Internet wirelessly when you don't have access to a Wi-Fi hot spot.

If you need to access the Internet wirelessly but will not be in a location with a convenient Wi-Fi hot spot, you can purchase an **aircard** such as the one shown in Figure 3.32. Aircards are devices that enable users to have wireless Internet access with mobile devices such as smartphones and notebooks. They require a service plan, similar to a cell phone plan. When considering purchasing an aircard and service plan, be sure to check the coverage and costs before deciding, because they vary among providers.

What are concerns with wireless? Most public hot spots are unsecured, so use caution when accessing the Internet from public locations. Although casually surfing the Internet is fine, it's best not to use your credit card, for example, to purchase items online from a public hot spot because your credit card information can be captured by a lurking identity thief. See additional information on wireless security in Chapter 7.

Dial-Up Connections

How does a dial-up connection work? A dial-up connection needs only a standard phone line and a modem. The word *modem* is short for *modulate/demodulate*.

How do we find information on the Web? Generally, we access Google or another search engine, type in the keyword or search phrase, and click the search button. As a result, millions of links to Web pages display. At best, we click on the first several links that seem reasonably relevant to our search. Rarely, if ever, do we explore all of the links that are found in the search results.

Similarly, think about all the other types of data on the Web that we access manually, such as contact information, appointment times, transportation schedules, entertainment schedules, medical treatments, and store types, locations, and hours. It would seem that computers would be helpful in plugging through all of this Web data, but oddly, that is not the case. Web pages are designed for people to read, not for computers to manipulate. Although computers can determine the parts and functionality of Web pages (headers, hyperlinks, etc.), as yet no reliable way exists for computers to process the *meaning* of the data so that they can use the information to see relationships or make decisions.

The Semantic Web is an evolving extension of the World Wide Web in which information is defined in such a way to make it more easily readable by computers. Tim Berners-Lee, the inventor of the World Wide Web, HTTP, and HTML, thought up the Semantic Web.

Right now, search engines function by recognizing keywords such as *treatment, dentist*, and *root canal,* but they cannot determine in which office and on what days Dr. Smith works and what his available appointment times are. The Semantic Web would enable computers to find and manage that type of information, and coordinate it with your other schedules and preferences.

Similarly, think about the convenience and efficiency that online shopping has brought to our lives. Then think about all the time we actually spend researching and comparing products, brands, stores, prices, and shipping options. Ultimately, after all that effort, we make the final buying decision and place the order. With the Semantic Web in place, you could enter your preferences into a computerized software agent, which would then search the Web for you, find the best option based on your criteria, and place the order. Additionally, the agent would be able to record the financial transaction into your personal bookkeeping software and arrange for a technician to help install your purchase, if needed.

The Semantic Web would use software agents that roam from page to page, completing sophisticated tasks. These agents would not read words, look at pictures, and process information as humans do, but rather would search through metadata. Metadata is machine-readable data that describes other data in such a way that the agents can identify and define what they need to know. Like Web page coding, which is now done in HTML, XML, and other formats, metadata would be invisible to humans reading pages on the Web, but would be clearly visible to computers, in essence turning the Web into a giant database.

The introduction of eXtensible Markup Language (XML) has helped make the user of the Web more of a participant. Web 2.0 technologies such as blogs, wikis, and social networking sites, as well as Web-based applications, are in part possible because of XML's tagging functionalities. RSS feeds also use technologies that are an underlying component of the Semantic Web.

The Semantic Web would build on this type of capability so that each Web site would have text and pictures (for people to read) and metadata (for computers to read) describing the information on the Web (see Figure 3.33). The metadata would contain all the attributes of the information, such as condition, price, or schedule availability, in a machine-readable format. Businesses, services, and software would all use the same categorization structures so that similar information would share the same attributes, ensuring consistency of metadata throughout the Web. Then, with Web data properly identified and categorized, computerized agents could read the metadata found on different sites, compare the information, and process the information based on user-defined criteria.

A **dial-up modem** is a device that converts (modulates) the digital signals the computer understands into analog signals that can travel over phone lines. The computer on the other end also must have a modem to translate (demodulate) the received analog signal back to a digital signal that the receiving computer can understand.

Modern desktop computers generally come with internal modems built into the system unit. Notebooks today usually have internal modems as well. If not, then small credit card–sized devices called **PC cards** (sometimes called **PCMCIA cards**), which can be inserted into a special slot on the notebook, function as external modems.

What are the advantages and disadvantages of dial-up? A dial-up connection is the least costly way to connect to the Internet. Although slower than broadband connections, dial-up connections are often fine for casual Internet users who do not need a fast connection. The major downside to dial-up is speed. Dial-up modems have a maximum data transfer rate that is much slower than that of a basic broadband connection. Although many Web pages can be sent without graphics as plain text, it still can take a long time to load a Web page, especially if it

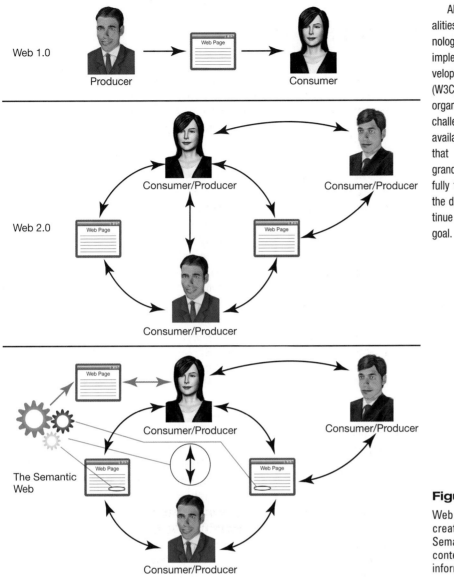

Web 1.0

Producer   Web Page   Consumer

Web 2.0

Consumer/Producer

Consumer/Producer

Web Page

Web Page

Consumer/Producer

The Semantic
Web

Web Page

Consumer/Producer

Web Page

Consumer/Producer

Web Page

Consumer/Producer

Although some of the Semantic Web functionalities are beginning to emerge in Web 2.0 technologies, the majority of the functionality and implementation of the Semantic Web is still in development. The World Wide Web Consortium (W3C), led by Tim Berners-Lee, is the primary organization leading the charge. The greatest challenge is recoding all the information currently available on the Web into the type of metadata that computers could recognize. The very grandeur of that task means that we will not see a fully functional Semantic Web until sometime in the distant future. In the meantime, we can continue to benefit from each small step toward that goal.

Figure 3.33

Web 2.0 technologies enable us to become creators and users of Internet content. The Semantic Web enables the computer to add context to Web content, providing meaning to information from different sources.

contains multimedia, which is the norm for most Web pages today. Similarly, if you visit many Web sites at the same time, or receive or send large files through e-mail, you'll find that a dial-up connection is especially slow. Another disadvantage of dial-up is that when you're on the Internet, you tie up your phone line if you don't have a separate line.

Choosing the Right Internet Connection Option

How do I choose which Internet connection option is best for me?
In 2007, approximately half of all U.S.

households connected to the Internet used some form of broadband connection. Depending on the area in which you live, you might not have a choice as to the type of broadband connection that is available. Check with your local cable TV provider, phone company, and satellite TV provider(s) to determine what broadband options are available where you live and what the transfer rates are in your area. It might also be good to check with your neighbors to see what kind of broadband connections they use. Speeds vary by neighborhood, sometimes exceeding advertised rates, so it's always good to check actual experiences.

Figure 3.34 | COMPARING CABLE, DSL, AND FIBER-OPTIC INTERNET CONNECTION OPTIONS

	DSL	Cable	Fiber-Optic
Maximum upload speeds	Average speeds of 1.5 Mbps, with a maximum of 6 + Mbps	Average speeds of 3 Mbps, with a maximum of 12 + Mbps	Average speeds of 20 Mbps, with a maximum speed of 30 Mbps
Pros	Lets you surf the Net and talk on the same phone line simultaneously.	Speeds are not dependent on distance from central office.	Increased speeds. Service is not shared or dependent on distance from central office.
Cons	Speed drops as you get farther from phone company's central office. Not every phone line will work; no easy way exists to find out if yours will.	Line is shared with others in neighborhood; speeds may vary. May require professional installation if cable not already present.	Cost, although this is a diminishing concern as the technology continues to be deployed and accepted. Not available in all areas.

Note: The data transfer rates listed in this table are approximations. As technologies improve, so do data transfer rates.

One factor to consider in choosing the right Internet connection is speed. **Data transfer rate** is the measurement of how fast data travels between computers. It is also informally referred to as *connection speed*. For example, dial-up modems have a maximum data transfer rate of 56 Kbps. This speed is usually referred to as *56K*. A kilobit is 1,000 bits and is normally used to represent the amount of data that is transferred in 1 second between two telecommunication points. Satellite Internet is faster than dial-up but is still slower than DSL and cable. Although DSL is catching up, cable wins out over DSL for speed. However, the availability of fiber-optic service through DSL providers can increase download rates to as high as 30 Mbps.

Finally, you may also need to consider which other services you want bundled into your payment, such as phone or TV. The table in Figure 3.34 compares several features of cable, DSL, and fiber-optic service to help you with your decision.

The Future of the Internet

The Internet of the future will have more bandwidth and offer increased services. Because of the prevalence of wireless technologies, the Internet will be more accessible, and we will become more dependent on it. However, because commerce and communication activities are increasingly dominating the Internet, the concern is that there will be no bandwidth left for one of the Internet's original purposes: exchange of scientific and academic research. Two major projects currently under way in the United States to develop advanced technologies for the Internet are the large scale networking (LSN) program and Internet2.

What are the large scale networking and Internet2 programs? Out of a project titled the Next Generation Internet (which ended in 2002), the U.S. government created the **large scale networking (LSN)** program. Large scale networking's aim is to fund the research and development of cutting-edge networking and wireless technologies and to increase the speed of networks.

The Internet2 is a research and development consortium of more than two hundred universities (supported by government and industry partners) that seeks to expand the possibilities of the Internet by developing new Internet technologies and disseminating them as rapidly as possible to the rest of the Internet community. Many of the current technologies of the commercial Internet are possible because of the research done by the Internet2 consortium. The Internet2 backbone supports extremely high-speed communications—up to 9.6 gigabits per second (Gbps)—and provides an excellent testing area for new data transmission technologies.

How else will the Internet become a more integral part of our lives? As this chapter explained, the Internet is already an integral part of our lives. It is the way we communicate, shop, research, entertain, and express ourselves. Many of the tools on the Web that have been described in this chapter—social networking sites, wikis, podcasts, and user content databases such as YouTube (for videos) and Flickr (for photos)—are part of a wave of Web-based services that emphasize online collaboration and sharing among users. The future Internet will continue to evolve with more Web-based applications driven by user input, interaction, and content.

In the future, you can expect to use the Internet to assist you with many day-to-day tasks that you now do manually. No longer will PCs and mobile devices be our primary access to the Internet. We can already see the convergence of the Internet with telephony, television, and gaming devices.

As other less obvious Internet-enabled devices become popular and more accessible to the common consumer, our lives will become more Internet dependent. For example, Internet-enabled appliances and household systems are now available that allow your home virtually to run itself. Today, there are refrigerators that can monitor their contents and go online to order more diet soda when they detect that the supply is getting low. Meanwhile, Internet heating and cooling systems can monitor weather forecasts and order fuel deliveries when supplies run low or bad weather is expected. These appliances will become more widespread as the price of equipment drops.

The uses of the Internet are limited only by our imaginations and the current constraints of technology. At some point, the Internet will no longer be a place we "go" to, but an integral part of our lives.

summary

1. What is the origin of the Internet?

The Internet is the largest computer network in the world, connecting millions of computers. Government and military officials developed the Internet as a reliable way to communicate in the event of war. Eventually, scientists and educators used the Internet to exchange research. Today, we use the Internet and the Web (which is a part of the Internet) to shop, research, communicate, and entertain ourselves.

2. How can I communicate through the Internet?

Communication was one of the reasons the Internet was developed and is one of the primary uses of the Internet today. E-mail allows users to communicate electronically without the parties involved being available at the same time, whereas instant messaging services are programs that enable you to communicate in real time with others who are online at the same time. Voice over Internet Protocol (VoIP) is a form of voice-based Internet communication that turns a standard Internet connection into a way to place phone calls. Other forms of group communication include chat rooms, newsgroups, and listservs.

3. How can I communicate and collaborate using Web 2.0 technologies?

Web 2.0 is a new trend of Web interactions among people, software, and data. Examples of these technologies include blogs, wikis, and more. Blogs are journal entries posted to the Web that are generally organized by a topic or area of interest and are publicly available. Generally, one person writes the blog, and others can comment on the journal entries. Video logs are personal journals that use video as the primary content in addition to text, images, and audio. Wikis are a type of Web site that allows users to change content by adding, removing, or editing it. A wiki is designed to allow many users to collaborate on the content. Podcasts are audio or video content that is broadcast over the Internet. Users subscribe to receive updates to podcasts. Social networking sites enable users to communicate and share information with existing friends as well as to meet and connect with others through common interests, experiences, or friends.

4. What are the various kinds of multimedia files found on the Web, and what software do I need to use them?

The Web is appealing because of its enriched multimedia content. Multimedia is anything that involves one or more forms of media in addition to text, such as graphics, audio, and video clips. Sometimes you need a special software program called a plug-in (or player) to view and hear multimedia files. Plug-ins are often installed in new computers or are offered free of charge at manufacturers' Web sites.

5. What is e-commerce, and what e-commerce safeguards protect me when I'm online?

E-commerce is the business of conducting business online. E-commerce includes transactions between businesses (B2B), between consumers (C2C), and between businesses and consumers (B2C). Because more business than ever before is conducted online, numerous safeguards have been put in place to ensure that transactions are protected.

6. What is a Web browser?

Once you're connected to the Internet, in order to locate, navigate to, and view Web pages, you need to install special software called a Web browser on your system. The most common Web browsers are Microsoft Internet Explorer, Mozilla, Firefox, and Safari. Google Chrome is the newest browser on the market.

7. What is a URL, and what are its parts?

You gain access to a Web site by typing in its address, called a Uniform Resource Locator (URL). A URL is composed of several parts, including the protocol, the domain, the top-level domain, and, occasionally, paths (or subdirectories).

8. How can I use hyperlinks and other tools to get around the Web?

One unique aspect of the Web is that you can jump from place to place by clicking on specially formatted pieces of text or images called *hyperlinks*. You can also use tools such as Back and Forward buttons, History lists, breadcrumb lists, and Favorites or Bookmarks to navigate the Web. Favorites, live bookmarks, and tagging help you return to specific Web pages without having to type in the URL and help you organize the Web content that is most important to you.

9. How do I search the Internet effectively?

A search engine is a set of programs that searches the Web using specific keywords you wish to query and then returns a list of the Web sites on which those keywords are found. Search engines can be used to search for images, podcasts, and videos in addition to traditional text-based Web content. A subject directory is a structured outline of Web sites organized by topic and subtopic. Metasearch engines search other search engines.

10. How do I evaluate a Web site?

Not all Web sites are equal, and some are better sources for research than others are. To evaluate whether it is appropriate to use a Web site as a resource, determine whether the author of the site is reputable and whether the site is intended for your particular needs. In addition, make sure that the site content is not biased, the information in the site is current, and all the links on the site are available and appropriate.

11. How does data travel on the Internet?

A computer connected to the Internet acts as either a client (a computer that asks for information) or a server (a computer that receives the request and returns the information to the client). Data travels between clients and servers along a system of communication lines or pathways. The largest and fastest of these pathways is the Internet backbone. To ensure that data is sent to the correct computer along the pathways, IP addresses (unique ID numbers) are assigned to all computers connected to the Internet.

12. What are my options for connecting to the Internet?

Home users have many options for connecting to the Internet. A dial-up connection, in which you connect to the Internet using a standard phone line, was at one time the standard way to connect to the Internet. Today's broadband connections are faster and have made dial-up a legacy connection technology. Broadband connections include cable, DSL, and fiber-optic. Satellite is a connection option for those who do not have access to faster broadband technologies. Wi-Fi allows users to connect to the Internet wirelessly.

13. What will the Internet of the future look like?

The Internet of the future will have faster connections and will be able to provide additional services as a result of projects such as the large-scale networking program and Internet2. The Internet will become more integrated into our daily lives as Internet-enabled appliances and household systems provide more remote-control features for our homes.

Word Bank

- blogs (weblogs)
- Bookmarks
- broadband
- DSL
- fiber-optic service (FiOS)
- hyperlink
- instant messaging (IM)
- keyword
- search engine
- social bookmarking
- social networking
- tag
- Uniform Resource Locators (URLs)
- Voice over Internet Protocol (VoIP)
- Web 2.0
- Web browser
- Wi-Fi
- wiki

Instructions: Fill in the blanks using the words from the Word Bank above.

Juan rests his new notebook on his lap and powers it up while waiting for his next class to begin. Using the (1) _____ access provided by his college, Juan is able to connect to the Internet wirelessly. Although the school's wireless access to the Internet is fast, it's not as fast as the (2) _____ connection at home, because his parents just switched to (3) _____, which transfers data at the speed of light.

Knowing he has only a few minutes before class, Juan launches Internet Explorer, the (4) _____ software from Microsoft that allows him to connect to the Internet. He quickly goes to Facebook, the (5) _____ site, to catch up on the activities of his friends. He also reads a few of the updates to the online journal Engadget.com, one of his favorite (6) _____. He's glad that the new (7) _____ technologies make such collaboration possible. Just before class begins, Juan's friend Marie, who is using her (8) _____ service, sees that Juan is available on her buddy list. She sends him a quick, real-time note to let him know she'll catch up with him after class.

At home Juan types in a (9) _____ in Google, the (10) _____, to find Web sites for a research paper. One of the first sites listed is Wikipedia, the online encyclopedia that takes advantage of the collaborative nature of (11) _____ technology. Because anyone can add, change, or edit content on Wikipedia, Juan knows that he can't rely completely on this information but finds that it is usually a pretty good starting point for his research. Juan clicks on a (12) _____, the specially coded text at the bottom of the Wikipedia article, which links him to another Web site. He adds a (13) _____ with a meaningful keyword in the (14) _____ site Delicious so he can return to it later. Finally, before going to bed, Juan uses (15) _____ technology to speak to his friend across the country with his Skype service.

becoming computer literate

Using key terms from the chapter, write a letter to the owners of your local coffee shop explaining why they should make it a Wi-Fi hot spot. Include in your letter the advantages Wi-Fi would bring to the customers and identify some security considerations that customers need to be aware of.

self-test three self-test

Instructions: Answer the multiple-choice and true–false questions below for more practice with key terms and concepts from this chapter.

Multiple Choice

1. Which of the following statements is NOT true about instant messaging?
   a. It is a popular form of communication.
   b. You communicate in real time.
   c. More than two people can IM at the same time.
   d. Unlike e-mail, IM is good for private conversations.

2. When you are shopping online, which of the following does NOT indicate that you have a secure connection?
   a. A closed padlock icon in the status bar
   b. A URL that begins with *https*
   c. The word "secure" in the title bar
   d. The VeriSign seal on the Web page

3. With a podcast, you can
   a. subscribe to video and audio content.
   b. have the most recent content "delivered" automatically.
   c. play the video and audio content on a portable media player.
   d. All of the above.

4. A Web page that enables online collaboration is
   a. a podcast.   c. a blog.
   b. a wiki.   d. an IM chat.

5. When searching the Internet, which of the following is true?
   a. All search engines provide the same results.
   b. A metasearch engine delivers the most specific results.
   c. Using advanced search pages broadens your results.
   d. Using words surrounded by quotation marks searches for those words in that exact order.

6. In the Web address **http://www.irs.gov**, which part is considered the top-level domain?
   a. www   c. http
   b. .gov   d. www.irs.gov

7. Which of the following broadband Internet connections transmits data at the speed of light?
   a. Cable   c. FioS
   b. DSL   d. Satellite

8. Which is an advantage to Web-based e-mail clients?
   a. They require you to download specific software to your computer.
   b. They offer more functionality than client-based software.
   c. They are accessible from any computer with an Internet connection.
   d. All of the above.

9. In evaluating Web sites as appropriate sources for research, which criteria you should consider?
   a. Authority, relevancy, bias, audience
   b. Authority, Web design, audience, links
   c. Relevancy, bias, Web design, audience
   d. Relevancy, Web design, audience, links

10. Which accurately defines an IP address?
   a. The means by which computers are identified on the Internet
   b. A set of four groups of numbers separated by dots
   c. A unique identification number assigned to a computer when it connects to the Internet
   d. All of the above

True–False

_____ 1. *Web* and *Internet* are interchangeable terms.

_____ 2. Social bookmarking is also known as *tagging*.

_____ 3. Because Google generates the most search results of any of the search engines, it is called a metasearch engine.

_____ 4. DSL, cable, and FiOS are all considered broadband Internet connections.

_____ 5. You cannot connect to the Internet wirelessly unless you're in a Wi-Fi hot spot.

making the transition to... next semester

1. Online Support Facilities

Your school most likely has many online support facilities. Do you know what they are? Go to your school's Web site and search for online support.

a. Is online tutoring available?
b. Can you reserve a book from the library online?
c. Can you register for classes online?
d. Can you take classes online?
e. Can you buy books online?

2. Plagiarism Policies

Does your school have a plagiarism policy?

a. Search your school's Web site to find the school's plagiarism policy. What does it say?
b. How well do you paraphrase? Find some Web sites that help test or evaluate your paraphrasing skills.

3. Searching Beyond Google

While Google is probably your first choice among search engines, there are many other very good search engines that are good to know about. Conduct searches for inexpensive travel deals for spring break by using the following search engines. Record your results and a summary of the differences among search engines. Would you choose to use any of these search engines again? Why or why not?

a. Clusty.com
b. Dogpile.com
c. Rollyo.com

4. Free Speech Online

Jeanne was suspended from school for several days because her posts on MySpace about her teacher and a few of her classmates were "vulgar" and "derogatory." Tom was expelled from his school because the picture he posted of himself was in violation of his school's code of conduct. Similarly, Bill, a local employer, changed his mind about a job offer to a recent graduate after seeing questionable content on the candidate's Facebook page.

a. Should a person be penalized for his or her content on any Web site?
b. Is the issue denial of free speech or prudent reactions to improper behavior?

5. Using Web 2.0 in Education

Social networking sites, blogs, and wikis are commonly referred to as Web 2.0 technologies. Sites that use Web 2.0 offer opportunities for collaboration, creativity, and enterprise. Describe how Web 2.0 sites such as Wikipedia, YouTube, Delicious, and Digg might change how you learn and manage information.

making the transition to... the workplace

1. Online Résumé Resources

Using a search engine, locate several Web resources that offer assistance in writing a résumé. For example, the University of Minnesota (**umn.edu/ohr/careerdev/resources/resume**) has a résumé tutor that guides you as you write your résumé.

   a. What other Web sites can you find that help you write a résumé?
   b. Do these sites all offer the same services and have the same features?

2. Online Cover Letter Resources

Your résumé will need to be accompanied by a cover letter. Research Web sites that offer advice for writing cover letters and samples of good ones.

   a. Which Web sites do you feel offer the best advice on how to write a cover letter? Which style cover letter works best for you?
   b. What do the Web sites say you should include in your cover letter, and why?

3. Evaluating Web Content

You have noticed that your co-workers are using the Internet to conduct research. However, they are not careful about checking the validity of the Web sites they find before using the information.

   a. Search the Internet for Web site evaluation guidelines. Print out your sources and findings.
   b. Using the material from step (a), create a scorecard or set of guidelines that will help others determine whether a Web site is reliable.

4. Internet Connection Option

Now that you've graduated, you are planning to move into your first apartment and leave behind the comforts of broadband access at the residence halls. Evaluate the Internet options available in your area.

   a. Create a table that includes information on broadband services in your area. The table should include the name of the provider, the cost of the service, information on bundled services (TV, Internet, phone), and the cost of bundled services.
   b. Based on the table you create, write a brief paragraph describing which service you would choose, and why.

5. Internet Connection Speed

You would like to know how fast your Internet connection speed is. Your co-worker in the information technology (IT) department recommended that you check out **bandwidthplace.com** and **pcpitstop.com**.

   a. Choose one of the recommended sites and test your connection speed. How is the test conducted? What is used to measure the connection speed?
   b. List reasons why you would be interested in measuring your Internet connection speed.

6. E-Mail Privacy

Take a moment to think about this statement: An e-mail is no more private than a postcard.

   a. Search the Web for resources that support and oppose the preceding statement. Print out sources for both sides of the argument.
   b. Write a paragraph that summarizes your position.

Instructions: Albert Einstein used *Gedankenexperiments*, or critical thinking questions, to develop his theory of relativity. Some ideas are best understood by experimenting with them in our own minds. The following critical thinking questions are designed to demand your full attention but require only a comfortable chair—no technology.

1. Internet and Society

The Internet was initially created in part to enable scientists and educators to share information quickly and efficiently. The advantages Internet access brings to our lives are evident, but does Internet access also cause problems?

a. What advantages and disadvantages does the Internet bring to your life?

b. What positive and negative effects has the Internet had on our society as a whole?

c. Some people argue that conducting searches on the Internet provides answers but does not inspire thoughtful research. What do you think?

d. Should use of the Internet be banned, or at least limited, for research projects in schools? Why or why not?

2. File Swapping Ethics

Downloading free music, movies, and other electronic media from the Internet, although illegal, still occurs on sites such as Limewire and Bit Torrents.

a. Do you think you should have the ability to download free music files of your choice? Do you think the musicians who oppose online music sharing have made valid points?

b. Discuss the differences you see between sharing music files online and sharing CDs with your friends.

c. The current price to buy a song online is about $1. Is this a fair price? If not, what price would you consider to be fair?

3. The Power of Google

Google is the largest and most popular search engine on the Internet today. Because of its size and popularity, some people claim that Google has enormous power to influence a Web user's search experience solely by its Web site ranking processes. What do you think about this potential power? How could it be used in negative or harmful ways?

a. Some Web sites pay search engines to list them near the top of the results pages. These sponsors therefore get priority placement. What do you think of this policy?

b. What effect (if any) do you think that Google has on Web site development? For example, do you think Web site developers intentionally include frequently searched words in their pages so that they will appear in more hits lists?

c. When you "google" someone, you type their name in the Google search box to see what comes up. What privacy concerns do you think such "googling" could present? Have you ever "googled" yourself or your friends?

4. Charging for E-Mail?

Should there be a charge for sending e-mail or having IM conversations? What would be an appropriate charge? If a fee were charged for e-mail and IM conversations, what would happen to their use?

5. Internet and Politics

What role has the Internet played in political campaigns? What role will it play in the future? Do you see the day when voting will happen through the Internet? Why or why not?

three team time

Comparing Internet Search Methods

Problem

With millions of sites on the Internet, finding useful information can be a daunting—and at times, impossible—task. However, there are methods to make searching easier, some of which have been discussed in this chapter. In this Team Time, each team will search for specific items or pieces of information on the Internet and compare search methodologies.

Process

Split your group into three or more teams, depending on class size. Each group will create a team wiki using free wiki software such as that found at **pbwiki.com**. To appreciate the benefits of wiki collaboration fully, each team should have at least five or six members.

1. Each team should come up with a theme for their wiki. Some suggestions include the following:

   Best computer technology Web sites

   Coolest new technology gadgets

   All-time greatest rock n' rollers

   All-time greatest athletes

   Best places to visit in the United States

   Best beaches in the United States

   Best skiing areas in the United States

2. Each student should pick one example to research and must design a wiki page highlighting that subject. For example, if the team chose all-time greatest rock n' rollers, one student could select Bruce Springsteen and create a wiki page on Bruce Springsteen. The wiki page should contain links to other Web sites and, if possible, images and videos.

3. After the team wikis are created, teams should make their wikis available to the other teams for comments.

Conclusion

After all the team wikis have been completed and shared, discuss the following with your class. What is the benefit of using wiki technology to create team pages? How did wikis help or hinder the team process? What other conclusions can the class draw about using wiki technology?

In addition to the review materials presented here, you'll find additional materials featured with the book's multimedia, including the *Technology in Action* Student Resource CD and the Companion Website (**pearsonhighered.com/techinaction**), which will help reinforce your understanding of the chapter content. These materials include the following:

Active Helpdesk

In Active Helpdesk calls, you'll assume the role of helpdesk operator, taking calls about the concepts you've learned in this chapter. You'll apply what you've learned and receive feedback from a supervisor to review and reinforce those concepts. The Active Helpdesk calls for this chapter are listed below and can be found on your Student Resource CD:

- Doing Business Online
- Getting Around the Web
- Using Subject Directories and Search Engines
- Connecting to the Internet

Sound Bytes

Sound Bytes are dynamic multimedia tutorials that help demystify even the most complex topics. You'll view video clips and animations that illustrate computer concepts and then apply what you've learned by reviewing with the Sound Byte Labs, which include quizzes and activities specifically tailored to each Sound Byte. The Sound Bytes for this chapter are listed below and can be found on your Student Resource CD:

- Creating a Web-Based E-mail Account
- Blogging
- Welcome to the Web
- Finding Information on the Web
- Connecting to the Internet

Companion Website

The *Technology in Action* Companion Website includes a variety of additional materials to help you review and learn more about the topics in this chapter. The resources available at **pearsonhighered.com/techinaction/** include:

- **Online Study Guide.** Each chapter features an online true–false and multiple-choice quiz. You can take these quizzes, automatically check the results, and e-mail the results to your instructor.
- **Web Research Projects.** Each chapter features several Web research projects that ask you to search the Web for information on computer-related careers, milestones in computer history, important people and companies, emerging technologies, and the applications and implications of different technologies.

Choice

EXIT NOW

Security

Computer Abuse

Information Technology

ethics

In this Technology in Focus section, we explore what ethics are, how your personal ethics develop, and how your personal ethics fit into the world around you. We'll also examine how technology and ethics affect each other and how technology can be used to support ethical conduct. Finally, we'll examine several key issues in technology ethics today, including the areas of social justice, intellectual property rights, privacy, Internet commerce, free speech, and computer abuse.

IN FOCUS

Gambling

Censorship

People speak of ethics—and the lack of ethics—casually all the time, but the ethical choices that individuals make are an extremely serious matter and can have a far-reaching impact. It is important to have a clear idea of what ethics are, what your personal ethics are, and how personal ethics fit into the world at large.

ETHICS IN COMPUTING

You just bought a new notebook computer. You know you can go to BitTorrent or LimeWire to download the latest summer blockbuster movie and its soundtrack. You also probably know this is unethical. Although pirating music and videos is a valid example of unethical behavior, it has been overused as an illustration of the ethical challenges of technology. There is a vast range of ethical issues surrounding technology (as shown in Figure 1), several of which we will discuss in this section. Many other issues are discussed in the Ethics in IT sections of each chapter throughout the book.

WHAT IS ETHICS?

Ethics is the study of the general nature of morals and of the specific moral choices made by individuals. Morals involve conforming to established or accepted ideas of right and wrong (as generally dictated by society), and are usually viewed as black and white. Ethical issues often involve subtle distinctions, such as the difference between fairness and equity. Ethical values are the guidelines you use to make decisions each day. For example, the person in front of you at the coffee shop drops a dollar on the floor and doesn't notice it. Do you tell him or her about it, or do you pick up the dollar and use it to pay for your coffee?

Doesn't everyone have the same basic ethics? There are many systems of ethical conduct. **Relativism** is a theory that holds that there is no universal moral truth and that instead there are only beliefs, perspectives, and values. Everyone has his or her own ideas of right and wrong, and so

who are we to judge anyone else? Another ethical philosophy is **situational ethics**, which states that decision making should be based on the circumstances of a particular situation and not on fixed laws.

Many other ethical systems have been proposed over time, some of which are defined by religious traditions. For example, the expression "Judeo-Christian ethics" refers to the common set of basic values shared across the Jewish and Christian religious traditions. These include behaviors such as respecting property and relationships, honoring one's parents, and being kind to others.

Are laws established to guide people's ethical actions? Laws are formal, written standards designed to apply to everyone. Laws are enforced by government agencies (such as the police, the Federal Bureau of Investigation, the Food and Drug Administration, and so on) and interpreted by the courts. It is not possible to pass laws that cover every possible behavior that human beings can engage in. Therefore, **societal ethics** provides a general set of unwritten guidelines for people to follow.

Rule utilitarianism is an ethical theory that espouses establishing moral guidelines through specific rules. The idea behind this system is that if everyone adheres to the same moral code, society as a whole will improve and people will be happier. Many societies follow this system in general terms, including the United States. For instance, laws against nudity in public places (except for a few nude beaches) in the United States help define public nudity as immoral.

Don't some people behave unethically? Although many valid systems of ethical conduct exist, sometimes people act in a manner that violates the beliefs they hold or the beliefs of the ethical system they say they follow. **Unethical behavior** can be defined as not conforming to a set of approved standards of social or professional behavior. For instance, using your phone to text message your friend during an exam is prohibited by most colleges' rules of student conduct. This behavior is different from **amoral behavior**, in which a person has no sense of right and wrong and no interest in the moral consequences of his or her actions.

Is unethical behavior a euphemism for illegal activity? Unethical behavior does not have to be illegal. An example of an

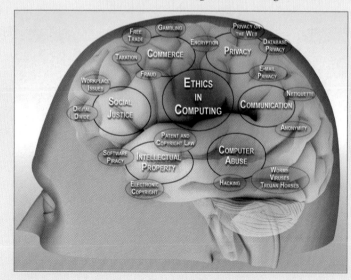

unethical but not illegal practice is supermarket slotting fees. These are fees that some supermarkets charge to produce companies and product manufacturers for the privilege of having their products placed on store shelves. This is considered unethical by many people because it puts smaller companies, which often don't have the financial resources to pay these fees, at a disadvantage.

Not all illegal behavior is unethical. Civil disobedience, which is manifested by intentionally refusing to obey certain laws, is used as a form of protest to effect change in extreme situations. Gandhi's nonviolent resistance to the British rule of India, which led to India's establishment as an independent country, is an example of civil disobedience. Although the British were ruling India, is it ever ethical for one country to control another country's people?

Which system of ethics works best?
There is no universal agreement on which is the best system of ethics. Most societies use a blend of different systems. Regardless of the ethical system of the society in which you live, all ethical decisions are greatly influenced by personal ethics.

PERSONAL ETHICS

What are personal ethics?
Every day you say certain things and take specific actions, and at each point you are making decisions based on some criterion. It may be that you are trying to care for the people around you, or are trying to eliminate a source of pain or anger in your life. Your words and actions may also be driven by a combination of criteria. As you choose your words and actions, you are following a set of personal ethics—a checklist of personal decisions you have compiled to organize your life. Some people have a clear, well-defined set of principles they follow. Others' ethics are inconsistent or are applied differently in similar situations.

It can be challenging to adhere to your own ethical system if the consequences of your decisions today might lead to an unhappy result for you in the short term. For instance, to get the job of your dreams, should you exaggerate a bit on your résumé and say you've already finished your college degree, even though you are

FIGURE 2

It would be nice if there were signposts to ethical conduct, but the issues are complex.

still one credit short? Is this lying? Is such behavior justified in this setting? After all, you do intend to finish that last credit, and you would work really hard for this company if you were hired. If you tell the truth and state that you haven't finished college yet, then you might be passed over for the position. Making this choice is an ethical decision (see Figure 2).

How do a person's ethics develop?
Many elements contribute to your ethical development (see Figure 3). Naturally, your family has a major role in establishing the values you cherish in your own life, and these might include a cultural bias toward certain moral positions. Your religious affiliation is

FIGURE 3

Many different forces shape your ethical worldview.

Family

Don't litter

Religion

Don't tell lies.

Your ethical behavior

Experience

Don't speed or you'll get a ticket.

Teacher

Don't cheat on tests or you'll fail.

another major influence in your ethical life, because most religions have established specific codes of ethical conduct. How these sets of ethics interact with the values of the larger culture is often challenging. Issues such as abortion, the death penalty, and war force confrontations between personal ethical systems and the larger society's established legal-ethical system.

As you mature, your life experiences also affect your personal ethics. Does the behavior you see around you make sense within the ethical principles that your family, your church, or your first-grade teacher taught you? Has your experience led you to abandon some ethical rules and adopt others? Have you modified how and when you apply these laws of conduct, depending on what is at stake?

What if I'm not sure what my personal ethics are? When you have a clear and firm idea of what values are most important to you, it may be easier to handle situations in your professional and your personal life that demand ethical action. Follow these steps to help define your personal ethics:

1. **Describe yourself.** Write down words that describe who you are, based on how others view you. Would a friend describe you as honest, or helpful, or kind?

2. **List your beliefs.** Make a list of all the beliefs that influence your decision making. For example, would you be comfortable working as a research assistant in a lab that infected dogs with diseases and used them for medical research? How important is it to you that you never tell a lie? Consider whether your answers to each of these questions are "flexible." Are there situations in which your answers might change (say, if a friend were ill or in danger)?

3. **Identify external influences.** Consider the places where you work and live and how you relate to the people you see during the day. Are there things that you would like to change about these relationships that would merit listing them in a code of ethics?

4. **Consider "why."** After writing down your beliefs, think about why you believe them. Have you accepted them without investigation? Do they stand up in the context of your real-world experiences? For which of these values would you make short-term sacrifices in order to uphold your beliefs?

5. **Prepare a statement of values.** It can be useful to distill what you have written into a short list. By having a well-defined statement of the values you hold most important in your own life, which you can refer to in times of challenge, it will be easier for you to make ethical decisions.

Are there tangible benefits to ethical living? Society has established its own set of rules of conduct in the form of laws. Ignoring or being inconsistent in following these principles can surely have an immediate impact. Whether it is complying with a law that affects the way your business is run, or with a law that affects your personal life (don't exceed the speed limit or you'll receive a fine), decision-making principles that work with society's legal boundaries can make your life much simpler.

More and more research is showing the health benefits of ethical living. When your day-to-day decisions are in conflict with the values you consider most important as a human being, you often develop stress and anger. Constant conflict between what you value and what actions you are forced to take can lead to a variety of types of mental and physical damage.

Perhaps even happiness itself is a result of living ethically (see Figure 4). "Positive psychology" is a new focus in the field of psychology.

Pioneered by Dr. Martin Seligman of the University of Pennsylvania, this field works to discover the causes of happiness instead of addressing the treatment of mental dysfunctions. Dr. Seligman's research has shown that, by identifying your personal strengths and values, and then aligning your life so that you can apply them every day, you can experience an increase in happiness (and a decrease in depression) equivalent to the effects of antidepressant medication and therapy. Thus, finding a way to identify and then apply your ethics and values to your daily life can have an impact on your health and happiness.

PERSONAL ETHICS AND YOUR WORLDVIEW

How do my personal ethics fit into the world at large?   All of your actions, words, and even thoughts are controlled by your personal ideas of right and wrong. But do your ethics shift when you go to work? Your employer expects you to follow the ethics and rules of conduct that the owner has established for the business. Although each person at your workplace may be trying to follow corporate ethical guidelines, each person will follow them differently based on his or her personal ethics. Person A may feel it is acceptable to tell white lies to get more funding for his project, whereas Person B might believe that telling the truth at all times is the best and only way that she can foster the teamwork and cooperation necessary to complete a project.

This doesn't mean that individuals need to blindly follow practices they feel are unethical or detrimental to society at large. Most **whistle-blowers** are people that report businesses to regulatory agencies for committing illegal acts. Other whistle blowers expose unethical (but still legal) acts by their employers by publicizing unethical behavior through various media outlets.

In summary, when you are working in a business environment, your ethics are guided by the ethical principles that are defined by the business owner or management, but you are still ultimately guided by your personal ethics.

How do employers affect personal ethics?   Should your employer have control (or even input) about your conduct outside of the office? Do behavior, integrity, and honesty off the job relate to job performance? They might. But even if they don't, your actions could reflect poorly on your employer from your employer's perspective. Consider Ellen Simonetti, who was fired by Delta Airlines for blogging. Even though Ms. Simonetti never mentioned Delta Airlines by name on her blog ("Queen of the Sky: Diary of a Dysfunctional Flight Attendant"), Delta Airlines objected to photos that she posted of herself and fellow flight attendants in their Delta uniforms. Delta Airlines felt that the photos were inappropriate and portrayed negative images of Delta Airlines employees. Another example is Jillian Tomlinson, the Australian surgeon who was suspended by her employer for discussing medical procedures, her work environment, and fellow employees, and for posting CAT scans of patients on her blog (although patient names were not revealed). Therefore, although your ethics might dictate one mode of behavior, you need to consider how your actions might be viewed by your employer (see Figure 5).

How does making ethical choices in a business setting differ from making personal ethical choices?   Most personal ethical decisions involve few people, unless the decision results in a significant impact on society. When making ethical choices

Is your boss watching you? Does that make you more or less inclined to behave ethically?

in the business world, give careful consideration to the stakeholders of the business. **Stakeholders** are those people or entities who are affected by the operations of a business. Before making an ethical choice for a business, you need to consider the effect that choice will have on all of the stakeholders. Typical stakeholders for most businesses are customers, suppliers, employees, investors (shareholders), financial lenders, and society.

For instance, suppose you decide to cut costs in your restaurant by hiring undocumented workers. While this might boost profits in the short term, the long-term impact on stakeholders can be severe. Potential employees who are eligible to work in the United States will be denied jobs. If you are caught using undocumented workers, fines will be levied against the business, which will cause investors to lose money and may affect the company's ability to repay lenders. The negative publicity from being caught may cause a downturn in business, which, in turn, might force layoffs of employees or even closure of the business. Your simple decision on cutting costs isn't as simple as it may seem!

TECHNOLOGY AND ETHICS: HOW ONE AFFECTS THE OTHER

In both good and bad ways, technology affects our community life, family life, work environment, education, and medical research, to name only a few areas of our lives. Because technology moves faster than rules can be formulated to govern it, how technology is used is often left up to the individual and the guidance of his or her personal ethics.

Technology constantly challenges our ethics as individuals and as a society. In the rest of this Technology in Focus feature, we will explore some issues involving the relationship between technology and ethics. Specifically, we will examine situations in which ethics and technology touch each other: social justice (benefits of technology), intellectual property (fair use), privacy (personal privacy and technology), e-commerce (online gambling), electronic communication issues (free speech), and computer abuse (protection versus access).

Ethical considerations are never black and white. They are complex, and reasonable people can have different yet equally valid views. We present alternative viewpoints in each setting for you to consider and discuss. Figure 6 summarizes these issues.

USING COMPUTERS TO SUPPORT ETHICAL CONDUCT

Although there are many opportunities to use computers and the Internet unethically, many more ways are available to use technology to support ethical conduct.

FIGURE 6

Ethics in Computing

Topic	Ethical Discussion	Debate Issue
Social justice	Can technology be used to benefit everyone?	Does technology provide economic opportunity for all?
Intellectual property	What is fair about fair use?	What kind of fair use standards are beneficial?
Privacy	Is personal privacy a casualty of the modern age?	Should personal privacy be protected?
E-commerce	Is online gambling a problem?	Should online gambling be banned or regulated?
Electronic communication	When does big business limit free speech?	Should companies allow the Chinese government to dictate when to curtail free speech?
Computer abuse	Does restricting access to online information protect children?	Is filtering or monitoring software helpful?

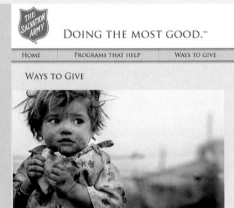

EVERYONE DESERVES A SECOND CHANCE.
NOT TO MENTION A FIRST.

FIGURE 7

Most major charities facilitate donations through the Internet.

Many charitable organizations use the Internet for fund-raising. When the Sichuan earthquake struck China in 2008, organizations such as the American Red Cross (see Figure 7) and other charities supporting relief efforts used their Web pages to help donors quickly, easily, and securely make contributions to aid earthquake victims. Using technology to garner contributions enables charities to raise billions of dollars quickly for relief efforts.

When you spot unethical behavior at your company, you need a fast, secure way to report it to the appropriate members of management. The Sarbanes–Oxley Act of 2002 requires companies to provide mechanisms for employees and third parties to report complaints, including ethics violations. These mechanisms are required to provide the employees with anonymity. In addition, many businesses are using their Web sites to allow whistle-blowers to report wrongdoing anonymously, replacing previous e-mail and telephone hotline systems, which did not shield employees from being identified. With an electronic system, it is easier for a company to sort and classify complaints and designate them for appropriate action.

Electronic systems such as intranets and e-mail are also excellent mechanisms for informing employees about ethics policies. Storing ethics guidelines electronically on a company intranet ensures that employees have access to information whenever they need it. By using e-mail, a company can communicate new policies, or changes to existing policies, to employees quickly and efficiently.

Throughout your life, you will encounter many ethical challenges relating to information technology. Your personal ethics—combined with the ethical guidelines your company provides and the general ethical environment of society—will guide your decisions.

For further information on ethics, check out the following Web sites:

- **ethics.csc.ncsu.edu**
- **ethicscenter.net**
- **business-ethics.com**
- **business-ethics.org**

Social Justice

Can Technology Be Used to Benefit Everyone?

SUMMARY OF THE ISSUE

Does our society have a responsibility to use technology to help achieve social justice? Freeman Dyson, an American physicist and mathematician, sparked discussion about this issue by saying that science is concentrating too much on "making toys for the rich" instead of addressing the needs of the poor (see Figure 8). There is great promise for financial reward from creating an even smaller cellular phone, but there is little incentive to find solar energy solutions that will help struggling rural communities. Dyson proposes the application of three technologies to turn poor rural areas into sources of wealth: solar energy, genetic engineering, and Internet access.

Solar energy is available virtually everywhere in the world. It could become cheap enough to compete with oil. The spiraling price of oil, which has been caused primarily by increased worldwide demand, has created a barrier to elevating poor rural communities above the poverty level.

Through genetic engineering, it might be possible to design new plants (or modify existing plants) to achieve novel biological processes such as converting sunlight into fuel efficiently. If plants could be engineered to improve their efficiency as sources of energy, or to provide other qualities that are in demand (such as making them better sources of protein and fiber when consumed), rural residents would be able to produce items with high market demand and would have greater opportunities to increase their standard of living.

The Internet can help businesses and farms in remote areas become part of the modern economy. Currently, it is difficult for rural farmers in Third World countries to determine the best place to take their crops to market. By consulting the Internet, however, they could obtain price quotes for markets within their reach and determine which ones would provide the best prices for their crops.

QUESTIONS TO THINK ABOUT AND RESEARCH

1. Are the types of technology suggested by Dyson plausible or out of the reach of current scientific methods?

2. Would Dyson's suggested use of technology help people or spark social revolution?

3. What impact would a widespread distribution of solar-powered cell phones have on a country that lacks the infrastructure for telephone and electrical wires? Has any country ever experienced such a leap in technology in a short period of time?

4. Dyson was a winner of the Templeton Prize in 2000. What kind of award is the Templeton, and what was the basis for Dyson's selection?

POINT

Technology Provides Economic Opportunity for All

The advocates of Dyson's position maintain that a lack of technology or resources is not what keeps the majority of the world's population in poverty. Instead, they argue, it is a lack of commitment to (and focus on) the problems of social justice that allows poverty to continue.

1. If people all agree that poverty is unacceptable, the world possesses the technology and resources to eliminate it.

2. Technology can improve the quality of life of poor countries (and poor people in rich countries) if scientists and business leaders join together.

3. Technology can be an ethical force to humanize us, giving us the ability to affect deeply the lives of all. Francis Bacon, the 16th- and 17th-century English philosopher, once wrote that science can "endow the human family with new mercies."

COUNTERPOINT

Technology Doesn't Provide Economic Opportunity for All

Dyson's critics maintain that his suggestions on using technology for social change are impractical and cannot be achieved with the current resources. They even feel his plan might be dangerous, inasmuch as it may have unforeseen scientific and political results.

1. No one can solve the problems of poverty. The proof is that it has never been done.

2. The problem of poverty is not an issue for technologists. It should be addressed by religious leaders, education experts, and politicians.

3. Genetic engineering may hold the promise of great benefits, but it should not be explored because of its potential risks.

4. Any move away from an oil-centered energy plan threatens the stability of the world's economies.

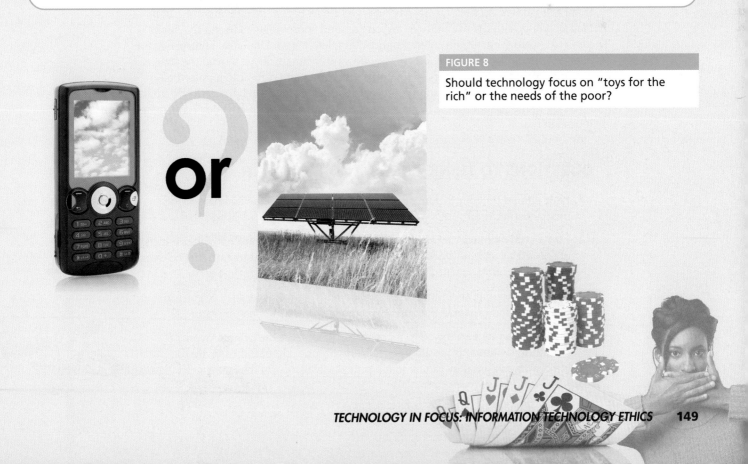

FIGURE 8

Should technology focus on "toys for the rich" or the needs of the poor?

Intellectual Property

What Is Fair about Fair Use?

SUMMARY OF THE ISSUE

Intellectual property (such as music, writing, and art) is protected through copyright law. This means that creative works such as songs, video productions, television programs, and written manuscripts cannot be reproduced without the permission of the creator, and usually not without payment to the copyright owner (see Figure 9).

Historically, the policy of fair use has allowed a range of exceptions to this copyright provision. Fair use is based on the belief that the public is entitled to use portions of copyrighted materials freely for certain purposes. If you wish to criticize a novelist, for example, under fair use, you have the freedom to quote a portion of the novelist's work without asking permission. Without this provision, copyright owners could prevent any negative comments about their work. Fair use decisions are guided by four criteria:

- What is the purpose of the fair use of the work? (For example, is it a for-profit use or an educational use?)
- What is the nature of the proposed work? (For example, will it be a published document or an unpublished product?)
- How much of the copyrighted material is being used?
- What is the effect of the fair use of the material? (For example, would it decrease the number of copies of the original that would be sold?)

In this age of easy digital media creation and distribution, the interpretation of fair use is being questioned. For example, Kevin Ryan found himself at odds with Dr. Seuss Enterprises. Ryan had created and recorded a set of songs, in the style of Bob Dylan, based on such Dr. Seuss classics as *Green Eggs and Ham* and *The Cat in the Hat*. He posted the MP3 files to a Web site, and soon bloggers found the songs and publicized them widely. A cease-and-desist letter from Dr. Seuss Enterprises for alleged copyright violations soon was issued, and Ryan quickly removed the material from his Web site (**dylanhearsawho.com**) rather than entering into a potentially lengthy legal battle. As this example shows, in today's fast-paced digital world, the question of the proper role of the fair use exclusion in copyright law may have to be reconsidered.

QUESTIONS TO THINK ABOUT AND RESEARCH

1. How should the four factors of fair use be interpreted in the age of electronic media distribution?

2. Can an online music reviewer post a song's audio to illustrate his or her criticism of the artist's album? Does that infringe on the artist's right to earn income from his or her work?

3. Should a documentary filmmaker be allowed to sample pieces of television interviews and organize them in a way that criticizes the person featured?

4. Should a parody be allowed to incorporate sections of the original work? By definition, a parody is negative or mocking in tone. Do parodies invite too much criticism now that they can be made publicly available on the Internet?

POINT

Liberal Fair Use Standards Are Beneficial

Artists and critics will be silenced if they are forced to fear legal action every time they use a portion of copyrighted material. The aggressive—and expensive—style of enforcement that copyright holders now use limits the free expression of ideas that is a cornerstone of most democratic societies.

1. Allowing an open interpretation of fair use encourages a wide dissemination of information.

2. Creative work and open criticism together allow the flourishing of a democratic, free society. If copyright owners can prohibit the use of any part of their works, then they have too much control over the creative process of others.

3. Although the existing laws on fair use worked well in the past, they cannot cope with the widespread dissemination of information that is possible with the modern Internet.

COUNTERPOINT

Strict Fair Use Standards Are Beneficial

Guidelines for what constitutes fair use already exist. Because these guidelines have worked well to protect the interests of creators of works as well as users and critics of those works, there is no need to modify them.

1. The existing laws on fair use have worked well for print media and do not need to be modified to reflect modern electronic distribution techniques.

2. Copyright holders are within their rights to be as aggressive as they wish in maintaining control of their own work. They should be allowed to set whatever licensing fees they wish. The artists or critics can still use the material, but must pay the licensing fee.

FIGURE 9

The issues of intellectual property have become critical because all the media we produce has become digital.

Privacy

Is Personal Privacy a Casualty of the Modern Age?

SUMMARY OF THE ISSUE

Like respect and dignity, privacy is a basic human right. What, exactly, is privacy? Simply stated, privacy is the right to be left alone to do as one pleases. The idea of privacy is often associated with hiding something (a behavior, a relationship, or a secret). However, privacy really means not being required to explain your behavior to others. With the advent of the digital society, is there any such thing as personal privacy (see Figure 10)? Like Hansel and Gretel, we leave a trail of electronic breadcrumbs almost everywhere we go.

Debit and credit cards are fast replacing cash, and they leave records of our purchases at merchants and our transactions at the bank. E-mail is fast replacing snail mail, so now your correspondence (and your secrets) may live on indefinitely in Web servers around the world. Have you visited a Web site lately? Chances are that the owner of that site kept track of what you looked at while you were visiting the site.

Can't we just modify our behavior to protect our privacy? We could, but a survey by the Ponemon Institute revealed that only about 7 percent of Americans are willing to change their behavior to protect privacy. Many people freely give personal information (such as their name, address, and phone number) to obtain buyer loyalty cards that qualify them for discounts at supermarkets and pharmacies. In addition, to obtain a discount on tolls and speed up their trips, many people sign up for electronic toll passes, which are actually radio frequency identification (RFID) devices that can be used to track where a driver was at a specific point in time. Information gathered by these programs could be used against you in a divorce case to prove you were a bad parent because you were routinely out in your car at 2 A.M. on school nights, or because you bought mostly junk food at the supermarket. Although many Americans say they are concerned about a loss of privacy, they have made few moves to preserve privacy rights in the United States.

QUESTIONS TO THINK ABOUT AND RESEARCH

1. Is privacy protected by the U.S. Constitution? If it isn't currently protected, would you be willing to join a group that was working toward a constitutional amendment on privacy?

2. Which is more important to you, protecting the United States from potential acts of terrorism by surrendering some personal privacy, or keeping all of your personal privacy rights?

3. Should U.S. citizens have the right to access personal information collected about them by companies and make corrections if the information is erroneous? How would you manage such a process if you ran a company that collected this information?

POINT

Protect Personal Privacy

The advocates of protecting privacy in the United States argue that the right to privacy is a basic human right that should be afforded to everyone. As long as individuals aren't hurting anyone or breaking any laws, people should be entitled to do what they want without fear of being monitored.

1. If I'm not doing anything wrong, then you have no reason to watch me.
2. If the government is collecting information by watching citizens, it might misuse or lose control of the data.
3. By allowing the government to determine what behaviors are right and wrong, we open ourselves to uncertainty because the government may arbitrarily change the definition of which behaviors are unacceptable.
4. Requiring national ID cards is reminiscent of the former Nazi and Soviet regimes.
5. Implementing privacy controls (such as national ID cards) or requiring passports for travel to Canada and Mexico is extremely expensive and a waste of taxpayer funds.

COUNTERPOINT

Reduced Privacy Is a Fact of Modern Life

Advocates for stronger monitoring of private citizens usually cite national security concerns and the prevention of terrorist activities. Inconvenience to ordinary people who are doing nothing wrong is just a price that everyone must pay to ensure that society is free from the malicious acts of a few malcontents.

1. If you aren't doing anything wrong, then you don't have anything to hide.
2. Electronic enhancements to identification documents are essential in the digital world we live in so that government agencies can more efficiently exchange information, thus facilitating the detection and apprehension of suspected terrorists.
3. Laws protect citizens from being abused or taken advantage of by overzealous government officials who are involved in monitoring activities.
4. It is not possible to put a price on freedom or security; therefore, projects such as a national ID system are worth the cost of implementation.

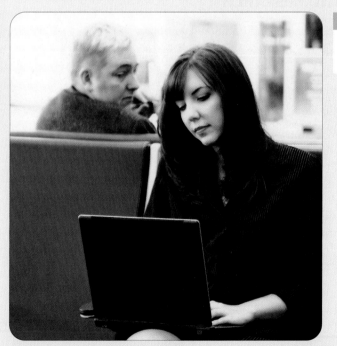

FIGURE 10

Is personal privacy possible any longer?

E-Commerce

Should Online Gambling Be Banned or Merely Regulated?

SUMMARY OF THE ISSUE

Internet gambling is currently a multibillion-dollar industry. Wireless Internet connectivity is increasingly available, and online gambling via cell phones will make online gambling even more accessible. The predominant online gambling activities are sports betting, casino games, lotteries, bingo, and poker (see Figure 11).

Hosting Internet gambling sites is already illegal in the United States. This means U.S. companies cannot run gambling sites. Gambling sites are any sites that allow participants to wager real money and withdraw any winnings. Legislation was passed in October 2006 to restrict U.S. citizens from participating in online gambling, but it remains a viable and growing industry worldwide. Because there are no boundaries to the Internet and Internet activity, restrictive legislation is not an effective way to ban gamblers from gambling or online casinos from offering gaming sites. The law, however, does make it more difficult for U.S. citizens to transfer money into online casinos. It prevents U.S. banks and credit card companies from transferring funds to overseas online casinos, thus making it more difficult for an online casino to serve U.S. customers. The debate remains whether such activity should continue to be banned altogether, or whether it should be allowed to operate legally but be subject to regulation by the U.S. government.

Internet gambling's characteristics have few parallels, and advocates of both sides of this issue acknowledge the obvious issues raised by online gambling. Online gambling, unlike gambling done in brick-and-mortar facilities, encourages gamblers to play 24 hours a day from home and facilitates addictive gambling. Betting with a credit card can undercut a player's perception of the value of cash, and may lead to gambling addiction, bankruptcy, and crime. In addition, children may play without sufficient age verification.

QUESTIONS TO THINK ABOUT AND RESEARCH

1. What are the important differences between online and traditional gambling?

2. In what ways can Internet gambling businesses be used to facilitate other illegal activities?

3. How might the prohibition of online gambling be compared to the prohibition of alcohol in the United States in the 1920s?

4. Why is online gambling legalized in other countries? How do those countries respond to the arguments presented by the opponents of legalized online gambling in the United States?

POINT

Ban Online Gambling

The advocates of continuing the ban on online gambling in the United States argue that thorough and extensive enforcement of the current prohibition would stop online gambling and hence eliminate the source of the problems.

1. Internet gambling is too easily accessible to minors and compulsive gamblers. In contrast, brick-and-mortar casinos enforce restrictions that help control access by minors and compulsive or addictive gamblers.

2. Offshore Internet gambling facilities could be used to support criminal activities such as illegal money laundering and identity theft.

3. Online gambling differs from gambling at physical facilities because it is difficult to put controls in place to ensure that online operations are honest. For example, how do you prevent odds being tweaked to favor the house unfairly, or money being collected from players but winnings never paid out?

4. Online gambling facilitates players' hiding of gambling addiction from family members, which may increase gambling's financial burden on families and society (loss of jobs, homes, and

COUNTERPOINT

Legalize Online Gambling

Advocates for legalizing online gambling in the United States argue that legalizing it will bring it out of the underworld and place stricter controls on the industry. Enforced governmental regulations placed on current onsite gambling facilities could be applied to online sites and eliminate the source of the problems.

1. Current multibillion-dollar public online gambling companies exist outside the United States. Increased regulatory action would bring to light the legitimate organizations that can and do protect consumers, restrict access by minors, and protect players at risk of developing a gambling addiction. Enhanced regulation would make the illegitimate operations more difficult to operate.

2. Online gambling is "transparent"; every transaction is logged and available for scrutiny.

3. Regulation would standardize the industry and bring in tax revenues to the U.S. government.

4. Online gambling is regulated in over 60 countries.

5. Prohibiting online gambling would send it underground and leave the vulnerable unprotected.

6. It's much easier to regulate online activity than prohibit it.

FIGURE 11

Online access to gambling makes it convenient. But how do you stop children from gambling in this environment?

Electronic Communication

When Does Big Business Limit Free Speech?

SUMMARY OF THE ISSUE

In early 2006, Google conceded to Beijing's demands that it self-censor its search engine. Google's Chinese site does not return search results for sites that the Chinese government believes contain illegal or objectionable content. Google was following in the footsteps of other large U.S. high-tech companies that had previously collaborated with the Chinese government in suppressing dissent in return for access to the booming Chinese Internet market. Corporate America's demonstration of the price it is willing to pay to obtain Chinese business has stirred up a vigorous controversy. Google justified its decision by stating that when a company decides to do business in a market, it must operate within the rules of that market.

Chinese policies include

- filters that block objectionable foreign Web sites.
- regulations that ban content that the Chinese government considers subversive or pornographic.
- a requirement that Internet service providers enforce government censorship.

How big is the Chinese Internet market? More than 298 million people in China are online, which is approximately 23 percent of the Chinese population. In comparison, 220 million people in the United States—72.5 percent of the U.S. population—are online. Although the number of Internet users in China currently almost equals the population of the United States, there is still considerable room for growth in Chinese Internet usage. Google and others decided to give in to the government's demands because otherwise they would have lost a huge market. History has shown that many businesses will give monetary gain (for shareholders) priority over protecting basic human rights such as free speech (see Figure 12).

QUESTIONS TO THINK ABOUT AND RESEARCH

1. Does the presence of U.S. tech companies in China contribute to increased access to information in China?

2. What kind of parallels can be drawn between the Chinese example and U.S. corporations' response to apartheid in South Africa in the 1970s?

3. Can U.S. government action help by pressing U.S. concerns on censorship during talks with foreign governments?

POINT

Google Acted Unethically

Those who protest Google's actions are individuals and groups that fight for human rights in many contexts. They feel that Google's compliant behavior only condones China's censorship policies and continues to thwart the effort to promote human rights initiatives in China.

1. Google sacrificed free speech for business. This action violates human rights, international law, and corporate ethics.

2. Cooperating with China violates human rights.

3. If international businesses can't stand up to China, how will China ever have an incentive to change?

4. Most other rights hang on the community's ability to have open discussions. Preventing that from happening is a serious assault on human rights.

5. If the policy were to make children work or to kill women, would the companies choose not to comply? Are human rights and freedom of speech any different?

COUNTERPOINT

Google's Actions Were Justified

The advocates of Google's actions tend to be businesses and others with large economic interests that can relate to Google's business predicament. They feel that Google acted in accordance with accepted business principles and should abide by the laws of local governments.

1. Companies are free to pursue profits as long as they follow a country's laws.

2. Withdrawing from China would further restrict free speech there.

3. Google's presence, as muted as it is, continues to advance the slow progress the Chinese government is making toward democracy. U.S. companies can ethically stay in China if they make an effort to improve human rights there. U.S. companies operating in China should agree on guidelines that respect human rights.

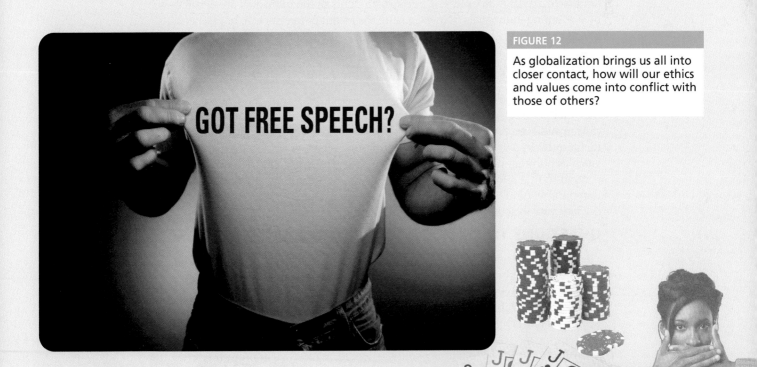

FIGURE 12

As globalization brings us all into closer contact, how will our ethics and values come into conflict with those of others?

Computer Abuse

Does Restricting Online Information Protect Children?

SUMMARY OF THE ISSUE

Computer abuse is loosely defined as using a computer or the Internet to harm another individual. By providing anonymity, the Internet facilitates such unsavory activities as

- the ability of sexual predators to contact potential victims.
- the distribution of pornography.
- cyberbullying (harassing individuals through electronic means).
- phishing (tricking individuals into revealing sensitive information).
- the dissemination of hate speech.

Although computer abuse is a threat to everyone, children are especially vulnerable because they tend to use technology more than adults do, are more trusting than many adults are, and may lack sufficient real-life experience to be able to identify malicious intent or behavior. No one argues that protecting children from harm is not a laudable goal; the question is how best to accomplish it. Laws restricting the Internet's content have largely failed, and they are often overturned by courts on the grounds that they violate free speech. Therefore, controlling access to objectionable material has been the avenue pursued.

Content-filtering software is designed to block objectionable content from view and is usually designed for shielding children (see Figure 13). Although software such as Net Nanny, illustrated here, is designed for home use by parents, content filtering software used in schools and libraries is similar. In exchange for providing affordable Internet access, the government requires schools and libraries to have filtering software on their computers. Problems have arisen when these types of public institutions have installed filtering software to protect children. When objectionable material is blocked, the free speech rights of the individual are affected—not by preventing individuals from exercising their right of free speech, but rather by infringing on their rights of free access to information. The courts have usually viewed access to information as a First Amendment (free speech) issue.

Filtering software presents a problem when it is unable to discriminate between information that should be blocked and information that is not objectionable but instead is informational. Blocking software has blocked informational sites such as the Safer Sex Page, groups supporting gay rights, sites with information about breast cancer, and even the home pages of politicians such as former Representative Richard (Dick) Armey (R–Texas). Furthermore, designers of objectionable Web sites (such as pornography sites) are often clever enough to disguise their objectionable content so that it fools the filters. The public has raised a huge outcry, demanding that publicly funded institutions protect children from objectionable content. What is the best way to satisfy this demand, if filtering isn't the answer?

QUESTIONS TO THINK ABOUT AND RESEARCH

1. Does your school use filtering software in computer labs on campus? Do you think your school should restrict objectionable content if it receives public funds?
2. Who should decide what types of sites should be blocked by filtering software? Educators? Librarians? Software programmers? The government?
3. If you have children (or if you have children in the future), will you install filtering software on computers in your home?
4. What alternatives to filtering software would be effective in protecting children from objectionable content?

POINT

Monitoring Software Protects Children

Most advocates of filtering software in publicly funded institutions cite the need to protect minors from material deemed objectionable by accepted public standards.

1. Because laws have proven ineffective, filtering software is the only way to protect children from objectionable material, such as pornography or violent content.

2. Parents need to be assured that publicly funded institutions such as schools and libraries are "safe havens" where their children will not be allowed to access or be exposed to objectionable material.

3. Publicly funded institutions have a right to uphold the moral standards of the public.

4. Filtering Internet content is a logical extension of the existing library screening process, whereby librarians decide what books to put on the shelves.

COUNTERPOINT

Monitoring Software Restricts Access to Information

Opponents of filtering software cite the First Amendment, which guarantees free speech and hence free access to information.

1. Filtering software routinely blocks Web sites with informational content as well as objectionable material.

2. Filtering software is akin to censorship, which violates the First Amendment.

3. Filtering software is not 100 percent reliable and fails to screen out a lot of objectionable material.

4. Filtering widens the "digital divide" by adversely affecting the poor. Wealthier individuals, who tend to have Internet access in their homes, are less affected by filters in public institutions.

5. Over the long run, educating children about using the Internet carefully and responsibly will be more effective than filtering software.

FIGURE 13

Net Nanny filtering software allows parents to exercise control over what their children can view.

four

application software:

programs that let you work and play

resources

Active Helpdesk

- Choosing Software **(p. 180)**
- Buying and Installing Software **(p. 191)**

Sound Bytes

- Creating Web Queries in Excel 2007 **(p. 165)**
- Using Speech-Recognition Software **(p. 174)**
- Enhancing Photos with Image Editing Software **(p. 175)**

Companion Website

The Companion Website includes a variety of additional materials to help you review and learn more about the topics in this chapter. Go to: *pearsonhighered.com/techinaction*

how cool is *this?*

There are millions of applications, and new ones are developed and released every day. How can you **find** the right application to meet your needs? What are the **cool new applications**, or the ones that just don't work? The editors and analysts at *PC Magazine* have put together AppScout (**appscout.com**), which provides **reviews** of the best software, Web sites, and Web applications. **AppScout** might be a good place to check first when you are in need of a new application.

The Nuts and Bolts of Software

A computer without software is like a sandwich without filling. Although a computer's hardware is critical, a computer system does nothing without software.

What is software? Technically speaking, the term **software** refers to a set of instructions that tells the computer what to do. An instruction set, also called a **program**, provides a means for us to interact with and use the computer, even if we lack specialized programming skills. Your computer has two basic types of software: system software and application software.

- **System software** includes software such as Windows Vista and Mac OS X, which help run the computer and coordinate instructions between application software and the computer's hardware devices. System software includes the operating system and utility programs (programs in the operating system that help manage system resources). We discuss system software in detail in Chapter 5.

- **Application software** is the software you use to do tasks at home, school, and work. You can do a multitude of things with application software, such as writing letters, sending e-mail, paying taxes, creating presentations, editing photos, and taking an online course, to name a few.

Figure 4.1 shows the various types of application software available. In this chapter, we look at each of these types in detail, starting with productivity software.

More Productivity at Home

One reason to have a computer is to make it easier to tackle the tasks you have in your daily life. Productivity software is all about helping you do that, making it easier to keep your budget, send letters, or keep track of the kids' school events. It's safe to say you regularly use some form of productivity software already. **Productivity software** includes programs that enable you to perform various tasks required at home, school, and business. This category includes word processing, spreadsheet, presentation, database, and personal information manager (PIM) programs.

Word Processing Software

What is the best software to use to create general documents? Most students use **word processing software** to create and edit documents such as research papers, letters, and résumés. Microsoft Word and Corel WordPerfect are popular word processing programs. Writer, a word processing program from the OpenOffice suite

Figure 4.1

Application software enables computer users to do a variety of tasks.

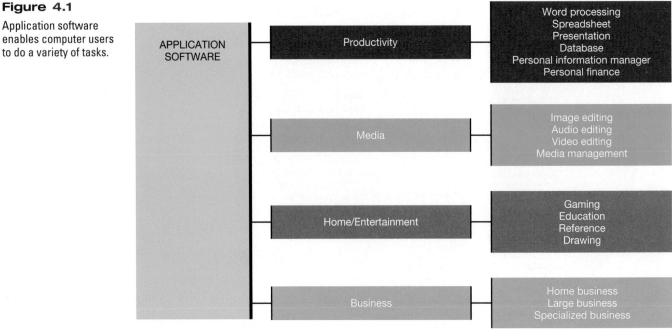

(**openoffice.org**), and AbiWord (**abiword. com**) are gaining in popularity because they are available as free downloads from the Internet. Both AbiWord and Writer have many of the same features as their higher-priced Word and WordPerfect competitors, making either a great choice for cost-conscious consumers.

Also gaining in popularity are several word processing programs that are Web-based, such as those found in Google Docs (**docs.google.com**), which can be accessed from any computer that has an Internet connection. Web-based applications are great for collaborating and coordinating input from a variety of users on a single document.

Because of its general usefulness, word processing software is the most widely used application. Word processing software has a key advantage over its ancestral counterpart, the typewriter: you can make revisions and corrections without having to retype an entire document. Instead, you can quickly and easily insert, delete, and move pieces of text, as well as move and insert text from one document into another seamlessly.

How do I control the way my documents look? Another advantage of word processing software is that you can easily

format, or change the appearance of, your document. As a result, you can produce professional-looking documents without having to send them to a professional. With formatting options, you can change fonts, font styles, and sizes; add colors to text; adjust margins; add borders to portions of text or entire pages; insert bulleted and numbered lists; and organize your text into columns. You also can insert pictures from your own files or from a gallery of images and graphics, such as clip art and SmartArt, which are included with the software. You also can enhance the look of your document by creating an interesting background or by adding a "theme" of coordinated colors and styles throughout your document. Figure 4.2 shows some of the formatting options found in many word processing applications. However, many of the open source and Web-based applications are not as fully featured as the proprietary applications.

Keep one thing in mind when you choose a free or Web-based software product: support. Unlike Microsoft Office and other proprietary applications, these applications offer no formal support. Instead, open source and Web-based applications are supported from their community of users across Web sites and newsgroups. For more

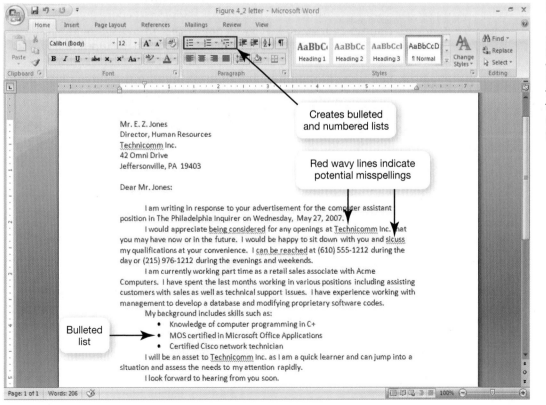

Figure 4.2

Nearly every word processing application has basic features to help you make your document look professionally formatted and to ensure that words are spelled correctly and used grammatically.

Looking for a Free or More Affordable Productivity Suite?

If you're looking for a more affordable alternative to proprietary software such as Microsoft Office, you may want to consider downloading a free open source productivity suite. **Open source software** is program code that is publicly available with few restrictions. The code can be copied, distributed, or changed without the stringent copyright protections of software products you purchase. OpenOffice is a popular open source software suite. In addition, some Web-based products are available free of charge. These Web-based applications, such as Google Docs and the Zoho suite, are accessible from wherever you are and are easily shared, so they are perfect for virtual workgroups.

Compared to Microsoft Office, you won't find all the features you're used to seeing, but OpenOffice offers most of the features required by the average user. And if you use OpenOffice, you can easily read, write, and edit files created in other applications, although you may lose some formatting when migrating or transferring files to OpenOffice. Similarly, users of other productivity suites can open files created in OpenOffice.

come with some form of spelling and grammar checker and a thesaurus, for example. Another popular tool is the search-and-replace tool that allows you to search for text in your document and automatically replace it with other text.

The average user is unaware of many interesting word processing software tools. For example, did you know that you could translate words or phrases to another language or automatically correct your spelling as you type? You also can automatically summarize key points in a text document. Writer, the word processing program in the OpenOffice suite, has many of the same tools you're used to seeing in Microsoft Word and Corel WordPerfect, as well as some unique ones (see Figure 4.3).

information on alternative software, see the Technology in Focus feature "Computing Alternatives" on page 252.

What special tools do word processing programs have? You're probably familiar with the basic tools of word processing software. Most applications

Spreadsheet Software

Why would I need to use spreadsheet software? Spreadsheet software—for example, Microsoft Excel and Open Office Calc—enables you to do calculations and numerical analyses easily. You can use spreadsheet software to track your expenses and create a simple budget. You also can use it to determine how much you should be paying on your student loans, car loan, or credit card bills each month. You know you should pay more than the minimum payment to spend less on interest, but how much more can you afford to pay, and for which loan? Spreadsheet software can help you evaluate different scenarios, such as planning the best payment strategy.

How do I use spreadsheet software? The basic element in a spreadsheet program is the worksheet, which is a grid consisting of columns and rows. As shown in Figure 4.4, the columns and rows form individual boxes called *cells*. Each cell can be identified according to its column and row position. For example, a cell in column A, row 1 is referred to as "cell A1." You can enter several types of data into a cell.

- **Text:** Any combination of letters, numbers, symbols, and spaces. Text is often used as labels to identify the contents of a worksheet or chart.
- **Values:** Numerical data that represent a quantity or an amount and are often the basis for calculations.

Designs and other visual effects

Bibliography tool organizes sources

Figure 4.3

Writer, the word processing program in the OpenOffice suite, has many of the same features as Word and WordPerfect as well as some unique ones.

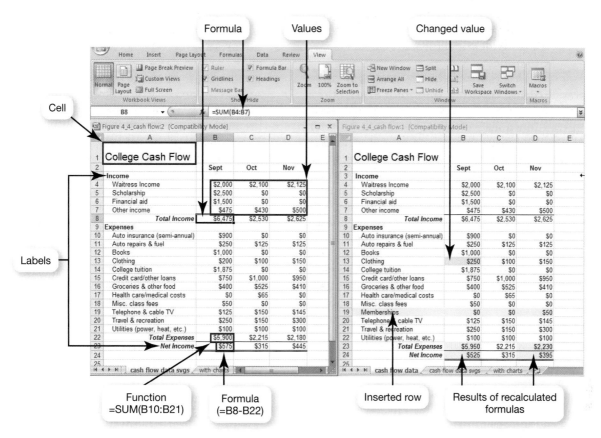

Formula | **Values** | **Changed value**

Cell

Labels

Function
=SUM(B10:B21)

Formula
(=B8-B22)

Inserted row | **Results of recalculated formulas**

Figure 4.4

Spreadsheet software enables you to calculate and manipulate numerical data easily with the use of built-in formulas.

- **Formulas:** Equations that you build yourself using addition, subtraction, multiplication, and division, as well as values and cell references. For example, in Figure 4.4, you would type the formula "=B8-B22" to calculate net income for September.

- **Functions:** Formulas that are preprogrammed into the spreadsheet software. Functions help you with calculations ranging from the simple (such as adding groups of numbers) to the complex (such as determining monthly loan payments), without your needing to know the exact formula. Therefore, in Figure 4.4, to calculate your average earned income in September, you could use the built-in AVERAGE function, which would look like this: =AVERAGE(B4:B7).

The primary benefit of spreadsheet software is its ability to recalculate all functions and formulas in the spreadsheet automatically when values for some of the inputs change. For example, as shown on the spreadsheet on the right side of Figure 4.4, you can insert an additional row (Memberships), change a value (September clothing expense), and then recalculate the results for Total Expenses and Net Income without having to redo the worksheet from scratch.

Because automatic recalculation enables you to see immediately the effects that different options have on your spreadsheet, you can quickly test different assumptions in the same analysis. This is called a *what-if analysis.* Look again at Figure 4.4 and ask, "What if I add $50 to my clothing budget? What impact will such an increase have on my budget?"

What kinds of graphs and charts can I create with spreadsheet software? Sometimes it's easier to see the meaning of numbers when they are shown in a graphical format such as a chart. As shown in Figure 4.5, most spreadsheet applications allow you to create a variety of charts, including basic column charts, pie charts, and line charts, with or without three-dimensional (3D) effects. In addition

SOUND BYTE

Creating Web Queries in Excel 2007

In this Sound Byte, you'll learn what Excel Web queries are, as well as how to use them effectively.

to these basic charts, you can use stock charts (for investment analysis) and scatter charts (for statistical analysis), or create custom charts.

Are spreadsheets used for anything besides financial analysis?

There are so many powerful mathematical functions built into spreadsheet programs that they can be used for serious numerical analyses or simulations. For example, an Excel spreadsheet could be designed to compute the output voltage at a point in an electrical circuit or to simulate customer arrival and wait times. In these settings, spreadsheet programs can often solve problems that formerly required custom programming. Many spreadsheet applications also have database capabilities and can sort, filter, and group data.

Figure 4.5

(a) Column charts show comparisons. (b) Pie charts show how parts contribute to the whole. (c) Line charts show trends over time.

Presentation Software

What software do I use to create presentations?

You've probably sat through presentations during which the speaker's topic was displayed in slides projected on a screen. These presentations can be the most basic of outlines, containing only a few words and simple graphics, or elaborate multimedia presentations with animated text, graphic objects, and colorful backgrounds. You use **presentation software** such as Microsoft PowerPoint, OpenOffice Impress, or Zoho Show (shown in Figure 4.6) to create these types of dynamic slide shows. Because these applications are simple to use, you can produce high-quality presentations without a lot of training.

How do I create a presentation?

Using the basic features included in

presentation software, creating a slide show is simple. To arrange text and graphics on your slides, you can choose from a variety of slide layouts. These layouts give you the option of using a single or double column of bulleted text, various combinations of bulleted text, and other content such as clip art, graphs, photos, and even video clips.

You also can lend a theme to your presentation by choosing from different design templates. You can use animation effects to control how and when text and other objects enter and exit each slide. Slide transitions add different effects as you move from one slide to the next during the presentation.

Database Software

How can I use database software?

Database software such as Oracle, MySQL, and Microsoft Access is basically a complex electronic filing system. As mentioned earlier, spreadsheet applications include many database features and are easy to use for simple database tasks such as sorting, filtering, and organizing data. However, you need to use a more robust, fully featured database application to manage larger and more complicated groups of data that contain more than one table; to group, sort, and retrieve data; and to generate reports.

Traditional databases are organized into fields, records, and tables, as shown in Figure 4.7. A field is a data category such as "First Name," "Last Name," or "Street Address." A record is a collection of related fields such as "Douglas Seaver, Printing Solutions, 7700 First Avenue, Topeka, KS, (888) 968-2678." A table groups related records such as "Sales Contacts."

How do you benefit when businesses use database software?

FedEx, UPS, and other shipping companies let customers search their online databases for tracking numbers, allowing customers to get instant information on the status of their packages. Other businesses use databases to keep track of clients, invoices, and personnel information. Often that information is available to a home computer user. For example, at Amazon.com you can use the company's Web site to access the entire history of all the purchases you have ever made.

Are there software programs to help students be more productive?

Popular programs are available to help students take notes during lectures and organize and maintain their lecture notes and the recordings they create from lectures. For example, Microsoft OneNote allows students who have Tablet PCs to write their notes directly onto the tablet, using it as an electronic notebook. Pieces of text can be easily moved around the page. With one click, Web links can be quickly integrated and audio or video recordings of lectures can be added. Students can search for a term across the full set of notebooks they have created during the term, helping them to find connecting ideas among their courses.

Personal Information Manager (PIM) Software

Which applications should I use to manage my time, contact lists, and tasks?
Most productivity suites contain some form of **personal information manager (PIM) software** such as

Microsoft Outlook or Lotus Organizer. Chandler (**chandlerproject.org**) is another PIM program that is open source and, therefore, free. These programs strive to replace the management tools found on a traditional desk—a calendar, address book, notepad, and to-do list, for example.

Figure 4.6

Several programs allow you to create presentation materials: (a) Microsoft Office PowerPoint 2007, (b) OpenOffice Impress, and (c) Zoho's Show.

Table

	ID ▾	FirstName ▾	LastName ▾	Company ▾	Street ▾	City ▾	State ▾	ZipCode ▾	Business
	1	Susan	Scantosi	eWidget Plus	363 Rogue Street	St. Louis	MO	63136	(612) 444
	2	Thomas	Mazeman	BooksRUs	2165 Piscotti Avenue	Springfield	IL	62702	(888) 234
	3	Douglas	Seaver	Printing Solutions	7700 First Avenue	Topeka	KS	66603	(888) 968
	4	Amir	Raviv	TechStands	1436 Riverfront Road	St. Louis	MO	63136	(877) 867
	5	Franklin	Scott	WorksSuite	8789 Ploughman Ave	Tulsa	OK	74101	(800) 864
	6	Ronald	Komeika	Creekside Financial	1264 Pond Hill Road	Toledo	OH	43601	(343) 332
	7	Barbara	Mitchell	Market Tenders	9823 Bridge Street	La Porte	IN	46350	(888) 283
*	(New)								

SalesContacts

Field

Record

Figure 4.7

In databases, information is organized into tables, fields, and records.

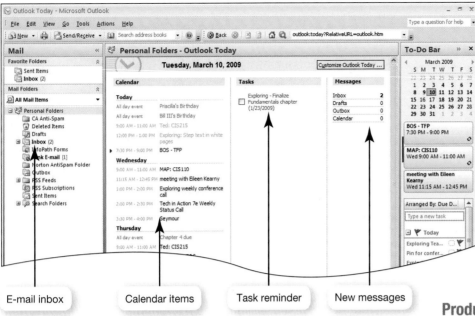

| E-mail inbox | Calendar items | Task reminder | New messages |

Figure 4.8

The Outlook Today feature in Microsoft Outlook includes common PIM features such as a summary of appointments, a list of tasks, and the number of new e-mail messages.

Some PIMs contain e-mail management features so that you not only can receive and send e-mail messages but also organize them into various folders, prioritize them, and coordinate them with other activities in your calendar (see Figure 4.8).

If you share a network at home or at work and are using the same PIM software as others on the network, you can use a PIM program to check people's availability before scheduling meeting times. Whether coordinating a team project or a family event, you can create and electronically assign tasks to group members by using a PIM. You can even track each person's progress to ensure that the tasks are finished on time.

Are there Web-based PIM programs? Many Web-based e-mail clients such as Yahoo!, Google, and AOL have developed coordinating calendar and contacts programs similar to Microsoft Outlook. Yahoo! includes Notepad for jotting down notes and tasks. Google's calendar and contacts sync with Outlook so that you can access your Outlook calendar information by logging into Google, giving you access to your schedule anywhere you have access to a computer and an Internet connection. AOL's Instant Messenger, AIM, has coordinated e-mail, calendar, and contact functions.

Productivity Software Features

What tools can help me work more efficiently with productivity software? Whether you are working on a word processing document, spreadsheet, database, or slide presentation, you can make use of several tools to increase your efficiency:

- A **wizard** is a systematic guide that walks you through the steps necessary to complete a complicated task. At each step, the wizard asks you questions. Based on your responses, the wizard helps you complete that portion of the task. When you install software, you are often guided by a wizard.
- A **template** is a predesigned form. Templates are included in many productivity applications. They provide the basic structure for a particular kind of document, spreadsheet, or presentation. Templates can include specific page layout designs, formatting and styles relevant to that particular document, and automated tasks (macros). Typical templates allow you to lay out a professional-looking résumé, structure a home budget, or communicate the results of a project in a presentation.
- A **macro** is a small program that groups a series of commands so they will run as a single command. Macros are best used to automate a routine task or a complex series of commands that must be run frequently. For example, a teacher may write a macro to sort the grades in her grade book automatically in descending order

Productivity Software Tips and Tricks

Looking for tips on how to make better use of your productivity software? Many Web sites send subscribers daily e-mails. Most of these services are free, although some require that you subscribe to an ancillary product full of tips, tricks, and shortcuts to their favorite software programs. Nerdy Books (**nerdybooks.com**), for example, sends a free tip each day to the e-mail accounts of its subscribers. (Note that it does not provide tips for Office 2007 users). Nerdy Books also publishes Bob's Blog, containing software tips, and podcasts for those tips that can't be written in just a few sentences. Dummies eTips (**etips.dummies.com**), based on the *For Dummies* series of help books, offers subscribers tips on a variety of topics, including using productivity applications.

and to highlight those grades that add up to less than a C average. Every time she adds the results of an assignment or test, she can set up the macro to run through that series of steps automatically.

Integrated Software Applications

What's an integrated software application? An **integrated software application** is a single software program that incorporates the most commonly used tools of many productivity software programs into a single integrated program. Note that integrated software applications are not substitutes for the full suite of applications they replace. Generally, because they don't include many of the more complex features of the individual productivity software applications, they can be thought of as "software lite." To have access to the full functionality of word processing and spreadsheet software, for example, you should get the individual applications or a suite that includes each of these applications.

Microsoft Works 9 is an example of an integrated software application. This integrated software application includes word processing, spreadsheet, and database functionality as well as templates, a calendar, a dictionary, and map features. iWork '09 is an integrated software application from Apple that includes word processing (Pages), presentation (Keynote), and spreadsheet (Numbers) functionality. Figure 4.9 shows the multifunctionality of Apple iWork. The Task Launcher is the first window that opens when you launch iWork.

Why would I use an integrated software application instead of individual stand-alone programs? Integrated software applications are perfect if you don't need the more advanced features found in the individual full versions of each program. Like stand-alone applications, integrated software programs provide templates for frequently developed documents such as résumés and invoices. An integrated software program is also less expensive than its individual, fully featured alternatives. If you find your needs go beyond the limited capabilities of an integrated program, you might want to consider buying the individual programs that meet your particular requirements or a software suite.

Software Suites

What's a software suite? A **software suite** is a group of software programs that have been bundled as a package. You can buy software suites for many different categories of applications, including productivity, graphics, and virus protection (see Figure 4.10). There are three primary developers of productivity software suites: Microsoft, Corel, and Lotus. Microsoft and Corel offer different packages with different combinations of applications, whereas Lotus (owned by IBM) offers only SmartSuite.

Which applications do productivity software suites contain? Most productivity software suites contain similar basic components, such as word processing, spreadsheet, presentation, and PIM software. However, depending on the version and man-

Figure 4.9

Although an integrated software application such as Apple iWork is one program, it contains the most commonly used features of several individual productivity applications.

Figure 4.10

Software suites provide users with a cheaper method of obtaining all of the software they want to buy in one bundle.

ufacturer, they may also include other types of applications, such as database programs and desktop publishing software. When you are shopping for software, it can be difficult to figure out which bundle is the right one for your needs. For example, Microsoft Office 2007 is bundled in eight different ways; four of these are described in the table in Figure 4.11. Be sure to research carefully the bundling options for software you are buying.

Why would I buy a software suite instead of individual programs? Most people buy software suites because doing so is cheaper than buying each program individually. In addition, because the programs bundled in a software suite come from the same company, they work well together (that is, they provide for better integration) and share common features,

toolbars, and menus. For example, when using applications in the Microsoft Office suite, you can seamlessly create a spreadsheet in Excel, import it into Access, and then link a query created in Access to a Word document. It would be much harder to do the same thing using different applications from a variety of software developers.

Personal Financial Software

What software can I use to prepare my taxes?

Everyone has to deal with taxes, and having the right computer software can make this burden much simpler and keep it completely under your control. **Tax preparation software** such as Intuit TurboTax and H&R Block TaxCut enable you to prepare your state and federal taxes on your own instead of hiring a professional. Both programs offer a complete set of tax forms and instructions, as well as videos that contain expert advice on how to complete each form. In addition, error-checking features are built into the programs to catch mistakes. TurboTax also can run a check for audit alerts, file your return electronically, and offer financial planning guidance to help you effectively plan and manage your financial resources in the following year (see Figure 4.12). Remember, however, that the tax code changes annually, so you must obtain an updated version of the software each year.

Figure 4.11 | A SAMPLING OF MICROSOFT OFFICE 2007 SUITES

Application	Function	Home and Student 2007	Standard 2007	Professional 2007	Ultimate 2007
Word	Word processing	X	X	X	X
Excel	Spreadsheet	X	X	X	X
PowerPoint	Presentation	X	X	X	X
Access	Database			X	X
Outlook	PIM		X	X	X
Publisher	Desktop publishing			X	X
OneNote	Note taking	X			X
InfoPath, Groove	Collaboration				X

Which software can I use to help keep track of my personal finances?
Financial planning software helps you manage your daily finances. Intuit Quicken and Microsoft Money are popular examples. Financial planning programs include electronic checkbook registers and automatic bill payment tools. With these features, you can print checks from your computer or pay recurring monthly payments, such as rent or student loans, with automatically scheduled online payments. The software records all transactions, including online payments, in your checkbook register. In addition, you can assign categories to each transaction and then use these categories to analyze your spending patterns. You even can set up a budget and review your spending habits.

Web-based programs such as Mint (**mint. com**) and Wesabe (**wesabe.com**) are rapidly gaining in popularity (see Figure 4.13). Although they do not offer bill-paying services or help track your investment portfolio like Quicken and Money do, they are great at analyzing your spending habits and offering advice on how to manage your spending better. Because they are Web-based, you can monitor and update your finances from any computer in a private and secure setting. Users also have access to a network of other users with whom to exchange tips and advice.

Financial planning applications also coordinate with tax preparation software. Quicken, for example, integrates seamlessly with TurboTax, so you never have to go through your checkbook and bills to find tax deductions, tax-related income, or expenses. Many banks and credit card companies also offer online services that download a detailed monthly statement into Quicken or Money. Quicken even offers a credit card. All of your purchases are organized into categories and are downloaded automatically to your Quicken file to streamline your financial planning and recordkeeping. You can also purchase Pocket Quicken to install on your smartphone so that your financial records are always at your fingertips.

More Media at Home

From movies and television to music and photography, the entertainment world is becoming digital. Your computer can help you create, organize, and modify digital images, songs, and movies, if you have the

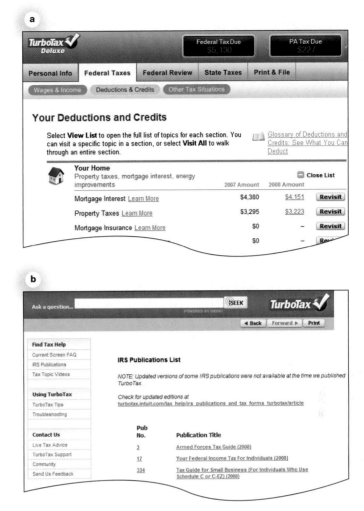

Figure 4.12

Tax preparation software, such as Intuit TurboTax, enables you to prepare and file your taxes using a guided, systematic process.

Figure 4.13

Wesabe.com is an online financial management tool. An extensive online community provides helpful tips and discussions with other people in similar situations.

Speech-Recognition Software

Dragon NaturallySpeaking is a leading **speech-recognition software** (or **voice-recognition software**) that translates your spoken words into typed text. With this software, you can dictate documents and e-mail messages, use voice commands to start and switch between applications, control the operating system, and even surf or fill out forms on the Web. Speech-recognition software is available in different language versions, including Dutch, French, German, Italian, and Spanish, as well as English. Accuracy levels of 95 percent to 99 percent can be achieved in quiet environments with a quality microphone.

Microsoft has incorporated a powerful speech-recognition system into Windows Vista. After starting speech recognition (from the Start menu, type "speech" in the search box and click on "Windows Speech Recognition"), the speech-recognition toolbar appears and indicates whether or not the computer is "listening" for voice input. Just click the microphone icon to make the computer listen to or ignore voice input. Figure 4.14 shows how you can use Vista's speech recognition functionality to instruct the software to run commands within an application. If you aren't sure which speech commands are available, just say, "What can I say?" to display the speech reference card.

Speech-recognition software is complicated. As you speak, the software divides each second of your speech into 100 individual *samples* (sounds). It then compares these individual sounds with a database

Figure 4.14

(a) Speech-recognition software allows you to create documents using simple voice commands.
(b) Speaking "What can I say?" brings up the speech reference card.

right software. **Multimedia software** includes image, video, and audio editing software; animation software; and other specialty software required to produce computer games, animations, and movies. In this section, we look at several popular types of multimedia software, as shown in Figure 4.15.

Digital Image Editing Software

What can I do with a digital image that I can't do with a photograph?

Once the image information is in a digital format (taken with a digital camera or scanned), you can use it easily with all your other software. For example, you can store a

b

Figure 4.14 (Continued)

(called a *codebook*) that contains samples of every sound a human being can make. When it finds a match, it gives your voice sound a number that corresponds to the number of the similar sound in the database.

After your voice sounds are assigned values, these values are matched with another database containing phonemes for the language being spoken. A *phoneme* is the smallest phonetic unit that distinguishes one word from another. For example, "b" and "m" are both phonemes that distinguish the words *bad* and *mad* from each other in the English language. Many languages, including English, are made up of thousands of different phonemes. Moreover, because of differences in pronunciation, some phonemes may actually have several different corresponding matching sounds.

Once all the sounds are assigned to phonemes, word and phrase construction can begin. The phonemes are matched against a word list that contains transcriptions of all known words in a particular language. Because pronunciation can vary (for example, the word *the* can be pronounced so that it rhymes with either *duh* or *see*), the word list must contain alternative pronunciations for many words. Each phoneme is worked

on separately; the phonemes are then chained together to form words that are contained in the word list. Because a variety of sounds can be put together to form many different words, the software analyzes all the possible values and picks the one value that it determines has the best probability of correctly matching your spoken word. The word is then displayed on the screen or is acted upon by the computer as a command.

However, there are problems with speech-recognition software. We don't always speak every word the same way, and accents and regional dialects produce great variation in pronunciations. Therefore, speech recognition is not perfect and requires training. Training entails getting the computer to recognize your particular way of speaking by reading prepared text into the computer so the phoneme database can be adjusted to your specific speech patterns.

Another approach to improve speech inconsistencies is to restrict the word list to a few keywords or phrases, and then have the computer guess the probability that a certain phrase is being said. This is how cell phones that respond to voice commands work. The phone doesn't really figure out that you said "call home" by breaking down the phonemes. It just determines how likely it is that you said "call home" as opposed to "call office." This reduces the processing power needed as well as the chance of mistakes. However, it also restricts the words you can use to achieve the desired results.

Though not perfect, speech-recognition software programs can be invaluable to individuals who don't type well or who have physical limitations that prevent them from using a keyboard or mouse. For those whose careers require a lot of typing, using speech-recognition software reduces their chances of incurring debilitating repetitive-strain injuries. In addition, because most people can speak faster than they can write or type, speech-recognition software can help individuals work more efficiently. Doctors are incorporating speech-recognition software into their practices to create a summary of the visit before the patient leaves the room. This eliminates the need for a dictated summary to be transcribed by a separate service, and increases the physician's in-office efficiency.

Speech-recognition software also can help you to be productive during generally nonproductive times. For example, you can dictate into a digital recording device while doing other things, such as driving, then download the digital file to your computer and let the program type up your words for you. Recently, voice recognition technologies have been incorporated into in-car communication and entertainment systems, such as Ford SYNC, which allows drivers to control mobile phones and digital music players with voice commands.

Speech recognition should continue to be incorporated into our daily lives. Aside from the obvious benefits to persons with disabilities, it will provide continued efficiencies to many others as well.

digital picture of each person in your Outlook contacts list or add a digital image you captured into a newsletter you are writing.

Products such as Microsoft Photo Story and Google Picasa, which are both free downloads, make it easy for you to use your collection of digital images in new ways. In Photo Story, you can add text, music, and

camera movement to create a fully featured slide show with your images. Using Picasa, you can create a poster or several different styles of collages from your images.

What software can I use to edit my photos? As its name implies, **image editing software** (sometimes called **photo editing software**) enables you to edit photo-

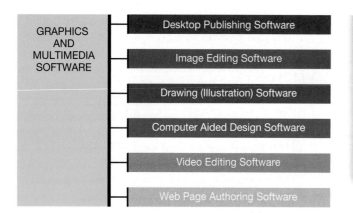

GRAPHICS AND MULTIMEDIA SOFTWARE

- Desktop Publishing Software
- Image Editing Software
- Drawing (Illustration) Software
- Computer Aided Design Software
- Video Editing Software
- Web Page Authoring Software

Figure 4.15

There are many varieties of graphics and multimedia software.

Figure 4.16

With some image editing software, you can take two individual pictures and combine them into one picture.

graphs and other images. Image editing software includes tools for basic modifications to digital images such as removing red-eye; modifying contrast, sharpness, and color casts; or removing scratches or rips from scanned images of old photos. Many of these software packages now also include an extensive set of painting tools such as brushes, pens, and artistic media (such as paints, pastels, and oils) that allow you to create realistic-looking images. Often graphic designers use digital photos and images as a basis for their design and then modify these images within image editing software to create their final products.

Adobe Photoshop and Corel Paint Shop Pro Photo are fully featured image editing applications. They each offer sophisticated tools for tasks like layering images (placing pictures on top of each other) and masking images (hiding parts of layers to create effects such as collages). As shown in Figure 4.16, these image editing applications offer sophisticated tools. Designers use these more sophisticated tools to create the enhanced digital images used commercially in logos, advertisements, and on book and CD covers.

Can a nonprofessional use image editing software? Image editing programs such as Adobe Photoshop Elements and Roxio PhotoSuite are geared toward the casual home user. Adobe also offers Adobe Photoshop Album Starter Edition, which is a free download. With these applications, you can perform the most common image editing tasks, such as taking out red-eye and cropping and resizing pictures. These programs enable you to add creative effects such as borders and frames. Some include templates so you can insert your favorite pictures into preformatted calendar pages or greeting cards. They may also have photo fantasy images that let you paste a face from your digital image onto the body of a professional athlete or other famous person.

If you want to use a program that offers more than basic features but is still easy to use, try Adobe Photoshop Elements (see Figure 4.17). With this program, you can improve the color balance of an image, touch up an image (by removing red-eye, for example), add creative effects to an image, or group images together to create montages. If you later decide to upgrade to the professional version of Adobe Photoshop, you will already be familiar with the user interface.

Digital Audio Software

Why would I have digital audio files on my computer? Best-selling novels, newspapers, and radio shows all can be purchased as audio files from sellers such as

Audible, Inc. (**audible.com**). Huge numbers of free audio files are also available through the phenomenon of *podcasting*, the distribution of audio files such as radio shows and music videos over the Internet. Offered by subscription, these audio files are delivered to your machine free with the release of each edition. You may also choose to extract (*rip*) your CD collection to store on your computer. In addition, with programs such as Magix Music Maker or Apple Garage-Band, you can compose your own songs or soundtracks with virtual instruments, voice recorders, synthesizers, and special audio effects. You may quickly have several gigabytes of audio files on your hard drive before you even know it!

Why are MP3 files so popular?

MP3 is a type of audio compression format that reduces the file size of traditional digital audio files so that they will take up less storage capacity. For example, a typical CD stores between 10 and 15 songs in uncompressed format, but with files in MP3 format, the same CD can store between 100 and 180. The smaller file size not only lets you store and play music in less space, but also allows quick and easy distribution over the Internet. You can find hundreds of digital audio applications that allow you to copy, play, edit, and organize MP3 files, and record and distribute your own music online. Most digital audio software programs support one of the following

functions. Others, such as iTunes, incorporate many of these capabilities into one multifunctional program:

- **MP3 recording** allows you to record directly from streaming audio and other software or microphone sources to MP3 format.
- **CD ripping** allows you to copy or extract CDs and encode to the MP3 format.
- **CD burning** allows you to create your own CDs from your MP3 collection.
- **Encoding and decoding** is done by *encoders*, programs that convert files to MP3 format at varying levels of quality. Most ripping software has encoders built in to convert the files directly into MP3 format.
- **Format conversion** programs allow you to convert MP3 files to other digital audio formats such as WAV (short for Waveform audio format), WMA (Windows Media Audio), and AIFF (Audio Interchange File Format).

Figure 4.17

Image editing software such as Adobe Photoshop Elements makes it easy to create (a) calendars, (b) greeting cards and postcards, (c) slide shows, and (d) more from your digital photos.

Video clips in clips pane

Window used to view or edit movie clips

Movie clips display in clip viewer

Trans icon controls transition effects between clips

Can I edit audio files? Audio editing software in-
cludes tools that make editing your audio files as easy as editing your text files. Software such as the open source Audacity (**audacity.sourceforge.net**) and Sony Sound Forge Audio Studio (**sonycreativesoftware. com**) enables you to perform such basic editing tasks as cutting dead air space from the beginning or end of the song or cutting a portion from the middle. You also can add special sound effects, such as echo or bass boost, and remove static or hiss from your MP3 files. Both of these applications support recording sound files from a microphone or any source you can connect through the input line of a sound card.

Digital Video Editing Software

What kind of software do I need to edit my digital videos? With the boom
of digital camcorders and the improved graphics capabilities on home computers, many people are experimenting with **digital video editing software**. Several video editing applications are available at a wide range of prices and capabilities. Although the most expensive products (such as Adobe Premiere Pro) offer the widest range of special effects and tools, some moderately priced video editing programs have enough features to keep the casual user happy.

Microsoft Movie Maker and Apple iMovie HD have intuitive drag-and-drop features that make it simple to create professional-quality movies with little or no training (see Figure 4.18). Microsoft Movie Maker is included with Windows XP and Vista. Other software developers offer free trial versions so that you can decide whether their product meets your needs before purchasing it.

Does video editing software support all kinds of video files?
Video files come in a number of formats. Many of the affordable video editing software packages support only a few types of video files. For example, one application may support Windows Media Player video files, whereas another may support Apple QuickTime or RealPlayer video files instead. Fortunately, software packaging lists which types of video files are supported by the software. You should buy the least expensive application that supports the greatest number of supported file formats.

For more information on video editing software, see the section "Video Editing" on page 380 of Chapter 8.

In what format are the videos I watch on my portable media player?
Videos that can be watched on portable media players, such as the fifth-generation iPod and iPod Touch, are in the MP4 (MPEG-4) video format. This format stores digital audio and digital video streams, as well as other items, such as text for subtitles

and still images. Similar to the MP3 format, MP4 compresses the audio and video content into a more manageable file size. Most MP4 files have the file extension .mp4. However, Apple has created other MPEG-4 extensions to identify specific content such as .m4b, which is often used to identify audiobook and podcast files, and .m4r, which is used to identify ringtone files for the iPhone.

Media Management Software

How do I manage the audio, video, and image files on my system?

Many people add hundreds or even thousands of files to their systems by purchasing music and downloading images and video. Your hard drive is a convenient place to store all your music and images, but only if you can find what you're looking for!

Software such as Windows Media Player, Nullsoft Winamp, and Apple iTunes allows you to organize audio and video files so that you can sort, filter, and search your music collection by artist, album, or category (see Figure 4.19). Using these programs, you can manage individual tracks, generate playlists, and even export the files to a database or spreadsheet application for further manipulation. Then you can burn the songs to a CD, and the program will print liner notes that you can place inside the CD case.

Are there Web-based programs available to edit, share, and store my photos? One great advantage of taking digital images is that you can easily share the images via the Internet. Initially, we had to send images as attachments—and our exuberance in sending several images at the same time often clogged someone's inbox. Several online photo sharing and photo storing sites, such as Snapfish (**snapfish. com**), Kodak (**kodak.com**), and Shutterfly (**shutterfly.com**), enable you to upload your digital images from your computer, create photo albums, and share them with friends and family. These sites offer printing services as well.

Flickr (**flickr.com**) is probably one of the best of these online photo management and photo sharing applications. It lets you organize your images and then share them publicly with millions of users, or just with your closest friends and family. Discussion boards are available so that groups can exchange comments about the images, just as you would if you were passing them around the dinner table. In addition, taking advantage of online mapping technologies, Flickr enables you to link your images to a map so that you can show exactly where you took the images or see where others took theirs.

Google Picasa (**picasa.google.com**) is another popular application in the online photo editing, storing, and sharing field.

Album covers flow by in a smooth display

Smart playlists select song lists based on criteria you specify

Figure 4.19

Software programs such as iTunes help you manage all the MP3 files on your computer. You can sort, filter, and search your collection by artist, album, or category, and you can create playlists.

Picasa helps you send images to your friends, your mobile devices, or your blog by automatically resizing a huge 5-megapixel image to a more manageable size for electronic transmission. With Picasa, you can then attach the image to an outgoing e-mail message, or transfer the image directly to your blog or to a mobile device such as an iPod or smartphone.

More Fun at Home

As the term implies, **entertainment software** is designed to provide users with thrills, chills, and all-out fun! Computer games make up the vast majority of entertainment software. These digital games began with Pong, Pac-Man, and Donkey Kong, and have evolved to include many different categories, including action, driving, puzzles, role-playing, card-playing, sports, strategy, and simulation games. Entertainment software also includes other types of computer applications, such as **virtual reality programs** that turn artificial environments into a realistic experience.

Figure 4.20

Computer controllers can be specialized. *Rock Band* controllers include a guitar, a drum set, and a microphone.

Gaming Software

Do I need special equipment to run entertainment software? As with any software, you need to make sure your system has enough processing power, memory (RAM), and hard drive capacity to run the program. Because games often push the limit of sound and video quality, be sure your system has the appropriate sound cards, video cards, speakers, monitor, and CD or DVD drives.

Some gaming software may require a special controller. Some games, such as *Steel Battalion, Rock Band*, and many games in the Nintendo Wii system, are sold with their own specialized controllers (see

Figure 4.20). These controllers also can be adapted to your computer. Complex simulation programs can benefit from configurable wireless controllers such as the Cyborg Evo.

How do I tell what computer games are appropriate for a certain user? The **Entertainment Software Rating Board (ESRB)** is a self-regulatory body established in 1994 by the Entertainment Software Association (**esrb.org**). The ESRB's rating system helps consumers choose the computer and video games that are right for their families by providing information about game content so they can make informed purchasing decisions. ESRB ratings have two parts: rating symbols that suggest age appropriateness, and content descriptors that indicate elements in a game that may have triggered a particular rating or be of interest or concern. It's important to check both the rating symbol (on the front of the game box) and the content descriptors (on the back of the game box). The rating symbols currently in use by the ESRB include E (Everyone), T (Teens), M (Mature), and AO (Adult Only).

Can I make video games? Now that video games represent an industry with revenue of more than $10 billion each year, designing and creating video games is emerging as a desirable career opportunity. Professionally created video games involve artistic storytelling and design, as well as sophisticated programming. Major production houses such as Electronic Arts use applications that are not easily available to the casual home enthusiast. However, you can use the editors and game engines available for games such as *EverQuest, Oblivion*, and *Unreal Tournament* to create custom levels and characters or to extend the game.

If you want to try your hand at creating your own video games, multimedia applications such as Adobe Flash CS4 and RPG Maker VX provide the tools you need to explore game design and creation. The program GameMaker (**yoyogames.com**) is a free product that allows you to build a game with no programming at all; key elements of the new game creation are dragged and dropped into place. Alice (**alice.org**) is another free environment to check out. It lets you easily create 3D animations and simple games and will soon include the actual Sims characters!

Educational Software

What kinds of educational applications are there? Although a multitude of educational software products are geared toward the younger set, software developers have by no means ignored adult markets. In addition to all the products relating to the younger audience, there are software products that teach users new skills such as typing, languages, cooking, and playing the guitar. Preparation software for students who will be taking the SAT, GMAT, LSAT, and MCAT exams is also popular. In addition, there are many computer and online brain training games and programs designed to improve the health and function of our brains. Lumosity (**luminosity. com**) is one such site that has a specific "workout" program. Brain Age (**brainage.com**) has software for the Nintendo DS and is designed for players of all ages.

What types of programs are available to train you to use software or special machines? Many programs provide tutorials for popular computer applications. These programs use illustrated systematic instructions to guide users through unfamiliar skills. Some training programs, known as **simulation programs**, allow users to experience or control the software as if it were the actual software or an actual event. Such simulation programs include commercial and military flight training, surgical instrument training, and machine operation training. Often these simulators can be delivered locally on CD or DVD or over the Internet.

One benefit of these simulated training programs is that they safely allow users to experience potentially dangerous situations such as flying a helicopter during high winds. Consequently, users of these training programs are more likely to take risks and learn from their mistakes—something they could not afford to do in real life. Simulated training programs also help prevent costly errors. Should something go awry, the only cost of the error is restarting the simulation program.

Do I need special software to take courses online? As long as you have a compatible Web browser, online classes will be accessible to you. Depending on the content and course materials, however, you may need a password or special plug-ins to view certain videos or demos.

Taking classes over the Internet is rapidly becoming a popular method of learning because it offers greater schedule flexibility for busy students. Although some courses are run from an individually developed Web site, many online courses are run using **course management software** such as Blackboard, Moodle, and Angel. These programs provide traditional classroom tools such as calendars and grade books over the Internet (see Figure 4.21). Special areas are available for students and professors to

Figure 4.21

Course management software such as Blackboard provides a method for doing traditional classroom tasks, such as participating in discussions and taking tests, in an online environment.

exchange ideas and information through the use of chat rooms, discussion forums, and e-mail. Other areas are available for posting assignments, lectures, and other pertinent class information.

Reference Software

How can I use software to research information? Encyclopedias are no longer those massive sets of books in the library. Now you can find full sets of encyclopedias such as World Book, Britannica, and Grolier on CDs and DVDs. In addition to containing all the information found in traditional paper encyclopedias, electronic encyclopedias include multimedia content such as interactive maps and video and audio clips. When researching famous sports figures, for example, not only can you read about Jackie Robinson, but you can also view a video of him in action.

Can I find reference information online? In addition to the traditional atlases, dictionaries, and thesauri available on CD and DVD, many other types of reference software are available online. Many traditional encyclopedias have online components. In addition, most of us are familiar with wiki-based online "encyclopedias" like Wikipedia (**wikipedia.org**) and Citizendium (**citizendium.org**). Other types of reference information are also available online. The American Sign Language dictionary, for example, is available online and includes video clips that show finger spelling and the modeling of each gesture. WebMD (**webmd.com**) offers medical information, and FindLaw (**findlaw.com**) provides basic legal information and forms that you previously would have had to pay a professional to obtain.

Drawing Software

What kind of software should I use for simple illustrations? Drawing software (or illustration software) lets you create or edit two-dimensional, line-based drawings. You can use drawing software to create technical diagrams or original nonphotographic drawings, animations, and illustrations using standard drawing and painting tools such as pens, pencils, and paintbrushes. You also can drag geometric objects from a toolbar onto the canvas area to create images and use paint bucket, eyedropper, and spray can tools to add color and special effects to the drawings.

Are there different types of drawing software? Drawing software is used in both creative and technical drawings. Applications such as Adobe Illustrator CS4 include tools that let you create professional-quality creative and technical illustrations. Illustrator's tools help you create complex designs, such as muscle structures in the human body, and use special effects, such as charcoal sketches. Its warping tool allows you to bend, stretch, and twist portions of your image or text. Because of its many tools and features, Illustrator is one of the preferred drawing software programs of most graphic artists.

There are many software packages to help plan the layout of rooms, homes, and landscapes, such as those offered by Broderbund. Microsoft Visio is a program used to create technical drawings, maps, basic block diagrams, networking and engineering flowcharts, and project schedules, but it can also be used by the more casual designer. Visio uses project-related templates with special objects that you drag onto a canvas. For example, by using the Visio floor template and dragging furniture and other interior objects onto it, you can create an interior design like the one shown in Figure 4.22. Visio also provides mindmapping templates to help you organize your thoughts and ideas.

Figure 4.22

The drawing program Visio lets you create different types of diagrams easily with drag-and-drop options.

Business Software

With the amount of power available in a typical home computer, you have more opportunities than ever to run a business from your home. No matter what service or product you provide, there are common types of software you'll want to consider. Accounting software will help manage the flow of money, and desktop publishing and Web page creation tools will help you market and develop your new enterprise. A number of software packages are designed to organize and help with the daily operations of a typical business. If you ever plan to run a business from your own home, or even if you are just a user of large business products and services, it is helpful to know what functions business software can perform.

Home Business Software

Which programs are good for people with small businesses? If you have a small business or a hobby that produces income, then you know the importance of keeping good records and tracking your expenses and income. **Accounting software** helps small-business owners manage their finances more efficiently by providing tools for tracking accounts receivable and accounts payable. In addition, these applications offer inventory management, payroll, and billing tools. Examples of accounting applications are Intuit QuickBooks and Peachtree by Sage. Both programs include templates for invoices, statements, and financial reports so that

small-business owners can create common forms and reports.

What software can I use to lay out and design newsletters and other publications? Desktop publishing (DTP) software allows you to incorporate and arrange graphics and text in your documents in creative ways. Although many word processing applications allow you to use some of the features that are hallmarks of desktop publishing, specialized desktop publishing software such as QuarkXPress and Adobe InDesign allows professionals to design books and other publications that require complex layouts (see Figure 4.23).

What tools do desktop publishing programs include? Desktop publishing programs offer a variety of tools with which you can format text and graphics. With text formatting tools, you easily can change the font, size, and style of your text and arrange text on the page in different columns, shapes, and patterns. You also can import files into your documents from other sources, including elements from other software programs (such as a chart from Excel or text from Word) and image files. You can readily manipulate graphics with tools that crop, flip, or rotate images or modify the image's color, shape, and size. Desktop publishing programs also include features that allow you to publish to the Web.

What software do I use to create a Web page? Web page authoring software allows even the novice to design interesting and interactive Web pages, without knowing any HyperText Markup Language (HTML) code. Web page authoring applications often include wizards, templates, and

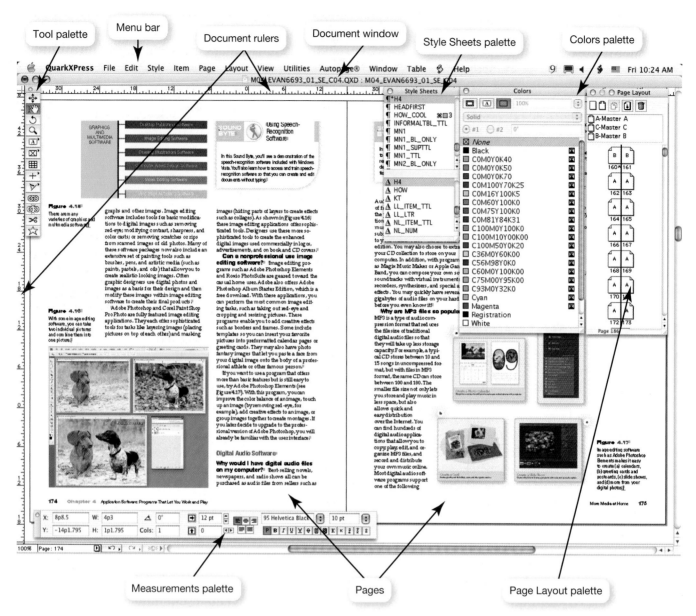

Tool palette | Menu bar | Document rulers | Document window | Style Sheets palette | Colors palette

Measurements palette | Pages | Page Layout palette

Figure 4.23

Major publishing houses use professional publishing programs such as QuarkXPress to lay out the pages of textbooks.

reference materials to help you easily complete most Web page authoring tasks. More experienced users can take advantage of these applications' advanced features, such as features that enable you to add headlines and weather information, stock tickers, and maps to make your Web content current, interactive, and interesting. Microsoft Expression Web and Adobe Dreamweaver are two of the programs to which both professionals and casual page designers turn.

Are there other ways to create Web pages? If you need to produce only the occasional Web page and do not need a separate page authoring program, you'll find that many applications include features

that enable you to convert your document into a Web page. For example, in some Microsoft Office applications, if you choose to save a file as a Web page, the application will automatically convert the file to a Web-compatible format.

Large Business Software

There is an application for almost every aspect of business. There are specialized programs for marketing and sales, finance, point of sale, general productivity, project management, security, networking, data management, e-commerce, and human resources, to name just a few. In the following sections, we discuss this seemingly endless list.

What software do businesses use for planning and management?

Planning is a big part of running a successful business. Software programs such as Palo Alto Software's Business Plan Pro and Marketing Plan Pro help users write strategic and development plans for general business and marketing needs. Another category of business planning software is **project management software**, such as Microsoft Project. This type of software helps project managers create and modify scheduling charts like the one shown in Figure 4.24, which help them plan and track specific tasks and coordinate personnel resources.

Customer relationship management (CRM) software stores sales and client contact information in one central database. Sales professionals use CRM programs to get in touch with and follow up with their clients. These programs also include tools that enable businesses to assign quotas and create reports and charts that document and analyze actual and projected sales data. Customer relationship programs coordinate well with PIM software such as Outlook and can be set up to work with smartphones. Gold-Mine from FrontRange Solutions is one example of a CRM program.

An **enterprise resource planning (ERP) system** lets a business consolidate multiple systems into one and improve coordination of these business areas across multiple departments. ERP systems are used to control many "back office" operations and processing functions such as billing, production, inventory management, and human resources management. These systems are implemented by third-party vendors and matched directly to the specific needs of a company. Oracle and SAP are well-known companies that sell ERP software.

What software helps business travelers?

Mapping programs such as DeLorme Street Atlas USA and Microsoft Streets & Trips are perfect for businesses that require employees to travel frequently. These programs provide street maps and written directions to locations nationwide, and users can customize maps to include landmarks and other handy traveling sites such as airports, hotels, and restaurants. More users now turn to an **online mapping service** such as MapQuest, Yahoo! Maps,

Google Maps, or Google Earth than to a more traditional mapping software program because the online services are easily accessible with any Internet connection and are updated more frequently than offline ones. Mapping programs, which can work in conjunction with a global positioning system (GPS), are available in versions for smartphones and for cars. Such programs help you navigate unfamiliar territory and are essential for sales representatives or delivery-intensive businesses. They are useful for nonprofessionals traveling to unfamiliar locations.

Is mapping software just used to assist with travel? Travel is only one of several applications that use mapping

Figure 4.24

A Gantt chart in Microsoft Project gives project managers a visual tool for assigning personnel and scheduling and managing tasks.

Need a Way to Share Files? Try PDF

Say you've created a file in Microsoft Excel, but the person to whom you want to send it doesn't have Excel, or any spreadsheet software, installed on his computer. Further, you do not want the contents of the original file to be changed. What do you do in these situations? One solution is to create a PDF file. Portable Document Format (PDF) is a file format you can create with Adobe Acrobat or Cutepdf Writer, a freeware program available from **cutepdf.com**. These programs transform any file, regardless of its application or platform, into a document that can be shared, viewed, and printed by anyone who has Adobe Reader. If you are using Microsoft Office 2007, OpenOffice, or Corel WordPerfect Office, you can create PDF files easily with a built-in feature. Adobe Reader (available from **adobe.com**.), the program you need to read all PDF files, is a free download.

Many graphics, animation, video, and gaming systems use applications from Autodesk called Autodesk 3ds Max and Autodesk Maya to create 3D models with complex textures and lighting models. Autodesk 3ds Max and Autodesk Maya are complex and rich programs. A slightly simpler package is the open source program Blender (**blender.org**.), which is available free of charge. A simple, Web-based, and fairly full-featured free 3D modeling application is Google's SketchUp. SketchUp designs coordinate well with other Google applications so, for example, you could easily import a 3D image of a deck you created in SketchUp into a Google Earth image of your home.

Digital elevation

Streets

Land use and cover

Topographic map

Digital line graph of rivers

Real world

Figure 4.25

A geographic information system (GIS) applies geographic data to provide solutions to complex business situations.

technologies to assist businesses in making complex decisions and managing complex systems. Many companies use a geographic information system (GIS) to assist with managing, analyzing, and displaying data, most often in spatial or map form (see Figure 4.25). These maps are used by power companies to manage electric grids, by water distribution companies to manage water distribution, by shipping and transportation companies to determine the most efficient routes, and even by school districts to manage the flow of students to the appropriate schools. Many of these systems are complex, proprietary ones such as those produced by ESRI. Google Earth and interactive maps like Google Maps are simple and free examples of basic forms of a GIS.

What software is used with e-commerce? It seems that every business has an online presence to display company information or products, handle online sales, or offer customer service and support. Depending on the size of the company and its specific needs, it may use products such as IBM's WebSphere, goEmerchant from William Bryan Company, and ProStores Business from ProStores (an eBay company). These products offer bundled Web site creation and hosting services, shopping cart setup, and credit card processing services. For larger businesses, specialized software to handle each aspect of e-commerce is available; alternatively, a large business might develop proprietary software tailored to its specific needs.

Specialized Business Software

Some applications are tailored to the needs of a particular company or industry. Software designed for a specific industry is

called **vertical market software**. For example, the construction industry uses software such as Sage Master Builder, which features estimating tools to help construction companies bid on jobs. It also integrates project management functions and accounting systems that are unique to the construction industry.

Other examples of vertical market software include property management software for real estate professionals; ambulance scheduling and dispatching software for emergency assistance organizations; and library automation software that combines cataloging, circulation, inventory, online catalog searching, and custom report printing.

In addition to these specific business applications, which companies can buy off the shelf, programs often are custom developed to address a company's specific needs. These custom applications are referred to as **proprietary software** because they are owned and controlled by the company that uses them.

What software is used to make 3D models? Computer-aided design (CAD) programs are a form of 3D modeling that engineers use to create automated designs, technical drawings, and model visualizations. Specialized CAD software such as Autodesk's AutoCAD is used in areas such as architecture, the automotive industry, aerospace, and medical engineering.

With CAD software, architects can build virtual models of their plans and readily visualize all aspects of design before actual construction. Engineers use CAD software to design everything from factory components to bridges. The 3D nature of these programs allows engineers to rotate their models and make adjustments to their designs where necessary, thus eliminating costly building errors.

CAD software also is being used in conjunction with GPS devices for accurate placement of fiber-optic networks around the country. The medical engineering community uses CAD to create anatomically accurate solid models of the human anatomy, allowing them to develop medical implants quickly and accurately. The list of CAD applications keeps growing as more and more industries realize the benefits CAD can bring to their product development and manufacturing processes.

Software can take us beyond what is familiar to us and into alternate realities. Virtual reality uses software to allow people to interact in a simulated three-dimensional environment that users can manipulate and explore as if they were in that world. Beyond video games, the applications of virtual reality are almost endless. Three-dimensional environments created by computers are getting better and better at helping people experience new things or experience familiar things in new ways.

Virtual environments are used in military training programs, the space program, and, as discussed in Chapter 1, in the medical field. Studies show that soldiers who have gone through virtual reality (VR) training are just as effective as those who have trained in traditional combat situations. Flight simulators are used by airlines to prepare commercial pilots to fly in a wide range of flight conditions; the military and NASA also use them. The obvious benefit of simulators and VR is that there is little machine or human expense when a mistake is made in virtual conditions—but there would be in "live" conditions.

Engineers and designers are also using virtual reality technologies. Car manufacturers build virtual prototypes of new vehicles, test them, and make alterations in design before producing a single physical part. Architects create virtual models of building plans so that clients or potential buyers can "walk through" and get a more realistic idea of what the completed building will be like.

Second Life, a virtual world launched in 2003 by Linden Research, Inc., has gained worldwide popularity. Users create avatars, or virtual representations of themselves, with which they interact in the virtual world. *Second Life* has its own economy, where users have created "in-world" businesses and residents can legally trade in the world's own currency, called Linden dollars.

Second Life has also begun to permeate the outside world. "Outside world" businesses now assist and advise "in-world" businesses. For example, real-world programmers build complex in-world projects for clients such as Dartmouth College, Major League Baseball, and Lego. Real-world accountants offer services to advise "in-world" businesses on finance, strategic planning, or budget forecasting. There is fertile ground for innovative and entrepreneurial thinkers both inside and outside *Second Life*.

Finally, businesses and educational institutions also recognize the marketing potential in *Second Life*, and they use the virtual world to test new ideas. Educational institutions such as Harvard, Princeton, and Ohio University have built virtual campuses with the intention of offering "virtual tours" to prospective students. At these "campuses," current students can take courses (see Figure 4.26), participate in student organizations, or meet and collaborate online just as they would if they met in the real-world student center.

Virtual worlds such as *Second Life* are innovative ways to hold distance learning classes. Online classes held in a virtual world environment give students the online convenience of not having to travel to class, while providing a more enjoyable and perhaps even more effective experience. In a virtual world, students are able to convene in traditional classrooms, on sandy Malibu beaches, or in open-air venues—environments limited only by the imagination of the instructor and the students. Given such enjoyable choices, students might be more inclined to make time to attend classes, thus increasing their productivity and the interactivity of the online classroom.

Virtual classroom environments may add an additional layer of experience that students may be able to bring into their professional lives. Seton Hall University, for example, uses *Second Life* in an emergency preparedness course that allows students to work in simulated catastrophic situations, which would otherwise be difficult to experience in the real world.

Just as in the real world, the virtual world has its problems. However, it is likely that virtual reality and virtual environments will continue to find uses in entertainment, education, distance learning, design, and manufacturing.

Figure 4.26

Virtual worlds are an innovative way to hold distance learning classes.

Getting Help with Software

If you need help while you are working with software, you can access several different resources to find answers to your questions. For general help or information about a product, many manufacturers' Web sites offer answers to **frequently asked questions (FAQs)**.

Where can I find help while I'm working in an application? Some programs offer online help and support. Online help may consist of documentation comparable to a user's manual. However, many applications' online help allows you to chat over the Internet with an online support team member. Some applications are context sensitive and offer task-specific help or screen tips to explain where your cursor is resting.

In Microsoft Office applications, you will see a question mark icon on the far top right of the program screen. This icon takes you to the main Help interface. **Integrated help** means that the documentation for the product is built directly into the software so you don't need to keep track of bulky manuals. You can type your question, search for a term, or browse the Help topics (see Figure 4.27). Like many software packages, Microsoft Office offers help documentation, which is installed locally on your machine, and online help resources, which are updated continually.

Finally, the Help menu, found on the menu bar of most applications, lets you choose to search an index or content outline to find out the nature of almost any Microsoft application feature.

Figure 4.27

Microsoft Office gives you tips on tasks you're working on and answers specific questions you have about using online and offline resources.

Click to open Help window

Access Help online or offline

Where do I go for tutorials and training on an application? If you need help learning how to use a product, the product's developer may offer online tutorials or program tours that show you how to use the software features. Often you can find good tutorials by searching the Internet. MalekTips (**malektips.com**), for example, includes a vast array of multimedia help files; you can find podcasts for applications such as Excel and Photoshop in iTunes; and even YouTube has some helpful videos.

Buying Software

These days, you no longer need to go to a computer supply store to buy software. You can find software in almost any retail environment. In addition, you can purchase software online, through catalogs, and at auctions.

Software Licenses

Don't I own the software I buy? Most people don't understand that, unlike other items they purchase, the software they buy doesn't belong to them. The only thing they're actually purchasing is a license that gives them the right to use the software for their own purposes as the *only* user of that copy. The application is not theirs to lend or copy for installation on another computer, even if it's another of their own machines.

What is a software license? A **software license** is an agreement between you, the user, and the software company. You accept this agreement before installing the software on your machine. It is a legal contract that outlines the acceptable uses of the program and any actions that violate the agreement. Generally, the agreement will state who the ultimate owner of the software is, under what circumstances copies of the software can be made, and whether the software can be installed on any other machine. Finally, the license agreement will state what, if any, warranty comes with the software.

Do you always buy just one license? Most individuals buy single licenses to cover their specific use. These licenses cannot be shared and you cannot "extend" the license to install the software on more than one of your computers.

However, Apple also offers a "family license" that permits a user to install some of its software legally on as many as five computers, and some versions of Microsoft Office come with three licenses. Businesses and educational institutions often buy multiuser licenses that allow more than one person to use the software. Some multiuser licenses are per-seat and limit the number of users overall, while others, called *concurrent licenses,* limit the number of users accessing the software at any given time.

Preinstalled Software

What application software comes with my computer? Virtually every new computer comes with some form of application software, although the particular applications depend on the hardware manufacturer and computer model. You usually can count on your computer having some form of productivity software preinstalled, such as Microsoft Works or Corel WordPerfect Office.

Multimedia-enriched computers also may offer graphics software or a productivity suite that includes page authoring software. Many new computers also include some software that is of interest to home users, such as image editing or financial planning software.

Can I get the manufacturer to install software before shipping? If you know you'll need a particular type of software not offered as standard on your new computer, you may want to see if the computer manufacturer has a special offer that will allow you to add that particular software at a reduced price. Sometimes, initially buying software through the hardware manufacturer is less expensive than buying software on the retail market. This is not always the case, so do some comparative pricing before you buy.

Web-Based Application Software

Does all application software require installation on my computer? Most application software you acquire, whether by purchasing a CD or DVD at a retail store or by downloading the software from a Web site, must be installed on your computer before use. However, Web-based software is

BITS AND BYTES — Applications on the Go

More and more of us carry some kind of mobile digital device that enables us to use software on the go. We can install productivity, entertainment, communication, and navigation software on our iPhones, Blackberries, iPods, and other mobile devices. The newest version of Microsoft Office is expected have modestly featured Web-based Word, Excel, and PowerPoint applications, so you'll have access to your productivity documents without having to worry about transferring files from one machine to another. Although mobile applications have been available for smartphones for a while, they have been limited in scope and content, in addition to being slightly pricey. One of the features that makes the iPhone and iPod Touch so popular is their ability to run small applications. Many of these applications are fun and free (such as the flashlight and Sudoku applications), while others (such as the Tip Calculator, the Remember the Milk list, or a connection to your online banking files) help you be more productive. The full list of available applications for the iPhone and iPod Touch is available on the iTunes music store Web site.

growing in popularity. **Web-based application software** is a program hosted on a Web site that does not require installation on your computer. In most cases, a Web-based application will not occupy space on your hard drive, but sometimes a small plug-in or control software module may need to be downloaded.

Is all Web-based software free? Web-based applications are run from software stored completely on a Web server instead of your hard drive. Web-based applications are a reflection of a movement toward a new software distribution model.

Although most Web-based software programs are free, some Web sites charge a fee for their online products. TurboTax Online (**turbotax.com**) is a version of the popular tax preparation software that you can access online to prepare your tax returns. In addition to saving you the hassle of software installation, TurboTax Online stores your information in a secure location so that you can retrieve it anytime.

More and more of your software needs might be met by some of the emerging Web-based providers. Many Web sites offer free Web-based applications, such as the mapping software Mapquest (**mapquest. com**) and Yahoo! Maps (**maps.yahoo.com**), which allow you to generate driving directions from point to point. Sites such as Zoho (**zoho.com**, see Figure 4.28), Think-Free (**thinkfree.com**), and Google (**docs.google.com**) offer Web-based applications that cover a range of word processing,

Figure 4.28
Zoho.com is one of the many emerging Web sites that offers free Web-based productivity software.

presentation, project management, and spreadsheet needs.

The features of these programs are generally a subset of what the installed versions offer, but they do offer other advantages. Google Docs, for example, is a free application with word processing, spreadsheet, and presentation capabilities. You can invite people to share your files and work together in real time, watching as others make changes to the document. As long as you have a Web browser, you can access your files, which are stored securely online. Although these free applications are not as fully featured as the products from Microsoft, they can read and export to many different file formats and be used with other software packages. Microsoft, in their newest release of Office, will provide Web-based Word, Excel, and PowerPoint applications that have limited functionality compared with the fully featured traditional version of the applications. It is expected that these will not be free, but will come as a part of the Office suite.

There is also a relatively new trend of on-demand software deployment, referred to as **Software as a Service (SaaS),** that many businesses are taking advantage of. Instead of the traditional model that requires software to be purchased and installed on individual machines or network servers, with the SaaS delivery model the application is hosted by the vendor and made available

to the customer over the Internet. Some examples include Intuit's Quick-Books online, Salesforce.com, and Citrix Online.

Discounted Software

Is it possible to buy software at a discount? Software manufacturers understand that students and educators often need to use software for short periods of time because of specific classes or projects. In addition, they want to encourage you to learn with their product, hoping you'll become a long-term user of their software. Therefore, if you're a student or an educator, you can purchase software that is no different from regularly priced software at prices that are sometimes substantially less than general consumer prices.

Campus computer stores and college bookstores sometimes offer discounted prices to students and faculty who possess a valid ID. Online software suppliers such as Journey Education Marketing (**journeyed.com**), CampusTech, Inc. (**campustech.com**), and Academic Superstore (**academicsuperstore.com**) also offer popular software to students at reduced prices.

Can I buy used software? Often you can buy software through online auction sites such as eBay. If you do so, be sure that you are buying licensed (legal) copies. Computer shows that display state-of-the-art computer equipment are generally good sources for software. However, here, too, you must exert a bit of caution to make sure you are buying licensed copies and not pirated versions.

Can I buy software directly from the Internet? As with many other retail products, you can buy and download software directly from many companies and retail Web sites such as Microsoft.com and Amazon.com. You also can use the Internet to buy software that is custom developed for your specific needs. Companies such as Ascentix Corporation (**ascentix.com**) act as intermediaries between you (the software user) and a software developer, who tweaks open source software code to meet your particular needs.

When buying software from the Internet, you should also request that the software be sent to you on CD or DVD, if this is available. Without a physical copy of the software, it is much more difficult to reinstall the software if you change computers or if your hard drive crashes. If a physical copy is not available, make sure you create a backup and keep it in a safe place.

The Microsoft .NET program (**microsoft. com/net**) offers software over the Internet for all devices—not just computers—that have a connection to the Internet. Therefore, you can download software specifically for your smartphone by using .NET. In addition, if you have a Microsoft .NET account (available free of charge at the Microsoft Web site), you can connect to any other .NET-connected device.

Freeware and Shareware

Can I get software for free legally?
Freeware is any copyrighted software that you can use for free. Plenty of freeware exists on the Web, ranging from games and screen savers to business, educational, graphics, home and hobby, and system utility software programs. To find free software, type "freeware" in your search engine. One good source of a large variety of freeware programs is Freeware Home (**freewarehome.com**).

Although they do not charge a fee, some developers release free software and request that you mail them a postcard or send them an e-mail message to thank them for their time in developing the software and to give them your opinion of it. Such programs are called *postcardware* and *e-mailware*, respectively.

Another option is to search for an open source program to fit your needs. Open source programs are free to use on the condition that any changes you make to improve the source code also must be distributed for free. SourceForge.net (**sourceforge.net**) is an excellent site to begin your hunt for a group that may already have built a solution that will work for you!

While many legitimate freeware exists, some unscrupulous people use freeware to distribute viruses and malware. Be cautious

BITS AND BYTES
Software 911

If your software problem is a technical one—the kind that might generate an error message—many resources are available on the Web. Most software manufacturers have support on their Web sites that include FAQs, discussion boards monitored by employees of the company, and collections of tutorials and troubleshooting advice. For example, to resolve problems with Microsoft products, check the Help and Support database located at **support.microsoft.com,** a collection of more than 250,000 articles written by Microsoft support professionals reflecting their resolution of customer issues and problems. To search Microsoft's Help and Support most effectively, use a search engine such as Google. To do so, go to Google (**google.com**) and select the Advanced Search option. Specify "support.microsoft.com" as the domain to be searched and then type your search terms. Technical communities, such as those from Microsoft (**microsoft.com/communities**) in the form of blogs, newsgroups, webcasts, and forums are also available on the Web and provide opportunities for you to interact with employees, experts, and peers.

when installing such programs, especially if you are unsure of the provider's legitimacy.

Can I try new software before it is really released?
Some software developers offer beta versions of their software free of charge. A **beta version** is an application that is still under development. By distributing free beta versions, developers hope users will report errors or bugs they find in their programs. Many beta versions are available for a limited trial period, and are used to help the developers correct any errors before they launch the software on the market at retail prices.

Is it still freeware if I'm asked to pay for the program after using it for a while?
One model for distributing software is to allow users to test software first by running it for a limited time, free of charge. Large corporations do this by offering free trial software products. These are fully functional packages, but they expire if not purchased within a certain timeframe. Small software developers also use this kind of distribution. This is referred to as **shareware**. Shareware software is distributed free, but with certain conditions. Sometimes the software is released on a trial basis only and must be registered after a certain period of time; in other cases, no support is available unless the software is registered. In some cases, direct payment to the author is required. Shareware is not freeware. If you use the software after the

initial trial period is over, then you are breaking the software license agreement.

Software developers put out shareware programs to get their products into users' hands without the added expense and hassle of marketing and advertising. Therefore, quite a few great programs are available as shareware, and they can compete handily with programs on retail shelves. For example, TechSmith Corporation (**techsmith.com**) offers screen capture and desktop recording applications as shareware, including SnagIt Screen Capture and Camtasia Studio, a screen recording and presentation application. You can try these products for free for a 30-day period, after which time you must purchase the software to continue using it. For a listing of other shareware programs, visit the CNET site Tucows (**tucows.com**), as shown in Figure 4.29, or the CNET site Shareware.com (**shareware.com**).

Can shareware programmers make me pay for their shareware once I have it? The whole concept of shareware assumes that users will behave ethically and abide by the license agreement. However, to protect themselves, many developers have incorporated code into the program to stop it from working completely or to alter the output slightly after the trial period expires.

Are there risks associated with installing beta versions, freeware, and shareware or downloading them from the Internet? Not all files available as shareware and freeware will work on your computer. You easily can crash your system, and may even need to reinstall your operating system as a result of loading a freeware or shareware program that was not written for your computer's operating system.

Of course, by their very nature, beta products are unlikely to be bug free, so you always run the risk of something going awry with your system. Unless you're willing to deal with potential problems, it may be best to wait until the last beta version is released. By that time, most of the serious bugs will have been worked out.

As a matter of precaution, you should be comfortable with the reliability of the source before downloading a freeware, shareware, or beta version of software. If it's a reliable developer whose software you are already familiar with, you can be more certain that a serious bug or virus is not hiding in the software. However, downloading software from an unknown source could potentially put your system at risk of contracting a virus. (We discuss viruses in detail in Chapter 9.)

A good practice to establish before installing any software on your system is to use the Windows Vista operating system's Restore feature and create a *restore point*. That way, if anything goes wrong during installation, you can restore your system to the way it was before you started. (We discuss the System Restore utility in Chapter 5.) Also, make sure that your virus protection software is up-to-date.

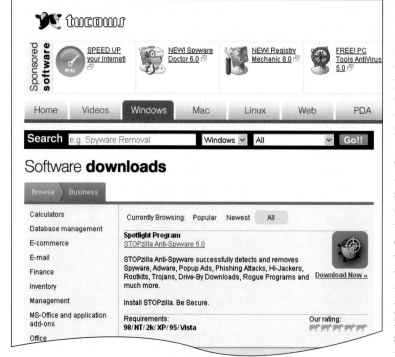

Figure 4.29

Tucows is a useful site for finding freeware applications. The site provides product reviews, hardware requirements, and details about the limitations of free versions of software.

Software Versions and System Requirements

What do the numbers after software names indicate? Software companies change their programs to repair problems (or bugs) or add new or upgraded features. Generally, they keep the software program's name but add a number to it to indicate that it is a different version. Originally, developers used numbers only to indicate different software versions (major upgrades) and releases (minor upgrades). Today, however, they also use years (such as Microsoft Office 2007) and letters (such as WordPerfect Office X3) to represent version upgrades.

When is it worth buying a newer version? Although software developers suggest otherwise, there is no need to rush out and buy the latest version of a software program every time one is available. Depending on the software, some upgrades may not be sufficiently different from the previous version to make it cost-effective for you to buy the newest version. Unless the upgrade adds features that are important to you, you may be better off waiting to upgrade every other release. You also should consider whether you use the software frequently enough to justify an upgrade and whether your current system can handle the new system requirements of the upgraded version.

If I have an older version of software and someone sends me files from a newer version, can I still open them? Software vendors recognize that people work on different versions of the same software. Vendors, therefore, make new versions backward compatible, meaning that they can recognize (open) files created with older versions. However, many software programs are not forward compatible, so older versions cannot recognize files created on newer versions of the same software. For example, when Microsoft came out with Office 2007, users of earlier versions of Microsoft Office could not read files created in Office 2007. Microsoft provided free conversion programs so users with earlier versions could read Office 2007 files. In addition, Microsoft incorporated a feature within Office 2007 that allows Office 2007 users to save documents so that they can be read by users of earlier versions.

 BITS AND BYTES Keeping Your Software Up-to-Date

Bugs in software occur all the time. Software developers are constantly testing their product, even after releasing the software to the retail market, and users report errors they find. In today's environment in which security is a large concern, companies test their products for vulnerabilities against hackers and other malicious users. Once a fix or patch to a bug or vulnerability is created, most software developers will put the repair in downloadable form on the Internet and make it available at no charge. You should check periodically for any software updates or service packs to ensure your software is up-to-date. For your convenience, many products have an automatic update feature that downloads and installs updates automatically.

How do I know whether the software I buy will work on my computer? Every software program has a set of **system requirements** that specify the minimum recommended standards for the operating system, processor, primary memory (RAM), and hard drive capacity. Sometimes there are other specifications for the video card, monitor, CD drive, and other peripherals. These requirements generally are printed on the software packaging or are available at the manufacturer's Web site. Before installing software on your computer, ensure that your system setup meets the minimum requirements by having sufficient storage, memory capacity, and processing capabilities.

Installing, Uninstalling, and Starting Software

Before you use your software, you must permanently place it, or install it, on your system. The installation process will differ slightly depending on whether you've

 ACTIVE HELP-DESK Buying and Installing Software

In this Active Helpdesk call, you'll play the role of a helpdesk staffer, fielding calls about how to best purchase software or get it for free, how to install and uninstall software, and where you can go for help when you have a problem with your software.

Figure 4.30
Part of the installation process in Windows Vista is a security check to confirm that the software is from a reliable source.

purchased the software from a retail outlet and have an installation CD or are downloading it from the Internet. Deleting or uninstalling software from your system requires that you take certain precautions to ensure you remove all associated programs as well.

How do I install software? When you purchase software, the program files may come on a CD or a DVD. For most programs created for installation on a PC, an installation wizard automatically opens when you insert the disc, as shown in Figure 4.30. By following the steps indicated by the wizard, you can install the application on your system. If the wizard doesn't open automatically for some reason, the best way to install the software is to go to the Programs and Features icon, located on the Control Panel on the Start menu. This feature locates and launches the installation wizard.

How is the installation process different for software I download from the Web? When you download software from the Web, you typically do not get an installation disc. Instead, everything you need to install and run the downloaded program is contained in one file that has been compressed (or zipped) to make the downloading process quicker. For the most part, these downloaded files unzip or de-compress themselves and automatically start or launch the setup program. During the installation and setup process, these

programs select or create the folder on your computer's hard drive in which most of the program files will be saved. Usually, you can select a different location if you desire. Either way, note the name and location of the files, because you may need to access them later.

What do I do if the downloaded program doesn't install by itself? Some programs you download do not automatically install and run on your computer. Although the compressed files may unzip automatically as part of the download process, the setup program may not run without some help from you. In this case, you need to locate the files on the hard drive (this is why you must remember the location of the files) and find the program that is controlling the installation (sometimes named *setup.exe* or *install.exe*). Files ending with the .exe extension are executable files or applications. All the other files in the folder are support, help, and data files. Once the setup program begins, you will be prompted to take the actions necessary to complete the installation.

What's the difference between a custom installation and a full installation? One of the first steps in the installation wizard asks you to decide between a full installation and a custom installation. A **full installation** will copy all the files and programs from the distribution disc to the computer's hard drive. By selecting **custom installation**, you can decide which features you want installed on the hard drive. Installing only the features you know you want allows you to save space on your hard drive.

Can I just delete a program to uninstall it? An application contains many different files—library files, help files, and other text files—in addition to the main file you use to run the program. By deleting only the main file, or only the icon on your desktop, you are not ridding your system of all the pieces of the program. In addition, some applications make changes to a variety of settings, and none of these will be restored if you just delete the desktop icon or remove the main file from your programs list.

Some programs place an Uninstall Program icon in the main program folder on the Start menu. Using this icon runs the proper cleanup routine to clear out all of the files associated with the application, and also restores any settings that have been changed. If you can't locate the uninstall program for a particular application, click the Start menu, click Control Panel, and then click Programs and Features. This will give you a list of applications installed on your system; from this list, you can choose which application you would like to uninstall.

Is there a best way to start an application?   The simplest way to start an application is by clicking its icon in the All Programs list found on the Start menu. Every program that you install on your system is listed on the Start menu. However, if you find you use only a few programs often, you can place a shortcut to those programs either on the Quick Launch toolbar on the taskbar or on your desktop. To place a program in the Quick Launch toolbar on the taskbar, right-click the program icon on your desktop or right-click the program name on the Start menu. From the shortcut menu that is displayed, select Add to Quick Launch. This places an icon for this program on the Quick Launch toolbar (see Figure 4.31a).

To create a shortcut on the desktop, right-click the icon of the desired program, click Send To, and select Desktop (see Figure 4.31b). This places the shortcut icon directly on the Desktop. You can identify a shortcut icon by the arrow in its lower left corner, as shown in Figure 4.31a.

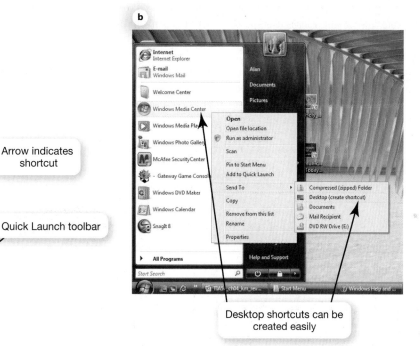

Figure 4.31

For quick access to an application you use often, you can place a shortcut in (a) the Quick Launch toolbar or (b) on your desktop.

A computer user who copies an application onto more than one computer is participating in **software piracy**, unless his or her license specifically provides for multiple distribution. What many software users do not realize, or do not think about, is that when they purchase software, they are actually purchasing a license to use it, rather than purchasing the actual software. That license is what tells you how many times you can install the software, so it is important to read it. If you make more copies of the software than the license permits, you are pirating. Historically, the most common way software has been pirated among computer users has been by supplementing each other's software library by borrowing installation CDs and installing the software on their own computers. Larger-scale illegal duplication and distribution by counterfeiters is quite common as well. In addition, the Internet provides various ways to copy and distribute pirated software illegally.

Is it really a big deal to copy a program or two? As reported by the Business Software Alliance, 40 percent of all software is pirated. Not only is pirating software unethical and illegal, but the practice has financial impacts on all software consumers. The dollars manufacturers lose when software is pirated decreases the amount of money available for further software research and development, while increasing the up-front costs to legitimate consumers.

To determine whether you have a pirated copy of software installed on your computer at work or at home, you can download a free copy of GASP (a suite of programs designed to help identify and track licensed and unlicensed software and other files) from the Business Software Alliance Web site (**bsa.org/usa**). A similar program is available at the Microsoft Web site (**microsoft.com/piracy**). These programs check the serial numbers of the software installed on your computer against software manufacturer databases of official licensed copies and known fraudulent copies. Any suspicious software installations are flagged for your attention.

As of yet, there's no such thing as an official software police force, but software piracy is so rampant that the U.S. government is taking steps to stop piracy worldwide. Efforts to stop groups that reproduce, modify, and distribute counterfeit software over the Internet are in full force. Software manufacturers also are becoming more aggressive in programming mechanisms into software to prevent repeated installations. For instance, with many Microsoft products, installation requires you to activate the serial number of your software with a database maintained at Microsoft. This is different from the traditional "registration" that enrolled you voluntarily and allowed you to be notified of product updates, for example. Activation is required, and failure to activate your serial number or attempting to activate a serial number that has been used previously results in the software going into a "reduced functionality mode" after the 50th time you use it. Therefore, without activation, you would not be able to save documents in Office—a strong motivator to let Microsoft watch how many times you install the software you purchased!

1. What's the difference between application software and system software?

System software is the software that helps run the computer and coordinates instructions between application software and the computer's hardware devices. System software includes the operating system and utility programs. Application software is the software you use to do everyday tasks at home, school, and work. Application software includes productivity software, such as word processing and finance programs; media software, such as applications used for image editing; home and entertainment software, such as games or educational programs; and business software.

2. What kinds of applications are included in productivity software?

Productivity software programs include word processing, spreadsheet, presentation, personal information manager (PIM), and database programs. You use word processing software to create and edit written documents. Spreadsheet software enables you to do calculations and numerical and what-if analyses easily. Presentation software enables you to create slide presentations. Personal information manager (PIM) software helps keep you organized by putting a calendar, address book, notepad, and to-do lists within your computer. Database programs are electronic filing systems that allow you to filter, sort, and retrieve data easily. Individuals can also use software to help with business-like tasks such as preparing taxes and managing personal finances.

3. What are the different types of multimedia software?

Multimedia software includes digital image, video, and audio editing software; animation software; and other specialty software required to produce computer games. Many software programs are available for playing, copying, recording, editing, and organizing multimedia files. Because modern users have so many audio, video, and image files, many software solutions are available for organizing and distributing these types of files.

4. What are the different types of entertainment software?

Beyond the games that most of us are familiar with, entertainment software includes virtual reality programs that use special equipment to make users feel as though they are actually experiencing the program in a realistic 3D environment.

5. What are the different types of drawing software?

Drawing software includes a wide range of software programs that help you create and edit simple line-based drawings or create more complex designs for both imaginative and technical illustrations. Floor plans, animations, and mind maps are some of the types of images that can be created.

6. What kinds of software do small and large businesses use?

Many businesses, including home businesses, use software to help them with finance, accounting, strategic planning, marketing, and Web-based tasks common to most businesses. In addition, businesses may use specialized business software (or vertical market software) that is designed for their specific industry.

7. What kind of software is available online?

Web-based software refers to programs that are hosted on a Web site and do not require installation on your computer. Many applications are available as Web-based software, including productivity, tax preparation, and financial planning software. Digital photos and videos can be manipulated, saved, and stored online. The features of many Web-based applications are not as robust as those of their downloadable counterparts, but this is likely to change.

8. Where can I go for help when I have a problem with software?

Most software programs have a Help menu built into the program with which you can search through an index or subject directory to find answers. Some programs group the most commonly asked questions into a single "frequently asked questions" (FAQ) document. In addition, many free and fee-based help and training resources are available on the Internet and through booksellers.

9. How can I purchase software or get it for free?

Almost every new computer system comes with some form of software to help you accomplish basic tasks. You must purchase all other software unless it is freeware or open source code, which you can download from the Web for free. You can also find special software called shareware you can run free of charge for a test period. Although you can find software in many stores, as a student you can purchase the same software at a reduced price with an academic discount.

10. How do I install, uninstall, and start software?

When installing and uninstalling software, it's best to use the specific Add or Remove Program feature that comes with the operating system. Most programs are installed using an installation wizard that walks you through the installation. Other software programs may require you to activate the setup program, which then will begin the installation wizard. Using the Add or Remove Programs feature when uninstalling a program will help you ensure that all ancillary program files are removed from your computer.

key terms

buzzwords four

Word Bank

- application software
- beta version
- freeware
- illustration software
- image editing software
- integrated help
- integrated software
- productivity software
- shareware
- software piracy
- software suite
- spreadsheet
- system requirements
- system software
- templates
- Web-based applications
- wizards
- word processing

Instructions: Fill in the blanks using the words from the Word Bank above.

Roxanne is so pumped! Her aunt is upgrading to a newer computer and is giving Roxanne her old one. Roxanne has just enrolled in college and knows she's going to need at least (1) a(n) _____ program to help her write papers and (2) a(n) _____ program to help her keep track of expenses while she is at school. Because both of these applications are part of a larger group of applications called (3) _____ , she knows she can buy them as a group. She's been told that it's cheaper to buy them as (4) a(n) _____ than to buy them individually. Because she knows she'll need the stable, tested versions of the software, she cannot get by using (5) a(n) _____ of the program. Roxanne is also aware of many interesting (6) _____ that are available from the Internet and that she can access anywhere she has an Internet connection.

As a graduation present, Roxanne received a new digital camera. She needs to install the (7) _____ that came with her camera to edit and manage her digital pictures. Although she's used the software a couple of times on her parents' computer, she is still glad for the (8) _____ feature to assist her with specific feature-related questions and the (9) _____ that provide systematic guides to help her do things.

Roxanne especially likes the decorative preformatted (10) _____ she can use to insert pictures and make them seem professional. She also knows of some (11) _____ games she can download without cost from the Internet and other (12) _____ programs that she could try but eventually pay for. She found some really useful utility programs under the category of (13) _____ programs, which she can download for no charge and would like to install and try out. It's tempting for her to borrow software from her friends, but she knows that it's considered (14) _____. She also knows that before installing any of the programs she must check the (15) _____ to determine if the software is compatible with her system as well as whether the system has enough resources to support the software.

becoming computer literate

Using key terms from this chapter, write a letter to one of your friends or relatives about which applications he or she may need to be able to work more productively. Also, include which application(s) that individual may need to modify, review, and store the pictures taken with a digital camera he or she just purchased.

self-test

Instructions: Answer the multiple-choice and true–false questions below for more practice with key terms and concepts from this chapter.

Multiple Choice

1. Application software
   a. is another name for system software.
   b. helps maintain the resources of the computer.
   c. includes products such as Microsoft Office, tax software, and editing packages.
   d. Both A and C.

2. Which of the following is an example of a software suite?
   a. Microsoft Word
   b. Google Docs
   c. WordPerfect Office X3
   d. None of the above

3. A Web-based software program is
   a. a stand-alone program developed to work exclusively for one company.
   b. an application designed specifically for a Web-based business or industry.
   c. a program that helps you design Web pages.
   d. an application that does not need to be installed but is run directly from the Web.

4. An integrated software application such as Microsoft Works is
   a. an individual program.
   b. meant only for business purposes.
   c. sold in specific collections, which reduces the price.
   d. only available in open source format.

5. The type of software you would use to help you coordinate many people on a single task is
   a. project management.
   b. spreadsheet.
   c. database.
   d. system.

6. What software is the best for creating a newsletter?
   a. Word processing software
   b. Desktop publishing software
   c. Computer-aided design software
   d. Media management software

7. Which is NOT true about Web-based applications?
   a. They are accessible from any computer that has an Internet connection.
   b. They are great for collaboration.
   c. They are typically more expensive than traditional applications.
   d. They are used to coordinate input from a variety of users on a single document.

8. Which of the following is true?
   a. MP4 files contain audio and video data.
   b. MP3 files are the only recognized format for digital audio.
   c. Windows Media player is able to organize large collections of audio files.
   d. Only A and C are true.

9. Where can you find help on how to use software and solve specific software problems?
   a. An index or subject directory found in the Help menu
   b. Documents containing frequently asked questions
   c. Resources on the Web
   d. All of the above

10. Which of the following best describes open source software?
    a. It is free and is as fully featured as similar proprietary applications.
    b. It is available from the Internet and can be virus ridden.
    c. It is freely available from the Internet, but has limited functionality when compared with proprietary products.
    d. It is freely available, but can only be used for a limited amount of time.

True-False

_____ 1. Software can be installed only from a CD or DVD.

_____ 2. Open source software such as Audacity is used to organize video files.

_____ 3. The best way to delete a program from your system is to delete the shortcut on the desktop.

_____ 4. When you buy software, it's yours to do whatever you'd like with, including making a copy for a friend.

_____ 5. Web-based application software will run from any computer without the need for any installation.

four

1. Installing Software

You have just spent $285 on a software package. You have a desktop computer that you use at home and a notebook that you use only at work.

a. Are you allowed to install the software on both computers? Should you be allowed to do that?
b. What if you wanted to install the software on two computers that you own and use exclusively at home?
c. Can you install the software on two computers if you use only one computer at a time?
d. Are you allowed to install the software package on your computer and also on a friend's computer if she is interested in buying her own copy but wants to test it first?

2. Software Training

You are most likely familiar with many applications, and you probably will use many more applications before your coursework is done. Make two lists. In one list, itemize by category the applications you are already familiar with. In the other list, identify at least three other applications you think you may need or would want to try in the future. Research the types of on-campus or online training or help features that may be offered for those programs you put on your second list.

3. Upgrading Software

You are trying to decide whether to upgrade some software that you used this past semester. How do the following items weigh into your decision to upgrade the software or not?

a. The cost of the upgrade
b. The length of time the upgrade has been available
c. Hardware requirements
d. Features of the upgrade versus the stability of your current system

4. Choices, Choices

There are many word processing software options. Describe the decision process you would use to choose among a free Web-based word processing application, an open source word processing application, and a standard packaged application if you are

a. traveling abroad for a semester, visiting 15 different cities, and not carrying a notebook with you.
b. staying at home for the term and compiling a capstone report using several hundred researched sources of information.
c. working with three people from other colleges on a joint paper that will be presented at a conference at the end of the term.

5. Choosing the Best Software

This past semester you spent a lot of time doodling, and created a comic strip character that all your friends love. You've decided to start a small newsletter, including some articles and a few comics each week. Which applications would be the best fit for the following tasks?

a. Designing and laying out the newsletter
b. Creating the text articles
c. Creating the comic strip

After the first five issues, the newsletter is clearly a smash. You decide to expand it into an Internet-delivered magazine. Which applications will you use now for the same tasks?

1. Surveying the Competition

You are asked to develop a departmental report that analyzes the key competitors in your market. You will need to take the following steps:

a. Identify the major competitors in your market.
b. Gather information on their companies, their sales, and the features of their products.
c. Organize your data so it can be easily sorted and filtered.
d. Analyze the trends in the marketplace and predict future direction of growth.
e. Create a final report and presentation to deliver to the department heads.

Identify what software products you would use to complete each of these tasks. How would you use them, and how would they work together to support your efforts?

2. Integrating Applications

Some applications work well together and some do not. Certainly, all of the applications within a given suite, such as Microsoft Office, are well integrated. Give an example of a business office need that would benefit from the following:

a. Integrating Excel with Word
b. Integrating Access with Excel
c. Integrating Access with Word

3. Choosing the Best Software for the Job

For each of the following positions, describe the set of applications you would expect to encounter if you were:

a. a photographer opening a new business to sell your own photography.
b. an administrative assistant to a college president.
c. a graphic designer at a large publishing house.
d. the publicity director of a new summer camp for children.
e. a presenter giving a program to elementary school students about a year spent living abroad.
f. a Web page designer for a small nonprofit organization.
g. a construction site manager.
h. a person in the career you are pursuing.

4. The Right Productivity Suite

You are asked to research the cost and use of productivity software for your small company. Until now, the company has been using Microsoft Works, but the need to expand to a full-fledged productivity suite is evident. Research the major productivity suites on the market. Look at cost, the ability to exchange files with customers and other employees easily (for example, does file type make a difference?), and the various features within each version of the software. Explore the major developers' products as well as the open source option OpenOffice and a set of Web-based packages. Which productivity suite would you recommend, and why? Be specific in your recommendation.

Instructions: Albert Einstein used *Gedankenexperiments* (critical thinking questions) to develop his theory of relativity. Some ideas are best understood by experimenting with them in our own minds. The following critical thinking questions are designed to demand your full attention but require only a comfortable chair—no technology.

1. Software Ethics 1

The cost of new software can be prohibitively high. You need to do a project for school that requires the use of an application you don't own, but your roommate has a copy that her dad gave her. He brought it home from his workplace, and she is letting you install it on your machine.

a. Is it okay for you to borrow this software?
b. Would it be okay if you uninstalled the application after you finished using it?
c. Would it be okay if the software was on the school's network and you could copy it from there?

2. Software Ethics 2

Currently, there is no accurate way to check for illegal installations of software programs. What kind of program or system do you think could be developed to do this type of checking? Who would pay to develop, run, and maintain the program: the developers or the software users?

3. Media Management

Less than a decade ago, home users had no media files on their computer systems. Today, many users have a library of music, a collection of digitized movies, personal photo collections, and even a large set of recorded television shows. Examine three different software packages on the market today for managing these materials. What features do they need to make the PC the primary entertainment device for a home? What would make users move their PC from the office into the living room?

4. Software and Microcredit

The 2006 Nobel Peace Prize was awarded to Muhammad Yunus, who created the Grameen Bank. This bank makes quite small loans to the poor of Bangladesh, without requiring collateral. Often these loans are smaller than $200, but they allow women to begin small businesses and climb out of poverty. How has software made the Grameen Bank productive and able to serve almost 7 million borrowers? What other ways could software make a difference to the struggling peoples of the world?

5. Software for the Hearing and Visually Impaired

The World Wide Web Consortium (W3C) currently has an initiative to ensure that all Web pages are accessible to everyone, including those with vision and hearing impairments. The W3C site has a list of currently available commercial and free Web accessibility evaluation tools (**w3.org/WAI/ER/tools**) that Web site developers can use to ensure their Web sites conform to the disability standards.

a. Pick a favorite Web site and see how it checks out by using one of the freeware programs on the W3C list. What changes would be necessary for that Web site to conform to W3C standards?
b. Can you think of other ways in which software might make the world a better place for those with vision and hearing impairments?
c. How might recommendations made by the W3C also benefit people without physical limitations?

four team time

Assessing Software Needs

Problem

Gizmos, Inc. is a start-up company in the business of designing, building, and selling the latest gizmos. You have been hired as director of information systems. As such, one of your responsibilities is to ensure that all necessary applications are purchased and installed on the company's server.

Task

Split your class into as many groups of four or five as possible. Each group is to perform the same activity. The groups will present and compare results with each other at the end of the project.

Process

1. Identify a team leader who will coordinate the project and record and present results.
2. Each team is to identify the various kinds of software that Gizmos, Inc. needs. Ensure that all activities and departments of the company have software to meet their needs. Consider software that employees will need for several tasks: software they can use to design the gizmos, productivity software they may need, and software the sales reps will need to help keep track of their clients. Also, consider software that human resources personnel can use to keep track of employee data, and that software product managers can use to track projects. Finally, think of other software that might be useful to Gizmos, Inc.
3. Create a detailed and organized list of required software applications. If possible, include licensing fees. Assume that the company has 50 users.

Conclusion

Software helps us do both the simplest and the most complex tasks every day. It's important to understand how dependent we are becoming on computers and technology. Compare your results with those of other team members. Were there applications that you didn't think about, but that other members did? How expensive is it to ensure that even the smallest company has all the software required to carry out daily activities?

In addition to the review materials presented here, you'll find additional materials featured with the book's multimedia, including the *Technology in Action* Student Resource CD and the Companion Website (**pearsonhighered.com/techinaction**), which will help reinforce your understanding of the chapter content. These materials include the following:

Active Helpdesk

In Active Helpdesk calls, you'll assume the role of helpdesk operator, taking calls about the concepts you've learned in this chapter. You'll apply what you've learned and receive feedback from a supervisor to review and reinforce those concepts. The Active Helpdesk calls for this chapter are listed below and can be found on your Student Resource CD.

- Choosing Software
- Buying and Installing Software

Sound Bytes

Sound Bytes are dynamic multimedia tutorials that help demystify even the most complex topics. You'll view video clips and animations that illustrate computer concepts and then apply what you've learned by reviewing it with the Sound Byte Labs, which include quizzes and activities specifically tailored to each Sound Byte. The Sound Bytes for this chapter are listed below and can be found on your Student Resource CD.

- Creating Web Queries in Excel 2007
- Using Speech-Recognition Software
- Enhancing Photos with Image Editing Software

Companion WebSite

The *Technology in Action* Companion Website includes a variety of additional materials to help you review and learn more about the topics in this chapter. The resources available at **pearsonhighered.com/techinaction** include:

- **Online Study Guide.** Each chapter features an online true–false and multiple-choice quiz. You can take these quizzes, automatically check the results, and e-mail the results to your instructor.
- **Web Research Projects.** Each chapter features several Web research projects that ask you to search the Web for information on computer-related careers, milestones in computer history, important people and companies, emerging technologies, and the applications and implications of different technologies.

chapter

five
using system software:
the operating system, utility programs, and file management

objectives

After reading this chapter, you should be able to answer the following questions:

resources

Active Helpdesk

Sound Bytes

Companion Website

The Companion Website includes a variety of additional materials to help you review and learn more about the topics in this chapter. Go to: *pearsonhighered.com/techinaction*

how cool is *this?*

Have you ever wanted to capture what appears on your **desktop**? You can use the PrtScr (print screen) key on your keyboard, but that captures the entire screen, and only onto the clipboard. You then need to crop and save the file for that **screen capture** to be useful. There are also screen capture software programs that you can purchase. However, Windows Vista and Windows 7 include a **Snipping Tool** to capture an entire screen image, or to take a freeform or rectangular "snip" of any window or object on the screen. Once snipped, you can **annotate**, save, or **share** the object. You can find the Snipping Tool by clicking the Start button, selecting All Programs, and then opening the Accessories folder. **Jing** (**jingproject.com**), a freeware tool from TechSmith, not only captures still screen shots, but also records video of on-screen action. You can share Jing files over the Web, or via instant messaging or e-mail.

System Software Basics

As you learned in the last chapter, there are two basic types of software on your computer: application software and system software. **Application software** is the software you use to do everyday tasks at home and at work. **System software** is the set of programs that help run the computer and coordinate instructions between application software and the computer's hardware devices. From the moment you turn on your computer to the time you shut it down, you are interacting with system software. System software consists of two primary types of programs: the operating system and utility programs.

What does an operating system do? The **operating system (OS)** is a group of programs that controls how your computer system functions. The OS manages the computer's hardware, including the processor (also called the central processing unit, or CPU), memory, and storage devices, as well as peripheral devices such as the monitor and printer. The OS also provides a consistent means for software applications to work with the CPU, and is responsible for the management, scheduling, and coordination of tasks as well as system maintenance. Your first interaction with the OS is the user interface—the features of the program that allow the user to communicate with the computer system.

System software also includes utility programs. A **utility program** is a small program that performs many of the general housekeeping tasks for the computer, such as system maintenance and file compression.

Do all computers have operating systems? Every computer, from the smallest notebook to the largest supercomputer, has an operating system. Even cell phones, game consoles, and some appliances have operating systems. The role of the OS is critical; the computer cannot operate without it. As explained more fully in the section of this chapter titled "What the Operating System Does," the operating system coordinates the flow of data and information through the computer system by coordinating the hardware, software, user interface, processor, and system memory.

"Every computer has an operating system."

Are all operating systems alike? Although most computer users can name only a few operating systems, many types exist. Some operating systems, such as those found in household appliances and car engines, don't require any user intervention at all. Some are proprietary systems developed specifically for the devices they manage. Some operating systems are available for personal and business use, and other operating systems coordinate resources for many users on a network. These operating systems were traditionally classified into categories, depending on the number of users they served (single user or multiple user) and the tasks they performed (single task or multitask). However, as devices begin to converge in their functionalities, and the operating systems continue to become more powerful, the distinction in the traditional categorization of operating systems begins to blur (see Figure 5.1).

For example, personal computers were at one time run by single-task, single-user operating systems such as the **Microsoft Disk Operating System (MS-DOS).** MS-DOS (or DOS) was the first widely installed operating system in personal computers. Compared to the operating systems we are familiar with today, DOS was a highly user-unfriendly OS. To use it, you needed to type specific commands, and didn't have the option to click on icons or choose from menus.

Eventually, single-user, multitasking operating systems, such as Apple's Mac OS and the Microsoft Windows operating systems, replaced DOS. These systems enabled the computer user to multitask (perform two or more tasks simultaneously). Then, networking capabilities were added to these personal computer operating systems to facilitate sharing peripheral devices and Internet access among multiple computers at home. These systems, while still traditionally used as single-user, multitask operating systems, technically became multiuser, multitask operating systems. Similar transitions are happening with mobile devices, as cell phones and PDAs converge and incorporate the functionalities of cameras and personal media players. Although these were initially single-task devices with combined functionalities, the newer devices are beginning to add multitasking capabilities.

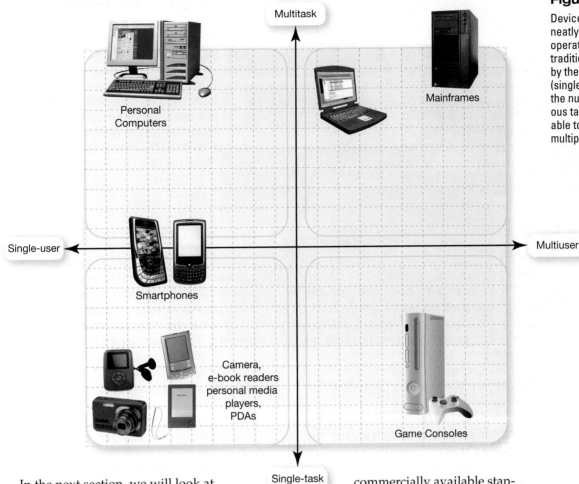

Figure 5.1
Devices no longer fit neatly into categories of operating systems, which traditionally were defined by the number of users (single or multiple) and the number of simultaneous tasks the device was able to perform (single or multiple).

In the next section, we will look at different types of operating systems that work with a variety of computers.

Types of Operating Systems

Operating systems can be categorized by the type of device in which they are installed, such as robots and specialized equipment, mainframes and network computers, mobile devices, and personal computers.

Real-Time Operating Systems

Why do machines with built-in computers need an operating system? Machinery that is required to perform a repetitive series of specific tasks in an exact amount of time requires a **real-time operating system (RTOS)**. Real-time operating systems require minimal user interaction. The programs are written specifically for the needs of the devices and their functions. Therefore, there are no commercially available standard RTOS software programs.

This type of operating system is a program with a specific purpose, and it must guarantee certain response times for particular computing tasks; otherwise, the machine is useless. Devices that must perform regimented tasks or record precise results—such as measurement instruments found in the scientific, defense, and aerospace industries—require real-time operating systems. Examples include digital storage oscilloscopes and the Mars Reconnaissance Orbiter.

Where else are RTOSs in use today? You also encounter real-time operating systems in everyday life. They are in devices such as fuel-injection systems in car engines, inkjet printers, VoIP phones, and some medical devices (see Figure 5.2). Real-time operating systems are also found in many types of robotic equipment. Television stations use robotic cameras with real-time operating systems that glide across a suspended cable system to record sports events from many angles.

Figure 5.2

Devices such as some cars, radiography devices, VoIP phones, and inkjet printers use real-time operating systems.

Operating Systems for Networks, Servers, and Mainframes

What kind of operating system do networks use? A **multiuser operating system** (also known as a **network operating system**) enables more than one user to access the computer system at one time by efficiently handling and prioritizing requests from multiple users. Networks (groups of computers connected to each other for the purposes of communicating and sharing resources) require a multiuser operating system because many users simultaneously access the **server**, which is the computer on a network that manages network resources such as printers.

The latest versions of Microsoft Windows and Mac OS X can be considered network operating systems, and enable users to set up networks in the home and for small businesses. (A more complete discussion of Microsoft Windows and Mac OS can be found in the "Operating Systems for Personal Computers" section.) In larger networks, a network operating system is installed on the server and manages all user requests, ensuring they do not interfere with each other. For example, on a network where users share a printer, the printer can produce only one document at a time. The OS is therefore responsible for managing all the printer requests and making sure they are processed

one at a time. Examples of network operating systems include Linux and UNIX.

What is UNIX? UNIX is a multiuser, multitask operating system used as a network operating system, primarily with mainframes, although it is also often found on PCs. Developed in 1969 by Ken Thompson and Dennis Ritchie of AT&T's Bell Labs, the UNIX code was initially not proprietary—in other words, no company owned it. Rather, any programmer was allowed to use the code and modify it to meet his or her needs. Later, AT&T licensed the UNIX source code to the Santa Cruz Operation Group. UNIX is a brand that belongs to the company The Open Group, but any vendor that meets testing requirements and pays a fee can use the UNIX name. Individual vendors then modify the UNIX code to run specifically on their hardware. HP/UX from Hewlett-Packard, Solaris from Sun, and AIX from IBM are some of the UNIX systems currently available in the marketplace.

What other kinds of computers require a multiuser operating system? Large corporations with hundreds or thousands of employees often use powerful computers known as mainframes. A **mainframe** is responsible for storing, managing, and simultaneously processing data from all users. Mainframe operating systems fall into the multiuser category. Examples include UNIX and IBM's i5/OS and z/OS.

Supercomputers also use multiuser operating systems. Scientists and engineers use supercomputers to solve complex problems or to perform massive computations. Some supercomputers are single computers with multiple processors, whereas others consist of multiple computers that work together.

Operating Systems for Mobile Devices

What kind of operating system controls a PDA or simple cell phone? A computer on which one user is performing just one task at a time requires a **single-user, single-task operating system**. In the days when cell phones and PDAs (personal digital assistants) were separate, single-function devices, they only required operating systems that could perform one task at a time. Cell phones had their own proprietary embedded operating systems, and PDAs were powered by operating systems such as Palm OS and Windows Mobile (see Figure 5.3). These operating systems were designed to look similar to desktop operating systems and included basic applications for personal information management, such as calendars, contact lists, and note pads. Microsoft's Windows Mobile also bundled application software, including versions of Word, Excel, PowerPoint, Outlook, Internet Explorer, and Windows Media Player. When PDAs began to include cell phone functionality (and became known as smartphones), these operating systems were expanded to have modest multitasking capabilities, so users can handle a phone call while accessing the calendar or contacts at the same time.

What kind of operating system do smartphones use? When cell phones and PDAs first came out, they were single-task devices. However, over the past several years, a convergence between the two devices has created the smartphone. A **smartphone** does more than let the user make and answer phone calls. It also has productivity features traditionally found on PDAs, in addition to features found on personal media players and cameras. The most current smartphones have the ability to connect to the Web. Examples of smartphones include BlackBerry devices and the iPhone. Initially, although multifunctional, smartphones were still primarily single-task devices and only capable of doing one task at a time. Now, most modern smartphones

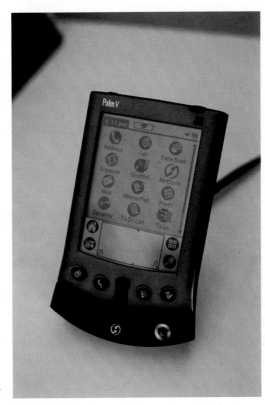

Figure 5.3

Some PDAs, like this older Palm V, used the Palm OS operating system, with which one user could perform only one task at a time. The OS was designed to look similar to that of a traditional desktop operating system.

have modest multitasking capabilities. The most common operating systems that can be found on smartphones include the Symbian OS, RIM's BlackBerry operating system, Windows Mobile, and the iPhone OS. Google's Android and Palm's webOS are the newest entries into this expanding market. The newest version of the iPhone and the Palm Pre have more multitasking capabilities, which let the user run more than one application concurrently.

Do gaming consoles and personal media players require an operating system? Gaming systems, like Microsoft's Xbox 360, the Nintendo Wii, and the Sony PlayStation, as well as personal media players like Microsoft's Zune, Apple's iPod, and SanDisk's Sansa, all require some form of customized system software that is developed specifically for the particular device. The system software includes system programs—also known as **firmware**—that control the device, as well as other programs that come with the personal media player or the gaming device. For example, the programs included with most portable media players allow users to manage music files on the player and to rip audio CDs. The operating systems on gaming consoles support Web browsing and file storage of media and photos as well as playing DVDs and games.

Operating Systems for Personal Computers

What type of operating system controls my personal computer?

Because personal computers—desktops, notebooks, and even tablet PCs—can handle only one person working on them at a time but can perform a variety of tasks simultaneously, one might think that they would use a **single-user, multitask operating system**. Indeed, the early versions of the Microsoft Windows and Macintosh operating systems were single-user, multitask operating systems. However, the newer versions, such as Mac OS X Snow Leopard and Windows 7, have networking capabilities, so technically they are considered multiuser operating systems.

Does it matter what operating system is on my computer? The type of processor in the computer determines which operating system a particular desktop computer uses. The combination of operating system and processor is referred to as a computer's **platform**. For example, Microsoft Windows operating systems are designed to coordinate with a series of processors from Intel Corporation and Advanced Micro Devices (AMD) that share the same or similar sets of instructions. Until a few years ago, Apple Macintosh operating systems worked primarily with processors from the Motorola Corporation and IBM that were designed specifically for Apple computers. Now Intel also makes processors for Apple computers.

Yet the two operating systems (Windows and Mac OS) are not interchangeable, even if both machines have Intel processors. If you attempted to load a Windows OS on a Mac computer, for example, the processor in the Mac would not understand the Windows operating system and would not function properly. Most application software is also platform dependent. For example, there are special Mac versions of Microsoft Office, Adobe Photoshop Elements, Intuit Quicken, and other "traditional" PC software applications.

Despite their inability to run the same software applications as PCs, Mac computers can be networked with PCs. Mac OS X Snow Leopard provides a variety of features and technologies that enable Macs and PCs running Windows to work seamlessly together. A utility called Boot Camp, available with OS X Snow Leopard, allows you to run Windows on a Mac while also running OS X. In addition, Macs and PCs can easily share files and even peripherals, such as printers, scanners, and cameras.

SOUND BYTE Customizing Windows

In this Sound Byte, you'll find out how to customize your desktop. You'll learn how to configure the desktop, set up a screen saver, change pointer options, customize the Start menu, and manage user accounts.

Microsoft Windows

What is the Microsoft Windows operating system? Microsoft Windows began as an operating environment that worked with MS-DOS and incorporated a graphical user interface like the one that was first introduced with the Mac OS. In 1995, Microsoft released Windows 95, a comprehensive update that made changes to the user interface and incorporated multitasking capabilities. Windows XP was the next major update; it provided networking capabilities in its consumer editions. The new **Windows 7** operating system builds upon the security and user interface upgrades that the Windows Vista release provided, and gives users with touch-screen monitors the ability to use touch commands to scroll, resize windows, pan, and zoom. What was once only a single-user, single-task operating system is now a powerful multiuser, multitask operating system. Over time, Windows improvements have concentrated on increasing user functionality and friendliness, improving Internet capabilities, and enhancing file privacy and security.

What is the difference between the various editions of Windows 7 operating systems? With each new version of its operating system, Microsoft continues to make improvements. However, it's still not a "one size fits all" operating system. Windows 7, the newest version, comes in a number of editions to accommodate different users: home users (Starter, Home Basic, Home Premium), business users (Professional and Enterprise), and combination users (Ultimate). Figure 5.4 outlines the features and benefits of each edition of Windows 7.

Mac OS

What is the Mac Operating System? In 1984, **Mac OS** became the first commercially available operating system to incorporate a graphical user interface (GUI) with user-friendly point-and-click technology into an affordable computer. Mac OS X Snow Leopard, the most recent version of the OS, is based on the UNIX operating system. Macs have long been recognized for their superior graphics display and processing capabilities. Users also attest to Mac's greater system reliability and superior file backup utilities. Despite these advantages, fewer software applications are available for the Mac platform than for Windows, and Mac systems tend to be more expensive than Windows-based PCs. For more information on Mac OS X, see the Technology in Focus feature "Computing Alternatives" on page 252.

How do the Mac and Windows operating systems compare?
Although the Apple Mac OS and the Windows operating system are not compatible, they are extremely similar in terms of functionality.

Both Windows and Mac operating systems have similar window-like work areas on the desktop that house individual applications and support users working in more than one application at a time. They both also have a streamlined user interface. Macs feature a Dock for the most commonly used programs and a Dashboard with widgets (a **widget** is a mini-application). These features enable quick access to frequently used tools and activities (such as stock prices, to-do lists, and games). The latest version of Windows has followed suit with a revised taskbar that has Dock-like capabilities and *gadgets* that provide functionality similar to that of the Mac widgets (see Figure 5.5). Despite their similarities, there are many subtle and not-so-subtle dif-

Figure 5.4 | WINDOWS 7 EDITIONS

Edition	Description
Windows 7 Starter	This edition is designed to run on small netbooks, and is for those users who have basic computing requirements. The user is limited to running three applications concurrently.
Windows 7 Home Basic	This edition is for users in emerging markets. It is not being distributed in the United States and Canada.
Windows 7 Home Premium	This edition incorporates multimedia functions as core components. No extra software is needed to run DVDs, and other audio and video files. Networking as well as file and peripheral sharing across PCs are included.
Windows 7 Professional	As its name implies, this edition is aimed at the business market, but is also appropriate for the advanced home user. This edition builds on Windows 7 Home Premium and features advanced networking capabilities.
Windows 7 Enterprise	This edition is geared to the large enterprise user and is available only through volume licensing.
Windows 7 Ultimate	This is the "ultimate" operating system for high-end PC users, gamers, multimedia professionals, and PC enthusiasts.

ferences that have created loyal fans for each operating system.

Linux

What is Linux? Linux is an open source operating system designed for use on personal computers and as a network operating system. Open source software is freely available for developers to use or modify as they wish. The Linux operating system is based on the central programming code of an operating system, and the rest of the code is from the GNU (pronounced

Figure 5.5

Although not compatible with each other, the Windows OS and the Mac OS have many similar features.

Widgets (Mac)/
Gadgets (Windows)

Files

Icons

Windows

Access to applications

Emerging Technologies: Open Source Software— Why Isn't Everyone Using Linux?

Proprietary software such as Microsoft Windows and Mac OS is developed by corporations and sold for profit. This means that the **source code**, the actual lines of instructional code that make the program work, is not accessible to the general public. Without being able to access the source code, it's difficult for a user to modify the software or see exactly how the program author constructed various parts of the system.

Restricting access to the source code protects companies from having their programming ideas stolen, and prevents customers from using modified versions of the software. However, in the late 1980s, computer specialists became concerned that large software companies (such as Microsoft) were controlling a large portion of market share and driving out competitors. They also felt that proprietary software was too expensive and contained too many bugs (errors).

These people felt that software should be developed without a profit motive and distributed with its source code free for all to see. The theory was that if many computer specialists examined, improved, and changed the source code, a more full-featured, bug-free product would result. Hence, the open source movement was born.

Open source software is freely distributed (no royalties accrue to the creators), contains the source code, and can in turn be redistributed freely to others. Most open source products are created by teams of programmers and are modified (updated) by hundreds of other programmers around the world. You can download open source products for free from the Internet. Linux is probably the most widely recognized name in open source software, but other products such as MySQL (a database program) and OpenOffice.org (a suite of productivity applications) are also gaining in popularity.

So, if an operating system such as Linux is free, why does Windows (which users must pay for) have such a huge market share (nearly 90 percent), and why does Linux have less than 1 percent of the desktop

market? One reason is that corporations and individuals have grown accustomed to one thing that proprietary software makers can provide: technical support. It is almost impossible to provide technical support for open source software because anyone can freely modify it; thus, there is no specific developer to take responsibility for technical support (see Figure 5.6). Similarly, corporations have been reluctant to install open source software extensively because of the cost of the internal staff of programmers that must support it.

Companies such as Red Hat have been combating this problem. Red Hat offers a free, open source operating system called Fedora. In addition, Red Hat has modified the original Linux source code and markets a version, Red Hat Enterprise Linux, as a proprietary program. Fedora is the testing ground for what eventually goes into this proprietary program. Red Hat Enterprise Linux 5 is the current system on the market, and comes in versions for servers and desktops. Purchasers of Red Hat Enterprise Linux receive a warranty and technical support. Packaging open source software in this manner has made its use much more attractive to businesses. As a result, many Web servers are hosted on computers running Linux.

When will free versions of Linux (or another open source operating system) be the dominant OSs on home computers? The answer is, maybe never. Most casual computer users won't feel comfortable without technical support; therefore, any open source products for home use will need to be marketed the way Red Hat markets Enterprise Linux. In addition, many open source products are not easy to maintain.

However, some companies are making easy-to-use visual interfaces, such as GNOME and KDE, which work with the Linux operating system. If one of these companies can develop an easy-to-use product and has the marketing power to challenge Microsoft, you may see more open source OSs deployed in the home computer market in the future.

Figure 5.6

Companies like Ubuntu and Xandros provide free (or low-cost) Linux software, but users must purchase technical support.

"g-noo") Project and other sources. Linux began in 1991 as a part-time project of Finnish university student Linus Torvalds, who wanted to create a free OS to run on his home computer. He posted his OS code to the Web for others to use and modify. It has since been tweaked by scores of programmers as part of the Free Software Foundation GNU Project (**gnu.org**).

Linux is gaining a reputation as a stable OS that is not subject to crashes or failures.

Because the code is open and available to anyone, Linux can be tweaked quickly to meet virtually any new operating system need. For example, when the Palm PDA emerged, the Linux OS was promptly modified to run on this new device. Similarly, only a few weeks were necessary to get the Linux OS ready for the Intel Xeon processor, a feat unheard of in proprietary OS development. Some Linux-based operating systems have been modified to run on iPods and gaming systems. Linux is also gaining popularity among computer manufacturers, which have begun to ship it with some of their latest PCs. Android, the new operating system developed by Google, is Linux-based. Because the overall size of Android is much smaller than that of Windows, many netbook users choose to use it in place of the factory-installed Windows operating system.

Where can I get Linux? You can download open source versions of Linux for free from the Internet. These free, open source Linux distributors include Mandriva, Ubuntu, Fedora, Suse, Debian GNU/Linux, and Gentoo Linux. However, several versions of Linux are more proprietary in nature and must be purchased. These versions come with support and other features that are not generally associated with the open source Linux. Red Hat has been packaging and selling versions of Linux since 1994 and is probably the best-known Linux distributor. For a full listing and explanation of all Linux distributors,

visit Distrowatch (**distrowatch.com**). For more information on Linux, see the Technology in Focus feature "Computing Alternatives" on page 252.

What the Operating System Does

As shown in Figure 5.7, the operating system is like a traffic cop. It coordinates the flow of data and information through the computer system. In doing so, the OS performs several specific functions:

- It provides a way for the user to interact with the computer.
- It manages the processor, or CPU.
- It manages the memory and storage.
- It manages the computer system's hardware and peripheral devices.
- It provides a consistent means for software applications to work with the CPU.

In this section, we look at each of these functions in detail.

Manages computer hardware and peripherals devices

Provides user interface

The Operating System

Manages memory and storage

Manages processor

Provides a consistent interaction between applications and CPU

Figure 5.7

The operating system is the traffic cop of your computer, coordinating its many activities and devices.

A Web-Based Operating System

Now that broadband Internet access is becoming commonplace, the concept of a more universal operating system, called a *Web-based OS*, is being discussed and some prototype sites are in their infancy. So what is a Web-based operating system? Actually, the terms *Web-based operating environment* or *portable desktop* might be more accurate. The concept behind this movement is to make the Web the primary application interface through which users can view content, manage data, and use various services (calendars, e-mail, and picture sharing and storage) on their local machine and on the Web without noticing any difference between interfaces.

Currently, most applications we use have been installed on a specific computer and can be used only on that computer. A Web-based operating environment would allow users access to applications and content via the Web, regardless of the machine they are using. This means business travelers would not need to lug their notebooks everywhere they went. Instead, they would only need to find a computer that had Internet access to be able to work on documents, see their calendar, read their e-mail, and so on. All of their settings and preferences (even a customized desktop image), as well as working documents, could be stored in an individual Web-based account for them to access anywhere and on any machine at any time. Google is the closest to having a complete Web-based system. Its Google Docs application and Chrome browser are the initial components of a completely Web-based operating environment, which is expected to come out by 2011. Because security measures have not been completely worked out, it's advisable that Web-based accounts not be used to store or manipulate personal or proprietary data and information. For more information, or to open your own account, check out the Web sites of the current Web-based OS innovators, including Google, eyeOS (**eyeos.org**), and GoGUI (**gogui.com**).

The User Interface

How does the operating system control how I interact with my computer? The operating system provides a **user interface** that enables you to interact with the computer. As noted earlier, the first

personal computers had a DOS operating system with a command-driven interface, as shown in Figure 5.8. A **command-driven interface** is one in which you enter commands to communicate with the computer system. The DOS commands were not always easy to understand; as a result, the interface proved to be too complicated for the average user. Therefore, PCs were used primarily in business and by professional computer operators.

The command-driven interface was later improved by incorporating a menu-driven interface, as shown in Figure 5.8. A **menu-driven interface** is one in which you choose commands from menus displayed on the screen. Menu-driven interfaces eliminated the need for users to know every command because they could select most of the commonly used commands from a menu. However, they were still not easy enough for most people to use.

What kind of interface do operating systems use today?

Current personal computer operating systems such as Microsoft Windows and Mac OS use a **graphical user interface**, or **GUI** (pronounced "gooey"). Unlike the command- and menu-driven interfaces used earlier, GUIs display graphics and use the point-and-click technology of the mouse and cursor, making them much more user-friendly. As illustrated in Figure 5.9, a GUI uses **windows** (rectangular boxes that contain programs displayed on the screen), **menus** (lists of commands that appear on the screen), and **icons** (pictures that represent an object such as a software application or a file or folder).

Unlike Windows or Mac OS, Linux does not have a single default GUI interface. Instead, users are free to choose among many commercially available and free interfaces, such as GNOME and KDE, each of which provides a different look and feel. For example, GNOME (pronounced "gah-NOHM")

Figure 5.8

(a) A command-driven interface. (b) A menu-driven interface.

actually allows you to select which desktop appearance (Windows or Mac) you'd like your system to have. This means that if you're using Linux for the first time, you don't have to learn a new interface; you just use the one you're most comfortable with already.

Processor Management

Why does the operating system need to manage the processor? When you use your computer, you are usually asking the CPU to perform several tasks at once. For example, you might be printing a Word document, waiting for a file to download from the Internet, listening to a CD on your CD drive, and working on a PowerPoint presentation—all at the same time, or at least what appears to be at the same time. Although the processor is the powerful brain of the computer, processing all of its instructions and performing all of its calculations, it needs the OS to arrange for the execution of all these activities in a systematic way, creating the appearance that everything is happening simultaneously.

To do so, the operating system assigns a slice of its time to each activity that requires the processor's attention. The OS must then switch among different processes thousands of times a second to make it appear that everything is happening seamlessly. Otherwise, you wouldn't be able to listen to a CD and print at the same time without experiencing delays in the process. When the OS allows you to perform more than one task at a time, it is said to be **multitasking**.

How exactly does the operating system coordinate all the activities? When you create and print a document in Word while also listening to a CD, for example, many different devices in the computer system are involved, including your keyboard, mouse, CD drive, and printer. Every keystroke, every mouse click, and each signal to the printer and from the CD drive creates an action, or **event**, in the respective device (keyboard, mouse, CD drive, or printer) to which the operating system responds.

Sometimes these events occur sequentially (such as when you type characters one at a time), but other events involve two or more devices working concurrently (such as the printer printing while you continue to type and listen to a CD). Although it looks as though the keyboard, CD drive, and printer are working at the same time, in fact, the OS switches back and forth among processes, controlling the timing of events the processor works on.

For example, assume you are typing and want to print a document. When you tell your computer to print your document, the printer generates a unique signal called an **interrupt** that tells the operating system that it is in need of immediate attention. Every device has its own type of interrupt, which is associated with an **interrupt handler**, a special numerical code that prioritizes the requests. These requests are placed in the interrupt table in the computer's primary memory (random access memory, or RAM). The operating system processes the task assigned a higher priority before processing a task that has been assigned a lower priority. This is called **preemptive multitasking**.

In our example, when it receives the interrupt from the printer, the operating system pauses the CPU from its typing activity and from the CD activity, and puts a "memo" in a special location in RAM called a *stack*. The memo is a reminder of what the CPU was doing before it started to work on the printer request. The CPU then retrieves the printer request from the interrupt table and begins to process it. On completion of the printer request, the CPU

Windows

Menu

Icons

Gadgets

Figure 5.9

Today's operating systems coordinate a user's experience through a graphical user interface.

Ethics: Sugar—The Sweet OS for Every Child

The Internet is a fantastic tool, but only if you can access it. In an effort to give children in developing countries a better opportunity to "learn, share, and create," the One Laptop per Child (OLPC) initiative was founded by Nicholas Negroponte and other faculty from MIT Media Lab, in conjunction with partners such as Google, AMD, and News Corporation. The mission of OLPC (**laptop.org**) is to ensure that all school-age children in lesser-developed communities receive their own personal computers so that they are no longer excluded from the educational, economic, and entertainment benefits that computers can provide. Laptops have been distributed to children in areas and countries such as the South Pacific, Uruguay, Mongolia, Nigeria, Ethiopia, and Rwanda.

This ambitious project to develop and distribute a low-cost notebook computer (currently, the cost is $199) would provide access to electronic textbooks and other learning aids—and eventually the Internet. The project has expanded to include a wide variety of professionals from academia, business, the arts, and technology. The main thrust of the project is to overcome the so-called digital divide (the gap between people who have access to computers and those who don't) and provide computing resources to everyone regardless of their financial means.

Figure 5.10

The revolutionary design of the XO-1 notebook is rugged yet child-friendly. The XO-1 can be easily converted from a traditional notebook to an e-book. It is extremely power-efficient but can also be self-powered.

The notebook itself is revolutionary in design (see Figure 5.10). Called the XO-1, the notebook is small and has a comfortable, child-sized, built-in handle. It also has a tablet-like monitor that can twist to turn the notebook into an electronic book (e-book) reader, which is critical in areas where books are hard to come by. The outside of the notebook is rugged and child-friendly. In addition, it is power efficient, running on less than one-tenth the power a standard notebook requires. Because access to electricity is minimal in many of the project's target areas, the notebook is self-powered by an easy-to-use pull-string.

At the core of the project is Sugar, the operating system. It is based on open source code components from Red Hat's Fedora Core 6 version of the Linux operating system, but has a user interface that is completely different from Windows, Mac OS, or Linux. Credit goes to the developers, who really thought about how the users of the notebook would interact with the device. The OLPC notebooks will most likely be the first computer that many of these children use. Because children have no idea of what to do with the machine and may not have anyone to tell them, the user interface was designed to be as intuitive as possible.

The operating system focuses on activities rather than applications. When the machine powers up, the first image is that of the XO man (an O on top of an X) in the

goes back to the stack, retrieves the memo it placed about the keystroke or CD activity, and returns to that task until it is interrupted again.

What happens if there is more than one document waiting to be printed? The operating system also coordinates multiple activities for peripheral devices such as printers. When the processor receives a request to send information to the printer, it first checks with the operating system to ensure that the printer is not already in use. If it is, the OS puts the request in another temporary storage area in RAM, called the *buffer*. The request then waits in the buffer until the **spooler**, a program that helps coordinate all print jobs currently being sent to the printer, indicates the printer is available. If more than one print job is waiting, a line (or *queue*) is formed so that the printer can process the requests in order.

Memory and Storage Management

Why does the operating system have to manage the computer's memory? As the operating system coordinates the activities of the processor, it uses RAM as a temporary storage area for instructions and data the processor needs. The processor then accesses these instructions and data from RAM when it is ready to process them. The middle of a circle. It is surrounded by icons that represent home, friends, and neighborhood. The computer includes a built-in microphone and webcam for children to create their own multimedia. For example, the multimedia tool allows children to add music to their drawings. Other activities include browsing the Internet, chatting, text editing, and playing games. At the core of each activity is the ability to collaborate, which facilitates the community learning experience. To enhance collaboration, the notebooks are all interconnected in a wireless mesh network, providing the potential for every activity to be a networked activity. Browsing, for example, would no longer be an isolated, individual activity; it could also be a collaborative group experience (see Figure 5.11). Wireless capabilities also help extend the community beyond its physical borders. These computers make it possible for a child in Africa, for example, to connect with another child in Europe.

In addition, the operating system uses a journaling technique for file management (see Figure 5.11). The file system records what the child has done (rather than just what the student has saved), working as a scrapbook of the student's interactions with the computer as well as with peers. The journal can be tagged, searched, and sorted in a variety of ways.

Another general concept behind the operating system is that children learn through doing, so the software puts an emphasis on tools for exploration and expression, as well as encouraging students to learn by helping each other. Because Sugar is built on an open source platform, it also encourages students to explore how it works and to modify the code to meet their individual preferences.

The OLPC is not the only organization interested in increasing the reach of technology to those in less-developed nations. Intel has gone forward with its own program and produced the Classmate PC. Although the Classmate PC is more closely aligned with the traditional Windows-based PC model—it runs on either Windows or the open source OS Mandriva Discovery 2007 (a version of Linux)—it offers some of the same user-friendly hardware features as the XO-1 machine does. Some reviewers and

Figure 5.11

(a) One student shares a browsing experience with several others. (b) The journaling file management system chronicles what the student saves as well as the student's interaction with the machine and with others.

followers of both projects have offered the opinion that the Classmate PC is better suited for the older student user, whereas the XO-1 laptop is geared toward a younger, less sophisticated user. With so many children waiting to be exposed to technology and to a more fun and intuitive learning process, there is most likely room in the market for both machines.

OS is therefore responsible for coordinating the space allocations in RAM to ensure that there is enough space for all of the pending instructions and data. It then clears the items from RAM when the processor no longer needs them.

Does the amount of RAM on a system control the type of OS I get? Until recently, the maximum amount of RAM found on most personal computers was 4 GB. That was considered a lot! Now, many personal computer systems that are reasonably priced provide for 8 GB or more of RAM. Systems that offer 4 GB or more of RAM will feature a 64-bit version of Windows. Compared to the more traditional 32-bit systems, a 64-bit

operating system provides the added responsiveness required by users who are running several applications at the same time, and are switching among them frequently. At the moment, the problem is that not all applications and devices are compatible with 64-bit systems. If you purchase a 64-bit system, you will need to make sure that all your hardware and software programs are updated to work well with the 64-bit version of your operating system. To assist you in this process, Microsoft has created the Windows 7 Upgrade Advisor. This downloadable free program checks to determine whether your computer is compatible in all respects with Windows 7, including the 64-bit compatibility.

Can my system ever run out of RAM? RAM has limited capacity. Like most users, over time you will expand how you use your computer by adding new software and new peripherals. Most computers sold for home use have between 1 and 4 GB of RAM. A system with 1 or 2 GB of RAM is usually sufficient if you're running several applications at the same time. If you're running Windows 7, however, the minimum requirement for the operating system using minimal capabilities is 1 GB of RAM. If you want to incorporate the translucent Aero user interface themes that are available in some versions of Windows 7, your system should have at least 2 GB of RAM and a video card with at least 128 MB of RAM. Systems that run Windows 7 may be challenged if they have only 1GB of RAM, especially if you run graphic-intensive programs such as Adobe Photoshop, many gaming applications, or even the latest version of Microsoft Office. As you add and upgrade software and increase your usage of the computer system, you will likely find that the amount of RAM you once found to be sufficient is no longer enough.

What happens if my computer runs out of RAM? When there isn't enough RAM for the operating system to store the required data and instructions, the operating system borrows room from the more spacious hard drive. This process of optimizing RAM storage by borrowing hard drive space is called **virtual memory**. As shown in Figure 5.12, when more RAM is needed, the operating system swaps out from RAM the data or instructions that have not been recently used and moves them to a temporary storage area on the hard drive called the **swap file** (or **page file**). If the data or instructions in the swap file are needed later,

the operating system swaps them back into active RAM and replaces them in the hard drive's swap file with less active data or instructions. This process of swapping is known as **paging**.

Can I ever run out of virtual memory? Only a portion of the hard drive is allocated to virtual memory. You can manually change this setting to increase the amount of hard drive space allocated, but eventually your computer system will become sluggish as it is forced to page more and more often. This condition of excessive paging is called **thrashing**. The solution to this problem is to increase the amount of RAM in your system so that it will not be necessary for it to send data and instructions to virtual memory.

How does the operating system manage storage? If it weren't for the operating system, the files and applications you save to the hard drive and other storage locations would be an unorganized mess. Fortunately, the OS has a file management system that keeps track of the name and location of each file you save and the programs you install. We will talk more about file management later in the chapter.

Hardware and Peripheral Device Management

How does the operating system manage the hardware and peripheral devices? Each device attached to your computer comes with a special program called a **device driver** that facilitates communication between the hardware device and the operating system. Because the OS must be able to communicate with every device in the computer system, the device driver translates the device's specialized commands into commands that the operating system can understand, and vice versa. Devices would not function without the proper device drivers because the OS would not know how to communicate with them.

Do I always need a driver? Today, most devices, such as flash drives, mice,

Figure 5.12

Virtual memory borrows excess storage capacity from the hard drive when there is not enough capacity in RAM.

Data and instructions not recently used

Data and instructions needed now

RAM

OS

Hard drive's swap file

keyboards, and many digital cameras, come with the driver already installed in Windows. The devices whose drivers are included in Windows are called Plug and Play devices. **Plug and Play (PnP)** is a software and hardware standard that Microsoft created with the Windows 95 OS. PnP is designed to facilitate the installation of new hardware in PCs by including in the OS the drivers these devices need in order to run. Because the OS includes this software, incorporating a new device into your computer system seems automatic. Plug and Play enables users to plug a new device into a port on the system unit, turn on the computer, and immediately play (use) the device. The OS automatically recognizes the device and its driver without any further user manipulations of the system.

What happens if the device is not Plug and Play? Some current devices, such as many types of printers and many older devices are not Plug and Play. When you install a non–PnP device, you will be prompted to insert the driver that was provided with the device. If you obtain a non–PnP device secondhand and do not receive the device driver, or if you are required to update the device driver, you can often download the necessary driver from the manufacturer's Web site. You can also go to Web sites such as DriverZone.com (**driverzone.com**) or Driver Guide (**driverguide.com**) to locate drivers.

Can I damage my system by installing a device driver? Occasionally, when you install a driver, your system may become unstable (that is, programs may stop responding, certain actions may cause a crash, or the device or the entire system may stop working). Although this is uncommon, it can happen. Fortunately, Windows has a Roll Back Driver feature that removes a newly installed driver, and replaces it with the last one that worked, to remedy the problem (see Figure 5.13). Roll Back Driver is found by accessing the Device Manager dialog box under System and Maintenance in the Control Panel.

Software Application Coordination

How does the operating system help application software run on the computer? Application software feeds

the CPU the instructions it needs to process data. These instructions take the form of computer code. Every computer program, no matter what its type or manufacturer, needs to interact with the CPU. For programs to work with the CPU, they must contain code that the CPU recognizes. Rather than having the same blocks of code for similar procedures in each program, the operating system includes the blocks of code—each called an **application programming interface (API)**—that application software needs in order to interact with the

Figure 5.13

The Roll Back Driver feature in Windows removes a newly installed driver and replaces it with the last one that worked.

>To access Device Manager, click the **Start** button, **Control Panel**, **Hardware** and **Sound Group**; then click the **Device Manager** link.

Locate drive in device list and click for device properties

Click to revert to previous driver

OS. Microsoft DirectX, for example, is a group of multimedia APIs built into the Windows operating system that improves graphics and sounds when you're playing games or watching video on your PC.

What are the advantages of using APIs? To create applications that can communicate with the operating system, software programmers need only refer to the API code blocks when they write an application. They don't need to include the entire code sequence in the application. APIs not only prevent redundancies in software code, but also make it easier for software developers to respond to changes in the operating system.

Large software developers such as Microsoft have many applications under their corporate umbrella and use the same APIs in all or most of their applications. Because APIs coordinate with the operating system, all applications that have incorporated these APIs have similar interface features, such as toolbars and menus. Therefore, many features of the applications have the same look. An added benefit to this system is that applications sharing these formats can easily exchange data with each other. As such, it's easy to create a chart in Microsoft Excel from data in Microsoft Access and incorporate the finished chart into a Microsoft Word document.

The Boot Process: Starting Your Computer

Although it only takes a minute or two, many things happen quickly between the time you turn on the computer and the time when it is ready for you to start using it. As you learned earlier, all data and instructions (including the operating system) are stored in RAM while your computer is on. When

you turn off your computer, RAM is wiped clean of all its data (including the OS). How does the computer know what to do when you turn it on if there is nothing in RAM? It runs through a special **boot process** (or start-up process) to load the operating system into RAM. The term *boot*, from *bootstrap loader* (a small program used to start a larger program), alludes to the straps of leather, called *bootstraps*, that men used in former times to help them pull on their boots. This is the source of the expression "pull oneself up by the bootstraps."

What are the steps involved in the boot process? As illustrated in Figure 5.14, the boot process consists of four basic steps:

1. The basic input/output system (BIOS) is activated by powering on the CPU.

2. The BIOS checks that all attached devices are in place (called a **power-on self-test** or **POST**).

3. The operating system is loaded into RAM.

4. Configuration and customization settings are checked.

How can I tell if my computer is entering the boot process? As the computer goes through the boot process in a Windows operating system, indicator lights on the keyboard and disk drives may illuminate, and the system may emit various beeps. If you have a version of Windows earlier than XP, text will scroll down the screen as well. When you boot up on a PC with Windows or on a Mac, you won't hear any beeps or see any keyboard lights illuminate, but you will most likely see the Windows or Mac OS logo display on the monitor, indicating the progress of the start-up process. Once the boot process has completed these steps, it is ready to accept commands and data. Let's look at each of these steps in more detail.

Step 1: Activating BIOS

What's the first thing that happens after I turn on my computer? In the first step of the boot process, the CPU activates the **basic input/output system (BIOS)**. BIOS (pronounced "bye-OSE") is a program that manages the exchange of data between the operating system and all the

ROM chip

CPU

STEP 1: CPU activates BIOS.

STEP 2: BIOS conducts power-on self-test.

STEP 3: BIOS loads OS to RAM.

STEP 4: Configuration and customization settings checked, and desktop displays.

Figure 5.14
The boot process.

input and output devices attached to the system, hence its name. BIOS is also responsible for loading the OS into RAM from its permanent location on the hard drive.

BIOS itself is stored on a special read-only memory (ROM) chip on the motherboard. Unlike data stored in RAM, data stored in ROM is permanent and is not erased when the power is turned off.

Step 2: Performing the Power-On Self-Test

How does the computer determine whether the hardware is working properly? The first job BIOS performs is to ensure that essential peripheral devices are attached and operational. As mentioned already, this process is called the power-on self-test, or POST. The POST consists of a test on the video card and video memory, a BIOS identification process, and a memory test to ensure that memory chips are working properly.

The BIOS compares the results of the POST with the various hardware configurations that are permanently stored in CMOS

(pronounced "see-moss"). CMOS, which stands for *complementary metal-oxide semiconductor*, is a special kind of memory that uses almost no power. A little battery provides enough power so that the CMOS contents will not be lost after the computer is turned off. CMOS contains information about the system's memory, types of disk drives, and other essential input and output hardware components. If the results of the POST compare favorably to the hardware configurations stored in CMOS, the boot process continues. If new hardware has been installed, this will cause the POST to disagree with the hardware configurations in CMOS, and you will be alerted that new hardware has been detected.

Step 3: Loading the Operating System

How does the operating system get loaded into RAM? When the previous steps are successfully completed, BIOS goes through a preconfigured list of devices in its search for the drive that contains the **system files**, which are the main files of the operating system. When it is located, the operating system loads into RAM from its permanent storage location on the hard drive.

Once the system files are loaded into RAM, the **kernel** (or **supervisor program**) is loaded. The kernel is the essential component of the operating system. It is responsible for managing the processor and all other components of the computer system. Because it stays in RAM the entire time your computer is powered on, the kernel is said to be *memory resident*. Other parts of the OS that are less critical stay on the hard drive and are copied over to RAM on an as-needed basis so that RAM is not entirely filled. These programs are referred to as *nonresident*. Once the kernel is loaded, the operating system takes over control of the computer's functions.

Step 4: Checking Further Configurations and Customizations

When are the other components and configurations of the system checked? CMOS checks the configuration of memory and essential peripherals in the beginning of the boot process. In this last phase of the boot process, the operating system checks the registry for the configuration of other system components. The **registry** contains all of the different configurations (settings) used by the OS and by other applications. It contains the customized settings you put into place, such as mouse speed and the display settings for your monitor and desktop, as well as instructions as to which programs should be loaded first.

Figure 5.15

If there is an error in the boot process, your system might boot into Safe mode. Safe mode offers functionality that is limited but sufficient to allow you to perform diagnostic testing.

Why do I sometimes need to enter a login name and password at the end of the boot process? In a networked environment, such as that found at most colleges, the operating system serves many users. To determine whether a user is authorized to use the system (for example, whether a user is a valid student or college employee), authorized users are given a login name and password. The verification of your login name and password is called **authentication**. The authentication process blocks unauthorized users from entering the system.

On your home computer, you also may need to input a password to log in to your user account on your computer after your computer has completely booted up. Even in a home environment, all users with access to a Windows computer (such as family members or roommates) can have their own user accounts. Users can set up a password to protect their account from being accessed by another user without permission. For more information on selecting a good password, see Chapter 9.

How do I know if the boot process is successful? The entire boot process takes only a minute or two to complete. If the entire system is checked out and loaded properly, the process completes by displaying the desktop. The computer system is now ready to accept your first command.

Handling Errors in the Boot Process

What should I do if my computer doesn't boot properly? Sometimes problems occur during the boot process. Fortunately, you have several options for correcting the situation. If you have recently installed new software or hardware, try uninstalling it. (Make sure you use the Add or Remove Programs feature in the Control Panel to remove the software.) If the problem no longer occurs when rebooting, you have determined the cause of the problem and can reinstall the device or software. If the problem does not go away, the first option is to restart your computer in Safe mode.

What is Safe mode? Sometimes Windows does not boot properly, and you end up with a screen that says "Safe Mode" in the corners, as shown in Figure 5.15. (Alternatively, you can boot directly into

Safe mode by pressing the F8 key during the boot process before the Windows logo appears.) **Safe mode** is a special diagnostic mode designed for troubleshooting errors. When the system is in Safe mode, only essential devices—such as the mouse, keyboard, and monitor—function. Even the regular graphics device driver will not be activated in Safe mode. Instead, the system runs in the most basic graphics mode, eliminating any desktop images and nonessential icons and resulting in a neutral screen. While in Safe mode, you can use the **Device Manager**, a feature in the operating system that lets you view and change the properties of all devices attached to your computer. Safe mode boots Windows with only the original Microsoft Windows drivers that are required to boot the computer.

If Windows detects a problem in the boot process, it will add **Last Known Good Configuration** to the Windows Advanced Options Menu (also accessible by pressing the F8 key during the boot process). Every time your computer boots successfully, a configuration of the boot process is saved. When you choose to boot with the Last Known Good Configuration, the operating system starts your computer by using the registry information that was saved during the last shutdown. Safe mode and Last Known Good Configuration are the two most widely used methods of booting into Windows when a user cannot do so with the current configuration. Finally, if all other attempts to reboot fail, try a System Restore to roll back to a past configuration. System Restore is covered in more detail later in the chapter.

What should I do if my keyboard or another device doesn't work after I boot my computer? Sometimes during the boot process, BIOS skips a device (such as a keyboard) or improperly identifies it.

> **"Safe mode is a special diagnostic mode designed for troubleshooting errors."**

Your only indication that this sort of problem has occurred is that the device won't respond after the system has been booted. When that happens, you can generally resolve the problem by rebooting. If the problem persists, you may want to check the operating system's Web site for any patches (or software fixes) that may resolve the issue. If there are no patches or the problem persists, then you may want to get technical assistance.

The Desktop and Windows Features

The **desktop** is the first interaction you have with the operating system and the first image you see on your monitor. As its name implies, your computer's desktop puts at your fingertips all of the elements necessary for a productive work session. They are items that are typically found on or near the top of a traditional desk, such as files and folders.

What are the main features of the desktop and Start menu? The very nature of a desktop is that it lets you customize it to meet your individual needs. As such, the desktop on your computer may be different from the desktop on your friend's computer, or even from the desktop of another account user on the same computer. In recent versions of Windows, many features that were once only found on the desktop have moved to the Start menu, including access to documents, programs, and computer drives and devices. You can always create shortcuts on your desktop to these features if you find that's more convenient (see Figure 5.16).

On the desktop you'll find:

- **Recycle Bin:** Location for deleted files and folders from the C: drive only. Deleted files from other locations do not go to the Recycle Bin; instead, they are permanently deleted. Deleted files in the Recycle Bin can be recovered easily before the Recycle Bin is emptied.

- **Sidebar and Gadgets:** The **Sidebar** is a pane on the right side of the Windows desktop where you can easily organize your Gadgets. A **Gadget** is an easy-to-

ACTIVE HELP-DESK

Starting the Computer: The Boot Process

In this Active Helpdesk call, you'll play the role of a helpdesk staffer, fielding calls about how the operating system helps the computer start up.

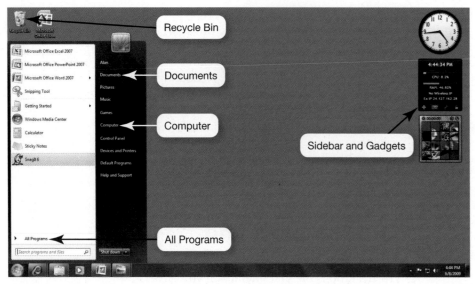

Figure 5.16

The Windows desktop puts the most commonly used features of the operating system at your fingertips.

Figure 5.17

Most windows in a graphical user interface have the same common elements.

use miniprogram that gives you information at a glance or quick access to frequently used tools including weather information, calendar items, calculators, games, photo albums, and system tools.

In the Start menu, you'll find:

- **Documents:** A convenient organizational tool that enables you to keep all your documents in one place. You can further organize your Documents folder with subfolders, similar to the way a traditional filing system is organized.
- **Computer:** Provides easy access to disk drives and system and network devices.

- **All Programs:** In the Start menu, this provides access to all programs available in the system. To prevent taking up valuable screen space, a limited number of programs displays. Use the scrollbar to gain access to programs not immediately visible. Instant Search can facilitate locating a program.

What are common features of a window? As noted earlier, one feature introduced in the graphical user interface is windows (with a lowercase w), the rectangular panes on your computer screen that display applications running on your system. Windows provide for a flexible, user-friendly, multitasking environment. Figure 5.17 illustrates some of the features of windows. They include **toolbars**, which are further organized into tabs that are displayed on the **Ribbon** (a grouping of icons collected for easy access) and **scrollbars** (bars that appear at the side or bottom of the screen that control which part of the information is displayed on the screen). Using the Minimize, Maximize and Restore, and Close buttons, you can open, close, and resize windows.

How can I see more than one window on my desktop at a time? You can easily arrange the windows on a desktop by arranging separate windows so that they sit next to each other either horizontally or vertically. You also can arrange windows by cascading them so that they overlap one another, or you can simply resize two open windows so that they appear on the screen at the same time.

Showing windows side by side or stacked on top of each other makes accessing two or more active windows more convenient. To do so, right-click the task bar and select "Show Windows Stacked" or "Show Windows

Side by Side." When you want to undo the arrangement, right-click the taskbar again and select "Undo Show Stacked" (or "Side by Side"). To bring a window back to its full size, click the Restore button in the top right corner of the window.

Windows Vista and 7 offer two more ways to navigate through open windows. To see live thumbnail images of open windows, press Alt + Tab to access Windows Flip. Pressing the Windows key + Tab initiates the Windows Flip 3D feature. You can then "flip" through open windows in a stack by using the scroll wheel on your mouse or the arrow keys on your keyboard. The open windows appear in a three-dimensional configuration as shown in Figure 5.18.

Can I move or resize the windows once they are tiled? Regardless of whether the windows are tiled, you can resize them and move them around the desktop. You can reposition windows on the desktop by using the mouse to point to the title bar at the top of the window and, while holding down the left mouse button, drag the window to a different location. To resize a window, place your mouse pointer over any side or corner of a window until it changes to a double-headed arrow [↕]. You can then left-click and drag the window to the new desired size.

Organizing Your Computer: File Management

So far you have learned that the operating system is responsible for managing the processor, memory, storage, and devices, and that it provides a mechanism whereby applications and users can interact with the computer system. An additional function of an operating system is to enable **file management**, which entails providing organizational structure to the computer's contents. The OS allows you to organize the contents of your computer in a hierarchical **directory** structure that includes files, folders, libraries, and drives. In this section, we discuss how you can use this hierarchical structure to make your computer more organized and efficient.

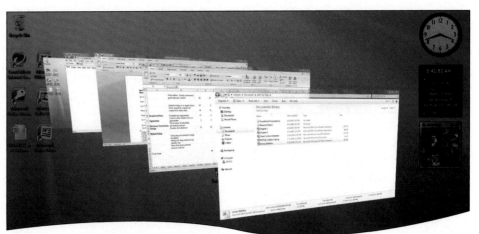

Organizing Your Files

What exactly is a file? Technically, a **file** is a collection of related pieces of information stored together for easy reference. A file in an operating system is a collection of program instructions or data that is stored and treated as a single unit. Files can be generated from an application such as a Word document or an Excel workbook. In addition, files can represent an entire

Figure 5.18
The Windows Flip 3D feature gives you the ability to move through live images of open windows.

 Upgrading Your Operating System

At some point, a new version of the operating system you are using will be released. You are then faced with the decision of whether to upgrade to the new version (such as going from Windows XP or Vista to Windows 7). Here are a few key things to consider before taking the plunge:

- **Are there significant features in the new version that will make your life easier?** If the only features the new version offers are ones you don't need, why bother upgrading?

- **Will your hardware work with the new OS?** Check the minimum operating requirements (required RAM, processor speed, hard drive space, etc.) of the new version to ensure that your computer can handle the workload of the new software. You will also need to make sure drivers for the new OS are available for all your hardware devices and peripherals to ensure they will work properly with the new OS.

- **Is your application software compatible with the new version of the OS?** Usually, application software works fine with a new version of an OS. Sometimes it doesn't. Check with the software vendors regarding compatibility.

- **Is your current operating system still supported?** When it deploys new versions of operating systems, the company may stop supporting older versions. If your version will not be supported, it's best to upgrade to a newer version.

Before starting the upgrade, you should back up all your data files. Upgrades are usually designed not to disturb data files, but upgrades do not always go smoothly. Make sure you have current backups of all your data files so you won't lose anything accidentally during the upgrading process.

application, a Web page, a set of sounds, or an image. Files are stored on the hard drive, a flash drive, or another permanent storage medium. As the number of files you save increases, it becomes more important to keep them organized in folders and libraries. A **folder** is a collection of files. Windows 7 introduces the concept of libraries. A **library** is a folder that gathers files from different locations and displays them as if they were all saved in a single folder, regardless of where they are actually physically stored.

How does the operating system organize files? Windows organizes the contents of your computer in a hierarchical structure comprising drives, folders, subfolders, and files. The hard drive, represented as the C drive, is where you permanently store most of your files. Other storage devices on your computer are also represented by letters. The A drive has traditionally been reserved for a floppy drive, which you may or may not have installed on your computer. Any additional drives (such as flash, CD, or DVD drives) found on your computer are represented by other letters (D, E, F, and so on).

How is the hard drive organized? The C drive, or hard drive, is like a large filing cabinet in which all files are stored. As such, the C drive is the top of the filing structure of the computer system and is referred to as the **root directory**. All other libraries, folders, and files are organized within the root directory. There are areas in the root directory that the operating system has filled with files and folders holding special OS files. The programs within these files help run the computer and generally

shouldn't be touched. The Windows operating system creates special folders, such as Documents, Pictures, Music, and Videos, where you may begin to store and organize your text, image, audio, and video files, respectively. However, users do not always carefully save their files in these special folders. Files are often stored all over the PC in various folders. For example, picture files may not just be stored in the Pictures folder, but might also be stored in the temporary folder, in a separate folder within the Documents folder, or even in remote storage, making finding all picture files difficult. Windows 7 tries to remedy this situation with the use of libraries. Recall, libraries gather files from different locations and display the files as if they were all saved in a single folder, regardless of where they are actually physically stored. Some libraries are created already in Windows, and Windows has defined specific folders to include in each standard library, but users can create other libraries to meet their special needs, or can modify the standard libraries, adding or deleting folders to meet their needs.

How can I easily locate and see the contents of my computer? If you use a Windows PC, **Windows Explorer** is the main tool for finding, viewing, and managing the contents of your computer. It shows the location and contents of every drive, folder, and file. As illustrated in Figure 5.19, Windows Explorer is divided into two panes, or sections.

The navigation pane on the left shows the contents of your computer in a traditional hierarchical tree structure. It displays all the drives of the system, as well as other commonly accessed areas such as the Desktop, Libraries, and Documents, Music, Pictures, and Video folders.

How should I organize my files? Creating folders is the key to organizing your files because folders keep related documents together. Again, think of your computer as a big filing cabinet that is filled with many folders. Those folders have the capacity to hold individual files, or even other folders that contain individual files. For example, you might create one folder called

Figure 5.19

Windows Explorer lets you see the contents of your computer.

>Click the **Windows Explorer** icon on the taskbar.

Navigation pane

File path

Files and folders in MGT 111

Libraries

Music folder

Opened MGT 111 folder

Classes to hold all of your class work. Inside the Classes folder, you could create folders for each of your classes (such as CIS 110, MGT 111, and HIS 112). Inside each of those folders, you could create subfolders for each class's assignments, completed homework, research, notes, and so on.

Grouping related files into folders makes it easier for you to identify and find files. Which would be easier—going to the MGT 111 folder to find a file or searching through the 143 individual files in Documents hoping to find the right one? Grouping files in a folder also allows you to move them more efficiently, so you can quickly transfer critical files needing frequent backup, for instance. Sometimes, it's not always possible to put all similar files into one folder. For example, you might have PowerPoint files stored in separate folders that correspond to each particular class. If you want to always have quick access to your PowerPoint files, you could create a PowerPoint Library and specify the folders where the PowerPoint files are located. The PowerPoint Library would then gather the PowerPoint files from the different locations and display them as if they were all saved in a single folder.

Viewing and Sorting Files and Folders

Are there different ways I can view and sort my files and folders? When you open any folder in Windows, the toolbar at the top displays a Views button. Clicking on the Views button offers you different ways to view the folders and files, which are discussed in more detail below. In some views, the folders are displayed as Live Icons, which is a feature that began in Windows Vista. Live Icons allows you to preview the actual contents of a specific file or folder without actually opening the file. Live Icons can be displayed in a variety of views.

- **Tiles view:** Displays files and folders as icons in list form. Each icon represents the application associated with the file, and also includes the file name and the file size, though the display information is customizable to include other data. The Tiles view also displays picture

Sort files and folders by clicking the headers

Figure 5.20

Details view enables you to sort and list your files in a variety of ways to enable quick access to the correct file.

dimensions, a handy feature for Web page developers.

- **Details view:** The most interactive view. Files and folders are displayed in list form, and the additional file information is displayed in columns alongside the file name. You can sort and display the contents of the folder by any of the column headings, so you can sort the contents alphabetically by file name or type, or hierarchically by date last modified or by file size (see Figure 5.20).

- **List view:** Another display of icons and file names that are even smaller than in Tiles view. This is a good view if you have a lot of content in the folder and need to see most or all of it at once.

- **Small and Medium Icons views:** These views also display files and folders as icons in list form, but the icons are either small- or medium-sized, respectively. Additional file information displays in a ScreenTip (the text that appears when you place your cursor over the file icon).

- **Large and Extra Large Icons views:** Large Icons view (see Figure 5.21) shows

Figure 5.21

The Large Icons view is an especially good way to display the contents of files and folders. The preview pane on the right enables you to see the first page of your document without first opening it.

>To access Large Icons view, from the command bar in any folder dialog box, click the **Views arrow**, and then select **Large Icons** view. To access the Preview Pane, click **Organize**, select **Layout**, and then **Preview Pane**.

Folders with live preview of contents

Preview pane allows viewing without opening file

Live preview of Excel and PowerPoint files

the contents of folders as small images. There is also Extra Large Icons view, which shows folder contents and other icons as even larger images. Large Icons and Extra Large Icons views are the best to use if your folder contains picture files, or for PowerPoint presentations, because the title slide of the presentation will display, making it easier for you to distinguish among presentations. You may use the scale feature to adjust the size of the icons further. Additionally, a preview pane is available in this view. It allows you to view the first page of the selected document without having to open it completely (see Figure 5.21).

For those folders that contain collections of MP3 files, you can download the cover of the CD or an image of the artist to display on any folder to identify that collection further.

What's the best way to search for a file? You've no doubt saved a file and forgotten where you saved it, or have downloaded a file from the Internet and then were not sure where it was saved. What's the quickest way to find a file? Looking through every file stored on your computer could take hours, even with a well-organized file management system. Fortunately, the newer

SOUND BYTE — File Management

In this Sound Byte, you'll examine the features of file management and maintenance. You'll learn the various methods of creating folders, how to turn a group of unorganized files into an organized system of folders, and how to maintain your file system.

versions of Windows include Instant Search, a search feature, found on the Start menu, which searches through your hard drive or other storage device (CD or flash drive) to locate files that match criteria you provide. Your search can be based on a part of the file name or just a word or phrase in the file. You can also narrow your search by providing information about the type of file, which application was used to create the file, or even how long ago the file was saved. (Mac OS Snow Leopard has a similar feature called Spotlight, known as Sherlock in earlier versions.) Instant Search can also find e-mails based on your criteria. Instant Search is found in Windows Explorer, too, and is used to search the contents of current folders.

Figure 5.22 | COMMON FILE NAME EXTENSIONS

Extension	Type of Document	Application
.doc	Word processing document	Microsoft Word 2003
.docx	Word processing document	Microsoft Word 2007
.wpd	Word processing document	Corel WordPerfect
.xlsx	Spreadsheet	Microsoft Excel 2007
.accdb	Database	Microsoft Access 2007
.pptx	PowerPoint presentation	Microsoft PowerPoint 2007
.pdf	Portable Document Format	Adobe Acrobat or Adobe Reader
.rtf	Text (Rich Text Format)	Any program that can read text documents
.txt	Text	Any program that can read text documents
.htm or .html	HyperText Markup Language for a Web page	Any program that can read HTML
.jpg	Joint Photographic Experts Group (JPEG) image	Most programs capable of displaying images
.gif	Graphics Interchange Format (GIF) image	Most programs capable of displaying images
.bmp	Bitmap image	Windows
.zip	Compressed file	WinZip

Select desired file format

Type file name

Change file type

Check to maintain compatibility with previous versions

Naming Files

Are there special rules I have to follow when I name files?
Files have names just like people. The first part of a file, or the **file name**, is similar to your first name, and is generally the name you assign to the file when you save it. For example, "bioreport" may be the name you assign a report you have completed for a biology class.

In a Windows application, an **extension**, or **file type**, follows the file name and a period or dot (.). Like a last name, this extension identifies what kind of family of files the file belongs to, or which application should be used to read the file. For example, if "bioreport" is a document created in Microsoft Works, it has a .wks extension and its name is "bioreport.wks." If the bioreport file is a Word 2007 document, then it has a .docx extension and its name is "bioreport.docx." Figure 5.22 lists some common file extensions and the types of documents they indicate.

Do I need to know the extension of a file to save it?
As shown in Figure 5.23, when you save a file created in most applications running under the Windows operating system, you do not need to add the extension to the file name; it is added automatically for you. Mac and Linux operating systems do not require file extensions. This is because the information as to the type of application the computer should use to open the file is stored inside the file itself. However, if you're using these operating systems and will be sending files to Windows users, you should add an extension to your file name so that Windows can more easily open your files. To ease the frustration

of users of previous versions of Office, when using any Office 2007 application, you can choose to save the file in either a 2007 format or a 2003 or earlier format.

Are there things I shouldn't do when naming my files?
Each operating system has its own naming conventions, or rules, which are listed in Figure 5.24. Beyond those conventions, it's important that you name your files so that you can easily identify them. A file name such as "research.docx" may be descriptive to you if you're only working on one research paper. However, if you create other research reports later and need to identify the contents of these files quickly, you'll soon wish

Figure 5.23

When you save a file in Microsoft Word 2007, you can first (a) select in what format you would like the file to be saved, and then (b) type the file name in the Save As dialog box.

>The Save As features are displayed by selecting the Office button and then selecting **Save As**.

Figure 5.24	FILE NAMING CONVENTIONS

	Mac OS	Windows
File and folder name length	As many as 255 characters*	As many as 255 characters
Case sensitive?	Yes	No
Forbidden characters	Colon (:)	" / \ * ? < < >	:
File extensions needed?	No	Yes
Path separator	Colon (:)	\

*Note: Although Mac OS X supports file names with as many as 255 characters, many applications running on OS X still support only file names with a maximum of 31 characters.

you had been more descriptive. Giving your files names that are more descriptive, such as bioresearch.docx or, better yet, bio101research.docx, is a good idea.

Keep in mind, however, that all files must be uniquely identified, unless they are saved in different folders or in different locations. Therefore, although files may share the same file name (such as "bioreport.docx" or "bioreport.xlsx") or share the same extension ("bioreport.xlsx" or "budget.xlsx"), no two files stored on the same device and folder can share *both* the same file name and the same extension.

How can I tell where my files are saved? When you save a file for the first time, you give the file a name and designate where you want to save it. For easy reference, the operating system includes default folders where files are saved unless you specify otherwise. In Windows, the default folders are "Documents" for files, "Downloads" for files downloaded from the Internet, "Music" for audio files, "Pictures" for graphic files, and "Videos" for video files. Although you can create your own folders, these default folders are the beginning of a well-organized system.

You can determine the location of a file by its **file path**. The file path starts with the drive in which the file is located and includes all folders, subfolders (if any), the file name, and the extension. For example, if you were saving a picture of Emily Brontë for a term paper for an English composition course, the file path might be C:\Users\Username\Documents\Spring 2010\English Comp\Term Paper\Illustrations\EBronte.jpg.

As shown in Figure 5.25, C is the drive on which the file is stored (in this case, the hard drive), and Documents is the file's primary folder. Spring 2010, English Comp, Term Paper, and Illustrations are successive subfolders within the Documents main folder. Last is the file name, EBronte, separated from the file extension (in this case, jpg) by a period. Notice that there are backslash characters (\) in between the drive, primary folder, subfolders, and file name. This backslash character, used by Windows and DOS,

ACTIVE HELP-DESK

Organizing Your Computer: File Management

In this Active Helpdesk call, you'll play the role of a helpdesk staffer, fielding calls about the desktop, windows features (such as scrollbars and the Minimize and Maximize buttons), and how the operating system helps keep the computer organized.

is referred to as a **path separator**. Mac files use a colon (:), whereas UNIX and Linux files use the forward slash (/) as the path separator.

Working with Files

How can I move and copy files? Once you've located your file with Windows Explorer, you can perform many other file-management actions such as opening, copying, moving, renaming, and deleting files. You open a file by double-clicking the file from its storage location. Based on the file extension, the operating system then determines which application needs to be started to open the requested file and opens the file within the correct application automatically. You can copy a file to another location using the Copy command. When you copy a file, a duplicate file is created and the original file remains in its original location. To move a file from one location to another, use the Move command. When you move a file, the original file is deleted from its original location.

Where do deleted files go? The **Recycle Bin** is a folder on the desktop where files deleted from the hard drive reside until you permanently purge them from your system. Unfortunately, files deleted from other drives (such as a CD/DVD drive, flash drive, external hard drive, or network drive) do not go to the Recycle Bin but are deleted from the system immediately. (Mac systems have something similar to the Recycle Bin, called Trash, which is represented by a wastebasket icon. To delete files on a Mac, drag the files to Trash on the Dock.)

Figure 5.25

Understanding file paths.

C:\Users\Username\Documents\Spring 2010\English Comp\Term Paper\Illustrations\EBronte.jpg

Drive — Primary Folder — Subfolders — File Name — Extension

How do I permanently delete files from my system? Files in the Recycle Bin or Trash are held only until they are permanently deleted. To delete your files from the Recycle Bin permanently, select Empty the Recycle Bin after right-clicking the desktop icon. On Macs, select Empty Trash from the Finder menu in OS X.

Utility Programs

You have learned that the operating system is the single most essential piece of software in your computer system because it coordinates all the system's activities and provides a means by which other software applications and users can interact with the system. However, there is another set of programs included in system software. Utility programs are small applications that perform special functions. Some utility programs help manage system resources (such as disk defragmenter utilities, or *defrag* utilities); others (such as screen savers) help make your time and work on the computer more pleasant; and still others (such as file compression utilities) improve efficiency.

Some of these utility programs are incorporated into the operating system. For example, Windows has its own firewall and file-compression utilities. Other utility programs, such as antivirus and security programs, are so large and require such frequent updating that they are sold as stand-alone programs or as Web-based services available for an annual fee. Sometimes utility programs, such as Norton SystemWorks, are offered as software suites, bundled with other useful maintenance and performance-boosting utilities. Still other utilities, like Lavasoft's Ad-Aware, are offered as freeware or shareware programs and are available as downloads from the Web.

Figure 5.27 illustrates some of the various types of utility programs available within the Windows operating system as well as those for sale as stand-alone programs. In general, the basic utilities designed to manage and tune the computer hardware are incorporated in the operating system. The stand-alone utility programs typically offer more features or an easier user interface for backup, security, diagnostic, or recovery functions.

In this section, we explore many of the utility programs you'll find installed on a

Imagine you are sending an e-mail to a diverse group of individuals. You are not sure what word processing software each of them uses, but you assume that there will be a mix of people who use Word, WordPerfect, and even Writer. How can you be sure that all users will be able to open the attachment regardless of the program installed on their computers? Save the file in Rich Text Format (.rtf), Portable Document Format (.pdf), or Text (.txt) format. Rich Text and Text files can be read by any modern word processing program, although some formatting may be lost when a document is saved in Text (.txt) format. Anyone can read a PDF file by downloading the Acrobat Reader from the Adobe Web site (**adobe.com**). To save files as RTF, PDF, or TXT files, simply change the file type when saving your file. In Microsoft Word, for example, you can select the file type in the Save As menu shown in Figure 5.26.

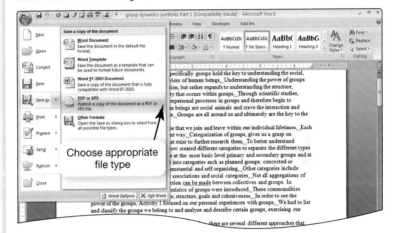

Choose appropriate file type

Figure 5.26

By changing a word processing file's type to PDF, RTF, or TXT (plain text), you can ensure that everyone can read your file, no matter which word processing program they are using.

Windows 7 operating system. Unless otherwise noted, you can find these utilities in the Control Panel or on the Start menu by selecting All Programs, Accessories, and then System Tools. (We also take a brief look at some Mac utilities.) We will discuss antivirus and personal firewall utility programs in Chapter 9.

Display Utilities

How can I change the appearance of my desktop? The Personalization icon, found in Appearance and Personalization on the Control Panel, has all the features you need to change the appearance of your desktop. It provides different options for the desktop background, screen savers, and window colors. Although Windows

Figure 5.27 | UTILITY PROGRAMS AVAILABLE WITHIN WINDOWS AND AS STAND-ALONE PROGRAMS

Windows Utility Program	Stand-Alone Windows Utility Program	Function
File Management		
Programs and Features		Properly installs and uninstalls software
Windows Explorer File Compression	WinZip	Reduces file size
Windows System Maintenance and Diagnostics		
Backup	Acronis True Image, Norton Ghost	Backs up important information
Disk Cleanup	CCleaner, McAfee Quick Clean	Removes unnecessary files from hard drive
Disk Defragmenter	Norton SystemWorks, Diskeeper	Arranges files on hard drive in sequential order
Error-checking (previously ScanDisk)		Checks hard drive for unnecessary or damaged files
System Restore	FarStone RestoreIT!, Norton Ghost	Restores system to a previous, stable state
Task Manager		Displays performance measures for processes; provides information on programs and processes running on computer
Task Scheduler		Schedules programs to run automatically at prescribed times

comes with many different background themes and screen saver options preinstalled, hundreds of downloadable options are available on the Web. Just search for "backgrounds" or "screen savers" on your favorite search engine to customize your desktop. Another way to access the background and screen saver options is to right-click an empty space on your desktop and choose Personalize from the shortcut menu.

Do I really need to use a screen saver? A **screen saver** is an animated image that appears on a computer monitor when no user activity has been sensed for a certain time. Originally, screen savers were used to prevent burn-in, the result of an image being burned into the phosphor inside the monitor's cathode ray tube when the same image was left on the monitor for long periods of time. Screen savers are now used almost exclusively for decoration.

You can control how long your computer sits idle before the screen saver starts. For example, if you don't want people looking at what's on your screen when you leave your computer unexpectedly for a time, you may want to program your screen saver to run after only a minute or two of inactivity. (Right-click on the Windows desktop, click Personalize, and then click Screen Saver on

BITS AND BYTES

Need to Recover a Deleted File?

Should you move a file to the Recycle Bin in error, you can immediately restore the deleted file by clicking Restore all Items from the Task pane in the Recycle Bin dialog box. Once you empty the Recycle Bin, getting the file back is difficult, but perhaps not impossible.

Because you don't see the file name anymore, it looks as if the file has been erased from the hard drive. However, only the reference to the deleted file is deleted permanently, so the operating system has no easy way to find the file. The file data actually remains on the hard drive until otherwise written over. For those files that have been deleted for a while, you can use a program such as FarStone's RestoreIT! or Norton Ghost. However, the longer you wait to recover a deleted file, the smaller your chances of a full recovery, because the probability increases that your file has been overwritten by other data.

SOUND BYTE

File Compression

In this Sound Byte, you'll learn about the advantages of file compression and how to use Windows to compress and decompress files. This Sound Byte also teaches you how to find and install file compression shareware programs.

the bottom right of the personalization window.) However, if you find that you tend to let your computer sit inactive for a while but need to look at the screen image—while you study or read a document or spreadsheet, for example—you may want to extend the period of inactivity.

The Programs and Features Utility

What is the correct way to add new programs to the system? These days, when you install a new program, the program automatically runs a wizard (a step-by-step guide) that walks you through the installation process. If a wizard does not start automatically, you should go to the Programs and Features utility found in the Programs folder in the Control Panel. This prompts the operating system to look for the setup program of the new software and starts the installation wizard.

What is the correct way to remove unwanted programs from my system? Some people think that deleting a program from the Program Files folder on the C drive is the best way to remove a program from the system. However, most programs include support files such as a help file, dictionaries, and graphics files that are not located in the main program folder found in Program Files. Depending on the supporting file's function, support files can be scattered throughout various folders within the system. You would normally miss these files by deleting only the main program file from the system. By selecting the Windows uninstaller utility, Programs and Features (found in the Control Panel), you delete not only the main program file but also all supporting files and most registry entries.

File Compression Utilities

What is file compression? A **file compression utility** is a program that takes out redundancies in a file to reduce the file size. File compression is helpful

because it makes a large file more compact, making it easier and faster to send over the Internet, upload to a Web page, or save onto a disc. As shown in Figure 5.28, Windows has built-in compression (or zip) file support. There are also several stand-alone freeware and shareware programs, such as WinZip (for Windows) and StuffIt (for Windows or Mac), that you can obtain to compress your files.

How does file compression work? Most compression programs look for repeated patterns of letters and replace these patterns with a shorter placeholder. The repeated patterns and the associated placeholder are cataloged and stored temporarily in a separate file called the *dictionary*. For example, in the following sentence, you can easily see the repeated patterns of letters.

The rain in Spain falls mainly on the plain.

Although this example contains obvious repeated patterns (**ain** and **the**), in a large document the repeated patterns may be more complex. The compression program's algorithm (a set of instructions designed to complete a solution in a step-by-step manner) therefore runs through the file several times to determine the optimal repeated patterns to use to obtain the greatest compression.

How effective are file compression programs? The effectiveness of file compression—that is, how much a file's size is reduced—depends on several factors, including the type and size of the individual

Figure 5.28

(a) File compression is a built-in utility of the Windows operating system. (b) Compressing the PowerPoint document reduced the file size from 1,935 KB to 1,453 KB.

>To access the Windows file compression utility, right-click the file or folder that is to be compressed, select **Send to** from the shortcut menu, and then select **Compressed (zipped) Folder**.

Compression reduces file size from 1935 KB to 1453 KB

STEP 1: Right-click zipped folder.

STEP 2: Select Extract All…

STEP 3: Browse to storage location.

STEP 4: Extracted file displays in selected location.

Figure 5.29

The Extraction Wizard in Windows makes unzipping compressed folders and files easy.

file and the compression method used. Current compression programs can reduce text files by as much as 50 percent. However, some files, such as PDF files, already contain a form of compression, so they do not need to be compressed further. Other file types, especially some graphics and audio formats, have gone through a compression process that reduces file size by permanently discarding data. For example, image files such as Joint Photographic Experts Group (JPEG), Graphics Interchange Format (GIF), and Portable Network Graphics (PNG) files discard small variations in color that the human eye may not pick up. Likewise, MP3 files permanently discard sounds that the human ear cannot hear. These graphic and audio files do not need further compression.

How do I decompress a file I've compressed? When you want to restore the file to its original state, you need to decompress the file so that the pieces of file that the compression process temporarily removed are restored to the document. Generally, the program you used to compress the file has the capability to decompress the file as well (see Figure 5.29).

System Maintenance Utilities

Are there any utilities that make my system work faster? **Disk Cleanup** is a Windows utility that cleans, or removes, unnecessary files from your hard drive. These include files that have accumulated in

the Recycle Bin as well as temporary files, which are files created by Windows to store data temporarily when a program is running. Windows usually deletes these temporary files when you exit the program, but sometimes it forgets to do this, or doesn't have time because your system freezes up or incurs a problem that prevents you from properly exiting a program. Disk Cleanup, found by clicking the Start button, then selecting All Programs, Accessories folder, and then the System Tools folder, also removes temporary Internet files (Web pages stored on your hard drive for quick viewing) as well as offline Web pages (pages stored on your computer so you can view them without being connected to the Internet). If not deleted periodically, these unnecessary files can hinder efficient operating performance.

How can I control which files Disk Cleanup deletes? When you run Disk Cleanup, the program scans your hard drive to determine which folders have files that can be deleted and calculates the amount of hard drive space that would be freed by doing so. You check off which type of files you would like to delete, as shown in Figure 5.30.

What else can I do if my system runs slowly? Over time, as you add and delete information in a file, the file pieces are saved in scattered locations on the hard drive. Locating all the pieces of the file takes extra time, making the operating system less efficient. Windows **Disk Defragmenter** regroups related pieces of files on the hard drive, thereby allowing the OS to work more efficiently. You can find the Windows Disk Defragmenter utility by clicking the Start menu, then All Programs, Accessories, and then System Tools. Using the Windows Disk Defragmenter Analyzer feature, you should check several times a year to determine whether your drive needs to be defragmented. Unfortunately, Macs do not have a defrag utility built into the system because developers thought that the file system used by Mac OS X was so efficient that defragging the hard drive would be unnecessary. Those users who feel the need to defrag their Mac can use iDefrag, an external program that can be purchased from Coriolis Systems.

Total space to be freed

Space freed with the selections

Description of folder contents

Figure 5.30

Using Disk Cleanup will help free space on your hard drive.

>Disk Cleanup is accessed by clicking **Start**, **All Programs**, **Accessories**, and then **System Tools**.

How do I diagnose potential errors or damage on my storage devices? **Error-checking**, once known as ScanDisk, is a Windows utility that checks for lost files and fragments as well as physical errors on your hard drive. Lost files and fragments of files occur as you save, resave, move, delete, and copy files on your hard drive. Sometimes the system becomes confused, leaving references on the **file allocation table** or **FAT** (an index of all sector numbers in a table) to files that no longer exist or have been moved. Physical errors on the hard drive occur when the mechanism that reads the hard drive's data (which is stored as 1s or 0s) can no longer determine whether the area holds a 1 or a 0. These areas are called *bad sectors*. Sometimes Error-checking can recover the lost data, but more often, it deletes the files that are unnecessarily taking up space. Error-checking also makes a note of any bad sectors so that the system will not use them again to store data.

Where can I find Error-checking? Starting with Windows XP, the Error-checking utility is located in Disk Properties. To locate Error-checking, after clicking Computer from the Start menu, right-click the disk you want to diagnose, select Properties, and select Tools. In earlier versions of the Windows operating system, Error-checking, known as ScanDisk, was located in System Tools. On Macs, you can use the Disk Utility to test and repair disks. You will find Disk Utility in the Utilities folder in the Applications folder on your hard drive.

How can I check on a program that has stopped running? If a program has stopped working, you can use the Windows **Task Manager utility** to check on the program or to exit the nonresponsive program. Although you can access Task Manager from the Control Panel, it is more easily accessible by pressing Ctrl + Alt and then the Delete key or by right-clicking an empty space on the taskbar at the bottom of your screen. The Applications tab of Task Manager lists all programs that you are using and indicates whether they are working properly (running) or have stopped improperly (not responding). You can terminate programs that are not responding by clicking the End Task button in the dialog box.

If you need outside assistance because of a program error, Dr. Watson for Windows, a tool that is included in Microsoft Windows XP, and Problem Reports and Solutions, a tool in Windows Vista and Windows 7, gather information about the computer when there is a program error. When an error occurs, these tools automatically create and save a text log. The log can then be viewed, printed, or delivered electronically to any technical support professional, who can then use this information to help diagnose the problem.

ACTIVE HELP-DESK

Using Utility Programs

In this Active Helpdesk call, you'll play the role of a helpdesk staffer, fielding calls about the utility programs included in system software and what these programs do.

To understand how disk defragmenter utilities work, you must first understand the basics of how a hard disk drive stores files. A hard disk drive is composed of several *platters*, or round, thin plates of metal, that are covered with a special magnetic coating that records the data. The platters are about 3.5 inches in diameter and are stacked onto a spindle. There are usually two or three platters in any hard disk drive, with data stored on one or both sides. Data is recorded on hard disks in concentric circles called tracks. Each **track** is further broken down into pie-shaped wedges, each called a **sector** (see Figure 5.31). The data is further identified by *clusters*, which are the smallest segments within the sectors.

When you want to save (or write) a file, the bits that make up your file are recorded onto one or more clusters of the drive. To keep track of which clusters hold which files, the drive also stores an index of all sector numbers in a table. To save a file, the computer will look in the table for clusters that are not already being used. It will then record the file information on those clusters. When you open (or read) a file, the computer searches through the table for the clusters that hold the desired file and reads that file. Similarly, when you delete a file, you are actually not deleting the file itself, but rather the reference in the table to the file.

How does a disk become fragmented? When only part of an older file is deleted, the deleted section of the file creates a gap in the sector of the disk where the data was originally stored. In the same way, when new information is added to an older file, there may not be space to save the new information sequentially near where the file was originally saved. In that case, the system writes the added part of the file to the next available location on the disk, and a reference is made in the table as to the location of this file fragment. Over time, as files are saved, deleted, and modified, the bits of information for various files fall out of sequential order and the disk becomes fragmented.

Disk fragmentation is a problem because the operating system is not as efficient when a disk is fragmented. It takes longer to locate a whole file because more of the disk must be searched for the various pieces, greatly slowing down the performance of your computer.

How can you make the files line up more efficiently on the disk? At this stage, the disk defragmenter utility enters the picture. The defragmenter tool takes the hard drive through a defragmentation process in which pieces of files that are scattered over the disk are placed together and arranged sequentially on the hard disk. Also, any unused portions of clusters that were too small to save data in before are grouped, increasing the available storage space on the disk. Figure 5.32 shows before and after shots of a fragmented disk that has gone through the defragmentation process.

For more about hard disks and defragmenting, be sure to check out the Sound Byte "Hard Disk Anatomy Interactive."

Figure 5.31

On a hard disk platter, data is recorded onto tracks, which are further broken down into sectors and clusters.

Figure 5.32

Defragmenting the hard drive arranges file fragments so that they are located next to each other. This makes the hard drive run more efficiently.

System Restore and Backup Utilities

Is there an undo command for the system?
Say you have just installed a new software program and your computer freezes. After rebooting the computer, when you try to start the application, the system freezes once again. You uninstall the new program, but your computer continues to freeze after rebooting. What can you do now?

The most recent versions of Windows have a utility called **System Restore** that lets you roll your system settings back to a specific date when everything was working properly. A System Restore point is made every day you use your computer. You also can create a custom restore point if needed, such as before installing new software or hardware. Should problems occur, if the computer was running just fine before you installed new software or a hardware device, you could restore your computer to the settings that were in effect before the software or hardware installation. System Restore does not affect your personal data files (such as Microsoft Word documents, browsing history, or e-mail), so you won't lose changes made to these files when you use System Restore. You can find System Restore by clicking Start, All Programs, Accessories, and then System Tools.

How does the computer remember its previous settings? Every time you start your computer or install a new application or driver, Windows automatically creates a snapshot of your entire system's settings. This snapshot is called a **restore point**. You also can create and name your own restore points at any time. Creating a restore point is a good idea before making changes to your computer such as installing hardware or software. If something goes wrong with the installation process, Windows can reset your system to the restore point. As shown in Figure 5.33, Windows includes a Restore Point Wizard that walks you through the process of setting restore points.

SOUND BYTE

Hard Disk Anatomy Interactive

In this Sound Byte, you'll watch a series of animations that show various aspects of a hard drive, including the anatomy of a hard drive, how a computer reads and writes data to a hard drive, and the fragmenting and defragmenting of a hard drive.

How can I protect my data in the event something malfunctions in my system? When you use the Windows **Backup and Restore utility** (found in the Control Panel), you can create a duplicate copy of all the data on your hard drive (or just the folders and files you specify) and copy it to another storage device, such as a DVD or external hard drive. A backup copy protects your data in the event your hard drive fails or files are accidentally erased. Although you may not need to back up every file on your computer, you should back up the files that are most important to you and keep the backup copy in a safe location. Mac OS X Snow Leopard includes a backup utility called Time Machine that will automatically back up your files to a specified location. Apple also offers backup hardware called Time Capsules, which are wireless devices designed to work with Time Machine and record your backup data. (For more information on backing up your files, see Chapter 9.)

The Task Scheduler Utility

How can I remember to perform all these maintenance procedures? To keep your computer system in top shape, it is important to run some of the utilities

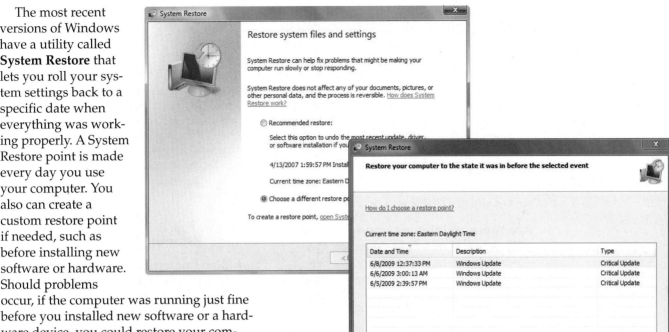

Figure 5.33

Setting a restore point is good practice before installing any hardware or software.

>The Restore Point Wizard is found by clicking **Start**, **All Programs**, **Accessories**, **System Tools**. In the System Tools folder, click **System Restore**. The System Restore wizard appears, with Restore Point shown on the first page of the Wizard.

described previously on a routine basis. Depending on your usage, you may want to defrag your hard drive or clean out temporary Internet files periodically. However, many computer users forget to initiate these tasks. Luckily, the Windows **Task Scheduler utility**, shown in Figure 5.34, allows you to schedule tasks to run automatically at predetermined times, with no additional action necessary on your part.

Accessibility Utilities

Are there utilities designed for users with special needs?   Microsoft Windows includes an Ease of Access Center, which is a centralized location for assistive technology and tools to adjust accessibility settings. In the Ease of Access Center, you can find tools to help you adjust the screen contrast, magnify the screen image, have screen contents read to you, and display an on-screen keyboard, as more fully explained in the following list. If you're not sure where to start or what settings might help, a questionnaire asks you about routine tasks and provides a personalized recommendation for settings that will help you use your computer (see Figure 5.35). Some of these features are described below.

- **High Contrast:** Allows you to select a color scheme setting in which you can control the contrast between text and background. Because some visually impaired individuals find it easier to see white text on a dark background, there are color schemes that invert screen colors.
- **Magnifier:** A utility that creates a separate window that displays a magnified portion of the screen. This feature makes the screen more readable for users who have impaired vision.

Figure 5.34

To keep your machine running in top shape, use Task Scheduler to schedule maintenance programs to run automatically at selected times and days.

>Task Scheduler is found by clicking **Start**, **All Programs**, **Accessories**, and then **System Tools**.

- **Narrator:** A very basic speech program that reads what is on screen, whether it's the contents of a window, menu options, or text you have typed. The Narrator coordinates with text utilities such as Notepad and WordPad as well as with Internet Explorer, but it may not work correctly with other programs. For this reason, Narrator is not meant for individuals who must rely solely on a text-to-speech utility to operate the computer.

- **On-Screen Keyboard:** Displays a keyboard on the screen. You type by clicking on or hovering over the keys with a pointing device (mouse or trackball) or joystick. This utility, which is similar to the Narrator, is not meant for everyday use for individuals with severe disabilities. A separate program with more functionality is better in those circumstances.

- **Windows Speech Recognition:** An effective tool that allows you to dictate text and control your computer by voice. The Speech Recognition utility is in the Ease of Access folder.

Whether you use Windows, OS X, Linux, or another operating system, a fully featured operating system is available to meet your needs. As long as you keep the operating system updated and regularly use the available utilities to fine-tune your system, you should experience little trouble from your OS.

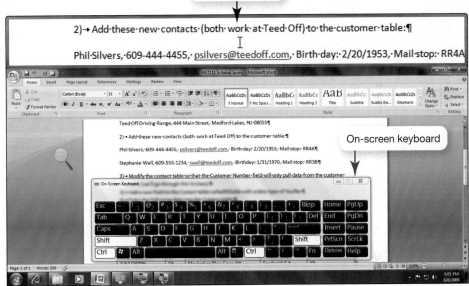

Figure 5.35

Microsoft Windows includes an Ease of Access Center to help users with disabilities. It has handy accessibility features such as a magnifier and an on-screen keyboard.

>The Ease of Access Center is found by clicking **Start**, **All Programs**, **Accessories**, **Ease of Access**.

1. What software is included in system software?

System software is the set of software programs that helps run the computer and coordinates instructions between application software and hardware devices. It consists of the operating system (OS) and utility programs. The OS controls how your computer system functions. Utility programs are programs that perform general housekeeping tasks for the computer, such as system maintenance and file compression.

2. What are the different kinds of operating systems?

Operating systems can be classified into four categories. Real-time operating systems (RTOSs) require no user intervention. They are designed for systems with a specific purpose and response time (such as robotic machinery). Single-user, single-task OSs are designed for computers on which one user is performing one task at a time (such as PDAs). Single-user, multitask OSs are designed for computers on which one user is performing more than one task at a time (such as desktop computers). Multiuser OSs are designed for systems in which multiple users are working on more than one task at a time (such as networks).

3. What are the most common operating systems?

Microsoft Windows is the most popular OS. It has evolved from being a single-user, single-task OS into a powerful multiuser operating system. The most recent release is Windows 7. Another popular OS is the Mac OS, which is designed to work on Apple computers. Apple's most recent release, Mac OS X Snow Leopard, is based on the UNIX operating system. You'll find various versions of UNIX on the market, although it is most often used on networks. Linux is an open source OS based on UNIX and designed primarily for use on personal computers, although it is often found as the operating system on servers.

4. How does the operating system provide a means for users to interact with the computer?

The operating system provides a user interface that enables users to interact with the computer. Most OSs today use a graphical user interface (GUI). Unlike the command- and menu-driven interfaces used earlier, GUIs display graphics and use the point-and-click technology of the mouse and cursor, making the OS more user-friendly. Common features of GUIs include windows, menus, and icons.

5. How does the operating system help manage resources such as the processor, memory, storage, hardware, and peripheral devices?

When you use your computer, you are usually asking it to perform several tasks at the same time. When the OS allows you to perform more than one task at a time, it is multitasking. To provide for seamless multitasking, the OS controls the timing of events the processor works on.

As the OS coordinates the activities of the processor, it uses RAM as a temporary storage area for instructions and data the processor needs. The OS is therefore responsible for coordinating the space allocations in RAM to ensure that there is enough space for the waiting instructions and data. If there isn't sufficient space in RAM for all the data and instructions, then the OS allocates the least necessary files to temporary storage on the hard drive, called virtual memory.

The OS manages storage by providing a file management system that keeps track of the names and locations of files and programs. Programs called *device drivers* facilitate communication between devices attached to the computer and the OS. Device drivers translate the specialized commands of devices to commands that the OS can understand and vice versa, enabling the OS to communicate with every device in the computer system. Device drivers for common devices are included in the OS software, whereas other devices come with a device driver that you must install or download off the Web.

6. How does the operating system interact with application software?

All software applications need to interact with the CPU. For programs to work with the CPU, they must contain code that the CPU recognizes. Rather than having the same blocks of code appear in each application, the OS includes the blocks of code to which software applications refer. These blocks of code are called *application programming interfaces (APIs)*.

7. How does the operating system help the computer start up?

When you start your computer, it runs through a special process called the *boot process*. The boot process consists of four basic steps. (1) The basic input/output system (BIOS) is activated when the user powers on the CPU. (2) In the POST check, the BIOS verifies that all attached devices are in place. (3) The operating system is loaded into RAM. (4) Configuration and customization settings are checked.

8. What are the main desktop and windows features?

The desktop provides your first interaction with the OS and is the first image you see on your monitor once the system has booted up. It provides you with access to your computer's files, folders, and commonly used tools and applications. Windows are the rectangular panes on your screen that display applications running on your system. Common features of windows include toolbars (or ribbons), scrollbars, and minimize, maximize and restore, and close buttons.

9. How does the operating system help me keep my computer organized?

The OS allows you to organize the contents of your computer in a hierarchical structure of directories that includes files, folders, libraries, and drives. Windows Explorer helps you manage your files and folders by showing the location and contents of every drive, folder, and file on your computer. Creating folders is the key to organizing files because folders keep related documents together. Following naming conventions and using proper file extensions are also important aspects of file management.

10. What utility programs are included in system software, and what do they do?

Some utility programs are incorporated into the OS; others are sold as stand-alone off-the-shelf programs. Common Windows utilities include those that enable you to adjust your display, add or remove programs, compress files, defragment your hard drive, clean unnecessary files off your system, check for lost files and errors, restore your system to an earlier setting, back up your files, schedule automatic tasks, and check on programs that have stopped running.

Word Bank

- Disk Defragmenter
- Error-checking
- file compression
- file management
- files
- folders
- Linux
- Mac OS
- platform
- system files
- system software
- Task Manager
- Task Scheduler
- tracks
- utility programs
- Windows
- Windows Explorer
- Windows 7

Instructions: Fill in the blanks using the words from the Word Bank above.

Veena was looking into buying a new computer and was trying to decide what
(1) _____ to buy—a PC or a Mac. She had used PCs all her life, so she was more
familiar with the (2) _____ operating system. Still, she liked the way the (3) _____
looked and was considering switching. Her brother didn't like either operating system, so
he used (4) _____, a free operating system instead.

After a little research, Veena decided to buy a PC. With it, she got the most recent version
of Windows, (5) _____. She vowed that with this computer, she'd practice better
(6) _____ because she often had a hard time finding files on her old computer. To view
all of the folders on her computer, she opened (7) _____. She made sure that she gave
descriptive names to her (8) _____ and placed them in organized (9) _____ and
libraries.

Veena also decided that with her new computer, she'd pay more attention to the
(10) _____, those little special-function programs that help with maintenance and
repairs. These special-function programs, in addition to the OS, make up the
(11) _____. Veena looked into some of the more frequently used utilities. She thought
it would be a good idea to run the (12) _____ on her hard drive regularly so that all the
files lined up in sequentially ordered (13) _____ and so that it was more efficient. She
also looked into (14) _____ utilities, which would help her reduce the size of her files
when she sent them to others over the Internet. Finally, she decided to use the Windows
(15) _____ utility to schedule tasks automatically so that she wouldn't forget.

becoming computer literate

Using key terms from the chapter, write a letter to your 70-year-old aunt who just received
her first computer, explaining the benefits of simple computer maintenance. First, explain
any symptoms her computer may be experiencing (such as a sluggish Internet connection);
then include a set of steps she can follow in setting up a regimen to remedy each problem.
Make sure you explain some of the system utilities described in this chapter, including but
not limited to Disk Defragmenter, Disk Cleanup, and Task Scheduler. Include any other
utilities she might need, and explain why she should have them.

Instructions: Answer the multiple-choice and true–false questions below for more practice with key terms and concepts from this chapter.

Multiple Choice

1. Smartphones use which category of operating system?
   a. Single-user, single-task
   b. Multiuser, multitask
   c. Single-user, multitask
   d. Real-time

2. Which best describes Gadgets and widgets?
   a. Smaller versions of traditional peripheral devices
   b. Mini programs that display on the desktop
   c. The most commonly used programs displayed at the bottom of the desktop
   d. Other names for icons and shortcuts

3. Virtual memory is
   a. unlimited in capacity.
   b. borrowed space on the hard drive.
   c. another name for RAM.
   d. synonymous with cache memory.

4. Plug and Play devices
   a. don't require drivers.
   b. have drivers included in the Windows OS.
   c. must be installed using Add or Remove Programs.
   d. None of the above.

5. Which is not a function of the operating system?
   a. Providing a means for the user to interact with the computer
   b. Enabling the processor to handle multiple operations, seemingly at the same time
   c. Carefully shutting the system down when RAM limits have been reached
   d. Facilitating installation of peripheral devices with the inclusion of drivers

6. The term that defines the condition that occurs when your system is running out of virtual memory is
   a. thrashing.   c. caching.
   b. multitasking.   d. paging.

7. Which view option would be best to sort picture or presentation files?
   a. Details   c. Large Icons
   b. Tiles   d. All of the above

8. Which of the following file names indicates a file created by a word processing program in the Office 2007 suite?
   a. bioreport.xls
   b. bioreport.docx
   c. bioreport.jpg
   d. All of the above

9. Which utility would you use to help manage your files and folders?
   a. System Restore
   b. Disk Defragmenter
   c. Windows Explorer
   d. Disk Cleanup

10. Which utility is NOT an accessibility utility?
   a. Magnifier
   b. Narrator
   c. Windows Speech Recognition
   d. File Compression

True–False

_____ 1. All computing devices need some form of operating system software.

_____ 2. Symbian OS is a common OS for smartphones.

_____ 3. Linux is not a common OS because it's more expensive than Windows or Mac OS.

_____ 4. Because of virtual memory, it is not possible for a computer to run out of memory.

_____ 5. Files deleted from a flash drive end up in the Recycle Bin.

1. Organizing Files and Folders

It's the beginning of a new semester and you promise yourself that you are going to keep all files related to your schoolwork more organized this semester. Develop a plan that outlines how you'll set up libraries, folders, and subfolders for each subject. Identify at least three different folders for each class. If time and schedule permit, discuss your organization scheme with your instructor.

2. OS Compatibility Issues

Your school requires that you purchase a notebook computer. All your other family members, as well as your school, use computers with Windows operating system. However, you really want a Mac notebook.

a. Research the compatibility issues between Mac and Windows computers.
b. How does a smartphone using Symbian OS fit into the equation?
c. Can you synchronize the smartphone with either or both machines?
d. Explore the application called Boot Camp. What does it do? Would it be helpful in this situation?

3. Understanding Safe Mode

It is the night before the major term paper for your philosophy class is due. Your best friend comes screaming down the hall, begging for help. His only copy of his draft paper is on his notebook, and the computer is suddenly booting up with the words "Safe Mode" in the corners of the screen. What would be the most useful questions to ask him? What steps would you take to debug the problem? If you cannot get the computer to come out of Safe mode, is there a way to retrieve the draft? How many times will you say, "Make backups!" that evening?

4. Software Requirements

This semester you upgraded to the most recent operating system and productivity software on your notebook to match what your college is using. You know which courses you'll be taking next semester, and you realize they will require the installation of more applications. A friend who is in a similar position tells you she's not worried about putting that much software on her computer because she has a really big hard drive.

a. Is hard drive storage your only concern? Should you also worry more about having sufficient RAM? How will your use of the software on your computer affect your answer?
b. Does virtual memory management by your operating system allow you to ignore RAM requirements?

5. Connecting Peripherals

You are considering upgrading to the latest version of Windows. Your current notebook computer is approximately three years old.

a. What concerns would you have about upgrading?
b. How would you determine if your peripheral devices would work with the new OS?
c. Would you consider switching to Linux instead? What are the pros and cons of this decision?

1. Organizing Files and Folders

You have started a new job and have a new computer. You never kept your files and folders organized on the computer you used when in college, but now you are determined to do a better job at keeping your files organized. You know you need folders for the several clients with whom you will be working. For each client, you'll need to have folders for billing information, client documents, and account information. In addition, you need folders for the MP3 files and video files you will listen to and watch when you're not working, as well as a folder for the digital pictures you'll take for personal and company reasons. Finally, you're working toward an advanced degree and will be taking business finance and introductory marketing courses at night, so you'll need folders for all the homework assignments for both courses.

Determine the file structure you would need to create to accommodate your needs. Start with the C drive and use the default Libraries in addition to using Documents, Pictures, Video, and Music as the default folders for documents, pictures, video, and music files, respectively. Also create any new libraries that you feel are necessary to further organize your data, and include references to whatever folders should be included in each library.

2. Using Mac Utility Programs

Your company has been having trouble with some of its Mac computers, which are running inefficiently. Your boss asks you to research the utility programs your company could use on its Macs to make them run more efficiently. In particular, your boss would like you to determine what utilities are available in the Mac OS and then determine what utilities the company may need to purchase. In addition, your boss wants to ensure the availability of a disk defragmenting utility, a file compression utility, and a diagnostic utility you could run to check the hard drive for errors. Using the Internet for your research, what utilities are already in the Mac OS, and what stand-alone utilities can you purchase? Will they run on all versions of the Mac OS?

3. Monitoring Activities with the OS

The company that you work for has just announced a new internal accounting structure. From now on, each department will be charged individually for the costs associated with computer usage, such as backup storage space and Internet usage.

a. Research how the operating system may be set up to monitor such activity by department.
b. What other activities do you think the operating system can be set up to monitor?

4. Choosing the Best OS

Your new boss is considering moving some of the department operations away from Windows-based computer systems. He asks you to research the advantages and disadvantages of moving to Linux or Mac OS X. How would these choices affect his department in the following areas?

a. Budget for technical support for the systems
b. Choice and budget for hardware for the systems
c. Costs of implementation
d. Possibility for future upgrades

Instructions: Albert Einstein used *Gedankenexperiments* or critical thinking questions, to develop his theory of relativity. Some ideas are best understood by experimenting with them in our own minds. The following critical thinking questions are designed to demand your full attention but require only a comfortable chair—no technology.

1. Open Source Pros and Cons

Open source programming embraces a philosophy that states programmers should make their code available to everyone rather than keeping it proprietary. The Linux operating system has had much success as an open source code. The chapter mentions some of the advantages of open source code, such as quicker code updates in response to technological advances and changes.

a. What are other advantages of open source code?
b. Can you think of disadvantages to open source code?
c. Why do you think that companies such as Microsoft maintain proprietary restrictions on their code?
d. Are there disadvantages to maintaining proprietary code?

2. The OS of the Future

Operating system interfaces have evolved from a text-based console format to the current graphical user interface. What direction do you think they will move toward next? How could operating systems be organized and used in a manner that is more responsive to humans and better suited to how we think? Are there alternatives to hierarchical file structures for storage? Can you think of ways in which operating systems could adapt and customize themselves based on your usage?

3. Which OS Would You Choose?

Suppose you are building a computer system from scratch and have complete discretion as to your choice of operating system. Which one would you install, and why?

4. The OS: With or Without Utilities?

Which do you think is better for consumers: to have companies develop smaller, more inexpensive operating systems and then allow competing companies to develop and market utility programs, or to have companies develop extremely large, full-featured operating systems that include most utilities as operating system features? Do you think that including utility programs with an operating system makes the cost of the operating system higher?

five team time

Choosing the Best OS

Problem

You have been hired to help set up the technology requirements for a small advertising company. The company is holding off on buying anything until it makes a decision as to the platform on which the computers should run. Obviously, one of the critical decisions is the choice of operating system.

Task

Recommend the appropriate operating system for the company.

Process

1. Break up into three teams. Each team will examine one of the three primary operating systems today: Windows, Mac, and Linux.
2. As a team, research the pros and cons of your operating system. What features does it have that would benefit your company? What features does it not have that your company would need? Why (or why not) would your operating system be the appropriate choice? Why is your OS better (or worse) than either of the other two options?
3. Develop a presentation that states your position with regard to your operating system. Your presentation should have a recommendation and include facts to back it up.
4. As a class, decide which operating system would be the best choice for the company.

Conclusion

Because the operating system is the most critical piece of software in the computer system, the selection should not be taken lightly. The OS that is best for an advertising agency may not be best for an accounting firm. It is important to make sure you consider all aspects of the work environment and the type of work that is being done to ensure a good fit.

In addition to the review materials presented here, you'll find additional materials featured with the book's multimedia, including the *Technology in Action* Student Resource CD and the Companion Website (**pearsonhighered.com/techinaction**), which will help reinforce your understanding of the chapter content. These materials include the following:

Active Helpdesk

In Active Helpdesk calls, you'll assume the role of helpdesk operator, taking calls about the concepts you've learned in this chapter. You'll apply what you've learned and receive feedback from a supervisor to review and reinforce those concepts. The Active Helpdesk calls for this chapter are listed below and can be found on your Student Resource CD:

- Managing Hardware and Peripheral Devices: The OS
- Starting the Computer: The Boot Process
- Organizing Your Computer: File Management
- Using Utility Programs

Sound Bytes

Sound Bytes are dynamic multimedia tutorials that help demystify even the most complex topics. You'll view video clips and animations that illustrate computer concepts and then apply what you've learned by reviewing with the Sound Byte Labs, which include quizzes and activities specifically tailored to each Sound Byte. The Sound Bytes for this chapter are listed below and can be found on your Student Resource CD:

- Customizing Windows
- File Management
- File Compression
- Hard Disk Anatomy Interactive
- Letting Your Computer Clean Up After Itself

Companion Website

The *Technology in Action* Companion Website includes a variety of additional materials to help you review and learn more about the topics in this chapter. The resources available at **pearsonhighered.com/techinaction** include:

- **Online Study Guide.** Each chapter features an online true–false and multiple-choice quiz. You can take these quizzes, automatically check the results, and e-mail the results to your instructor.
- **Web Research Projects.** Each chapter features several Web research projects that ask you to search the Web for information on computer-related careers, milestones in computer history, important people and companies, emerging technologies, and the applications and implications of different technologies.

Computing|Alternatives

You may think that there are no viable alternatives to buying computers that run Microsoft Windows and use Microsoft Office applications such as Word and Excel. In this Technology in Focus feature, we explore software and hardware alternatives to Microsoft products, many of which may provide you with less expensive and more flexible options. Let's get started by looking at alternatives to Microsoft Office products.

Application Software Alternatives

Proprietary (or commercial) software is developed by corporations such as Microsoft and Apple to be sold for a profit. Opponents of proprietary software contend that software should be developed without profit motive and that the source code (the actual lines of instructional code that make the program work) should be made available so that others may modify or improve the software.

Open source software is freely distributed (no royalties accrue to the creators), contains the source code, and can in turn be distributed to others. Therefore, you can download open source software for free from various Web sites, install it on as many computers as you wish, make changes to the source code if you know how to do this, and redistribute it to anyone you wish (as long as you don't charge for distributing it). In this section, we look at some open source software that you can download and use on your computer. For a list of open source resources available on the Web, visit **sourceforge.net**.

PRODUCTIVITY SOFTWARE ALTERNATIVES: OPENOFFICE

As mentioned in Chapter 4, the Open-Office.org suite (which we'll refer to as OpenOffice) is a free suite of productivity software programs that provides functionality similar to that of Microsoft Office. Versions of OpenOffice are available for a variety of operating systems, including Windows, Linux, and Mac. It currently offers support in more than 100 languages besides English, with more being added all the time by the development community. You can download the installation file you'll need to run OpenOffice at **openoffice.org**. The minimum system requirements for installing OpenOffice 3 in a Windows environment are less than those required for Microsoft Office.

The main components of OpenOffice are word processing (Writer), spreadsheet (Calc), presentation (Impress), and database (Base) programs. These provide functionality similar to that of the Word, Excel, PowerPoint, and Access applications you might be familiar with in Microsoft Office.

The OpenOffice 3 suite also includes additional programs. Draw provides the most common tools needed to communicate using graphics and diagrams, and Math creates equations and formulas for your documents.

The great advantage of OpenOffice is its compatibility with most programs. This means that if your friend uses Microsoft Office and you send her an OpenOffice file, she can still read it, and you can read all of her Microsoft Office files, too. OpenOffice 3 is able to open Microsoft Office 2007 or 2010 files without the need for a conversion program. Although the individual applications in OpenOffice are not as fully featured as those in Microsoft Office, and do not have the ribbon interface found in the newest versions of the Office applications, it is still a powerful productivity software suite, and the price is right.

When you launch OpenOffice via the **Quickstarter** icon (see Figure 1), you can choose a file type from the list displayed in the Templates and Documents dialog box. Once you select the appropriate file type (such as spreadsheet, presentation, or text) and click Open, the appropriate application and a new, blank document will open so that you can begin working.

FIGURE 1

Clicking the OpenOffice Quickstarter icon (in the system tray on the bottom right) displays a list of file types from which you can choose to begin working on your project.

Writer

Writer, the OpenOffice word processing application, is extremely similar in look and feel to Microsoft Word 2003 (see Figure 2). As is the case in Word, you can easily change text appearance in Writer by altering font type, style, alignment, and color. You can also easily insert graphics (pictures or clip art), tables, and hyperlinks into documents. Writer's wizards provide you with several templates you can use to create standard documents such as faxes, agendas, and letters. Special tools in Writer also allow you to create bibliographic references, indexes, and tables of contents.

When saving a document in Writer, the default file format has an .odt extension. By using the Save As command, you can save files in other formats, such as various versions of Word (.doc and .docx), Pocket Word (.psw) for mobile devices, Rich Text Format (.rtf), Text (.txt), and HTML Document (.htm). The handy Export Directly as PDF icon in Writer allows you to save documents as PDF files.

Calc

Once you open a Calc spreadsheet, you enter text, numbers, and formulas into the appropriate cells, just as you would in Microsoft Excel. You also can apply a full range of formatting options (font size, color, style, and so on) to the cells, making it easy to create files such as the monthly budget spreadsheet shown in Figure 3. Built-in formulas and functions simplify the job of creating spreadsheets, and Calc's Function Wizard guides you through the wide range of available functions, providing suggestions as to which function to use.

When saving a document in Calc, the default file format has an .ods extension. You can also save files in other formats, such as Excel (.xls and .xlsx) and Pocket Excel (.pxl) for use on mobile devices. The handy Export Directly as PDF icon is also available in Calc.

Impress

When you select Presentation from the OpenOffice start-up interface, a wizard is displayed that offers you the option of creating a blank Impress presentation or building one from supplied templates. Compared to the vast array of stunning templates in Microsoft PowerPoint, the templates supplied with Impress are less than impressive. Still, it is easy to construct attractive slides and save them as templates. You can also "Google" the words "OpenOffice.org Impress Templates." You'll find a wide variety of templates for Impress that others have created and that you can download free of charge. To help you in the search, OpenOffice installation includes the option of installing the Google search bar (Web or Desktop), which will appear in the taskbar, making it easy to access while you are working in any of the OpenOffice applications.

FIGURE 2

Writer provides similar functionality and icons to Microsoft Word.

FIGURE 3

Calc offers many of the same features as Microsoft Excel.

Web-Based Alternatives

Open source alternatives to Microsoft Office applications are attractive because they are free, and they are also convenient because of their availability. Like most other applications, though, you can only use these programs with the computer on which they were installed. For ultimate accessibility and transferability, consider using Web-based Office software alternatives. With only a computer and an Internet connection, you can be productive almost anywhere because you access these programs from the Internet without having to install the software on your computer. Moreover, with Web-based applications you can collaborate on a document online with others, thus avoiding the coordination mess that generally occurs when transferring documents among colleagues or classmates via e-mail. As mentioned in Chapter 4, Google Docs includes Web-based word processing, spreadsheet, and presentation applications. These applications, while useful for sharing and creating basic documents, lack many of the more robust features that Microsoft Office and other proprietary programs have.

Zoho (**zoho.com**) is another great Web-based productivity suite that features project management software, customer relationship management software, and other business solutions in addition to the traditional productivity applications. ThinkFree Office Live (**thinkfree.com**) is an online productivity suite comprising word processing (ThinkFree Write), spreadsheets (ThinkFree Calc), and presentations (ThinkFree Show). ThinkFree also offers ThinkFree Office for desktops and ThinkFree Mobile for smartphones and other mobile devices. Many of the features are available to you without your having to register and create an account, and Web services are supported in English and many Asian languages. Like Google and Zoho, ThinkFree applications are fully compatible with Microsoft Office—including the latest formats—and run on Mac, Windows, and Linux platforms.

Base

If you want to create or just manipulate databases, Base enables you to create and modify tables, forms, queries, and reports by using wizards, design views, and SQL views. Base is similar to Microsoft Access and SQL Server, and works seamlessly with files created in most database applications, although you will need a separate converter to work with Microsoft Access 2007.

DATABASE SOFTWARE ALTERNATIVES: MYSQL

While Base, the OpenOffice database program described above, is perfectly functional, if you're interested in getting your hands on a free high-end SQL database application, the most popular open source option is MySQL (**mysql.com**). Sporting many of the features contained in SQL Server and Oracle Database 11g, MySQL is a powerful database program you can use to develop serious database applications. The two main components you should download and install with MySQL are the Database Server and the Query Browser (see Figure 4). You

use the Database Server to create tables for your database and enter your data. The Query Browser provides a visual interface for the database to display the results of queries you create.

FIGURE 4

MySQL is a free open source database alternative to Microsoft Access.

Although it is more difficult to learn and use than Microsoft Access, many books and online tutorials are available to help you get MySQL up and running.

E-MAIL CLIENT ALTERNATIVES: THUNDERBIRD AND EUDORA

If you are exploring other choices for Microsoft Office productivity applications, don't overlook other e-mail clients as alternatives to Microsoft Outlook. Mozilla Thunderbird is an open source e-mail client that has many enhancements that allow you to organize e-mail with tagging, folders, search, and saved search features. The latest version, Mozilla Thunderbird 2, has increased security and privacy measures so that messages received and sent remain safe. Plenty of add-ons, including a blog editor, calendar, calculator, and multimedia tools, are available from the Mozilla Web site (**mozilla.org**). Thunderbird can run on Windows, Mac, and Linux platforms. Eudora, another popular e-mail client, is currently being retrofitted by Qualcomm and other contributors into an open source application. Eudora8 is in beta testing at the time of this writing and is based on the same technology as Mozilla Thunderbird.

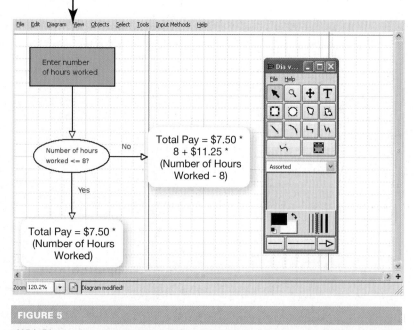

FIGURE 5

With Dia, you can create simple flowcharts, which a computer programmer might use in developing algorithms.

DRAWING SOFTWARE ALTERNATIVES: DRAW AND DIA

Microsoft Visio is a popular program for creating flowcharts and diagrams. However, Visio is not inexpensive. As mentioned previously, OpenOffice includes a program called Draw that allows you to create simple graphs, charts, and diagrams. Another option is Dia, a free program that allows you to create Visio-like diagrams and charts (see Figure 5). You can download a Windows-compatible version of Dia from **live.gnome.org/Dia**. The Web site also offers a tutorial to get you up and running.

Google offers yet another charting option. SketchUp (**sketchup.google. com**) is a full-featured 3D modeling software application. SketchUp comes in two versions. SketchUp7 is a free program that you can use to create, modify, and share 3D models. SketchUp Pro 7 is more fully featured and is available for less than $500.

WEB PAGE AUTHORING SOFTWARE ALTERNATIVES: SEAMONKEY

Although Microsoft Word and OpenOffice Writer can save documents as HTML files, sometimes you need a more versatile tool for creating Web pages, especially for larger sites with many linked pages. Adobe Dreamweaver is a popular commercial package for building Web sites, and Expression Web is a Web authoring application that is complementary to the Microsoft Office 2007 suite. Both of those solutions are proprietary applications that you must purchase. If you are looking for an open source alternative, SeaMonkey Composer, part of the SeaMonkey all-in-one Internet application suite (**seamonkey-project.org**), is a free, open source WYSIWYG ("what you see is what you get") Web authoring application that is compatible with the Windows, Mac, and Linux platforms. SeaMonkey Composer (see Figure 6) supports cascading style sheets, positioned layers, and dynamic image and table resizing. The SeaMonkey suite also includes a Web browser, e-mail and newsgroup client, and IRC chat.

IMAGE EDITING SOFTWARE ALTERNATIVES: GIMP

Do you need to create or edit some digital art but can't afford a high-end package such as Adobe Photoshop, or even a consumer package such as Adobe Photoshop Elements? Download a free copy of GIMP (short for GNU Image Manipulation Program) at **gimp.org** and you'll find a set of tools almost as powerful as Photoshop. GIMP is available for systems running Windows, Mac, Linux, and UNIX. Many good tutorials, available at **gimp.org/ tutorials**, can turn you into an accomplished user in no time.

Here are some handy things you can do with GIMP in five minutes or less:

- Crop or change the size of an image (see Figure 7).
- Reduce the file size of an image by decreasing its quality.
- Flip an image or rotate an image 90 degrees.

GIMP also enables you to use advanced techniques such as applying image filters, creating textures and gradients, drawing digital art, creating animated images through layer manipulation, and changing a photo into a painting or sketch.

Operating System Alternatives

Installing open source application software such as OpenOffice on a Windows machine is simple. Changing your OS from Windows to an open source OS such as Linux is a bit more complex. Why would you want to switch to Linux if you already own Windows?

Before Windows XP, many people felt Windows was not stable. Citing lockups and forced reboots, many users searched for an OS that would not crash as often. Starting with Windows XP, Microsoft has done a great deal to address stability issues.

Because Windows is the most widely used OS, with 90 percent of the market share, it's a prime target for viruses and other annoyances. From a virus creator or hacker's perspective, nuisances that spread via Windows have the greatest chance of causing the most aggravation. A lot of spyware, computer viruses, and other hacker

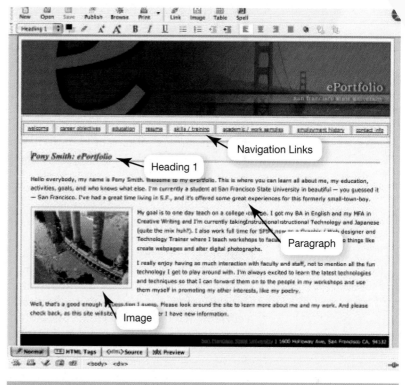

FIGURE 6

SeaMonkey Composer is an open source Web page authoring program that contains many features similar to those of leading commercial packages and is available at no cost.

FIGURE 7

GIMP is a freely available software application for image editing.

Photo Management Software Alternatives: JAlbum

If you're like many people, you have gigabytes of digital photos on your hard drive. How can you easily organize photos for display on a Web site so that you can share them with friends and family? An open source option is JAlbum (**jalbum.net**), a program that allows you to create Web albums of your digital images easily using drag-and-drop tools. JAlbum is available for the Windows, Mac, Linux, and UNIX operating systems, and supports 30 languages.

JAlbum provides significant advantages over some commercial photo management systems because it provides a high degree of control over the look and feel of the album you create. It offers many templates if you don't have the time, energy, or artistic flair to create your own. You also can use JAlbum to create index and slideshow pages. The software even uploads your album to the Internet. Best of all, your friends and family don't need any software other than a current Web browser to view your album. (You can also choose to burn your album onto a CD for sharing.)

nuisances are designed to take advantage of security flaws in Windows. An open source OS alternative, such as Linux, that is not as widely used as Windows is less of a target for these annoyances.

Another reason to install an open source OS is portability. Depending on which version of Linux you use, you may be able to take it with you on a CD or flash drive and use it on almost any computer. This portability feature appeals to people who use many different computers (such as lab computers at school). Instead of getting used to a new configuration every time you're away from your home computer, wouldn't it be nice to have the same environment you're used to everywhere you go? Such portability also offers an additional level of protection for users of public computers. As explained in Chapter 9, using an open source OS that's installed on a portable flash drive helps reduce your risk of picking up viruses and malware from public computers. In addition, it enhances privacy, because temporary Internet files are stored on the portable device on which the OS is installed, rather than on the hard drive of the public computer you are using. Lastly, many users of netbooks, the lightest, smallest category of notebook computers, have opted to install Linux because it takes up less space on the hard drive and runs faster than the proprietary software that was installed

originally by the manufacturer. In the next section, we explore the different varieties of Linux and explain how to install them.

WHICH LINUX TO USE

Linux is available for download in various packages known as **distributions**, or **distros**. Think of distros as being like different makes and models of cars. Distros include the underlying Linux kernel (the code that provides Linux's basic functionality) and special modifications to the OS, and may also include additional open source software (such as OpenOffice). Which distro is right for you?

A good place to start researching distros is **distrowatch.com**. This site tracks Linux distros and provides helpful tips for beginners on choosing one. Figure 8 lists some popular Linux distros and their home pages.

Before you can decide which distro is right for you, there are a few things to consider. The overall requirements to run Linux are relatively modest:

- A 1.2 GHz processor
- 384 MB of RAM (text mode) and 192 MB RAM (graphical mode)
- 8 GB of hard drive space
- VGA graphics card capable of 640 × 480 resolution

Just like any other software program, however, Linux performs better with a faster processor and more memory. Depending on how much additional software is deployed in the distro you choose to use, your system requirements may be higher, and you may need more hard drive space. Check the specific recommendations for the distro you're considering on that distro's Web site.

EXPERIMENTING WITH LINUX

Some Linux distros (such as Ubuntu and PCLinuxOS) are designed to run from a CD or DVD. This eliminates the need to install files on the computer's hard drive. Therefore, you can boot up from a DVD on an existing Windows PC and run Linux without disturbing the existing Windows installation. If you're looking to do this with a public computer, please note that some public computers do not allow access to the CD or DVD drive. Additionally, depending on the distro you use, you may not have full access to the files on your Windows hard drive.

Booting your existing computer from a CD- or DVD-based version of Linux is a low-risk way to experiment with Linux and see how well you like it. Ubuntu, for example, uses an extremely familiar-looking, Windows-like desktop. When you access Ubuntu, you get the Firefox browser as well as GIMP, OpenOffice, and many other software packages, including utilities and games. The minimum system requirements to run Ubuntu are:

- An Intel-compatible CPU (including 64-bit PCs and Intel-based Macs)
- At least 4 GB of hard drive space (if you are installing Ubuntu and not just running it from a CD or DVD)
- 256 MB of RAM for the alternative installation CD, or 384 MB to use the live, CD-based installer
- A bootable CD/DVD-ROM drive
- A standard graphics card

Figure 9 shows Ubuntu in action. After you connect to the Internet from your home network via a high-speed connection, the computer boots from the Ubuntu disc when it detects it in the optical disc drive. As part of the installation sequence, Ubuntu automatically detects components of the computer (such as the network card) and

FIGURE 8	Linux Distributions
Distro	**Home Page**
Debian GNU/Linux	**debian.org**
Fedora Core (Red Hat)	**fedoraproject.org**
Gentoo Linux	**gentoo.org**
Mandriva Linux	**mandriva.com**
PCLinuxOS	**pclinuxos.com**
Slackware Linux	**slackware.com**
Ubuntu	**ubuntu.com**

configures Linux to recognize them. You will have no trouble browsing the Internet because Firefox, a Web browser, is included with the Ubuntu distro. You can also save any files you create with the included OpenOffice suite to a flash drive.

Mandriva Linux offers several versions of its OS. Mandriva Linux One 2009 Spring is the company's most recent and most basic product. It is free, remains true to the original open source principles, and is installable. Alternatively, you can try Mandriva in the "live" mode, which doesn't require installation. Other versions with more features are available for a fee, including PowerPack 2009 Spring, which offers a more complete package that includes added multimedia and gaming software. In addition, for a small fee, you can get Mandriva Flash. Flash is Mandriva's portable OS option, and is installed on a convenient 8 GB flash drive.

FIGURE 9

The Ubuntu user interface resembles the Windows desktop.

FIGURE 10

The Mandriva operating system has an innovative 3D desktop environment.

When you install the Mandriva OS, you also get other open source applications, such as OpenOffice, the Firefox browser, and the KMail e-mail manager, as well as several multimedia programs including applications for managing photo albums and digital music collections.

In addition to all this, Mandriva includes security features. The OS divides security levels into five rankings that range from "Poor" to "Paranoid." Your choice depends on how you're using the system. (Select "Paranoid" if you're running business transactions through your computer.) You also can set up a simple-to-configure firewall called Shorewall to prevent unauthorized Internet users from accessing your personal network.

If you don't like Mandriva Linux or Ubuntu, head out to distrowatch.com and find another free Linux distro to install. With hundreds of distros available, you're sure to find one that fits your needs.

Hardware Alternatives

Tired of your Windows-based PC? Is your old computer too slow for your current needs and not worth upgrading? If so, you may be in the market for some new hardware. Before you head off to the store to buy another Windows-based computer, why not consider two alternatives: (1) moving to an Apple platform or (2) building your own computer.

This portable version does not make changes on the host computer, so you can bring your computer environment anywhere you go. Mandriva Flash takes up one-quarter of the flash drive, leaving the remaining 6 GB free so you can conveniently store and take with you all your office work and Internet and multimedia files Mandriva also offers Metisse, an innovative 3D desktop environment (see Figure 10).

APPLE COMPUTERS

The best way to decide whether a Mac is right for you is to get your hands on one and take it for a test drive. Chances are that someone you know has a Mac. Alternatively, your school might have a Mac lab or have Macs in the library. If not, then Apple has retail stores chock full of employees who are very happy to let you test out the equipment. You also can test Macs at Best Buy. Be sure to check out the entry-level Macs (see Figure 11). The MacBook Air is Apple's thinnest notebook. It weighs less than three pounds, and includes a 13-inch screen and a full-sized keyboard. The MacBook weighs in at five pounds and features the Intel Core 2 Duo processor and a

FIGURE 11

(a) The MacBook Air. (b) The MacBook.
(c) The iMac.

13-inch screen. The iMac line features sleek, space-saving desktop units sporting fast Intel Core 2 Duo processors.

Some people are switching to Macs because they love their iPods so much. Apple is leveraging the popularity of these digital devices by designing software to let its computers work seamlessly with the iPods. In addition, many Apple fans think Macs are more user-friendly and stylish than their PC competitors. Professionals such as digital artists and graphic designers who create or edit computer images change to Macs because the applications these users rely on deliver superior features on the Apple platform.

Mac OS X Snow Leopard

Many Mac users have switched from Windows because of the operating system, Mac OS X. The latest version, Snow Leopard, has many slick and innovative features that are tempting to even the most loyal Windows users. If you've been using Windows for a while, you shouldn't have any problem making the transition to Snow Leopard. You'll notice immediately that the Mac OS uses the same desktop metaphors as Windows, including icons for folders and a Trash Can (similar to a Recycle Bin) to delete documents. It also includes a window-based interface like the one you're already accustomed to using in Windows.

Like earlier versions of Mac OS, Snow Leopard is based on the UNIX OS, which is exceptionally stable and reliable. Aside from stability, security and safety are great reasons to switch to the Mac OS because it does not seem as vulnerable as Windows is to the exploitation of security flaws by hackers. This doesn't necessarily mean that the Mac OS is better constructed than Windows; it could just be that because Windows has a lead in market share, it is a more attractive target for hackers. Regardless of the reason, you're probably somewhat less likely to be inconvenienced by viruses, hacking, and spyware if you're running Mac OS. Of course, you won't have any better protection from spam, phishing, or other Internet scams than you would with Internet Explorer, so you still need to stay alert. Snow Leopard offers a 3D desktop environment as well as an automated backup utility called Time Machine (see Figure 12).

When you boot up a Mac, a program called the Finder automatically starts. This program is like Windows Explorer and

FIGURE 12

Time Machine, an automated backup and restore utility, is one of the features in Mac OS X.

controls the desktop and the windows with which you interact. It's always running when the Mac is on. With the Quick Look feature, it is possible for you to view the contents of a file without ever opening it. This allows you to flip through multipage documents, watch videos, and view an entire presentation with just a single click of the mouse. Spaces is the name of another feature, which helps to keep order when projects pile up. With Spaces, you can group your application windows.

Snow Leopard has kept other features from previous versions, such as Spotlight, a desktop search feature that allows you to find anything on your computer from one spot. The Dashboard and widgets enable you to have easy access to many mini-applications that allow you to perform common tasks and get quick access to real-time information such as weather, stock prices, and sports updates.

At the top of the desktop is the menu bar. The options on the menu bar change according to which program is "active" (that is, foremost on your screen) at the moment. When you click the Apple icon in the upper left corner, a drop-down menu displays, from which you can select several options. The Dock is similar to the Taskbar in Windows and includes a strip of icons that displays across the bottom of the desktop.

Each Finder window has an area on the left known as the Sidebar (see Figure 13).

The Sidebar holds any folders you specify (such as the PageOneEditing folder shown here).

>To access the Sidebar, double-click the hard drive icon on the desktop.

The Sidebar holds any folders you specify (even though the icons don't look like folders). This makes navigation easier and faster. You can choose to view the contents of files and folders in three different views: icon view, list view, and column view. As shown in Figure 13, the sidebar shows that the PageOneEditing folder is selected. The files

Much like the Control Panel in Windows, the System Preferences window allows you to customize and configure Mac OS X.

>To get to System Preferences, click the **Apple** menu icon in the top left corner of the screen and choose **System Preferences**.

and subfolders in the PageOneEditing folder display in the next two columns. A display window shows a thumbnail preview of the selected file. Navigating around a Finder window and copying and moving files work almost exactly the same way as they do in Windows.

Configuring a Mac

In Windows, you make changes to settings and preferences through the Control Panel. In Mac OS X Snow Leopard, you use System Preferences, which is an option on the Apple menu. Selecting System Preferences from the Apple menu displays the window shown in Figure 14.

Protecting Your Mac

Although Macs tend to be attacked less frequently by viruses and other hacker nuisances than PCs running Windows are, you can still be vulnerable if you don't take precautions. Snow Leopard comes with a firewall, but you should take the necessary steps to configure it properly before connecting to the Internet for the first time, because the firewall is set, by default, to allow all incoming connections. As shown in Figure 15, to block all connections except those that are critical to your computer's operation, select "Allow only essential services." If you'd rather set up your firewall on a per-application basis, select the Access for specific services and applications option.

In addition, hackers may be creating viruses and other nuisances to exploit security holes in the Mac OS. Mac users, like Windows users, should keep their software up to date with the latest fixes and software patches by setting their system to check automatically for software updates on a periodic basis. On Macs, this feature is available through the System Preferences window. Figure 16 shows the options you should choose to keep the Mac OS up to date. The Check Now button enables you to check for immediate updates, which is a great thing to do when you first set up your computer. Then, you can choose to have your computer check for updates regularly by scheduling software updates to run automatically at a time convenient to you. Make sure you choose to have the updates downloaded automatically. This feature alerts you when updates are ready to be installed. In addition to these precautions, antivirus software such as Norton is available for Snow Leopard.

Utility Programs

Just like Windows, the Mac OS contains a wide variety of utility programs to help users maintain and evaluate their computers. In Macs, utility programs are located in a folder named Utilities within the Applications folder on the hard drive.

If you're a Windows user, you know that the Windows Task Manager utility can help you determine how your system is performing. In Macs, a similar utility, shown in Figure 17, is called the Activity Monitor. It shows what programs (processes) are currently running and how much memory they're using. The CPU, System Memory, Disk Activity, Disk Usage, and Network buttons indicate the activity in each of these crucial areas.

Like the Systems Properties box in Windows, the Mac OS System Profiler shown in Figure 18 displays all the hardware (and software) installed in a Mac, including the type of processor, the amount of RAM installed, and the amount of VRAM on the video card.

As you can see, operating a Mac is fairly simple and is similar to working in the Windows environment. If you need more help beyond what we provide in this Technology in Focus feature, there are many books that will help you make a smooth transition to using an Apple computer.

DO IT YOURSELF!

The do-it-yourself craze has swept across America, so why not stop repainting the house and apply those do-it-yourself skills to building a computer? Of course, building a computer isn't for everyone, but for those who enjoy working with their hands and don't mind doing some up-front research, it can be a rewarding experience.

Many Web sites can provide guidance for building your own Windows-based computer. PC Mechanic (**pcmech.com/byopc**) is a good place to start. Just Google "How to build your own computer" and you'll find plenty of online help and advice. To start, you need a list of parts. Here's what you'll typically need:

FIGURE 15

Macs have a firewall, but be sure to configure the firewall before you connect to the Internet.

>Click on the **Security** icon under the **Personal** section of the **System Preferences** window. When the Security window opens, click on the **Firewall** button to display the Firewall configuration screen.

FIGURE 16

Keeping the Mac OS up to date with the latest software fixes and patches greatly decreases your chances of being inconvenienced by hackers.

From the **Apple** menu, choose **System Preferences**, and then click **Software Update**.

1. **Case:** Make sure the case you buy is an ATX-style case, which accommodates the newest motherboards, and that it includes an adequate cooling fan. Also, be sure there are enough drive bays in the case to handle the hard drive and

Running processes and memory usage displayed

Graphical representation of CPU usage

CPU display

FIGURE 17

Similar to the Task Manager in Windows, the Activity Monitor analyzes the performance of a Mac.

>Go to the **Utilities** folder found in the **Applications** folder on your hard drive and double-click **Activity Monitor** to open the utility.

FIGURE 18

The System Profiler is similar to the Systems Properties dialog box in Windows and reveals a wealth of information about the hardware and software in the computer.

>To launch System Profiler, from the **Apple** menu, click **About this Mac**, and then click the **More Info** button.

any other peripheral drives (CD, DVD, and so on) you'll be installing.

2. **Power Supply:** A power supply provides power to the computer. Some cases come with a power supply installed. Make sure to get a power supply with adequate wattage to handle the load generated by all of the computer's components.

3. **Processor (CPU):** Get the fastest one you can afford, because it will help to extend the life of your computer. Many processors come with a fan installed to cool the unit; if not, you'll need to purchase a processor cooling fan.

4. **Motherboard:** Many motherboards come with sound, video, and network cards. These work fine for basic computing, but if you're building a PC for gaming, opt for a motherboard into which you can plug higher-end graphics and sound cards. Also make sure that the motherboard you buy can accommodate the CPU you have chosen. The motherboard needs to have expansion slots (PCI slots and a separate AGP) for high-end video and sound cards and Internet connectivity.

5. **USB ports:** Make sure that your motherboard has at least two USB ports, and install a separate bay with USB and FireWire ports for flash drives and other devices. Other devices, such as your monitor and keyboard, may also incorporate USB ports for additional flexibility.

6. **RAM:** Check your motherboard specifications before buying RAM to ensure you buy the correct type and an amount that will fit into the available slots. In addition, make sure that the amount of RAM you choose is supported by your operating system (32 bit vs. 64 bit).

7. **Video Card:** Low-end cards with 128 or 256 MB of video memory are fine for normal computer use, but for gaming or displaying high-end graphics or videos, get a card with 512 MB or more, depending on your budget. If you will be using a digital LCD monitor or hooking your gaming system to your computer, make sure that the video card has a DVI connection or an HDMI port.

8. **Sound card:** Make sure to get a PCI card that is compatible with Sound Blaster (the standard for sound cards).

9. **Optical drives (CD, DVD, and Blu-ray):** A CD or DVD drive is necessary for software installation. You can install individual drives or a combination drive that has CD and DVD capabilities. If you want portable storage, make sure the CD or DVD drive has the capability to write CDs and DVDs. You may want to install a Blu-ray drive to view your favorite movies using high-definition technology, or a Blu-ray burner to archive large volumes of data.

10. **Hard drive:** The price per gigabyte has been rapidly coming down in recent years, so get a large-volume drive. For optimal performance, choose a hard drive with the fastest RPM you can afford.

11. **Network interface card:** Network cards for wired or wireless Internet connectivity are sometimes integrated with the motherboard, so check before you buy one.

In addition to these components, you'll need a keyboard, a mouse or other pointing device, a monitor, and OS software.

You can buy these components at reputable Web sites such as Tiger Direct (**tigerdirect.com**), CompUSA (**compusa.com**), or New Egg (**newegg.com**). Once you have the components, it is almost as simple as bolting them into the case and connecting them properly. Make sure you read all the installation instructions that come with your components before beginning installation. Don't forget to check YouTube or the Web sites of component manufacturers for handy how-to videos and step-by-step installation guides. Then read a complete installation tutorial such as the one found at the Tech Report Web site (**techreport.com**), which provides an excellent visual guide to assembling a computer. Now, grab your screwdriver and get started. You'll be up and running in no time. The advantages and disadvantages of building your own Windows-based computer are shown in Figure 19.

As you can see, there are many computing options other than a Windows-based computer running commercial software applications. We hope you spread your wings and try a few of them.

FIGURE 19 Considerations When Building Your Own Computer

Advantages	Disadvantages
You get exactly the configuration and features you want.	There is no technical support when things go wrong.
You have the option of using components other than those that are used in mass-produced computers.	You'll need to examine more complex technical specifications (such as which CPU works with the motherboard you want), which may overwhelm the average computer user.
If you succeed, you will get a feeling of satisfaction from a job well done.	You will not necessarily save money.

six

understanding and assessing hardware:

evaluating your system

objectives

After reading this chapter, you should be able to answer the following questions:

1. How can I determine whether I should upgrade my existing computer or buy a new one? *(pp. 268–272)*

2. What does the CPU do, and how can I evaluate its performance? *(pp. 272–276)*

3. How does memory work in my computer, and how can I evaluate how much memory I need? *(pp. 276–281)*

4. What are the computer's main storage devices, and how can I evaluate whether they match my needs? *(pp. 281–286)*

5. What components affect the output of video on my computer, and how can I evaluate whether they match my needs? *(pp. 287–289)*

6. What components affect my computer's sound quality, and how can I evaluate whether they match my needs? *(pp. 290–291)*

7. How can I improve the reliability of my system? *(pp. 291–293)*

resources

Active Helpdesk

- Evaluating Your CPU and RAM **(p. 276)**
- Evaluating Computer System Components **(p. 287)**

Sound Bytes

- Using Windows 7 to Evaluate CPU Performance **(p. 276)**
- Memory Hierarchy Interactive **(p. 278)**
- Installing RAM **(p. 279)**
- CD, DVD, and Blu-ray Reading and Writing Interactive **(p. 285)**
- Installing a Blu-ray Drive **(p. 286)**

Companion Website

The Companion Website includes a variety of additional materials to help you review and learn more about the topics in this chapter. Go to: *pearsonhighered.com/techinaction*

how cool is *this?* The **Phobos** com-

puter system is designed to work as a media entertainment unit or a high-performance business system. It features a **touch-panel LCD** on the front of the system unit that reports system performance parameters, controls music content, and presents a summary of storage and memory usage. There is also an integrated iPod/iPhone **docking station** on the top of the system unit. It is designed so all of the cables exit from the bottom of the unit instead of the back for a cleaner appearance.

With four hard drive bays, a front slot-loading Blu-ray drive, and an RF remote to control it all, the Phobos works well as a **media center**. Because of its 12 GB of DDR3 RAM and Intel i7 processor, the Phobos works well, too, as a powerhouse business computer.

Is It the Computer or Me?

After saving up for a computer, Natalie took the leap a couple of years ago and bought a new desktop PC. Now she is wondering what to do. Her friends with newer computers are burning DVDs and Blu-ray discs, and they're able to hook their digital cameras directly to their computers and create multimedia files. They seem to be able to do a hundred things at once without their computers slowing down at all.

Natalie's computer can't do any of these things—or at least she doesn't think it can. Lately it seems to take longer to open files and scroll through Web pages. Making matters worse, her computer freezes often and takes a long time to reboot. Now she's wondering whether she should buy a new computer, but the thought of spending all that money again makes her think twice. As she looks at ads for new computers, she realizes she doesn't know what such things as "CPU" and "RAM" really are, or how they affect her system. Meanwhile, she's heard it's possible to upgrade her computer, but the task seems daunting. How will she know what she needs to do to upgrade, or whether it's even worth it?

Are you in the same situation? How well is your computer meeting your needs? Do you ever wonder whether your computer is fine and you just need more training to get it to work smoothly? Is that true, or do you really need a more sophisticated computer system? In this chapter, you'll learn how to evaluate your computer system to determine whether it is meeting your needs. You'll start by figuring out what you want your ideal computer to be able to do. You'll then learn more about important components of your computer—its CPU, memory, storage devices, audio and video devices, and ports—and how these components affect your system. Along the way, you'll find worksheets to help you conduct a system evaluation, and multimedia Sound Bytes that will show you how to install various components in your system and increase its reliability. You'll also learn about the various utilities available to help speed up and clean up your system. If you don't have a computer, this chapter will provide you with important information you will need about computer hardware to make an informed purchasing decision.

Is now a good time to buy a new computer? There never seems to be a perfect time to buy. It seems that if you can just wait a year, computers will inevitably be faster and cost less. Is this actually true?

As it turns out, it is true. In fact, a rule of thumb often cited in the computer industry, called **Moore's Law**, describes the pace at which CPUs (central processing units)—the small chips that can be thought of as the "brains" of the computer—improve. Named for Gordon Moore, the cofounder of the CPU chip manufacturer Intel, this rule predicts that the number of transistors inside a CPU will increase so fast that CPU capacity will double every 18 months. (The number of transistors on a CPU chip helps determine how fast it can process data.)

As you can see in Figure 6.1, this rule of thumb has held true since 1970, when Moore first published his theory. Imagine finding a bank that would agree to treat your money in this way. If you put 10 cents in that kind of savings account in 1965, you would have a balance of more than $100 million today! Moore himself, however, has predicted that around the year 2020 CPU chips will be manufactured in a different way, thus changing or eliminating the effects of Moore's Law altogether.

In addition to the CPU becoming faster, other system components also continue to improve dramatically. For example, the capacity of memory chips such as dynamic random access memory (DRAM)—the most common form of memory found in personal computers—increases about 60 percent every year. Meanwhile, hard drives have been growing in storage capacity by some 50 percent each year.

Figure 6.1

Moore's Law predicts that CPUs will continue to get faster.

Source: Adapted from the Moore's Law animated demo at **Intel.com**.

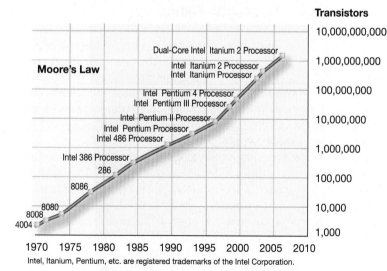

Intel, Itanium, Pentium, etc. are registered trademarks of the Intel Corporation.

So, with technology advancing so quickly, how do you make sure you have a computer that matches your needs? No one wants to buy a new computer every year just to keep up with technology. Even if money weren't a consideration, the time it would take to transfer all of your files and reinstall and reconfigure your software would make buying a new computer every year terribly inefficient. Extending the life of a computer also reduces or postpones the environmental and security concerns involved in the disposal of computers.

No one wants to keep doing costly upgrades that won't significantly extend the life of a system, either. How can you determine if your system is suitable or if it just needs to be upgraded? Moreover, how can you know which is the better option—upgrading or buying a new computer? The first step is figuring out what you want your computer to do for you.

> **"To determine your ideal system, consider what you want to be able to do with your computer."**

What Is Your Ideal Computer?

As you decide whether your computer suits you, it's important to know exactly what you would want your ideal computer system to be able to do. Later, as you perform a system evaluation, you can compare your existing system to your ideal system. This will help you determine whether you should purchase hardware components to add to your system or buy a new system.

But what if I don't have a computer? Even if you're a new computer user and are looking to buy your first system, you will still need to evaluate what you want your system to do for you before you purchase a computer. Being able to understand and evaluate computer systems will make you a more informed buyer. You should be comfortable answering questions such as "What kinds of CPUs are there, and how does the CPU affect system performance?" and "How much RAM do I need, and what role will it play in my system?" It's important for you to be able to answer such questions before you buy a computer.

How do I know what my ideal system is? To determine your ideal system, consider what you want to be able to do with your computer. For example, do you need to bring your computer to school or work with you? Do you want to be able to edit digital photos? Do you want to watch and record Blu-ray discs? Or are you just using your computer for word processing? The worksheet in Figure 6.2 lists a number of ways in which you may want to use your computer. In the second column, place a check next to those computer uses that apply to you. Also, set a priority of high, medium, or low in the rightmost column so that you can determine which features are most important to you.

Next, look at the list of desired uses for your computer and determine whether your current system can perform these activities. If there are things it can't do, you may need to purchase additional hardware or a better computer. For example, if you want to play and burn CDs and DVDs, all you need is a DVD–RW drive. However, you need a Blu-ray burner if you want to burn (record) the higher capacity Blu-ray discs. Likewise, if you plan to edit digital video files or play games that include a lot of sounds and graphics with large files, you may want to add more memory, buy a better set of speakers, add a high-speed hard drive, and possibly invest in a new monitor. Depending on the costs of the individual upgrade components, you may be better off buying a new system.

BITS AND BYTES

Moving to a New Computer Doesn't Have to Be Painful

Are you ready to buy a new computer but dread the prospect of transferring all your files and redoing all of your Windows settings? You could transfer all those files and settings manually, but Windows stores much information in the registry files, which can be tricky to update. So what do you do? Windows 7 incorporates Windows Easy Transfer, which lets you migrate files and settings from a Windows Vista system to a Windows 7 system via a network connection by using a flash drive or external hard drive or using optical media such as a CD or DVD.

Alternatively, other PC migration software is available, such as Acronis Migrate Easy 7.0 and PCmover, both of which are designed to make the transition to a new computer easier. For the latest information on such utilities, search on migration software at PCmag (**pcmag.com**). You'll be ready to upgrade painlessly in no time. If you prefer to avoid the do-it-yourself option, support technicians at retail stores (such as the Geek Squad at Best Buy) will often perform the migration for a nominal charge.

Figure 6.2 | WHAT SHOULD YOUR IDEAL COMPUTER SYSTEM BE ABLE TO DO?

Computer Uses	Can Your System Do This Now?	Do You Want Your System to Do This?	Priority (High, Medium, Low)
Portability Uses			
Take your computer with you			
Access the Internet wirelessly			
Entertainment Uses			
Access the Internet, send e-mail			
Play and record CDs and DVDs			
Play and record Blu-ray discs			
Record and edit digital videos			
Record and edit digital music			
Edit digital photos			
Play graphics-intensive games			
Transfer digital photos (or other files) to your computer using flash memory cards			
Connect all your peripheral devices to your computer at the same time			
Purchase music or videos from the Internet			
Talk with friends and family with live video and audio			
Other			
Educational Uses			
Perform word processing tasks			
Use educational software			
Access library and newspaper archives			
Create multimedia presentations			
Create backups of all your files			
Other			
Business Uses			
Create spreadsheets or databases			
Work on multiple software applications quickly and simultaneously			
Conduct online banking, pay bills online, or prepare your taxes			
Conduct online job searches or post résumés			
Synchronize your mobile device (smartphone, or portable media player) with your computer			
Conduct online meetings with video and audio			
Other			

Note that you also may need new software and training to use new system components. Many computer users forget to consider the training they'll need when they upgrade their computer. Missing any one of these pieces might make the difference between your computer enriching your life and its becoming another source of stress.

How do I know if I need training? Although computers are becoming increasingly user-friendly, you still need to learn how to use them to your best advantage. Say you want to edit digital photos. You know image editing software exists, but how do you know if your computer's hardware can support the software? What will happen if you can't get it installed or don't know how to use it? If you have questions like these, you know you need training. Training shouldn't be an afterthought. Consider the time and effort involved in learning about what you want your computer to do before you buy hardware or software. If you don't, you may have a wonderful computer system but lack the skills necessary to take full advantage of it.

Choosing Either a Desktop or Notebook System

The first step in evaluating your system needs is determining whether you want a desktop or a notebook. In this discussion, we'll only be considering full-size desktops and notebooks. If your main need is Internet connectivity, not processing power, and a small screen and small keyboard are acceptable, a netbook may be a workable option. Netbooks are discussed in more detail in Chapter 8.

To make the best decision, it's important to evaluate how and where you will use the computer. The main distinction between desktops and notebooks is portability. If you indicated in the chart in Figure 6.2

Figure 6.3

ExpressCards add functionality to your notebook.

that you need to take your computer with you to work or school, or even want the flexibility to move from room to room in your house, a notebook is the best choice. If portability is not an absolute factor, you should consider a desktop. Here are additional factors to consider in the decision.

How does a notebook compare to a desktop for value? Desktop systems are invariably a better value than notebooks in terms of computing power gained for your dollar. Because of the notebook's small footprint (the amount of space it takes up on the desk), you pay more for each component. Each piece has had extra engineering time invested to make sure it fits in the smallest space. In addition, a desktop system offers more expandability options. It's easier to add new ports and devices because of the amount of room available in the desktop computer's design.

Desktop systems also are more reliable. Because of the amount of vibration that a notebook experiences and the added exposure to dust, water, and temperature fluctuations that portability provides, notebooks do not last as long as desktop computers. Manufacturers offer extended warranty plans that cover accidental damage and unexpected drops; however, such plans may be costly.

How long will a notebook be useful to me? The answer to that question depends on how easy it is to upgrade your system. Take note of the maximum amount of memory you can install in your notebook because that cannot be changed a few years down the road. Internal hard drives are not easy for novices to install in a notebook, but if you have a fast transfer port like **eSATA** (external SATA) or USB 2.0 on your notebook, you can easily add an external hard drive for more storage space.

Notebooks that are also equipped with an ExpressCard slot. **ExpressCard** (shown in Figure 6.3) can add fax modems, network connections, wireless adapters, USB 2.0 and

Figure 6.4 | DESKTOP VERSUS NOTEBOOK COMPUTERS—WHICH FITS YOU?

Notebooks	Desktops
Portable	Best value: more speed, memory, and storage capacity for lower price
Take up less physical space	More difficult to steal, less susceptible to damage from dropping or mishandling
Easier to ship or transport if the system needs repair	Easier to expand and upgrade

FireWire ports, and other capabilities to your system. You can add an ExpressCard that allows you to read flash memory cards such as CompactFlash, Memory Sticks, and Secure Digital cards. As new types of ports and devices are introduced, many will be manufactured in ExpressCard formats so you can make sure your notebook does not become obsolete before its time. Figure 6.4 summarizes the advantages and disadvantages of each style of computer.

Assessing Your Hardware: Evaluating Your System

With a better picture of your ideal computer system in mind, you can make a more informed assessment of your current computer. To determine whether your computer system has the right hardware components to do what you ultimately want it to do, you need to conduct a **system evaluation**. To do this, you look at your computer's subsystems, see what they do, and check how they perform. These subsystems include the following:

- CPU subsystem
- Memory subsystem (the computer's random access memory, or RAM)
- Storage subsystem (hard drive and other drives)
- Video subsystem (video card and monitor)
- Audio subsystem (sound card and speakers)
- Computer ports

In the rest of this chapter, we will examine each subsystem. At the end of each section, you'll find a small worksheet you

can use to evaluate each subsystem on your computer. *Note:* This chapter discusses tools you can use to assess a Windows-based PC. For information on how to assess a Mac, refer to the Technology in Focus feature "Computing Alternatives" on page 252.

Evaluating the CPU Subsystem

Early in the process of determining whether your computer system adequately meets your needs, you'll want to consider the type of processor in your system. As mentioned in chapter 2, your computer's central processing unit (CPU or processor) is critically important because it processes instructions, performs calculations, manages the flow of information through a computer system, and is responsible for turning raw data into valuable information through processing operations. The CPU is located on the motherboard, the primary circuit board of the computer system. There are several types of processors on the market including Intel processors (such as the Core family with the i7, Core 2 Quad and Core 2 Duo, and the Centrino line) and AMD processors (such as the Athlon and Phenom, both of which are used on PCs). The Intel Core i7 is the most advanced desktop CPU ever made by Intel. Figure 6.5 shows the Core i7 as well as the CPU used in the Microsoft Xbox 360 gaming console, the PowerPC.

How does the CPU work? The CPU is composed of two units: the control unit and the arithmetic logic unit (ALU). The control unit coordinates the activities of all the other computer components. The ALU is responsible for performing all the arithmetic calculations (addition, subtraction, multiplication, and division). The ALU also makes logic and comparison decisions such as comparing items to determine if one is greater than, less than, equal to, or not equal to another.

Every time the CPU performs a program instruction, it goes through the same series of steps. First, it fetches the required piece of data or instruction from RAM, the temporary storage location for all the data and instructions the computer needs while it is running. Next, it decodes the instruction into something the computer can understand. Once the CPU has decoded the instruction, it executes the instruction and stores the result to RAM before fetching the next instruction. This process is called a machine cycle. (We will discuss the machine cycle in more detail in the Technology in Focus feature "Under the Hood" on page 340.)

What makes one CPU different from another? The primary distinction between CPUs is processing power, which is determined by a number of factors. One such factor is the design of the CPU in terms of the number of cores. A **core** is a complete processing section from a CPU embedded into one physical chip. In addition to core design, other factors differentiate CPUs, including how quickly the processor can work (called its **clock speed**) and the amount of immediate access memory the CPU has (called its cache memory).

How will a multiple-core CPU help me? CPUs began to execute more than one instruction at a time quite a while ago, when hyperthreading was introduced. **Hyperthreading** provides quicker processing of information by enabling a new set of instructions to start executing before the previous set has finished. The most recent design innovation for PC processors, an improvement upon hyperthreading, is the use of multiple cores on one CPU chip. With core technology, two or more processors reside on the same chip, enabling the execution of two sets of instructions at the same time. Now applications that are always running behind the scenes, such as virus

protection software and your operating system, can have their own processor, freeing the other processor to run other applications such as a Web browser, Word, or iTunes more efficiently. Figure 6.6 shows these different approaches.

In Figure 6.6c, hyperthreading allows two different programs to be processed at one time, but they are sharing the computing resources of the chip. With multiple cores, each program has the full attention of its own processing core (see Figure 6.6a and Figure 6.6b). This results in faster processing and smoother multitasking. It is possible to design a CPU to have multiple cores *and* hyperthreading. The Intel i7 has four cores, each one using hyperthreading, so it simulates having eight processors!

Figure 6.5

(a) The Intel Core i7 is the most advanced desktop CPU ever made by Intel. (b) The Microsoft Xbox 360 gaming console uses a custom PowerPC–based CPU to perform 115 billion calculations per second.

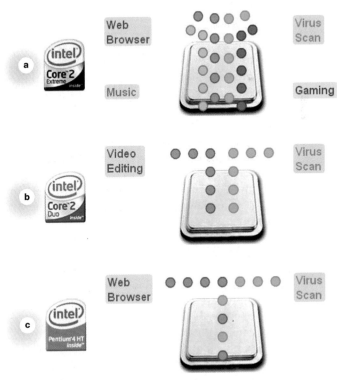

Figure 6.6

(a) The Intel Core 2 Extreme is a four-core processor, able to run four programs simultaneously. (b) The Intel Core 2 Duo is a two-core processor. (c) The Intel Pentium 4 Hyperthreading operates with only one core but it hyperthreads (working on two processes at once).

Figure 6.7 | PROCESSOR SPECIFICATIONS

		Number of Cores	Max Clock Speed	Max FSB	Max L2Cache
Desktop Processors	Core 2 Duo	2	3.33 GHz	1333 MHz	6 MB
	Core 2 Quad	4	3 GHz	1333 MHz	12 MB
	Core 2 Extreme	4	3.20 GHz	1600 MHz	12 MB
Notebook Processors	Celeron	1	2.16 GHz	666 MHz	1 MB
	Core 2 Solo	1	1.40 GHz	800 MHz	3 MB
	Core 2 Duo	2	2.93 GHz	1066 MHz	6 MB
	Core 2 Quad	4	3 GHz	1333 MHz	12 MB
	Core 2 Extreme	4	3.06 GHz	1066 MHz	12 MB

How do I pick the fastest processor? While clock speed is an important consideration when determining processor performance, CPU performance also is affected by the amount of cache memory and the speed of the front side bus (FSB). **Cache memory** is a form of random access memory that is more accessible to the CPU than regular RAM. Because of its ready access to the CPU, cache memory gets data to the CPU for processing much faster than bringing the data in from RAM.

There are several levels of cache memory. These levels are defined by a chip's proximity to the CPU. Level 1 cache is a block of memory that is built onto the CPU chip for the storage of data or commands that have just been used. Level 2 cache is located on the CPU chip but is slightly farther away from the CPU, or it's on a separate chip next to the CPU and therefore takes somewhat longer to access. Level 2 cache contains more storage area than does level 1 cache.

The **front side bus** (FSB) connects the processor (CPU) in your computer to the system memory. Think of the front side bus as the highway on which data travels between the CPU and RAM. With a wider highway, traffic can move faster because more cars can travel at the same time. Consequently, the faster the FSB is, the faster you can get data to your processor. The faster you get data to the processor, the faster your processor can work on it. FSB speed is measured in megahertz (MHz). The speed of the front side bus is an important consideration that determines CPU performance.

Modern processors are defined by the combination of processor speed, front side bus speed, and the amount of cache memory. For example, Intel's Core 2 Duo processors come in a range of clock speeds, cache memory sizes, and front side bus speeds, as seen in Figure 6.7. Even within one processor family, there is a variety of choices. For example, the E8500 Core 2 Duo processor has a 3.16 GHz processor speed, 6 MB L2 cache, and 1333 MHz front side bus, whereas the E6700 Core 2 Duo processor has a 2.66 GHz processor speed, 4 MB L2 cache, and a 1066 MHz front side bus.

There are many factors that influence CPU design, so picking the fastest CPU for the kind of work you do often involves researching some performance benchmarks. **Benchmarks** are measurements used to compare CPU performance between processors. Benchmarks are generated by running software programs specifically designed to push the limits of CPU performance. Articles are often published comparing a number of chips, or complete systems, based on their benchmark performance. Investigate a few, like **cpubenchmark.net**, before you select the chip that is best for you.

Why are there different CPU choices for notebooks and desktops? Both Intel and AMD make processors that are specifically designed for notebook computers. Notebook processors not only need to perform quickly and efficiently, like their desktop counterparts, but also need better power savings to improve battery life. Hardware used in notebooks includes Intel's Centrino 2 processor technology, which is a combination of a Core 2 Duo series processor with specialty hardware that supports long battery life and more flexible wireless connectivity options. AMD features notebook processors like the Turion 64 Mobile and the Mobile AMD Sempron. Desktop processors include Intel's Core i7, Core 2 Extreme, Quad, and Duo, and AMD's Athlon, Phenom, and Sempron.

What CPU does my current computer have? You can easily identify the type of CPU in your current system by accessing the system properties. As shown in Figure 6.8, you can view basic information about your computer, including which CPU is installed in your system as well as its speed. More detailed information, like the FSB speed and the amount of cache memory, is not shown in this screen. You can find those values by checking the manufacturer's Web site for the specific model number of CPU shown. For example, the CPU illustrated here is the Intel Core2 Duo, version E8400.

How can I tell whether my CPU is meeting my needs? As shown in Figure 6.9, several factors determine whether your CPU is meeting your needs. Although speed determines how fast your CPU is capable of performing operations, you also need to determine if that speed is capable of handling the tasks you need to perform. Even though your CPU meets the minimum requirements specified for a particular software application, if you're running other software (in addition to the operating system, which is always running), you'll need to check to see how well the CPU is handling the entire load. You can tell whether your CPU speed is limiting your system performance if you periodically watch how busy it is as you work on your computer. Keep in mind that the workload your CPU experiences will vary considerably depending on what you're doing. Even though it might run Word just fine, it may not be able to

handle running Word, a Web browser, iTunes, and IM at the same time. The percentage of time that your CPU is working is referred to as **CPU usage**.

A utility that measures information such as CPU usage and RAM usage is incredibly useful, both for considering whether you should upgrade and for investigating if your computer's performance suddenly seems to drop off for no apparent reason. On Windows systems, a program called Task Manager gives you easy access to all this data. Mac OS X has a utility similar to Task Manager called Activity Monitor, which is located in the Utilities folder in your Applications folder.

To view information on CPU usage, right-click an empty area of the taskbar, select Start Task Manager, and click the Performance tab, as shown in Figure 6.10. The CPU Usage graph records your CPU usage for the past several seconds. Of course, there will be periodic peaks of high CPU usage, but if you see that your CPU usage levels are greater than 90 percent during most of your work session, a faster CPU will contribute a great deal to your system's performance. If you are using the Windows Sidebar, there is a CPU Meter gadget you can add to track

Figure 6.8

The System Properties window identifies which CPU you have, as well as its speed.

>Click the **Start** button and then click **Computer** on the right panel of the **Start** menu. On the top toolbar, click **System Properties**.

Figure 6.9 | DO YOU NEED TO UPGRADE YOUR CPU?

	Current System	My Ideal System
What is my computer's CPU speed?		
How much cache memory is on the CPU*?		
What is the FSB speed*?		
What kind of multilevel processing does the CPU have—quad core, dual core, hyperthreaded, etc.?		
Is the CPU usage value below 90% during most of my daily tasks?		

*You can find these by checking the manufacturer's specifications for your model of CPU.

Using Windows 7 to Evaluate CPU Performance

In this Sound Byte, you'll learn how to use the utilities provided by Windows 7 to evaluate your CPU's performance. You'll also learn about shareware utilities (software that you can install and try before you purchase it) that expand on the capabilities the Task Manager utility provides.

both CPU and RAM usage. To see exactly how to use the Task Manager and the Sidebar gadget, watch the Sound Byte "Using Windows 7 to Evaluate CPU Performance."

Will improving the performance of the CPU be enough to improve my computer's performance? You may think that if you have the best processor, you will have a system with the best performance. However, upgrading your CPU will affect only the processing portion of the system performance, not how quickly data can move to or from the CPU. Your system's overall performance depends on many other factors, including the amount of RAM installed as well as hard drive speed. Therefore, your selection of a CPU may not offer significant improvements to your system's performance if there is a bottleneck in processing because of insufficient RAM or hard drive capacity.

Figure 6.10

The Performance tab of the Windows Task Manager utility shows you how busy your CPU actually is.

>In an empty area of the taskbar, right-click, select **Start Task Manager**, and click the **Performance** tab.

Current CPU usage level

CPU usage over time

Total RAM installed

Percentage of RAM in use

Evaluating RAM: The Memory Subsystem

Random access memory (RAM) is your computer's temporary storage space. Although we refer to RAM as a form of storage, it really is the computer's short-term memory. As such, it remembers everything that the computer needs to process the data into information, such as data that has been entered and software instructions, but only when the computer is on. RAM is an example of **volatile storage**. When the power is off, the data stored in RAM is cleared out. This is why, in addition to RAM, systems always include **nonvolatile storage** devices for permanent storage of instructions and data when the computer is powered off. ROM memory, for example, holds the critical startup instructions. Hard drives provide the greatest nonvolatile storage capacity in the computer system.

Why not use a hard drive to store the data and instructions? It's about one million times faster for the CPU to retrieve a piece of data from RAM than from a hard drive. The time it takes the CPU to retrieve data from RAM is measured in nanoseconds (billionths of seconds), whereas retrieving data from a fast hard drive takes an average of 10 milliseconds (ms), or thousandths of seconds. Figure 6.11 shows the various types of memory and storage that are distributed throughout your system: CPU registers, cache, RAM, and hard drive. Each of these has its own tradeoff of speed vs. price. Because the fastest memory is so much more expensive, systems are designed with much less of it. This principle is influential in the design of a balanced computer system and can have a tremendous impact on system performance.

Are there different types of RAM? Like most computer components, RAM has gone through a series of transitions. In current systems, the RAM used most often

ACTIVE HELP-DESK

Evaluating Your CPU and RAM

In this Active Helpdesk call, you'll play the role of a helpdesk staffer, fielding calls about what the CPU does and how to evaluate its performance. You'll also field calls about how memory works and how to evaluate how much memory a computer needs.

Figure 6.11

A computer system's memory has many different levels, ranging from the small amounts in the CPU to the much slower but more plentiful storage of a hard drive.

Fast access but very little storage

CPU Registers

Level 1 cache

Level 2 cache

Level 3 cache

Physical RAM

Virtual Memory

Optical Disk Drives

Hard Drive

Huge amounts of storage but slow speeds

Hard drive

RAM

CPU registers and L1, L2 cache

comes in the form of double data rate 2 (DDR2) memory modules. Double data rate 3 memory (DDR3), which has an even faster data transfer rate, is seen in high-performance systems. In older systems, other types of RAM may have been used, including DRAM, static RAM (SRAM), and synchronous DRAM (SDRAM). RAM appears in the system on **memory modules** (or **memory cards**), small circuit boards that hold a series of RAM chips and fit into special slots on the motherboard (see Figure 6.12). Most memory modules in today's systems are called *dual inline memory modules (DIMMs)*.

Types of RAM are slightly different from each other in how they function and in the speed at which they access memory. On high-end systems, manufacturers may offer an option to purchase Corsair Dominator DDR3 modules. These are tested to high levels to guarantee optimum performance. A special heat exchanger is designed into the RAM module to help it operate at a lower temperature, making it more stable and more reliable. All of these factors boost the performance of the memory and make it popular with demanding video gamers.

If you're adding RAM to any system, you must determine what type your system needs. Consult your user's manual or the manufacturer's Web site. In addition, many online RAM resellers, such as Crucial (**crucial.com**), can help you determine the type of RAM that is compatible with your

Figure 6.12

Memory modules hold a series of RAM chips and fit into special slots on the motherboard.

system based on the model number and brand of your computer.

How can I tell how much RAM is installed in my computer? The amount of RAM that is actually sitting on memory modules in your computer is your computer's **physical memory**. The easiest way to see how much RAM you have is to look in the System Properties window. (On the Mac, choose About This Mac from the Apple menu.) This is the same tab you looked in to determine your system's CPU type and speed, and is shown in Figure 6.8. RAM capacity is measured in gigabytes (GB), and most machines sold today, especially those running Windows, have at least 2 GB of RAM. The computer in Figure 6.10 has 4094 MB (or 4.00 GB) of RAM installed.

More detailed information on physical memory is displayed in the Physical Memory table in the Performance tab of Windows Task Manager, shown in Figure 6.13. The Physical Memory table shows the total amount of physical memory you have installed as well as the available physical memory you have. If you are used to using Windows XP, when you have only a couple of applications running, you might expect to see lots of available memory. When using Windows Vista or Windows 7, even with just one application running, it will appear

SOUND BYTE

Memory Hierarchy Interactive

In this Sound Byte, you'll learn about the different types of memory used in a computer system.

that you have little available memory, because these versions of Windows manage memory differently from previous versions of the Windows OS. Windows now uses a memory-management technique known as SuperFetch. SuperFetch monitors which applications you use the most and preloads these into your system memory so they'll be ready.

Because RAM is so much faster to access than the hard drive that you have in your computer, it would be helpful to have as much information as possible about the programs you are currently using in RAM so your computer will respond faster. Windows 7 manages memory by anticipating what information you will need next and storing it in RAM instead of in cache memory or on your hard drive. For example, if you have Word running, Windows 7 stores as much of the information related to Word in RAM as it can, thereby almost filling up your RAM. Don't worry, because as other needs arise (if you start Excel, for instance), the operating system reallocates the contents of RAM to account for your use of multiple programs.

How much memory does the operating system need to run? The memory that your operating system uses is referred to as **kernel memory**. This memory is listed in a separate Kernel Memory table in the Performance tab. In Figure 6.13, the Kernel Memory table tells you that approximately 555 MB (total kernel memory) of the total 4 GB of RAM is being used to run the operating system.

As you know from Chapter 5, the operating system is the main software application that runs the computer. Without it, the computer does not work. At a minimum, the system needs enough RAM to run the operating system. Therefore, the amount of kernel memory that the system is using is the absolute minimum amount of RAM that your computer can run on. However, because you run additional applications, you need to have more RAM than the minimum.

How much RAM do I need?
Because RAM is the temporary holding space for all the data and instructions that the computer uses while it's on, most computer users need quite a bit of RAM. In fact, systems running all the new features of Windows 7 should have a minimum of 1 GB of RAM, but for peak performance, systems are recommended to have at least 2 GB of RAM. Ultimately, the amount of RAM your system needs depends on how you use it. At a minimum, you need enough RAM to run the operating system (as explained earlier), plus whatever other software applications you're using, and then a bit of additional RAM to hold the data you're inputting.

To determine how much RAM you need, list all the software applications you might be running at one time. Figure 6.14 shows an example of RAM requirements. In this example, if you are running your operating system, word processing and spreadsheet programs, a Web browser, a music player, and photo editing software simultaneously, then you will need a minimum of 2.15 GB of RAM. It's always best to check the system requirements of any software program before you buy it to make sure your system can handle it. System requirements can be found on the software packaging or on the manufacturer's Web site.

It's a good idea to have more than the minimum amount of RAM you need now, so you can use more programs in the future. Remember, too, that these are the minimum values recommended by the manufacturers,

Figure 6.13

The Performance tab of the Windows Task Manager shows you how much physical memory is installed in your system, as well as how much is currently being used and how much is available.

>In the **Taskbar** area, right-click. Select **Start Task Manager**. Click the **Performance** tab.

Memory required to run the operating system

Figure 6.14 | SAMPLE RAM REQUIREMENTS

Application	Minimum RAM Required
Windows 7	1,000 MB
Microsoft Office Professional 2007	256 MB
Internet Explorer 8	128 MB
iTunes	256 MB
Adobe Photoshop Elements	512 MB
Total RAM required to run all programs simultaneously	2,152 MB (2.15 GB)

and having more RAM often helps programs run more efficiently. When upgrading RAM, the rule of thumb is to buy as much as you can afford but no more than your system will handle.

Virtual Memory

Would adding more RAM improve my system performance?   You should consider several factors when determining if your system needs more RAM. When there's not enough RAM installed in your system, it will become sluggish, freeze more often, or just shut down when you perform certain tasks. When this happens, the system becomes **memory bound**—that is, limited in how fast it can send data to the CPU, because there is not enough memory. If this is the case, then adding more RAM to your system will immediately improve performance.

How do I know whether my system is memory bound?   As you recall from Chapter 5, if you don't have enough RAM to hold all of the programs you're currently trying to run, then the operating system will begin to store the data that doesn't fit in RAM in a space on the hard drive called **virtual memory**. When it is using virtual memory, your operating system builds a file called the **page file** on the hard drive to allow processing to continue. This enables the system to run more applications than can actually fit in your computer's RAM.

So far, this system of memory management sounds like a good idea, especially because hard drives are much cheaper than RAM per gigabyte of storage. The drawback

is speed. Remember that accessing data from the hard drive to send it to the CPU is more than one million times slower than accessing data from RAM. Another drawback is that some applications do not run well on virtual memory. Therefore, using virtual memory is a method of last resort.

If your system is often using virtual memory, then adding more RAM will dramatically increase performance. You can monitor how often you are exceeding your installed physical RAM by running the System Information program. In the Search box, type "system information". The System Summary tells you how much physical RAM is installed, how much is free, how much virtual memory is set up, and how much virtual memory is free. Do this at several points during the day and you will build a picture of how memory bound your system is.

Adding RAM

Is there a limit to how much RAM I can add to my computer?   Every computer is designed with a maximum limit on the amount of RAM it can support. Each computer is designed with a specific

Figure 6.15 | DO YOU NEED TO UPGRADE YOUR RAM?*

	Application	Current System	Ideal System
What is the maximum amount of RAM I need in my system for the applications I currently run?			
How much RAM is in my system?			
What is the maximum amount of RAM the system can hold*?			
Would I be willing to upgrade a 32-bit operating system to a 64-bit operating system to support having 4 GB or more of RAM?			

*Check the manufacturer's specifications for your system.

Figure 6.16

Adding RAM to a computer is quite simple and relatively inexpensive.

number of slots on the motherboard into which the memory cards fit, and each slot may have a limit on the amount of RAM it can support. To determine your specific system limits, check your owner's manual or the manufacturer's Web site.

In addition, the operating system running on your machine imposes its own limit. For example, the maximum amount of RAM for the 32-bit version of Windows 7 is 4 GB, while the 64-bit version of Windows 7 Ultimate can address up to 192 GB.

Once you know how much RAM your computer can support, you can determine the best configuration of memory modules to achieve the greatest amount of RAM. For example, say you have a total of four memory card slots: Two are already filled with 512 MB RAM cards and the other two are empty. The maximum RAM allowed for your system is 4 GB. This means you can buy two more 512 MB RAM modules for the two empty slots, for a total of 2 GB (4 × 512 MB) of RAM. Alternatively, you could throw away the 512 MB cards you have and purchase four new 1 GB cards, filling the system up to its capacity of 4 GB.

Review the considerations presented in Figure 6.15 to see if your system could benefit from an upgrade of additional RAM.

Is it hard to add RAM? Adding RAM to a computer is fairly easy (see Figure 6.16). RAM comes with installation instructions, which you should follow carefully. RAM is also relatively inexpensive compared with other system upgrade options. Still, the cost of RAM fluctuates in the marketplace as much as 400 percent over time, so if you're considering adding RAM, you should watch the prices of memory in online and print advertisements.

Adding RAM to a personal computer is quite simple and relatively inexpensive. You simply line up the notches and push in the memory module. Just be sure that you're adding a memory module that's compatible with your computer. For a video demonstration and more details, watch the Sound Byte, "Installing RAM."

Evaluating the Storage Subsystem

As you've learned, there are two ways data is saved on your computer: temporary storage and permanent storage. RAM is a form of temporary (or volatile) storage. Thus, anything that resides in RAM is not saved permanently. It's critical to have the means to store data and software applications permanently.

Fortunately, several storage options exist within every computer system. Storage devices for a typical personal computer include the hard drive, USB flash drives, optical drives, and external hard drives. When you turn off your computer, the data

stored to these devices is saved. These devices are therefore referred to as *nonvolatile* storage devices. Of all the nonvolatile storage devices, the hard drive is used the most.

The Hard Drive

What makes the hard drive the most popular storage device? With storage capacities exceeding 2 terabytes (TB), a **hard drive** has the largest storage capacity of any storage device. The hard drive is also a much more economical device than other storage options, because it offers the most gigabytes of storage per dollar. Most system units are designed to support more than one internal hard drive. The Apple Mac Pro, shown in Figure 6.17, has room for four hard drives. Each one simply slides into place when you want to upgrade.

Another reason the hard drive is so useful for storage is that the hard drive's **access time**, the time it takes a storage device to locate its stored data and make it available for processing, is faster than that of other

Figure 6.17
The Mac Pro allows you to slide a new hard drive into place easily. In all, the Mac Pro can hold up to 4 TB.

Empty cover removed

New 1 TB hard drive

Hard drive #2 slides into place

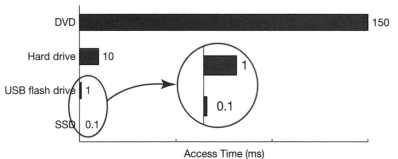

Figure 6.18

Access times for non-volatile storage options.

permanent storage devices, like optical drives. Hard drive access times are measured in milliseconds (ms), meaning thousandths of seconds. For large-capacity drives, access times of approximately 9.5 milliseconds—that's less than one-hundredth of a second—are typical. A DVD drive can take over 150 milliseconds to access data.

Solid state drives offer even faster access times. A **solid state drive** (SSD) uses the same kind of memory that flash drives use, but whereas flash drives have access times of about 1 ms, SSD drives can reach data in only a tenth of that time (around 0.1 ms). Because there are no spinning platters or motors needed, SSDs run with no noise, very little heat, and require very little power. As the prices for SSDs continue to drop, you'll start to see them in a wide range of systems.

Figure 6.18 provides a listing of the various storage options and compares their access times.

Another key performance specification for a hard drive is the speed at which it can transfer data to other computer components (such as RAM). This speed of transfer is referred to as **data transfer rate**. Depending on the manufacturer, the rate is expressed in either megabits or megabytes per second.

How is data stored on a hard drive?
A hard drive is composed of several coated round, thin plates of metal stacked on a spindle. Each plate is called a **platter**. When data is saved to a hard drive platter, a pattern of magnetized spots is created on the iron oxide coating of each platter. When the spots are aligned in one direction, they represent a 1; when aligned in the other direction, the represent a 0. These 0s and 1s are bits (or binary digits) and are the smallest pieces of data that computers can understand. When data stored on the hard drive platter is retrieved (or read), your computer translates these patterns of magnetized spots into the data you have saved.

How do I know how much storage capacity I need? Typically, hard drive capacity is measured in gigabytes (GB), although some high-end systems have a hard drive with capacity in the terabytes (TB). To check how much total capacity your hard drive has, as well as how much is being used, click the Start button and select Computer from the right side of the Start menu. Windows displays the hard drives, their capacity, and usage information, as seen in Figure 6.20. To get a slightly more detailed view, select a drive; then right-click and choose Properties.

To determine the storage capacity your system needs, calculate the amount of storage required by all the types of files you will be keeping on your system. If you have a large digital music library, that alone could require 30 to 50 GB. Do you keep all of your photographs on your hard drive? You may need another 40 GB or more for them. If you store digital video of television shows and movies, that could easily be 100 to 200 GB more, even higher if the videos are all high definition. Of course, the operating system also requires storage space. The demands on system requirements have grown with new versions of operating systems. Windows 7, the latest Microsoft operating system, can require up

---

BITS AND BYTES

HDTV on Your Notebook

If you are moving through your day with a notebook in tow, why not use it to pull up your favorite television shows? There are now several USB devices that allow your notebook or desktop to receive the high-definition television (HDTV) signals whizzing by in the airwaves.

Devices like the Hauppauge HDTV stick (see Figure 6.19) are USB digital TV tuners. One end plugs into any available USB port. The other end connects to the provided digital antenna. Software is included that allows you to schedule shows to record onto your hard drive, so your notebook essentially becomes a time-shifting digital video recorder. If you are at home, you can remove the antenna and connect to your home cable television signal. It's enough to make you think about buying a larger hard drive on your next computer!

Figure 6.19

The Hauppauge HDTV stick allows you to watch and record high-definition television shows on your computer.

to 20 GB of available hard drive capacity, depending on the configuration.

In addition to having space for the operating system, you need enough space to store the software applications you use, such as Microsoft Office, music, and games. Figure 6.21 shows an example of hard drive requirements for someone storing a few programs on a hard drive.

Are some hard drives faster than others? There are several types of hard drives. Integrated Drive Electronics (IDE), which is also called *parallel advanced technology attachment (PATA)*, is an older style that uses wide cables to connect the hard drive to the motherboard. **Serial Advanced Technology Attachment (Serial ATA)** hard drives use much thinner cables, and can transfer data more quickly than IDE drives. A slower drive is fine if you use your computer primarily for word processing, spreadsheets, e-mail, and the Internet. However, "power users" such as graphic designers and software developers will benefit from the faster Serial ATA hard drive.

Another factor that affects a hard drive's performance is access time (the speed with which it locates data for processing). As noted earlier, access time is measured in milliseconds. The faster the access time the better, although many hard drives have similar access times.

The latest and fastest hard drive option is the solid state drive (SSD). These are popular in the netbook market because they require so little power to run and are so cool and quiet. With access times of merely a tenth of a millisecond, SSDs can deliver data many times more quickly than mechanical hard drives. SSD drives as large as 1 TB are available, but right now, all SSD drives are still much more expensive than mechanical drives. Watch for the integration of SSD drives into most systems as the cost of SSDs continues to drop.

Evaluate hard drive transfer rate when looking for the best performing drive. The **data transfer rate** is the speed at which a hard drive can transfer data to other computer components (such as RAM). Depending on the manufacturer, the rate is expressed in either megabits or megabytes per second. You can compare the average read and write data transfer rates of hard drives at sites that do performance benchmarking, like Tom's Hardware (**tomshardware.com**).

If you are adding an external hard drive to your system, there are two popular ports

to use. Many hard drives use a USB 2.0 port to connect, which limits the transfer rate of data to 400 Mbps. In addition, some computer systems now offer an eSATA port, shown in Figure 6.22. This is an external SATA port that will connect to some external hard drive models. It allows much faster data transfer—up to 3 Gbps.

Optical Storage

Optical drives are disc drives that use a laser to store and read data. Data is saved to a compact disc (CD), digital video discs (DVD), or **Blu-ray disc (BDs)** within established tracks and sectors, just like on a hard drive. However, unlike hard drives, which store their data on magnetized platters, optical discs store data as tiny pits that are burned into the disc by a high-speed laser. These pits are extremely small. For CDs and DVDs, they are less than 1 micron in

Figure 6.20

In Windows, the free and used capacity of each device in the computer system are shown in the Computer window. The General tab of the Properties dialog box gives you information that is more detailed.

>To view the Computer window, click **Start**, and click **Computer**. To view the pie chart, right-click the C drive, and select **Properties**.

Figure 6.21 | SAMPLE HARD DRIVE REQUIREMENTS

Application	Hard Drive Space Required
Windows 7	16–20 GB
MS Office 2007 Professional	2 GB
Adobe Photoshop Elements	2 GB
Roxio Easy Media Creator 9	1 GB installation space and as much as 9 GB to copy CDs or DVDs
Total required	21–33 GB

diameter, so nearly 1,500 pits fit across the top of a pinhead. The pits on a Blu-ray disc are only 0.15 microns in diameter, more than twice as small as the pits on a DVD. As you can see in Figure 6.23, data is read from a disc by a laser beam, with the pits and nonpits (called *lands*) translating into the 1s and 0s of the binary code computers understand. CDs and DVDs use a red laser to read and write data. Blu-ray discs get their name because they are read with a blue laser light. All of them collectively are referred to as **optical media**.

Figure 6.22

An eSATA port allows you to connect an external hard drive that can transfer data at much greater speeds than those a USB port supports.

Why can I store data on some discs but not others? All forms of optical media come in prerecorded, recordable, and rewritable formats. The prerecorded discs—known as CD-ROM, **DVD-ROM**, and **BD-ROM discs**—are read-only optical discs, meaning you can't save any data onto them. Pre-recorded CDs usually contain audio content, software programs, or games, whereas DVD-ROMs and BD-ROMs typically contain movies or prerecorded TV shows in regular or high definition, respectively. Recordable formats such as CD-R, DVD-R, and BD-R allow data to be written (saved or burned) to them. If you want to be able to use a form of optical media repetitively, writing and rewriting data to it many times, read/writeable formats such as CD-RW, DVD-RW, and BD-RE are available.

Do I need separate players and burners for CD, DVD, and now BD formats? Although CDs and DVDs are based on the same optical technology, CD drives cannot read DVDs. If your system has only a CD drive, you will need to add a DVD drive to view DVDs. However, if your system has a DVD drive, that is all you need, even just to listen to CDs, because DVD drives can read them. Although Blu-ray discs are read with a different type of laser than CDs and DVDs, most Blu-ray players are backward compatible and can play DVDs and CDs. There are different types of optical drives for playing or recording to discs. If you want to record to CDs, DVDs, or Blu-ray discs, you need to make sure your drive is capable of recording (or burning) and not just playing. Because recording drives are also backward compatible, you do not need separate burners for each form of media. A DVD burner will also record CDs, and a Blu-ray burner will most likely record both CDs and DVDs (although there may be some compatibility issues).

Are there different standards of optical media? Unfortunately, technology experts have not agreed on a standard DVD format. Currently, there are multiple

To read information stored on a disc, a laser inside the disk drive sends a beam of light through the spinning disc.

Laser beam

Non-scattered reflected light = 1

Scattered reflected light = 0

Laser beam

If the light reflected back is scattered in all directions (which happens when the laser hits a pit), the laser translates this into the binary digit 0.

If non-scattered light is reflected back to the laser (which happens when the laser hits an area in which there is no pit), the laser translates this into the binary digit 1.

Spinning CD

In this way, the laser reads the pits and non-pits as a series of bits (0s and1s), which the computer can then process.

Figure 6.23

Data is read from a CD using focused laser light.

The thin metal platters that make up a hard drive are covered with a special magnetic coating that enables the data to be recorded onto one or both sides of the platter. Hard drive manufacturers prepare the disks to hold data through a process called *low-level formatting*. In this process, concentric circles, each called a **track**, and pie-shaped wedges, each called a **sector**, are created in the magnetized surface of each platter, setting up a gridlike pattern that identifies file locations on the hard drive. A separate process called *high-level formatting* establishes the catalog that the computer uses to keep track of where each file is located on the hard drive. More detail on this is presented in the Dig Deeper feature "How Disk Defragmenter Utilities Work" on page 238.

Hard drive platters spin at a high rate of speed, some as fast as 15,000 revolutions per minute (rpm). Sitting between the platters are special "arms" that contain read/write heads (see Figure 6.24). A **read/write head** moves from the outer edge of the spinning platter to the center, as frequently as 50 times per second, to retrieve (read) and record (write) the magnetic data to and from the hard drive platter. As noted earlier, the average total time it takes for the read/write head to locate the data on the platter and return it to the CPU for processing is called its access time. A new hard drive should have an average access time of approximately 10 ms.

Access time is mostly the sum of two factors: seek time and latency. The time it takes for the read/write heads to move over the surface of the disk, moving to the correct track, is called the **seek time**. (Sometimes people incorrectly refer to this as access time.) Once the read/write head locates the correct track, it may need to wait for the correct sector to spin to the read/write head. This waiting time is called **latency** (or *rotational delay*). The faster the platters spin (or the faster the rpm), the less time you'll have to wait for your data to be accessed. Currently, most hard drives for home systems spin at 7,200 rpm. Some people design their systems to have a faster hard drive run the operating system, such as the Western Digital Velociraptor, which spins at 10,000 rpm. They then add a slower drive with greater capacity for storage.

The read/write heads do not touch the platters of the hard drive; rather, they float above them on a thin cushion of air at a height of 0.5 microinches. As a matter of comparison, a human hair is 2,000 microinches thick and a particle of dust is larger than a human hair. Therefore, it's critical to keep your hard drive free from all dust and dirt, because even the smallest particle could find its way between the read/write head and the disk platter, causing a **head crash**—a stoppage of the hard drive that often results in data loss.

Capacities for hard drives in personal computers can exceed 2000 GB (2 TB). Increasing the amount of data stored in a hard drive is achieved either by adding more platters or by increasing the amount of data stored on each platter. How tightly the tracks are placed next to each other, how tightly spaced the sectors are, and how closely the bits of data are placed affect the measurement of the amount of data that can be stored in a specific area of a hard drive platter. Modern technology continues to increase the standards on all three levels, enabling massive quantities of data to be stored in small places.

Read/write head

Arms

Platters

Figure 6.24

The hard drive is a stack of platters enclosed in a sealed case. Special arms fit in between each platter. The read/write heads at the end of each arm read from and save data to the platters.

recognized formats, **DVD-R/RW** (pronounced "DVD dash") and **DVD+R/RW** (pronounced "DVD plus"). **DVD-RAM** is a third format. You can record, erase, and rewrite on DVD-RAM, as you can with the plus and minus formats, but DVD-RAM discs are generally encased in a plastic cartridge. Web sites such as Video Help (**videohelp. com**) list the compatibility of various DVD players with the various DVD formats.

SOUND BYTE CD, DVD, and Blu-ray Reading and Writing Interactive

In this Sound Byte, you'll learn about the process of storing and retrieving data from CD-RW, DVD, and Blu-ray discs. You'll be amazed to see how much precision engineering is required to burn MP3 files onto a disc.

Taking Care of Optical Discs

The following guidelines will help you keep your optical discs safe:

- Exercise care in handling your optical discs. Dirt or oil on CDs, DVDs, and BDs can keep data from being read properly, and large scratches can interrupt data completely. Hold the disc by the edge or the center ring only.
- To keep CDs, DVDs, and BDs from warping, avoid placing them near heat sources and store them at room temperature.
- Clean CDs, DVDs, and BDs by taking a bit of rubbing alcohol on a cotton ball and wiping them from the center to the edge of the disc in long swipes. Don't rub the optical disc in a circular motion, because you may cause more scratches.
- Use a felt-tip marker to identify optical discs and write on the area provided. Don't put stickers or paper labels on optical discs unless they're specifically designed for that purpose.

However, you must make sure you purchase blank DVD discs that match the type of drive you own. Most new systems come equipped with a DVD + / − RW drive, that supports both the plus and minus formats.

There were "format wars" like this for high-definition discs as well. Blu-ray competed against another storage format called HD-DVD (high-definition DVD). Some movie companies would only provide their films on HD discs, while other films were exclusive to Blu-ray. Different players were required to view each kind of disc. In 2008, HD-DVDs were retired, and HD discs and players are no longer in production.

SOUND BYTE

Installing a Blu-ray Drive

In this Sound Byte, you'll learn how to install a Blu-ray drive in your computer.

Are some CD and DVD drives faster than others? When you buy an optical drive, knowing the drive speed is important. Speeds are listed on the device's packaging. Record (write) speed is always listed first, rewrite speed is listed second (except for CD-R drives and DVD-R, which cannot rewrite data), and playback speed is listed last. For example, a CD-RW drive may have speeds of 52X32X52X, meaning that the device can record data at 52X speed, rewrite data at 32X speed, and play back data at 52X speed. For CDs, the X after each number represents the transfer of 150 KB of data per second. For example, a CD-RW drive with a 52X32X52X rating records data at 52 times 150 KB per second, or 7,800 KB per second.

DVD drives are much faster than CD drives. For example, a 1X DVD-ROM drive provides a data transfer rate of approximately 1.3 MB of data per second, which is roughly equivalent to a CD-ROM speed of 9X. CD and DVD drives are constantly getting faster. If you're in the market for a new CD or DVD burner, then you'll want to investigate the drive speeds on the market and make sure you get the fastest one you can afford.

Blu-ray drives are the fastest optical devices on the market. Blu-ray technology defines 1X speed as 36 MB per second. Because BD movies require data transfer rates of at least 54 MB per second, most Blu-ray disc players have a minimum of 2X speeds (72 MB per second). Many units are available with 6X speeds.

So how do my storage devices measure up? The table in Figure 6.25 will help you determine if your computer's storage subsystem needs upgrading.

Figure 6.25 | DO YOU NEED TO UPGRADE YOUR STORAGE SUBSYSTEM?

	Current System	Ideal System
What is my current hard drive capacity?		
Do I have a DVD-ROM drive?		
Can I burn DVDs (i.e., do I have a DVD-/+RW drive)?		
Can I play Blu-ray discs (i.e., do I have a Blu-ray drive)?		
Can I burn my own Blu-ray discs (i.e., do I have a Blu-ray burner installed)?		
Do I have a working data backup solution such as external backup drives or remote data storage?		
Do I use any portable storage devices such as flash drives or portable hard drives?		

Processor covered by heat sink and fan

Video memory chips

Video memory chip

Connects to a monitor

HDMI port to Xbox 360

S-video port to TV, stereo, or VCR

Digital Video Interface (DVI) port to LCD monitor

Video memory chip

Clips into motherboard

Figure 6.26

Video cards have grown to be highly specialized subsystems.

Evaluating the Video Subsystem

How video is displayed depends on two components: your video card and your monitor. It's important that your system have the correct monitor and video card to meet your needs. If you are considering loading Windows 7 on your system, or using your computer system to display files that have complex graphics, such as videos on Blu-ray or from your camcorder, or even playing graphics-rich games with a lot of fast action, you may want to consider upgrading your video subsystem.

Video Cards

What is a video card? A **video card** (or **video adapter**) is an expansion card that is installed inside your system unit to translate binary data into the images you view on your monitor. Modern video cards like the ones shown in Figure 6.26 and Figure 6.27 are extremely sophisticated. They include ports that allow you to connect to different video equipment such as the DVI ports for digital LCDs, HDMI ports to connect to high-definition TVs or gaming consoles, lower-resolution S-video ports for connecting your computer to a TV, and Super VGA ports for CRT and analog LCD monitors. In addition, video cards include their own RAM, called **video memory**. Several standards of video memory are available, including graphics double data rate 3 (GDDR3) memory and the newer graphics double data rate 5 (GDDR5) memory. Because displaying graphics demands a lot of the

Figure 6.27

Because of the large amount of graphics memory and the fast graphics processing units on modern video cards, they have their own fan to remove heat.

Fan built into graphics card

ACTIVE HELP-DESK

Evaluating Computer System Components

In this Active Helpdesk call, you'll play the role of a helpdesk staffer, fielding calls about the computer's storage, video, and audio devices and how to evaluate whether they match your needs, as well as how to improve the reliability of your system.

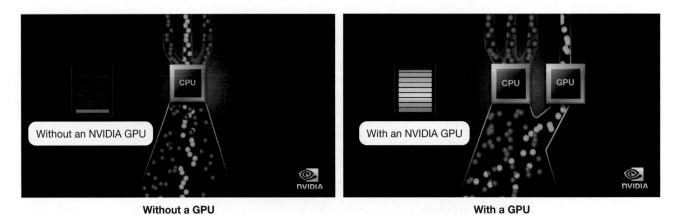

| Without a GPU | With a GPU |

Figure 6.28

The graphics processing unit (GPU) is specialized to handle processing of photos, videos, and video game images. It frees the CPU to work on other system demands.

CPU, video cards also come with their own graphics processing units (GPUs). When the CPU is asked to process graphics, those tasks are redirected to the GPU, significantly speeding up graphics processing.

Is a GPU different from a CPU?
The **graphics processing unit (GPU)** performs the same kind of computational work that a CPU performs. However, a GPU is specialized to handle 3-D graphics and image and video processing speedily. Figure 6.28 shows that the CPU can run much more efficiently when a GPU does all of the graphics computation.

Special lighting effects can be achieved with a modern GPU. Designers can now change the type of light, the texture, and the color of objects based on complex interactions. Some GPU designs incorporate dedicated hardware to allow high-definition movies to be decoded.

Does the GPU live on the motherboard or on the video card? Basic video processing is sometimes integrated into the motherboard. However, high-end video cards that have their own GPUs

are separate from the motherboard. These sophisticated video cards connect through the ultrafast PCI Express bus. The ATI Radeon HD 4870 X2, a top-end card, is a multi-GPU card with two GPUs that work together to add even more processing punch. Cards like this one carry their own processing RAM space, which can range between 512 MB and 2 GB, depending on the model. Together they provide an unprecedented level of realism and detail in gaming environments (see Figure 6.29).

How can I tell how much memory my video card has? Information about your system's video card can be found in the Advanced Settings of the Screen resolution dialog box. To get to the Screen resolution dialog box, right-click on your desktop and select Screen resolution. In the Screen resolution dialog box, click the Advanced Settings link. A window will appear that shows you the type of graphics card installed in your system, as well as memory information including total available graphics memory, dedicated video memory, system video memory, and shared system memory. The documentation that came with your computer should also contain specifications for the video card, including the amount of video memory it has installed.

How much memory does my video card need? The amount of memory your video card needs depends on what you want to display on your monitor. If you work primarily in Microsoft Word and conduct general Web searches, 128 MB is a realistic minimum. For the serious gamer, a 512 MB or greater video card is essential, although cards with as much as 1 or 2 GB are available in the market and are preferred. These high-end video cards, which have greater amounts

Figure 6.29

These two images show the difference in displayed gaming environments with a basic video card and one with an advanced GPU. The Nvidia GeForce GPU allows more detailed water ripples, shadowing effects, and more realistic terrain texture.

of memory, allow games to generate smoother animations and more sophisticated shading and texture. Before purchasing new software, check the specifications to ensure your video card has enough video memory to handle the load.

How many video cards can I add to a system? For users who are primarily doing text processing or spreadsheet work, one video card is certainly enough. However, computer gamers and users of high-end visualization software often take advantage of the ability to install more than one video card at a time. Two or even three video cards can be used in one system. The two major video card manufacturers, Nvidia and ATI, have each developed their own standards supporting the combining of multiple video cards. For Nvidia this standard is named SLI and for ATI it is called CrossFire. When the system is running at very high video resolutions, such as 1920 × 1200 or higher, multiple video cards working together provide the ultimate in performance. If you are buying a new system and might be interested in employing multiple video cards, be sure to check whether the motherboard supports SLI or CrossFire.

What else does the video card do? The video card also controls the number of colors your monitor can display. The number of bits the video card uses to represent each pixel (or dot) on the monitor, referred to as **bit depth**, defines the color quality of the image displayed. The more bits, the better an image's color detail. A 4-bit video card displays 16 colors, the minimum number of colors your system works with (referred to as Standard VGA). Most video cards today are 24-bit cards, displaying more than 16 million colors. This mode is called *true color mode* (see Figure 6.30).

Figure 6.30 | BIT DEPTH AND COLOR QUALITY

Bit Depth	Color Quality Description	Number of Colors Displayed
4-bit	Standard VGA	16
8-bit	256-color mode	256
16-bit	High color	65,536
24-bit	True color	16,777,216
32-bit	True color	16,777,216 plus 8 bits to help with transparency

The most recent generation of video cards can add some great features to your computer if you are a TV fan. Multimedia cards such as the ATI All-In-Wonder X1900 can open a live TV window on your screen, including features such as picture-in-picture. Using this video card, you can record programs to your hard drive or pause a live TV broadcast. The card even comes with a wireless remote control.

So how do I know if I need a new video card? If your monitor takes a while to refresh when you are editing photos, surfing the Web, or playing a graphics-rich game, then the video card could be short on memory. You also may want to upgrade if added features such as television viewing or importing analog video are important to you. If you want to use two monitors at the same time, you also may need to upgrade your video card. Review the considerations listed in Figure 6.31 to see if it might be time for you to upgrade. On a desktop computer, replacing a video card is fairly simple: just insert the new video card in the correct expansion slot on the motherboard.

Figure 6.31 | DO YOU NEED TO UPGRADE YOUR VIDEO CARD?

	Current System	Ideal System
Is my video card able to refresh the screen fast enough for the videos and games I play?		
What is the total amount of video memory on my video card?		
How many monitors can this card support?		
Can I import video through my video card?		
Can I send a cable television signal to my video card?		

Decades ago, when the electronic photocopier made its debut, book publishers and others who distributed the printed word feared they would be put out of business. They were worried that people would no longer buy books and other printed matter if they could simply copy someone else's original. Years later, when audiocassette and VCR players and recorders arrived on the market, those who felt they would be negatively affected by these new technologies expressed similar concerns. Now, with the arrival of CD-RW, DVD-RW, and BD-RE technology, the music and entertainment industries are worried because users can copy CDs, DVDs, and Blu-ray discs in a matter of minutes.

Although photocopiers and VCRs certainly didn't put an end to the industries they affected, some people still say the music and entertainment industries will take a significant hit with CD-RW, DVD-RW, and BD-RE technology. Industry insiders are claiming that these technologies are unethical, and they're pressing for increased federal legislation against such copying. It's not just the CD-RW, DVD-RW, BD-RE technology that's causing problems, either, because "copies" are not necessarily of the physical sort. Thanks to the Internet, file transfers of copyrighted works—particularly music and films—is now commonplace. According to Music United (**musicunited.org**), more than 243 million files are downloaded illegally every month, and about one-quarter of all Internet users worldwide have downloaded a movie from the Internet.

In a separate survey, the Recording Industry Association of America (RIAA), a trade organization that represents the interests of recording giants such as Sony, Capitol Records, and other major producers of musical entertainment, reported that 23 percent of music fans revealed they were buying less music because they could download it or copy a CD-ROM from a friend.

As you would expect, the music and entertainment industries want to be fairly compensated for their creative output. They blame the technology industry for the creation of means by which artists, studios, and the entertainment industry in general are being "robbed." Although technology that readily allows consumers to transfer and copy music and videos exists, the artists who produce these works do not want to be taken advantage of. However, others claim that the technology industry should not bear the complete burden of protecting entertainment copyrights. The RIAA sums up the future of this debate nicely: "Goals for the new millennium are to work with [the recording] industry and others to enable technologies that open up new opportunities but at the same time to protect the rights of artists and copyright owners."

Evaluating the Audio Subsystem

Computers output sound by means of speakers (or headphones) and a sound card. For many users, a computer's preinstalled speakers and sound card are adequate for the sounds produced by the computer itself—the beeps and so on that the computer makes. However, if you're listening to music, viewing DVDs, hooking into a household stereo system, or playing games with sophisticated sound tracks, you may want to upgrade your speakers or your sound card.

Sound Cards

What does the sound card do? Like a video card, a **sound card,** is an expansion card that attaches to the motherboard inside your system unit. Just as the video card enables your computer to produce images on the monitor, a sound card enables the computer to produce sounds. Most systems have a separate sound card, although low-end computers often have integrated the job of managing sound onto the motherboard itself.

Can I hook up a surround-sound system to my computer? Many computers ship with a basic sound card, which is often a **3D sound card**. The 3D sound technology advances sound reproduction beyond traditional stereo sound (where the human ear perceives sounds as coming from the left or the right of the performance area) and is better at convincing the human ear that sound is omnidirectional, meaning that you can't tell from which direction the sound is coming. This tends to produce a fuller, richer sound than stereo sound. However, 3D sound is not surround sound.

What is surround sound then? **Surround sound** is a type of audio processing that makes the listener experience sound as if it were coming from all directions. The current surround sound standard is from Dolby. There are many formats available, including Dolby Digital EX and Dolby Digital Plus for high-definition audio. Dolby TrueHD is the newest standard. It features high-definition and lossless technology, in which no data is lost in the compression process. To create surround sound, Dolby takes digital sound from a medium (such as a DVD-ROM) and reproduces it in eight channels. Seven channels cover the listening field with placement to the left front, right front, and center of the audio stage, as well as the left rear and right rear, and then two extra side speakers are added, as shown in Figure 6.32. The eighth channel holds extremely low-frequency sound data and is sent to a subwoofer, which can be placed anywhere in the room. To set up surround sound on your computer, you need two things: a set of surround-sound speakers and, for the greatest surround-sound experience, a sound card that is Dolby Digital–compatible.

I don't need surround sound on my computer. Why else might I need to buy an upgraded sound card? Most basic sound cards contain the following input and output jacks (or ports): microphone in, speaker out, and line in. This allows you to hook up a set of stereo speakers and a microphone. But what if you want to hook up a right and left speaker individually, or attach other audio devices to your computer? To do so, you need more ports, which are provided on upgraded sound cards like the one shown in Figure 6.33.

With an upgraded sound card, you can connect portable minidisc players, portable media players, portable jukeboxes, headphones, and CD players to your computer. Musicians also create music on their computers by connecting special devices (such as keyboards) directly to sound card ports. To determine whether your audio subsystem is meeting your needs, review the table in Figure 6.34.

Evaluating System Reliability

Many computer users decide to buy a new system not necessarily because they need a faster CPU, more RAM, or a bigger hard drive, but because they are experiencing problems such as slow performance, freezes, and crashes. Over time, even normal use can cause your computer to build up excess files and to become internally disorganized. This excess, clutter, and disorganization can lead to deteriorating performance or, far worse, system failure. If you think your system is unreliable, see if the problem is one you can fix before you buy a new machine. Proper upkeep and maintenance also may

Figure 6.32
Dolby Digital 7.1 surround sound gives you better-quality audio output.

postpone an expensive system upgrade or replacement.

What can I do to ensure my system performs reliably? Here are several procedures you can follow to ensure your system performs reliably:

1. **Clean out your Startup folder.** Some programs install themselves into your Startup folder and run automatically each time the computer reboots, whether you are using them or not. This unnecessary load causes extra stress on RAM. Check your Startup folder by clicking Start > All Programs. Then click on the Startup folder and make sure all the programs listed are important to you. Right-click on any unnecessary program and select Delete to remove it from the Startup folder. Make sure you delete *only* programs you are absolutely

Figure 6.33

In addition to improving sound quality, upgraded sound cards can provide additional ports for your audio equipment.

Analog/Digital Output

Line Input Signal

Microphone Input

Line Output

Rear Speaker Output

FireWire (IEEE 1394)

sure are unnecessary. Another way programs sneak their way in is to load themselves into your system tray. Keep an eye on how many icons are in the system tray and uninstall any that you do not use frequently.

2. **Clear out unnecessary files.** Temporary Internet files can accumulate quickly on your hard drive, taking up unnecessary space. Running the Disk Cleanup utility is a quick and easy way to ensure your temporary Internet files don't take up precious hard drive space. Likewise, you should delete any unnecessary files from your hard drive regularly, because they can make your hard drive run more slowly.

3. **Run spyware and adware removal programs.** These often detect and remove different pests and should be used in addition to your regular antivirus package. You can find more details on how to keep your system safe from spyware, adware, and viruses in Chapter 9.

4. **Run the Disk Defragmenter utility on your hard drive.** When your hard drive becomes fragmented, its storage capacity is negatively affected. When you defragment (defrag) your hard drive, files are reorganized, making the hard drive work more efficiently. For a more complete discussion of the Disk Defragmenter, refer to Chapter 5.

The utilities that need to be run more than once, like Disk Cleanup, Disk Defragmenter, and the antivirus and spyware programs, can be configured to run automatically at any time interval you want. You can set up a sequence of programs to run one after the other every evening while you sleep, and wake up each day to a reliable, secure system.

My system crashes often during the day. What can I do? Computer systems are complex. It's not unusual

Figure 6.34 | DO YOU NEED TO UPGRADE YOUR AUDIO SUBSYSTEM?

	Current System	Ideal System
Is the speaker quality high enough for the way I am using my computer?		
Is my sound card capable of 3D sound?		
Does my sound card support Dolby Digital surround sound?		
Do I have 5.1-channel surround sound or 7.1-channel surround sound?		
Do I have an HDMI port on the audio card?		

to have your system stop responding occasionally. If rebooting the computer doesn't help, you'll need to begin troubleshooting:

1. Check that you have enough RAM, which you learned how to do in the section "Evaluating RAM: The Memory Subsystem" earlier in this chapter. Systems with insufficient amounts of RAM often crash.

2. Make sure you have properly installed any new software or hardware. If you're using a Windows system, use the System Restore utility to "roll back" the system to a time when it worked more reliably. (To find System Restore, just type "restore" into the Start menu search box.) For Mac systems, Mac OS X Time Machine, shown in Figure 6.35, provides automatic backup and enables you to look through and restore (if necessary) files, folders, libraries, or the entire system.

3. If you see an error code in Windows, visit the Microsoft Knowledge Base (**support.microsoft.com**), an online resource for resolving problems with Microsoft products. This may help you determine what the error code indicates and how you may be able to solve the problem. If you don't find a satisfactory answer in the Knowledge Base, try copying the entire error message into Google and searching the larger community for solutions.

Can my software affect system reliability? Having the latest version of software products makes your system much more reliable. You should upgrade or update your operating system, browser software, and application software as often as new patches (or fixes) are reported for resolving errors. Sometimes these errors are performance-related; sometimes they are potential system security breaches.

How do I know whether updates are available for my software? You can configure Windows so that it automatically checks for, downloads, and installs any available updates for itself, Internet Explorer, and other Microsoft applications such as Microsoft Office. Many other applications now also include the ability to check for updates. Check under the Help menu of

Figure 6.35

Mac's Time Machine restores files, folders, libraries and, if necessary, the entire system.

the product, and often you will find a Check for Updates command.

What if none of this helps? Is buying a new system my only option? If your system is still unreliable after these changes, then you have two options:

1. **Upgrade your operating system to the latest version.** There are substantial increases in reliability with each major release of a new operating system. However, upgrading the operating system may require hardware upgrades such as additional RAM, an updated graphics processor, and an even larger hard drive. The Microsoft Windows 7 Upgrade Advisor (a free download from (**microsoft.com**) will scan your system to determine what upgrades might be required before you convert to Windows 7. Be sure to examine the *recommended* (not required) specifications of the new operating system.

2. **Reinstall the operating system.** As a last resort, you might need to reinstall the operating system. To do so, you'll want to back up all of your data files before the installation and be prepared to reinstall all your software after the installation. Make sure you have all of the original discs for the software installed on your system, along with the product keys, serial numbers, and any other activation codes so that you can reinstall them.

What happened to your last computer? If you threw it away hoping it would be safely recycled with your empty water bottles, think again. Mercury in LCD screens, cadmium in batteries and circuit boards, and flame retardant in plastic housings all are toxic. An alarming, emerging trend is that discarded machines are beginning to create an e-waste crisis.

Instead of throwing your computer away, you may be able to donate it to a nonprofit organization. Many manufacturers, such as Dell, offer recycling programs and have formed alliances with nonprofit organizations to help distribute your old technology to those who need it. You can also take your computer to an authorized computer recycling center in your area (see Figure 6.36). The Telecommunications Industry Association provides an e-cycling information site you can use to find a local e-cycling center (**eiae.org**).

However, before donating or recycling a computer, make sure you carefully remove all data from your hard drive, or you may end up having your good deed turn bad by becoming the victim of identity theft. Credit card numbers, bank information, Social Security numbers, tax records, passwords, and personal identification numbers (PINs) are just some of the types of sensitive information that we casually record to our computers' hard drives. Just deleting files that contain proprietary personal information is not protection enough. Likewise, reformatting or erasing your hard drive does not totally remove data, as was proved by two MIT graduate students. In 2003, they bought more than 150 used hard drives from various sources. Although some of the hard drives had been reformatted or damaged so the data was supposedly irrecoverable, the two students were able to retrieve medical records, financial information, pornography, personal e-mails, and more than 5,000 credit card numbers!

The U.S. Department of Defense suggests a seven-layer overwrite for a "secure erase." In other words, they suggest that you fill your hard drive *seven times over* with a random series of 1s and 0s. Fortunately, several programs exist for PCs running Windows, such as Active@ KillDisk, Eraser, and CyberScrub. Wipe is available for Linux, and Shredit X can be used for OS X. These programs provide secure hard drive erasures, either of specific files on your hard drive or of the entire hard drive.

Keep in mind that even these data erasure programs can't provide the ultimate level in security. Computer forensic specialists or supercybercriminals can still manage to retrieve some data from your hard drive if they have the right tools. The ultimate level of protection comes from destroying the hard drive altogether. Suggested methods include drilling holes in the hard drive, burning or melting it, or just taking an old-fashioned sledgehammer to it! For large companies that need to upgrade large quantities of computers and have the options of destroying or recycling their old computers, the problem becomes much worse. In these cases, recycling isn't a good option, and throwing the computers away can create an environmental hazard. Companies such as GigaBiter (**gigabiter.com**) eliminate security and environmental risks associated with electronic destruction by first delaminating the hard drive and then breaking down the computer e-waste into recyclable products. The result of the final step is a sandlike substance that is 100 percent recyclable.

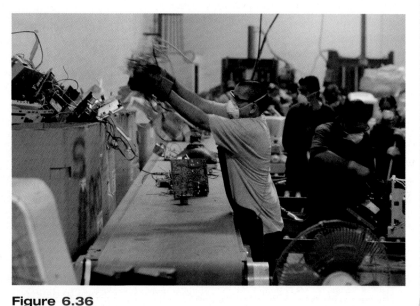

Figure 6.36

An electronics scrap recycler "demanufactures" printers, computers, and other electronics and then resells the usable parts.

Making the Final Decision

Now that you have evaluated your computer system, you need to shift to questions of *value*. How closely does your system come to meeting your needs? How much would it cost to upgrade the system you have to match what you'd ideally like your computer to do, not only today but also a few years from now? How much would it cost to purchase a new system that meets these specifications?

To decide whether upgrading or buying a new system has better value for you, you need to price both scenarios. Figure 6.37

Figure 6.37 | UPGRADE/NEW PURCHASE COMPARISON WORKSHEET

Needs	Hardware Upgrade Cost	Included on New System?	Additional Expense If Not Included on New System
Portability			
Wireless connectivity			
CPU and Memory Subsystems			
CPU upgrade			
RAM upgrade			
Storage Subsystem			
Hard drive upgrade			
SSD drive			
DVD+/-RW drive			
DVD+/-RW burner			
Blu-ray drive			
Blu-ray burner			
Video and Audio Subsystems			
Video card upgrade			
Sound card upgrade			

provides an upgrade worksheet you can use to evaluate both the upgrade path and the new purchase path. Be sure to consider what benefit you might obtain by having two systems if you were to buy a new computer. Would you have a use for the older system? Would you donate it to a charitable organization? Would you be able to give it to a family member? Purchasing a new system is an important investment of your resources, and you want to make a well-reasoned, well-supported decision.

six summary

1. How can I determine whether I should upgrade my existing computer or buy a new one?

To determine whether you need to upgrade your system or purchase a new one, you need to define your ideal system and what you want it to do. Then you need to perform a system evaluation to assess the subsystems in your computer, including the CPU, memory, storage, video, and audio. Finally, you need to determine if it's economical to upgrade, or whether buying a new computer would be better.

2. What does the CPU do, and how can I evaluate its performance?

Your computer's CPU processes instructions, performs calculations, manages the flow of information through the computer system, and is responsible for processing the data you input into information. CPU speed is measured in gigahertz (billions of machine cycles per second). You can tell whether your CPU is limiting your system performance by watching how busy it is as you work on your computer. The percentage of time that your CPU is working is referred to as CPU usage, which you can determine by checking the Task Manager. Benchmarking software offers direct performance comparisons of different CPUs.

3. How does memory work in my computer, and how can I evaluate how much memory I need?

RAM is your computer's short-term memory. It remembers everything that the computer needs to process data into information. However, it is an example of volatile storage. When the power is off, the data stored in RAM is cleared out. The amount of RAM sitting on memory modules in your computer is your computer's physical memory. The memory your OS uses is kernel memory. At a minimum, you need enough RAM to run the OS plus the software applications you're using, plus a bit more to hold the data you will input.

4. What are the computer's main storage devices, and how can I evaluate whether they match my needs?

Storage devices for a typical computer system may include a hard drive, an SSD drive, a flash drive, and CD and DVD drives. Blu-ray drives are gaining in popularity for viewing and burning high-density media. When you turn off your computer, the data stored in these devices is saved. These devices are referred to as *nonvolatile* storage devices. Hard drives have the largest storage capacity of any storage device and are the most economical. Newer SSD drives have the fastest access time and data transfer rate of all nonvolatile storage options. CDs and DVDs have capacities from 700 MB to 17 GB, while Blu-ray discs can hold up to 50 GB. Portable flash drives allow easy transfer of 64 GB or more of data from machine to machine. To determine the storage capacity your system needs, calculate the amount of storage your software needs to reside on your computer. To add more storage or to provide more functionality for your system, you can install additional drives, either internally or externally.

5. What components affect the output of video on my computer, and how can I evaluate whether they match my needs?

How video is displayed depends on two components: your video card and your monitor. A video card translates binary data into the images you see. These cards include their own RAM (video memory) as well as ports that allow you to connect to video equipment. The amount of video memory you need depends on what you want to display on the monitor. A more powerful card will allow you to play graphics-intense games and multimedia.

6. What components affect the quality of sound on my computer, and how can I evaluate whether they match my needs?

Your computer's sound depends on your speakers and sound card. A sound card enables the computer to produce sounds. Users upgrade their sound cards to provide for 3D sound, surround sound, and additional ports for audio equipment.

7. How can I improve the reliability of my system?

Many computer users decide to buy a new system because they are experiencing problems with their computer. However, before you buy a new system because you think yours may be unreliable, make sure the problem is not one you can fix. Make sure you have installed any new software or hardware properly, check that you have enough RAM, run system utilities such as Disk Defragmenter and Disk Cleanup, clean out your Startup folder, remove unnecessary files from your system, and keep your software updated with patches. If you continue to have troubles with your system, reinstall or upgrade your OS, and, of course, seek technical assistance.

six key terms

key terms

Word Bank

- access time
- Blu-ray disc
- cache memory
- CPU usage
- data transfer rate
- eSATA
- express cards
- front side bus
- GPU
- hard drive
- memory bound
- memory module
- Moore's law
- sound card
- SSD
- surround sound
- system evaluation

Instructions: Fill in the blanks using the words from the Word Bank above.

Joe already has a PC but just heard about a great deal on a new one. He decides to perform a(n) (1) _____ on his computer to see whether he should keep it or buy the new one. First, he runs the Task Manager in Windows. By doing so, he can check the history of (2) _____ as he works through his day. Because he is often over 90 percent, he begins to suspect his system is (3) _____ memory bound. He has room for an additional two (4) _____ memory module(s) on his motherboard. Adding RAM is something he learned how to do this semester, but would that be enough to make this machine do all he needs?

He visits the Intel Web site to check two other important factors on his model of CPU: the amount of (5) _____ memory and the speed of the (6) _____. It looks like the newer i7 processor would be much faster overall. It seems each generation of processors is so much faster than the last. That rule, (7) _____, is still holding true!

He continues to evaluate his system by checking out which components he has and which ones he'll need. He notes the storage capacity of the (8) _____. Recently, he has been wishing his system had a(n) (9) _____ port because adding an external hard drive would give him enough space to start to record HD television shows. As it is, he is running out of space to store files. But the (10) _____, or the amount of time it takes to retrieve data from the disk drive, on any mechanical drive is slow compared to the (11) _____ in the new computer he's eyeing, which has no moving parts at all. Joe also notes that he is unable to do a complete backup of his music library onto optical media now that he has 40 GB of music data. His current system can't burn a (12) _____, but the new system could. The new system would also include a(n) (13) _____ that would allow him to connect his Xbox 360 using the HDMI cable. It would be great if he could take advantage of the 5.1 (14) _____ that is on the soundtrack of most of the movies he watches on DVD.

He also has a lot of friends who play video games on their computer systems. However, his current system doesn't meet the minimum requirements for a video card. Newer cards have blindingly fast (15) _____, and some cards even have multiple processors. Overall, with prices dropping, it seems like time to go buy that new system!

becoming computer literate

Jen lives across the hall from you. She heard you worried last semester that your PC wasn't fast enough. Between the simulation program for math, the reports you did for English, and your programming class, your computer was running slowly and you were out of storage space. She's offered to help you upgrade your system, but she needs you to tell her what you want upgraded and why.

Instructions: Using the preceding scenario, write a letter to Jen using key terms from the chapter. Be sure your sentences are grammatically correct and technically meaningful.

Instructions: Answer the multiple-choice and true–false questions below for more practice with key terms and concepts from this chapter.

Multiple Choice

1. The amount of RAM recommended for most systems today is measured in
  a. gigabytes.   c. megahertz.
  b. gigahertz. d. kilobytes.

2. When evaluating CPU performance, which is NOT a feature you need to consider?
  a. Amount of cache memory
  b. Speed of the processor
  c. Speed of the front side bus
  d. Size of the processor

3. RAM is classified as what kind of storage in a computer system?
  a. Volatile   c. Permanent
  b. Nonvolatile d. Flash

4. SSD technology involves
  a. fast, cool hard drives that have no moving parts.
  b. surround-sound devices that support multichannel audio.
  c. hard drives that are expandable beyond 2 TB.
  d. faster transfer speeds in the front side bus.

5. From which location is it slowest to get data to the CPU for processing?
  a. RAM
  b. Cache memory
  c. Hard drive
  d. Virtual memory

6. Multicore CPUs are
  a. not common in notebook computers.

  b. available in only a dual-core configuration.
  c. available in two- or four-core designs.
  d. available in seven- or eight-core designs.

7. eSATA is a high-speed port used for
  a. video processing.
  b. attaching external hard drives.
  c. communication with printers.
  d. adding RAM.

8. Blu-ray technology is required to store what kind of media?
  a. Standard definition video
  b. High-definition video
  c. Analog audio
  d. Digital audio

9. Evaluating your computer system is important when
  a. your system has stopped working altogether.
  b. you are planning to purchase a new system.
  c. you are wondering if you should upgrade your system.
  d. All of the above.

10. Which of the following should you do to ensure the reliability of your system?
  a. Run Disk Defragmenter.
  b. Run Disk Cleanup.
  c. Install software upgrades and patches.
  d. All of the above.

True–False

_____ 1. The task manager provides information for the windows operating system about programs and processes running on your computer.

_____ 2. Installing a second hard drive in your system will have an immediate impact on system performance if your system is memory bound.

_____ 3. Data is stored using motors and spinning platters on hard drives, CDs, and solid state drives.

_____ 4. A video card has its own memory and its own processor.

_____ 5. CPU performance is affected by the clock speed, the cache size, and the transfer speed of the front side bus.

making the
transition to...
next semester

six chapter

making the
transition to...
next semester

1. Evaluating Your System

A small worksheet follows the end of each section in this chapter to guide you as you evaluate your own system. These smaller worksheets have been combined into one complete worksheet that is on the book's Companion Website (**pearsonhighered.com/ techinaction**). Download the worksheet and fill it in based on the computer you are currently using.

a. Research the costs of replacement parts for those components you feel should be upgraded.
b. Research the cost of a new system that would be roughly equivalent to your current computer after upgrades.
c. Determine whether it would be more cost effective to upgrade your computer or buy a new one.

2. Your Software Needs

What software do you need for the courses you're taking this semester? Will you need any different software for next semester? How many of these software applications do you run at one time? Examine the requirements for those software packages. Prepare a table that lists the software applications you are currently using as well as any you may need to use in the future. For each, list the minimum RAM and hard drive space requirements. How does your system measure up against those requirements?

3. Campus Computer Use

What kinds of computers do students use in college, and how do different people budget for their computer needs? To find an answer to these questions, interview several people who started college in different years. Ask them the following questions:

a. Did you need your own computing equipment, or did you use your college's equipment when you first started school? Would you recommend I do the same?
b. Did you need to upgrade your computer before you came to college? How did you do this?
c. Was the computer you used in your first year of college able to handle your workload in later years?
d. If you used one computer throughout college, what upgrades did you need to perform?
e. If you had to buy a new computer during college, how much money did you budget and how much did you spend? What did you do with your old computer?

4. Buying Computers Online

Visit an online seller of computer systems and components such as Cool Computing (**coolcomputing.com**), Price Watch (**pricewatch.com**), Newegg (**newegg.com**), or Tiger Direct (**tigerdirect.com**) and answer the following questions:

a. What is the current cost of RAM?
b. How much additional RAM could you add to your system?
c. What are the prices of the most popular CPU chips?
d. How much would you need to spend to upgrade to a new operating system?
e. How would each of these help you in your work?

5. Comparing CPU Benchmark Results

You want to purchase a new system but need to decide which CPU best fits your needs. Using the Web, research several different CPU benchmarking reports. Compare specifications for the CPUs, including number of cores, clock speed, cache size, front side bus transfer rates, and cost. From your list, identify the one CPU you would choose and explain why. Be sure to try to find benchmarking reports that simulate the types of programs you would be using most often.

making the
transition to...
the workplace

1. Using Your Computer for Education and Business

As you move from an educational environment to a business environment, how you use your computer will inevitably change. Write one or two paragraphs that describe what your computer system is like now. Then write one or two paragraphs that describe what your ideal computer system would be like after you've graduated and entered the workforce. What different components, if any, would your ideal system need? Could you upgrade your current system to incorporate these new components, or would you need to buy a new system? Make sure you defend the position you take with information covered in this chapter. To help you in your decision, fill out the worksheet, similar to Figure 6.2, that is available on the book's companion Website (**pearsonhighered.com/techinaction**).

2. Assessing Memory Use

Your home office computer is running a bit sluggishly, and you want to determine which application is the memory hog so you can either avoid using it or use it without any other programs running to preserve RAM. You've been told you can do this in the Processes tab in the Task Manager utility. On your computer, open the Task Manager utility and determine which currently running application is using the most memory. Can you tell how much it is using? Note that because the names of the programs have been shortened (for example, Microsoft Word is referred to as *winword.exe*), you may not immediately recognize the program names.

3. IT Support at Work

When you are evaluating potential employers, one consideration will be how well they support you as an employee and provide the environment you need to do productive work. What questions would you ask in an interview to determine what kind of IT support you can expect in your new position?

4. Web Programming Software at Home

You are a Web programmer and you often work from home. You need to investigate whether your home computer will be able to run the three programs you use most frequently at work: Adobe Photoshop, Microsoft Visual Basic .NET, and Microsoft Word. Use the Web to research RAM and hard drive requirements for these programs. Will your computer be able to handle the load?

5. Build an Ideal System

Imagine that a client tells you she wants a system that has at least 8 GB of RAM, the fastest processor on the market, and enough storage space to edit hours of video and music files. In table format, compare the components and pricing of three systems that would meet the client's needs by visiting manufacturer Web sites such as Maingear.com (**maingear.com**), Falcon Northwest (**falcon-nw.com**), and Alienware (**alienware.com**). Make a final selection and justify why this is the best solution.

Instructions: Albert Einstein used *Gedankenexperiments*, or critical thinking questions, to develop his theory of relativity. Some ideas are best understood by experimenting with them in our own minds. The following critical thinking questions are designed to demand your full attention but require only a comfortable chair—no technology.

1. Your Ideal System

If you could buy any new system on the market, not worrying about the price, what would you buy? What kind of video card(s) would you have? How much RAM would you have installed, and which model of CPU would you request? Which sound card would fit your needs? Would you know how to use your ideal system?

2. Future Systems

Given current trends in technology, what kind of system can you imagine upgrading to or buying new in 10 years? Which components would change the most? Which components would need to stay the same, if any? What do you imagine the entire system would look like?

3. Impacts of New Technology

We are constantly being bombarded with new technology. We hear of new tools and system improvements from our friends, relatives, and advertisements almost daily. This chapter talks about upgrading current systems so that we can take advantage of some of the newer technology. There are some improvements we may absolutely need (more RAM, perhaps), whereas there are others that we may simply want (such as a Blu-ray burner). What do you think are the societal, economic, and environmental impacts of our wanting to have the latest and greatest computers? Do you think the push toward faster and more powerful machines is a good thing?

4. Recycling Computers

Mercury in LCD monitors and switches and cadmium in batteries and circuit boards are environmentally toxic metals. Discarded machines are beginning to create an e-waste crisis. Who do you think should assume the cost of recycling computers? Should it be the consumer, the government, or the industry? What other options are there besides throwing older computers away?

5. System Longevity

If you purchase a computer system for business purposes, the Internal Revenue Service (IRS) allows you to depreciate its cost over five years. The IRS considers this a reasonable estimate of the useful lifetime of a computer system. What do you think most home users expect in terms of how long their computer systems should last? How does the purchase of a computer system compare with other major household appliances in terms of cost, value, benefit, life span, and upgrade potential?

Meeting a Corporation's Computing Needs

Problem

In a large organization, whether it is a company or a college, the IT department often has to install several different types of computing systems. There would be advantages to having every computer be identical, but because different departments have different needs and items are purchased at different times, it is typical for there to be significant differences between two computers in the same corporation.

Process

Split your class into teams.

1. Select a department or computer lab on campus (or one within your company or at the public library). *Note:* If you are physically unable to go to a lab, describe the type of components that would be needed by that particular department. (For example, if you choose the computer art department, you know you will need good graphics software. You also know you will need certain levels of RAM and other functionalities to accommodate that graphics software.)

2. Following the worksheet in Figure 6.2, analyze the computing needs of that particular computer lab.

3. Using the System Evaluation worksheet (found on the book's Companion Website at **pearsonhighered.com/techinaction**), develop a complete systems evaluation of the computers at the lab.

4. Consider which upgrades to hardware, software, and peripherals would make this lab better able to meet the needs of its users.

5. Write a report that summarizes your findings. If purchasing a new system is more economical, then recommend which system the lab should buy.

Conclusion

The pace of technological change can make computer science an uncomfortable field for some. For others, it is precisely the pace of change that is exciting. Being able to evaluate a computer system and match it to the current needs of its users is an important skill.

In addition to the review materials presented here, you'll find additional materials featured with the book's multimedia, including the *Technology in Action* Student Resource CD and the Companion Website (**pearsonhighered.com/techinaction**), which will help reinforce your understanding of the chapter content. These materials include the following:

Active Helpdesk

In Active Helpdesk calls, you'll assume the role of helpdesk operator, taking calls about the concepts you've learned in this chapter. You'll apply what you've learned and receive feedback from a supervisor to review and reinforce those concepts. The Active Helpdesk calls for this chapter are listed below and can be found on your Student Resource CD:

- Evaluating Your CPU and RAM
- Evaluating Computer System Components

Sound Bytes

Sound Bytes are dynamic multimedia tutorials that help demystify even the most complex topics. You'll view video clips and animations that illustrate computer concepts and then apply what you've learned by reviewing with the Sound Byte Labs, which include quizzes and activities specifically tailored to each Sound Byte. The Sound Bytes for this chapter are listed below and can be found on your Student Resource CD:

- Using Windows 7 to Evaluate CPU Performance
- Memory Hierarchy Interactive
- Installing RAM
- CD, DVD, and Blu-ray Reading and Writing Interactive
- Installing a Blu-ray Drive

Companion Website

The *Technology in Action* Companion Website includes a variety of additional materials to help you review and learn more about the topics in this chapter. The resources available at **pearsonhighered.com/techinaction** include:

- **Online Study Guide.** Each chapter features an online true–false and multiple-choice quiz. You can take these quizzes, automatically check the results, and e-mail the results to your instructor.
- **Web Research Projects.** Each chapter features several Web research projects that ask you to search the Web for information on computer-related careers, milestones in computer history, important people and companies, emerging technologies, and the applications and implications of different technologies.

seven
networking
connecting computing devices

resources

Active Helpdesk

Sound Bytes

Companion Website

The Companion Website includes a variety of additional materials to help you review and learn more about the topics in this chapter. Go to: **pearsonhighered.com/techinaction**

how cool is *this?* Configuring a

network using Windows networking tools can often be a **confusing** task for beginners. Network Magic from Cisco is a software package designed to simplify configuring network components. The **Network Magic** software guides you through tasks such as sharing devices, such as printers, among multiple computers; configuring folders, such as ones containing music and digital images, for sharing; setting up **security alerts** to warn you of intruders on your network; and repairing damaged network connections. The software provides a **visual map** of your network so you can easily see which devices are online and change the configuration of any device quickly and easily.

Networking Fundamentals

Even if you do not have a home network, you use and interact with networks all the time. In fact, every time you use the Internet you're interacting with the world's largest network. But what, exactly, *is* a network? A computer **network** is simply two or more computers that are connected via software and hardware so that they can communicate with each other. Devices connected to a network are referred to as **nodes**. A node can be a computer, a peripheral (such as a printer), a game console (such as an Xbox 360 or a Wii), a digital video recorder (such as a TiVo), or a communications device (such as a modem). The main function for most networks is to facilitate information sharing, but networks provide other benefits.

What are the benefits of networks? There are several benefits to installing a network. First of all, networks allow users to share peripherals. For example, in Figure 7.1a, the computers are not networked. Computer 1 is connected to the printer, but Computer 2 is not. To print files from Computer 2, users have to transfer them using a flash drive or another storage medium to Computer 1, or they have to disconnect the printer from Computer 1 and connect it to Computer 2. By networking Computer 1 and Computer 2, as shown in Figure 7.1b, both computers can print from the printer attached to Computer 1 without transferring files or moving the printer (although Computer 1 must be powered on). Allowing two people to share a printer saves the cost of buying one printer for each computer.

By networking computers, you can transfer files from one computer to another without using external storage media such as flash drives. In addition, you can set up shared folders in Windows or OS X that allow the user of each computer on the

Figure 7.1

(a) Computers 1 and 2 are not networked, and Computer 2 cannot access the printer. (b) Networking allows sharing of the printer.

network to store files that other computers on the network may need to access, as shown in Figure 7.2.

This Windows network has two computers attached to it, ALAN-PC and PAT, which are running different Windows operating systems. In this example, both the Public and the SharedDocs folders do the same thing: they enable file sharing. When viewing files in Windows Explorer, Alan can easily access files located in the SharedDocs directory on Pat's computer, such as the file called One Yellow Rose.

Can I use a network to share an Internet connection? If you install a device called a *router* on your network, you can share broadband Internet connections. Although you could share a dial-up Internet connection, the resulting speed of the networked connection would be painfully slow and would make surfing the Internet almost impossible. We'll discuss routers in detail later in the chapter.

Network Architectures

The term **network architecture** refers to the design of a network. Network architectures are classified according to the way in which they are controlled and the distance between their nodes.

Describing Networks Based on Network Administration

What do we mean by networks being "administered"? A network can be administered (managed) in either of two main ways: locally or centrally. A peer-to-peer network is the most common example of a locally administered network. The most common type of centrally administered network is a client/server network.

What are peer-to-peer networks? In a **peer-to-peer (P2P) network**, each node connected to the network can communicate directly with every other node on the network instead of having a separate device control the network centrally. Thus, all nodes on this type of network are peers (equals). When printing, for example, a computer on a P2P network doesn't have to go through the computer that's connected to the printer. Instead, it can communicate directly with the printer. Figure 7.1b shows a very small peer-to-peer network.

Because they are simple to set up, P2P networks are the most common type of home network. We discuss different types of peer-to-peer networks that are popular in homes later in this chapter.

What are client/server networks? Very small schools and offices may have P2P networks. However, most networks that have 10 or more nodes are client/server networks. A **client/server network** contains two different types of computers: clients and servers. A **client** is a computer on which users accomplish specific tasks (such as construct spreadsheets) and make specific requests (such as printing a file). The **server** is the computer that provides information or resources to the client computers on the network. The server on a client/server network also provides central administration for functions on the network (such as printing). Figure 7.3 illustrates a client/server network in action.

As you learned in Chapter 3, the Internet is an example of a client/server network. When your computer is connected to the Internet, it is functioning as a client computer. When it accesses the Internet through an Internet service provider (ISP), your computer connects to a

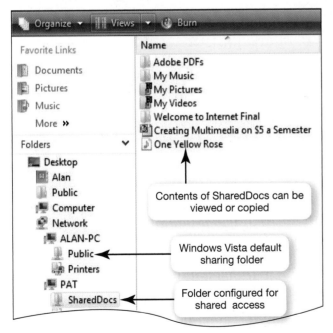

Figure 7.2

Windows Explorer showing shared folders on two computers.

server computer maintained by the ISP. The server "serves up" resources to your computer so that you can interact with the Internet.

Are client/server networks ever used as home networks? Although client/server networks can be configured for home use, P2P networks are more often used in the home because they cost less than

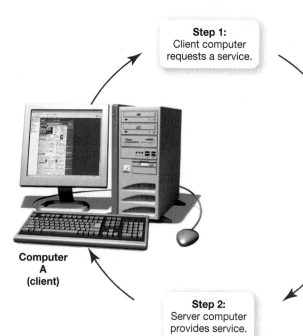

Step 1:
Client computer requests a service.

Computer
A
(client)

Step 2:
Server computer provides service.

Computer
B
(server)

Figure 7.3

In a client/server network, a computer acts either as a client making requests for resources or as a server providing resources.

client/server networks and are easier to configure and maintain. To set up a client/server network in your home, you have to buy an extra computer to act as the server. Although a computer could function both as a server and as a client, its performance would be significantly degraded because of the complexity of the server-related functions it would have to perform. Therefore, it is impractical to use a single computer as both a client and a server. In addition, you need training to install and maintain the special software required by client/server networks. The major benefits a client/server network provides (such as centralized security and administration) are not necessary in most home networks.

However, because of the proliferation of media files from digital cameras, camcorders, and music downloads on home computers, home server options are now being marketed. Windows Home Server and Hewlett Packard's MediaSmart servers, although not as fully featured as servers

used in business networks, are increasingly popular choices for managing an entire family's personal media. We'll discuss servers designed for home networks later in the chapter.

Describing Networks Based on Distance

How does the distance between nodes define a network? The distance between nodes on a network is another way to describe a network. A **local area network (LAN)** is a network in which the nodes are located within a small geographic area. Examples include a network in a computer lab at school or at a fast-food restaurant. A **home area network (HAN)** is a network located in a home. HANs are used to connect all of its digital devices, such as computers, peripherals, phones, cameras, digital video recorders (DVRs), and televisions.

Is it possible to connect LANs together? A **wide area network (WAN)** is made up of LANs connected over long distances. Say a school has two campuses (east and west) located in different towns. Connecting the LAN at the east campus to the LAN at the west campus by telecommunications lines would allow the users on the two LANs to communicate. The two LANs would be described as a single WAN.

Are wireless networks that cover large portions of cities considered WANs? Technically, wireless networks like the one deployed in Minneapolis, which provides Internet access to city residents and visitors, are WANs. However, when a network is designed to provide access to a specific geographic area, such as an entire city, the network is usually called a **metropolitan area network (MAN)**. Many cities in the United States are now deploying MANs to provide Internet access to residents and provide convenience for tourists.

Network Components

To function, all networks must include (1) a means of connecting the nodes on the network (cables or wireless technology),

Labels in figure:

Networking software running on each computer

Computer 2 network node

Printer network node

Transmission media (wires or radio waves) connecting network nodes

Computer 1 network node

External network adapter

Internal network adapter (network interface card)

Router

Wireless access point

Network adapter attached to or inserted in each network node

Specialized network navigation devices (used on some networks)

Figure 7.4

Network components.

(2) special devices that allow the nodes to communicate with each other and to send data, and (3) software that allows the network to run. We discuss each of these components next (see Figure 7.4).

Transmission Media

How are nodes on a network connected? All network nodes (computers and peripherals) are connected to each other and to the network by **transmission media**. A transmission medium establishes a communications channel between the nodes on a network and can take several forms:

1. Networks can use additional cable to connect nodes, such as twisted-pair cable, coaxial cable, or fiber-optic cable. You have probably seen twisted-pair and coaxial cable. Normal telephone wire is **twisted-pair cable**. It is made up of copper wires that are twisted around each other and surrounded by a plastic jacket. If you have cable TV, the cable running into your TV or cable box is **coaxial cable**. Coaxial cable consists of a single copper wire surrounded by

layers of plastic. **Fiber-optic cable** is made up of plastic or glass fibers that transmit data at extremely fast speeds.

2. Wireless networks use radio waves instead of wires or cable to connect nodes.

3. Networks can use existing wiring, such as power lines, to connect nodes.

What media should I use to ensure my network transfers data quickly? Different types of transmission media transmit data at different speeds. **Data transfer rate** (also called **bandwidth**) is the maximum speed at which data can be transmitted between two nodes on a network. **Throughput** is the actual speed of data transfer that is achieved. It is usually less than the data transfer rate. Data transfer rate and throughput are usually measured in megabits per second (Mbps). A megabit, when applied to data transfer rates, represents 1 million bits. Twisted-pair cable, coaxial cable, and wireless media provide enough bandwidth for most home networks, whereas fiber-optic cable is sometimes used in client/server networks.

Network Adapters

How do the different nodes on the network communicate? Network adapters are devices connected to or installed in network nodes that enable the nodes to communicate with each other and to access the network. Most desktop and notebook computers (and many peripherals) sold today contain network adapters installed *inside* as expansion cards. This type of adapter is referred to as a **network interface card (NIC)**.

What if I don't have a network adapter installed inside my computer or peripheral? Network adapters are also available as external devices that plug into an available USB port. These are often used to provide older computing devices or other devices (such as TiVo digital video recorders) with wireless connectivity. We discuss network adapters in more detail throughout the chapter.

Network Navigation Devices

How is data sent through a network? Data is sent over transmission media in bundles. Each bundle is called a **packet**. For computers to communicate, these packets of data must be able to flow between computers. A **network navigation device** helps make this data flow possible. These devices, which are attached to the network, enable the transmission of data. Some simple peer-to-peer networks do not require network navigation devices because the network adapters serve that purpose. Networks that are more sophisticated need specialized navigation devices.

What network navigation devices might I use on my home network? The two most common specialized navigation devices are routers and switches. A **router** transfers packets of data between two or more networks. For example, if a home network is connected to the Internet, a router is required to send data between the two networks (the home network and the Internet). A **switch** is a "traffic cop" on a network. Switches receive data packets and send them to their intended nodes on the same network (not between different networks). Most routers sold for home use have switches integrated into them. We discuss routers and switches in more detail later in the chapter.

> **"What software do home networks require?"**

Networking Software

What software do home networks require? Home networks need operating system (OS) software that supports peer-to-peer networking. The most common versions of Windows used in the home (Windows 7, Vista, and XP) support P2P networking. You can connect computers running any of these OSs to the same network. Mac OS X and the various versions of Linux also support P2P networking. Moreover, computers using OS X and Windows can communicate with each other on the same network.

Is the same software used in client/server networks? Client/server networks are controlled by a central server that has specialized **network operating system (NOS)** software installed on it. This software handles requests for information, Internet access, and the use of peripherals for the rest of the network nodes. Examples of NOS software include Windows Server 2008 and SUSE Linux Enterprise.

Types of Peer-to-Peer Networks

The most common type of network you will probably encounter in the home is a peer-to-peer network, because this is the type of network you would set up in your home. Therefore, we'll focus on P2P networks in this chapter. There are three main types of P2P networks:

1. Wired Ethernet networks
2. Wireless Ethernet networks
3. Power-line networks

SOUND BYTE

Installing a Home Computer Network

Installing a network is relatively easy if you've seen someone else do it. In this Sound Byte, you'll learn how to install the hardware and configure Windows for a wired or wireless home network.

The major differences among these networks are the transmission media by which the nodes are connected and the bandwidth each achieves. In the following sections, we will look at these networks and how each one is set up.

Wired Ethernet Networks

What are Ethernet networks? An **Ethernet network** is so named because it uses the Ethernet protocol as the means (or standard) by which the nodes on the network communicate. The Ethernet protocol was developed by the Institute of Electrical and Electronics Engineers (IEEE). This nonprofit group develops many standard specifications for electronic data transmission that are adopted throughout the world. Each standard the IEEE develops is numbered, with 802.3 being the standard for wired Ethernet networks. The Ethernet protocol makes Ethernet networks extremely efficient at moving data. However, to achieve this efficiency, the algorithms for moving data through an Ethernet network are complex.

Because of this complexity, Ethernet networks require additional devices such as switches and routers. A **wired Ethernet network** is slightly more complicated to set up than other home network options (such as the direct connection of two Windows computers), but these networks are faster, more reliable, and less expensive, making them the most popular choice for home networks. Although 100 Mbps Ethernet networks are most commonly installed in homes, prices are falling quickly on 1-gigabit-per-second (1 Gbps, or 1,000 Mbps) Ethernet components. The potential high throughput of Gigabit Ethernet is useful if you're moving large files, such as downloaded movies, around your home network.

How do I create an Ethernet network? An Ethernet network requires you to install or attach network adapters to each computer or peripheral you want to connect to the network. Because Ethernet networks are so common, most computers sold today come with Ethernet adapters preinstalled. To see if you have a network adapter installed in your Windows computer

Network adapters

Figure 7.5

This Windows device manager shows a wireless and a wired network adapter installed in a computer.

(and check whether the adapter is working), click on the Hardware and Sound Group and then access Device Manager from the Control Panel (see Figure 7.5). Click on the Network adapters section to display installed adapters.

As noted earlier, such internal network adapters are referred to as *network interface cards (NICs)*. Modern Ethernet NICs are usually 10/100/1000 Mbps cards (see Figure 7.6a). This means they can handle the old 10 Mbps and 100 Mbps data transfer rates as well as the newer 1 Gbps data transfer rate.

If your computer doesn't have a NIC (or the NIC installed in your motherboard fails), you can buy one and install it or you can use a USB adapter, which plugs into any

Figure 7.6

Ethernet network adapters come in a variety of versions, including (a) a 10/100/1000 NIC, which is installed in an expansion slot inside the system unit, (b) a USB adapter, and (c) an ExpressCard.

open USB port on the system unit (see Figure 7.6b). Although you can use USB versions in notebooks, ExpressCard versions of Ethernet NICs are made especially for notebooks (see Figure 7.6c). ExpressCards are about the size of a flash drive and fit into specially designed slots on a notebook. There are several different configurations of ExpressCards, so make sure you are purchasing the correct one for your computer. However, most new notebooks include built-in wired and wireless Ethernet adapters.

How are nodes connected on wired Ethernet networks? The most popular transmission media option for wired Ethernet networks is **unshielded twisted-pair (UTP) cable**. UTP cable is composed of four pairs of wires that are twisted around each other to reduce electrical interference. You can buy UTP cable in varying lengths with RJ-45 connectors (Ethernet connectors) already attached. RJ-45 connectors resemble standard phone connectors (called *RJ-11 connectors*) but are slightly larger and have contacts for eight wires (four pairs) instead of four wires (see Figure 7.7). You must use UTP cable with RJ-45 connectors on an Ethernet network because a phone cable will not work.

Do all wired Ethernet networks use the same kind of UTP cable? Figure 7.8 lists the three main types of UTP cable you would consider using in home-wired Ethernet networks—Cat 5E, Cat 6, and Cat 7—and their data transfer rates. Although Cat 5E cable is the cheapest and is sufficient for many home networking tasks, installing **Cat 6 cable** will allow you to run a Gigabit Ethernet network. Gigabit networks support throughput that is designed to handle data-intensive file transfers, such as digital movies. Cat 7 cable is designed for Ultra-Fast Ethernet (10 Gigabit Ethernet)

networks that run at speeds as fast as 10 Gbps. Installing a 10 Gigabit Ethernet network in the home is probably unnecessary because today's home applications don't require this rate of data transfer. However, if the cost of installing Cat 7 cable is not significantly more than installing Cat 6 cable, you may want to consider using it as a hedge against higher bandwidth requirements of future networking applications.

Is UTP cable difficult to install? UTP cable is no more difficult to install than normal phone cable. You just need to take a few precautions. Avoid putting sharp bends into the cable when running it around corners because this can damage the copper wires inside and lead to breakage. Also, run the cable around the perimeter of the room (instead of under a rug, for example) to prevent damage to wires from foot traffic.

How long can an Ethernet cable run be? Cable runs for Ethernet networks using UTP cable can't exceed 100 meters (328 feet) or the signal starts to degrade. For cable runs of more than 100 meters, you can use a **repeater**, a device that is installed on long cable runs to amplify the signal. In effect, repeaters act as signal boosters. Repeaters can extend run lengths to 600 feet, but they do add to the cost of a network. Whenever possible, use continuous lengths of cable. Although two cables can be spliced together with a connecting jack, this creates a point of failure for the cable, because connectors can loosen in the connecting jack and moisture or dust can accumulate on the contacts. Usually, extending your wired network using wireless technology is a better option than using repeaters or splicing cable.

If I only have notebook computers, why would I even consider using a wired network? Because the whole idea of notebooks is portability, it seems natural to connect them to a network using wireless media. However, most wired networks achieve a much higher rate of data throughput than wireless networks. When engaging in large file transfers (such as downloading digital movies), it may be very desirable to connect your notebook to your network using a cable to take advantage of faster data transfer rates. Fortunately, most wireless routers sold for the home market include an option for creating wired

Figure 7.7

(a) An RJ-45 (Ethernet) connector, which is used on UTP cables; and (b) a typical RJ-11 connector, which is used on standard phone cords.

connections as well. Therefore, you can get the best of both worlds by using your notebook in wireless mode most of the time and connecting it to your network via a wired connection when you need increased throughput.

Figure 7.8 | DATA TRANSFER RATES FOR POPULAR HOME NETWORK CABLE TYPES

UTP Cable Category	Data Transfer Rate
Category 5E (Cat 5E)	100 to 1,000 Mbps
Category 6 (Cat 6)	1,000 Mbps (1 Gbps) and higher
Category 7 (Cat 7)	10 Gbps and higher

Ethernet Switches

How do Ethernet networks use switches?

Data is transmitted through the wires of an Ethernet network in packets. Imagine the data packets on an Ethernet network as cars on a road. If there were no traffic signals or rules of the road (such as driving on the right-hand side), we'd see a lot more collisions between vehicles, and people wouldn't get where they were going as readily (or at all). Data packets can also suffer collisions. If data packets collide, the data in them is damaged or lost. In either case, the network doesn't function efficiently. The routers you buy for home networks have a switch integrated into them, so you won't need to buy a stand-alone switch for your home network.

As shown in Figure 7.9, a switch in an Ethernet network acts like a traffic signal (or a traffic cop) by enforcing the rules of the data road on the transmission media. The switch keeps track of the data packets and, in conjunction with network interface cards, helps the data packets find their destinations without running into each other. This keeps the network running efficiently.

Switches are often mistakenly referred to as *hubs*. A **hub** is a network navigation device that merely retransmits a signal to all other nodes attached to it. Switches are essentially "smart hubs" because they

transmit data only to the node to which it should be sent. When Ethernet networks first came out, switches were much more expensive than hubs, so many home networks used hubs, but today there is virtually no cost difference. Therefore, most navigation devices sold for home networks are switches (even if they are mistakenly referred to as hubs).

How many computers and peripherals can be connected to a switch?

Switches are differentiated by the number of ports they have for connecting network devices. Four- and eight-port switches are often used in home networks. A four-port switch can connect a maximum of four devices to the network, whereas an eight-port switch can handle eight devices. You should buy a switch that has enough ports for all the devices you want to connect to the network. Many people buy switches with more ports than they currently need so that they can expand their network in the future.

A wonderful feature of switches is that you can daisy-chain them together. Usually, one port on a switch is designated for plugging into a second switch. You can chain two four-port switches together to

Figure 7.9

A simplified explanation is that switches (working in conjunction with NICs) act like traffic signals or traffic cops. They enforce the rules of the data road on an Ethernet network and help prevent data packets from crashing into each other.

Switch

Data packet 1

Data packet 2

Data packet 3

Data packet 4

ETHERNET MEDIA

ETHERNET MEDIA

provide connections for a total of six devices. Most switches can be chained to provide hundreds of ports, which would far exceed the needs of most home networks, but may provide you with needed expandability in a small business network.

Ethernet Routers

How is data from an Ethernet network shared with the Internet or another network? As mentioned earlier, routers are devices that transfer packets of data between two or more networks. If a home network is connected to the Internet, you need a router to send data between the home network and the Internet.

Because so many people are sharing Internet access in home networks, manufacturers are making devices that combine switches and routers and are specifically designed to connect to DSL or cable modems. Such devices are often referred to as **DSL/cable routers**. If you want your Ethernet network to connect to the Internet through a DSL or cable modem, obtaining a DSL/cable router is essential. Because you already need a switch to connect multiple devices on an Ethernet network, these routers (which include switching capabilities) fulfill a dual role by controlling your network traffic and allowing your Internet connection to be shared. Figure 7.10 shows an example of an Ethernet network configured using a DSL/cable router.

Besides computers, what other devices can I attach to a router? Because sharing peripherals is a major benefit of installing a network, many peripheral devices, such as scanners and printers, now come with built-in Ethernet capability. Such devices are usually described as network-ready devices. A **network-ready device** can be connected directly to a router instead of to a computer on the network. These devices can then be accessed by any computer on the network. If a printer were connected

Figure 7.10

Two desktop computers and a notebook connected to a DSL/cable router.

INTERNET

DSL/Cable modem

DSL/Cable router

Computer #1

Computer #2

Computer #3

directly to another computer on the network instead of to the router, that computer would need to be switched on so other computers could access the printer. With a network-ready printer, only the printer needs to be powered on for any computer on the network to print to it. Many network-ready printers contain wireless NICs so they can be easily installed on wireless networks.

Network attached storage (NAS) devices are also becoming popular in home networks. People are generating tremendous quantities of digital data today with digital cameras and camcorders, and these digital files need to be stored. Although data can always be stored on individual hard drives in computers on a network, NAS devices provide for centralized data storage and access.

Popular for years on business networks, NAS devices are specialized computing devices designed to store and manage data. You can think of them as specialized external hard drives. NAS devices, like the My Book series from Western Digital, connect directly to the network through a router or switch. Specialized software can then be installed on computers attached to the network to ensure that all data saved to an individual computer is also stored on the NAS as a backup. We'll discuss backing up your data in more detail in Chapter 9.

Aside from creating backups, NAS devices facilitate the sharing of files such as movies, music, and digital photos. Some NAS devices, such as those in the Western Digital My Book line (see Figure 7.11), are accessible over the Internet, making it possible to retrieve your data wherever you have an Internet connection.

A **digital media receiver (DMR)**, which can also be called a *media extender* or a *media adapter,* is often connected to a home network. DMRs are specialized entertainment devices that are specifically designed to retrieve digital media (music, movies, or pictures) from computers or storage devices on a network and display them on televisions or home theater systems. Some DMRs include their own displays and speakers, while others must be connected to a television or stereo system.

Home network servers, such as a computer configured with Windows Home

Figure 7.11

The My Book drives from Western Digital feature NAS devices that can store 2 TB of data in a device the size of a small book.

Ethernet port for easy connection to a router

Server, can also be connected to the router on a home network. Home servers do not necessarily convert a home peer-to-peer network into a client/server network, but the servers do take charge of a variety of tasks that are often performed centrally in a client/server network. Home servers often handle the following tasks:

- Back up files for all computers connected to the network.
- Act as a repository for files to be shared across the network (such as music and video files).
- Function as an access gateway to allow any computer on the network to be accessed from a remote location via the Internet.

All of these devices can usually be attached to a network via either wired or wireless transmission media as the situation demands.

Wireless Ethernet Networks

What is a wireless network? A **wireless network** uses radio waves instead of wires or cables as its transmission media. Just as it established the 802.3 standard for wired Ethernet networks, the IEEE has established standards for wireless Ethernet networks. Any current **wireless Ethernet network** in the United States will be based on the **802.11 standard**, which was established in 1997. The 802.11 standard is also known as **Wi-Fi**. Four standards are currently defined under 802.11: 802.11a, 802.11b, 802.11g, and 802.11n. The last of these was ratified in 2009 and is quickly becoming the most popular standard in home networks. The main differences among these standards are the maximum data transfer rates and the types of security that they support. For home networking, 802.11g and 802.11n are the standards most commonly used today.

The 802.11g standard, which supports a data transfer rate of 54 Mbps, is a well-established standard for home use because it is much faster than the original 802.11b standard. Devices using the newly ratified 802.11n standard use multiple transmitter and receiver antennas to achieve higher throughput and increased signal range. Devices using the 802.11n standard are more costly than 802.11g devices. However, 802.11n devices usually achieve a data transfer rate that usually exceeds 200 Mbps. Since the signals produced by 802.11n devices also cover a wider area than 802.11g devices, they can be used effectively even in large houses. Therefore, you may want to spend the extra money on 802.11n equipment to achieve good wireless coverage throughout your home.

Do all my devices need to use the same wireless networking standard? When new standards are designed, they are made to be backward compatible with previous standards (work with previous standards). For instance, 802.11n will recognize and work with 802.11g equipment. However, to achieve 802.11n speeds, you need to ensure that your computers have 802.11n network adapters installed in them or connected to them so they can function efficiently with an 802.11n router. A notebook computer with an 802.11g adapter in it can connect to an 802.11n router, but will function at the lower 802.11g speeds. If you were buying 802.11n equipment to upgrade your network, it

would be a good idea to buy all the components (adapters, routers, etc.) from one manufacturer to ensure they work correctly together. Sometimes manufacturers make proprietary tweaks to their equipment, usually to boost throughput. This may keep it from functioning efficiently with another manufacturer's equipment.

What do I need to set up a wireless network? Just like other networks, each node on a wireless network requires a **wireless network adapter**. If not built into the motherboard of the computer, these adapters are available as NICs that are inserted into expansion slots on the computer (see Figure 7.12a) or as USB devices that plug into an open USB port (see Figure 7.12b). Most notebooks today come with a built-in 802.11g or 802.11n wireless/wired network adapter.

Wireless network adapters differ from other network adapters in that they contain transceivers. A **transceiver** is a device that translates the electronic data that needs to be sent along the network into radio waves and then broadcasts these radio waves to other network nodes. Transceivers serve a dual function because they also receive the signals from other network nodes. As shown in Figure 7.12, many add-on wireless network adapters have antennae poking out of them. Antennae are necessary for the transmission and reception of these radio waves.

Do all nodes on the wireless network have to be computers? A node on a wireless network can also be a peripheral device such as a printer, storage device, or scanner. The peripheral will need to be connected to

Figure 7.12

Wireless network adapters are available as (a) NICs, which are inserted into an open expansion slot on the computer, or (b) USB devices, which plug into an open USB port.

a wireless network adapter so that other nodes on the network can communicate with it.

How do I share an Internet connection on a wireless network?

Just like wired Ethernet networks, wireless Ethernet networks require the installation of a router to share an Internet connection. A **wireless router** (sometimes called a **gateway**) is a device that combines the capabilities of a wired router with the ability to receive wireless signals. Don't buy a wireless access point (which we discuss later) by mistake when you need a wireless router, because a wireless access point does not perform the same function.

What types of problems can I run into when installing wireless networks?

The maximum range of wireless devices under the 802.11g standard is about 250 feet. However, as the distance between nodes increases, throughput decreases markedly. Equipment that meets the 802.11n standard provides greater bandwidth over longer distances.

Note that 802.11g devices work on a bandwidth of 2.4 GHz. This is the same bandwidth that many cordless phones use, so your phone and wireless network may interfere with each other. The best solution is to buy a cordless phone that uses a bandwidth of 5 GHz, or else purchase 802.11n equipment, which uses the 5 GHz band.

Obstacles between wireless nodes also decrease throughput. Walls and large metal objects are the most common sources of interference with wireless signals. For example, placing a computer with a wireless network adapter next to a refrigerator may prevent the signals from reaching the rest of the network. Similarly, a node that has four walls between it and the Internet connection will most likely have lower-than-maximum throughput. The 802.11n devices have a range up to three times as far as 802.11g

devices and are less susceptible (but not immune) to interference.

What if a node on the network can't communicate with other nodes, or with the router?

Repositioning a node or wireless network adapter within the same room (sometimes even just a few inches from the original position) can often affect communication between nodes. If this doesn't work, try moving the computer closer to the router or to other rooms in your house. Many newer routers support the addition of external antennae, which are either directional ones that focus the signal in a certain direction, or omnidirectional ones that spread the signal out over a wide area. If you have a single problem area, plugging a directional antenna into your router, placing the antenna as close to the problem area as possible, and facing directly toward it may solve the reception problem.

If these solutions don't work, then you may need to add a wireless access point. A **wireless access point (WAP)** is a device that attaches to a network and provides wireless nodes (such as a notebook with a wireless NIC installed) with a means of wirelessly connecting to the network. When you have connection problems (for example, the notebook on your porch can't connect to the wireless router), adding a WAP to the network will often solve the problem. Essentially, you're extending the range of the wireless network by providing a second point at which nodes can connect to the network. The WAP must be connected to the network either directly to the switch on the router or to another node within range of the router.

For example, as you can see in Figure 7.13, Notebook C on the back porch and the wireless router (connected to

BITS AND BYTES

Wireless Hot Spots: How to Find One on the Go

Wireless hot spots are places where you can connect to the Internet via a computing device with wireless networking capability (such as your notebook computer). Providers of wireless hot spots may provide free access, or they may charge a fee, which is usually based on connection time (such as a set fee per hour of access). So aside from randomly cruising around searching for a place to connect, how do you find out where the hot spots are? Directories have popped up on the Internet to help you locate hot spots in the areas in which you'll be traveling. Check out JiWire (**jiwire.com**), Wi-Fi FreeSpot (**wififreespot.com**), and Wi-Fi Hotspot List (**wi-fihotspotlist.com**) to locate a hot spot near you.

| Bedroom | Den | Back porch |

Wireless router

Information from A to C

Information from A to C

Wireless access point

Computer A with wireless network adapter

Computer B with wireless access point

Notebook C with wireless network adapter

Figure 7.13

Because a wireless access point is installed on Computer B, data can travel from Notebook C on the back porch to the wireless router in the bedroom.

Figure 7.14

Wired and wireless connections in the same home network.

Computer A in the bedroom) can't make contact. However, Notebook C can connect to Computer B in the den. By connecting a WAP to Computer B, all traffic from Notebook C is relayed to the wireless router through the WAP connected to Computer B. It is a good idea to set up appropriate wireless security for your WAP so that strangers can't connect to your network without your knowledge. (We cover wireless security later in this chapter.)

Can I have wired and wireless nodes on one network? Many users want to create a network in which some computers (such as desktops) connect to the network with wires, whereas other computers (such as

notebooks) connect to the network wirelessly. Most wireless DSL/cable routers allow you to connect wireless and wired nodes to the same network. This type of router contains both a WAP and ports that allow you to connect wired nodes to the router. Figure 7.14 shows an example of a network with a wireless DSL/cable router attached. As you can see, the notebook maintains a wireless connection to the router, whereas the other two computers are connected by wires. Using this type of router is a cost-effective way to have some wireless connections while preserving the high-speed attributes of wired Ethernet where needed.

INTERNET

Wireless DSL/Cable router

Computer in bedroom with wired connection

Notebook on back porch with wireless connection

Computer in den with wired connection

Power-Line Networks

What are power-line networks?

Power-line networks use the existing electrical wiring in your home to connect the nodes in the network. Thus, in a power-line network, any electrical outlet provides a network connection. The HomePlug Power Line Alliance (**homeplug.org**) sets standards for home power-line networking. The original power-line networks had a maximum data transfer rate of 14 Mbps. However, currently available power-line networks have data transfer rates approaching 200 Mbps, which can make them a viable alternative to wireless or wired Ethernet in certain situations.

How do I create a power-line network?

To create a power-line network, you connect a power-line network adapter (similar to a network adapter in an Ethernet network) to each computer or peripheral that you're going to attach to the network (see Figure 7.15). You can buy power-line network adapters in either USB or Ethernet versions. After you attach a network adapter to each node on the network, you plug the adapters into an electrical outlet. Most power-line network adapters will be recognized automatically by the Windows operating system.

Why would I use a power-line network instead of an Ethernet network?

Because of the low bandwidth of the original power-line networks and the lower costs of Ethernet networks, power-line networks declined in popularity. However, with the introduction of power-line equipment that supports much higher data throughput, power-line networks are becoming popular again. Modern power-line networks can sometimes exceed speeds of wireless Ethernet networks, especially where there is a lot of interference on the wireless network. Therefore, if you're in a situation in which running new wires is impractical and you're experiencing too much interference to run a wireless network, you may want to consider installing a power-line network.

Choosing a Peer-to-Peer Network

If you're setting up a home network, the type of network you should choose will depend on your particular needs. In general, consider the following questions in determining your network type:

- Is existing wiring available?
- Do you want wireless communications?
- How fast do you want your network connection to be?
- How much money can you spend on your network?

What if I want to use existing wiring for my home network?

As noted earlier, you can use power lines (electrical wiring) as media for a home network. Obviously, you need to have an electrical outlet available in each room in which you want to connect a node to the network. Because you have to plug most nodes (computers, printers, and so on) into an electrical outlet to operate them anyway, connecting a power-line network is usually convenient. However, these networks might be more expensive than wired or wireless Ethernet networks.

What are the pros and cons of wireless networks?

Wireless networks free you from having to run wires in your home. In addition, your ability to move around is not impaired or restricted by wires. However, wireless networks may not work effectively in every home, so you need to install and test the wireless network to figure out whether it will work. To avoid unnecessary expenses, make sure you can

Plug into electrical outlet

Ethernet connection

Figure 7.15

Power-line adapters plug into any electrical outlet and can then connect to your computer (or peripheral) via an Ethernet cable.

return equipment for a refund if it doesn't work properly in your home.

Which network type provides the highest data transfer rate? Most routine home computing tasks such as Web browsing and e-mailing require minimal throughput (less than 10 Mbps is sufficient). However, if high-speed data transmission is important (for example, if you play computer games or exchange large files), then you may want a network with high throughput. With data transfer rates as high as 1,000 Mbps, wired Ethernet networks are the fastest home networks. You may want to consider a Gigabit network if you engage in a lot of multiplayer gaming or video transfer. Without high throughput, streaming video can appear choppy, games can respond slowly, and files can take a long time to transfer.

What cost factors do I need to consider in choosing a network? You may need to consider your budget when deciding what type of network to install. Figure 7.16 lists the approximate costs of installing the various types of peer-to-peer networks and their advantages and disadvantages.

Do I need to consider the type of broadband connection I have? Whether you connect to the Internet by DSL, cable, or satellite makes no difference in terms of the type of network you select. The differences occur with your particular network's hardware and software requirements.

Configuring Software for Your Home Network

Once you install the hardware for your network, you need to configure your operating system software for networking on your computers. In this section, you'll learn how to do just that using special Windows tools. Although configuration is different with Mac OS X, the setup is quick and easy. Linux is the most complex operating system to configure for a home network, though the difficulties are not insurmountable.

Is configuring software difficult? Windows makes configuring software relatively simple by virtually automating the entire process of setting up a network using various wizards. As you learned in Chapter 4, a wizard is a utility program included with software that you can use to help you accomplish a specific task. You can launch the Windows wizards from the Network and Sharing Center, which can be accessed via the Network and Internet group in the Control Panel. Before running any wizards, you should do the following:

1. Install network adapters on each node.

2. For a wired network, plug all the cables into the router, network adapters, and so on.

Figure 7.16 | COMPARISON OF MAJOR TYPES OF HOME NETWORKS

	Wired			Wireless	
	100 Mbps Ethernet	Gigabit Ethernet	Power Line	802.11g	802.11n
Maximum data transfer rate (bandwidth)	100 Mbps	1,000 Mbps or 1 Gbps	200 Mbps	54 Mbps	540 Mbps
Actual expected throughput	50 to 60 Mbps	500 to 600 Mbps	100 Mbps	15 to 25 Mbps	150 to 200 Mbps
Operational frequency	N/A	N/A	N/A	2.4 GHz	5 GHz
Cost of basic access point, router or switch	$40 to $60 (switch)	$100 to $200 (switch)	$100 to $200 (adapter or router)	$30 to $60	$80 and up
Pros	Mature, proven technology; low cost	Fastest practical home technology available	No additional wiring required	Mature, proven technology; low cost	Significantly faster than 802.11g
Cons	Can be expensive to install hidden wiring.	Cat 6 wiring required. Can be expensive to install hidden wiring.	May not have outlets in the correct locations.	Interference from walls and other structures can cause signal to degrade (especially over greater distances).	Same as 802.11g, but to a lesser extent.

Source: Table adapted from "Pump Up Your Home Network" by Erik Rhey, *PC Magazine*, October 3, 2006.

3. Make sure your cable/DSL modem is connected to your router and that it is connected to the Internet.

4. Turn on your equipment in the following order (allowing the modem and the router about one minute each to power up and configure):
   a. your cable/DSL modem,
   b. your router, and

c. all computers and peripherals (printers, scanners, and so on).

By completing these steps, you enable the wizards to make decisions about how best to configure your network. After you have completed these steps, open the Network and Sharing Center from the Control Panel (see Figure 7.17a). You can see the network to which you are currently connected on

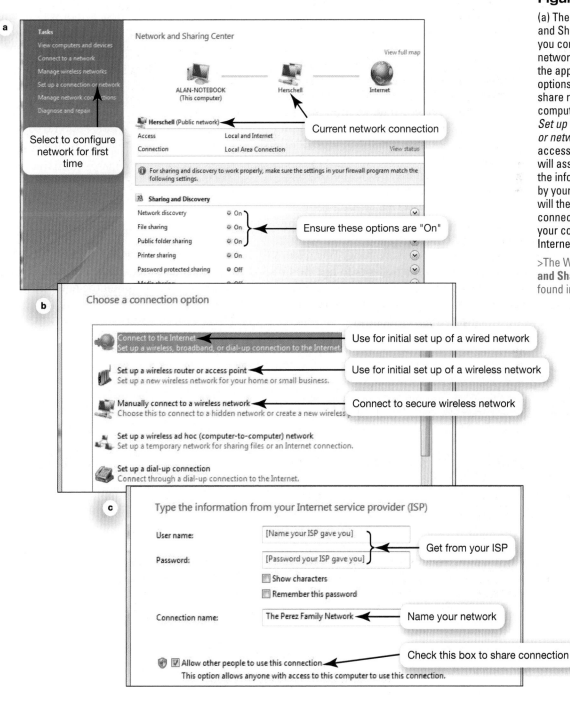

Figure 7.17

(a) The Windows Network and Sharing Center helps you configure your home network. (b) Selecting the appropriate sharing options allow others to share resources on your computer. (c) Selecting *Set up a new connection or network* provides access to wizards that will assist you. (d) Fill in the information provided by your ISP. The wizard will then set up your connection and connect your computer to the Internet.

>The Windows **Network and Sharing Center** is found in the **Control Panel**.

this screen. On the lower portion of the Network and Sharing Center screen, you can set sharing options for your network. Ensure that network discovery is shown as "on," because this allows your computer to locate other computers and peripherals on the network. You should also verify that the options for file and printer sharing and public folder sharing are shown as "on" to enable file and printer sharing with other computers. From the Network and Sharing Center, select *Set up a new connection or network* to access the Windows networking wizards (see Figure 7.17b). *Note:* If you already have a wired network set up and are connected to the Internet, plugging your Windows computer into the router is all you need to do. Windows will automatically detect an existing wired network.

Select the Connect to the Internet wizard to configure your network to use your cable/DSL modem to connect to the Internet for the first time. This wizard also configures your wired network. On the information screen (see Figure 7.17c) enter and access information provided by your ISP. Enter a memorable name for your network and check the box to allow other people to use the Internet connection you are establishing. This will allow all users on the network to use the same connection.

After running this wizard, run the Set Up a Wireless Router wizard to configure your wireless network. If you set up a secured wireless network, use the Manually Connect to a Wireless Network wizard to connect computers to the secure network.

What if I don't have the same version of Windows on all my computers? Windows 7, Windows Vista, and Windows XP are the most common OSs for home use that support P2P networking. Fortunately, you can network computers using any of these versions of Windows. If you have one computer with Windows 7 but your other computers run on other versions of Windows, then you should set up your Windows 7 computer first. Windows 7 and Vista can automatically detect computers running other versions of Windows on your network; however, you may have to make adjustments to the Windows XP computers on your network (such as installing Windows XP Service Pack 3) to enable them to see the networked Windows 7 and Vista computers. Check the Microsoft Web site for instructions.

How do I differentiate the computers on my network? When you set up your Windows computer, you gave it a name. Each computer on a network needs a name that is different from the names of all other computers on the network so that the network can identify it. This unique name ensures that the network knows which computer is requesting services and data and can deliver data to the correct computer.

Figure 7.18

Accessing the System screen allows you to check your computer and workgroup names and change them if necessary.

>The **Windows System** screen can be accessed by clicking the **System and Security** link in the **Control Panel**.

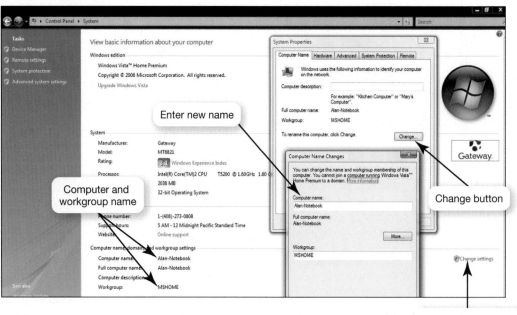

Computers on a network can be located in various workgroups. For simplicity on a home network, you should assign all your computers to the same workgroup. If you don't recall your computer's name or the workgroup to which it is assigned, open the Control Panel, click the System and Security link and then click the System icon (see Figure 7.18). The current name of your computer and the workgroup to which it belongs is shown. You can change the name of the computer or the workgroup by clicking the Change Settings link, which launches the System Properties dialog box. Clicking the Change button on the Computer Name tab will launch the Computer Name Changes dialog box, where you can rename your computer or assign it to a different workgroup.

Is that it?　Assuming you installed and configured everything properly, your home network should now be up and running, allowing you to share files, Internet connections, and peripherals. Most routers will work right out of the box. However, with some routers you may have to alter the configuration to connect to the Internet. Check the instructions that came with your router or refer to the router manufacturer's Web site for guidance.

How do I set up my router so that I can use it to connect to the Internet?　First, contact your ISP and find out about any special settings that you may need to configure your router to work with your ISP. Next, access your router from Internet Explorer (or another Web browser) by entering the router's IP address or default URL. You can usually find this information in the documentation that came with the router. You'll also need a username and password to log on to the router. You'll probably find these, too, in the documentation that came with the router.

Many routers feature their own wizard (different from the Windows Networking wizards) that takes you through special configuration screens. A sample screen from a router is shown in Figure 7.19. The documentation that came with your router will provide a URL to use to log on to the router. If you're unsure of any information that needs to be entered to configure the router (such as whether IP addresses are assigned dynamically—meaning you are assigned a new IP address by your ISP each time you connect to the Internet), contact your ISP and ask for guidance.

How can I test my Internet connection speed?　Your ISP may have promised you certain speeds of downloading and uploading data. How can you tell if you are getting what was promised? There are numerous sites on the Internet, such as **Speedtest.net** (see Figure 7.20), where you can test the speed of downloading files to your computer and uploading files to other computers. You can then see how your results compare to those of

NETGEAR Router - Microsoft Internet Explorer

File　Edit　View　Favorites　Tools　Help

Back　Search　Favorites

Address　http://www.routerlogin.net　←　URL for router logon　　Go　Norton Internet Security

Setup Wizard

Setup
Basic Settings
Wireless Settings
Content Filtering
Logs
Block Sites
Block Services
Schedule
E-mail
Maintenance
Router Status
Attached Devices

Basic Settings

Does Your Internet Connection R
○ Yes
◉ No

Get logon information from ISP

Account Name (If Required)　WGR614v6
Domain Name (If Required)

Internet IP Address
◉ Get Dynamically From ISP　←　Most IP addresses assigned dynamically
○ Use Static IP Address

Help

The Basic Settings pages allow you to configure, upgrade and check the status of your NETGEAR Wireless Router.

Click an item in the leftmost column. The current settings or information for that area appear in the center column.

Helpful information related to the selected Settings page appears in this column. If you are using Internet Explorer, you may click an item in the

Figure 7.19

Although setups differ from router to router, you will need basic information such as the logon information and the type of IP addressing to configure the router to work with your network and your ISP.

Figure 7.20

Speed test showing a download speed of 8.38 megabits, which is fast for a home Internet connection.

other users in your state and across the United States. Many factors can influence your Internet speeds, so be sure to run the test at several different times during the day over the course of a week before complaining to your ISP about not getting your promised speed.

Securing Wireless Networks

All computers that connect to the Internet (whether or not they are on a network) need to be secured from intruders. This is usually accomplished by using a **firewall**, which is a hardware or software solution that helps shield your network from prying eyes. We discuss firewalls at length in Chapter 9. Wireless networks present special vulnerabilities; therefore, you should take additional specific steps to keep your wireless network safe.

Why is a wireless network more vulnerable than a wired network? With a wired network, it is fairly easy to tell if a **hacker** (someone who breaks into computer systems to create mischief or steal valuable information) is using your network. However, wireless networks, especially those using 802.11n equipment, have wide ranges that may extend outside of your house. This makes it possible for a hacker to access your network without your knowledge.

Why should I be worried about someone logging onto my wireless network without my permission? Some use of other people's wireless

networks is unintentional. Houses are built close together. Apartments are clustered even closer together. Wireless signals can easily reach a neighbor's residence. Most wireless network adapters are set up to access the strongest wireless network signal detected. If your router is on the east side of your house and you and your notebook are on the west side, then you may get a stronger signal from your neighbor's wireless network than from your own. **Piggybacking** is connecting to a wireless network (other than your own) without the permission of the owner. This practice is illegal in many jurisdictions but often happens inadvertently between neighbors.

Your neighbor probably isn't a hacker, but he might be using a lot of bandwidth—your bandwidth! If he's downloading a massive movie file while you're trying to do research for a term paper, he's probably slowing you down. In addition, when some less-than-honest neighbors discover they can log onto your wireless network, they may cancel their own Internet service to save money by using yours. Some neighbors might even be computer savvy enough to penetrate your unprotected wireless network and steal personal information, just as any other hackers would.

In addition, because computer criminal activities are traceable, hackers love to work their mischief from public computers (such as those in a library or college) so they can't be identified. If a hacker is sitting in her car outside your house and logging on to your wireless network, any cyberattacks she launches might be traced back to your computer, and you might find law enforcement officials knocking on your door.

How is my wireless network vulnerable? Packets of information on a wireless network are broadcast through the airwaves. Savvy hackers can intercept and decode information from your transmissions that may allow them to bypass any standard protections, such as a firewall, which you have set up on your network. Therefore, to secure a wireless network, you should take the additional precautions described in the Sound Byte "Securing Wireless Networks" and as summarized below:

1. **Change your network name (SSID).** Each wireless network has its own name to identify it. Unless you change this name when you set up your router,

SOUND BYTE

Securing Wireless Networks

In this Sound Byte, you'll learn what "war drivers" are and why they could potentially be a threat to your wireless network. You'll also learn some simple steps to secure your wireless network against intruders.

the router uses a default network name (also known as the **service set identifier** or **SSID**) that all routers from that manufacturer use (such as "Wireless"). Hackers know the default names and access codes for routers. If you haven't changed the SSID, it's advertising the fact that you probably haven't changed any of the other default settings for your router, either.

2. **Disable SSID broadcast.** Most routers are set up to broadcast their SSIDs so that other wireless devices can find them. If your router supports disabling SSID broadcasting, turn it off. This makes it more difficult for a hacker to detect your network.

3. **Change the default password on your router.** Hackers know the default passwords of most routers, and if they can access your router, they can probably break into your network. Change the password on your router to something hard to guess. (Use at least eight characters that are a combination of letters, symbols, and numbers.)

4. **Turn on security protocols.** Most routers ship with security protocols such as Wired Equivalent Privacy (WEP) or Wi-Fi Protected Access (WPA). Both use encryption (a method of translating your data into code) to protect data in your wireless transmissions. WPA is a much stronger protocol than WEP, so enable WPA if you have it; enable WEP if you don't. When you enable these

protocols, you are forced to create a security encryption key (passphrase). When you attempt to connect a node to a security-enabled network for the first time, you'll be required to enter the encryption key. The encryption key (see Figure 7.21) is the code that computers on your network need to decrypt (decode) data transmissions. Without this key, it is extremely difficult, if not impossible, to decrypt the data transmissions from your network (see Figure 7.22). This prevents unauthorized access to your network because hackers won't know the correct key to use. The Windows 7 Connect to a network dialog box shows all wireless networks within range (see Figure 7.22). Clicking on one allows you to connect to it, or prompts you for more information such as the SSID name and security key.

5. **Implement media access control.** Each network adapter on your network has a unique number (like a serial number) assigned to it by the manufacturer. This is called a **media access control (MAC) address**, and it is a number printed right on the network adapter. Many routers allow you to restrict access to the network to only certain MAC addresses. This helps ensure that only authorized devices can connect to your network.

6. **Limit your signal range.** Most modern routers allow you to adjust the

Figure 7.21

By running your router configuration wizard, you can configure the security protocols available on your router and change the SSID, which helps protect your wireless network.

Setup Wizard			
Setup	**Wireless Settings**		Create and enter unique SSID here
Basic Settings			
Wireless Settings	**Wireless Network**		
Content Filtering	Name (SSID):	Herschell	
Logs	Region:	United States ▼	
Block Sites	Channel:	11 ▼	
Block Services	Mode:	g and b ▼	
Schedule			
E-mail	**Security Options**		
Maintenance	⚪ Disable		
Router Status	⚪ WEP (Wired Equivalent Privacy)		
Attached Devices	⦿ WPA-PSK (Wi-Fi Protected Access Pre-Shared Key)		Select a security protocol
Backup Settings	**Security Encryption (WPA-PSK)**		
Set Password	Passphrase: traSk35wE12SAwY	(8-63 characters)	
Router Upgrade	Key Lifetime: 60 (minutes)		

Create hard-to-guess passphrase

Figure 7.22

(a) The Windows 7 Connect to a network dialog box. (b) Manually connecting to a wireless network allows you to establish a connection if you know the network encryption key and the SSID name.

>You can access the **Connect to a network** dialog box by right-clicking the **Network Connection** icon on the taskbar and selecting **Connect to a network** from the shortcut menu. You can access the **Manually connect to a wireless network** dialog box by accessing the **Control Panel**, clicking on **Network and Internet**, selecting **Network and Sharing Center**, choosing the **Set up a connection or network** option, and then clicking on **Manually connect to a wireless network**.

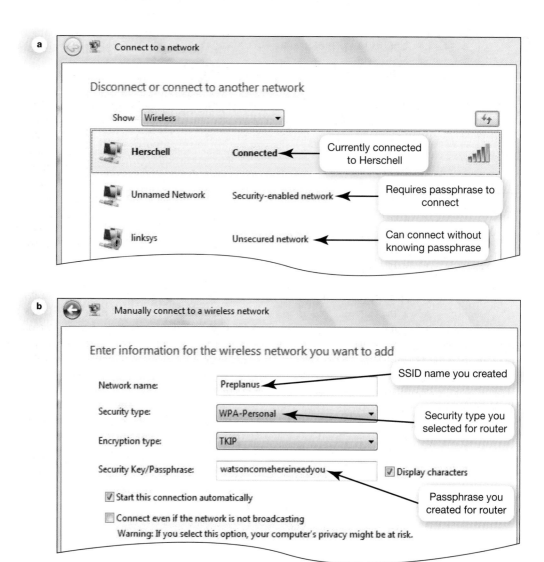

transmitting power to low, medium, or high. Cutting down the power to low or medium could prevent your signal from reaching too far away from your home, making it tougher for interlopers to poach your signal.

7. **Apply firmware upgrades.** Your router has read-only memory that has software written to it. This software is known as **firmware**. As bugs are found in the firmware (which hackers might exploit), manufacturers issue patches, just as the makers of operating system software do. Periodically check the manufacturer's Web site and apply any necessary upgrades to your firmware.

If you follow these steps, you will greatly improve the security of your wireless network. In Chapter 9, we'll explore many other ways to keep your computer safe from malicious individuals on the Internet and ensure that your digital information is secure.

Ethics: Sharing Your Internet Connection with Your Neighbors: Legal? Ethical? Safe?

With the advances in wireless equipment, signals can travel well beyond the range of your home. This makes it possible in an apartment or single family home (where homes are close together) for a group of neighbors to share a wireless signal and potentially save money by splitting the cost of one Internet connection among them. However, before jumping into this venture, you need to weigh a few issues carefully.

You probably aren't legally prohibited from sharing an Internet connection, but you should check on the state and local laws. Most laws are designed to prohibit piggybacking, which is using a network without the account holder's consent. However, if you are giving neighbors permission to share your connection, you probably don't violate any piggybacking laws.

Of course, your ISP might not permit you to share your Internet access with anyone. You probably have a personal account that is designed for one household. The terms of your agreement with the cable company might prohibit you from sharing your connection with people outside your household. If you aren't allowed to share the type of account you have now, your ISP probably offers a type of account (such as a small business account) that will allow you to share a connection, but it will most likely be more expensive. The ISPs know that the more people that share an account, the more likely that account is to use bandwidth; so they price their accounts accordingly. You might be able to share a personal account without being detected by your ISP, but that certainly would be unethical because you should be paying for a higher level of access. Therefore, make sure to check with your ISP to determine that you have the right account.

The next thing you need to consider is whether the shared access should be open to all neighbors, or just to the neighbors that are contributing to the cost of the Internet connection. You could leave the connection open (like the connections at Panera Bread are) and let anyone who finds it log on and surf. You might consider this a very ethical action, because you are providing free Internet access for anyone who needs it. You could register your free hot spot with a service like JiWire, and then people would know where it is. However, your neighbors who are helping pay the cost might have a different viewpoint and not want to fund free surfing for everyone. Make sure you work this out before proceeding.

If you are going to host a free and open hot spot, you still need to make sure that you set it up safely. You want to maintain a secure network for you and your neighbors while still allowing the occasional visiting surfer to use the connection. There are Wi-Fi sharing services (see Figure 7.23) such as Fon (**fon.com/en**), Whisher (**whisher.com**, now owned by **wifi.com**), and WeFi (**wefi.com**) that can provide you with special hardware (a router) or software that allows you to configure your hot spot so your network remains secure.

While offering free access to anyone will earn you lots of good karma, additional risks exist because you don't know what mischief or criminal activities someone might engage in while connected to the Internet through your account. Think very carefully before you proceed down the sharing path, and make sure you set your hot spot up to protect your internal network.

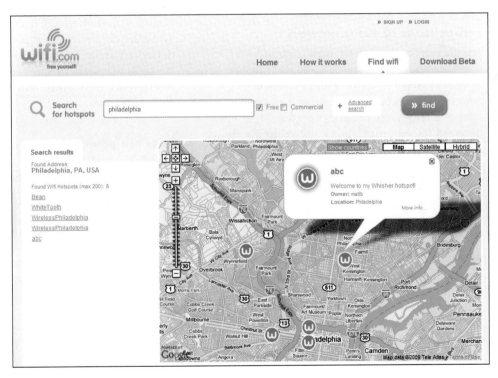

Figure 7.23
At Wifi.com you can search and find free hot spots hosted by other Whisher users.

1. What is a network, and what are the advantages of setting one up?

A computer network is simply two or more computers that are connected using software and hardware so that they can communicate. Networks allow users to (1) share peripherals, (2) transfer files easily, and (3) share an Internet connection.

2. What is the difference between a client/server network and a peer-to-peer network?

In peer-to-peer networks, each node connected to the network can communicate directly with every other node instead of having a separate device exercise central control over the network. P2P networks are the most common type of network installed in homes. Most networks that have 10 or more nodes are client/server networks. A client/server network contains two types of computers: a client computer on which users perform specific tasks and a server computer that provides resources to the clients and central control for the network.

3. What are the main hardware components of every network?

To function, any network must contain four components: (1) transmission media (cables or radio waves) to connect and establish communication between nodes, (2) network adapters that allow the nodes on the network to communicate, (3) network navigation devices (such as routers and switches) that move data around the network, and (4) software that allows the network to run.

4. What are the most common home networks?

The two most common home networks are wired Ethernet and wireless Ethernet. Modern power-line networks, boasting faster data throughput, are now a viable option in certain situations. The major difference among these network types is the transmission media by which the nodes are connected.

5. What are wired Ethernet networks, and how are they created?

Ethernet networks use the Ethernet protocol as the means by which the nodes on the network communicate. This protocol makes Ethernet networks efficient but also slightly complex. Because of this complexity, additional devices (switches or routers) are required in Ethernet networks. To create a wired Ethernet network, you connect or install network adapters or NICs to each network node. Network adapters connect via cables to a central network navigation device such as a switch or a router. Data flows through the navigation device to the nodes on the network.

6. What are wireless Ethernet networks, and how are they created?

A wireless network uses radio waves instead of wires or cable as its transmission medium. Current wireless protocols provide for networks with data transfer rates in excess of 100 Mbps. To create a wireless network, you install or attach wireless network adapters to the nodes that will make up the network. If the nodes are unable to communicate because of distance, you can add a wireless access point to the network to help relay data between nodes. Wireless networks are susceptible to interference from other wireless devices such as phones.

7. How are power-line networks created, and are they a viable alternative to Ethernet networks?

Power-line networks use the electrical wiring in your home to connect the nodes in the network. To create a power-line network, you connect special network adapters to each node on the network. These adapters are then plugged into an electrical outlet, and data is transmitted through the electrical wires. Modern power-line networks can often exceed the throughput achieved in wireless Ethernet networks, making them a viable option when interference with wireless signals is present.

8. How do I configure my computer's software to set up a network?

Windows 7, Vista, and XP all feature software wizards that facilitate the setup of both wired and wireless networks. Plug in the modem, routers, and all cables, and then switch on the modem, router, and computers (in that order). Run the wizards, which should guide you through the process. Make sure each computer has a distinct name and ensure that all computers are in the same workgroup.

9. Why are wireless networks more vulnerable than wired networks, and what special precautions are required to ensure my wireless network is secure?

Wireless networks are even more susceptible to hacking than wired networks because the signals of most wireless networks extend beyond the walls of your home. Neighbors may unintentionally (or intentionally) connect to the Internet through your wireless connection, and hackers may try to access it. To prevent unwanted intrusions into your network, you should change the default password on your router to make it tougher for hackers to gain access, use a hard-to-guess SSID (network name), turn off SSID broadcasting to make it harder for outsiders to detect your network, and enable security protocols such as WPA or WEP.

key terms

Word Bank

- Cat 6 cable
- client/server
- data transfer rate
- hacker(s)
- hub
- LAN

- network adapter(s)
- network-ready
- peer-to-peer (P2P)
- coaxial cable
- piggybacking
- router

- switch
- throughput
- WAN
- wired Ethernet
- wireless access point
- wireless Ethernet

Instructions: Fill in the blanks using the words from the Word Bank above.

Cathi needed to network three computers for herself and her roommates, Sharon and Emily. She decided that a(n) (1) _____ network was the right type to install in their dorm suite because a (2) _____ network was too complex. Because they all liked to download digital movies, they needed high (3) _____. Because they knew that they would never achieve the promised (4) _____ in any network they installed, they decided to use the fastest type of home network, a(n) (5) _____ network. However, because they wanted to use their notebooks wherever they were in their suite, they needed their network to also be a(n) (6) _____ network. Therefore they needed to buy a (7) _____ with wireless capability that would allow them to share the high-speed Internet access that Sharon already had through the cable TV company. This device would also double as a(n) (8) _____, preventing the need to purchase a separate device. Fortunately, all their computers already had (9) _____ installed, making it easy to connect the computers to the network. Cathi knew they would need to purchase some (10) _____ for the wired part of the network because this would provide them with a fast data transfer medium.

Cathi's roommate Emily wanted to know if they could hook into the (11) _____ (small network) that was already deployed for the students in the dorm. This student network was already hooked into the college's (12) _____ (large network), which spanned all three of the college's campuses. She knew they would need to be careful when connecting to the network, because some students from the dorm had accidentally been illegally (13) _____ on a network from the deli across the street. As the connectivity for notebooks in the lounge at the end of the hall was very poor, they needed to consider purchasing a (14) _____ to extend the range of the wireless signal. As a final detail, Emily suggested they get a (15) _____ printer that would plug right into the router and allow them all to print whenever they needed to do so.

becoming computer literate

While attending college, you are working at the Snap-Tite company, a small manufacturer of specialty fasteners. Currently, the employees must copy files to flash drives to transfer them among the four PCs the company owns. Only the company president has access to the Internet. The accounts payable clerk is the only one who has a printer. He is constantly being interrupted by other employees when they want to print their files. Your boss heard that you were taking a computer course and asked you to create a solution.

Instructions: Using the preceding scenario, draft a networking plan for Snap-Tite, using as many of the keywords from the chapter as you can. Be sure that the company president, who is unfamiliar with many networking terms, can understand the report.

Instructions: Answer the multiple-choice and true–false questions below for more practice with key terms and concepts from this chapter.

Multiple Choice

1. Which type of sharing is not a benefit of installing a home network?
   a. Peripheral
   b. Router
   c. Media
   d. Internet connection

2. Which of the following is a reason peer-to-peer networks are generally installed in homes?
   a. Peer-to-peer networks are more expandable than client/server networks.
   b. Client/server networks aren't designed to handle wireless networking, which is required by most home users.
   c. Client/server networks do not provide the level of security needed in a home network.
   d. The expense of a server is difficult to justify for most home networks

3. All networks contain the following elements except
   a. hubs.
   b. networking software.
   c. network adapters.
   d. transmission media.

4. Which is an example of a network navigation device required to move data around a single network?
   a. Wireless signal sender
   b. Switch
   c. Router
   d. Cat 6 cable

5. Wired Ethernet networks are superior to wireless networks because
   a. they generally provide faster data throughput.
   b. they have fewer security vulnerabilities.

   c. they are less susceptible to signal interference.
   d. they are significantly cheaper to install.

6. Power-line networks are desirable to install for all of the following reasons except
   a. Running Cat 6 cable would be too expensive.
   b. They are considerably cheaper to deploy than wireless networks.
   c. There is significant wireless signal interference.
   d. Lower throughput is acceptable.

7. A wireless network set up by a city to provide access to residents and visitors is usually referred to as a:
   a. LAN   c. HAN
   b. MAN   d. WAN

8. The throughput of a network
   a. is usually lower than the data transfer rate.
   b. is usually higher than the data transfer rate.
   c. is equal to the data transfer rate.
   d. is equal to the data transfer rate divided by bandwidth.

9. Which network navigation device is designed to move data between two networks?
   a. Hub   c. Router
   b. Repeater   d. Switch

10. The newest wireless Ethernet standard, which also provides the fastest data transfer rate, is
   a. 802.11g.   c. 802.11a.
   b. 802.11n.   d. 802.11b.

True–False

_____ 1. Actual data throughput is usually lower on wireless networks.

_____ 2. All home networks require each computer on the network to be equipped with its own network navigation device.

_____ 3. To facilitate sharing an Internet connection between computers on an Ethernet network, you should install a router.

_____ 4. LANs cover a larger geographic area than WANs.

_____ 5. Modern wireless Ethernet networks are immune to signal interference.

1. Dormitory Networking

Dave, Jerome, and Thomas were sitting in the common room of their campus suite staring at $100 piled up on the coffee table. Selling last semester's books back to the bookstore had been a good idea. As they waited for Phil, their other roommate, to come home, Dave said, "Wouldn't it be cool if we could network our notebooks? Then we could play Ultra Super Robot Kill-Fest in team mode!" Jerome pointed out it would be even more useful if they could all have access to Dave's laser printer because he owned the only one. "And Jerome's always bugging me to use my scanner when I'm trying to sleep," remarked Thomas. "And I can't believe the only high-speed Internet connection is out here in the lounge!" The three roommates ran down the hall and rapped on your door looking for some guidance. Consider how you would answer their questions:

a. Is $100 enough to set up a wireless network for four notebooks in four separate rooms? (Assume each computer contains a wireless network adapter already.)

b. Can the roommates share a printer and a scanner if they set up a wireless network? Will they need any additional equipment for the printer and the scanner to share them across the network if they are already connected to one of the notebook computers?

c. How would they share the one high-speed Internet connection wirelessly?

d. Phil just returned from the campus post office with a check from his aunt for $75. Do the roommates now have enough money to set up a network attached storage (NAS) device that would allow them to have their files automatically backed up?

To answer these questions, use the chapter text and the following resources: **coolcomputing.com**, **pricewatch.com**, **westerndigital.com**, **netgear.com**, **bestbuy.com**, and **tigerdirect.com**.

2. Connecting Your Computer to Public Networks

In the course of your education, you are constantly connecting your notebook to various wireless public networks such as those in the school library and the neighborhood coffee shop. As you know from reading this chapter, you are more vulnerable to hackers when connected to a wireless network. Conduct research on the Internet about surfing at public hot spots and prepare a list of sensible precautions for you and your classmates to take when surfing on an open network.

3. Adding a Hard Drive for Backups to Your Network

You know that adding a network-ready external hard drive to your network would facilitate sharing of your digital media and would make backing up data files easier. You need to consider the following questions when selecting an appropriate hard drive:

1. What is the volume of shared media that you need to store? (In other words, how many MP3 files, movies, and other media files do you have?)

2. What are the sizes of the hard drives of the computers on your network (for backup purposes)?

3. Do you need to access files on the hard drive when you are away from home?

Research network-ready hard drives using sites such as **wdc.com** and **buffalotech.com** to select one that is appropriate for your home network. Prepare a summary of your findings. Include the reasons for your selection.

1. Wireless LAN for a Small Business

You are working for a local coffee shop. The owner of the shop thinks that adding a wireless network and providing free Internet access to customers would be a good way to increase business. The owner has asked you to research this idea and prepare a report of your findings. Consider the following:

a. Price out business Internet connectivity with local phone and cable providers. Which vendor provides the most cost effective solution for a coffee shop? Are there any limitations on bandwidth or the number of people that can access the Internet at one time through the business account connection?

b. What potential problems could you foresee with providing unrestricted free access to the Internet? What policies would you suggest to keep people from abusing the free Internet access? (An example of abuse is someone who sits all day and surfs for free without purchasing any coffee.)

2. Public Wireless Access

Many corporations are using wireless technology to enhance or drive their businesses. Assume you are opening a local coffee shop in your town. Investigate the following:

a. Starbucks (**starbucks.com**) currently provides wireless access (for a fee) in many of its locations. Using **jwire.com** or **wi-fihotspotlist.com**, find the closest Starbucks to your home that features wireless access. Will this store compete with your proposed store, or is it too far away?

b. Visit your local Starbucks (or check **starbucks.com**) and find out the cost of its wireless access. Use the Internet to research whether wireless access is profitable for Starbucks and whether it drives customers to their stores. (Many articles have been written about this.) Compare Starbucks' model with that of Panera Bread, which offers free wireless access to its customers. Why does one company charge for Internet access while another does not?

c. As part of your business plan, write one or two paragraphs explaining why you will (or will not) offer wireless connectivity at your coffee shop and whether it will be a pay service or a free service.

d. Can you find any free wireless access points within a 10-mile radius of your proposed store location? How will this affect your decision to offer wireless connectivity at your business?

3. Testing Your Internet Connection Speed

Visit **speedtest.net** and **speakeasy.net/speedtest** and test the speed of your Internet connection at your home and in the computer lab at your school. Try to repeat the test at two different times during the day.

a. What did you find out about download speeds at your home? Are you getting as much speed as was promised by your ISP? Would this speed be sufficient for a home-based business? What type of business packages does your ISP offer, and what speeds could you expect when paying for a business package?

b. How does the connection speed at your school compare to the speed at your home? Where do you think you should have a faster connection—at your school or at your home? Why might the connection speed at your school be slower than you think it should be?

Instructions: Albert Einstein used *Gedankenexperiments,* or critical thinking questions, to develop his theory of relativity. Some ideas are best understood by experimenting with them in our own minds. The following critical thinking questions are designed to demand your full attention but only require a comfortable chair—no technology.

1. **Protecting Your Wireless Home Network**

   Many people have installed wireless networks in their homes. Consider the wireless network installed in your home (or in a friend's home if you don't have wireless).

   a. Is your network set up to provide adequate protection against hackers? If not, what would you need to do to make it secure?
   b. Are there other wireless networks within range of your home? If so, are they set up with an adequate level of security, or can you connect to them easily? How would you go about informing your neighbors that their networks are vulnerable?

2. **Upgrading Your Wireless**

   You have just finished purchasing and installing a new wireless network in your home. A new wireless standard of networking will be launched next month that is 10 times as fast as the wireless network you installed.

   a. What types of applications would you need to be using heavily to make it worth upgrading to the new standard?
   b. Suppose your neighbor upgraded to the new standard but does not have his network secured. Is tapping into your neighbor's wireless connection ethical? Is it illegal where you live?

3. **Evaluating Your Home Networking Needs**

   You might have a network installed in your home already, or perhaps you are still considering whether it is necessary to install one. Consider these issues:

   a. Who uses computing devices in your home? How many computers (notebooks and desktops) are currently in your home? Are the computers networked? If not, should they be networked? What advantages would your family gain by networking its computers?
   b. Which computer peripheral devices does your family own? Which family members need to use which peripherals? Are the peripherals network-ready or are they connected to individual computers? How easy is it to share these peripherals? Which peripherals don't your family own that would be beneficial? (Make sure to explain why.) How would you go about connecting new peripherals to your network?
   c. Does your home network have network attached storage or a home server? Would your family benefit from having this technology on your home network? What types of media do your family members routinely share? What other types would they share if they had the means?

4. **Sharing a Home Internet Connection**

   Perhaps you have considered whether sharing a home Internet connection with your neighbors would save you money. Consider the following issues:

   a. How many neighbors would be within range (say, within 350 feet of your router) of an 802.11n signal that came from your house or apartment? Do you think your neighbors would be amenable to sharing the cost of your Internet connection and your bandwidth? Why or why not?
   b. Is it permissible to share an Internet connection with neighbors under your ISP's terms of use for the type of connection you purchased? If not, what type of plan would you need to upgrade to in order to share a connection with your neighbors? Would the increased cost of upgrading your connection still make it economically feasible to share a connection?
   c. Do you think any of your neighbors would use significantly more bandwidth than others would? If so, do you think they should pay for a greater portion of the monthly Internet fees? What would you do if one of the neighbors were constantly hogging most of the bandwidth that you all were sharing?

Creating a Wireless Network

Problem

Wireless technology is being adopted by leaps and bounds, both in the home and in the workplace. Offering easy access free of physical tethers to networks seems to be a solution to many problems. However, wireless computing also has problems, ranging from poor reception to hijackers stealing your bandwidth.

Task

You are volunteering for a charity that installs wireless networks in homes for needy families. Many of these installations are done in older homes, and some recipients of the networks have reported poor connectivity in certain areas of their residences and extremely low bandwidth at other times. You have volunteered to research the potential problems and to suggest solutions to the director of the program.

Process

Break the class into three teams. Each team will be responsible for investigating one of the following issues:

1. **Detecting poor connectivity:** Research methods that can be used to find areas of poor signal strength, including signal sniffing software (**netstumbler.com**) and handheld scanning devices such as Wi-Fi Finder (**us.kensington.com**). Investigate maximum distances between access points and network nodes and make appropriate recommendations. (Equipment manufacturers such as **netgear.com** and **linksys.com** provide guidelines.)
2. **Signal boosters:** Research ways to increase signal strength in access points, antennae, and wireless cards. Signal boosters are available for access points. You can purchase or construct replacement antennae or antenna enhancements. Wi-Fi cards that offer higher power than conventional cards are now available.
3. **Security:** "War drivers" (people who cruise neighborhoods looking for open wireless networks from which to steal bandwidth) may be the cause of the bandwidth issues. Research appropriate measures to keep wireless network traffic secure from eavesdropping by hackers. In your investigation, look into the new Wi-Fi Protected Access (WPA) standard developed by the Wi-Fi Alliance. Check out the security section on the Wi-Fi Alliance Web site to start (**weca.net**).

Present your findings to your class and discuss possible causes of and ways to prevent the problems encountered at the residences. Provide your instructor with a report suitable for eventual presentation to the CEO of the charity.

Conclusion

As technology improves, wireless connectivity should eventually become the standard method of communication between networks and network devices. As with any other technology, security risks exist. Understanding those risks and how to mitigate them will allow you to participate in the design and deployment of network technology and provide peace of mind for your network users.

In addition to the review materials presented here, you'll find additional materials featured with the book's multimedia, including the *Technology in Action* Student Resource CD and the Companion Website (**pearsonhighered.com/techinaction**), which will help reinforce your understanding of the chapter content. These materials include the following:

Active Helpdesk

In Active Helpdesk calls, you'll assume the role of helpdesk operator, taking calls about the concepts you've learned in this chapter. You'll apply what you've learned and receive feedback from a supervisor to review and reinforce those concepts. The Active Helpdesk call for this chapter is listed below and can be found on your Student Resource CD:

- Understanding Networking

Sound Bytes

Sound Bytes are dynamic multimedia tutorials that help demystify even the most complex topics. You'll view video clips and animations that illustrate computer concepts and then apply what you've learned by reviewing with the Sound Byte Labs, which include quizzes and activities specifically tailored to each Sound Byte. The Sound Bytes for this chapter are listed below. They can be found on your Student Resource CD.

- Installing a Home Computer Network
- Securing Wireless Networks

Companion Website

The *Technology in Action* Companion Website includes a variety of additional materials to help you review and learn more about the topics in this chapter. The resources available at **pearsonhighered.com/techinaction** include:

- **Online Study Guide.** Each chapter features online true–false and multiple-choice quizzes. You can take these quizzes, automatically check the results, and e-mail the results to your instructor.
- **Web Research Projects.** Each chapter features several Web research projects that ask you to search the Web for information on computer-related careers, milestones in computer history, important people and companies, emerging technologies, and the applications and implications of different technologies.

TECHNOLOGY

Under the Hood

SOME PEOPLE ARE DRAWN TO UNDERSTANDING things in detail, but many folks are happy just to have things work. If you use a computer, you may not have ever been tempted to "look under the hood." However, without understanding the hardware inside, you'll be faced with some real limitations. You'll have to pay a technician to fix or upgrade your computer. This won't be as efficient as fine-tuning it yourself, and you may find yourself buying a new computer sooner than necessary. If you're preparing for a career in information technology, understanding computer hardware will affect the speed and efficiency of the programs you design. And what about all those exciting advances you hear about? How do you evaluate the impact of a new type of memory or a new processor? A basic appreciation of how a computer system is built and designed is a good start.

We'll build on what you've learned about computer hardware in other chapters and go under the hood, looking at the components of your system unit in more detail. Let's begin by looking at the building blocks of computers: switches.

Switches

The **system unit** is the box that contains the central electronic components of the computer. But how, exactly, does the computer perform all of its tasks? How does it process the data you input? The CPU performs functions like adding, subtracting, moving data around the system, and so on using nothing but a large number of on/off switches. In fact, a computer system can be viewed as an enormous collection of on/off switches.

ELECTRICAL SWITCHES

Computers work exclusively with numbers, not words. To process data into information, computers need to work in a language they understand. This language, called **binary language**, consists of just two numbers: 0 and 1. Everything a computer does, such as processing data or printing a report, is broken down into a series of 0s and 1s. **Electrical switches** are devices inside the computer that can be flipped between these two states: 1 and 0, signifying "on" and "off." Computers use 0s and 1s to process data because they are electronic, digital machines. They only understand two states of existence: on and off. Inside a computer these two possibilities, or states, are represented using the binary switches (or digits) 1 and 0.

You use various forms of switches every day. The on/off button on your DVD player is a mechanical switch: pushed in, it represents the value 1 (on), whereas popped out, it represents the value 0 (off). Another switch you use each day is a water faucet. As shown in Figure 1, shutting off the faucet so that no water flows could represent the value 0, whereas turning it on could represent the value 1.

Because computers are built from a huge collection of switches, using buttons or water faucets obviously would limit the amount of data computers could store. It would also make computers huge and cause them to run at extremely slow speeds. Thus, the history of computers is really a story about creating smaller and faster sets of electrical switches so that more data can be stored and manipulated quickly.

Vacuum Tubes

The earliest generation of electronic computers used devices called **vacuum tubes** as switches. Vacuum tubes act as computer switches by allowing or blocking the flow of electrical current. The problem with vacuum tubes is that they take up a lot of space, as you see in Figure 2. The first high-speed digital computer, the Electronic Numerical Integrator and Computer (ENIAC), was deployed in 1945. It used nearly 18,000 vacuum tubes as switches and filled approximately 1,500 square feet of floor space. That's about one-half the size of a standard high school basketball court! In addition to being large, the

FIGURE 1

Water faucets can be used to represent binary switches.

vacuum tubes produced a lot of heat and burned out frequently. Thus, vacuum tubes are impractical to use as switching devices in personal computers because of their size and reliability.

Since the introduction of ENIAC's vacuum tubes, two major revolutions have occurred in the design of switches, and consequently computers, to make them smaller and faster: the invention of the transistor and the fabrication of integrated circuits.

Transistors

Transistors are electrical switches that are built out of layers of a special type of material called a **semiconductor**, which is any material that can be controlled to either conduct electricity or act as an insulator (to prohibit electricity from passing through). Silicon, which is found in common sand, is the semiconductor material used to make transistors.

By itself, silicon does not conduct electricity particularly well, but if specific chemicals are added in a controlled way to the silicon, it begins to behave like a switch (see Figure 3). The silicon allows electrical current to flow easily when a certain voltage is applied; otherwise, it prevents electrical current from flowing, thus behaving as an

FIGURE 2

Computers can be constructed using vacuum tubes (see inset). The difference in size achieved by moving from tubes to transistors allowed computers to become desktop devices.

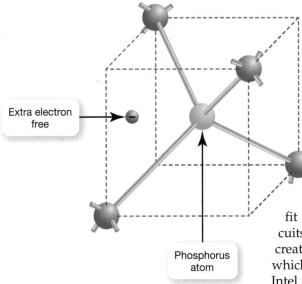

FIGURE 3

In "doping," a phosphorous atom is put in the place of a silicon atom. Because phosphorous has five electrons instead of four, the extra electron is free to move around.

on/off switch. This kind of behavior is exactly what is needed to store digital information, the 0s (off) and 1s (on) in binary language.

Early transistors were built in separate units as small metal rods, with each rod acting as a single on/off switch. These first transistors were much smaller than vacuum tubes, produced little heat, and could quickly be switched from on to off, thereby allowing or blocking electrical current. They also were less expensive than vacuum tubes.

It wasn't long, however, before transistors reached their limits. Continuing advances in technology began to require more transistors than circuit boards could reasonably handle at the time. Something was needed to pack more transistor capacity into a smaller space. Thus, integrated circuits, the next technical revolution in switches, were developed.

FIGURE 4

Integrated circuits use advanced fabrication techniques to fit millions of transistors into a quarter inch of silicon. This is an integrated circuit with areas marked out in black to show memory units, logic sections, and input/output blocks.

Integrated Circuits

Integrated circuits (or **chips**) are tiny regions of semiconductor material such as silicon that support a huge number of transistors (see Figure 4). Along with all the many transistors, other components critical to a circuit board (such as resistors, capacitors, and diodes) are also located on the integrated circuit. Most integrated circuits are no more than a quarter inch in size. Because so many transistors can fit into such a small area, integrated circuits have enabled computer designers to create small yet powerful **microprocessors**, which are the chips that contain a CPU. The Intel 4004, the first complete microprocessor to be located on a single integrated circuit, was released in 1971, marking the beginning of the true miniaturization of computers. The Intel 4004 contained slightly more than 2,300 transistors. Today, more than 500 million transistors can be manufactured in a space as tiny as the nail of your little finger!

This incredible feat has fueled an industry like no other. In 1951, the Univac I computer was the size of a large room. The processor memory unit itself was 14 feet long by 8 feet wide by 8.5 feet high and could perform about 1,905 operations per second. Thanks to advances in integrated circuits, the IBM PC released 30 years later took up just 1 cubic foot of space, cost $3,000, and performed 155,000 times more quickly. (For more information about computer history, see the Technology in Focus feature "The History of the PC" on page 36.)

Computers use on/off switches to perform their functions. But how can these simple switches be organized so that they let you use a computer to pay your bills online or write an essay? How can a set of switches describe a number or a word, or give a computer the command to perform addition? Recall that to manipulate the on/off switches, the computer works in binary language, which uses only two digits, 0 and 1. To understand how a computer works, let's first look at the special numbering system called the *binary number system*.

THE BINARY NUMBER SYSTEM

A **number system** is an organized plan for representing a number. Although you may not realize it, you are already familiar with one number system. The **base 10 number system**, also known as **decimal notation**, is the system you use to represent all of the numeric values you use each day. It's called base 10 because it uses 10 digits, 0 through 9, to represent any value.

To represent a number in base 10, you break the number down into groups of ones, tens, hundreds, thousands, and so on. Each digit has a place value depending on where it appears in the number. For example, using base 10, in the whole number 6,954, there are 6 sets of thousands, 9 sets of hundreds, 5 sets of tens, and 4 sets of ones. Working from right to left, each place in a number represents an increasing power of 10, as shown here:

$$6,954 = 6 * (1,000) + 9 * (100) + 5 * (10) + 4 * (1)$$
$$= 6 * 10^3 + 9 * 10^2 + 5 * 10^1 + 4 * 10^0$$

Note that in this equation, the final number 1 is represented as 10^0 because any number raised to the zero power is equal to 1.

Anthropologists theorize that humans developed a base 10 number system because we have 10 fingers. However, computer systems, with their huge collections of on/off switches, are not well suited to thinking about numbers in groups of 10. Instead, computers describe a number in powers of 2 because each switch can be in one of two

FIGURE 5

The joke here is that the decimal value 2 is written as 10 in binary.

positions: on or off. This numbering system is referred to as the **binary number system**.

The binary number system is also referred to as the **base 2 number system**. Even with just two digits, the binary number system can still represent all the values that a base 10 number system can (see Figure 5). Instead of breaking the number down into sets of ones, tens, hundreds, and thousands, as is done in base 10 notation, the binary number system describes a number as the sum of powers of 2. Binary numbers are used to represent every piece of data stored in a computer: all of the numbers, all of the letters, and all of the instructions that the computer uses to execute work.

Representing Integers

In the base 10 number system, a whole number is represented as the sum of ones, tens, hundreds, and thousands—that is, sums of powers of 10. The binary system works in the same way, but describes a value as the sum of groups of 1s, 2s, 4s, 8s, 16s, 32s, 64s, etc—that is, powers of 2: 1, 2, 4, 8, 16, 32, 64, and so on.

Let's look at the number 67. In base 10, the number 67 would be six sets of 10s and seven sets of 1s, as follows:

$$\text{Base 10: } 67 = 6 * 10^1 + 7 * 10^0$$

One way to figure out how 67 is represented in base 2 is to find the largest possible power of 2 that could be in the number 67. Two to the eighth power is 256, and there are no groups of 256 in the number 67. Two to the seventh power is 128, but that is bigger than 67. Two to the sixth power is 64, and there is a group of 64 inside a group of 67.

67 has	1 group of	64	That leaves 3 and
3 has	0 groups of	32	
	0 groups of	16	
	0 groups of	8	
	0 groups of	4	
	1 group of	2	That leaves 1 and
1 has	1 group of	1	And now nothing is left

So, the binary number for 67 is written as 1000011 in base 2:

$$Base\ 2:\ 67 = 64 + 0 + 0 + 0 + 0 + 2 + 1$$
$$= (1 * 2^6) + (0 * 2^5) + (0 * 2^4) + (0 * 2^3) + (0 * 2^2) + (1 * 2^1) + (1 * 2^0)$$
$$= (1000011)\ base\ 2$$

It is easier to have a calculator do this for you! Some calculators have a button labeled DEC (for decimal) and another labeled BIN (for binary). Using Windows, you can access the Scientific Calculator that supports conversion between decimal (base 10) and binary (base 2) by choosing Start, All Programs, Accessories; then clicking Calculator; and then

clicking the View menu to select Scientific. Instead of the default setting of DEC (decimal), switch to BIN (binary) and enter your calculation.

A large integer value becomes a very long string of 1s and 0s in binary! For convenience, programmers often use **hexadecimal notation** to make these expressions easier to use. Hexadecimal is a base 16 number system,

meaning it uses 16 digits to represent numbers instead of the 10 digits used in base 10 or the 2 digits used in base 2. The 16 digits it uses are the 10 numeric digits, 0 to 9, plus six extra symbols: A, B, C, D, E, and F. Each of the letters A through F corresponds to a numeric value, so that A equals 10, B equals 11, and so on (see Figure 6). Therefore, the value

FIGURE 6 Sample Hexadecimal Values

Decimal Number	Hexadecimal Value	Decimal Number	Hexadecimal Value
00	00	08	08
01	01	09	09
02	02	10	0A
03	03	11	0B
04	04	12	0C
05	05	13	0D
06	06	14	0E
07	07	15	0F

67 in decimal is 1000011 in binary or 43 in hexadecimal notation. It is much easier for computer scientists to use the two-digit 43 than the seven-digit string 1000011. The Scientific Calculator in Windows also can perform conversions to hexadecimal notation. (You can watch a video showing you how to perform conversions between bases using the Windows Calculator in the Sound Byte titled "Where Does Binary Show Up?")

Representing Characters: ASCII

We have just been converting integers from base 10, which *we* understand, to base 2 (binary state), which the computer understands. Similarly, we need a system that converts letters and other symbols that *we* understand to a binary state that the computer understands. To provide a consistent means for representing letters and other characters, certain codes dictate how to represent characters in binary format. Older mainframe computers use Extended Binary-Coded Decimal Interchange Code (EBCDIC, pronounced "Eb-sih-dik"). However, most of today's personal computers use the American National Standards Institute (ANSI, pronounced "An-see") standard code, called the **American Standard Code for Information Interchange** (**ASCII**, pronounced "As-key"), to represent each letter or character as an 8-bit (or 1-byte) binary code.

Each binary digit is called a **bit** for short. Eight binary digits (or bits) combine to create one **byte**. We have been converting base 10 numbers to a binary format. In such cases, the binary format has no standard length.

For example, the binary format for the number 2 is two digits (10), whereas the binary format for the number 10 is four digits (1010). Although binary numbers can have more or fewer than 8 bits, each single alphabetic or special character is 1 byte (or 8 bits) of data and consists of a unique combination of a total of eight 0s and 1s.

The ASCII code represents the 26 uppercase letters and 26 lowercase letters used in the English language, along with many punctuation symbols and other special characters, using 8 bits. Figure 7 shows several examples of ASCII code representation of printable letters and characters.

Representing Characters: Unicode

Because it represents letters and characters using only 8 bits, the ASCII code can assign only 256 (or 2^8) different codes for unique characters and letters. Although this is enough to represent English and many other characters found in the world's languages, ASCII code cannot represent all languages and symbols, because some languages require more than 256 characters and letters. Thus, a new encoding scheme, called **Unicode**, was created. By using 16 bits instead of the 8 bits used in ASCII, Unicode can represent nearly 1,115,000 code points and currently assigns more than 96,000 unique character symbols (see Figure 8). The first 128 characters of Unicode are identical to ASCII, but because of its depth, Unicode is also able to represent the alphabets of all

FIGURE 7 ASCII Standard Code for a Sample of Letters and Characters

ASCII Code	Represents This Symbol	ASCII Code	Represents This Symbol
01000001	A	01100001	a
01000010	B	01100010	b
01000011	C	01100011	c
01011010	Z	00100011	#
00100001	!	00100100	$
00100010	"	00100101	%

Note: For the full ASCII table, see **asciitable.com.**

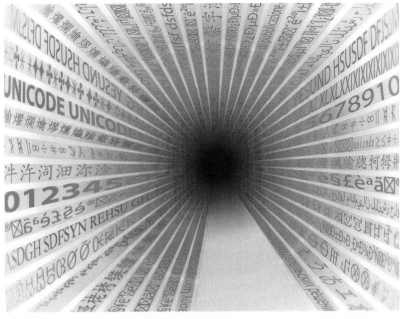

FIGURE 8

The written languages of the world require thousands of different characters, shown here. Unicode provides a system allowing digital representation of over 1,100,000 unique characters.

modern and historic languages and notational systems, including such languages and writing systems as Tibetan, Tagalog, Japanese, and Canadian Aboriginal syllabics. As we continue to become a more global society, it is anticipated that Unicode will replace ASCII as the standard character formatting code.

Representing Decimal Numbers

The binary number system also can represent a decimal number. How can a string of 1s and 0s capture the information in a value such as 99.368? Because every computer must store such numbers in the same way, the Institute of Electrical and Electronics Engineers (IEEE) has established a standard called the *floating-point standard* that describes how numbers with fractional parts should be represented in the binary number system. Using a 32-bit system, we can represent an incredibly wide range of numbers. The method dictated by the IEEE standard works the same for any number with a decimal point, such as the number –0.75. The first digit, or bit (the sign bit), is used to indicate whether the number is positive or negative. The next eight bits store the magnitude of the

number, indicating whether the number is in the hundreds or millions, for example. The standard says to use the next 23 bits to store the value of the number.

Interpretation

All data inside the computer is stored as bits. Positive and negative numbers can be stored using signed integer notation, with the first bit (the sign bit) indicating the sign and the rest of the bits indicating the value of the number. Decimal numbers are stored according to the IEEE floating-point standard, and letters and symbols are stored according to the ASCII code or Unicode. All of these different number systems and codes exist so that computers can store different types of information in their on/off switches. No matter what kind of data you input in a computer—a color, a musical note, or a street address—that data will be stored as a string of 1s and 0s. The important lesson is that the interpretation of 0s and 1s is what matters. The same binary pattern could represent a positive number, a negative number, a fraction, or a letter.

How does the computer know which interpretation to use for the 1s and 0s? When your brain processes language, it takes the sounds you hear and uses the rules of English, along with other clues, to build an interpretation of the sound as a word. If you are in New York City and hear someone shout, "Hey, Lori!" you expect someone is saying hello to a friend. If you are in London and hear the same sound—"Hey! Lorry!"—you jump out of the way because a truck is coming at you! You knew which interpretation to apply to the sound because you had some other information—that you were in England.

Likewise, the CPU is designed to understand a specific language or set of instructions. Certain instructions tell the CPU to expect a negative number next or to interpret the following bit pattern as a character. Because of this extra information, the CPU always knows which interpretation to use for a series of bits.

The CPU Machine Cycle

Any program you run on your computer is actually a long series of binary code describing a specific set of commands the CPU must perform. These commands may be coming from a user's actions or may be instructions fed from a program while it executes. Each CPU is somewhat different in the exact steps it follows to perform its tasks, but all CPUs must perform a series of similar general steps. These steps, illustrated in Figure 9, are referred to as a CPU **machine cycle** (or **processing cycle**).

1. FETCH: When any program begins to run, the 1s and 0s that make up the program's binary code must be "fetched" from their temporary storage location in random access memory (RAM) and moved to the CPU before they can be executed.

2. DECODE: Once the program's binary code is in the CPU, it is decoded into the commands the CPU understands.

3. EXECUTE: Next, the CPU actually performs the work described in the commands.

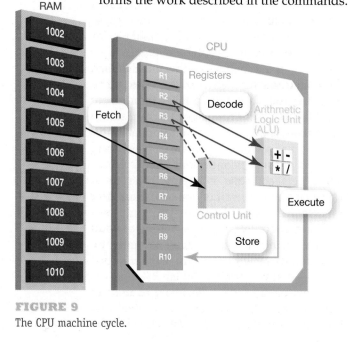

FIGURE 9
The CPU machine cycle.

Specialized hardware on the CPU performs addition, subtraction, multiplication, division, and other mathematical and logical operations at incredible speeds.

4. STORE: The result is stored in **registers**, special memory storage areas built into the CPU, which are the most expensive, fastest memory in your computer. The CPU is then ready to fetch the next set of bits encoding the next instruction.

No matter what program you are running, be it a Web browser or a word processing program, and no matter how many programs you are using at one time, the CPU performs these four steps over and over at incredibly high speeds. Shortly, we'll look at each stage in more detail so that you can understand the complexity of the CPU's design, how to compare different CPUs on the market, and what enhancements you can expect in CPU designs of the future. But first, let's examine a few of the CPU's other components that help it perform its tasks.

THE SYSTEM CLOCK

To move from one stage of the machine cycle to the next, the motherboard uses a built-in **system clock**. This internal clock is actually a special crystal that acts like a metronome, keeping a steady beat and thereby controlling when the CPU will move to the next stage of processing.

These steady beats or "ticks" of the system clock, known as the **clock cycle**, set the pace by which the computer moves from process to process. The pace, known as **clock speed**, is measured in hertz (Hz), a unit of measure that describes how many times something happens per second. Today's system clocks are measured in gigahertz (GHz), each of which represents one billion clock ticks per second. Therefore, in a 3 GHz system, there are three billion clock ticks each second. Computers with older processors would sometimes need one or more cycles to process one instruction. Today, however, CPUs are designed to handle more instructions more efficiently, and are, therefore, capable of executing more than one instruction per cycle.

THE CONTROL UNIT

The CPU, like any part of the computer system, is designed from a collection of switches. How can simple on/off switches "remember" the fetch-decode-execute-store sequence of the CPU machine cycle? How can they perform the work required in each of these stages?

The **control unit** of the CPU manages the switches inside the CPU. It is programmed by CPU designers to remember the sequence of processing stages for that CPU and how each switch in the CPU should be set (i.e., on or off) for each stage. With each beat of the system clock, the control unit moves each switch to the correct on or off setting and then performs the work of that stage.

Let's now look at each of the stages in the machine cycle in a bit more depth.

STAGE 1: THE FETCH STAGE

The data and program instructions the CPU needs are stored in different areas in the computer system. Data and program instructions move between these areas as they are needed by the CPU for processing. Programs (such as Microsoft Word) are permanently stored on the hard drive because it offers nonvolatile storage, meaning the programs remain stored there even when you turn the power off. However, when you launch a program (that is, when you double-click an icon to execute the program), the program, or sometimes only the essential parts of a program, is transferred from the hard drive into RAM.

The program moves to RAM because the CPU can access the data and program instructions stored in RAM more than one million times faster than if they are left on the hard drive. In part, this is because RAM is much closer to the CPU than the hard drive is. Another reason for the delay in transmission of data and program instructions from the hard drive to the CPU is that the hard drive is a mechanical device. The hard drive has read/write heads that have to sweep over the spinning platters, which takes time. RAM is faster because it's electronic, not mechanical.

As specific instructions from the program are needed, they are moved from RAM into registers (the special storage areas located on the CPU itself), where they wait to be executed.

The CPU's storage area is not big enough to hold everything it needs to process at the same time. If enough memory were located on the CPU chip itself, an entire program

could be copied to the CPU from RAM before it was executed. This certainly would add to the computer's speed and efficiency, because there would be no delay while the CPU stopped processing operations to fetch instructions from RAM to the CPU. However, including so much memory on a CPU chip would make these chips extremely expensive. In addition, CPU design is so complex that only a limited amount of storage space is available on the CPU itself.

Cache Memory

The CPU doesn't actually need to fetch every instruction from RAM each time it goes through a cycle. There is another layer of storage, called **cache memory**, that has even faster access than RAM. The word *cache* is derived from the French word *cacher*, which means "to hide." Cache memory consists of small blocks of memory located directly on and next to the CPU chip. These memory blocks are holding places for recently or frequently used instructions or data that the CPU needs the most. When these instructions or data are stored in cache memory, the CPU can retrieve them more quickly than would be the case if it had to access the instructions or data in RAM.

Taking data you think you'll be using soon and storing it nearby is a simple idea but a powerful one. This is a strategy that shows up in other places in your computer system. For example, when you are browsing Web pages, it takes longer to download images than text. Your browser software automatically stores images on your hard drive so that you don't have to wait to download them again if you want to go back and view a page you've already visited. Although this cache of files is not related to the

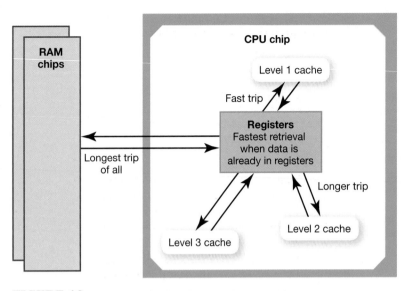

FIGURE 10

Modern CPUs have two or more levels of cache memory, which leads to faster CPU processing.

cache storage space designed into the CPU chip, the idea is the same.

Modern CPU designs include several types of cache memory. If the next instruction to be fetched is not already located in a CPU register, instead of looking directly to RAM to find it, the CPU first searches Level 1 cache. **Level 1 cache** is a block of memory that is built onto the CPU chip to store data or commands that have just been used.

If the command is not located in Level 1 cache, the CPU searches Level 2 cache. Depending on the design of the CPU, **Level 2 cache** is either located on the CPU chip but is slightly farther away from the CPU, or is on a separate chip next to the CPU and therefore takes somewhat longer to access. Level 2 cache contains more storage area than does Level 1 cache. For the Intel Core 2 Duo, for example, the Level 1 cache is 32 kilobytes (KB) and the Level 2 cache is 6 megabytes (MB).

Only if the CPU doesn't find the next instruction to be fetched in either Level 1 or Level 2 cache will it make the long journey to RAM to access it.

The current direction of processor design is toward increasingly large multilevel CPU cache structures. Therefore, some newer CPUs, such as Intel's Xeon processor for workstations and servers, have an additional third level of cache memory storage called **Level 3 cache**. On computers with Level 3 cache, the CPU checks this area for instruc-tions and data after it looks in Level 1 and Level 2 cache, but before it makes the longer trip to RAM (see Figure 10). The Level 3 cache holds between 2 and 8 MB of data. With 8 MB of Level 3 cache, there is storage for some entire programs to be transferred to the CPU for execution.

As an end user of computer programs, you do nothing special to use cache memory. In fact, you are not even able to see that caching is being used—nothing special lights up on your system unit or keyboard. The advantage of having more cache memory is that you'll experience better performance because the CPU won't have to make the longer trip to RAM to get data and instructions as often. Unfortunately, because it is built into the CPU chip or motherboard, you can't upgrade cache: It is part of the original design of the computer system. Therefore, as with RAM, it's important when buying a computer to consider buying the one, everything else being equal, with the most cache memory.

STAGE 2: THE DECODE STAGE

The main goal of the decode stage is for the CPU's control unit to translate (or **decode**) the program's instructions into commands the CPU can understand. A CPU can understand only a tiny set of commands. The collection of commands a specific CPU can execute is called the **instruction set** for that system. Each CPU has its own unique instruction set. For example, the AMD Athlon 64 X2 Dual-Core processor in an Alienware Aurora gaming computer has a different instruction set than does the Intel Core 2 Duo used in a Dell Inspiron notebook. The control unit interprets the code's bits according to the instruction set the CPU designers laid out for that particular CPU. Based on this process of translation, the control unit then knows how to set up all the switches on the CPU so that the proper operation will occur.

Because humans are the ones who write the initial instructions, all of the commands in an instruction set are written in a language called **assembly language**, which is easier for humans to work with than binary. Many CPUs have similar assembly commands in their instruction sets, including the commands listed here:

ADD	Add
SUB	Subtract
MUL	Multiply
DIV	Divide
MOVE	Move data to RAM
STORE	Move data to a CPU register
EQU	Check if equal

CPUs differ in the choice of additional assembly language commands selected for the instruction set. Each CPU design team works to develop an instruction set that is both powerful and speedy.

However, because the CPU knows and recognizes only patterns of 0s and 1s, it cannot understand assembly language directly, so these human-readable instructions are translated into long strings of binary code. The control unit uses these long strings of binary code called **machine language** to set up the hardware in the CPU for the rest of the operations it needs to perform. Machine language is a binary code for computer instructions, much like the ASCII code is a binary code for letters and characters. Similar to each letter or character having its own unique combination of 0s and 1s assigned to it, a CPU has a table of codes consisting of combinations of 0s and 1s for each of its commands. If the CPU sees a particular pattern of bits arrive, it knows the work it must do.

Figure 11 shows a few commands in both assembly language and machine language.

STAGE 3: THE EXECUTE STAGE

The **arithmetic logic unit (ALU)** is the part of the CPU designed to perform mathematical operations such as addition, subtraction, multiplication, and division and to test the comparison of values such as *greater than, less than*, and *equal to*. For example, in calculating an average, the ALU is where the addition and division operations would take place. The ALU also performs logical OR, AND, and NOT operations. For example, in determining whether a student can graduate, the ALU would need to ascertain whether the student had taken all required courses AND obtained a passing grade in each of them. The ALU is specially designed to execute such calculations flawlessly and with incredible speed.

The ALU is fed data from the CPU's registers. The amount of data a CPU can process at a time is based in part on the amount of data each register can hold. The number of bits a computer can work with at a time is referred to as its **word size**. Therefore, a 64-bit processor can process more information faster than a 32-bit processor.

STAGE 4: THE STORE STAGE

In the final stage, the result produced by the ALU is stored back in the registers. The instruction itself will explain which register should be used to store the answer. Once the entire instruction has been completed, the next instruction will be fetched, and the fetch-decode-execute-store sequence will begin again.

FIGURE 11 Representations of Sample CPU Commands

Human Language for Command	CPU Command in Assembly Language (Language Used by Programmers)	CPU Command in Machine Language (Language Used in the CPU's Instruction Set)
Add	ADD	1110 1010
Subtract	SUB	0001 0101
Multiply	MUL	1111 0000
Divide	DIV	0000 1111

Making CPUs Even Faster

Knowing how to build a CPU that can run faster than the competition can make a company rich. However, building a faster CPU is not easy. A new product launch must take into consideration the time it will take to design, manufacture, and test that processor. When the processor finally hits the market, it must be faster than the competition if the manufacturer hopes to make a profit. To create a CPU that will be released 36 months from now, it must be built to perform at least twice as fast as anything currently available.

Gordon Moore, the cofounder of processor manufacturer Intel, predicted more than 40 years ago that the number of transistors on a processor would double every 18 months. Known as **Moore's Law**, this prediction has been remarkably accurate—but only with tremendous engineering ingenuity. The first 8086 chip had only 29,000 transistors and ran at 5 MHz. Advances in the number of transistors on processors through the 1970s, 1980s, and 1990s continued to align with Moore's prediction.

However, there was a time near the turn of the 21st century when skeptics questioned how much longer Moore's Law would hold true. These skeptics were proved wrong with the microprocessor's continued growth in power. Today's Penryn chip (for notebook computers) has 820 million transistors and runs at 2.6 GHz—more than 200 times faster than its original counterpart. Moreover, Intel's Tukwila flaunts a whopping 2 billion transistors! How much longer can Moore's prediction hold true? Only time will tell.

Processor manufacturers can increase CPU performance in many different ways. One approach is to use a technique called *pipelining* to boost performance. Another approach is to design the CPU's instruction set so that it contains specialized, faster instructions for handling multimedia and graphics. In addition, some CPUs, such as Intel's i7 processors, now have four independent processing paths inside, with one CPU chip doing the work of four separate CPU units. Some heavy computational problems are attacked by large numbers of computers actually clustered together to work at the same time.

PIPELINING

As an instruction is processed, the CPU runs sequentially through the four stages of processing: fetch, decode, execute, and store. **Pipelining** is a technique that allows the CPU to work on more than one instruction (or stage of processing) at a time, thereby boosting CPU performance.

For example, without pipelining, it may take four clock cycles to complete one instruction (one clock cycle for each of the four

DOES YOUR COMPUTER NEED MORE POWER? TEAM IT UP!

The history of computing shows us that processing power increases tremendously each year. One strategy in use now for continuing that trend is cluster computing. If one computer is powerful, then two are twice as powerful—if you can get them to work together. A **computing cluster** is a group of computers, connected by specialized clustering software, that works together to solve complex equations. Most clusters work on something called the *balancing principle,* whereby computational work is transferred from overloaded (busy) computers in the cluster to computers that have more computing resources available. Computing clusters, although not as fast as supercomputers (single computers with extremely high processing capabilities), can perform computations faster than one computer working alone and are used for complex calculations such as weather forecasting and graphics rendering. You can now rent time on computing clusters through services like PurePowua (**purepowua.com**), where you can upload and remotely control your job from your desktop as it runs on a cluster of computers.

processing stages). However, with a four-stage pipeline, the computer can process four instructions at the same time. Like an automobile assembly line, instead of waiting for one car to go completely through each process of assembly, painting, and so on, you can have four cars going through the assembly line at the same time. When every component of the assembly line is done with its process, the cars all move on to the next stage.

Pipelined architectures allow several instructions to be processed at the same time. The ticks of the system clock (the clock cycle) indicate when all instructions move to the next process. The secret of pipelining is that the CPU is allowed to be fetching one instruction while it is simultaneously decoding another, executing a third, storing a fourth, and so on. Using pipelining, a four-stage processor can potentially run up to four times faster because some instruction is finishing every clock cycle rather than waiting four cycles for each instruction to finish.

In Figure 12a, a non-pipelined instruction takes four clock cycles to be completed, whereas in Figure 12b, the four instructions have been completed in the same time using pipelining.

The number of stages in a pipeline depends entirely on design decisions. Earlier we analyzed a CPU that went through four stages in the execution of an instruction. The Intel Pentium 4 with hyperthreading features a 31-stage pipeline, and the PowerPC G5 processor uses a 10-stage pipeline. Thus, similar to an assembly line, in a 31-stage pipeline, as many as 31 different instructions can be processed at any given time, making the processing of information much faster. However, because so many aspects of the CPU design interact, you cannot predict performance based solely on the number of stages in a pipeline.

There is a cost to pipelining a CPU as well. The CPU must be designed so that each stage (fetch, decode, execute, and store) is independent. This means that each stage must be

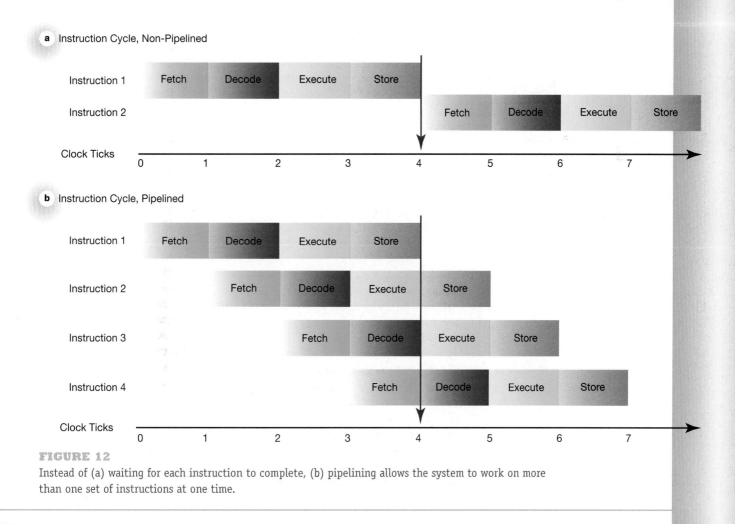

FIGURE 12

Instead of (a) waiting for each instruction to complete, (b) pipelining allows the system to work on more than one set of instructions at one time.

able to run at the same time that the other three stages are running. This requires more transistors and a more complicated hardware design.

SPECIALIZED MULTIMEDIA INSTRUCTIONS

Each design team that develops a new CPU tries to imagine what users' greatest needs will be in four or five years. Currently, several processors on the market reflect this consideration by incorporating specialized multimedia instructions into the basic instruction set.

Hardware engineers have redesigned the chip so that the instruction set contains new commands that are specially designed to speed up the work needed for video and audio processing. For example, Intel has integrated the Streaming Single Instruction Multiple Data (SIMD) Extensions 3 set of commands into its processor designs, adding a special group of 157 commands to the basic instruction set. These multimedia-specific instructions work to accelerate video, speech, and image processing in the CPU.

MULTIPLE PROCESSING EFFORTS

Many high-end server systems employ a **dual-processor design** that has two completely separate CPU chips on one motherboard. Often, these server systems can later be scaled so that they can accommodate four, six, or even eight processors. Some of the most powerful mainframes support as many as 32 processors!

Meanwhile, Intel is promoting a technology called *multi-core processing* in its Core 2 Duo line of chips. Chips with dual-core processing capabilities have two separate parallel processing paths inside them, so they are almost as fast as two separate CPUs. Dual-core processing is especially helpful because antivirus software and other security programs often run in the background as you use your system. A dual-core processor enables these multiple applications to execute much more quickly than with traditional CPUs. Quad-core processors, like the Intel i7, are appearing in high-performance home-based systems now as well, executing four separate processing paths.

Multiprocessor systems are often used when intensive computational problems need to be solved in such areas as computer simulations, video production, and graphics processing. Having two processors allows the work to be done almost twice as quickly, but not quite. It is not quite twice as fast because the system must do some extra work to decide which processor will work on which part of the problem and to recombine the results each CPU produces.

Certain types of problems are well suited to a parallel-processing environment. In **parallel processing**, there is a large network of computers, with each computer working on a portion of the same problem simultaneously. To

TODAY'S SUPER-COMPUTERS: THE FASTEST OF THE FAST

Supercomputers are the biggest and most powerful type of computer. Scientists and engineers use these computers to solve complex problems or to perform massive computations. Some supercomputers are single computers with multiple processors, whereas others consist of multiple computers that work together.

One of the fastest supercomputers today is the Roadrunner, developed by IBM for the U.S. Department of Energy, which uses it for computing the safety of the nation's nuclear weapons stockpile. It operates at a peak of more than 1,400 teraflops (or 1,400 trillion operations per second). That's almost 700,000 times faster than the average personal computer! Of course, the Roadrunner does use more than 129,000 separate processors at the same time. The supercomputer Columbia uses its 10,000 processors to compute the impact of space shuttle damage on the craft's orbit. This takes 24 hours, instead of the three months required by older systems. Check out the current crop of the world's fastest supercomputers at the Top 500 site (**top500.org**).

be a good candidate for parallel processing, a problem must be one that can be divided into a set of tasks that can be run simultaneously. If the next step of an algorithm can be started only after the results of the previous step have been computed, parallel processing will present no advantages.

A simple analogy of parallel processing is a laundromat. Instead of taking all day to do five loads of laundry with one machine, you can bring all your laundry to a laundromat, load it into five separate machines, and finish it all in approximately the same time it would have taken you to do just one load on a single machine. In real life, parallel processing is used in complex weather forecasting to run calculations over many different regions around the globe; in the airline industry to analyze customer information in an effort to forecast demand; and by the government in census data compilation.

Thus, what you can continue to expect from CPUs in the future is that they will continue to get smaller and faster and consume less power. This fits with the current demands of consumers for more powerful portable computing devices.

At the most basic level of binary 1s and 0s, computers are systems of switches that can accomplish impressive tasks. By understanding the hardware components that make up your computer system, you can use your system more effectively and make better buying decisions.

YOUR DNA AS A CPU?

Israeli scientists have devised a computer that runs on DNA molecules and enzymes instead of silicon chips. Although it has no practical applications just yet, the computer is extremely fast—in fact, it can perform 330 trillion operations per second, approximately 100,000 times as fast as any personal computer on the market today. Whereas silicon chips are reaching their limit of miniaturization, DNA computers can be constructed using only a few molecules. You don't get much smaller than that! As shown in Figure 13, DNA computers are combinations of DNA and specially constructed enzymes. Within a single drop of this special fluid, chemical reactions are taking place in billions of DNA computers that generate data and perform rudimentary calculations.

DNA computers use chemical reactions caused by mixing enzymes and DNA molecules. The reactions are designed to provide data and the needed energy for any calculations. Because chemical reactions can be measured precisely and their outcomes predicted reliably, there is no need for conventional hardware and software. All information can be passed at the molecular level. Although DNA computing is today in its infancy, doctors envision devices constructed from DNA computers that will patrol our bodies and make repairs (such as clearing plaque from arteries) as soon as a problem is detected.

FIGURE 13

Here you see a representation of the inside of a DNA-based computer. The double-stranded DNA is combined with enzymes, and together they become the CPU for this biological computing device.

eight
digital lifestyle:
managing digital data and devices

resources

Active Helpdesk

- Keeping Your Data on Hand **(p. 369)**
- Using Portable Media Players **(p. 375)**

Sound Bytes

- Smartphones Are Really Smart **(p. 363)**
- Connecting with Bluetooth **(p. 364)**

Companion Website

The Companion Website includes a variety of additional materials to help you review and learn more about the topics in this chapter. Go to: *pearsonhighered.com/techinaction*

how cool is *this?*

TiVo is not the only game in town! PVR (personal **video recorder**) software is now available, free of charge, for every style of operating system. Using a PVR, you can record standard or HD television broadcasts on your **hard drive** and then watch them when you have the time. Free programs like XBMC Media Center and MeediOS let you pause and rewind live TV shows and include features that allow you to automatically detect and **skip commercials**. You even have access to a TV listings guide and can schedule your PVR from any location using the **Web**.

A Digital Lifestyle

Computers today are central to everyday life. Which part of your life isn't touched by some sort of computer or digital technology? Computer-like devices (such as smartphones and iPods) are everywhere. Much of your entertainment—playing games, watching movies and television, and downloading songs—is probably delivered via the Internet.

Do you really understand how all this digital technology works? Do you know all of your options so you can enjoy the digital devices you purchase to the fullest extent? In this chapter, we explore the key aspects of your digital life—digital communication, digital entertainment, and digital mobility—and help you understand how the related technologies work so you can use them to your best advantage.

When did everything go "digital"? It used to be that everything was analog. Today, no matter what you're interested in—music, movies, television, radio, stock prices—digital information is the key. All forms of entertainment have migrated to the digital domain (see Figure 8.1). MP3 files encode digital forms of music, and digital cameras and video camcorders are now commonplace. In Hollywood, some feature films are now being shot entirely with digital equipment, and many movie theaters use digital projection equipment. Satellite radio systems such as Sirius Satellite Radio and HD Radio are broadcast in digital formats.

Phone systems and television signals are now digital streams of data.

What is special about digital? Any kind of information can be digitized (measured and converted to a stream of numeric values). Consider sound. It is carried to your ears by sound waves, which are actually patterns of pressure changes in the air. Images are our interpretation of the changing intensity of light waves around us. These sound and light waves are called **analog** waves or continuous waves. They illustrate the loudness of a sound or the brightness of the colors in an image at a given moment in time. They are continuous signals because you would never have to lift your pencil off the page to draw them; they are just long, continuous lines.

First-generation recording devices such as vinyl records and analog television broadcasts were designed to reproduce these sound and light waves. A needle in the groove of a vinyl record vibrates in the same pattern as the original sound wave. Analog television signals are actually waves that tell an analog TV how to display the same color and brightness as is seen in the production studio. However, it's difficult to describe a wave, even mathematically. The simplest sounds, such as that of middle C on a piano, have the simplest shapes, like the one shown in Figure 8.2. However, something like the word *hello* generates a highly complex pattern, like the one shown in Figure 8.2.

What advantages do digital formats have over analog ones? Digital formats describe signals as long strings of numbers. This digital representation gives us a simple way to describe sound and light waves exactly, so that sounds and images can be reproduced perfectly each time. In addition, we already have easy ways to distribute digital information (on CDs and DVDs and using e-mail, for example). Thus, digital information can be reproduced exactly and distributed easily. Both give it huge advantages over analog.

How can a sequence of numbers express complicated analog shapes? The answer is provided by something called analog-to-digital conversion. In analog-to-digital conversion, the incoming analog signal is measured many times each second. The strength of the signal at each measurement is recorded as a simple number. The series of numbers

Figure 8.1 | ANALOG VERSUS DIGITAL ENTERTAINMENT

	Analog	Digital
Music	Vinyl record albums Cassette tapes	CDs MP3 files
Photography	35-mm single lens reflex (SLR) cameras Photos stored on film	Digital cameras, including digital SLRs Photos stored as digital files
Video	8-mm, Hi8, and VHS camcorders Film stored on VHS tapes	Digital video (DV) camcorders Film stored as digital files; often distributed on DVD and Blu-ray discs
Radio	AM/FM radio	HD Radio Sirius/XM Radio
Television	Conventional broadcast analog TV	Digital television (DTV)

produced by the analog-to-digital conversion process gives us the digital form of the wave. Figure 8.3 shows analog and digital versions of the same wave. In Figure 8.3a, you see the original, continuous analog wave. You could draw that wave without lifting your pencil from the page. In Figure 8.3b, the wave has been digitized and is no longer a single line; instead, it is represented as a series of points or numbers.

How has the change from analog to digital technologies affected our lifestyle? When the market for communication devices for entertainment media—like photographs, music, and video—switched over to a digital standard, we began to have products with new and useful capabilities. Small devices can now hold huge collections of a variety of types of information. We can interact with our information any time we like, in ways that, prior to the conversion to digital media, had been too expensive or too difficult to learn. The implications of the shift to digital media are continually evolving. Let's examine the many ways in which digital media has already changed our lifestyles.

Figure 8.2

(a) This is an analog wave showing the simple, pure sound of a piano playing middle C. (b) This is the complex wave produced when a person says "Hello."

Figure 8.3

(a) A simple analog wave. (b) A digitized version of the same wave.

Digital Telephony: Communicating with Bits

Communication has changed radically in the digital age. Chapter 3 discussed the use of wikis, blogs, RSS feeds, and other Web-based tools for connecting people and their ideas. All of these software applications are dependent on digital information.

Hardware devices that support communication also have evolved because of digital technologies. **Telephony**, the use of equipment to provide voice communications over a distance, has shifted from an analog science to a digital one. In this section, we examine cell phones, smartphones, and Voice over Internet Protocol (VoIP) devices to see how they are changing to meet modern communication needs.

What are cell phones and smartphones? The **cellular phone** (or **cell phone**) has evolved from a clunky, boxlike device to a compact, fully featured communication and information storage device. Cell phones offer all of the features available on a traditional telephone system, including automatic redial, call timers, and voice mail capabilities. Some cell phones also feature voice-activated dialing, which is important for hands-free operation. In addition, many cell phones offer Internet access, text messaging, personal information management (PIM) features, voice

recording, GPS services, and digital image and video capture. The most fully featured and powerful cellular phones are found in the **smartphone** category. A smartphone often requires a data plan from the provider. This is logical because a smartphone user is likely to spend a lot of time accessing the Internet to upload and download e-mail and data. Some smartphones have enough computing power to run versions of programs like Microsoft Excel and PowerPoint.

How do cell phones use digital signals? When you speak into a cell phone, the sound enters the microphone as a sound wave. Because analog sound waves need to be digitized (that is, converted into a sequence of 1s and 0s that the cell phone's processor can understand), an **analog-to-digital converter chip** converts your voice's sound waves into digital signals. Next, the digital data must be compressed, or squeezed, into the smallest possible space so that it will transmit more quickly to another phone. The processor cannot perform the mathematical operations required at this stage quickly enough, so a specialized chip called the **digital signal processor** is included in the cell phone to handle the compression work. Finally, the digital data is transmitted as a radio wave through the cellular network to the destination phone.

When you receive an incoming call, the digital signal processor decompresses the incoming message. An amplifier boosts the signal to make it loud enough, and it is then passed on to the speaker.

What's "cellular" about a cell phone? A set of connected "cells" makes up a cellular network. Each cell is a geographic area centered on a **base transceiver station**, which is a large communications tower with antennas, amplifiers, receivers, and transmitters. When you place a call on a cell phone, a base station picks up the request for service. The station then passes the request to a central location called a **mobile switching center**. (The reverse process occurs when you receive an incoming call on a cell phone.) A telecommunications company builds its network by constructing a series of cells that overlap in an attempt to guarantee that its cell phone customers have coverage no matter where they are.

As you move during your phone call, the mobile switching center monitors the strength of the signal between your cell phone and the closest base station. When the

Figure 8.4

Inside your cell phone, you'll find a CPU, a memory chip, input devices such as a microphone and a keypad, and output devices such as a display screen and a speaker.

Speaker

Liquid crystal display

Keypad

Microphone

Memory chip

CPU

signal is no longer strong enough between your cell phone and the base station, the mobile switching center orders the next base station to take charge of your call. When your cell phone "drops out," it may be because the distance between base stations was too great to provide an adequate signal.

Are cell phones and smartphones considered to be computers? Cell phones and smartphones are so advanced that they have many of the same components as a computer: a processor (central processing unit, or CPU); memory; and input and output devices, as shown in Figure 8.4. Cell/smartphones also require software and have their own operating systems (OSs).

What does the processor inside a cell/smartphone do? Although the processor inside a cell/smartphone is obviously not as fast or as high-powered as a processor in a desktop computer, it is still responsible for a great number of tasks. The processor coordinates sending all of the data among the other electronic components inside the phone. It also runs the cell/smartphone's operating system, which provides a user interface so that you can change phone settings, store information, play games, and so on. Popular processors for cell/smartphones include the Samsung SC, the Texas Instruments OMAP, and the Marvell XScale processor. Some processors use dual-core processing technology, which is also used in some desktop processors.

Remember to be well prepared when shopping, and use published mobile phone benchmarking results to compare performance. These are often published on the PC Magazine Web site (**pcmag.com**) or at Wired (**wired.com**).

Is there a standard operating system for cell/smartphones? Each cell/smartphone manufacturer makes its own tweaks to an operating system and designs its own user interface. This can make switching phones daunting because you have to learn how to use a different set of commands and icons for each cell/smartphone you use.

There are a number of operating systems in the cell/smartphone market now. One popular OS is the Symbian, from the Symbian Foundation. Many smartphones use the Windows Mobile operating system. Apple's iPhone uses a version of the OS X operating system that is used in Apple's personal computers, while the Palm Pre uses its own Palm-developed webOS. These operating systems are required to translate the user's commands into instructions for the processor.

There now are free operating systems that a manufacturer can use as a base for its cell/smartphone operating system. One open source project to develop a free cell/smartphone operating system is Openmoko. Another is the Android collection developed by Google. The goal of an open source mobile operating system is to leverage the creativity of many developers in creating great applications and new phone designs. Figure 8.5 illustrates some of the different and creative user interfaces

Figure 8.5

(a) Openmoko, (b) Windows Mobile, and (c) Android are all cell/smartphone operating systems.

Figure 8.6

You can insert additional memory by installing a micro SD flash card in a smartphone.

featured in modern cell/smartphone operating systems.

What does the memory chip inside a cell/smartphone do? The operating system and the information you save in your cell/smartphone (such as phone numbers and addresses) need to be stored in memory. The operating system is stored in read-only memory (ROM) because the phone would be useless without that key piece of software. As you learned earlier, there are two kinds of memory used in computers: volatile memory, which requires power to save data, and nonvolatile memory, which stores data even when the power is turned off. ROM is nonvolatile, or permanent, memory. This means that when you turn off your phone, the data that is stored in ROM (including the operating system) remains in memory.

Other phone data, such as ring tones, is stored in separate internal memory chips. Full-featured cell

phones have as many as 200 MB of internal memory (with some smartphones carrying 1 GB internally) and support additional memory through micro SD flash cards that can store up to 32 GB. Micro SD cards are easy to install in a phone, as shown in Figure 8.6. You can use that storage for contact data, ring tones, images, songs, videos, and even software applications such as a currency converter or a world clock. Not every cell/smartphone allows memory upgrades in this way, however. For example, the iPhone series does not allow you to add any memory.

What input and output devices do cell/smartphones use? The primary input devices for a cell/smartphone are a microphone and a keypad. Some phones, such as the Samsung Impression (see Figure 8.7), feature both a hidden keyboard (to make sending e-mail or text messages more efficient) and a touch-sensitive screen. The Apple iPhone uses its touch-sensitive screen to offer a software-based keyboard (see Figure 8.7) that supports more than 40 languages.

Cell/smartphones often include a digital camera. The Sony Ericsson Cyber-Shot C510 offers a high-quality 3.2-megapixel camera with flash and smile shutter feature. (The shutter goes off once the camera detects a smile.) Most cameras on cell/smartphones can record video as well as take still shots. Picture and video messaging is popular with many cell/smartphone users. They can transmit photos and video files via e-mail, post the files to Web sites such as Facebook, or send them directly to other cell/smartphones.

Cell/smartphone output devices include a speaker and a liquid crystal display (LCD). Higher-end models include full-color, high-resolution LCD screens. Newer on the market are OLED (organic light-emitting diode) displays, which allow very bright, sharp imaging and draw less power. High-resolution displays are becoming increasingly popular because more people are using their cell phones to send and receive the digital images included in multimedia text messages and e-mail, and even to watch TV (see Figure 8.8). Cell phone and cable providers are teaming up to deliver broadcast TV programs directly to cell phones through services such as Verizon V Cast and Sprint TV Live. A developing standard named Mobile DTV allows

Figure 8.7

(a) The Samsung Impression includes a touch screen and a built-in QWERTY keyboard. (b) The Apple iPhone has a touch keyboard that supports over 40 languages and a range of character sets.

cell/smartphones to receive free broadcasts from television stations using the M-DTV technology. At the time of this writing, affiliates of NBC, CBS, and PBS are testing this system.

What cell phone and smartphone software is available? Most devices come with a standard collection of software such as a to-do list, contact manager, and calendar. Modified versions of application software such as Microsoft Word, Excel, Outlook, and PowerPoint are available for some high-end smartphones. A variety of games, tools, and reference applications are available from numerous software companies. A good source to locate software applications for your phone is PDA Street (**pdastreet.com**). In addition, Web sites such as download.com (**download.com**) and Tucows (**tucows.com**) feature plenty of shareware and freeware applications for mobile platforms. Some manufacturers have Web-based software stores, like iTunes for the Apple iPhone and the BlackBerry App World for RIM's BlackBerry devices (see Figure 8.9). The Android developer community has held competitions to spur the creation of new software applications for Android-based phones. Many software applications are available for Android though the Web and the Android Market.

How do I move music from my computer to my cell/smartphone? On the 32 GB micro SD cards available for smartphones, there is room for thousands of songs, videos, or data files. You can transfer files between your phone and your computer easily. Some phones are designed with a flash card that can be easily removed

Figure 8.8

Mobile DTV receiver chips are appearing in a number of phones, like this model from LG.

and slipped directly into a flash card reader on the computer. Almost all phones are designed with a USB port. Some have a mini-USB connector, while other models require a special cable to connect the phone to a standard USB port (see Figure 8.10). Once connected using a USB data cable, your phone will appear on your computer like an additional flash drive, and you can drag and drop files to it. You can also charge your cell/smartphone through the USB cable.

How do I synchronize a cell phone with a computer? Cell/smartphones let you coordinate the changes you make to your to-do lists, schedules, and other files with the files on your home or office computer. This process of updating your data so that the files on your cell phone and computer are the same is called **synchronizing**. To synchronize your computer and the device, simply place the cell phone in its cradle (or attach it to the computer via a USB cable) and touch a "sync" button. This begins the process of data transfer that updates both sets of files to the most current version.

Microsoft has recognized the vast increase in portable computing devices by integrating synchronization into the

Figure 8.9

The Blackberry App World is one of many online stores delivering software for smartphones.

Figure 8.10

A USB data synch cable connects your cell phone to your computer for data transfer.

Figure 8.11

The Windows Sync Center makes it easy to arrange for synchronization of all your mobile devices.

> To launch Sync Center, click the **Start** button, select **Control Panel**, and double-click the **Sync Center** icon.

Windows operating system. The Sync Center (see Figure 8.11), which is accessed from the Control Panel, allows you to set up automatic or manual synchronization. Ensure that the device for which you are trying to set up synchronization parameters is connected to your computer and then launch the Sync Center. Select the *Set up new sync partnerships* option to view available devices and configure their synchronization options.

Can I transfer files wirelessly? **Bluetooth** technology uses radio waves to transmit data signals over short distances (approximately 30 feet for Bluetooth 1 and 60 feet for Bluetooth 2 and 3). Bluetooth 3 devices is expected to hit the market in 2010. Distance is expected to be about the same, but throughput is increased. Most cell phones on the market today are Bluetooth-enabled, meaning they include a small Bluetooth chip that allows them to transfer data wirelessly to any other Bluetooth-enabled device. One benefit Bluetooth has over infrared, a wireless connection used in the past, is that a direct line of sight does not have to be present between two devices for them to communicate. You also can use Bluetooth to synchronize your device with your computer. Bluetooth accessories such as earpieces, mice, keyboards, and even stereo headsets are now available.

Text Messaging

What is text messaging? Short message service (SMS)—often just called *text messaging*—is a technology that allows you to send short text messages (comprising up to 160 characters) over mobile networks. To send SMS messages from your cell phone, you use the keypad or a pre-saved template and type your message. You can send SMS messages to other mobile devices (such as cell phones or pagers) or to any e-mail address. You also can use SMS to send short text messages from your home computer to mobile devices such as your friend's cell phone.

How does SMS work? SMS uses the cell phone network to transmit messages. When you send an SMS message, an SMS calling center receives the message and delivers it to the appropriate mobile device using something called *store-and-forward* technology. This technology allows users to send SMS messages to any other SMS device in the world.

Many SMS fans like text messaging because it can be cheaper than a phone call and allows the receivers to read messages when it is convenient for them. In fact, in some countries such as Japan, text messaging is more popular than voice messaging. There are several companies that provide useful services based on text messaging (see Figure 8.12).

If you plan to do a lot of texting, look for a phone with a good text prediction algorithm. With such an algorithm, typing a single letter pulls up a list of popular words beginning with that letter, saving you typing time. For example, the T9 algorithm also "learns" from your usage patterns and displays the most-used word first.

The Apple iPhone offers some unique services. You can rent movies from the iTunes store and have them delivered directly to your phone. In addition, Apple and Starbucks have teamed up to develop the Now Playing service. When in a participating Starbucks, iPhone users can enter the iTunes store online and identify, purchase, and download the song they are currently listening to at their Starbucks location.

Can I send and receive multimedia files over a cell/smartphone? SMS technology allows you to send only text messages. However, an extension of SMS called **multimedia message service (MMS)** allows you to send messages that include text, sound, images, and video clips to other phones or e-mail addresses. MMS messages actually arrive as a series of messages; you view the text, then the image, and then the sound, and so on. You can then choose to save just one part of the message (such as the image), all of it, or none of it. MMS users can subscribe to financial, sports, and weather services that will "push" information to them, sending it automatically to their phones in MMS format.

BITS AND BYTES

411 for Answers

Most phone services charge as much as $2.00 for a 411 call for information on a phone listing or address. Now there is competition. The Google 411 service is a free way to find out the address of, directions to, or phone number of a business or person. A call to 1-800-GOOG-411 gets you this information at no charge. If you say "text" into the phone, it kicks back a text message with the address and a map.

If you are looking for a different kind of information, try the ChaCha service. You can either call (1-800-2chacha) or text (242 242) with any kind of question, and real human "guides" will find the answer and send it back to you. So, answers to questions like

- How many calories are there in a slice of pizza?
- When is *American Idol* on tonight?
- Is there a way to get acrylic paint out of jeans?

are just a free call or text away!

Internet Connectivity

How do I get Internet service for my cell/smartphone? Just as you have an Internet service provider (ISP) for Internet access for your desktop or notebook computer, you must have a **wireless Internet service provider** (or **wireless ISP**) to connect your cell/smartphone to the Internet. Phone companies that provide cell/smartphone calling plans (such as T-Mobile, Verizon, and AT&T) usually double as wireless ISPs. An Internet connectivity plan or text messaging plan is usually known as a **data plan**. Data charges are separate from phone calling charges and are provided at rates different from voice calls. Before subscribing to a data plan, you should assess your data needs: How often do you download new wallpaper, ring tones, or games? Do you use your cell/ smartphone's Internet access to download

---

Figure 8.12 | TEXT MESSAGING SERVICES

SMS Code	Service Name	Web Site	Description
466453 (google)	Google SMS	**google.com/sms**	Obtains information such as addresses, phone numbers, driving directions, sports scores, and movie listings from the Google search engine.
44636 (4Info)	4INFO	**4info.net**	Similar to Google SMS, but also handles flight information and horoscopes.
242 242 (cha cha)	ChaCha	**chacha.com**	Human "guides" provide answers to any question in conversational English.
3109043113	411sms	**411sms.com**	Offers many services, including address and phone listings, turn-by-turn directions, movie show times, stock quotes, hot spot locations, dictionary definitions, horoscopes, and foreign language translations.

Make Your Cell/Smartphone Deliver

Carriers offer many additional services for your cell/smartphone. MusicID, for example, allows you to identify a song easily. Just hold your phone close to the radio's speaker for 15 seconds. You will then receive a text message with the name of the artist and the song. MusicID has a database of more than 3 million songs, so you can be the first to grab those new titles.

Other services can be added to your cell/smartphone plan. For example, you can subscribe to high-definition radio stations over your cell phone. The extra fee allows you to stream more than 50 channels of commercial-free digital radio through your phone. Many phones are equipped for navigation services such as TeleNav Navigator. TeleNav delivers turn-by-turn instructions to you over your phone and displays real-time traffic information.

files from e-mails or from your company Web site? Begin by estimating how many kilobytes of data you transfer up and down from the Internet each month. Then select a plan that provides adequate service at a good price.

At what speed is digital information transferred to my cell/smartphone? A cell/smartphone connection often is slower than the one you have at your home. Although broadband speeds of 50 megabits per second (Mbps) are achievable at home using a cable or fiber-optic connection, your cell/smartphone will connect at a much lower speed (see Figure 8.13).

Providers have introduced many cell/smartphones based on two standards that support faster data transfer technologies: EDGE (short for enhanced data rate for global evolution) and 3G. EDGE and 3G have brought mobile devices much faster data transfer—as high as 1.7 Mbps (or more) under ideal conditions. If you use a cell/smartphone that supports EDGE or 3G, and have a phone plan that allows data transfer, both uploading information (such as e-mail messages that include photos) and

downloading information (such as from a company intranet or the Internet) can take place much more quickly. Of course if you are in range of a WiFi signal, that is going to be a much faster transfer option. EDGE and 3G have advantages over WiFi, however. They are more reliable and less susceptible to interference. Moreover, you won't have to hunt for a WiFi hot spot, because these technologies are used to blanket major urban areas with connectivity.

As of this writing, 4G networks are beginning to be tested in two cities. The promise of 4G is incredible: mobile connection speeds of up to 100 Mbps. The expansion of 4G will usher in a new generation of mobile devices and applications that will continue to expand how we think of mobile computing.

How is the Internet displayed on a cell/smartphone? On cell/smartphones that have a limited amount of screen space, it is difficult to view Web pages without a great deal of horizontal scrolling. This is because most Web sites are designed for viewing on desktop monitors, which have much wider pixel widths than mobile screens. To enhance your Internet browsing experience on mobile devices, special microbrowser software runs on your phone. **Microbrowser** software provides a Web browser that is optimized to display Web content effectively on the smaller screen (see Figure 8.14). Popular versions of microbrowser software include Internet Explorer Mobile (included with the Windows Mobile OS) and Opera Mobile. Opera Mobile uses special small-screen rendering technology to reformat the Web images to fit on your cell/smartphone screen, eliminating the need for horizontal scrolling. For the best Web experience, consider a phone that has a large screen, such as the Samsung Omnia 2, which boasts a 3.7-inch diagonal measure screen.

More and more Web sites are being created with content specifically designed for wireless devices. This specially designed content, which is text based and contains no graphics, is written in a format called **Wireless Markup Language (WML)**. Content is designed so that it fits the smaller display screens of handheld mobile devices.

Can I keep my e-mail up to date using my cell/smartphone? A popular feature of cell/smartphones with Internet access lets users check e-mail. BlackBerry

Figure 8.13 | CELLULAR CONNECTION SPEEDS

Network	Availability	Connection Speed (Mbps)
Edge	13,000 cities	0.1
3G	300 major markets	1.7
WiFi	WiFi hot spots	5.0
4G	2 cities in trial	50.0

Note: Speeds will vary. This data was measured using an iPhone over the AT&T network.

handhelds were the first devices that were optimized to check e-mail. BlackBerry pioneered the "push" technology that delivers your e-mail automatically to your phone, whether you want it or not. Now many other systems also offer "push" technology. BlackBerry devices are still an excellent option, but they aren't the only option. With Internet access, users can always e-mail through Web-based e-mail accounts like Gmail or Yahoo!

If checking and sending e-mail while on the go is mission critical for you, check out cell/smartphones with larger displays and integrated keyboards that make it easier to read and respond to messages.

Voice over Internet Protocol

Cell phone service is still not 100 percent reliable. Dropped calls and poor reception are a problem in many areas. In addition, the call quality of landline phone service is often superior to cell phone call quality. Therefore, many people who run home businesses or make business calls from their home maintain a landline to ensure high voice quality of calls. In many instances, landline phone plans can be cheaper than cell phone plans, especially for international calls. Therefore, you may want to consider a style of landline phone service called VoIP (voice over Internet protocol).

How is VoIP different from regular telephone service? Voice over Internet Protocol (VoIP) is a form of voice-based Internet communication that turns a standard Internet connection into a means to place phone calls, including long- distance calls. Traditional telephone communications use analog voice data and telephone connections. In contrast, VoIP uses technology similar to that used in e-mail to send your voice data digitally over the Internet.

What do I need to use VoIP? For the simplest and least costly VoIP service, you need speakers, a microphone, an Internet connection, and a VoIP provider (see Figure 8.16). Depending on the provider you choose, you also may need to install software or a special adapter. Creating a VoIP account with Skype (**skype.com**) is similar to creating an instant messaging account. Skype requires that both callers and

Figure 8.14

Microbrowser software on phones like the Palm Pre let you work with (a) one window or (b) several live browser windows.

 How Do You Find Your WiFi?

Detecting a nearby WiFi signal is important if you are looking for Internet connectivity while you are on the move. Some notebooks have a built-in WiFi scanner that displays a row of lights on the case whenever a WiFi signal is available. Keychain fobs that light up when they detect WiFi signals in the vicinity are also available.

If you are running Windows 7, the Connect to a Network dialog box (accessible from the Network and Sharing Center) shows the strength of all wireless networks within range of your computer.

At ThinkGeek (**thinkgeek.com**), you may find the most easy-to-use WiFi detector ever. The WiFi Detector t-shirt has a logo that lights up to indicate the signal strength of a nearby WiFi network (see Figure 8.15). Find your WiFi and look . . . well, look geeky while doing so!

Figure 8.15

The WiFi Detector T-shirt makes a statement—a geeky statement.

receivers have the company's free software installed on their computers. Another similarity to IM is that with Skype you can

Phoning Home—Accessing Your Home Computer from Your Cell Phone

An estimated 1 billion cellular phones that aren't considered smartphones currently are deployed. But don't count your cheap phone out of the running if it doesn't have advanced software capabilities. You can still use it to access your home computer remotely and retrieve that big presentation you need for this afternoon. Remote access services such as GoToMyPC (**gotomypc.com**) and LogMeIn (**logmein.com**) can help and are free of charge. As long as you have a browser on your cell phone and a data plan with your provider, you can access the files on your computer from your phone without installing any software on the cell phone. You may not have to trade in that low-end cell phone yet. Just try getting it to work a little harder!

change your online status, look at your contact list, and decide whom you want to talk to. Other VoIP services, such as Vonage (**vonage.com**), are a bit more complicated to set up and are not free. You can use your own telephone by connecting your phone to a special adapter that the company provides, or you can buy a special IP phone that connects to your broadband Internet connection or to a USB port on your computer.

One limitation of VoIP used to be that when you made a call, you had to be at your computer. WiFi (wireless Internet) IP phones, however, make it possible to place VoIP calls from any WiFi hot spot location.

What are the advantages and disadvantages of VoIP? For people who make many long-distance phone calls, the advantage of VoIP is its free or low cost. Portability is another advantage because all

you need is an Internet connection. With Internet accessibility so abundant, you can keep in touch with friends and family no matter where you are. As long as you are covered by a WiFi signal, you can plug in your headset or IP phone, sign on to your VoIP service, and make your call.

Although VoIP is affordable and convenient, it does have drawbacks. Some people regard sound quality and reliability issues as VoIP's primary disadvantages. Another drawback is the loss of service if power is interrupted. Although many traditional phones do not depend on electricity, your Internet connection and IP phone do. One serious drawback when VoIP service was first offered to the public was the inability for 911 calls to be traced back to the caller, unlike with a traditional phone. The FCC now requires all VoIP providers to provide traceable 911 services.

Another issue with VoIP is security. Security risks are similar to the risks associated with e-mail (such as spam) and fraud (such as where a hacker breaks into a VoIP system to make unauthorized calls). These are real risks but they are avoidable if you take proper precautions. In addition, encryption services (similar to those used with e-mail) that convert data into a form that is not easily understood by unauthorized people are being deployed to help protect the very nature of calls made over the Internet. Despite these concerns, VoIP continues to enjoy explosive growth, and the technology will continue to improve.

Figure 8.16

Depending on your VoIP service, you can hold conversations through a computer, a special VoIP telephone, or a regular telephone with an adapter.

Computer

VoIP phone

INTERNET

DSL/Cable modem

Phone adapter

Computer

Phone

What new features come with having an Internet-based digital phone at home? Once you are using an Internet-based digital phone system, new features become possible. You can have your telephone messages automatically bundled up as e-mails and sent to your account. If you are watching television and a call comes in, it can be displayed on the screen with caller ID information. Many cable delivery companies are bundling digital phone services in for free if you already purchase cable and television through them, so the price may be attractive.

Cell Phone/Smartphone Security

Can I get a virus on my cell/smartphone? Although viruses can already infect cell phones, manufacturers and software engineers are bracing themselves for a tidal wave of viruses targeted to cell/smartphones. With half of users reporting that they send confidential e-mails using their phones and one-third of users indicating that they access bank account or credit card information, cell/smartphones are the next most likely realm of attack by cybercriminals. The potential of cell/smartphone viruses ranges from the mildly annoying (certain features of your phone stop working) to the expensive (your phone is used without your knowledge to make expensive calls).

How can I prevent cell/smartphone viruses? Symantec, McAfee, and F-Secure are the leading companies currently providing antivirus software for mobile devices. Products are designed for specific cell/smartphone operating systems; for example, Symantec Mobile Security for Symbian is designed for cell/smartphones running the Symbian OS. Often businesses will have their information technology department install and configure an antivirus solution like this for all the phones used in the organization. Although viruses plaguing cell/smartphones have not yet reached the volume of viruses attacking PC operating systems, with the proliferation of mobile devices it is expected that such virus attacks will increase. If no antivirus program is available for your phone's operating

"How do I keep my cell/smartphone number private?"

system, the best precautions are common sense ones. Check the phone manufacturer's Web site frequently to see whether your cell/smartphone needs any software upgrades that could patch security holes. In addition, remember that you should not download ring tones, games, or other software from unfamiliar Web sites.

How do I keep my cell/smartphone number private? It seems that every time you fill out a Web form someone is asking for your phone number. If you are concerned about widely distributing your cell/smartphone number and potentially inviting lots of unwanted solicitation calls, you should consider using a virtual phone number. A virtual phone number is a phone number you create that can be assigned to ring on existing phone numbers (such as your cell phone). Companies such as Telusion (**tossabledigits.com**) provide these virtual numbers. Then, when you are filling out a registration form for some Web service, you can input your virtual phone number in the Web form instead of giving out your number. When you set up the virtual account, you can restrict the hours that you will receive calls from that number (no more 2:00 A.M. telemarketing calls), and if you are receiving many unwanted calls, you can disable the virtual number without affecting your cell/smartphone service.

Digital Media

The entertainment industry has become an all-digital field. Today, videos, music, and photographs are created using digital recording devices, processed using digital software systems, and delivered over digital distribution channels. What does this mean

Singer playing music

Analog wave

ADC

Digital format
28,36,42,
84,120,126,
120,98,98...

CD or DVD

DAC

28,36,42,
84,120,126,
120,98,98...

Speaker

Figure 8.17

During the complete recording process, information changes from analog form to digital data and then back again to analog sound waves.

for you and your use of music, photography, and video?

How is digital media created? All digital media, whether an image, a song, or a video, has the same basis—digitized information. Figure 8.17 shows the process of creating digital information for a musical selection. This process is described below:

1. Playing music creates analog waves.

2. A microphone feeds the sound waves into a chip called an *analog-to-digital converter (ADC)* inside the recording device.

3. The ADC digitizes the waves into a series of numbers.

4. This series of numbers can be recorded onto CDs and DVDs or sent electronically.

5. On the receiving end, a playback device such as a CD player or DVD player is fed that same series of numbers. Inside the playback device is a digital-to-analog converter (DAC), a chip that converts the digital numbers to a continuous analog wave.

6. That analog wave tells the receiver how to move the speaker cones to reproduce the original waves, resulting in the same sound as the original.

More precisely, the digital wave will be *close* to exact. How accurate it is, or how close the digitized wave is in shape to the original analog wave, depends on the sampling rate of the ADC. The **sampling rate** specifies the number of times the analog

wave is measured each second. The higher the sampling rate, the more accurately the original wave can be re-created. However, higher sampling rates also produce much more data, and therefore result in bigger files. For example, sound waves on CDs are sampled at a rate of approximately 44,000 times a second. This produces a huge list of numbers for even a single minute of a song!

When sounds or image waves are digitized, it means that analog data is changed into digital data—from a wave into a series of numbers. The digital data is perfectly reproducible and can be distributed easily on CDs and DVDs or through the airwaves. The data also can be easily processed by a computer.

Digital Music

How can I carry music files easily? Portable media players (PMPs) are small portable devices (such as an iPod) that enable you to carry your MP3 files around with you. Many PMPs handle video and still images, as well as music files. Many smartphones are capable of storing and playing media files, but for the best experience, a dedicated media player, such as a portable media player, is often the optimal choice because PMPs tend to offer more features and storage.

Depending on the player, you can carry several hours of music or video—or possibly your entire CD collection—in an incredibly small device. For example, an Apple iPod classic with a 160 GB hard drive is 4.1 inches by 2.4 inches (and only 0.41 inch thick), yet it can hold as many as 40,000 songs, or 200 hours of video. The most compact players are slightly larger than a flash drive (although they hold far less music than the iPod). Figure 8.18 shows several models of PMPs, all of which connect to computers via USB 2.0 ports.

Are all music files MP3 files? The letters at the end of a file name (the file extension) indicate how the data in the file is organized. MP3 is the name of just one type of file format used to store digital music, but many others exist, such as AAC and WMA. There are also many video formats such as DivX, MPEG-4 (which usually has an .mp4 extension), WMV, and XviD. All file

Figure 8.18 | SOME PORTABLE MEDIA PLAYERS AND THEIR CHARACTERISTICS

	Media Capacity	Built-In Flash Memory	Hard Drive Capacity	Connection to Computer	Other Features
Sansa® Fuze™ Player	2000 songs or 24 hours of video	512 MB to 1 GB	None but 16 GB mSD card supported	USB 2.0 port	FM radio, voice recorder and available "radio" cards prefilled with 1000 songs
Oregon Scientific MP121	Up to 32 hours of music	1 GB	None	USB 2.0 port	Waterproof to 3 feet, built-in pedometer, built-in FM radio, and equalizer.
Apple iPod touch	As many as 14,000 songs or 80 hours of video	8 GB to 64 GB	None	USB 2.0 port	Weighs only 4.05 ounces; flash memory enables skip-free playback.
Apple iPod classic	As many as 40,000 songs or 200 hours of video	None	160 GB	USB 2.0 port	Has calendar feature that syncs with Outlook; can serve as a small, portable hard drive.
Archos 7	As many as 190,000 songs or 400 movies	None	320 GB	USB 2.0 port	Includes 7" screen display, Wi-Fi, and touch screen.

formats compete on sound and video quality and *compression,* which relates to how small the file can be and still provide high-quality playback. If you buy a song from the iTunes Music Store, for example, you receive an .aac format file. AAC files can be played only on iPods but can be converted to the more widely seen MP3 or Windows Media Audio (WMA) formats. WMA files can be played on a wide variety of MP3 players. Most PMPs that support video playback can play a wide range of video formats.

Are PMP devices the only choice for portable media management?
PMP devices are not the only choice for portable media management. A number of electronic devices now incorporate the capability to carry electronic files and play music and video files. Some models of digital cameras, such as the Samsung NV3, have support for playing both music and videos. Gaming devices such as the Sony PlayStation Portable (PSP) allow you to play video games, play music and video files, and browse the Internet.

In the last few years, stand-alone **GPS (global positioning system)** devices have dropped dramatically in price and size. Now these small, handheld units organize music and photos as well as deliver turn-by-turn instructions and real-time traffic

Figure 8.19

The Garmin Nuvi series GPS devices are also able to provide Internet services.

information. Full-featured GPS models such as the Garmin Nuvi 705 series include MP3 players, audio book players, and the capability to display photos and connect to the Internet (see Figure 8.19). Using Internet services such as MSN Direct, your GPS can keep you informed about the weather, traffic backups, local movie times, and even local gas prices.

How do I know how much digital media a PMP can hold? The number of songs or hours of video a portable media

---

The Power of GPS ... and the Threats

Most people know where the closest supermarket is in relation to their home. But if you are out of town, how can you find a local supermarket when you get a craving for potato chips? Many people aren't whizzes at geography, but knowing your current location and the location of your destination can often come in handy. Luckily for those who are "directionally impaired," GPS technology enables users to carry a powerful navigational aid in a pocket.

You've probably heard of GPS, but what is it exactly and how does it work? Built and operated by the U.S. Department of Defense, the global positioning system is a network of 21 satellites (plus 3 working spares) that constantly orbit the Earth. GPS devices use an antenna to pick up the signals from these satellites and use special software to transform those signals into latitude and longitude. Using the information obtained from the satellites, GPS devices can tell you what your geographical location is anywhere on the planet to within 10 feet (see Figure 8.20). Because they provide such detailed positioning information, GPS devices are now used as navigational aids for aircraft, recreational boats, and automobiles, and they even come in handheld models for hikers.

Although this precise positioning information clearly redefines the fields of surveying and search-and-rescue operations, it also has changed other fields. Wildlife researchers now tag select animals, watch their migration patterns, and observe how populations are distributed. GPS also was important to the two teams that created the Chunnel, the tunnel under the English Channel that connects England to France. One team worked from France toward England and the other from England toward France. They used GPS information along the way to make sure they were on target. In 1990, the two sections were joined to become the first physical link between England and the continent of Europe since the Ice Age.

GPS units are available with a wide range of features. Garmin, for example, offers a wide range of services on its line of GPS units. A Map mode displays your location on a map that is updated in real time as you drive. Enter a series of destinations, and an optimal route is developed for you. A voice warns you of lane changes and approaching turns, giving you directions using the actual street name ("Turn right on Hancock

Figure 8.20

GPS computes your location anywhere on Earth from a system of orbiting satellites.

Avenue"). If you miss a turn, the unit automatically recalculates the required route and gives you directions to get back on course. Flip to player can hold depends on how much storage space it has. Most PMPs use built-in **flash memory**, a type of nonvolatile memory, to store files. Most PMPs that support video use a hard drive instead of flash memory and can store a much greater amount of music and video. Less expensive PMPs use flash memory (ranging from 1 GB to 32 GB), whereas models that are more expensive use built-in hard drives, which provide as much as 160 GB of storage. Some of the PMPs that use flash memory allow you to add storage capacity by purchasing removable flash memory cards.

Another factor that determines how much music a player can hold is the quality of the MP3 music files. The size of an MP3 file depends on the digital sampling of the song. The same song could be sampled at 320 kbps or 64 kbps. The size of the song file will be five times larger if it is sampled at 320 kbps rather than the lower sampling rate of 64 kbps. The higher the sampling rate, the better quality the sound—but the larger the file size.

How do you control the size of an MP3 file? If you are *ripping*, or converting, a song from a CD into a digital MP3 file,

Figure 8.21

A cell/smartphone can now use a GPS service to give you turn-by-turn directions and current traffic conditions.

another screen, and it shows you how far you have to drive to the next gas station, restaurant, or hospital. Some models automatically mark the location of your car when you remove them from the vehicle, and can give you step-by-step directions back to your car.

Most automotive companies now offer GPS systems as installed options in their vehicles. However, GPS navigation can be added to any vehicle using a portable GPS device or a PDA/smartphone equipped with GPS (see Figure 8.21), or by adding GPS software and accessories to your notebook.

But Who Is Watching?

Having the ability to locate and track an object anywhere on Earth does bring with it societal implications, however. The Federal Communications Commission (FCC) mandated that every cell/smartphone had to include a GPS chip by the end of 2005. This enabled the complete rollout of the Enhanced 911 (E911) program. E911 automatically gives dispatchers precise location information for any 911 call. It also means your phone records may include this precise tracking information, which indicates where you are when you make a call. Is that information something you would want the government, or other people, to know? Consider if you were at a park playing baseball with your friends and you made a phone call. At the same time, in another part of the park, an organization with suspected terrorist ties was holding a rally. Would you want the government to assume that because you made a phone call from the park, you are a member of that organization?

Because phones now have GPS chips, cellular phone providers offer plans (for a monthly fee) that allow you to track where a phone is at any given time via a Web site. This could be a real boon for tracking a lost child who wandered off into the woods during a group hike. But are other uses of the technology ethical? Did your daughter really go to the library, or is she actually at the local skate park hanging with her friends? Is your spouse really working late at the office—or at the ballpark watching the baseball game with friends? Now, with a few clicks of the mouse, you can tell where a family member's phone is located. Is this an invasion of privacy? Is it ethical to track the whereabouts of your family members? This is something that you need to decide.

GPS technology begs several questions: What limits and supervision of the government need to be in place to ensure the ethical use of GPS technologies? In what ways could the tracking information provided by GPS devices be used unethically? If GPS tracking information is recorded in people's phone data, should the criteria for allowing government agencies to subpoena phone records be changed? Should users be allowed to disable the location information feature on their phones? Location records such as these were used to determine that *New York Times* reporter Jayson Blair had been fabricating stories, a determination that resulted in his resignation. Car rental companies such as Acme Car Rental of New Haven, Connecticut are using GPS records to fine customers for speeding violations. As a nation, we now need to decide how we should balance the benefits and costs (to our privacy) of using this new level of tracking information.

you can select the sampling rate yourself. You decide by considering what quality sound you want, as well as how many songs you want to fit onto your MP3 player. For example, if your player had 1 GB of storage and you have ripped songs at 192 kbps, you could fit about 694 minutes of music onto the player. The same 1 GB could store 2,083 minutes of music if it were sampled at 64 kbps. Whenever you are near your computer, you can connect your player and download a different set of songs, but you always are limited by the amount of storage your player has.

What if I want to store more music or video than the memory on my PMP allows?   Some PMPs allow you to add memory by inserting removable flash memory cards. Flash memory cards are noiseless and featherlight, use tiny amounts of power, and slide into a special slot in the player. If you've ever played a video game on PlayStation or Xbox and saved your progress to a memory card, then you have used flash memory. Because flash memory is nonvolatile, when you store data on a flash memory card, you won't lose it when you turn off the player. In addition, flash memory can be erased and rewritten with new data. PMPs use a variety of different types of flash cards. Check your manual and then review the coverage on flash media in Chapter 2 for more details.

How do I transfer media files to my portable media player?   All portable media players come with software that enables you to transfer audio and video files from your computer to the player. As noted earlier, players that hold thousands of songs and hours of video use internal hard drives to store the files. For example, devices such as Apple iPods can hold several gigabytes of data. To move large volumes of data between your computer and your PMP, you want a high-speed port. Most PMPs use a USB 2.0 port, but some players may use FireWire ports, which provide comparable throughput. Using a USB 2.0 port, you can transfer two dozen MP3 files to the iPod in less than 10 seconds.

What if I want a lot of people to listen to my digital music?   PMPs are great for individual listening, but to share

> **"Audio receivers now come with a port to connect a PMP device directly."**

music from a PMP, you have to connect it to an alternative device. Many audio receivers now come with a port or a dock so that you can connect a PMP device directly to them as another audio input source, like a CD player or a television. Most new cars are equipped with at least an auxiliary input to the speaker system to support connecting a PMP; others have a fully integrated software system that displays and runs the PMP playlists. There are alarm clocks and home speaker docks that can mate with a PMP and broadcast brilliant sound.

How did the shift to digital music impact the music industry?   The initial MP3 craze was fueled by sites such as MP3.com, which originally stored its song files on a public server with the permission of the original artists or recording companies. Therefore, you were not infringing on a copyright by downloading songs from sites such as MP3.com (which still exists and now provides free music in streaming format).

Napster was a file exchange site created to correct some of the annoyances found by users of MP3.com. One such annoyance was the limited availability of popular music in MP3 format. With the MP3 sites, if you found a song you wanted to download, the link to the site on which the file was found often no longer worked. Napster differed from MP3.com because songs or locations of songs were not stored in a central public server, but instead were "borrowed" directly from other users' computers. This process of users transferring files between computers is referred to as **peer-to-peer (P2P) sharing**. Napster also provided a search engine dedicated to finding specific MP3 files. This direct search and sharing eliminated the inconvenience of searching links only to find them unavailable.

The problem with Napster was that it was so good at what it did. Napster's convenient and reliable mechanism to find and download popular songs in MP3 format became a huge success. The rapid acceptance and use of Napster—at one point, it had nearly 60 million users—led the music industry to sue the site for copyright infringement, and Napster was closed in June 2002. Napster has since reopened as a music site that sells music downloads and is sanctioned by the recording industry.

The reaction of the record industry was to continue to enforce its absolute ownership over digital forms of its music. The industry even filed legal actions against individuals who had downloaded large amounts of music from Internet sites. This heavy-handed reaction to the new era of digital music ultimately backfired and left the music industry scrambling. Overall music sales in 2009 were about half what they were at the industry's peak. The record industry is still trying to counter losing CD sales to digital forms of music. The approach they took early on did not allow them to adapt quickly enough to the new business models required by the shift to digital technologies.

So if I don't pay for a music download, is it illegal? Although you need to pay for most music you download, some artists post songs for free. Business models are still evolving as artists and recording companies try to meet audience needs while also protecting their own intellectual property rights. Several different approaches exist. One is to deliver something called *tethered downloads* in which you pay for the music and own it, but are subject to restrictions on its use.

Another approach is to offer *DRM-free* music, which is music without any digital rights management. These song files can be moved freely from system to system. For example, Apple's iTunes store currently sells only DRM-free types of music. A DRM-free song can be placed on as many computers or players as you wish. Other sites offer subscription services. For a monthly fee, Napster to Go allows you to download as many songs as you like to your MP3 player. These songs will be usable, however, only as long as you are paying the monthly subscription fee.

Why buy any music if peer-to-peer (P2P) sharing sites are still operating? When Napster was going through its legal turmoil, other P2P Web sites were quick to take advantage of a huge opportunity. Napster was "easy" to shut down because it used a central index server that queried other Napster computers for requested songs. Current P2P protocols (such as LimeWire and BearShare) differ

from Napster in that they do not limit themselves to sharing only MP3 files. Video files are obtainable easily on P2P sites. More importantly, these sites don't have a central index server. Instead, they operate in a true P2P sharing environment in which computers connect directly to other computers. This makes them a prime source of unwanted viruses and spyware.

The argument these P2P networks make to defend their legality is that they do not run a central server like the original Napster, but only facilitate connections between users. Therefore, they have no control over what the users choose to trade. Note that not all P2P file sharing is illegal. For example, it is legal to trade photos or movies you have created with other folks over a P2P site.

People who oppose such file-sharing sites contend that the sites know their users are distributing files illegally and breaking copyright laws. Be aware that having illegal content on your computer, deliberately or by accident, is a criminal offense in many jurisdictions.

Will PMPs eliminate radio stations? Radio stations have always had certain advantages: early access to new music, and personalities and conversations that add to the listening experience.

However, the Internet allows artists to release new songs to their fans immediately (on sites such as mp3.com) and without relying on radio airtime. This opens up new channels for artists to reach an audience and changes the amount of power radio stations have in the promotion of music. Many radio stations have increased listenership by making their stations available through Internet sites and by broadcasting in high-definition quality.

Another development that competes with radio (and television) is *podcasting,* which allows users to download audio and video content and then listen to those broadcasts on their PMPs whenever they want. Podcasting is paving the way for anyone to create a radio or television show at home and distribute it easily to an audience. Using free software such as Audacity (**audacity. sourceforge.net**) and a microphone, you can record voice-overs, sequence songs, and "publish" your show to the Internet. Loyal fans can use podcasting software such as Juice (**juicereceiver.sourceforge.net**) or iTunes (for Windows or Mac) to find a podcast's latest episode and automatically transfer it to their portable media players. Plugging your iPod into a data port on your computer causes the iPod to search iTunes for new content and automatically transfers the new files to your iPod. Podcasts are easy to subscribe to and download using iTunes (see Figure 8.22).

Digital Photography

What is "analog" photography?
Before digital cameras hit the market, most people used some form of 35-mm single-lens reflex (SLR) camera. When you take a picture using a traditional SLR camera, a shutter opens, creating an aperture (a small window in the camera) that allows light to hit the 35-mm film inside. Chemicals coating the film react when exposed to light. Later, additional chemicals develop the image on the film, and the image is printed on special light-sensitive paper. A variety of lenses and processing techniques, special equipment, and filters are needed to create printed photos from traditional SLR cameras.

What is different about digital photography?
Digital cameras do not use film. Instead, they capture images on electronic sensors called *charge-coupled device (CCD) arrays* and then convert those images to digital data, long series of numbers that represent the color and brightness of millions of points in the image. Unlike traditional cameras, digital cameras allow you to see your images the instant you shoot them. Most camera models can now record digital video as well as digital photos.

How do I select a digital camera?
With hundreds of models to choose from, where do you begin? The first question to answer is whether you want a compact "point-and-click" model camera or a more serious digital SLR. The larger digital SLR cameras allow you to switch among different lenses and offer features important to serious amateur and professional photographers (such as depth-of-field previewing). Although having such flexibility in moving up to a larger zoom lens is a great advantage, these cameras are also larger, heavier, and use more battery power than the tiny point-and-click models. Think about how you will be using your camera and decide which model will serve you best in the long run.

Figure 8.22

iTunes makes it easy to subscribe to and manage podcasts.

Consider this scenario: You were in Washington, D.C. over spring break and you took a lovely photograph of the Washington Monument at sunset. You posted the photo on your Facebook page so your family and friends could see it. One morning you pop open your e-mail and there is an offer from a magazine to feature your photo on the cover. (An editor saw it on Facebook.) Before accepting the offer, you need to be aware of your digital rights concerning your photograph.

As you learned in Chapter 3, copyright is a bundle of rights that are granted to creators of original works such as literary materials, music, and photographs. For photographs, the photographer usually owns the copyright to the photo. The rights you have over your photograph of the Washington Monument include the right to publish, to display (such as on your Facebook page), or to sell copies of the work. Therefore, posting the photograph on your Facebook page, as well as selling it to the magazine, are probably within your rights.

In the United States, you are free to take photographs in public places such as streets, public parks, or sidewalks without asking anyone's permission. However, property owners can prohibit photography on their premises or place restrictions on the use of photographs taken on their property. For instance, museums usually restrict the photographic rights of buildings and works of art on display. If you had taken a photograph of *Coast of Normandy* (a painting by Claude Monet), which is displayed at the Philadelphia Museum of Art, you would not be able to use the photograph for commercial purposes (for example, sell it to a magazine) without the consent of the museum. When taking photographs on private property, you should always inquire about restrictions on the use of photographs.

In the case of a national monument, which is a public place, there are generally no restrictions to copyright on photographs you take. Nevertheless, for our example, you should check with the National Park Service (which administers the Washington Monument) just to be on the safe side.

But what if two of your friends and three complete strangers, who were all standing in front of the Washington Monument, are prominently featured in your photograph? Generally speaking, people in photographs do not have any rights or partial ownership of the copyright of the photo.

However, in the United States, the Fourth Amendment to the Constitution and various other laws and court cases have recognized Americans' rights to certain amounts of privacy. Being photographed without your consent is considered a violation of privacy. Your friends essentially gave their permission to be photographed by jumping in front of your camera and posing. However, the three strangers didn't give their permission.

Usually, when photographers know they will use a photograph for commercial purposes, they have all people in the photograph sign a *model release*. A model release grants the photographer the rights to use an image of the model (the person in the photo) commercially. Be aware there are many instances where you grant your approval to have your image used commercially. For example, most tickets to amusement parks have a clause on the back that states that by entering the park you grant the park permission to use your image in marketing and publicity materials.

On the other hand, if a picture of you is published without your consent, you may have the basis for a lawsuit. Consider the case of teenager Alison Chang, who was photographed at a church-sponsored car wash. The photographer posted the photograph on Flickr, stating that anyone was free to use his photos as long as they identified him as the photographer. An advertising agency in Australia saw the photograph on Flickr and used it in a billboard advertising campaign for a cell phone company. All of a sudden, Alison was the "friend" you could dump when you became cool and bought a cell phone. When Alison found out about this unauthorized use of her image, her family promptly filed a lawsuit seeking damages. Although the photographer was able to give away his rights to the photograph, he couldn't give away Alison's rights without her permission.

Therefore, for your Washington Monument photo, you should obtain model releases from your friends before selling the photo to the magazine. You should also inform the magazine that you do not possess model releases for the three strangers in the photo so the magazine can remove those people from the image before publication. You need to respect the rights of others, and exercise discretion when taking and displaying photographs, so you don't end up on the wrong side of a lawsuit.

Next, you'll want to evaluate the quality of the camera on a number of levels. One great resource to use is Digital Photography Review (**dpreview.com**). The site's camera reviews evaluate a camera's construction as well as its features, image quality, ease of use, and value for the cost. In addition, the site provides comparisons to similar camera models by other manufacturers and feedback from owners of those models. Links are provided to several resellers, making it easy to compare prices as well.

Why not just use the camera on my cell/smartphone? Many cell/smartphones include a digital camera. These cameras often provide lower resolutions than stand-alone models and inferior lenses. Many features that photographers rely on are not often available in the cameras included on phones, such as different types of autofocus, image stabilization algorithms, and *smile shutter*, which waits to take a shot until your subject is smiling.

What determines the image quality of a digital camera? Part of what determines the image quality of a digital camera is its **resolution**, or the number of data points it records for each image captured. A

Figure 8.23
Digital camera resolutions.

Canon Lumix G1 (12.1 MP)

Kodak V1273 (12 MP)

Canon EOS-1Ds (21.9 MP)

Sony Cybershot
DSC-T900R (12.1 MP)

digital camera's resolution is measured in megapixels (MP). The prefix *mega* is short for millions. The word *pixel* is short for picture element, which is a single dot in a digital image. Point-and-click models typically offer resolutions from 8 MP to 15 MP. Professional digital SLR cameras, such as the Canon EOS-1Ds Mark III, can take photos at resolutions as high as 21.1 MP, but they sell for thousands of dollars. Figure 8.23 shows some popular digital camera models and the number of pixels they record at their maximum resolution.

If you're interested in making only 5" × 7" or 8" × 10" prints, a lower-resolution camera is fine. However, low-resolution images become grainy and pixelated when pushed to make larger-size prints. For example, if you tried to print an 11" × 14" enlargement from a 2 MP image taken using your cell phone's camera, the image would look grainy; you would see individual dots of color instead of a clear, sharp image. The 8 MP to 15 MP cameras on the market now have plenty of resolution to guarantee sharp, detailed images even with enlargements as big as 11" × 14".

What file formats are used for digital images? To fit more photos on the same size of flash memory card, digital cameras allow you to choose from several different file types in order to compress, or squeeze, the image data into less memory space. When you choose to compress your images, you will lose some of the detail, but in return, you'll be able to fit more images on your flash card. The most common file

types supported by digital cameras are raw uncompressed data (RAW) and Joint Photographic Experts Group (JPEG). Raw files have different formats and extensions depending on the manufacturer of a particular camera. The raw file records all of the original image information, so it is larger than a compressed JPEG file. JPEG files can be compressed just a bit, keeping most of the details, or compressed a great deal, losing some detail. Most cameras allow you to select from a few different JPEG compression levels.

Often cameras also support a very low-resolution storage option, enabling you to create files that you can easily attach to e-mail messages. This low-resolution setting typically provides images that are not useful for printing but are so small in size that they are easily e-mailed. Even people who have slow Internet connections are able to quickly download and view such images on-screen.

How do I move photos to my computer? If you just want to print your photos, you may not need to transfer them to your computer. Many photo printers can make prints directly from your camera or from a flash memory card, and many retailers, like CVS and Wal-Mart, provide photo printing machines that can read directly from your memory card. However, transferring the photos to your computer does allow you to store them and frees your flash card for reuse.

Digital cameras have a built-in USB 2.0 port. (Some high-end models may also include a FireWire port.) Using a USB 2.0 cable, you can connect the camera to your computer and copy the converted images as uncompressed files or in a compressed format as JPEG files. Another option is to transfer the flash card from your camera directly to the built-in memory card reader on your computer. Some camera models support wireless network connections so that you can transfer the images without the fuss of putting a cable in place. The Panasonic Lumix TZ50 goes a step further. It uses its integrated WiFi to connect to Google's online photo service, Picasa, and uploads your images to a Picasa Web photo album automatically.

Can I make my old photos digital?

Obviously, not every document or image you have is in an electronic form. What about all the photographs you have already taken? What about an article from a magazine or a hand-drawn sketch? How can these be converted into digital format?

Digital scanners such as the ones shown in Figure 8.24 convert paper text and images into digital formats. You can place any flat material on the glass surface of the scanner and convert it into a digital file. Most scanner software allows you to store the converted images as RAW files or in compressed form as JPEG files. Some scanners include hardware that allows you to scan film negatives or slides as well or even insert a stack of photos to be scanned in sequence.

Scanner quality is measured by its resolution, which is given in dots per inch (dpi). Most modern scanners can digitize a document at resolutions as high as 4,800 × 9,600 dpi, in either color or grayscale mode. You can easily connect a scanner to your computer using USB 2.0 or FireWire ports. Scanners also typically come with software that supports optical character recognition (OCR). OCR software converts pages of handwritten or typed text into electronic files. You can then open and edit these converted documents with traditional word processing programs such as Microsoft Word. In addition, many scanners have a copy function that allows you to scan and print documents, taking the place of a copy machine.

How do I print a digital image?

You can print a digital image using a professional service or your own printer. Most photo printing labs, including the film processing departments at stores such as Wal-Mart and Target, offer digital printing services, as do many high-end online processing labs. The paper and ink used at processing labs are higher quality than what is available for home use and produce heavier, glossier prints that won't fade. You can send your digital photos directly to local merchants such as CVS and Walgreens for printing using Windows Live Photo Gallery. Online services, such as Flickr (**flickr.com**) and Shutterfly (**shutterfly.com**), store your images and allow you to organize them into photo albums or to create hard-copy prints, mugs, T-shirts, or calendars.

Photo printers for home use are available in two technologies: inkjet and dye sublimation (see Figure 8.25). The most popular and inexpensive ones are inkjet printers. As noted in Chapter 2, some inkjet printers are capable of printing high-quality color photos, although they vary in speed and quality. Some include a display window so that you can review the image as you stand at the printer, whereas others are portable, allowing you to print your photos wherever you are. Some printers even allow you to crop the image right at the printer without having to use special image editing software.

Unlike inkjet printers, which use an inkjet nozzle, dye-sublimation printers produce images using a heating element. The heating element passes over a ribbon of translucent film that has been dyed with bands of colors. Depending on the temperature of the element, dyes are vaporized from a solid into a gas. The gas vapors penetrate the photo paper before they cool and return to solid form, producing glossy, high-quality images. If you're interested in a printer to use for printing only

Figure 8.24

Scanners are available in a variety of shapes, but all of them can convert paper documents, photo prints, and strips of film negatives into digital data.

Figure 8.25

(a) The Kodak EasyShare inkjet system allows you to transfer and print pictures quickly and easily. (b) The Sony DPP-FP90 dye-sublimation printer produces professional-quality images that resist fading, water stains, and fingerprints.

photographs, a dye-sublimation printer is a good choice. However, some models print only specific photo sizes, such as 4″ × 6″ prints, so be sure the printer you buy will fit your long-term needs.

Transferring images to a printer is similar to transferring them to your computer. If you have a direct-connection camera, you can plug the camera directly into the printer with a cable. Some printers have slots that accept different types of flash memory cards. Of course, you also can transfer your images to the printer from your computer if you have stored them there.

Do I need to print out my photos? You may decide not to print your photos at all. As noted earlier, online albums let you share your photos without having to print them. Portable devices, such as Apple's iPod and cell phones, also enable you to carry and display your photos. The iPod, for example, can be connected to a TV and deliver slide shows of your photographs, complete with musical soundtracks you have selected.

Digital Video

Where does digital video come from? Digital video that you watch comes from several sources, but now people often create their own digital videos. As a video creator, you may purchase dedicated digital camcorders to record digital video. Most cell phones can record video, and digital cameras take video as well as digital still shots. Webcams also work as inexpensive devices for creating digital video.

There are many other sources of digital video available to you now. Television is broadcasting in digitally formatted signals.

The Internet delivers a huge amount of digital video through Google Video, YouTube, communities like Vimeo (**vimeo.com**), and webcasting sites like Ustream (**ustream.tv**). Many pay services are available to deliver digital video to you. These include on-demand streaming from cable providers, iTunes, Netflix's Instant Watch films, and Amazon's Video On Demand download service.

How do I record my own digital video? Video equipment for home use stores information in the digital video (DV) format. This allows the cameras to be incredibly small and light. Such cameras don't require any tapes at all; they store hours of video on built-in hard drives or flash cards. Some models even record directly to DVD discs.

You can easily transfer video files to your computer and, using video editing software, edit the video at home, cutting out sections, resequencing segments, and adding titles. To do the same with analog videotape would require expensive and complex audio/video equipment available only in video production studios. You can save (or *write*) your final product on a CD or DVD and play it in your home DVD system or on your computer. For true videophiles, cameras and burners are now available for high-definition video format.

What if I decide to add some special effects and a sound track? Video editing software presents a storyboard or *timeline* with which you can manipulate your video file, as shown in Figure 8.26. You can review your clips frame by frame or trim them at any point. You can order each segment on the timeline in whichever sequence you like and correct segments for color balance, brightness, or contrast.

In addition, you can add transitions to your video such as those you're used to seeing on TV—fades to black, dissolves, and so on. Just select the type of transition you want from the drop-down list and drag that icon into the timeline where you want the transition to occur.

Video editing software also lets you add titles, animations, and audio tracks to your video, including background music, sound effects, and additional narration. You can adjust the volume of each audio track to switch from one to the other or have both playing together. Finally, you can preview all of these effects in real time.

There is a lot to learn about digital video editing, and with the number of choices available, it is easy to be overwhelmed. Examine online tutorial resources such as Izzy Video podcasts (**izzyvideo.com**) to learn how to make the most impact with the editing and effects you apply to your raw video footage.

What kinds of files will I end up with? Once you're done editing your video file, you can save (or export) it in a variety of formats. Figure 8.27 shows some of the popular video file formats in use today, along with the file extensions they use.

Your choice of file format for your finished video will depend on what you want to do with your video. For example, the QuickTime streaming file format is a great choice if your file is really large and you plan to post it on the Web. The Microsoft AVI format is a good choice if you're sending your file to a wide range of users, because it's extremely popular and is commonly accepted as the standard video format for the Windows Media Player.

You also can try different compression choices to see which one does a better job of compressing your particular file. A **codec** (**c**ompression/**dec**ompression) is a rule,

Figure 8.26

Adobe Premiere Elements allows you to build a movie from video clips and add sound tracks and special effects.

Figure 8.27 | TYPICAL FILE FORMATS FOR DIGITAL VIDEO

Format	File Extension	Notes
QuickTime	.mov .qt	You can download QuickTime player without charge from **apple.com/quicktime**. The pro version allows you to build your own QuickTime files.
Moving Picture Experts Group (MPEG)	.mpg .mpeg .mp4	MPEG-4 video standard adopted internationally in 2000; recognized by most video player software.
Windows Media Video	.wmv	Microsoft file format recognized by Windows Media Player (included with the Windows OS).
Microsoft Video for Windows	.avi	Microsoft file format recognized by Windows Media Player (included with the Windows OS).
RealMedia	.rm	Format from RealNetworks; popular for streaming video. You can download the player for free at **real.com**.
Adobe Flash Video	.flv	Adobe Flash video format, sometimes embedded in Shockwave files (*.swf).

So you just returned from your trip to the Grand Canyon and all your friends are raving about the high quality of the photographs you took. You decide to put the photographs out on Flickr so your friends can see them. You also think that maybe someone might see your photos and want to use them in a commercial publication such as a magazine. Wouldn't that be cool? Because you own the copyright to your photos, you control how they can be used—and you want to protect your rights. You add a disclaimer to Flickr indicating that all rights are reserved on your photos. Anyone who wants to use them will need to contact you and request permission.

All of a sudden, you are bombarded by dozens of requests for permission to use your photographs for all sorts of purposes. A high school student in Illinois wants to feature one of your photos on her travel blog. A church in Georgia wants to use a photo for their newsletter to illustrate a story about a church member's trip to Arizona. An advertising agency in Seattle wants to modify your sunrise photo by inserting a family on a camping trip into the photo. You want to protect your rights (maybe the ad agency might even pay you!), but isn't there an easier way to manage photo permission requests?

Copyleft, a play on the word copyright, is designed for this situation. Copyleft is a term for various licensing plans that enable copyright holders to grant certain rights to the work while retaining other rights. The GNU General Public License is a popular copyleft license that is used for software. For other works, the Creative Commons, a nonprofit organization, has developed a range of licenses that can be used to control rights to works.

Creative Commons has various types of licenses available based on the rights you wish to grant. The company provides a simple form to assist you with selecting the proper license for your work. Creative Commons provides two licenses at **creativecommons.org/about/licenses** that could simplify your life. An *attribution license* permits others to copy, distribute, and display your copyrighted work, but only if they give you credit in the way you specify. Under this license, the high school student could use one of your photos as long as he or she gave you credit.

A *noncommercial license* allows anyone to copy, distribute, and display your work, but only for noncommercial purposes. The church in Georgia could use one of your photos under this license because it is not profiting from its use.

Both of these licenses can also be used to cover derivative works. A **derivative work** is based on the original work (one of your photos) but is modified in some way. The ad agency that wants to modify one of your photos is seeking permission to create a derivative work. If you had used an attribution license, the ad agency could use your work for a derivative purpose, but only if it attributed the original work to you as the author. If you had used a noncommercial license, the ad agency could not use your work to make a profit for itself.

The obvious advantage to using these Creative Commons licenses is that people won't constantly annoy you with permission requests to use your work. These licenses explain exactly how you are willing to have your work be used. Also, many advocates of copyleft schemes feel that creativity is encouraged when people are free to modify other people's work instead of worrying about infringing on copyright.

Opponents of Creative Commons licenses often complain that these licenses have affected their livelihoods. If millions of images are out on Flickr with Creative Commons licenses that permit free commercial use, professional photographers might have a tougher time selling their work. Furthermore, Creative Commons licenses are irrevocable. If you make a mistake and select the wrong license for your work, or you later find out a work is valuable and you've already selected a license that allows commercial use, you're out of luck.

Many people find listings of Creative Commons licenses confusing. If there is a Creative Commons disclaimer at the bottom of a group of photos, does that mean all the photos are available under that license, or just some of them? What actually constitutes commercial use? Is displaying Google Adsense ads on your blog commercial use?

You need to carefully consider the value of your intellectual property and decide how best to protect your rights. You should proceed carefully before giving up some of your rights under any copyleft license, especially if it is irrevocable. Nevertheless, using a copyleft scheme may be appropriate if it greatly simplifies your life in regards to managing permission requests.

---

implemented in either software or hardware, that squeezes the same audio and video information into less space. Some information will be lost using compression, and there are several different codecs to choose from, each claiming better performance than its competitors. Commonly used codecs include MPEG-4, H.264, and DivX. There is no one codec that is always superior—a codec that works well for a simple interview may not do a good job compressing a live-action scene.

What if I want a DVD with a menuing system? If you want a DVD with a menuing system, you can use special DVD authoring software such as Pinnacle Studio or Adobe Encore DVD. These DVD software packages often include preset selections for producing video for mobile devices (like the Apple iPod or the Sony PSP). These programs can also create final DVDs that have animated menu systems and easy navigation controls, allowing the viewer to move quickly from one movie or scene to another. Home DVD players as well as gaming systems such as PlayStation and Xbox can read these DVDs.

What is the quickest way to get my video out to viewers? Because of the popularity of videos on the Web, products and services are now available that let you quickly upload your videos. One such product is the Flip video camcorder from Pure Digital Technologies, shown in Figure 8.28.

The Flip camcorder, which retails at about $200, can record 60 minutes of video. After recording, simply flip out the USB connector and plug it into your computer. Flip has built-in software that lets you transfer the video file directly to YouTube (**youtube.com**) or e-mail the file. It's a simple solution that takes advantage of the easy Web-based distribution of video.

YouTube has a special Mobile Upload Profile that you can set up for your account. Once your unique e-mail address has been assigned, you can submit a video that you have on your phone to YouTube by e-mailing the file to the account address. Of course, it is illegal for you to upload videos you do not own. You also cannot take a piece of a copyrighted video and post it publicly. The Ethics in IT section in this chapter presents several legal and ethical situations that it is important for you to be aware of as a content creator in the digital age.

Figure 8.28

The Flip video camcorder is an inexpensive way to capture 60 minutes of HD video and post it on YouTube.

Webcasting, or broadcasting your video live to an audience, is another option that has become simpler. Inexpensive webcams (costing from $25 to $100) can be easily attached to your desktop or notebook computer. Many models of monitors have built-in webcams. Webcam models that are more expensive have motors that allow you to automatically rotate to track the sound, so you are always in the frame even if you are moving around the room. Services such as YouTube offer Quick Capture buttons, so with one click, your video can be shot and delivered to the Internet.

How can I distribute my video to the greatest number of viewers? Sites like **justin.tv** or **ustream.tv** let you quickly set up to webcast your video as it is captured to a live Internet audience. You can also display an interactive chat next to the video feed. Both the chat and the video are captured and archived for viewers who missed the live broadcast. iTunes offers free distribution of video podcasts, so you can build a following there for your video work.

Are the television shows and movies I watch digital? There are a number of ways you can create video content yourself; but probably most of the video you consume in a typical week was created by someone else—movie studios, television studios, or other students. The number of sources we have for video has increased dramatically since digital video appeared. Because the hardware for capturing video and the software for doing professional-level editing have become so inexpensive, there are few barriers to anyone making video. Further, because the opportunities for distributing video have broadened so much and become so instantaneous, there is an ever-growing market for more video.

Is all video digital video now? The switch to digital video as a broadcasting medium has happened over the past few years. As of June 13, 2009, all television stations were required to make the move to digital signal broadcasting. **DTV.gov** is a site that keeps consumers current on using conversion boxes to allow older television sets to operate with the new digital signal.

Movie production studios have also been moving toward digital video for many years. George Lucas, a great proponent of digital technology, filmed *Star Wars Episode II: Attack of the Clones* completely in digital format way back in 2002. It played in a special digital release at digital-ready theaters. And in January 2005, the digital film *Rize*, by David LaChapelle, premiered at the Sundance Film Festival. It was streamed from computers in Oregon to a full-size cinema screen in Park City, Utah, beginning a new age of movie distribution.

Since the conversion to digital TV signals, are there any more "free" television signals? Digital television signals now flood the air around you and can be picked up by a digital antenna. If you live in an area with good "over-the-air"

NTSC

HDTV

Extra image area

Letterbox

Figure 8.29

(a) Standard definition television has a more "square" aspect ratio, while (b) high-definition television matches the 16:9 ratio used in the motion picture industry without resorting to (c) letterboxing.

(OTA) reception, you can pick up crisp, high-quality digital versions of all the shows on local network affiliates for free.

How is HD different from "plain" digital? HD stands for *high definition*. It is a standard of digital television signal that guarantees a specific level of resolution and a specific *aspect ratio,* which is the rectangular shape of the image. A 1080 HD TV displays 1,920 vertical lines and 1,080 horizontal lines of video on the screen, which is over six times as many pixels as standard definition. The aspect ratio used is 16:9, which makes the screen wider, giving it the same proportions as the rectangular shape of a movie theater screen (see Figure 8.29). This allows televisions to play movies in the widescreen format that they were created for, instead of "letterboxing" the film with black bars on the top and the bottom of the screen.

What types of connectivity are provided on modern television sets? As video sources have increased, so have the number and types of connectors on a television. A typical HD set has at least three HDMI connectors, allowing game consoles, Blu-ray players, and cable boxes to be connected and produce the highest-quality output. HDMI is a single cable, with just one plug, that carries all of the video and all of the audio information. That means there is one connector, not three for different parts of the video signal and another two for the stereo sound signals!

Many sets have a built-in SD card reader. This allows users to display slide shows of photographs captured by their digital cameras. A PC VGA port is also included on most sets. This allows you to feed your computer's output video signal directly to the television so you can display an Internet browser or work on your files on the big screen. Some sets are now incorporating a wireless network adapter so the set can stream video from the Internet without having a separate computer connected. The Sony Bravia Internet Video link can deliver content on demand from a number of free sources (see Figure 8.30).

What advantages are there to watching digital video? Because the signal can be stored into computer memory as it is delivered, a digital video television show can be paused, or can be rewound in real time. Other information services can be integrated with the broadcast; so if a telephone call came through during the show, a pop-up could appear identifying the caller. The Sony Bravia series of televisions, for example, has Internet video capabilities that let you select "widgets" you can position on the screen to display the latest news, weather, sports, or other Internet downloads. In the future, there will be more interactivity integrated so you can participate in live polls or chats onscreen as the show is broadcast.

In movie studios, digital video is ushering in the age of "remixable" films. The components of these feature films—from production footage to soundtrack, dialogue, and sound effects—are available to the audience online, and each person is able to interact with and modify the film, creating a new plotline or a different ending. The MOD

Films site (**modfilms.com**) is one place where remixers gather.

Can I record the digital video that comes over my television? There are a variety of digital video recorders (DVRs) available to record the digital video from your television. These can record in either standard or HD quality and store the information on a hard drive. Useful features include being able to record two shows at once, being able to download movie purchases or rentals from the Internet directly to the DVR unit, and easily moving stored content to a mobile device like an iPod or a notebook. Using a DVR, you can pause live TV or set up a schedule to capture every episode of a series, no matter when it airs. Models like TiVo even recommend new shows you might like based on what you have been watching. If you don't want to purchase a DVR or pay the monthly subscription fee for DVR service, you can install PVR (personal video recording) software on your computer. When connected to your cable signal, programs like BeyondTV (**snapstream.com**) and SageTV (**sagetv.com**) turn your computer itself into a DVR.

How else can I get digital video to my TV? In addition to the broadcast content coming in to your TV, there are a number of streaming sources of digital video. Cable providers offer a wide range of on-demand video services. Many older films, as well as shows such as exercise classes, are offered free of charge. Other premium content, like new-release movies, is offered for a fee. Just one click and you can instantly watch any offered movie for 24 hours, with full control—stopping, starting, and rewinding. Other providers, like Netflix, also offer streaming video content. While Netflix's basic business model is to ship members DVDs physically in the mail, they now also offer Watch Instantly. Thousands of movies and TV series are available with just a click. You can view these shows on a television through an Xbox gaming console, a PC, or a specialized device like the Roku digital video player.

Figure 8.31

Slingbox can send your digital television content to your notebook or phone, wherever that may be.

Can I get digital video to watch on my portable device? Yes. Many DVR units, like TiVo, support software that allows you to transfer recorded shows to files on your PC and format them for viewing on an iPod, a PlayStation Portable, or another mobile device. There are also devices like Slingbox that take the video from your television and broadcast it to you over the Internet. With Slingbox, you can be in another room, or another country, and control and watch your home television on your notebook or your smartphone (see Figure 8.31).

Digital Mobility and Access

Once you are comfortable with digital communication and digital media, you'll want to be able to communicate and to access your music, files, and videos whether you are in front of a desktop at home or in an airport while traveling. Access to your digital assets is required in a modern business environment and is a great benefit for personal lifestyles. Earlier chapters discussed expensive solutions like notebook computers; but now there is a much wider range of devices that grant you access to your media and data wherever you are.

Selecting the Right Device

Do I need access to my digital assets all the time? Figure 8.32 presents a checklist of the factors you need to consider

Figure 8.30

Sony Bravia televisions use a wireless network adapter to stream digital video from a number of online sources.

Figure 8.32 | HOW IMPORTANT IS ACCESS TO DIGITAL ASSETS TO YOU?

Consideration	Yes	No
When I'm away from my desk, I need to **communicate** with others using both voice and e-mail.		
I need access to **my electronic files** wherever I am.		
I need access to **the Internet** wherever I am.		
The added **convenience and productivity** of mobile devices are important to me.		
My needs match the **limitations** of mobile devices (such as short battery life, small display screens, and slower Internet connection speeds).		
Most of my living and travel locations are **covered** by wireless Internet access.		
It is worth the added **expense** for me to go mobile.		

when deciding if you need a digital device when you are on the go. Do your needs to communicate and to access electronic information and the Internet when you're away from your desk make mobile devices a good investment?

How do I select the right device for my needs? There are a wide range of computing devices on the market today that give you varying access to digital

communication and digital media. A **netbook** runs a fully featured operating system but weighs in at 2 pounds or less. An **Internet tablet** is another type of very light, very portable device. Internet tablets do not offer full-size keyboards. Netbooks and Internet tablets can carry files, music, and videos as well as providing specialized services. Then there is the full range of notebooks and tablet computers. Figure 8.33 lists

Figure 8.33 | MOBILE DEVICES: PRICE, SIZE, WEIGHT, AND CAPABILITIES

Device	Relative Price	Approximate Size	Approximate Weight	Standard Capabilities
Cell phone	$$ (Includes cost for the phone, a monthly plan, and Internet access)	5″ × 2″ × 0.5″	0.25 lb.	Voice, e-mail, some application software, and Internet connectivity
PMP	$$–$$$	3″ × 2″ × 0.5″	0.25 lb. or more	Storage of digital music, video, and other digital files
Smartphone	$$–$$$	4.5″ × 2″ × .75″;	0.25 lb.	PIM capabilities, access to application software, and access to the Internet
Internet tablet	$$	3″ × 5″ × 0.5″	0.5 lb	Webcam, GPS, phone calls using Skype, sharp resolution, and widescreen display
Netbook	$$$$	7″ × 5″	1–2 lbs.	8″ to 10″ screens and run full-featured operating systems and applications
Tablet PC	$$$$$	10″ × 8″ × 1″	3 lbs.	PIM capabilities, access to application software, access to the Internet, and special handwriting- and speech-recognition capabilities
Notebook	$$$$–$$$$$	10″ × 13″ × 2″	5 to 8 lbs.	All the capabilities of a desktop computer plus portability

Emerging Technologies: Nanotubes—The Next Big Thing Is Pretty Darn Small!

In the classic 1967 film *The Graduate*, Dustin Hoffman is a young man uncertain about which career he should embark on. At a cocktail party, an older gentleman provides him with some career advice, telling him, "I've got just one word for you … plastics!" This made sense at the time because plastics were coming on strong as a replacement for metal. If *The Graduate* were remade today, the advice would be, "I've got just one word for you … nanotubes!"

As you learned in Chapter 1, nanoscience involves the study of molecules and structures (called *nanostructures*), whose size ranges from 1 nanometer to 100 nanometers (or one-billionth of a meter). Using nanotechnology, scientists are hoping to one day build resources from the molecular level by manipulating individual atoms instead of using raw materials already found in nature (such as wood or iron ore). This would allow us to create microscopic computers—the ultimate in portable devices. Imagine nano-sized robotic computers swimming through your arteries, clearing them of plaque. Consider carrying a supercomputer the size of a pencil eraser—or, even better, having the power of your desktop computer implanted in your body as a nano-sized chip.

The possibilities of miniaturization are endless, but what materials would be used to construct the computer circuits for these devices? Carbon nanotubes are poised to be the building blocks of the future. You're familiar with carbon from pencils. The graphite core in a pencil is composed of sheets of carbon atoms laid out in a honeycomb pattern. Individual sheets of graphite are extremely strong but don't bond well to other sheets. This makes them ideal for use in a pencil because, as you write, the graphite flakes off and leaves marks on the paper. Unfortunately, graphite doesn't conduct electricity well. This inability, coupled with the lack of strong bonding principles, makes graphite unsuitable as a material to manufacture circuits.

There needs to be a way to rearrange the carbon to give it just the behaviors we want. Carbon nanotubes, discovered in the 1950s, are the answer. A nanotube is essentially a sheet of carbon atoms (much like graphite) laid out in a honeycomb pattern but rolled into a spherical tube, as shown in Figure 8.34. Arranging the carbon in a tube increases its strength astronomically. It is estimated that carbon nanotubes are as much as 10 to 100 times stronger per unit of weight than steel. This should make them ideal for constructing many types of devices and building materials. Someday we may have earthquake-proof buildings constructed from nanotubes or virtually indestructible clothing woven from nanotube fibers.

How does this help us build a computer? Aside from strength, the most interesting property of nanotubes is that they are good conductors of electricity. Nanotubes are actually classified as *semimetal*, meaning they can have properties that are a cross between semiconductors (such as silicon, which is used to create computer chips) and metals. In fact, depending on how a nanotube is constructed, it can change from a semiconductor to a metal along the length of the tube. These properties make nanotubes vastly superior to silicon for the construction of transistor pathways in computer chips because they provide engineers with more versatility.

In addition, although the smallest silicon transistors that are likely to be produced in the future will be millions of atoms wide, scientists believe that transistors constructed of nanotubes would be only 100 to 1,000 atoms wide. This represents a quantum leap in miniaturization that surpasses even the original invention of the transistor. Just imagine what can be done when nanotube transistors replace silicon transistors!

So, when can you buy that pencil eraser–sized computer? Not for quite a while. At this point, researchers can manufacture nanotubes only in extremely small quantities at a large cost. However, the U.S. government and many multinational corporations are expected to pour billions of dollars into nanoscience research over the next decade. It is hoped that the ongoing research will lead to breakthroughs in manufacturing technology that will result in nano-scale computers within your lifetime.

Figure 8.34

Here is a highly magnified close-up of a carbon nanotube. Rolling the sheets of carbon atoms into a tube shape gives them incredible strength.

the main features of several different mobile devices.

What if I don't need a phone but do need Internet access? New offerings are hitting the market regularly. Tiny Internet-enabled devices are appearing that don't bother to include cell phone features at all. The Nokia N810 Internet tablet series

Figure 8.35

The Nokia N810 series Internet tablet features a touch screen and keypad and is designed primarily for Web surfing and sending e-mail.

(see Figure 8.35), for example, uses Skype or Gizmo for voice communications instead of a cell phone service. It has a high-resolution screen and WiFi connectivity so you can stream audio and video, use Web e-mail clients, and access Web sites. It features an RSS reader so you can peruse the latest from the sites you are following. Memory expands with SD expansion cards.

What if I need a larger screen and keyboard? If you require a larger screen and more processing power, then look at a category of emerging computer systems known as *netbooks* or *subnotebooks*. Examples include the Asus Eee PC and the Dell Inspiron Mini 9 (see Figure 8.36). Netbooks pack major computing power into a tiny package, and manufacturers try to extend battery life as long as possible. Screen sizes are typically between 8" to 10", and keyboards are less than full sized. No optical drive is integrated but one can be connected as a separate peripheral via the USB port. Netbooks often come with a Windows operating system. Some users opt to install a flavor of Linux, however, because Linux requires fewer resources than Windows. Solid-state hard drives are a good choice because they use

Figure 8.36

Subnotebooks like the Asus Eee PC weigh in at less than two pounds but run fully featured operating systems.

less power and produce less heat. Many models include integrated webcams as well as Bluetooth, so while netbooks are small and light, they still can serve many functions.

What if all I really need is to bring my books with me? For avid readers of e-books (books stored as electronic files), the Amazon Kindle DX (see Figure 8.37) or the Sony Reader Digital Book could be what you are looking for. These feature internal RAM, but also support flash memory cards for more storage. You can get approximately 7,500 turned pages on one charge, so on long plane flights this may be the device you use most. Color e-books are appearing as well. The Fujitsu FLEPia e-book reader has a color touch screen that can display 260,000 colors. It also can support e-mail, spreadsheets, and Web browsing, so it is part e-book and part computer.

Are portable gaming systems able to do any real work? Many portable gaming systems are very sophisticated. The Sony PlayStation Portable (PSP) can play video games but also includes a Web browser, Skype, and an RSS reader. It uses Sony Memory Sticks to store data files, videos, music, and images. The screen is a 4.3" widescreen design with great clarity and brightness. The PSP can even connect over the Internet to your PlayStation 3 system at home and display the videos or music stored there for you wherever you are.

Ubiquitous Computing

What is in the future for our digital lifestyles? Mark Weiser, a researcher at Xerox's PARC laboratories, has predicted that "computing will be woven into the fabric of everyday life until it is indistinguishable from it." This concept is called

Figure 8.37

The Amazon Kindle DX is designed to store as many as 3,500 e-books and is about 1/3" thick.

ubiquitous computing (or *ubicom*). More and more styles of digital devices are being introduced, but there is a second force at work. Digital computing devices are increasingly embedded in appliances, clothing, cars—all the items we physically interact with in our day. The era of "smart things" is just beginning.

How will our lifestyles change as computing becomes everywhere and invisible? Researchers and inventors like Mike Kuniavsky of ThingM are creating devices that exploit the new digital nature of our world to make tasks easier. The WineM product from ThingM is a good example (see Figure 8.38). WineM is a "smart" wine rack. Each bottle is labeled with a radio frequency identification (RFID) tag

when it is stored by the owner. When it is time to pick the perfect bottle for dinner, the owner can ask the wine rack to show just the Chardonnay, and LEDs light up just those bottles. WineM can also display which wines are ready to drink, or if any of your friends has a similar wine collection, or if the winery is having a sale. It updates information automatically and will e-mail or text you an alert when a bottle of wine is removed from the rack.

The evolution of information to a digital form is allowing us to change our relationship to objects. Items like bicycles and cars can become "subscriptions" instead of large one-time purchases. Call a Bike is a program run in Germany. At most major street corners, there is a rack of Call a Bikes

Figure 8.38

The smart WineM Rack answers queries from its controller, (a) like "Show me all of the California wines I have that are ready to drink and under $50 in value." (b) In response WineM lights up the bottles that fit the criteria.

Figure 8.39

Call a Bike uses digital technology to change our lifestyle from one of ownership to one of "subscription."

(see Figure 8.39). Place a call to the phone number printed on the bike, and it texts you a code you can use to unlock the bike lock. Ride the bike to where you're going. When you arrive, re-lock it. The amount of time you rode it automatically is billed (by the minute) to your phone.

City CarShare is another system using the digital communication of information to change our lifestyle habits. Many cities, like San Francisco and Philadelphia, now offer a City CarShare program. Residents sign up for the program and receive a key that has an RFID chip in it. All cars are connected to a central network. You can open a City CarShare car and start the engine only when your specific key is scheduled to open and start it. GPS technology is used to track where the car is, whether it has been dropped off at the right location, and how far it has been driven. The entire process is transparent to City CarShare members. Members have 24/7 access to a vehicle—a truck, a hybrid, a convertible—when they need it, with very little advance notice, for a cost of about $6.00 an hour. Gas and insurance are included.

With the rise of portable computing devices, the idea of ubiquitous networking has been generating a lot of interest. Ubiquity in computing essentially means (a) being able to have access to and exchange information wherever you happen to be, and (b) having access to the key information that you need when you need it. How can networking move us closer to that goal? There are two popular approaches.

The Network Is Watching You (Hello, Big Brother!)

Instead of having to move the files and programs you need onto mobile devices, how about having a network that "watches" your movements and moves the data so that it follows you? Researchers at telecommunications companies such as the AT&T Laboratories at Cambridge University are attempting to make this possible by creating a detection system that can track your location within a building, moving your files wherever you go. To take advantage of the network, users will carry a small device called a "bat," shown in Figure 8.40. This device will have a unique ID number and contain a radio transceiver and transmitter. A detection system (or central controller) installed in the building will keep track of the physical location of the bats (and of the people who carry them).

How does this system work? Suppose you go into a conference room that contains a computer and a phone. The controller is tracking the bat you have in your pocket, so it knows you have entered the conference room and therefore routes all your phone calls to the phone in the conference room. It also sends your files and desktop settings to the computer in the conference room.

What if two people are in the conference room at the same time? The controller assigns available devices to the

first person who enters the room. However, using interactive buttons on your bat, you can indicate to the controller that you wish to take temporary possession of a device assigned to another person.

Take Your Computer's Soul with You

Another option would be to take not just your data files with you (say, on a flash drive), but instead to take your entire computer with you (virtually, of course). IBM is conducting a research project called SoulPad that attempts to achieve this miracle of portability. Using a portable storage device (IBM has used iPods in its testing), you save a suspended image of your computer, including all desktop settings and data files (essentially the "soul" of your computer), before leaving your main computer. When you arrive at another computer, you attach the portable storage device. Your computer data and settings then are loaded onto the remote computer so that you can pick up exactly where you left off. In testing, this has been piloted on computers running Windows and Linux. What is making this technology possible is the availability of tiny, high-capacity storage devices, high-speed data transfer (via FireWire or USB 2.0), and virtualization software. Eventually, it will probably be possible to deploy the SoulPad on a smartphone. This is convergence at the next level!

As we achieve ubiquity in computing, we will have to rethink our territorial approach to work and living spaces, as well as some of our ideas about privacy. In the future, because our data might follow us around (or we'll take it all with us), access to our personal information may always be right where we are.

Figure 8.40

Bats are about the size of a pager and therefore are small enough to be carried comfortably. They allow the detection system to locate the bat owners wherever they roam in the facility.

1. What are the changes that have brought us a digital lifestyle?

The increased use of digital information has led to a period of greater creativity and control of our data. In a digital format, information is easy to carry, manipulate, and exchange. This has led to revolutionary changes in communication, entertainment media, and mobile computing.

2. How has the move to digital information affected the communication tools important to both the business world and life outside of work?

The age of digital information has brought new opportunities and challenges to businesses. Some have had to struggle to shift their business models to the new style of information. Because information can be shared so easily, issues of copyright and intellectual property have become critical. In our personal lives, we see products that allow us to interact with information in ways that had been too expensive or difficult before.

3. How do cell/smartphone components resemble a traditional computer, and how do they work?

Like a traditional computer, a cell/smartphone has a central processor, memory, and an operating system. These components work in the same way as in a computer to process information and support communications, software applications, and other services.

4. Why would I use VoIP, and what does it offer that is unique?

VoIP allows inexpensive communication using a computer or a WiFi-enabled phone. Because it is based on a digital format for information, it can support services like on-screen caller ID with your television or automatic delivery of phone messages to an e-mail account.

5. How is digital media different from analog?

Digital media is based on a series of numeric data comprising number values that were measured from the original analog waveform. As a string of numbers, a digital photo or video file can be easily processed by modern computers.

6. What can I carry in a portable media player, and how does it store data?

Most PMPs can store any kind of digital information—photos, videos, or music files as well as data files. Some PMPs store data on a hard drive, while others use flash memory. Some also allow the amount of memory to be upgraded, while others have a fixed amount of memory.

7. What ways are there for me to create and to watch digital video?

You can create digital video using any digital camera, webcam, or digital camcorder. Digital editing software allows you to add transitions, effects, and sound tracks. There are a great many sources of digital video, including free sources like YouTube and JustIn, as well as pay-per-view services like Amazon Video On Demand or cable providers' streaming video options.

8. What changes does ubiquitous computing bring to our lifestyles?

As computers become smaller and less obvious, they will begin to integrate into our lifelike appliances rather than complicated tools. Ubiquitous computing is beginning to allow us to move some objects from an ownership model to a subscription service model.

key terms

Word Bank

- analog-to-digital converter
- Bluetooth
- cell phone
- GPS
- Internet tablet
- microbrowser
- MMS
- netbook
- P2P
- PMP
- sampling rate
- smartphone
- SMS
- synchronize
- telephony
- ubiquitous computing
- VoIP
- WML

Instructions: Fill in the blanks using the words from the Word Bank above.

Elizabeth knows that everything seems to be "digital" these days. In the past, she carried a traditional SLR camera but now she uses her simple (1) _____ to take photos. She can connect wirelessly to the computer to transfer the images because the phone supports (2) _____. Sometimes she doesn't bother to do that because she has already sent a(n) (3) _____ message to a friend with the image. Her old phone couldn't do that because it only supported (4) _____. If she upgraded to a(n) (5) _____, she could actually make many refinements and edits to the image without transferring it to the computer at all.

Pete is a real fan of technology, and so he has selected a(n) (6) _____ instead of a cell phone. He's always near a WiFi signal, so he doesn't need an actual phone. He doesn't even pay for traditional phone service at home, where he uses (7) _____ instead of a land-line. He's fallen in love with his new device for many reasons. It can give him driving directions with its built-in (8) _____. The (9) _____ software displays full HTML Web pages right on the device. To keep this device coordinated with the data on his computer, he makes sure to (10) _____ the data each night.

Niti can't quite decide what device will work best for his new life. He's moving to California and plans to be outside a lot, so he wants something very light. He thinks the two-pound (11) _____ might be ideal because he doesn't really need a full keyboard or a huge screen. When he's out biking, he'll just wear his (12) _____ on his arm to keep the tunes flowing. He downloads free songs offered by bands that are just starting out from a(n) (13) _____ site. The songs have a much lower (14) _____ than he usually demands, but at least they don't take up much space on his hard drive. He's heard that electronics are merging with clothing more and more, so maybe soon (15) _____ will lead to a T-shirt that can take care of his mobile music needs!

becoming computer literate

Instructions: Write a report providing answers to the question posed below, using as many of the key terms from the chapter as you can. Be sure the sentences are grammatically and technically correct.

You have a limited budget to spend on technology tools and toys in the years you will be a student. You are considering communication, entertainment media, and your need to be able to work and connect with your information when you are not at home. Which digital media services and products would you definitely invest in? How would you justify their value? What kinds of services and products would you use that are free or low cost? Has the migration to a digital lifestyle given you more freedom and creativity or just caused you more annoyance and expense?

Instructions: Answer the multiple-choice and true–false questions below for more practice with key terms and concepts from this chapter.

Multiple Choice

1. Digital communication is useful only in professions
    a. that don't rely on Internet access.
    b. where work requires intensive graphics and large display screens.
    c. where work requires intensive computer processing power.
    d. None of the above.

2. Currently, cell phones contain ALL of the following except
    a. a CPU.
    b. output devices.
    c. hard drives.
    d. input devices.

3. Cell phones store data
    a. on memory cards.
    b. in RAM.
    c. in ROM.
    d. All of the above.

4. To fit more songs on a personal media player, you can
    a. decrease the sampling rate of digitized music files.
    b. install additional ROM in the PMP.
    c. increase the sampling rate of digitized music files.
    d. install a larger hard drive in the PMP.

5. Digital video allows us to
    a. create our own high-definition videos and distribute them.
    b. create our own personalized endings to films.
    c. deliver our recorded television shows to our phone.
    d. All of the above.

6. A Nokia N810 Internet tablet is useful to consider when
    a. you need an inexpensive cell phone.
    b. you plan to create computationally intensive graphics.
    c. you need Internet access and a large screen, and can use Skype to communicate.
    d. you need to have a full-sized keyboard.

7. GPS chips are
    a. installed in all newly manufactured automobiles.
    b. installed in all newly manufactured cell/smartphones.
    c. reliable only when installed in a stand-alone GPS device.
    d. available only for smartphones.

8. For Internet access, you should obtain
    a. a smartphone.
    b. a cell phone.
    c. a netbook.
    d. All of the above support Internet access.

9. "Ubiquitous computing" is a phrase that means
    a. Ubisoft is the best gaming company.
    b. Computers have the capability to do everything.
    c. You should be using a computer to do every task.
    d. Computers are small enough to be integrated invisibly into our lives.

10. Netbooks have become very popular because
    a. they have such large, clear screens.
    b. they feature full-sized keyboards with numeric keypads.
    c. they run fully featured operating systems but weigh less than two pounds.
    d. they do only one thing—connect to the Internet—but they do it very well.

True-False

_____ 1. VoIP will soon be available to homes and not just businesses.

_____ 2. PMPs with a hard drive are able to carry fewer songs than those with flash memory.

_____ 3. Intellectual property rights always favor the consumer of the content.

_____ 4. Some digital cameras feature wireless file transfer and automatic upload of images to the Internet.

_____ 5. Smartphones run Windows 7 as an operating system.

making the
transition to...
next semester

eight chapter

making the
transition to...
next semester

1. Choosing Devices to Fit Your Needs

As a student, which devices discussed in this chapter would have the most immediate impact on the work you do each day? Which would provide the best value (that is, the greatest increase in productivity and organization per dollar spent)? Consider the full range of devices, from cell phones to notebook systems.

2. Keeping Your Content

As a student, you create large numbers of products each semester—papers, videos, software programs, presentations. How do you organize and display them? Will they be available to you if you transfer to another school or apply for a job? How do you store, organize, and use those files to show the growth of your skills and abilities? Are there devices or services discussed in this chapter that would support you in doing that?

3. Do You Still Need a Phone?

Explore Skype (**skype.com**) as an alternative to paid telephone service. What equipment would you need to use Skype as your everyday communication medium? Skype now works on the iPhone. When would this be useful? What telephone services and features would you lose if you went to Skype?

4. Choosing the Best Phone

Your friend wants to trim down the number of different devices that she carries. Visit the most popular cellular providers' Web sites and research options. Which phone would you recommend to your friend, and why? Compare at least three different models of phones and list their price, music storage capacity, built-in memory, and expandability options.

a. Which of the three models you compared is the best value for your friend?
b. What special features does the phone you chose have? What accessories would you recommend your friend buy to make the phone more useful?
c. Would you suggest buying a refurbished phone? Why or why not?

5. iTunes U

Download a free copy of iTunes software. In the iTunes Store, explore the iTunes U podcast directory, which contains free audio and video lectures published by major universities.

a. Look for the MIT Open Courseware video podcasts. How many lectures are available from MIT (Massachusetts Institute of Technology)?
b. If each lecture were 90 minutes on average and approximately 200 MB in size, how much storage would it take to save all of the video lectures in every course published by MIT?
c. Is there a mobile device that can store and play that much content? What devices could store the lectures from all of the courses in mathematics offered by MIT Open Courseware?

making the transition to ... the workplace

1. Corporate Mobile Communications Needs

Imagine your company is boosting its sales force and looking to the future of mobile technology. Your manager has asked you to research the following issues surrounding mobile communications for the company:

a. Do mobile communication devices present increased security risks? What would happen if you left a cell phone at a meeting and a competitor picked it up? Are there ways to protect your data on mobile devices?

b. Can viruses attack cell phones? Is there any special software on the market to protect mobile devices from viruses? How much would it cost to equip 20 devices with virus protection?

c. Is there a role for mobile communication devices even if employees don't leave the building? Which devices would be important for a company to consider for use within corporate offices? Are there software solutions that would work as well?

d. Should employees be allowed to use mobile phones provided by the company for personal use even though files related to personal use might eat up potentially valuable memory and space? What restrictions should be put on personal use to protect the privacy of proprietary company information contained on the devices?

2. 3G Communications

The current generation of telecommunications (nicknamed "3G" for third generation) allows the speed of cellular network transmissions to hit 3 Mbps. How does that compare to dial-up and cable modem access over wired networks? What implications does it have for information access and e-commerce? What download speed would be ideal? Upload speed?

3. Subscription versus Ownership

Consider the examples of Call-a-Bike and CarShare. Are there other businesses you can identify that would be able to take advantage of digital information and become subscription services instead of vendors of a physical product? What are the advantages to the consumer of subscription over ownership? What are the drawbacks?

4. Too Much Media?

Imagine you are a manager of 18 employees, all of whom work with constant Internet access. As a manager, what concerns might you have about their use of corporate bandwidth to download and view media files? Do you think it would benefit your business to block any MP3 file transfers? Should you put in place a block to prevent access to sites that store huge numbers of streaming videos? As a manager, are there concerns you might have if employees have digital cameras on their cell phones? What would you do if an employee records a meeting with you on his cell phone without your knowledge?

5. Mobile Devices on the Highway

Mobile devices used in vehicles are becoming the norm in today's society. Consider the following:

a. Several car manufacturers provide Bluetooth option packages for their vehicles. What advantages are there to having Bluetooth connectivity in your car? Are there any disadvantages?

b. Examine the Microsoft Sync software package. List the features and services it provides. If you were a salesperson with a territory that you covered by car, how would Sync help you?

Instructions: Albert Einstein used *Gedankenexperiments*, or critical thinking questions, to develop his theory of relativity. Some ideas are best understood by experimenting with them in our own minds. The following critical thinking questions are designed to demand your full attention but require only a comfortable chair—no technology.

1. Digital Entertainment

Can you name a style of media that has not made the shift to digital? What advantages does digital photography offer? Digital video? What disadvantages come along with a digital format for entertainment media? Has the growth in digital media promoted an increased understanding between people or has it created more isolation?

2. The Ultimate Style

As ubiquitous computing continues to evolve, devices become lighter and smaller, and we are beginning to see a convergence of computing and clothing.
a. What would the ultimate convergent mobile clothing be for you? Is there a limit in weight, size, or complexity?
b. Can you imagine uses for technology in fashion that would support better health? Better social relationships? A richer intellectual life?

3. Protecting Intellectual Property

The recording industry, recording artists, the motion picture industry, and consumers find themselves in a complex discussion when the topic of peer-to-peer sharing systems is brought up.
a. Have you ever downloaded music, movies, or software from the Web? Did you download in a legal manner? Did the media you downloaded have any associated DRM (digital rights management)? Do you think peer-to-peer download sites should be allowed to exist in their current form?
b. Now, imagine yourself as a video creator. You spend hours on your home computer producing a short weekly cartoon video that you are hoping will lead to a career in animation. How can you build an audience for your work? How could you expand your audience and still garner some income from the cartoon series?

4. Next Wave Is Nano

As nanotechnology continues to mature as a science, what impacts will we begin to see on our digital lifestyle? How will communications change? How might our consumption of digital media change? What new privacy and intellectual property rights challenges may appear?

5. Privacy Concerns: GPS Tracking at Home

Consider the following questions related to GPS security risks:
a. Your spouse carries a GPS-enabled cell phone. The GPS chip inside allows a private service (**ulocate.com**) to gather information on your spouse's last location, the path he or she took to get there, and his or her average speed from point to point. Would you use the service to check on your spouse's activities? What if your spouse was monitoring you?
b. Would you agree to insert a GPS-enabled tracking device into your pet? Your child? What legislation do you think should be required if tracking data was available about you? Would you be willing to sell that information to marketing agencies? Should that data be available to the government if you were suspected of a crime?

6. Electronic Publishing

Explore the specifications of the Sony Portable Reader and the Amazon Kindle. How would your study habits change if your textbooks were only delivered to you in electronic format on one of these E-reader machines? What unique advantages would there be? What disadvantages would there be? How would using an E-reader compare with just receiving the book as an electronic file, such as a PDF document?

Assisting with the Move to a Digital Lifestyle

Problem

You have formed a consulting group that advises clients on how to move their businesses and personal lives into the age of the digital lifestyle.

Task

Each team will be defined as an expert resource in one of the digital areas presented in this chapter: digital communication, digital media, or digital mobility. For each scenario described by a client, the group should assess the kinds of technologies that will meet and enhance the client's needs.

Process

Divide the class into three or four teams and assign each group a different digital lifestyle focus (communication, media, or mobility).

1. Research the current digital technologies emerging in the area your team has been assigned.
2. Consider the following three clients:
   - A retired couple who now travel for pleasure a great deal. They want to be involved in their grandchildren's lives and will need support for their health and personal care as they age.
   - A young family with two children, two working parents, and a tight budget.
   - A couple in which each individual is a physician and both adore technology.
3. Make two recommendations for your client in terms of digital technologies that will enhance their business or their lifestyle. Discuss the advantages and disadvantages of each technology. Consider value, reliability, computing needs, and communication needs, as well as expandability for the future.
4. As a group, prepare a final report that considers the costs, availability, and unique features of the recommendations you have made for each client.
5. Bring the research materials from the individual team meetings to class. Looking at the clients' needs, make final decisions as to which digital technologies are best suited for each client.

Conclusion

Digital information has allowed the development of a new style of living, both at home and at work. With so many digital solutions on the market today, recommending digital communication, media management, and mobility options depends on factors such as value, reliability, expandability, and the needs of the client.

In addition to the review materials presented here, you'll find additional materials featured with the book's multimedia, including the *Technology in Action* Student Resource CD and the Companion Website (**pearsonhighered.com/techinaction**), which will help reinforce your understanding of the chapter content. These materials include the following:

Active Helpdesk

In Active Helpdesk calls, you'll assume the role of helpdesk operator, taking calls about the concepts you've learned in this chapter. You'll apply what you've learned and receive feedback from a supervisor to review and reinforce those concepts. The Active Helpdesk calls for this chapter are listed below and can be found on your Student Resource CD:

- Keeping Your Data on Hand
- Using Portable Media Players

Sound Bytes

Sound Bytes are dynamic multimedia tutorials that help demystify even the most complex topics. You'll view video clips and animations that illustrate computer concepts and then apply what you've learned by reviewing with the Sound Byte Labs, which include quizzes and activities specifically tailored to each Sound Byte. The Sound Bytes for this chapter are listed below and can be found on your Student Resource CD.

- Smartphones Are Really Smart
- Connecting with Bluetooth

Companion Website

The *Technology in Action* Companion Website includes a variety of additional materials to help you review and learn more about the topics in this chapter. The resources available at **pearsonhighered.com/techinaction** include

- **Online Study Guide.** Each chapter features an online true–false and multiple-choice quiz. You can take these quizzes, automatically check the results, and e-mail the results to your instructor.
- **Web Research Projects.** Each chapter features several Web research projects that ask you to search the Web for information on computer-related careers, milestones in computer history, important people and companies, emerging technologies, and the applications and implications of different technologies.

nine

digital lifestyle:

protecting digital data and devices

resources

Active Helpdesk

Sound Bytes

Companion Website

The Companion Website includes a variety of additional materials to help you review and learn more about the topics in this chapter. Go to: *pearsonhighered.com/techinaction*

how cool is *this?*

Protect your surfing like a pro. When you use **public hotspots** to surf, your Internet activity is subject to **snooping** by prying eyes. Hotspot Shield (**hotspotshield.com**) is a free **software utility** that ensures all of your data is transmitted across the Internet through a virtual private network (VPN). A VPN is a secure Internet pathway that large corporations use to protect sensitive data. Using the VPN **shields your data**, such as information in forms you fill out, credit card data, instant messages, and Web browsing activities, from the prying eyes of hackers. So install Hotspot Shield today and surf with confidence.

Keeping Your Data Safe

The media is full of stories about computer viruses damaging computers, criminals stealing people's identities online, and attacks on corporate Web sites that have brought major corporations to a standstill. These are examples of **cybercrime**, which is defined as any criminal action perpetrated primarily through the use of a computer. The existence of cybercrime means that computer users must take precautions to protect themselves (see Figure 9.1).

Who perpetrates computer crimes? **Cybercriminals** are individuals who use computers, networks, and the Internet to perpetrate crime. Anyone with a computer and the wherewithal to arm him- or herself with the appropriate knowledge can be a cybercriminal.

What kind of cybercrimes are conducted over the Internet? The Internet Crime Complaint Center (IC3) is a partnership between the Federal Bureau of Investigation (FBI) and the National White Collar Crime Center (NW3C). In 2008, the latest year for which data is available, IC3 processed more than 275,000 complaints related to Internet crime. Many complaints were fraud-related, such as auction fraud, nondelivery of ordered items, and credit and debit card fraud. Non-fraud–related complaints pertained to issues such as computer intrusions, unsolicited e-mail, and child pornography. The majority of complaints (more than 58 percent) were related to three key areas: Internet auction fraud, nondelivery of merchandise, and failure to pay. Much of this credit card fraud was perpetrated when credit card numbers were stolen by phishing (tricking people into revealing sensitive information) or by virus programs that gather credit card data.

Are computer viruses a type of cybercrime? Creating and disseminating computer viruses is one of the most widespread types of cybercrimes. Tens of thousands of new viruses or modified versions of old viruses are released each year. The effect of a computer virus varies widely. Some cause only minor annoyances, while others cause wanton destruction of data. Many viruses are now designed to gather sensitive information such as credit card numbers. The Conficker virus that broke out in late 2008 infected an estimated 15 million computers in a few weeks, which illustrates how serious a threat a virus can pose to your digital security. You need to make sure your data is protected from viruses and other malicious software attacks.

Does cybercrime include the theft of computing devices? Although theft of computer equipment is not classified as a cybercrime (rather, it is considered larceny), the theft of notebook computers, cell phones, iPods, and other portable computing devices is on the rise. The resale value for used electronic equipment is high, which contributes to demand for stolen merchandise. The ease with which equipment can be sold online also fuels this problem.

In this chapter, we discuss serious threats to your digital security (such as computer viruses and other activities of cybercriminals), less serious annoyances (such as spyware and spam), and good security practices to keep yourself from undermining your digital security. We also discuss methods for protecting your digital assets from attacks and damage.

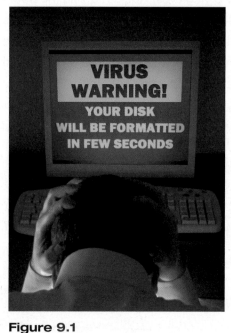

Figure 9.1

Cybercrimes, including virus attacks, are a serious problem for Web surfers.

Computer Threats: Computer Viruses

One of the most serious threats to digital security is computer viruses. A computer **virus** is a computer program that attaches itself to another computer program (known as the *host program*) and attempts to spread to other computers when files are exchanged. Viruses normally attempt to hide within the code of a host program to avoid detection.

What do computer viruses do? A computer virus's main purpose is to replicate itself and copy its code into as many other files as possible. Although virus replication can slow down networks, it is not usually the main threat. The majority of viruses have secondary objectives or side effects, ranging from displaying annoying messages on the computer screen to destroying files or the contents of entire hard drives. Because computer viruses cause disruption to computer systems, including data destruction and information theft, virus creation and deployment is a form of cybercrime.

How does my computer catch a virus? If your computer is exposed to a file infected with a virus, the virus will try to copy itself and infect a file on your computer. If you never expose your computer to new files, it will not become infected. However, this would be the equivalent of a human being living in a bubble to avoid catching viruses from other people—quite impractical.

Downloading infected audio and video files from peer-to-peer file sharing sites is a major source of virus infections. Shared disks or flash drives are also a common source of virus infection, as is e-mail, although many people have misconceptions about how e-mail infection occurs. Just opening an e-mail message will not infect your computer with a virus. Downloading or running a file that is attached to the e-mail is how your computer becomes infected. Thus, be extremely wary of e-mail attachments, especially if you don't know the sender. Figure 9.2 illustrates the steps by which computer viruses are often passed from one computer to the next.

1. A hacker writes a virus program disguised as an MP3 file of a popular music group's new hit song to a file sharing site.

Figure 9.2

Computer viruses are passed from one unsuspecting user to the next.

Step 1: Virus creation.

Hacker's computer

File sharing server

Step 2: Initial virus infection.

Bill's computer

Coworker's computer

Coworker's computer

Fred's work computer

Step 3: Virus spreads to another computer.

Step 4: Virus spreads to work computer.

Step 5: Other computers susceptible to infection.

Fred's home computer

2. Unsuspecting Bill downloads the "music file" and infects his computer.

3. Bill sends his cousin Fred an e-mail with the infected "music file" and contaminates Fred's computer.

4. Fred saves the MP3 file to a flash drive and then copies it to his work computer and infects that machine as well.

5. Everyone who copies files from Fred's infected computer at work, or whose computer is networked to Fred's computer, is at risk to spread the virus.

Types of Viruses

Although thousands of computer viruses and variants exist, they can be grouped into six broad categories based on their behavior and method of transmission.

Boot-Sector Viruses

What are boot-sector viruses? A **boot-sector virus** replicates itself into a hard drive's master boot record. The **master boot record** is a program that executes whenever a computer boots up, ensuring that the virus will be loaded into memory immediately, even before some virus protection programs can load. Boot-sector viruses are often transmitted by a flash drive left in a USB port. When the computer boots up with the flash drive connected, the computer tries to launch a master boot record from the flash drive, which is usually the trigger for the virus to infect the hard drive. Boot-sector viruses can be extremely destructive.

Logic Bombs and Time Bombs

What is a logic bomb? A **logic bomb** is a virus that is triggered when certain logical conditions are met—such as opening a file, or starting a program a certain number of times. A **time bomb** is a virus that is triggered by the passage of time or on a certain date. For example, the Michelangelo virus, first launched in 1992, was a famous time bomb that was set to trigger every year on March 6, Michelangelo's birthday. The BlackWorm virus (otherwise known as Kama Sutra, Mywife, or CME-24), another time bomb, spreads

through e-mail attachments. Opening the attachment infects the computer, and on the third day of every month, the virus seeks out and deletes certain file types (such as executable or EXE files) on Windows computers. The effects of logic bombs and time bombs range from display of annoying messages on the screen to reformatting of the hard drive, which causes complete data loss.

Worms

What is a worm? A **worm** is slightly different from a virus in that a worm attempts to travel between systems through network connections to spread an infection. A virus infects a host file and waits until that file is executed on another computer to replicate. A worm, however, works independently of host file execution and is much more active in spreading itself. The Conficker worm broke out in November 2008 and quickly infected an estimated 9 to 15 million individual computers. This worm spread through vulnerabilities in the Windows code and compromised computers by disabling certain software services and utility programs (such as Windows Update). Fortunately, it is easy to protect yourself from most worms. Installing antivirus software and a firewall is a good start. You also should apply software patches (code issued by the manufacturers of software such as Windows that repairs known security problems) to your computer whenever they are issued. We discuss protective measures later in the chapter.

Script and Macro Viruses

What are script and macro viruses? Some viruses are hidden on Web sites in the form of scripts. A **script** is a series of commands—actually, a miniprogram—that is executed without your knowledge. Scripts are often used to perform useful, legitimate functions on Web sites such as collecting name and address information from customers. However, some scripts are malicious. For example, say you receive an e-mail encouraging you to visit a Web site full of useful programs and information. When you click a link to display a video on the Web site you were directed to, a script runs that infects your computer with a virus without your knowledge

A **macro virus** is a virus that attaches itself to a document (such as a Word or Excel file) that uses macros. A macro is a short series of commands that usually automates repetitive tasks. However, macro languages are now so sophisticated that viruses can be written with them. In March 1999, the Melissa virus became the first major macro virus to cause problems worldwide. It attached itself to a Word document.

The Melissa virus was also the first practical example of an **e-mail virus**. E-mail viruses use the address book in the victim's e-mail system to distribute the virus. Anyone opening an infected document triggered the virus, which infected other Word documents on the victim's computer. Once triggered, the Melissa virus sent itself to the first 50 people in the address book on the infected computer. This helped ensure that Melissa became one of the most widely distributed viruses ever released.

Encryption Viruses

What are encryption viruses?

Encryption viruses are the newest form of virus. When these viruses infect your computer, they run a program that searches for common types of data files (such as Microsoft Word and Excel files) and compresses them using a complex encryption key that renders your files unusable. You then receive a message that asks you to send money to an account if you want to receive the program to decrypt your files. The flaw with this type of virus, which keeps it from being widespread, is that law enforcement officials can trace the payments to an account and may possibly be able to catch the perpetrators. Still, we see these types of viruses from time to time.

Avoiding Computer Viruses

In this Active Helpdesk call, you'll play the role of a helpdesk staffer, fielding calls about different types of viruses and what users should do to protect their computer from them.

Virus Symptoms

If your computer displays any of the following symptoms, it may be infected with a virus:

1. Existing program icons or files suddenly disappear. (Viruses often delete specific file types or programs.)
2. Changes appear in your browser. If you fire up your browser and it takes you to an unusual home page (one you didn't set) or it has new toolbars, then you may have a virus.
3. Odd messages or images are displayed on the screen or strange music or sounds play.
4. Data files become corrupt. Although files become corrupt for many reasons, a virus is one cause.
5. Programs don't work properly. This could be caused by either a corrupted file or a virus.

If you think you have a virus, boot up your computer with an antivirus software DVD (or CD) in your DVD/CD drive. This allows you to run the antivirus software before potential viruses load on the computer. Are you looking for free antivirus software? Consider downloading AVG Antivirus Free Edition (**free.avg.com**).

Virus Classifications

How else are viruses classified?

Viruses can also be classified by the methods they take to avoid detection by antivirus software:

- A **polymorphic virus** changes its own code (or periodically rewrites itself) to avoid detection. Most polymorphic viruses infect one type of file (.exe files, for example).
- A **multipartite virus** is designed to infect multiple file types in an effort to fool the antivirus software that is looking for it.
- **Stealth viruses** temporarily erase their code from the files where they reside and then hide in the active memory of the computer. This helps them avoid detection if only the hard drive is being searched for viruses. Fortunately, antivirus software developers are aware of, and have designed software to watch for, these tricks.

Given the creativity of virus programmers, you can be sure we'll see other types of viruses emerge in the future. In the next section, we discuss preventing virus infections.

Computer Safeguard: Antivirus Software and Software Updates

Certain viruses merely present minor annoyances, such as randomly sending an ambulance graphic across the bottom of the screen, as is the case with the Red Cross virus. Other viruses can significantly slow down a computer or network, or destroy key files or the contents of entire hard drives. The best defense against viruses is to install **antivirus software**, which is specifically designed to detect viruses and protect your computer and files from harm. Norton, Kaspersky, AVG, and McAfee are among the companies that offer highly rated antivirus software packages.

Although you can buy stand-alone antivirus software, antivirus protection is included in comprehensive Internet security packages such as Norton Internet Security, Kaspersky Internet Security, or McAfee Total Protection. These software packages will help protect you from other threats as well as from computer viruses.

Antivirus Software

How often do I need to run antivirus software? Although antivirus software is designed to detect suspicious activity on your computer at all times, you should run an active virus scan on your entire system at least once a week. By doing so, all files on your computer will be checked for undetected viruses. Because these checks take time, you can configure the software to run them automatically when you aren't using your system—for example, late at night (see Figure 9.3). Alternatively, if you suspect a problem, you can launch a scan and have it run immediately.

How does antivirus software work? Most antivirus software looks for virus signatures in files. A **virus signature** is a portion of the virus code that is unique to a particular computer virus. Antivirus software scans files for these signatures and thereby identifies infected files and the type of virus that is infecting them.

The antivirus software scans files when they're opened or executed. If it detects a virus signature or suspicious activity (such as the launch of an unknown macro), it stops the execution of the file and virus and notifies you that it has detected a virus. It also places the virus in a secure area on your hard drive so that it won't spread infection to other files. This procedure is known as **quarantining**. Usually the antivirus software then gives you the choice of deleting or repairing the infected file. Unfortunately, antivirus programs can't always fix infected files to make them usable again. You should keep backup copies of critical files so that you can restore them in case a virus damages them irreparably.

Most antivirus software will also attempt to prevent infection by inoculating key files on your computer. In **inoculation**, the antivirus software records key attributes about files on your computer (such as file size and date created) and keeps these statistics in a safe place on your hard drive. When scanning for viruses, the antivirus software compares the files to the attributes it previously recorded to help detect attempts by virus programs to modify your files.

Does antivirus software always stop viruses? Antivirus software catches known viruses effectively. Unfortunately, new viruses are written all the time. To combat unknown viruses, modern antivirus programs search for suspicious viruslike activities as well as virus signatures. However, virus authors know how antivirus software works. They take special measures to disguise their virus code and hide the effects of a virus until just the right moment. This helps ensure that the virus spreads faster and farther. Thus, your computer can be attacked by a virus that your antivirus

Figure 9.3

In Norton Internet Security, complete virus scans can be set up to run automatically. This computer will be scanned every Tuesday at 8 P.M.

software doesn't recognize. To minimize this risk, you should keep your antivirus software up to date.

How do I make sure my antivirus software is up to date? Most antivirus programs have an automatic update feature that downloads updates for virus signature files every time you go online (see Figure 9.4).

What should I do if I think my computer is infected with a virus? Boot up your computer with the antivirus installation DVD/CD in your DVD drive. (Note: If you download your antivirus software from the Internet, it is a good idea to copy your antivirus software to a DVD in case you have problems in the future.) This should prevent most virus programs from loading and will allow you to run the antivirus software directly from the DVD drive. If the software does detect viruses, you may want to research them further to determine whether your antivirus software will eradicate them completely or whether you will need to take additional manual steps to eliminate the virus. Most antivirus company Web sites, such as the Symantec site (**symantec.com**), contain archives of information on viruses, and provide step-by-step solutions for removing viruses.

Are instant messenger programs safe from virus attacks? Virus attacks and other forms of malicious hacking are being perpetrated at an alarming rate via instant messenger (IM) programs such as AOL Instant Messenger and Windows Live Messenger. Even if you have antivirus protection installed, people still could contact you for the purposes of trying to trick you into revealing sensitive information. Therefore, you should try to hide your instant messaging activity from everyone except people that you know. To keep your IM sessions safe, follow these precautions:

1. **Allow contact only from users on your Buddy or Friends List.** This prevents you from being annoyed by unknown parties. On the settings screen for your IM program (Figure 9.5), select Allow only users on my Buddy List. And, of course, don't put anyone you don't know and trust on your buddy list.

2. **Never automatically accept transfers of data.** Although file and video transfers are potentially useful for swapping files over IM (see Figure 9.5), they are a common way of transmitting malicious

Click to check for updates

Figure 9.4

Antivirus software, such as Norton Internet Security, provides for automatic updates to the software installed on the computer.

files, which can then infect your computer with viruses. Enabling auto-acceptance of data transfers is never a good idea.

3. **Avoid using instant messaging programs on public computers.** If you use a shared computer, such as one in a computer lab at school, be sure you don't select any features that remember your password or connect you automatically. The next person who uses the computer might be able to connect to the instant messaging service with your screen name and impersonate you.

Software Updates

Is there anything else I should do to protect my system? Many viruses exploit weaknesses in operating systems. Malicious Web sites can be set up to attack your computer by downloading harmful software

SOUND BYTE Protecting Your Computer

In this Sound Byte, you'll learn how to use a variety of tools to protect your computer, including antivirus software and Windows utilities.

Figure 9.5

When you use instant messenger programs, check all of the preference screens for appropriate settings.

your operating system as easy as updating your antivirus program. Windows provides an automatic update utility called Windows Update. When you enable automatic updates, your computer searches for Windows updates on the Microsoft Web site every time it connects to the Internet. OS X has a similar utility for gathering updates.

Do updates only happen automatically? Although many people decide to receive updates automatically, there are several options you can choose from in Windows, as shown in

onto your computer. According to research conducted by Google, this type of attack, known as a **drive-by download**, is common and affects almost one in one thousand Web pages. To combat these threats, make sure your antivirus software and your operating system are up to date and contain the latest security patches. You can make updating

Figure 9.6. The following options are noteworthy:

- Option 1: **Install updates automatically:** Selecting this option will automatically download and install updates at a time you have specified. We strongly recommend that you select this option.

- Option 2: **Download updates but let me choose whether to install them:** Although this option automatically downloads updates, they are not installed until you instruct Windows to install them. We don't usually recommend this option because you may forget to install important updates.

- Option 3: **Check for updates but let me choose whether to download and install them:** This is an appropriate choice if you have low bandwidth Internet access. Because downloads over dial-up can take a long time due to low bandwidth, you need to control when downloads will occur so they don't interrupt your workflow.

- Option 4: **Give me recommended updates:** This option ensures you receive recommended (optional) updates as well as critical (necessary) updates.

- Option 5: **Microsoft Update:** This option ensures you receive updates for other Microsoft products besides Windows (such as Microsoft Office).

Figure 9.6

The Windows Update screen makes it easy for users to configure Windows to update itself.

>To enable automatic updates, click **Start**, select **Control Panel**, select **System and Security**, click the **Windows Update** link, and then click the **Change Settings** link.

In the next section, we explore another major threat to your digital security—hackers.

Computer Threats: Hackers

Although there is a great deal of disagreement as to what a hacker actually is (especially among hackers themselves), a **hacker** is most commonly defined as anyone who unlawfully breaks into a computer system—either an individual computer or a network (see Figure 9.7).

Are there different kinds of hackers?

Some hackers are offended by being labeled as criminals and therefore attempt to classify different types of hackers. A hacker who breaks into systems just for the challenge of it (and who don't wish to steal or wreak havoc on the systems) may refer to him- or herself as a **white hat hacker**. These individuals tout themselves as experts who are performing a needed service for society by helping companies uncover the vulnerabilities in their systems.

White hat hackers look down on those hackers who use their knowledge to destroy information or for illegal gain. A term for these more villainous hackers is **black hat hacker**. (The terms *white hat* and *black hat* are references to old Western movies in which the heroes wore white hats and the outlaws wore black hats.) Regardless of the hackers' opinions, the laws in the United States and in many other countries consider any unauthorized access to computer systems a crime.

What about the teenage hackers who are caught every so often?

These amateur hackers are often referred to as **script kiddies**. Script kiddies don't create the programs they use to hack into computer systems; instead, they use tools created by skilled hackers that enable unskilled novices to wreak the same havoc as professional hackers. Although these tools can be found on the Web, using such tools

(even ones created by someone else) to penetrate computer systems is a crime.

Fortunately, because the users of these programs are amateurs, they're usually not proficient at covering their electronic tracks. Therefore, it's relatively easy for law enforcement officials to track them down and prosecute them. Script kiddies nevertheless can cause a lot of disruption and damage to computers, networks, and Web sites before they're caught.

Why would a hacker be interested in breaking into my home computer?

Some hackers just like to snoop. They enjoy the challenge of breaking into systems and seeing what information they can find. Other hackers are hobbyists seeking information about a particular topic wherever they can find it. Because many people keep proprietary business information on their home computers, hackers bent on industrial espionage may break into home computers. For other hackers, hacking is a way to pass time.

What Hackers Steal

Could a hacker steal my credit card number? If you perform financial transactions online, such as banking or buying goods and services, then you probably do so using a credit (or debit) card. Credit card

Figure 9.7

Although they do not necessarily destroy civilization, hackers can cause problems for corporations and individuals alike.

Be Careful When Joining Social Networking and Video Sites

Making contacts and meeting friends online has never been easier. Social networking services such as MySpace (**myspace.com**) and Facebook (**facebook.com**) are signing up users at a rapid pace. Another site, YouTube (**youtube.com**), allows you to post videos of yourself and your friends. These services have you list personal information about yourself (interests, hobbies, photos, what school you attend, and so on) and encourage you to list connections to your friends. When your friends log on and view your profile, they can see themselves and long chains of other acquaintants. The idea is that your friends can see who else you know and get you to make appropriate introductions (or do it themselves).

Although the sites offer fairly tight protection of personal information (such as not revealing last names), think carefully about making your personal information visible on a site and be wary of disclosing additional information to people you meet online. Often children and young adults, who account for a large percentage of the users on these sites, are too trusting about revealing personal information. Cybercriminals are combing these sites with the sole purpose of using the information to perpetrate identity theft. Therefore, always avoid giving out personal information such as your full name, address, Social Security number, or financial information to people you have never met. Also, be careful when uploading videos of yourself or your friends. Identity thieves often like to steal younger people's identities because the identity theft of minors takes longer to detect.

Finally, be wary of accepting computer files from people you've met online, because these files could contain viruses or other destructive software. Just because you meet someone who is a friend of a friend of your second cousin doesn't mean that person isn't a hacker or a scam artist. So, enjoy meeting new people, but exercise the appropriate amount of caution.

not enable encryption of data when they set up their wireless networks (covered in Chapter 7). This makes it easy for hackers to intercept and read sensitive information transmitted in plain text, such as credit card numbers or the contents of e-mails.

What do hackers do with the information they "sniff"? Once a hacker has your credit card information, he or she can either use it to purchase items illegally or sell the number to someone who will. If a hacker steals the login ID and password to an account where you have your credit card information stored (such as eBay or Amazon), he or she can also use your account to purchase items and have them shipped to him- or herself instead of to you. If hackers can gather enough information in conjunction with your credit card information, they may be able to commit identity theft. **Identity theft** is characterized by someone using personal information about you (such as your name, address, or Social Security number) to assume your identity for the purpose of defrauding others.

Although this sounds scary, you can easily protect yourself from packet sniffing by installing a firewall (which we discuss later in this chapter) and using data encryption on a wireless network (which was covered in Chapter 7).

and bank account information can thus reside on your hard drive and may be detectable by a hacker. Also, many sites require you to provide a login ID and password to gain access. Even if this data is not stored on your computer, a hacker may be able to capture it when you're online by using a packet sniffer.

What's a packet sniffer? Data travels through the Internet in small pieces, each called a **packet**. The packets are identified with an IP address, in part to help identify the computer to which they are being sent. Once the packets reach their destination, they are reassembled into cohesive messages. A **packet sniffer** is a program that looks at (or sniffs) each packet as it travels on the Internet—not just those that are addressed to a particular computer, but all packets. Some packet sniffers are configured to capture all the packets into memory, whereas others capture only packets that contain specific content (such as credit card numbers). Wireless networks can be particularly vulnerable to this type of exploitation because many people do

Trojan Horses

Besides stealing information, what other problems can hackers cause if they break into my computer? Hackers often use individuals' computers as a staging area for mischief. To perpetrate widespread computer attacks, for example, hackers need to control many computers at the same time. To this end, hackers often use Trojan horses to install other programs on computers. A **Trojan horse** is a program that appears to be something useful or desirable (like a game or a screen saver), but while it runs does something malicious in the background without your knowledge. The term *Trojan horse* derives from Greek mythology and refers to the wooden horse that the Greeks used to sneak into the city of Troy and conquer it. Therefore, computer programs that contain a hidden (and usually dreadful) "surprise" are referred to as Trojan horses.

What damage can Trojan horses do? Often, the malicious activity perpetrated by a Trojan horse program is the installation of a **backdoor program** that allows hackers to take almost complete control of your computer without your knowledge. Using a backdoor program, hackers can access and delete all the files on your computer, send e-mail, run programs, and do just about anything else you can do with your computer. A computer that a hacker controls in this manner is referred to as a **zombie**. Zombies are often used to launch denial-of-service attacks on other computers.

Denial of Service Attacks

What are denial-of-service attacks?

In a **denial-of-service (DoS) attack**, legitimate users are denied access to a computer system because a hacker is repeatedly making requests of that computer system through a computer he or she has taken over as a zombie. A computer can handle only a certain number of requests for information at one time. When it is flooded with requests in a denial-of-service attack, it shuts down and refuses to answer any requests for information, even if the requests are from a legitimate user. Thus, the computer is so busy responding to the bogus requests for information that authorized users can't gain access.

Couldn't a DoS attack be traced by to the computer that launched it?

Launching a DoS attack on a computer system from a single computer is easy to trace. Therefore, most savvy hackers use a **distributed denial-of-service (DDoS) attack**, which launches DDoS attacks from more than one zombie (sometimes thousands of zombies) at the same time. Figure 9.8 illustrates how a DDoS attack works. A hacker creates many zombies (sometimes hundreds or thousands) and coordinates them so that they begin sending bogus requests to the same computer at the same time. Administrators of the victim computer often have a great deal of difficulty stopping the attack because it comes from so many computers. Often the attacks are coordinated automatically by botnets. A **botnet** is a large group of software programs (called *robots* or *bots*) that runs autonomously on zombie computers. Some botnets have been known to span 1.5 million computers.

DDoS attacks are a serious problem. In January 2008, Scientology Web sites became the victims of DDoS

Figure 9.8

Zombie computers are used to facilitate a distributed denial-of-service (DDoS) attack.

Hacker launches DDoS by activating zombies (red lines)

Hacker's computer

Academic computer (zombie)

Government computer (zombie)

Home computer (zombie)

Corporate computer (zombie)

ISP computer (zombie)

Zombie computers attack target system (blue lines)

Victim of DDoS

Prevention of Identity Theft . . . Don't Overlook Photocopiers!

We are constantly bombarded with identity theft warnings regarding suspicious e-mail, phishing sites, and telephone scams. Many people are unaware that photocopiers, too, present a risk of identity theft. This is because most photocopiers manufactured today contain hard drives, just as computers do. Documents are scanned, stored on the hard drive, and then printed by the copier. So, unless the copier has been specially configured to have the hard drive overwritten to destroy data or to use encryption, copies of your tax return may be lurking on the public copier at your local library or copy shop that you used before you mailed your return to the Internal Revenue Service. A clever hacker could retrieve a wealth of potential information off just one public copy machine.

So what should you do to protect yourself? Ask the local copy shop or public library, or the IT department at your office, about the security measures they have set up on their copiers before you use them to copy sensitive documents. If you are buying a copier for your business, investigate security options that are available to protect your employees. For small copying jobs (such as your tax return), consider buying an all-in-one device (combining a printer, copier, scanner, and fax machine) for your home office because you can more easily keep that machine protected from wily hackers.

remove key components (such as the power cord) when strangers such as repair personnel are in your house and may be unobserved for periods of time. You might also set up your computer so that it requires a password for a user to gain access to your desktop.

The most likely method a hacker will use to access a computer is to enter indirectly through its Internet connection. When connected to the Internet, your computer is potentially open to attack by hackers. Many people forget that their Internet connection is a two-way street. Not only can you access the Internet; people on the Internet can also access your computer.

Think of the computer as a house. Common sense tells you to lock your doors and windows to deter theft when you aren't home. Hooking your computer up to the Internet is like leaving the front door to your house wide open. Anyone passing by can access your computer and poke around for valuables. Your computer obviously doesn't have doors and windows like a house, but it does have logical ports.

What are logical ports? Logical **ports** are virtual—that is, not physical—communications gateways or paths that allow a computer to organize requests for information (such as Web page downloads or e-mail routing) from other networks or computers. Unlike physical ports (USB, FireWire, and so on), you can't see or touch a logical port; it is part of a computer's internal organization.

Logical ports are numbered and assigned to specific services. For instance, logical port 80 is designated for hypertext transfer protocol (HTTP), the main communications protocol (or standard) for the Internet. Thus, all requests for information from your browser to the Web flow through logical port 80. E-mail messages sent by simple mail transfer protocol (SMTP), the protocol used for sending e-mail on the Internet, are routed through logical port 25. Open logical ports, like open windows in a home, invite intruders, as illustrated in Figure 9.9. Unless you take precautions to restrict access to your logical ports, other people on the Internet may be able to access your computer through them.

Fortunately, you can thwart most hacking problems by installing a firewall.

attacks by a group that called itself "Anonymous," and whose members were linked to an anti-Scientology campaign called Project Chanology. In April 2009, the International Federation of the Phonographic Industry (IFPI) and Motion Picture Association of America (MPAA) Web sites were subjected to DDoS attacks in protest of the conviction of the owners of The Pirate Bay (a notorious file-sharing site) on charges of assisting in copyright infringement. Because many Web sites receive revenue from users, either directly (such as via subscriptions to online games) or indirectly (such as when Web surfers click on advertisements), DDoS attacks can be financially distressing for the owners of the affected Web sites.

How Hackers Gain Access

How exactly does a hacker gain access to a computer? Hackers can gain access to computers directly or indirectly. Direct access involves sitting down at a computer and installing hacking software. It is unlikely that such an attack would occur in your home. However, to deter unauthorized use, you may want to lock the room that your computer is in or

Restricting Access to Your Digital Assets

Keeping hackers at bay is often just a matter of keeping them out. This can be achieved either by preventing them from accessing your computer (usually through your Internet connection), by protecting your digital information in such a way that it can't be accessed (with passwords, for example), or by hiding your activities from prying eyes. In the next section, we explore strategies for protecting access to your digital assets and keeping your Internet surfing activities from being seen by the wrong people.

Although installing either a software or a hardware firewall on your home network is probably sufficient, you should consider installing both for maximum protection.

What software firewalls are there? Firewalls for home networks are mostly offered through comprehensive security packages such as Norton Internet Security, McAfee Internet Security, and ZoneAlarm Internet Security Suite. Most current operating systems also include reliable firewalls. These products are easy to set up and include options that allow the software to make security decisions for you based on the level of security you request. These programs also come with monitoring systems that alert you if your computer is under attack. The newest versions of these programs have "smart agents" that automatically stop attacks as they are detected by closing the appropriate logical ports or disallowing the suspicious activity.

What are hardware firewalls? You can also buy and configure hardware firewall devices. For example, when buying a router for your network, make sure to buy one that also acts as a firewall. Manufacturers such as Linksys, Belkin, and Netgear make routers that double as firewalls. Just like software firewalls, the setup for

Figure 9.9

FTP (Port 21) — YOUR COMPUTER — DNS (Port 53) — HTTP (Port 80) — E-mail (Port 25) — Telnet (Port 23) — WEB SITE REQUEST

Open logical ports are an invitation to hackers.

Firewalls

A **firewall** is a program or hardware device designed to keep computers safe from hackers. A firewall specifically designed for home networks is called a **personal firewall**. Personal firewalls are made to be easy to install. By using a personal firewall, you can close open logical ports to invaders and potentially make your computer invisible to other computers on the Internet.

Firewalls are named after a housing construction feature. When houses were first being packed densely into cities, they were attached to each other with common walls. Fire was a huge hazard because wood (the major construction component for houses) burns readily. An entire neighborhood could be lost in a single fire. Thus, builders started building common walls of nonflammable or slow-burning material to stop, or at least slow, the spread of fire. These came to be known as firewalls.

Types of Firewalls

What kinds of firewalls are there?

As noted earlier, firewalls can be configured using either software or hardware devices.

ACTIVE HELP-DESK — Understanding Firewalls

In this Active Helpdesk call, you'll play the role of a helpdesk staffer, fielding calls about how hackers can attack networks and what harm they can cause, as well as what a firewall does to keep a computer safe from hackers.

Firewalls are designed to restrict access to a network and its computers. Firewalls protect you in two major ways: by blocking access to logical ports and by keeping your computer's network address secure.

To block access to logical ports, firewalls examine data packets that your computer sends and receives. Data packets contain information such as the address of the sending and receiving computers and the logical port the packet will use. Firewalls can be configured so that they filter out packets sent to specific logical ports. This process is referred to as **packet filtering**.

For example, file transfer protocol (FTP) programs are a typical way in which hackers access a computer. Hackers can disguise their requests for information as legitimate packets that appear to be FTP requests authorized by your computer. If a firewall is configured to ignore *all* incoming packets that request access to port 21 (the port designated for FTP traffic), no FTP requests will get through to your computer. This process is referred to as **logical port blocking**. If port 21 were a window at your home, you : would probably lock it so that a burglar 'couldn't get in. If you needed port 21 for a legitimate purpose, you could instruct the firewall to allow access to that port for a specified period of time or by a certain user.

For the Internet to share information seamlessly, data packets must have a way of getting to their correct locations. Therefore, every computer connected to the Internet has a unique address called an **Internet Protocol address** (or **IP address**). As noted earlier, data packets contain the IP address of the computer to which they are being sent. Routing servers on the Internet make sure the packets get to the correct address. This is similar to the way addresses work on a conventional letter. A unique street address (such as 123 Main St., Anywhere, CA 99999) is placed on the envelope and the postal service routes it to its correct destination. Without such addressing, data packets, like letters, would not reach the intended recipients.

IP addresses are assigned in a procedure known as **dynamic addressing** when users log on to their Internet service provider (ISP). This is illustrated in Figure 9.10. IP addresses are assigned out of a pool of available IP addresses licensed to the ISP in this manner:

1. When you connect to your ISP, your computer requests an IP address.
2. The ISP's Web server consults its list of available IP addresses and selects one.
3. The selected IP address is communicated to your computer. The address remains in force for as long as you are connected to the ISP.
4. Once on the Internet, your Web browser requests access to ABC Company's Web site.
5. The ABC Company server consults an IP address listing and determines that the IP address of your computer is assigned to your ISP. It then forwards the requested information to the ISP's Web server.
6. The ISP's Web server knows to whom it assigned the IP address and, therefore, forwards the requested information to your computer.

Because hackers use IP addresses to find victims and come back to their computers for more mischief, frequently switching IP addresses helps make users less vulnerable to attacks. Periodically switching off your modem and rebooting it will cause a different IP address to be assigned dynamically to your

Figure 9.10

How dynamic addressing works.

---

hardware firewalls is designed for novices, and the default configuration keeps unnecessary logical ports closed. Documentation accompanying the firewalls can assist users with more experience in adjusting the settings to allow access to specific ports if needed.

Knowing Your Computer Is Secure

How can I tell if my computer is at risk? For peace of mind (and to ensure that your firewall setup was successful), you can visit several Web sites that offer free services that test your computer's vulnerability. One popular site is Gibson Research (**grc.com**). The company's ShieldsUP and LeakTest programs are free, easy to run, and can pinpoint security vulnerabilities in a system that is connected to the Internet. If you get a clean report from these programs, your system is probably not vulnerable to attack. Figure 9.12 shows the results screen

Step 1 **Step 2**

Step 4 **Step 3**

Router IP address:
111.22.3.44

Your computer's internal
IP address: 112.11.4.13

ABC Company
Web server

Hacker

Figure 9.11

Network address
translation in action.

modem by your ISP. This tends to enhance your security.

However, because many broadband (cable and DSL) users leave their modems on for long periods of time (consecutive days or weeks), their IP addresses tend to change less frequently than those of dial-up users. This is similar to having an IP address assigned by **static addressing**. In static addressing, your IP address is always the same and is assigned by your ISP. This process is often used by businesses who are hosting a Web site. When a broadband user has a static address, the user is more vulnerable to hackers because the hackers have a more permanent IP address with which to locate the computer. It also makes it easier for hackers to make repeated visits to a computer.

To combat the problems associated with static addressing, firewalls use a process called **network address translation (NAT)** to assign internal IP addresses on a network. These internal IP addresses are only shared with devices that are part of the network, so the addresses are safe from hackers. Figure 9.11 shows how NAT works. Your computer's internal IP address is assigned to your computer by the router. This IP address is used only on the internal network and therefore cannot be detected by other Internet users. Here's how it works:

1. Your computer's Web browser requests access to the ABC Company's Web site. This request travels through the router, which is configured as a firewall.

2. The router forwards the browser request to the ABC Company Web server and directs that server to send the data back to the router IP

address (in this example, 111.22.3.44). The internal IP address of your computer (assigned by NAT) is not revealed to computers outside your network.

3. The ABC Company Web server processes the request and sends the data back to the router IP address (111.22.3.44). This is the IP address the ISP assigned to your router, and it can be detected by other users on the Internet.

4. The router then passes the requested data to the IP address of the computer that requested it (in this example, 112.11.4.13).

The router's IP address is assigned by your ISP. Only the router's IP address can be detected by other users on the Internet. For hackers to access your computer, they must know your computer's IP address. With a NAT capable router/firewall installed on your network, hackers are unable to access the internal IP address assigned to your computer, so your computer is safe.

You can use NAT in your home by purchasing a hardware firewall with NAT capabilities. As noted earlier, many routers sold for home use are also configured as firewalls, and many feature NAT as well.

143	IMAP	Closed	Your computer has responded that this port exists but is currently closed to connections.
389	LDAP	Closed	Your computer has responded that this port exists but is currently closed to connections.
443	HTTPS	Closed	Your computer has responded that this port exists but is currently closed to connections.
445	MSFT DS	Stealth	There is NO EVIDENCE WHATSOEVER that a port (or even any computer) exists at this IP address!
1002	ms-ils	Closed	Your computer has responded that this port exists but is currently closed to connections.
1024	DCOM	Closed	Your computer has responded that this port exists but is currently closed to connections.
1025	Host	OPEN!	One or more unspecified Distributed COM (DCOM) services are opened by Windows. The exact port(s) opened can change, since queries to port 135 are used to determine... ...here. As is the rule for all exposed Intern... ...close this port to external access so tha... ...curity or privacy exploits can not succeed against your system.

Ports safe from attack

Port subject to attack

Figure 9.12

ShieldsUP common ports test results

from a ShieldsUP port probe test, which checks which logical ports in your computer are vulnerable. This test was run on a computer connected to the Internet with no firewall installed. Ports reported as closed or in stealth mode are safe from attack. Ports reported as open (such as port 1025) are subject to exploitation by hackers. Installation of a hardware or software firewall should close any open ports.

What if I don't get a clean report from the testing program? If the testing program detects potential vulnerabilities and you don't have a firewall, you should install one as soon as possible. If the firewall is already configured and common ports (such as those shown in Figure 9.13) are identified as being vulnerable, consult your firewall documentation for instructions on how to close or restrict access to those ports.

Preventing Bluetooth Attacks

What are the security vulnerabilities of Bluetooth devices? Bluetooth is a transmission medium for exchanging data wirelessly over short distances. Most smartphones are Bluetooth enabled. Although progress is being made, Bluetooth hardware and software still are riddled with security holes, especially on smartphones. If you have a Bluetooth-enabled device, you are susceptible to two severe types of mischief:

- **Bluesnarfing:** Bluesnarfing involves exploiting a flaw in the Bluetooth access software for the purpose of accessing a Bluetooth device and stealing the

information contained on it. Think how much valuable information is contained on your smartphone (names, contact information, and meeting notes) that might be valuable to a business competitor. Unfortunately, Bluesnarfing is relatively easy (and cheap) because a lot of Bluesnarfing software is available on the Internet.

- **Bluebugging:** Although much more difficult and expensive to execute, Bluebugging presents more serious dangers. The process involves a hacker actually taking control of a Bluetooth-enabled device. Once a hacker gains control of the device, he or she can make phone calls; establish Internet connections; read phonebook entries; set call forwarding; or send, receive, and read short message service (SMS) messages.

- This is a major risk in Europe because Bluetooth and SMS are wildly popular there, but the rise of Bluetooth usage in the United States is making it a risk here as well. Many cars in the United States are now equipped with Bluetooth so that owners can connect their mobile devices (such as phones and GPS units) to the car's systems. Many Europeans use their phones to make micropayments (small purchases from merchants that eventually appear on their cell phone bill) by a process known as *reverse SMS*. If a hacker Bluebugs your phone, he could potentially send payments to fake accounts he or she controls, using reverse SMS.

How can I protect myself from Bluetooth attacks? Most devices with Bluetooth capability give you the option of making your device invisible to unauthorized Bluetooth devices. This does not affect your ability to use two Bluetooth devices you own together (such as a wireless headset paired with a phone). When you pair your headset with your phone, the headset (which has a unique serial number) becomes an authorized Bluetooth device for your phone. Moreover, by making your device invisible to unauthorized devices (such as hackers' headsets), you prevent hackers from connecting to your equipment (your phone) because their headsets are not

Figure 9.13 │ COMMON LOGICAL PORTS

Port Number	Protocol Using the Port
21	FTP (file transfer protocol) control
23	Telnet (unencrypted text communications)
25	SMTP (simple mail transfer protocol)
53	DNS (domain name system)
80	HTTP (hypertext transfer protocol)
443	HTTPS (HTTP protocol with transport layer security [TLS] encryption)

authorized devices for your phone. When vulnerabilities are discovered, smartphone manufacturers issue software patches. Antivirus software is also available for mobile devices, so you may wish to purchase this for your smartphone. You must ensure that you update the software in your mobile devices just as you do your computer's OS and antivirus software. For more information on securing your Bluetooth devices, go to the Bluetooth Technology Web site (**bluetomorrow.com**).

Password Protection and Password Management

Passwords, used in conjunction with login IDs, are the major way we restrict access to computers, networks, and online accounts. You no doubt have many passwords that you need to remember to access your digital life. However, creating strong passwords— ones that are difficult for hackers to guess— is an essential piece of security that individuals sometimes overlook. Password cracking programs have become more sophisticated lately. In fact, some commonly available programs, such as John the Ripper, can test more than 1 million password combinations per second! Creating a secure password is therefore more important than ever.

Creating Passwords

What constitutes a strong password?
Strong passwords are difficult for someone to guess. They should not contain easily deduced components related to your life such as parts of your name, your pet's name, your street address, or your telephone number. To create strong passwords, follow the basic guidelines shown here:

- Your password should contain at least 14 characters and include numbers, symbols, and upper- and lowercase letters.

- Your password should not be a single word or any word found in the dictionary.

- Ideally, it should be a combination of several words with strategically placed uppercase characters.

- Your password should not be easily associated with you (such as your birth date, the name of your pet, or your nickname).

- Use a different password for each system or Web site you need to access. This prevents access to other accounts you maintain if one of your passwords is discovered. (If you can't remember them all, use the password management feature of Windows or of the Firefox browser.)

- Never tell anyone your password or write it down in a place where others might see it.

- Change your password on a regular basis (say every month) and change it sooner if you think someone may know it.

Figure 9.14 shows some possible passwords and explains why they are strong or weak candidates.

How can I check the strength of my passwords? You can use online password strength testers, such as The

Are Klingonese Passwords Safe?

Many computer users are diehard science fiction fans. *Star Trek*, *Star Wars*, and *Battlestar Galactica* have provided computer users with loads of planet names, alien races, alien vocabulary (Klingon words from the *Star Trek* series are especially popular), and starship names to use as passwords. Unfortunately, hackers are onto this ploy. Recently developed hacking programs use dictionaries of "geek-speak" to attempt to break passwords. Although "Qapla" (Klingonese for "success"; also used as "goodbye") might seem like an unbreakable password, don't bet your data on it! You can still use these words if you incorporate multiple words into a password that also contains symbols and numbers.

Password Meter (**passwordmeter.com**) or Microsoft's test (**microsoft.com/protect/yourself/password/checker.mspx**), to evaluate your passwords (see Figure 9.15). The Password Meter provides guidelines for good passwords and shows you how integrating various elements (such as symbols) affects the strength score for your password.

You should make sure you change your passwords on a regular basis (such as monthly or quarterly). Your school or your employer probably requires you to change your password regularly. This is also a good idea for your personal passwords. You should also not use the same password for every account that you have. Because remembering constantly changing strong passwords for numerous accounts can be a

challenge, you should use password management tools, as described below, to make the process easier to handle. If you have trouble thinking of secure passwords, there are many password generators available for free, such as Perfect Passwords (**grc.com/passwords.htm**) and the Bytes Interactive Password Generator (**goodpassword.com**).

Can I use a password to restrict access to my computer? Windows has built-in password protection for files as well as the entire desktop. If your computer is set up for multiple users with password protection, the Windows login screen requires you to enter a password to gain access to the desktop. You are also asked to enter a password hint to remind you in case you forget your password. The computer can be set to default back to the Welcome screen after it is idle for a set period of time. This forces a user to reenter a password to regain access to the computer. If someone attempts to log on to your computer without your password, that person won't be able to gain access. It is an especially good idea to use passwords on notebook computers or any computer that may be unattended for periods of time. Figure 9.16 shows the Control Panel screen used to set up a password on a user account.

There are two types of users in Windows: administrators and standard users. Setting up a password on a standard user account prevents other standard users from being

Figure 9.14 | STRONG AND WEAK PASSWORD CANDIDATES

Strong Password	Reason
L8t2meGaNDalf351	Uses letters and numbers to come up with memorable phrase "Late to me" and adds it to a character name from *Lord of the Rings* plus a random number.
IwaLR8384GdY	First initials of first line of Green Day song *I Walk a Lonely Road* plus a random number and an abbreviation for Green Day
P1zzA244WaterShiPDowN	Easily remembered word with mix of alphanumeric characters and upper- and lowercase letters, your locker number at your gym, plus the title of a book that you like (with upper- and lowercase letters)
S0da&ICB3N&J3RRY	Mix of numbers, symbols, and letters. Stands for soda and ice cream and the names of famous ice cream makers with the number 3 instead of the letter E

Weak Password	Reason
Jsmith	Combination of first initial and last name
4smithkids	Even though this has alphanumeric combination, it is too descriptive of a family.
Brown5512	Last name and last four digits of phone number are easily decoded.
123MainSt	A street address is an easily decoded password.

able to access that user's files. However, users with administrator privileges can still see your files if you are a standard user. So be aware that your files may not be safe from all prying eyes!

Managing Your Passwords

How can I remember all of my complex passwords? Good security practices suggest that you have different passwords for different Web sites that you access and that you change your passwords frequently. The problem with well-constructed passwords is that they can be hard to remember. Fortunately, password management tools are now widely available. This takes the worry out of forgetting passwords because the password management software does the remembering for you.

Where can I obtain password management software? Windows, Norton 360 (and other Internet security packages), and the Firefox browser make it easy to keep track of passwords by providing password management tools. From the Tools menu in Firefox, select Options, and then click the Security icon (the closed padlock) shown in Figure 9.17. In the Passwords section, check **Remember passwords for sites** to have Firefox remember passwords when you log onto Web sites. Check **Use a master password**, which causes a dialog box to appear, and enter a well-designed, secure password. The next time you go to a Web site that requires a login, Firefox will a dialog box prompting you to have Firefox remember the login name and password for this site. Then, when you return to the site and select a login option, enter the master password and the Firefox Password Manager will fill in the login and password information for you.

You also can see a list of sites maintained by the Firefox Password Manager by clicking the Show Passwords button, which displays the Remember Passwords dialog box (see Figure 9.17). Passwords for each site are displayed after you click the Show Passwords button and enter the master password.

Even though you only need to remember the master password, you still need to make sure that is a secure password (according to the rules we discussed earlier) and that you change it on a regular basis. Password

Figure 9.15
The Password Meter objectively evaluates your passwords.

Figure 9.16
Windows provides additional security for your files by locking unauthorized users out of your account.

>Click **Start**, click **Control Panel**, click **User Accounts and Family Safety**, click **User Accounts**, and then click **Create a password for your account**.

managers are useful on the machine that you use on a regular basis. However, if you need to access your accounts from another computer (such as one at school), you will still need to know the individual passwords for each site you wish to access.

So start using secure passwords and let your browser relieve you of the problem of trying to remember them all.

Figure 9.17

(a) The security tab in the Firefox browser options screen provides access to password management tools.

(b) The Firefox Remember Passwords dialog box displays all sites for which login information is saved.

>From the **Tools** menu, select **Options**. In the **Options** dialog box, click the **Show Passwords** button.

Anonymous Web Surfing: Hiding from Prying Eyes

Should I be concerned about surfing the Internet on shared or public computers?

If you use shared computers in public places such as libraries, coffee shops, or college student unions, you should be concerned about a subsequent user of a computer spying on your surfing habits. You never know what nefarious tools have been installed by hackers on a public computer. When you browse the Internet, traces of your activity are left behind on that computer, often as temporary files. A wily hacker can glean sensitive information long after you have finished your latte and your surfing session.

What tools can I use to protect myself when using public computers?

Google Chrome and Internet Explorer 8 both include privacy tools that help you surf the Internet anonymously. Google Chrome's Incognito feature allows you to open a special version of the Google browser window. When surfing in this window, records of

Figure 9.18

Portable privacy devices help to protect your privacy when you work on computers away from your home or office.

Web sites you visit and files you download do not appear in the Web browser's history files. Furthermore, any new cookies that were generated in that browsing session are deleted when you exit the Incognito window. The InPrivate feature of Internet Explorer 8 offers similar security features.

Portable privacy devices, such as the IronKey (**ironkey.com**) shown in Figure 9.18, provide an even higher level of surfing privacy. Simply plug the device into an available USB port on the machine on which you will be working. All sensitive Internet files, such as cookies, Internet history, and browser caches, then will be stored on the privacy device, not on the computer you are using. Privacy devices such as these often come preloaded with software such as Anonymizer Safe Surfing Suite (**anonymizer.com**), which shields your IP address from prying eyes, making it difficult (if not impossible) for hackers to tell where you are surfing on the Internet. These privacy devices also have password management tools that store all of your login information and encrypt it so it will be safe if your privacy device falls into someone else's hands.

Another free practical solution is to take the Linux OS with you on a flash drive and avoid using the public computer's operating system. The interfaces of many Linux builds,

Figure 9.19

Ubuntu is a version of Linux that has a Windows-like interface and familiar browser tools like Firefox.

such as Ubuntu (see Figure 9.19), look almost exactly like Windows and are easy to use.

There are several advantages to using a Linux-based operating system on a public computer. First, your risk of picking up viruses and other malware is significantly reduced because when you boot a public computer from a flash drive, you completely eliminate any interaction with the public computer's operating system. This, in turn, significantly reduces the chance that your flash drive will become infected by any malware running on the public computer.

Next, virus and hacking attacks against Linux are far less likely than attacks against Windows. Because Windows has an over 90 percent share of the operating system market, people who write malware tend to target Windows systems. Finally, when you run software from your own storage medium (flash drive), you avoid reading and writing to the hard disk of the public computer. This significantly enhances your privacy because you don't leave traces of your activity behind.

Pendrivelinux.com (**pendrivelinux.com**) is excellent resource that offers many different versions of Linux for download and includes step-by-step instructions on how to install them on your flash drive. If you are a Mac user, there is an option for you, too! gOS is a version of Linux that provides

a close approximation of OS X, so you can feel right at home.

Biometric Authentication Devices

Besides passwords, how else can I restrict the use of my computer? A biometric authentication device is a device that reads a unique personal characteristic such as a fingerprint or the iris pattern in your eye and converts its pattern to a digital code. When you use the device, your pattern is read and compared to the one stored on the computer. Only users having an exact fingerprint or iris pattern match are allowed to access the computer.

Because no two people have the same biometric characteristics (fingerprints and iris patterns are unique), these devices provide a high level of security. They also eliminate the human error that can occur in password protection. You might forget your password, but you won't forget to bring your fingerprint to the computer! Some notebooks feature built-in fingerprint readers, and Figure 9.20a shows a mouse that includes a fingerprint reader. Another useful device is the APC Touch Biometric Pod Password Manager (see Figure 9.20b); after it identifies you by your fingerprint, the device provides login information to password-protected Web sites you need to access. The device also stores all your login names and passwords so that you don't have to keep track of them. As many as 20 users can use the same device, making it perfect for shared computers. Other biometric devices, which include voice authentication and face pattern–recognition systems, are now widely offered in notebook computers.

Make sure to utilize some (or all) of these methods to keep your activities from prying eyes and to restrict access to your digital information.

Managing Online Annoyances

Surfing the Web, sending and receiving e-mail, and chatting online have become a common part of most of our lives.

Figure 9.20

(a) The SecuGen Opti-Mouse III is a two-button mouse with a scroll wheel that includes a digital fingerprint reader. (b) The APC Touch Biometric Pod Password Manager employs a fingerprint reader to recognize authorized users.

Fingerprint reader

Unfortunately, the Web has become fertile ground for people who want to advertise their products, track our Web browsing behaviors, or even con people into revealing personal information. In this section, we'll look at ways in which you can manage, if not avoid, these and other online headaches.

Malware, Adware, and Spyware

What is malware? Malware is software that has a malicious intent (hence the prefix *mal*). There are three primary forms of malware: adware, spyware, and viruses (which we have already discussed). Adware and spyware are not destructive like viruses and worms are. Known collectively as grayware, most are intrusive, annoying, or objectionable online programs that are downloaded to your computer when you install or use other online content such as a freeware program, game, or utility.

Figure 9.21

The Internet Explorer pop-up blocker settings dialog box.

>Pop-up Blocker is found in the **Tools** menu on the Internet Explorer toolbar.

What is adware? Adware is software that displays sponsored advertisements in a section of your browser window or as a pop-up ad box. It is considered a legitimate (though sometimes annoying) means of generating revenue for those developers who do not charge for their software or information. Pop-up windows (small boxes that open up automatically on your screen) have been referred to as the billboards of the Internet because they appear and display advertisements or other promotional information when you install freeware programs or access certain Web sites. These pop-up windows, at one point, were so common that they were incredibly irritating and annoying.

Some pop-ups, however, are legitimate and increase the functionality of the originating site. For example, your account balance may pop up on your bank's Web site. Fortunately, because Web browsers such as Firefox, Safari, and Internet Explorer have pop-up blockers built into their browsers, the occurrence of annoying pop-ups has been greatly reduced. You can access the pop-up blockers settings in your browser (see Figure 9.21) and add Web sites for which you will allow pop-ups. Whenever a pop-up is blocked, the browser displays an information bar at the top of the browser window or plays a sound to alert you. If you feel the pop-up is legitimate, you can then choose to accept it.

What is spyware? Some adware programs are more intrusive than the ones just discussed. Without your knowledge, they transmit information about you, such as your Internet surfing habits, to the owner of the adware program so that the information can be used for marketing purposes. In these

Ethics: Big Brother Is Watching . . . But Should He Be Allowed to Do So?

Think you aren't being closely watched by your employer? Think again! A survey of employers by the American Management Association and the ePolicy Institute revealed that of the employers surveyed:

- 73 percent monitored e-mail messages
- 66 percent monitored Web surfing
- 48 percent monitored activities using video surveillance
- 45 percent monitored keystrokes and keyboard time
- 43 percent monitored computer files in some other fashion

There is a high probability that you are being monitored while you work and when you access the Internet via your employer's Internet connection.

The two most frequently cited reasons for employee monitoring are to prevent theft and to measure productivity. Monitoring for theft isn't new, because monitoring cameras have been around for years, and productivity monitoring has been a consistent process for assembly line workers for decades. However, the rise of the Internet has led to a new type of productivity drain that is of concern to employers. **Cyberloafing**, or cyberslacking, means doing anything with a computer, while you are being paid to do your job, that is *not* an approved function of your job. Examples of cyberloafing activities are playing games, reading personal e-mail, checking sports scores, watching videos, and buying personal-use products on e-commerce sites. Estimates of business productivity losses due to cyberloafing top $50 billion annually. While many employers don't mind if workers answer the occasional personal e-mail while at work, they would probably not appreciate it if they spent four hours of their workday playing World of Warcraft online!

Like most other Americans, you probably feel you have a right to privacy in the workplace. Unfortunately, the laws in the United States don't support a worker's right to privacy. Laws such as the 1986 Electronic Communications Privacy Act (ECPA), which prohibits unauthorized monitoring of electronic communications, have been interpreted by the courts in favor of employers. The bottom line is that when the employer is paying for equipment and software (such as Internet access and e-mail), the employer has the legal right to monitor its usage.

Is it ethical for employers to monitor employees? Just because an action is *legal* doesn't mean it is *ethical*. It is difficult to argue that an employer doesn't have the right to take measures to prevent theft and detect low productivity. The ethical issue here is whether or not the employees are made aware that they are being monitored. An ethical employer should treat employees with respect and dignity and inform the employees that they are being monitored. Employers have an ethical responsibility (and a legal one as well, depending on the jurisdiction) not to place monitoring devices in sensitive locations such as bathrooms and dressing areas. However, in many states, the employer does not need to inform the employees in advance that they are being monitored. Conscientious employers include monitoring disclosures in published employee policies to avoid confusion and conflict. If you aren't sure whether your employer monitors employees, check with the company's human resources department.

Employers use a variety of software programs to monitor employee computer usage. Certain software packages keep track of every Web site you visit and the duration of your stay. Checking the baseball scores might take only three seconds and go unnoticed, but spending two hours updating your fantasy football team may be flagged. Keystroke loggers were originally used to monitor performance for people with input-intensive jobs, like clerks and secretaries. Now these programs have the potential to be used to invade your privacy, because they can record everything you type, even that nasty e-mail about the boss that you thought better of sending and deleted!

In addition to monitoring keystrokes, computer software can also be used to monitor the contents of your hard drive, so you don't want to collect 4,823 illegal MP3 files on your work computer. Some programs even keep track of how long your computer is idle, which can give your manager a good idea of whether you were working or taking a three-hour lunch.

Since your employer might not tell you that your computer use is being monitored, you should assume that anything you do on your company-provided computer is subject to scrutiny. If you need to do personal work on your lunch hour or other breaks, you may be able to use your personal laptop to avoid the monitoring. Check with your employer to be sure you can connect personal computers to the corporate network or Internet connection. Note that courts in some jurisdictions have ruled that e-mails sent from third-party systems, such as Yahoo! and Gmail, are subject to monitoring if they are sent from employer-provided computer systems. Instant messaging is also subject to monitoring. Therefore, the best defense against monitoring of personal instant messaging or e-mail is to use your own computing device to send the communications.

People who monitor employees have a duty to protect their right to privacy and not to disclose any information that they may inadvertently see during the course of monitoring. The acceptable computer use policies at most companies include guidelines for network administrators and other people who have high levels of access to sensitive information. When monitoring employees' work habits, management must ensure that compliance with the policies is tested periodically. Periodic reviews of procedures and compliance help ensure that established company policies are working as designed. An ethical employer strives to prevent misuse of personal data and accidental data loss. This helps a company maintain the trust of its employees. However, you can't always be certain that everyone who monitors you will behave in an ethical manner. Therefore, you need to think very carefully about exactly what personal tasks you are willing to risk engaging in on company computer systems.

So, do your employers have an ethical right to monitor your activities? Certainly, they have a right to ensure they are getting a fair day's work from you, just as you have an ethical obligation to provide a fair effort for a fair wage. However, employers should also be willing to respect the privacy rights of their employees and treat them as professionals, unless there is some indication of wrongdoing. Because employers may have a legal right to monitor you in the workplace, you should work under the assumption that everything you do on your work computer is subject to scrutiny, and behave accordingly. Do your online shopping at home!

instances, such adware is more malicious in intent and can be considered spyware. **Spyware** is an unwanted piggyback program that usually downloads with other software you want to install from the Internet. It runs in the background of your system. Many spyware programs use tracking cookies to collect information, whereas others are disguised as benign programs that are really malicious programs (such as Trojan horses). One type of spyware program (known as a **keystroke logger**) monitors keystrokes with the intent of stealing passwords, login IDs, or credit card information.

Can I prevent spyware? Many Internet security suites now include antispyware software. However, you can also obtain stand-alone spyware removal software and run it on your computer to delete unwanted spyware. Because there are so many variants of spyware, your Internet security software may not detect all types that attempt to install themselves on your computer. Therefore, it is a good idea to install one or two additional stand-alone antispyware programs on your computer.

Because new spyware is created all the time, you should update and run your spyware removal software regularly. Windows comes with a program called Windows Defender, which scans your system for spyware and other potentially unwanted software. Ad-Aware and Spybot–Search & Destroy (both available from **download.com**) and CA Anti-Spyware (**ca.com**) are other programs that are easy to install and update. Figure 9.22 shows an example of Ad-Aware and Spybot in action. They detect unwanted programs and allow you to delete the offending software easily.

Spam

How can I best avoid spam? Companies that send out **spam**—unwanted or junk e-mail—find your e-mail address either from a list they purchase or with software that looks for e-mail addresses on the Internet. (Unsolicited instant messages are also a form of spam, called *spim*.) If you've used your e-mail address to purchase anything online, open an online account, or participate in a social network such as Facebook, your e-mail address eventually will appear on one of the lists that spammers get.

One way to avoid spam in your primary account is to create a free Web-based e-mail address that you use only when you fill out forms or purchase items on the Web. For example, both Office Live Mail and Yahoo! allow you to set up free e-mail accounts. If your free Web-based e-mail account is saturated with spam, then you can abandon that account with little inconvenience. It's much less convenient to abandon your primary e-mail address.

Another way to avoid spam is to filter it. A **spam filter** is an option you can select in your e-mail account that places known or suspected spam messages into a folder other than your inbox. Most Web-based e-mail

Figure 9.22

After performing a routine scan of a computer, Ad-Aware and Spybot each return a log of problems found on the system.

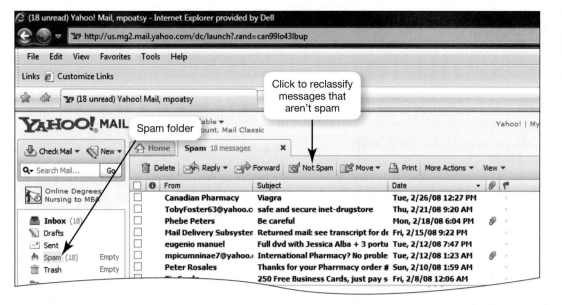

Figure 9.23

In Yahoo! Mail, messages identified as spam are directed into a folder called "Spam" for review and deletion.

services, such as Office Live Mail and Yahoo!, offer spam filters (see Figure 9.23). Files perceived to be spam are segregated in a special folder (often named "Spam"). Microsoft Outlook also features a spam filter. Third-party programs that provide some control over spam include SPAM-fighter and Cactus Spam Filter, both of which can be obtained at download.com.

How do spam filters work? Spam filters and filtering software can catch as much as 95 percent of spam by checking incoming e-mail subject headers and senders' addresses against databases of known spam. Spam filters also check your e-mail for frequently used spam patterns and keywords (such as "for free" and "over 21"). E-mail that the filter identifies as spam does not go into your inbox, but rather to a folder set up for spam. Spam filters aren't perfect, and you should check the spam folder before deleting its contents because legitimate e-mail might end up there by mistake. Most programs provide you with a tool to reclassify e-mails that have been misidentified as spam.

How else can I prevent spam? There are several additional ways you can prevent spam.

1. Before registering on a Web site, read its privacy policy to see how it uses your e-mail address. Don't give the site permission to pass on your e-mail address to third parties.

2. Don't reply to spam to remove yourself from the spam list. By replying, you are confirming that your e-mail address is active. Instead of stopping spam, you may receive more.

3. Subscribe to an e-mail forwarding service such as Emailias (**emailias.com**) or Sneakemail.com (**sneakemail.com**). These services screen your e-mail messages, forwarding only those messages you designate as being okay to accept.

Cookies

What are cookies? Cookies are small text files that some Web sites automatically store on your computer's hard drive when you visit them. When you log on to a Web site that uses cookies, a cookie file assigns an ID number to your computer. The unique ID is intended to make your return visit to a Web site more efficient and better geared to your interests. The next time you log on to that site, the site marks your visit and keeps track of it in its database.

What do Web sites do with cookie information? Cookies provide Web sites with information about your browsing habits, such as the ads you've opened, the products you've looked at, and the time and duration of your visits. Companies use this information to determine the traffic flowing through their Web site and the effectiveness of their marketing strategy and placement on Web sites. By tracking such information, cookies enable companies to identify different users' preferences.

Can companies get my personal information when I visit their sites? Cookies do not go through your hard drive in search of personal information such as passwords or financial data. The only personal information a cookie obtains is the information you supply when you fill out forms online.

Do privacy risks exist with cookies? Some sites sell the personal information their cookies collect to Web advertisers that are building huge databases of consumer preferences and habits, collecting personal and business information such as phone numbers, credit reports, and the like. The main concern is that advertisers will use this information indiscriminately, thus infiltrating your privacy.

Should I delete cookies from my hard drive? Because cookies pose no security threat (it is virtually impossible to hide a virus or malicious software program in a cookie), take up little room on your hard drive, and offer you small conveniences on return visits to Web sites, there is no great reason to delete them. Deleting your cookie files could actually cause you the inconvenience of reentering data you have already entered into Web site forms. However, if you're uncomfortable with the accessibility of your personal information, you can periodically delete cookies or configure your browser to block certain types of cookies, as shown in Figure 9.24. Software such as Cookie Pal (**kburra.com**) also can help you monitor cookies.

Figure 9.24

Tools are available, either through your browser (Internet Explorer is shown here) or as separate applications, to distinguish between cookies you want to keep and cookies you don't want on your system.

>On the Internet Explorer menu toolbar, click **Tools**, and then click **Internet Options**. The cookie settings are on the **Privacy** tab.

Protecting Yourself . . . From Yourself!

People are often too trusting or just plain careless when it comes to protecting private information about themselves or their digital data. When was the last time you created a copy of your digital data (such as the thousands of photographs you have stored on your hard drive)? The hard drive in your computer is likely to fail at some point, which may render all the data on it useless. What strategy do you have in place to protect your data from damage?

If you have a MySpace or Facebook account, you are probably constantly revealing information about your likes and dislikes, such as what movie you saw this weekend, which concert you attended last night, the presents you received for your birthday, and so on. You might even be revealing information about where you live. Have you ever filled out an online form to enter a contest? Have you ever applied for a customer loyalty card at your local supermarket or electronics store? Think about how much information you voluntarily give up all the time in the course of running your digital life. Con artists and scammers take advantage of people's tendency to reveal information freely to compromise their privacy and commit theft.

In this section, we discuss ways to keep your data safe from damage (either accidental or intentional) and to keep unscrupulous individuals from tricking you into revealing sensitive information.

Backing Up Your Data

How might I damage the data on my computer? The data on your computer faces three major threats: unauthorized access, tampering, and destruction. As noted earlier, a hacker can gain access to your computer and steal or alter your data. However, a more likely scenario is that you will lose your data unintentionally. You may accidentally delete files. You may drop your notebook on the ground, causing the hard drive to break down, resulting in complete data loss. A virus from an e-mail attachment you opened may destroy your original file. Your house or dorm many catch fire and your computer be destroyed. Because many of these factors are beyond your control, you should have a strategy for backing up your files. Backups are especially important if you are running a small business. (The backup strategy for small businesses is quite similar to the procedures recommended for individuals.)

> **"The data on your computer faces three major threats: unauthorized access, tampering, and destruction."**

What exactly is a meant by backing up data? **Backups** are copies of files that you can use to replace the originals if they are lost or damaged. To be truly secure, backups must be stored away from your home or office. You wouldn't want a fire or a flood destroying the backups along with the original data. Removable storage media, such as external hard drives, DVDs, CDs, and flash drives, are popular choices for backing up files because they hold a lot of data and can be transported easily.

Do I need to back up all the files on my computer? Two types of files need backups—program files and data files.

A **program file** is used to install software and usually comes on CDs or DVDs or is downloaded from the Web. If any programs came preinstalled in your computer, then you may have received a CD or DVD that contains the original program. As long as you have the original media in a safe place, you shouldn't need to back up these files. If you have downloaded a program file from the Internet, however, you should make a copy of the program installation files on a removable storage device as a backup. If you didn't receive discs for installed programs with your computer, then see the next section for suggested strategies for backing up your entire computer.

A **data file** is a file you have created or purchased. Data files include such files as research papers,, spreadsheets, music files, movies, contact lists, address books, e-mail archives, and your Favorites list from your browser.

How often should I back up my files? You should back up your data files frequently. How frequently will depend on how much work you cannot afford to lose. You should always back up data files when you make changes to them, especially if those changes involve hours of work. It may not seem important to back up your history term paper file when you finish it, but do you really want to do all that work again if your computer crashes before you have a chance to turn in your paper?

To make backups easier, store all your data files in one folder on your hard drive. For example, in Windows and most other operating systems, on your hard drive you will find a folder called Documents. You can create subfolders (such as History Homework, Music Files, and so on) within the Documents folder. If you store all your data files in one place, to back up your files, you simply copy the Documents folder and all of its subfolders onto an alternative storage medium.

For Mac OS X users, backups are much easier. The Time Machine feature (in Mac OS X Snow Leopard and previous versions) detects when an external hard drive is attached to the computer. You are then asked if you want this to be your backup drive. If you answer yes, all of your files (including operating system files) are automatically backed up to the external drive. You even have the option to go back in time and see what your computer looked like on a specific date. This is very handy for recovering a file that you wish you hadn't deleted.

Figure 9.25

(a) The General tab in Cobian Backup lets you choose the type of backup. (b) The Schedule window makes it easy to schedule backups on a regular basis. (c) You simply drag and drop files or folders that need to be backed up from Windows Explorer to the storage location.

How do I actually perform a file backup? The simplest method would be to open Windows Explorer and copy the files you need to back up to another medium, such as an external hard drive. Of course, this method relies on your remembering to back up files and update the backups when you make changes to the original file. Many people use backup software with features that allow them to schedule backups of key files or directories automatically at specified times. Additionally, some backup software can be configured to make backups of data files automatically as soon as they are created or when they are changed. This resolves the problem of forgetting to perform backups. Many external hard drives are sold with backup software.

Windows 7 includes a backup utility that provides a quick and easy way to schedule backups of files on a regular basis. This utility allows you to select certain folders or directories for backup, although it does not allow you to select individual files. A better choice for Windows users is backup software such as Norton Ghost, Genie Backup Manager, or a free product called Cobian Backup (which you can download from the CNet download site (**download.cnet.com/windows/**), shown in Figure 9.25. Cobian allows you to easily configure backup tasks and select directories or individual files to back up on a regular basis. A **full backup** will back up all files in a specified location. An **incremental backup** will back up only files that have changed since the last time a backup was performed on the files.

What backups should I perform in case of a total hard drive failure? Your OS and software applications also need to be protected by backups. Although you can create restore points in Windows to take your system back to the time before it had a problem, this doesn't help in the case of a hard drive failure. If you have the media to reinstall Windows and your application programs, then you should be in good shape—although this process may take more time than you think. Windows has many settings that may need to be reinstated to get your machine functioning the way you had it set up. Working with these settings can be intimidating for the average user and just plain time consuming for experienced users. In addition, all of your applications would need to be reinstalled, which could take hours (or days), assuming you can locate all of the CDs and DVDs for your software and re-download all of the applications you purchased over the Internet. If you are running a small business, the time you lose reconfiguring the computers probably means lost revenue.

For complete protection, you should use backup software such as Genie Backup Manager (**genie-soft.com**) or Safety Drill, which comes with Maxtor external hard drives. These products create an **image backup** of your entire system. Windows 7 backup utilities also give you the option of making a copy of your system image for restoration purposes. Taking an image of your entire system and storing it on another hard drive provides you with the ultimate protection. With a backup of your entire hard drive, including your system image, you won't need to reinstall all of the program software from the original media. Instead, you just replace the broken hard drive with the backup hard drive (or copy the contents of the backup drive to a new drive).

Where is a safe place to store my backups? Taking the backup media (external hard drive, DVDs, etc.) to a location other than where the original files are located is usually a sufficient solution. You could store the backups at a friend's house or dorm room. However, if you want an extremely secure location you can store backups of your files online, which is often the most convenient solution for small businesses. For a fee, companies such as Iron Mountain (**backup.ironmountain.com**) and IBackup (**ibackup.com**) can provide you with such online storage. If you store a backup of your entire system on the Internet, then you won't need to buy an additional hard drive for backups. This method also takes the worry out of finding a safe place to keep your backups because they're always stored in an area far away from your computer (on the backup company's server). However, if you'd like to store your backups online, make sure you have high-speed Internet access.

Should I back up my files that are stored on my school's network? Most likely, if you're allowed to store files on your school's network, these files are backed up on a regular basis. You should check with your school's network administrators to determine how often they're backed up and how you would go about requesting that files be restored from the backup media if they're damaged or deleted. But don't rely on these network backups to bail you out if your data files are lost or damaged. It may take days for the network administrators to get around to restoring your files. It is better to keep backups of your data files yourself (especially homework and project files) so that you can immediately restore them. Buy a large-capacity flash drive and carry it with you!

> **"Where is a safe place to store my backups?"**

Social Engineering: Fooling the Unwary

What is social engineering? **Social engineering** is any technique that uses social skills to generate human interaction that entices individuals to reveal sensitive information. Social engineering often doesn't involve the use of a computer or face-to-face interaction. For example, telephone scams are a common form of social engineering because it is often easier to manipulate someone when you don't have to look at them.

How does social engineering work? Most social engineering schemes use a pretext to lure their victims. **Pretexting** involves creating a scenario that sounds legitimate enough that someone will trust you. For example, you might receive a phone call during which the caller says he is from the bank and that someone tried to use your account without authorization. The caller then tells you he needs to confirm a few personal details such as your birth date, Social Security number, bank account number, and whatever other information he can get out of you. The information he obtains can then be used to empty your bank account or commit some other form of fraud. Often pretexting is used to gain access to corporate computer networks. People will sometimes call random extensions in a large business, claiming to be from technical support. Eventually, the caller will find someone who has a problem and is happy that someone is willing to help. The scam artist will then elicit information such as logins and passwords from the victim as part of the

TRENDS IN IT

Computers in Society: Identity Theft—Is There More Than One You Out There?

You've no doubt heard of identity theft. A thief steals your name, address, Social Security number, and bank account and credit card information and runs up debts in your name. This leaves you holding the bag, and you're hounded by creditors collecting on the fraudulent debts. It sounds horrible—and it is. In fact, one of the authors of this textbook had his identity stolen and spent about 50 hours filing police reports, talking to credit agencies, closing bogus accounts, and convincing companies that the $25,000 of debt run up on six phony credit card accounts was done by an identity thief. Many victims of identity theft spend months (or even years) trying to repair their credit and eliminate fraudulent debts. Worse yet, if an identity thief uses your identity to obtain medical services at a hospital, you may be denied coverage at a later date because the thief's treatment has exceeded the limit of covered services on your policy.

Stories of identity thieves—such as the New York. Man accused of stealing more than 30,000 identities—abound in the media, and should serve to make the public wary. However, many media pundits would have you believe that the only way your identity can be stolen is by a computer. This is simply not true. The Federal Trade Commission (**ftc.gov**) has identified other methods thieves use to obtain others' personal information. These include (1) stealing purses and wallets, in which people often keep unnecessary valuable personal information such as their ATM PIN codes, (2) stealing mail or looking through trash for bank statements and credit card bills, which provide valuable personal information; and (3) posing as bank or credit card company representatives and tricking people into revealing sensitive information over the phone.

Obviously, you're at risk from online attacks, too, such as phishing and pharming. Once identity thieves obtain your personal information, they can use it in many different ways. Identity thieves often request a change of address for your credit card bill or bank statement. By the time you realize that you aren't receiving your statements, the thieves have rung up bogus charges on your account or emptied your bank account.

The thieves can open new credit card and bank accounts in your name. They then will write bad checks and not pay the credit card bills, which will ruin your credit rating.

Even worse, the identity thieves may counterfeit debit cards or checks for your legitimate accounts and empty them of funds. They might even take out a mortgage in your name and then disappear with the proceeds, leaving you with the debt.

Although foolproof protection methods don't exist, there are precautions that will help you minimize your risk. You should never reveal your password or your PIN code to anyone or place it in an easy-to-find location. Also, never reveal personal information unless you're sure that a legitimate reason exists for a business to know the information, and you can confirm you're actually dealing with a legitimate representative (don't fall for phishing schemes). If someone calls or e-mails asking you for personal information, decline and call the company with which you opened your account.

Obviously, you should create secure passwords for your online accounts. When shopping online, be wary of unfamiliar merchants that you can't contact through a mailing address or phone number, or businesses whose prices are too good to be true. These can be attempts to collect your personal information for use in fraudulent schemes.

If you have been the victim of identity theft, most states now allow you to freeze your credit history so that no new accounts can be opened until you lift the credit freeze. Even if you live in a state where you can't freeze your account, you can still place an extended fraud alert on your credit history for seven years, which also warns merchants that they should check with you (at your home address or phone number) before opening an account in your name.

Using common sense and keeping personal information in the hands of as few people as possible are the best defenses against identity theft. For additional tips on preventing identity theft or for procedures to follow if you are a victim, check out the U.S. government site on identity theft (**consumer.gov/idtheft**).

---

process for "solving the problem." The most common form of pretexting in cyberspace is phishing.

Phishing and Pharming

How are phishing schemes conducted? **Phishing** (pronounced "fishing") lures Internet users to reveal personal information such as credit card numbers, Social Security numbers, or other sensitive information that could lead to identity theft. The scammers send e-mail messages that look like they are from a legitimate business such as an online bank. The e-mail states that the recipient needs to update or confirm his or her account information. When the recipient clicks the provided link, he or she goes to a Web site. The site looks like a legitimate site but is really a fraudulent copy the

scammer has created. Once the e-mail recipient confirms his or her personal information, the scammers capture it and can begin using it.

Is pharming a type of phishing scam? Pharming is much more insidious than phishing. Phishing requires a positive action by the person being scammed, such going to a Web site mentioned in an e-mail and typing in your bank account information. **Pharming** is when malicious code is planted on your computer that alters your browser's ability to find Web addresses. Users are directed to bogus Web sites even when they enter the correct address of the real Web site or follow a bookmark that they previously had established for the Web site. So instead of ending up at your bank's Web site when you type in its address, you end up at a fake Web site that looks like your bank's site but is expressly set up for the purpose of gathering information.

How can I avoid being caught by phishing and pharming scams? You should never reply directly to any e-mail asking you for personal information. Never click on a link in an e-mail to go to a Web site. Instead, type the Web site address in the browser. Check with the company asking for the information and only give the information if you are certain it is needed.

Also, never give personal information over the Internet unless you know the site is secure. Look for the closed padlock, https, or a certification seal such as VeriSign to indicate that the site is secure. The latest versions of Firefox, Chrome, and Internet Explorer have phishing filters built in, so each time you access a Web site, the phishing filter checks for the site's legitimacy and warns you of possible Web forgeries.

Finally, make sure you have Internet security software installed on your computer and that it is constantly being updated. Most Internet security packages can detect and prevent pharming attacks. The major Internet security packages—for example, McAfee and Norton (see Figure 9.26)—also offer phishing protection tools. When you have the Norton Toolbar displayed in your browser, you are constantly informed about the legitimacy of the site you are visiting. In fact, if you have an Internet security package installed, you can turn off the phishing filter in your browser to speed up the loading of Web pages.

Another way to protect yourself is never to use your credit card number when you shop online. Although it sounds impossible, credit card providers such as Citibank are offering services such as "Virtual Account Numbers" for their customers. Before purchasing a product online, you visit an online site, where you are assigned a new virtual account number each time you visit. This number looks like a regular credit card number and is tied to your real credit card account. However, the virtual account number can be used only once. That means that if the number is stolen, it's no good to thieves. They can't use the virtual account number, because you've already used it.

Hoaxes

What is a hoax? A **hoax** is an attempt to make someone believe something that is

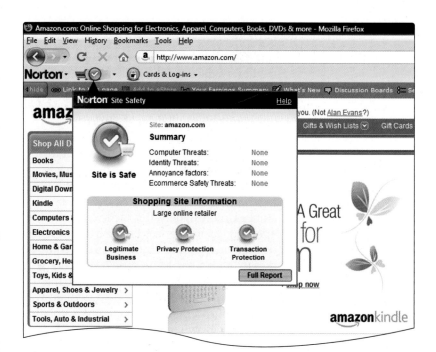

Figure 9.26

Not sure whether you are on the Amazon Web site or a cleverly disguised phishing site? Norton Site Safety reassures you that all is well.

untrue. Hoaxes target a large audience and are generally perpetrated as practical jokes, instruments of social change (which poke fun at an established norm in an effort to change it), or merely ways to waste people's valuable time. Although there are hoax Web sites such as Pacific Northwest Tree Octopus (**zapatopi.net/treeoctopus/**), most cyberspace hoaxes are perpetrated by e-mail.

Why do people concoct e-mail hoaxes? As opposed to garnering financial rewards (like in a phishing fraud), the motives of e-mail hoax creators can be more complex. Many people start an e-mail hoax just for the challenge of seeing if their "brainchild" can be spread globally. Other hoaxes start as innocent practical jokes between friends but then take on a life of their own via the fast communication available on the Internet. Many hoaxes become so well known that they are accepted by society as true events even though they are false. Once this happens to a hoax, it becomes known as an **urban legend**. An example is the phony story about the man who woke up in a bathtub full of ice water and found he had had his kidney stolen. Hoaxes may be compared to acts of real-world vandalism like graffiti. Graffiti artists "make their mark" on the world, physically; hoaxers may consider they are making a similar mark when a bogus e-mail they have created becomes widespread.

Sometimes hoaxes are based on misinformation or are a way to vent frustration. An e-mail hoax that reappears every time there is a spike in gasoline prices is the Gas Boycott (Gas War) hoax. To boost the scheme's credibility, the e-mail touts it as having been invented by reputable businesspeople. The e-mail explains how boycotting certain gasoline companies will drive the price of gasoline down and urges recipients of the e-mail to join the fight. The originator of this hoax was probably frustrated by high gas prices and, armed with a poor understanding of economics, distributed this brainstorm. Unfortunately, this tactic can have no effect on gasoline prices because it only shifts demand for gasoline from certain oil companies to other sources. Because it does not reduce the overall demand for gasoline, the price of gas will not decline. Did you receive this e-mail and think it sounded like a plausible idea? How many people did you forward it to?

How can I tell if an e-mail is a hoax? Sometimes it is difficult to separate fact from fiction. Many hoax e-mails are well written and crafted in such a way that they sound very real. Before using the Forward button and sending an e-mail to all your friends, check it out at one of the many Web sites that keep track of and expose e-mail hoaxes. Check sites such as Snopes (**snopes.com**), Hoax Slayer (**hoax-slayer.com**, shown in Figure 9.27), or TruthOrFiction.com (**truthorfiction.com**). These sites are searchable, so you can enter a few keywords from an e-mail you suspect may be a hoax and quickly find similar e-mails, with an explanation of whether they are true or false. Checking out e-mails before

forwarding them on to friends, family, and co-workers will save other people's time and help end the spread of these time wasters.

Protecting Your Physical Computing Assets

Your computer isn't useful to you if it is damaged. Therefore, it's essential to select and ensure a safe environment for it. This includes protecting it from environmental factors, power surges, power outages, and theft.

Environmental Factors

Why is the environment critical to the operation of my computer equipment? Computers are delicate devices and can be damaged by the adverse effects of being kept in a poor environment or abused. Sudden movements (such as a fall) can damage your notebook computer or mobile device's internal components. You should make sure that your computer sits on a flat, level surface, and, if it is a notebook, carry it in a padded case to protect it. If you do drop your computer, have it professionally tested by a computer repair facility to check for any hidden damage.

Electronic components do not like excessive heat or excessive cold. Unfortunately, computers generate a lot of heat, which is why they have fans to cool their internal components. Make sure that you place your computer where the fan's input vents (usually found on the rear of the system unit) are unblocked so that air can flow inside. And don't leave computing devices in a car during especially hot or cold weather, because components can be damaged by extreme temperatures. Naturally, a fan drawing air into a computer also draws in dust and other particles, which can wreak havoc on your system. Therefore, keep the room in which your computer is located as clean as possible. Even in a clean room, the fan ducts can become packed with dust, so vacuum it periodically to keep a clear airflow into your computer. Finally, because food crumbs and liquid can damage keyboards and other computer components, consume food and beverages away from your computer.

Figure 9.27

Sites like Hoax-Slayer help you research potential hoaxes.

Power Surges

What is a power surge? Power surges occur when electrical current is supplied in excess of normal voltage (120 volts in the United States). Old or faulty wiring, downed power lines, malfunctions at electric company substations, and lightning strikes can all cause power surges. A **surge protector** is a device that protects your computer against power surges (see Figure 9.28). To use a surge protector, you simply plug your electrical devices into the outlets of the surge protector, which in turn plugs into the wall.

How do surge protectors work? Surge protectors contain two components that are used to protect the equipment that is connected to them. Metal-oxide varistors (MOVs) bleed off excess current during minor surges and feed it to the ground wire, where it harmlessly dissipates. The MOVs can do this while still allowing normal current to pass through the devices plugged into the surge protector. Because the ground wire is critical to this process, it is important to plug the surge protector into a grounded (typically 3-prong) power outlet.

During major surges that overwhelm the MOVs, a fuse inside the surge protector blows, which stops the flow of current to all devices plugged into the surge protector. After a major surge, the surge protector will no longer function and must be replaced.

Over time, the MOVs lose their ability to bleed off excess current, which is why you should replace your surge protectors every 2 to 3 years. Buy a surge protector that includes indicator lights. Indicator lights illuminate when the surge protector is no longer functioning properly. (Don't be fooled by old surge protectors that can still function as multiple-outlet power strips,

Metal-oxide varistors (MOVs) bleed off excess current

Fuse blows during major surges

Figure 9.28

Anatomy of a surge protector.

delivering power to your equipment without protecting it.) A power surge could ruin your computer and other devices if you don't protect them. At $20 to $40, a quality surge protector is an excellent investment.

Besides my computer, what other devices need to be connected to a surge protector? All electronic devices in the home that have solid-state components, such as TVs, stereos, computers, printers, and phones, should be connected to a surge protector. Printers and other computer peripherals all require protection. However, it can be inconvenient to use individual surge protectors on everything. A more practical method is to install a **whole-house surge protector** (see Figure 9.29). Whole-house surge protectors function like other surge protectors, but they protect *all* electrical devices in the house. Typically, you will need an electrician to install a whole-house surge protector, which will cost $200 to $300 (installed).

Data lines (transmission media), such as the coaxial cable that attaches to your modem, also can carry surges. Installing a **data line surge suppressor** for each data line connected to your computer through another device (such as a modem) will provide additional protection (see Figure 9.30). A data line surge suppressor is connected to the data line at a point before it reaches the modem or

Surge protector

Figure 9.29

A whole-house surge protector usually is installed at the breaker panel or near the electric meter.

other device. In this way, it intercepts surges on the data line before they reach sensitive equipment.

Is my equipment 100 percent safe when plugged into a surge protec-tor? Surge pro-tectors won't necessarily guard against all surges. Lightning strikes can generate such high voltages that they can overwhelm a surge protector. As tedious as it sounds, unplugging com-puters and peripherals during an electrical storm is the only way to achieve absolute protection.

How can I prevent my computers from losing power during a power outage? Like power surges, power outages can wreak havoc on a system. Computers can de-velop software glitches caused by a loss of power if not shut down properly. Mission-critical computers such as Web servers often are pro-tected by an **uninterruptible power supply**

(UPS), as shown in Figure 9.31. A UPS is a device that contains surge protection equipment and a large battery. When power is interrupted (such as during a blackout), the UPS continues to send power to the attached computer from its battery. Depending on the battery capacity, you have between about 20 minutes and 3 hours to save your work and shut down your computer properly.

Figure 9.30

American Power Conversion (APC), a large manufacturer of surge protection devices, makes a wide range of data line surge suppressors to accommodate almost any type of data line.

Deterring Theft

Because they are portable, notebooks are easy targets for thieves. Common sense dic-tates that you shouldn't leave your notebook unattended or in a place where it can be stolen easily (such as in a hotel room or coffee shop). Even though they are not considered portable, desktop computers are also subject to theft. Three approaches to deterring computer theft include alarming them, locking them down, or installing devices that alert you (or destroy data) when the computer is stolen.

Figure 9.31

A UPS device should not be mistaken for a fat surge protector!

Alarms

What type of alarm can I install on my notebook computer? To prevent your notebook from being stolen, you can attach a motion alarm to it (see Figure 9.32). When you leave your notebook, you use a small device called a *key fob activator* to acti-vate the alarm. If your notebook is moved while the alarm is activated, it emits a wail-ing 85-decibel sound. The fact that the alarm is visible acts as an additional theft deter-rent, just like a "Beware of Dog" sign in a front yard.

Figure 9.32

A notebook alarm sends out an ear-piercing sound if your notebook is moved before you deactivate the alarm.

Alarm

Locks and Surrounds

How can I lock up a notebook computer? Chaining a notebook to your work surface can be another effective way to prevent theft. As shown in Figure 9.33, a special locking mechanism is attached to the notebook (some notebooks are even manufactured with locking ports), and a hardened steel cable is connected to the locking mechanism. The other end of the cable is looped around something large and heavy, such as a desk. The cable lock requires the use of a key or combination to free the notebook. You should consider taking a cable lock with you when traveling to help deter theft from hotel rooms.

Many people associate computer theft only with notebooks or mobile devices. Desktop computers are vulnerable to theft also, especially theft of internal components such as RAM. Your school most likely has the desktop computers in the lab secured in some fashion. Cable locks connect through special fasteners on the back of desktop computers, but components can still be stolen because these cables often don't prevent the system unit case from being opened. A more effective theft deterrent for desktops is a surround (or cage) such as the one shown in Figure 9.34. A surround is a metal box that encloses the system unit, making it impossible to remove from the cage while still allowing access to ports and devices such as DVD players.

Figure 9.33

Cable locks are an effective deterrent to theft.

Software Alerts

How can my computer alert me when it is stolen? You've probably heard of LoJack, the theft-tracking device used in cars. Car owners install a LoJack transmitter somewhere in their vehicle. If the vehicle is stolen, police activate the transmitter and use its signal to locate the car. Similar systems now exist for computers. Tracking software such as Computrace Complete, Computrace LoJack for Laptops (**absolute.com**), PC PhoneHome, and Mac PhoneHome (**pcphonehome.com**) enables the computer it is installed on to alert authorities as to the computer's location if it is stolen. This software can be installed in either notebook or desktop computers.

To enable your computer to help with its own recovery, install the tracking software on your hard drive. The software contacts a server at the software manufacturer's Web site each time you connect to the Internet. If your computer is stolen, you notify the software manufacturer. The software manufacturer instructs your computer to transmit tracking information (such as an IP address) that will assist authorities in locating and retrieving the stolen computer.

What if the thieves find the tracking software and delete it? The files and directories holding the software are not visible to thieves looking for such software, so they probably won't know the software is there. Furthermore, the tracking software is written in such a way that even if the thieves tried to reformat the hard drive, it would detect the reformat and hide the software code

Figure 9.34

Computer surrounds deter theft by making access to the internal components of the computer difficult while still allowing access to ports and drives.

in a safe place in memory or on the hard drive. (Some sectors of a hard drive are not rewritten during most reformattings.) That way, it can reinstall itself after the reformatting is completed.

Are there ways to protect data contained on mobile devices? Smartphones can be vulnerable to unauthorized access if they are left unattended or are stolen. Although some devices offer basic protection features (such as password protection), sensitive business information often requires an additional level of protection. Security software such as TealLock from TealPoint Software (**tealpoint.com**) offers additional protection features such as data encryption and protection against attempts to break into a device through "brute force" attacks (running a program to guess all possible passwords). Most programs feature optional data self-destruct modes (sometimes known as **bomb software**) that destroy data on both internal memory and external data cards if repeated attempts are made to crack passwords.

How can I ensure that I've covered all aspects of protecting my computer? The checklist in Figure 9.35 is a guide to ensure you didn't miss any critical aspects of security. If you've addressed all of these issues, you can feel reasonably confident that your Internet access will be secure and free from problems.

Taking a few precautions regarding your data security can provide huge benefits such as peace of mind and the avoidance of time spent correcting problems. So enjoy your computing experiences, but do so safely.

Figure 9.35 | COMPUTER SECURITY CHECKLIST

	Yes	No
Virus and Spyware Protection		
Is antivirus and antispyware software installed on all your computers?		
Is the antivirus and antispyware software configured to update itself automatically and regularly?		
Is the software set to scan your computer on a regular basis (at least weekly) for viruses and spyware?		
Firewall		
Do all your computers have firewall software installed and activated before connecting to the Internet?		
Is your router also able to function as a hardware firewall?		
Have you tested your firewall security by using the free software available at **grc.com**?		
Wireless Security (see Chapter 7 for additional details)		
Have you changed the default password for your router?		
Have you changed the name (SSID) of your network and turned off SSID broadcasting?		
Have you enabled WPA or WEP encryption for your network?		
Software Updates		
Have you configured your operating systems (Windows, OS X) to install new software patches and updates automatically?		
Is other software installed on your computer (such as Microsoft Office) configured for automatic updates?		
Is the Web browser you are using the latest version?		

With billions of dollars spent on e-commerce initiatives every year, companies have a vested interest in keeping their information technology (IT) infrastructures humming along. The rise in terrorism has shifted the focus slightly—from protecting virtual assets and access, to protecting these plus physical assets and access points. The increased need for virtual and physical security measures means there should be a robust job market ahead for computer security experts.

The National Security Agency and the Office of Homeland Security are both encouraging information security professionals to be proficient in information assurance. As defined by the NSA, **information assurance** is "the set of measures intended to protect and defend information and information systems by ensuring their availability, integrity, authentication, confidentiality, and non-repudiation. This includes providing for restoration of information systems by incorporating protection, detection, and reaction capabilities." The five key attributes of secure information systems are as follows:

1. **Availability:** The extent to which a data-processing system is able to receive and process data. A high degree of availability is usually desirable.

2. **Integrity:** A quality that an information system has if the processing of information is logical and accurate and the data is protected against unauthorized modifications or destruction.

3. **Authentication:** Security measures designed to protect an information system against acceptance of a fraudulent transmission of data by establishing the validity of a data transmission or message, or the identity of the sender.

4. **Confidentiality:** The assurance that information is not disclosed to unauthorized persons, processes, or devices.

5. **Nonrepudiation:** A capability of security systems that guarantees that a message or data can be proven to have originated from a specific person and was processed by the recipient. The sender of the data receives a receipt for the data, and the receiver of the data gets proof of the sender's identity. The objective of nonrepudiation is to prevent either party from later denying having handled the data.

The Global Information Assurance Certification, or GIAC (**giac.org**), is an industry-recognized certification that provides objective evidence (through examinations) that security professionals have mastered key skills in various aspects of information assurance.

What skill sets will be most in demand for security professionals? In addition to information assurance technical skills (with an emphasis on network engineering and data communications), broad-based business experience is also extremely desirable. IT security professionals need to understand the key issues of e-commerce and the core areas of their company's business (such as marketing, sales, and finance). Understanding how a business works is essential to pinpointing and correcting security risks that could be detrimental to a company's bottom line. Because of the large number of attacks by hackers, security and forensic skills and related certifications also are in high demand. Working closely with law enforcement officials is essential to rapidly solving and stopping cybercrime.

Another important attribute of security professionals is the ability to lead and motivate teams. Security experts need to work with diverse members of the business community, including customers, to forge relationships and understanding among diverse groups. Security professionals must conduct skillful negotiations to ensure that large project implementations are not unduly delayed by security initiatives or pushed through with inadequate security precautions. Diplomacy is therefore a sought-after skill.

Look for more colleges and universities to roll out security-based degree and certificate programs as the demand for security professionals increases. These programs will most likely be appropriate for experienced networking professionals who are ready to make the move into the IT security field. If you're just starting to prepare for a career, consider a degree in network engineering, followed by network security training while you're working at your first job. A degree program that is also designed to prepare you for security certification exams is particularly desirable. Networking and security degrees, combined with passing grades on certification exams, should help you make a smooth transition into the exciting world of cybersecurity.

summary

1. From which types of viruses do I need to protect my computer?

A computer virus is a program that attaches itself to another program and attempts to spread to other computers when files are exchanged. Computer viruses can be grouped into five categories: (1) boot-sector viruses, (2) logic bombs and time bombs, (3) worms, (4) scripts and macros, and (5) encryption viruses. Once run, they perform their malicious duties in the background, and are often invisible to the user.

2. What can I do to protect my computer from viruses?

The best defense against viruses is to install antivirus software. You should update the software on a regular basis and configure it to examine all e-mail attachments for viruses. You should periodically run a complete virus scan on your computer to ensure that no viruses have made it onto your hard drive.

3. How can hackers attack my computing devices, and what harm can they cause?

A hacker is defined as anyone who breaks into a computer system unlawfully. Hackers can use software to break into almost any computer connected to the Internet (unless proper precautions are taken). Once hackers gain access to a computer, they can potentially (1) steal personal or other important information; (2) damage and destroy data; or (3) use the computer to attack other computers.

4. What is a firewall, and how does it keep my computer safe from hackers?

Firewalls are software programs or hardware devices designed to keep computers safe from hackers. By using a personal firewall, you can close open logical ports to invaders and potentially make your computer invisible to other computers on the Internet.

5. How do I create secure passwords and manage all of my passwords?

Secure passwords contain a mixture of upper- and lowercase letters, numbers, and symbols, and are at least 14 characters long. Passwords should not contain words that are in the dictionary or easy-to-guess personal information (like your pet's name). Online password checkers can be used to evaluate the strength of your passwords. Utilities built into Web browsers and Internet security software can be used to manage your passwords and alleviate the need to remember numerous complex passwords.

6. How can I surf the Internet anonymously and use biometric authentication devices to protect my data?

The current versions of the popular browsers include tools (such as Chrome's Incognito feature) that hide your surfing activities by not recording Web sites that you visit, or files that you download, in your browser's history files. Biometric authentication devices use a physical attribute (such as a fingerprint) that is not easily duplicated to control access to data files or computing devices. Some notebooks today feature fingerprint readers and facial recognition software to control access.

7. How do I manage online annoyances such as spyware and spam?

The Web is filled with annoyances such as spam, pop-ups, cookies, spyware, and scams such as phishing that make surfing the Web frustrating and sometimes dangerous. Software tools help to prevent or reduce spam, adware, and spyware, while exercising caution can prevent serious harm caused by phishing, pharming, and other Internet scams and hoaxes.

8. What data do I need to back up, and what are the best methods for doing so?

Data files created by you (such as Word and Excel files) or purchased by you (such as music files) need to be backed up in case they are inadvertently deleted or damaged. Application software (such as Microsoft Office) may need to be reinstalled if files are damaged, so backups (usually the DVDs or CDs the application came on) must be maintained. External hard drives are popular choices for holding backup copies of files. Various backup software packages are available to automate the backup tasks.

9. What is social engineering, and how do I avoid falling prey to phishing and hoaxes?

Social engineering schemes use human interaction, deception, and trickery to fool people into revealing sensitive information such as credit card numbers and passwords. Phishing schemes usually involve e-mails that direct the unwary to a Web site that appears to be legitimate (such as a bank site) but is specifically designed to capture personal information for committing fraud. To avoid phishing scams, you should never reply directly to any e-mail asking you for personal information, and never click on a link in an e-mail to go to a Web site. You can research topics you believe to be hoaxes at sites such as Snopes (**snopes.com**).

10. How do I protect my physical computing assets from environmental hazards, power surges, and theft?

Computing devices should be kept in clean environments free from dust and other particulates and should not be exposed to extreme temperatures (either hot or cold). You should protect all electronic devices from power surges by hooking them up through surge protectors, which will protect them from most electrical surges that could damage the devices. Notebook computers can be protected from theft either by attaching alarms to them or by installing software that will help recover the computer, if stolen, by reporting the computer's whereabouts when it is connected to the Internet.

chapter nine
key terms

buzzwords

Word Bank

- adware
- antivirus software
- backup(s)
- distributed denial-of-service (DDoS)
- firewall
- hacker(s)
- identity theft
- information assurance
- keystroke logger(s)
- logical port(s)
- phishing
- social engineering
- spyware
- virus
- zombie(s)

Instructions: Fill in the blanks using the words from the Word Bank above.

Emily learned a lot about computer security in her computer literacy class. She already knew it was important to exercise caution when using the Internet because she had been the victim of (1) _____, which destroyed her credit rating. A(n) (2) _____ had obtained her credit card information by posing as an employee of her bank, using a method known as (3) _____. In her class, Emily learned that hackers could install (4) _____, a type of software that will capture everything she types, to steal her personal information. And one of Emily's classmates received a (5) _____ e-mail that directed her to a fake Web site that looked like her bank's Web site and resulted in her bank account information being stolen. The computers in the lab at school had just been cleaned of (6) _____ software that was displaying annoying pop-up advertisements. The computer technician who fixed this problem indicated that (7) _____ software, which was monitoring computer user activity, was often inadvertently installed on lab computers by students downloading files.

Emily found out that her router could be configured as a(n) (8) _____ to repel malicious hacking mischief and assist in providing (9) _____ for the data on her computer. Turning off the unused (10) _____ would repel most attacks on her home network. With this protection, it was unlikely that a hacker would turn her PC into a(n) (11) _____ to launch (12) _____ attacks. However, after the scare with the Conficker (13) _____, Emily was careful to warn her family not to open files from untrusted sources. She also made sure all of the computers in her home had (14) _____ installed to protect them from viruses. For extra security, Emily installed an external hard drive so that she could create (15) _____ of her data files.

becoming computer literate

While attending college, you are working at the Snap-Tite company, a small manufacturer of specialty fasteners. Recently, the company computers have been behaving strangely and running slowly. You suspect that viruses and spyware might be present on the computers, as it appears most of the computers lack any sort of protection. Your boss heard that you are taking a computer course and has asked you to suggest a solution.

Instructions: Using the preceding scenario, draft an antivirus and antispyware plan for Snap-Tite using as many of the keywords from the chapter as you can. Be sure that the company president, who is unfamiliar with many computer terms, can understand the report.

Instructions: Answer the multiple-choice and true–false questions below for more practice with key terms and concepts from this chapter.

Multiple Choice

1. Computer viruses that are triggered when a certain condition is met are known as
   a. logic bombs.
   b. time bombs.
   c. stealth viruses.
   d. multipartite viruses.

2. Viruses that periodically change their code to avoid detection are called
   a. stealth viruses.
   b. script viruses.
   c. polymorphic viruses.
   d. macro viruses.

3. Portions of virus code that are unique to a particular computer virus are known as
   a. master boot records.
   b. virus signatures.
   c. virus footprints.
   d. virus traces.

4. Hackers who break into systems just for the challenge, or to bring system vulnerabilities to light for the greater good, are called
   a. black hat hackers.
   b. script kiddies.
   c. valiant hackers.
   d. white hat hackers.

5. Programs that allow hackers to take almost complete control of a computer without the owner's knowledge are known as
   a. Trojan horses.
   b. backdoor programs.
   c. stealth viruses.
   d. None of the above.

6. Techniques that use verbal or written communication to generate human interaction that tricks individuals into revealing sensitive information are collectively known as
   a. phishing.
   b. pharming.
   c. pretexting.
   d. social engineering.

7. When hackers use computers to launch an attack on another computer, the computers used to stage the attack are known as
   a. drones.
   b. zombies.
   c. packet sniffers.
   d. Trojan horses.

8. Which is NOT a benefit of firewalls?
   a. They make it harder for a hacker to locate specific computers on a network.
   b. They repeatedly change the IP address of the router.
   c. They close unused logical ports to decrease network vulnerability.
   d. They filter out unauthorized requests for data.

9. Planting code on your computer that alters your browser's ability to find Web addresses is a type of cyberannoyance known as
   a. phishing.
   b. keystroke logging.
   c. logic bombing.
   d. pharming.

10. Viruses that attempt to travel between systems through network connections to spread their infections are called
   a. worms.
   b. stealth viruses.
   c. logic bombs.
   d. macro viruses.

True–False

_____ 1. Viruses that render your files unusable in an attempt to extort money to have them restored are known as stealth viruses.

_____ 2. A properly installed surge protector will protect a computer from all power surges.

_____ 3. Installing a firewall on your network will not stop most viruses from being planted on your network.

_____ 4. E-mails designed to trick you into revealing information (such as bank account numbers) are a type of phishing scam.

_____ 5. If you have designed strong passwords, there is never a need to change them.

making the
transition to...
next semester

nine chapter

making the
transition to...
next semester

1. Backup Procedures

After reading this chapter, you know you should have a good backup strategy in place for your key data. Consider the following and prepare answers in an appropriate format as directed by your instructor.

a. How often do you back up critical data files such as homework files? What type of device do you use for backing up files? Where do you store the backups to ensure they won't be destroyed if a major disaster (such as a fire) destroys your computer?

b. List the applications (such as Microsoft Office) that are currently installed on your computer. Where is the media (DVDs, CDs) for your application software stored? For any software you purchased in an Internet download, have you burned a copy of the installation files to DVD/CD in case you need to reinstall the software?

c. Have you ever made an image backup of your entire system? If so, what software do you use for image backups, and where are the image backups stored? If not, research image backup software on the Internet and find an appropriate package to use. Will you need to purchase an additional backup device to hold your image backup or does your current device have room for an image backup? If you need a new device, find one on the Internet that is appropriate. What is the total cost of the software and hardware you will need to implement your image backup strategy?

2. Connecting Your Computer to Public Networks

In the course of your education, you are constantly connecting your notebook to various wireless public networks such as those in the school library and neighborhood coffee shop. As you know from reading this chapter, you are more vulnerable to hackers when connected to a wireless network in a public place such as a coffee shop. Conduct research on the Internet about surfing at public hot spots and prepare a list of sensible precautions for you and your classmates to take when surfing on an open network.

3. Identity Theft Awareness

Two students in your residence hall have recently been the victims of identity theft. You have been assigned to create a flyer telling students how they can protect themselves from identity theft in their residence hall. Using the information found in this chapter, materials you find on the U.S. government Web site on identity theft (**consumer.gov/idtheft**), and other Web resources, create a flyer that lists 5 to 10 ways in which students can avoid having their identities stolen.

1. Antivirus Protection

Your employer recently installed high-speed Internet access at the office where you work. There are 50 workstations connected to the network and the Internet. Within a week, half the computers in the office went down because of a virus that infected a screen saver. In addition, network personnel from a university in England contacted the company, claiming that your employer's computer systems were being used as part of a denial-of-service (DDoS) attack on their Web site.

a. Price security suite software on the Internet and determine the most cost-effective package for the company to use to implement protection on 50 workstations.
b. Write a "virus prevention" memo to all employees that suggests strategies for avoiding computer virus infections.
c. Draft a note to the CEO to explain how a firewall could prevent DDoS attacks from being launched on the company network.

2. Securing Customer Data

Many corporations are collecting vast amounts of sensitive data (such as credit card numbers, birth dates, etc.) about their customers. Assume you are working for a business that accepts orders for merchandise through a Web site. Answer the following questions:

a. What security measures should you implement on your Web site to ensure that customers' data is protected (or encrypted) from the prying eyes of hackers?
b. Your company would like to send e-mails to customers on their birthdays, offering them a special discount on merchandise purchased within one week of their birthday. How would you explain to customers why you are collecting their birthdates, and what measures would you need to take to keep this data secure?
c. How would you ensure that information shared with third parties (such as delivery companies) is kept secure?

3. Testing Your Computer

Visit Gibson Research (**grc.com**) and run the company's ShieldsUP and LeakTest programs on your computer.

a. Did your computer get a clean report? If not, what potential vulnerabilities did the testing programs detect?
b. How could you protect yourself from the vulnerabilities these programs can detect?

Instructions: Albert Einstein used *Gedankenexperiments*, or critical thinking questions, to develop his theory of relativity. Some ideas are best understood by experimenting with them in our own minds. The following critical thinking questions are designed to demand your full attention but only require a comfortable chair—no technology.

1. Protecting Your Home Network

Many people have networks in their homes. Consider the network installed in your home (or in a friend's home if you don't have a network).

a. Is your network set up to provide adequate protection against hackers? If not, what would you need to do to make it secure?

b. Are the computers on your home network protected against viruses and malware? Is the software used for protection updated on a regular basis? Have you ever had problems from a virus or spyware infestation? If so, how did you resolve the problem?

2. Password Protection

You know from reading this chapter that secure passwords are essential to protecting your digital information. Consider the following:

a. How many online accounts do you have that have passwords? List them. Are the passwords for these accounts secure, based on the suggestions proposed in this chapter? Do you change your passwords on a regular basis?

b. How do you keep track of all of your passwords? Do you use password management software? If so, what product are you using? How often do you change your master password? If you don't use password management software, what methodology do you use for remembering and tracking your passwords? Do you think password management software would improve your password security?

3. Ethical Hacking?

Hackers and virus authors cause millions of dollars worth of damage to PCs and networks annually. However, hacking is a highly controversial subject. Many hackers believe they are actually working for the "good of the people" or "exercising their freedom" when they engage in hacking activities. However, in most jurisdictions in the United States, hacking is punishable by stiff fines and jail terms.

a. Hackers often argue that hacking is for the good of all people because it points out flaws in computer systems. Do you agree with this? Why or why not?

b. What should the punishment be for convicted hackers? Why?

c. Who should be held accountable at a corporation whose network security is breached by a hacker?

4. Keeping Networks Safe from Cyberterrorists

Many of us rely on networks every day, often without realizing it. Whether you are researching a term paper on the Internet, ordering a book from Amazon.com, or accessing your college e-mail from home, you are relying on networks to relay information. But what if terrorists destroyed key components of the Internet or other networks on which we depend?

a. What economic problems would result from DDoS attacks launched by terrorists on major e-commerce sites?

b. Research the precautions that the U.S. military and intelligence agencies such as the Departments of Homeland Security and Commerce, the FBI, and the CIA are taking to ensure that networks involving national defense remain secure from terrorist attacks. What else should they do?

Protecting Your Local Real Estate Office

Problem

Computer networks with high-speed connections to the Internet are common in most businesses today. However, along with easy access to computing devices and the Web comes the danger of theft of digital assets.

Task

A recent graduate of your school has opened a 15-person real estate office in a neighboring town. He approached your instructor for help in assuring that his computers are adequately protected from viruses, malware, and hackers. Because he is currently low on funds, he is hoping that there may be free software available that can adequately shield his company from harm.

Process

Break the class into three teams. Each team will be responsible for investigating one of the following issues:

1. **Firewalls:** Research free firewall software and locate at least three software options that can be deployed at the business. Be sure to concentrate on software that is easy to configure and requires little or no user interaction to be effective.

2. **Antivirus software:** Research alternatives that can be used to protect the computers in the office from virus infection. Find at least three alternatives and support your recommendations with reviews (from publications such as *PC Magazine* or *Consumer Reports*) that evaluate the free packages and compare them to commercial solutions.

3. **Anti-malware software:** Research free packages that will offer protection from malware. Locate at least three alternatives and determine whether the recommended software can be updated automatically. (Many free versions require manual updates.) Most companies that provide free malware protection also offer commercial packages (for a fee) that provide automatic updates. You may need to recommend that the company purchase software to ensure that a minimum of employee intervention is needed to keep the software up to date.

Present your findings to your class and discuss the pros and cons of free and commercial software. Provide your instructor with a report suitable for eventual presentation to the owner of the real estate office.

Conclusion

With the proliferation of viruses and malware, it is essential to protect business (and home) computers and networks from destruction and disruption. Free alternatives might work, but you should ensure that you have done adequate research to determine the best possible protection solution for your particular situation.

In addition to the review materials presented here, you'll find additional materials featured with the book's multimedia, including the *Technology in Action* Student Resource CD and the Companion Website (**www.pearsonhighered.com/techinaction**), which will help reinforce your understanding of the chapter content. These materials include the following:

Active Helpdesk

In Active Helpdesk calls, you'll assume the role of helpdesk operator, taking calls about the concepts you've learned in this chapter. You'll apply what you've learned and receive feedback from a supervisor to review and reinforce those concepts. The Active Helpdesk calls for this chapter are listed below and can be found on your Student Resource CD:

- Avoiding Computer Viruses
- Understanding Firewalls

Sound Bytes

Sound Bytes are dynamic multimedia tutorials that help demystify even the most complex topics. You'll view video clips and animations that illustrate computer concepts and then apply what you've learned by reviewing with the Sound Byte Labs, which include quizzes and activities specifically tailored to each Sound Byte. The Sound Bytes for this chapter are listed below and can be found on your Student Resource CD:

- Protecting Your Computer
- Installing a Personal Firewall
- Surge Protectors

Companion Website

The *Technology in Action* Companion Website includes a variety of additional materials to help you review and learn more about the topics in this chapter. The resources available at **www.pearsonhighered.com/techinaction** include:

- **Online Study Guide.** Each chapter features an online true–false and multiple-choice quiz. You can take these quizzes, automatically check the results, and e-mail the results to your instructor.
- **Web Research Projects.** Each chapter features several Web research projects that ask you to search the Web for information on computer-related careers, milestones in computer history, important people and companies, emerging technologies, and the applications and implications of different technologies.

Careers in IT

It's hard to imagine an occupation in which computers are not used in some fashion. Even such previously low-tech industries as junkyards and fast food use computers to manage inventories and order commodities. In this Technology in Focus feature, we explore various information technology (IT) career paths open to you.

What to Consider First: Job Outlook

If you want to investigate a career with computers, the first question you probably have is, "Will I be able to get a job?" With all the media hoopla surrounding the loss of IT jobs, many people think the boom in computer-related jobs is over. However, current projections by the U.S. Department of Labor's Bureau of Labor Statistics report that 3 out of the top 17 fastest-growing occupations from 2006 through 2016 are still in computer fields (see Figure 1). Recently, *Money* magazine rated the top 10 best jobs in the United States; computer IT analysts came in at number 7, and software engineers were number 1! *Money* projects growth rates for these jobs over the next 10 years at 36.1 percent and 46.07 percent, respectively. A 2009 survey conducted by Polachi, Inc., a Framingham, Massachusetts–based executive search firm, found that more than 50 percent of the senior IT managers were hiring and that 93 percent of the survey respondents felt the overall demand for IT professionals would increase or remain the same.

After five years of declining enrollment, students pursuing computer science degrees finally began to increase in 2008 (up 6.2 percent in the Taulbee survey). This marks a reversal of a trend that developed mainly because of the intense media discussion about the demise of Internet start-up companies in the early 2000s. Because of low enrollment during the current decade, critical shortages of computing professionals in the

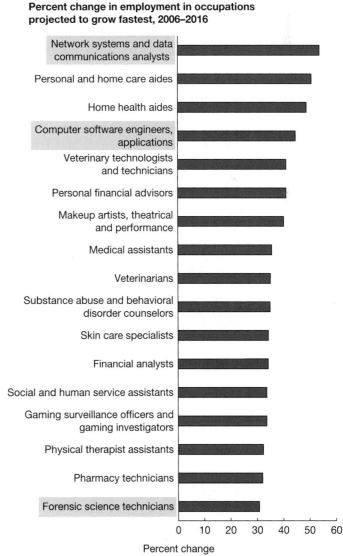

FIGURE 1

As this chart shows, huge growth is expected in three different computer-related occupations, according to the Bureau of Labor Statistics.

Percent change in employment in occupations projected to grow fastest, 2006–2016

- Network systems and data communications analysts
- Personal and home care aides
- Home health aides
- Computer software engineers, applications
- Veterinary technologists and technicians
- Personal financial advisors
- Makeup artists, theatrical and performance
- Medical assistants
- Veterinarians
- Substance abuse and behavioral disorder counselors
- Skin care specialists
- Financial analysts
- Social and human service assistants
- Gaming surveillance officers and gaming investigators
- Physical therapist assistants
- Pharmacy technicians
- Forensic science technicians

Percent change

United States are projected over the next 5 to 10 years. In terms of job outlook, this is a perfect time to consider an IT career.

Regardless of whether you choose to pursue a career in IT, you should visit the Bureau of Labor Statistics site (**bls.gov**). One of the site's most useful features is the *Occupational Outlook Handbook*. Aside from projecting job growth in various career fields, it describes typical tasks that workers perform, the amount of training and education needed, and salary estimates.

In the global economy in which we now operate, job outlook also includes the risk of jobs being outsourced, possibly to other countries (a process known as *offshoring*). **Outsourcing** is a process whereby a business hires a third-party firm to provide business services (such as customer-support call centers) that were previously handled by in-house employees. **Offshoring** occurs when the outsourcing firm is located (or uses employees) outside the United States. India was the first country to offer its workforce and infrastructure for offshoring, and countries such as China, Romania, and other former Eastern Bloc countries now vie for a piece of the action. The big lure of outsourcing and offshoring is cost savings: The outsourcing firm can do the work more cheaply than in-house employees can. Considering that the standard of living and salaries are much lower in many countries than they are in the United States, offshoring is an attractive option for many U.S. employers. It may also be faster to hire outside assistance if a business does not already employ workers with the required skill set.

However, outsourcing and offshoring do not always deliver the vast cost savings that chief executive officers (CEOs) envision. TPI, a global sourcing advisory firm, conducted a survey that showed that the average cost savings from outsourcing was only 15 percent. Furthermore, other less-tangible factors can outweigh the cost savings from outsourcing. Some helpdesk jobs are being brought back to the United States because companies have experienced a backlash from consumers who have had difficulty understanding the employees with foreign accents who staff the support lines. Communications problems can arise between internal and external employees, for example, and cultural differences between the home country and the country doing the offshoring can result in software code that needs extensive rework by in-house employees to make it usable. Data also can be less secure in an external environment, or during the transfer between the company and an external vendor. A study by Deloitte Consulting found that 70 percent of survey participants had "negative experiences" with overseas outsourcing, and 44 percent of participants saw no cost savings as a result of outsourcing. Although outsourcing and offshoring won't be going away, companies are approaching it with more caution.

So, what IT jobs will be staying in the United States? According to *InformationWeek* magazine, most of the jobs in these three categories (see Figure 2) will stay put:

1. **Customer facing:** Jobs that require direct input from customers or that involve systems with which customers interface daily.

FIGURE 2 Jobs That Should Remain Onshore

Customer Interaction	Software and Systems	Hardware/Networking
Web application developers	Business process analysts	Network security
Web interface designers	Application developers (when customer interaction is critical)	Network installation technicians
Database and data warehouse designers/developers	Project managers (for systems with customers and business users who are located predominantly in the United States)	Network administrators (engineers)
Customer relationship management (CRM) analysts		Wireless infrastructure managers and technicians
Enterprise resource planning (ERP) implementation specialists		Disaster recovery planners and responders

2. **Enablers:** Jobs that involve getting key business projects accomplished, often requiring technical skills beyond the realm of IT and good people skills.

3. **Infrastructure jobs:** Jobs that are fundamental to moving and storing the information that U.S.–based employees need to do their jobs.

Common Myths About IT Careers

Many people have misconceptions about pursuing a career in IT that scare them away from considering a career in computing or convince them

to pursue a computing career for the wrong reasons. Review the myths listed in the boxed feature. Do you share any of these misconceptions?

Is an IT Career Right for Me?

A career in IT can be a difficult path. Before preparing yourself for such a career, consider the following.

1. **Salary range:** What affects your salary in an IT position? Your skill set and your experience level are obvious answers, but the size of an employer and its geographic location are also factors. Large companies

COMMON MYTHS ABOUT IT CAREERS

MYTH 1: Getting a computer science degree means you're going to be rich. Computer-related careers often offer high salaries, but choosing a computer career isn't a guarantee you'll get a high-paying job. Just as in other professions, you probably will need years of training and on-the-job experience to earn a high salary. However, starting salaries in certain IT professions are robust.

MYTH 2: You have three professional certifications—so you're ready to work. Many freshly minted technical school graduates sporting IT certifications feel ready to jump into a job. However, employers routinely cite experience as being more desirable than certification. Experience earned through an internship or a part-time job will make you much more marketable when your certification program is complete.

MYTH 3: Women are at a disadvantage in an IT career. Currently, women make up less than 25 percent of the IT workforce. This presents a huge opportunity for women who have IT skills because many IT departments are actively seeking to diversify their workforces. In addition, although a salary gender gap (the difference between what men and women earn for performing the same job) exists in IT careers, it's smaller than in many other professions.

MYTH 4: People skills don't matter in IT jobs. Despite what many people think, IT professionals are not locked in lightless cubicles, basking in the glow of their monitors. Most IT jobs require constant interaction with other workers, often in team settings. People skills are important, even when you work with computers.

MYTH 5: Mathematically impaired people need not apply. It is true that a career in programming involves a fair bit of math, but even if you're not mathematically inclined, you can explore other IT careers. IT employers also value such attributes as teamwork, creativity, leadership ability, and artistic style.

MYTH 6: Working in IT means working for a computer company or in an IT department. Computers and information systems are used across all industries and in most job functions. For example, as an accounting major, if you minor in IT, employers may be more willing to consider hiring you because working in accounting today means constantly interfacing with management information systems and manipulating data.

MYTH 7: All of the jobs are going offshore. Although many IT jobs have been lost to international competition over the past decade, most networking, analyst (business, systems, and database)\and creative (digital media creation and game development) jobs have stayed in the United States. As demand for IT professionals has increased overseas, foreign wages have been driven up, making offshoring of jobs less attractive. The bottom line is that plenty of IT jobs remain in the United States.

Resolving myths is an important step toward considering a job in IT. However, you need to consider other issues related to IT careers before you decide to pursue a particular path.

HOW MUCH WILL I EARN?

Like many other professionals, IT employees can earn a very good living. Although starting salaries for some IT positions (computer desktop support and helpdesk analysts) are in the modest range ($34,000 to $38,000), starting salaries for students with bachelor's degrees in computer science are fairly robust. *Money* magazine profiles the best jobs in the United States on a regular basis. Their last profile showed that the highest annual starting salaries belong to engineers (chemical, electrical, and mechanical). Coming in at a respectable fourth place, however, is computer science, with salaries of slightly more than $50,000.

IT salaries vary widely, depending on experience level and the geographic location of the job. To obtain the most accurate information, research salaries yourself. Job posting sites such as **Monster.com** can provide guidance, but **Salary.com** provides a wizard to help you determine what IT professionals in your area are making compared with national averages. Figure 3 shows that for an entry-level programming position in Scottsdale, Arizona, you could expect to earn a median salary of approximately $52,027

FIGURE 3

The salary wizard at Salary.com is easy to tailor to your location and job preferences.

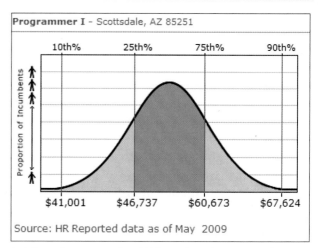

(midway between the 25th and 75th percentiles). Hundreds of IT job titles are listed so that you can fine-tune your search to the specific job in which you're interested.

tend to pay more, so if you're pursuing a high salary, set your sights on a large corporation. But remember that making a lot of money isn't everything—be sure to consider other quality-of-life issues such as job satisfaction.

2. **Gender bias:** Many women view IT departments as *Dilbert*-like microcosms of antisocial geeks and don't feel they would fit in.

Unfortunately, some mostly male IT departments do suffer from varying degrees of gender bias. Although some women may thrive on the challenge of enlightening these male enclaves and bringing them into the 21st century, others find it difficult to work in such environments.

3. **Location:** In this case, *location* refers to the setting in which you work. IT jobs can be office based, field based, project based, or

FIGURE 4 Where Do You Want to Work?

Type of Job	Location and Hours	Special Considerations
Office based	Report for work to the same location each day and interact with the same people on a regular basis Requires regular hours of attendance (such as 9 A.M. to 5 P.M.)	May require working beyond "normal" working hours May also require workers to be on call 24/7
Field based	Travel from place to place as needed and perform short-term jobs at each location	Involve a great deal of travel and the ability to work independently
Project based	Work at client sites on specific projects for extended periods of time (weeks or months) Examples: contractors and consultants	Can be especially attractive to individuals who like workplace situations that vary on a regular basis
Home based (telecommuting)	Work from home	Involve very little day-to-day supervision and require an individual who is self-disciplined

MATCHING A CAREER TO YOUR SKILLS

Are you unsure about what career you would like to pursue? Online tools such as the ISEEK Skills Assessment (**iseek.org**) can help you identify careers based on your skills. This tool asks you to assess your skills (see Figure 5) in six broad categories. The program then evaluates the skills matrix and suggests job titles for you to explore.

FIGURE 5

"People Skills" is one of six categories on the ISEEK skills matrix, a survey that you can complete to help you assess which career paths match your talents.

ISEEK Skills Assessment
Tell us what you like to do. We'll tell you about jobs you might like.

⌄ Share   🖶 Print

1. Basic Skills
2. Management Skills
3. People Skills
4. System Skills
5. Technical Skills
6. Results: Matching Jobs

Start a new assessment

Step 3 of 6: People Skills

◀ Previous: Management Skills   Next: System Skills ▶

How important is it to you to do the following things in your job?

Being Aware of Others ❓

○ 1   ○ 2   ○ 3   ● 4   ○ 5
Not Important   Extremely Important

Coordinating with Others ❓

○ 1   ○ 2   ○ 3   ○ 4   ● 5
Not Important   Extremely Important

Helping Others ❓

○ 1   ○ 2   ○ 3   ○ 4   ● 5
Not Important   Extremely Important

Negotiating ❓

○ 1   ○ 2   ○ 3   ● 4   ○ 5
Not Important   Extremely Important

---

home based. Not every situation is perfect for every individual. Figure 4 summarizes the major job types and their locations.

4. **Changing workplace:** In IT, the playing field is always changing. New software and hardware are constantly being developed. It's almost a full-time job to keep your skills up to date. You can expect to spend a lot of time in training and self-study trying to learn new systems and techniques.

5. **Stress:** Whereas the average American works 42 hours a week, a survey by *InformationWeek* shows that the average IT staff person works 45 hours a week and is on call for another 24 hours. On-call time (hours an employee must be available to work in the event of a problem) has been increasing in recent years because more IT systems (such as e-commerce systems) require 24/7 availability.

The good news is that despite the stress (see Figure 6) and changing nature of the IT environment, most computing skills are portable from industry to industry. A networking job in the clothing manufacturing industry uses the same primary skill set as a networking job for a supermarket chain. Therefore, if something disastrous happens to the industry you're in, you should be able to switch to another industry with little trouble.

FIGURE 6

Stress comes from multiple directions in IT jobs.

Emails from 63 customers complaining about new Web site design

Marketing department needs new Web page by Friday

Supervisor needs quarterly budget report yesterday!

Sales staff at annual golf outing in Scottsdale can't access their sales reports

What Realm of IT Should I Work In?

Figure 7 provides an organizational chart for a modern IT department that should help you understand the careers currently available and how they interrelate. The chief information officer (CIO) has overall responsibility for the development, implementation, and maintenance of information systems and infrastructure. Usually the CIO reports to the chief operating officer (COO).

The responsibilities below the CIO are generally grouped into two units: development and integration (responsible for the development of systems and Web sites) and technical services (responsible for the day-to-day operations of the company's information infrastructure and network, including all hardware and software deployed).

FIGURE 7

This is a typical structure for an IT department at a large corporation.

In large organizations, responsibilities are distinct and jobs are defined more narrowly. In medium-sized organizations, there can be overlap between position responsibilities. At a small shop, you might be the network administrator, database administrator, computer support technician, and helpdesk analyst all at the same time. Let's look at the typical jobs found in each department.

Working in Development and Integration

Two distinct paths exist in this division: Web development and systems development. Because everything involves the Web today, there is often a great deal of overlap between these paths.

Web Development

When most people think of Web development careers, they usually equate them with being a *webmaster*. However, today's webmasters usually are supervisors with responsibility for certain aspects of Web development. At smaller companies, they may also be responsible for

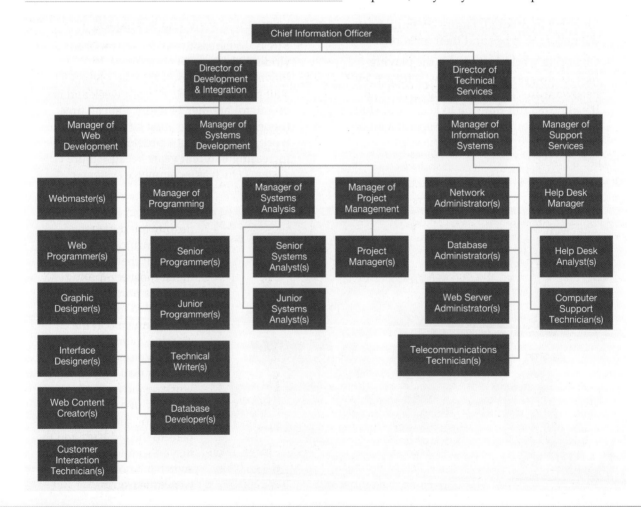

tasks that the other individuals in a Web development group usually do:

- **Web content creators** generate the words and images that appear on the Web. Journalists, other writers, editors, and marketing personnel prepare an enormous amount of Web content, whereas **video producers**, **graphic designers**, and **animators** create Web-based multimedia. **Interface designers** work with graphic designers and animators to create a look and feel for the site and make it easy to navigate. Content creators have a thorough understanding of their own fields as well as HTML/XHTML and JavaScript. They also need to be familiar with the capabilities and limitations of modern Web development tools so that they know what the Web publishers can accomplish.

- **Web publishers** build Web pages to deploy the materials that the content creators develop. They wield the software tools (such as Adobe Dreamweaver and Microsoft Expression) that develop the Web pages and create links to databases (using products such as Oracle and SQL Server) to keep information flowing between users and Web pages. They must possess a solid understanding of client- and server-side Web languages (HTML/XHTML, XML, Java, JavaScript, ASP, and PERL) and development environments such as the Microsoft .NET Framework.

- **Customer interaction technicians** provide feedback to a Web site's customers. Major job responsibilities include answering e-mail, sending requested information, funneling questions to appropriate personnel (technical support, sales, and so on), and providing suggestions to Web publishers for site improvements. Extensive customer service training is essential to work effectively in this area.

As you can see in Figure 8, many different people can work on the same Web site. The education required varies widely for these jobs. Web programming jobs often require a four-year college degree in computer science, whereas graphic designers often are hired with two-year art degrees.

Systems Development

Ask most people what systems developers do and they will answer, "programming." However, programming is only one aspect of systems development. Because large projects involve many people, there are many job opportunities in systems development. An explanation of each key area follows.

- **Systems analysts** spend most of their time in the beginning stages of the system development life cycle (SDLC). They talk with end users to gather information about problems and existing information systems. They document systems and propose solutions to problems. Having good people skills is essential to success as a systems analyst. In addition, systems analysts work with programmers during the development phase to design appropriate programs to solve the problem at hand. Therefore, many organizations insist on hiring systems analysts who have both solid business backgrounds and

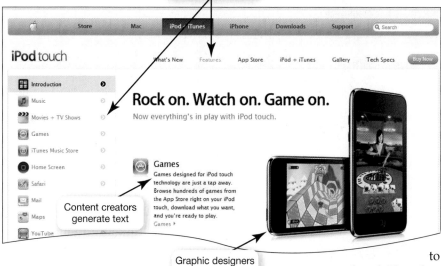

Interface designers create navigation schemes

Content creators generate text

Graphic designers create art

FIGURE 8

As you can see, it takes a team to create and maintain a Web site.

previous programming experience (at least at a basic level). For entry-level jobs, a four-year degree is usually required. Many colleges and universities offer degrees in management information systems (MIS) that include a mixture of systems development, programming, and business courses.

- **Programmers** participate in the SDLC, attending meetings to document user needs and working closely with systems analysts during the design phase. Programmers need excellent written communication skills because they often generate detailed systems documentation for end-user training purposes. Because programming languages are mathematically based, it is essential for programmers to have strong math skills and an ability to think logically. Programmers should also be proficient at more than one programming language. A four-year degree is usually required for entry-level programming positions.
- **Project managers** usually have years of experience as programmers or systems analysts. This job is part of a career path upward from entry-level programming and systems analyst jobs. Project managers manage the overall systems development

process: assigning staff, budgeting, reporting to management, coaching team members, and ensuring deadlines are met. Project managers need excellent time management skills because they are pulled in several directions at once. Many project managers obtain master's degrees to supplement their undergraduate degrees in computer science or MIS.

In addition to these key players, the following people are also involved in the systems development process:

- **Technical writers** generate systems documentation for end users and for programmers who may make modifications to the system in the future.
- **Network engineers** help the programmers and analysts design compatible systems, because many systems are required to run in certain environments (UNIX or Windows, for instance) and must work well in conjunction with other programs.
- **Database developers** design and build databases to support the software systems being developed.

Large development projects may have all of these team members on the project. Smaller projects may require an overlap of positions (such as a programmer also acting as a systems analyst). The majority of these jobs require four-year college degrees in computer science or management information systems. As shown in Figure 9, team members work together to build a system.

It is important to emphasize that all systems development careers are stressful. Deadlines are tight for development projects, especially if they involve getting a new product to market ahead of the competition. Nevertheless, if you enjoy challenges and can endure a fast-paced, dynamic environment, there should be

FIGURE 9

This is a flowchart of an order processing system. Each member of the systems development team performs functions critical to the development process (as shown in the red boxes).

GET IN THE GAME: CAREERS IN GAME DEVELOPMENT

The video gaming industry in the United States has surpassed the earning power of the Hollywood movie industry. In 2008, U.S. consumers bought over $21 billion worth of video games and accessories, whereas Hollywood took in just under $10 billion. Although some aspects of game development, such as scenery design and certain aspects of programming, are being sent offshore, the majority of game development requires a creative team whose members need to work in close proximity to each other. Therefore, it is anticipated that most game development jobs will stay in the United States. The release of the Xbox 360 and PlayStation 3 consoles have doubled development budgets for games because the new consoles support games that are more sophisticated. Because the majority of development costs are personnel related, which translates into more job opportunities.

Game development jobs usually are split along two paths: designers and programmers. Game designers tend to be artistic and are responsible for creating 2D and 3D art, game interfaces, video sequences, special effects, game levels, and scenarios. Game designers must master software packages such as Autodesk 3ds Max, Autodesk Maya, NewTek LightWave 3D, Adobe Photoshop, and Adobe Flash (see Figure 10).

FIGURE 10

LightWave is a popular package that is used to create realistic graphics for games such as the one shown here.

Programmers are then responsible for coding the scenarios developed by these designers. Using languages such as C, C++, Assembly, and Java, programmers build the game and ensure that it plays accurately.

Aside from programmers and designers, play testers and quality assurance professionals play the games with the intent of breaking them or discovering bugs within the game interfaces or worlds. *Play testing* is an essential part of the game development process because it assists designers in determining which aspects of the game are most intriguing to players and which parts of the game need to be repaired or enhanced.

No matter what job you may pursue in the realm of gaming, you will need to have a two- or four-year college degree. If you're interested in gaming, then look for a school with a solid animation or 3D art program or a computer game programming curriculum. Programming requires a strong background in mathematics and physics to enable you to realistically program environments that mimic the real world. Proficiency with mathematics (especially geometry) also helps with design careers. For more information on gaming careers, check out the International Game Developers Association site (**igda.org**) and Game Career Guide (**gamecareerguide.com**).

plenty of opportunities for good systems developers in the decade ahead.

Working in Technical Services

Technical services jobs are vital to keeping IT systems running. The people in these jobs install and maintain the infrastructure behind the IT systems and work with end users to make sure they can interact with the systems effectively. These also are the *least likely* IT jobs to be outsourced because hands-on work with equipment and users is required on a regular basis. The two major categories of technical services careers are information systems and support services.

Information Systems

The information systems department keeps the networks and telecommunications up and running at all times. Within the department, you'll find a variety of positions.

- **Network administrators** (sometimes called *network engineers*) install and configure servers, design and plan networks, and test new networking equipment (see Figure 11).

- **Database administrators (DBAs)** install and configure database servers and ensure that the servers provide an adequate level of access to all users.
- **Web server administrators** install, configure, and maintain Web servers and ensure that the company maintains Internet connectivity at all times.
- **Telecommunications technicians** oversee the communications infrastructure, including training employees to use telecommunications equipment. They are often on call 24 hours a day.

Support Services

As a member of the support services team, you interface with users (external customers or employees) and troubleshoot their computer problems. These positions include the following:

- **Helpdesk analysts** staff the phones, respond to Internet live chat, or respond to e-mail and solve problems for customers or employees, either remotely or in person.

FIGURE 11

At smaller companies, you may be fixing a user's computer in the morning, installing and configuring a new network operating system in the afternoon, and troubleshooting a router problem (shown here) in the evening.

Often helpdesk personnel are called upon to train users on the latest software and hardware.

- **Computer support technicians** go to a user's physical location and fix software and hardware problems. They also often have to chase down and repair faults in the network infrastructure.

As important as these people are, they often receive a great deal of abuse by angry users whose computers are not working. When working in support services, you need to be patient and not be overly sensitive to insults!

Technical services jobs often require two-year college degrees or training at trade schools or technical institutes. At smaller companies, job duties tend to overlap between the helpdesk and technician jobs. These jobs are in demand. A survey of 1,400 chief information officers sponsored by Robert Half Technology identified Windows administration, wireless network management, and database management (SQL) as the top skills needed by U.S. IT departments.

How Should I Prepare for a Job in IT?

A job in IT requires a robust skill set and formal training and preparation. Most employers today have an entry-level requirement of a college degree, a technical institute diploma, appropriate professional certifications, experience in the field, or a combination of these. How can you prepare for a job in IT?

1. **Get educated.** Two- and four-year colleges and universities normally offer three degrees to prepare students for IT careers: computer science, MIS, and computer engineering (although titles vary). Alternatives to colleges and universities are privately licensed technical (or trade) schools. Generally, these programs focus on building skill sets rapidly and qualifying for a job in a specific field. The main advantage of technical schools is that their programs usually take less time to complete than college degrees. However, to have a realistic chance of employment in IT fields other than networking or Web development, you should attend a degree-granting college or university.

SO YOU WANT TO BE A NETWORK ADMINISTRATOR?

You know that network administrators are the people who design, install, and maintain the network equipment and infrastructure. But what *exactly* do they do?

Network administrators are involved in every stage of network planning and deployment. They decide what equipment to buy and what type of media to use, and they determine the correct topology for the network. They also often develop policies regarding network usage, security measures, and hardware and software standards.

After the planning is complete, network administrators help install the network (either by supervising third-party contractors or by doing the work themselves). Typical installation tasks include configuring and installing client computers and peripherals,

running cable, and installing wireless media devices. Installing and configuring security devices and software are also critical jobs.

When equipment and cables break, network administrators must locate the source of the trouble and fix the problem. They also obtain and install updates to network software, and evaluate new equipment to determine whether the network should be upgraded. In addition, they monitor the network performance to ensure that users' needs are met.

Because of the importance of the Internet to most organizations, network administrators ensure that the Internet connection is maintained at all times, which usually is a high priority on their to-do list. Finally, network administrators plan disaster recovery strategies (such as what to do if a fire destroys the server room).

2. **Investigate professional certifications.** Certifications attempt to provide a consistent method of measuring skill levels in specific areas of IT. Hundreds of IT certifications are available, most of which you get by passing a written exam. Software and hardware vendors (such as Microsoft and Cisco) and professional organizations (such as the Computing Technology Industry Association) often establish certification standards. Visit **microsoft.com**, **cisco.com**, **comptia.org**, and **sun.com** for more information on certifications.

Employees with certifications generally earn more than employees who aren't certified. However, most employers don't view a certification as a substitute for a college degree or a trade school program. You should think of certifications as an extra edge beyond your formal education that will make you more attractive to employers. To ensure you're pursuing the right certifications, ask employers which certifications they respect, or explore online job sites to see which certifications are listed as desirable or required.

3. **Get experience.** In addition to education, employers want you to have experience, even for entry-level jobs. While you're still completing your education, consider getting an internship or part-time job in your field of study. Many colleges will help you find internships and allow you to earn

credit toward your degree through internship programs.

4. **Do research.** Find out as much as you can about the company and the industry it is in before going on an interview. Start with the company's Web site and then expand your search to business and trade publications such as *Business Week* and *CIO* magazines.

How Do I Find a Job in IT?

Training for a career is not useful unless you can find a job at the end of your training. Here are some tips on getting a job.

1. **Visit your school's placement office.** Many employers recruit at schools, and most schools maintain a placement office to help students find jobs. Employees in the placement office can help you with résumé preparation and interviewing skills, and provide you with leads for internships and jobs.

2. **Visit online employment sites.** Most IT jobs are advertised online at sites such as Monster (**monster.com**) and Career Builder (**careerBuilder.com**). Most of these sites allow you to store your resume online, and CareerBuilder (see Figure 12) matches your resume to jobs that require your skill set.

FIGURE 12
Employment sites such as CareerBuilder.com enable you to search for specific jobs within a defined geographic area.

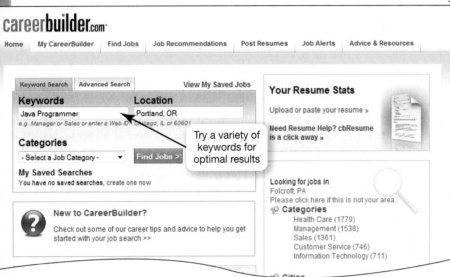

postings detail the skill sets employers require. Focusing on coursework that will provide you with desirable skill sets will make you more marketable

3. **Start networking.** Many jobs are never advertised but instead are filled by word of mouth. Seek out contacts in your field and discuss job prospects with them. Find out what skills you need, and ask them to recommend others in the industry with whom you can speak. Professional organizations such as the Association for Computing Machinery (ACM) offer one way to network. These organizations often have chapters on college campuses and offer reduced membership rates for students. The contacts you make there could lead to your next job. Local user groups that are made up of working professionals with similar interests (such as Microsoft programmers or Linux administrators) also are good sources of contacts. Figure 13 lists major professional organizations you should consider investigating.

Other sites also offer career resources, including **computerjobs.com**, **jobcircle.com**, **techcareers.com**, **justtechjobs.com**, **linkedin.com**, **computerwork.com**, **dice.com**, and **gamasutra.com**. Begin looking at job postings on these sites early in your education, because these job

If you are a woman and are thinking about pursuing an IT career, there are many

FIGURE 13 Professional Organizations

Organization Name	Purpose	Web Site
Association for Computing Machinery (ACM)	Oldest scientific computing society. Maintains a strong focus on programming and systems development.	acm.org
Association for Information Systems (AIS)	Organization of professionals who work in academia and specialize in information systems.	aisnet.org
Association of Information Technology Professionals (AITP)	Heavy focus on IT education and development of seminars and learning materials.	aitp.org
Institute of Electrical and Electronics Engineers (IEEE)	Provides leadership and sets engineering standards for all types of network computing devices and protocols.	ieee.org
Information Systems Security Association (ISSA)	Not-for-profit, international organization of information security professionals and practitioners.	issa.org

FIGURE 14 Resources for Women in IT

Organization Name	Purpose	Web Site
Anita Borg Institute for Women and Technology	Organization whose aim is to "increase the impact of women on all aspects of technology."	**anitaborg.org**
Association for Women in Computing (AWC)	A not-for-profit organization dedicated to promoting the advancement of women in computing professions.	**awc-hq.org**
Center for Women and Information Technology (CWIT)	Established at the University of Maryland, Baltimore County (UMBC), the organization is dedicated to providing global leadership in achieving women's full participation in all aspects of IT.	**umbc.edu/cwit**
Diversity/Careers in Engineering & Information Technology	An online magazine whose articles cover career issues focused on technical professionals who are members of minority groups, women, or people with disabilities.	**diversitycareers.com**
Women in Technology International (WITI)	A global trade association for tech-savvy, professional women.	**witi.com**

resources and groups that cater to female IT professionals and students. The oldest and best-known organization is the Association for Women in Computing, founded in 1978. Figure 14 provides a list of resources to investigate.

4. **Check corporate Web sites for jobs.** Many corporate Web sites list current job opportunities. For example, Apple features a searchable site (see Figure 15) that you can tailor to a specific job type. Check the sites of companies in which you are interested and then do a search on the sites for job openings or, if provided, click their Employment links.

The outlook for IT jobs should continue to be positive in the future. We wish you luck with your education and job search.

FIGURE 15

Corporate Web sites often list available jobs. The Apple site arranges jobs into broad categories and then provides easy search tools to help you zero in on the right job for you.

Job Opportunities

Apple Pro

Are you an experienced pro? New college grad? We're looking for the best. Explore the groups below for more information.

Mac Hardware Engineering
Join the team of ingenious engineering minds that design and develop Apple's revolutionary products. Mac hardware engineering looks for people with disciplines in electrical, mechanical, and specialized engineering, industrial design, and quality assurance.

Software Engineering
Make the move to Apple's software engineering team—and move the industry forward at the blazing pace of innovation. Software engineering is the division behind cutting-edge software like QuickTime, Spotlight, and iChat; the system-level software for iPhone and Apple TV; Mac OS X; and more.

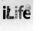
Applications
Each Apple application is managed by a dedicated team of programmers, marketers, and project managers. Their passion for music, photography, and film is showcased in innovative applications such as iTunes, iPhoto, and Final Cut Pro.

iPod Engineering
This is team that delivers many of Apple's cutting-edge consumer electronics. The talented iPod engineers, project managers, and designers are driving the digital music revolution with products such as the new iPod and iPod nano.

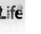
Marketing
This team creates the imaginative strategies-in product marketing, marketing communications, and public relations-that represent our products to the world. Their innovative point-of-view is an integral part of the product development process.

Sales
The Sales team-including field and education sales, enterprise sales, the online store, and more-manages relationships with our resellers and customers. Our sales reps have the right combination of passion and product knowledge to deliver the Apple experience worldwide.

Operations
Operations' role is to ensure that Apple's state-of-the-art designs become industry-leading products, delivered on time and on spec. They drive Apple's manufacturing process as well as worldwide procurement and fulfillment.

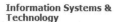
Information Systems & Technology
These Mac experts use their creativity to design solutions for customers and ensure that every computer, phone, server farm, and network inside Apple is up and running, 24/7.

objectives

After reading this chapter, you should be able to answer the following questions:

1. What is a system development life cycle, and what are the phases in the cycle? *(pp. 466–468)*

2. What is the life cycle of a program? *(p. 470)*

3. What role does a problem statement play in programming? *(pp. 470–472)*

4. How do programmers create algorithms? *(pp. 472–478)*

5. How do programmers move from algorithm to code, and in what categories of language might they code? *(pp. 478–482)*

6. How does a programmer move from code in a programming language to the 1s and 0s the CPU can understand? *(pp. 483–485)*

7. How is a program tested? *(pp. 486–487)*

8. What steps are involved in completing the program? *(p. 487)*

9. How do programmers select the right programming language for a specific task? *(p. 488)*

10. What are the most popular programming languages for Windows and Web applications? *(p. 488–494)*

resources

Active Helpdesk

- Understanding Software Programming **(p. 487)**
- Selecting the Right Programming Language **(p. 489)**

Sound Bytes

- Programming for End Users **(p. 471)**
- Looping Around the IDE **(p. 485)**
- 3D Programming the Easy Way **(p. 495)**

Companion Website

The Companion Website includes a variety of additional materials to help you review and learn more about the topics in this chapter. Go to: *pearsonhighered.com/techinaction*

how cool is *this?* If you want to take a quick

look at programming, why not try out Kudo, an **Xbox 360 game** (research.
microsoft.com/en-us/projects/kodu)?

This game is actually a programming tool that lets players create their own
video game by dragging and dropping individual programming elements, like
decisions, loops, and button controls. When the game is complete, the "developer"
can distribute his or her creation to other players using the **Xbox Live** network.

If you are interested in more detailed video game programming, take a look at the
Microsoft XNA Game Studio. This platform uses the C# programming language to develop video games for both Windows and the Xbox 360 game
system. Tour the XNA **Creators Club** (creators.xna.com/
en-US) to see the types of games players from all over the world
have created!

Understanding Software Programming

Every day we face a wide array of tasks. Some tasks are complex and need a human touch; others require creative thought and higher-level organization. However, some tasks are routine, such as alphabetizing a huge collection of invoices. Tasks that are repetitive, work with electronic information, and follow a series of clear steps are candidates for automation with computers.

Why would I ever need to create a program? Well-designed computer programs already exist for many tasks. For example, if you want to write a research paper, Microsoft Word allows you to do just that. The program has already been designed to translate the tasks you want to accomplish into computer instructions. To do your work, you need only be familiar with the interface of Word; you do not have to create a program yourself.

However, for users who cannot find an existing software product to accomplish a task, programming is mandatory. For example, imagine that a medical company comes up with a new smart bandage that is designed to transmit medical information about a wound directly to a diagnostic computer. (These devices are currently under development.) No software product on the market is designed to accumulate and relay information in this manner. Therefore, the company will need to deploy a team of software developers to generate the appropriate software if this bandage is to function as designed.

If I'm not going to be a programmer, why do I need to know some programming? Even if you'll never create a program of your own, knowing the basics of computer programming is still helpful. For example, most modern software applications enable you to customize and automate various features by using custom-built mini-programs called *macros*. By creating macros, you can ask the computer to execute a complicated sequence of steps with a single command. Understanding how to program macros enables you to add custom commands to Word or Excel, for example, and to automate frequently performed tasks, providing a huge boost to your productivity.

> **"Why do I need to know some programming?"**

Understanding programming is therefore an important piece of getting the most out of your computer system. If you plan to use only off-the-shelf (existing) software, having a basic knowledge of programming enables you to understand how application software is constructed and to add features that support your personal needs. If you plan to create custom applications from scratch, having a detailed knowledge of programming will be critical to the successful completion of your projects. Thus, in this behind-the-scenes chapter, we explore the stages of program development and survey the most popular programming languages.

The Life Cycle of an Information System

Generally speaking, a system is a collection of pieces working together to achieve a common goal. Your body, for example, is a system of muscles, organs, and other organized groups of cells working together. The college you attend is a system, too, in which administrators, faculty, students, and maintenance personnel work together. An **information system** includes data, people, procedures, hardware, and software. You interact with information systems all the time, whether you are at a grocery store, bank, or restaurant. In any of these instances, the parts of the system work together toward a similar goal. Because teams of individuals are required to develop such systems, they need to follow an organized process (set of steps) to ensure that development proceeds in an orderly fashion.

This set of steps is usually referred to as the **system development life cycle (SDLC)**. Systems theory came long before programming: everything is a part of something larger and something smaller. If you change one part of a system, other parts of the system also change. In this section, we provide you with an overview of systems development and show you how programming fits into the cycle.

System Development Life Cycle

Why do I need a process to develop a system? If you have programming skills, you can sit down in a day, perhaps, to write a little program to balance your checkbook or organize your CD collection. If you don't have such skills or the time or inclination to write a program, you can buy one. However, one person does not develop in a day the types of programs you buy in a store. Those programs are generally far more complex than the ones you would write yourself, and they require many phases to make the product complete and saleable. Therefore, an entire team of people and a systematic approach are necessary. That approach is often referred to as the *system development life cycle (SDLC)*.

What steps constitute the SDLC?
All six steps of the SDLC are shown in Figure 10.1. As the figure shows, this system is sometimes referred to as a "waterfall" system because each step is dependent on the previous step being completed first. A brief synopsis of each step follows.

1. **Problem and Opportunity Identification:** Corporations are always attempting to break into new markets, develop new sources of customers, or launch new products. For example, when the founders of eBay developed the idea of an online auction community, they needed a system that could serve customers and allow them to interact with each other. At other times, systems development is driven by a company's desire to serve its existing customers more efficiently or to respond to problems with a current system. For example, when traditional brick-and-mortar businesses want to launch e-commerce sites, they need to develop systems for customers to purchase products.

   Whether solving an existing problem or exploiting an opportunity, corporations usually generate more ideas for systems than they have the time and money to implement. Large corporations typically form a development steering committee to evaluate systems development proposals. The committee reviews ideas and decides which projects to take forward based on available resources such as personnel and funding.

2. **Analysis:** In this phase, analysts explore in depth the problem to be solved and develop a program specification. The program specification is a clear statement of the goals and objectives of the project. It is also at this stage that the first feasibility assessment is

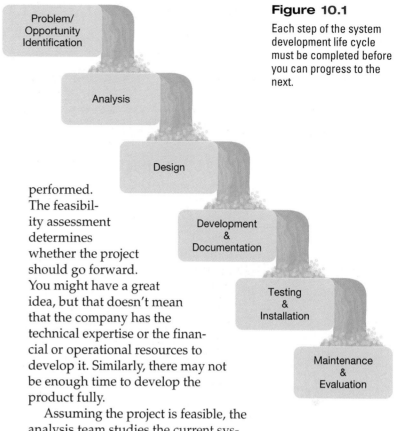

Figure 10.1

Each step of the system development life cycle must be completed before you can progress to the next.

performed. The feasibility assessment determines whether the project should go forward. You might have a great idea, but that doesn't mean that the company has the technical expertise or the financial or operational resources to develop it. Similarly, there may not be enough time to develop the product fully.

Assuming the project is feasible, the analysis team studies the current system (if there is one) and defines the user requirements of the proposed system. Finally, the analysts recommend a solution or plan of action, and the process moves to the design phase.

3. **Design:** Before a house is built, blueprints are developed so that the workers have a plan to follow. The design phase of the SDLC has the same objective: generating a detailed plan for programmers to follow. The current and proposed systems are documented using flowcharts and data-flow diagrams. Flowcharts are visual diagrams of a process, including the decisions that need to be made along the way. Data-flow diagrams trace all data in an information system from the point at which data enters the system to its final resting place (storage or output). The data-flow diagram in Figure 10.2 shows the flow of concert ticket information.

The ultimate goal of the design phase with respect to software development is to design documents that programmers can follow in developing the actual system. It is also in this phase that the "make or buy" decision is made. Once the system plan is

Figure 10.2

Data-flow diagrams illustrate the way the data travels in a system. Here the diagram documents the top-level view of a ticketing information system. More detailed diagrams for each portion of the system would show other information being tracked, such as customer name and payment information.

designed, a company evaluates existing software packages (off-the-shelf software) to determine whether it needs to develop a new piece of software or can buy something already on the market and adapt it to fit its needs. For instance, if it wants to start an online auction site to compete with eBay, it might not have to build its own system. Numerous online auction software packages that are for sale now might meet its needs. If the company cannot find an existing package that meets its needs, then it would have to develop its own system. Alternatively, it could outsource (hire someone outside the corporation) to develop the program it needs.

4. **Development and Documentation:** It is during this phase that actual

programming takes place. This phase is also the first part of the program development life cycle (PDLC), described in detail in the rest of the chapter.

5. **Testing and Installation:** The next step in the SDLC is testing the program to ensure it works properly and then installing the program so that it can be used.

6. **Maintenance and Evaluation:** Once the system is installed, its performance must be monitored to determine whether it is still meeting the needs of the end users. Bugs (errors) that were not detected in the testing phase but that the users discover subsequently must be corrected. Additional enhancements that users request are evaluated so that appropriate program modifications can be made.

The waterfall model is an idealized view of software development. Most developers follow some variation of it, however. For example, a design team may "spiral," so a group that is supporting the work of another group will work concurrently with that group on development. (This contrasts with workflows in which the groups work independently, one after the other.) Often there is a "backflow" up the waterfall, because even well-designed projects can require redesign and specification changes midstream.

Some people criticize the waterfall model for taking too long to feed actual running code back to the client. This may contribute to scope creep, an ever-changing set of requests from the clients for additional features as they wait longer and longer to see a

The More Minds the Better

In each phase of the software development life cycle, a style of interaction named *joint application development (JAD)* is useful in creating successful, flexible results. JAD is popular because it helps designers adapt to changes in program specifications quickly. In JAD, the customer is intimately involved in the project right from the beginning. Slow communication and lengthy feedback time is one reason the traditional development process is so time-consuming. In JAD "workshops," there are no communication delays. Such workshops usually include end users, developers, subject experts, observers (such as senior managers), and a facilitator. The facilitator enforces the rules of the meeting to make sure all voices are heard and agreement is reached as quickly as possible. Also called *accelerated design* or *facilitated team techniques*, JAD's goal is to improve design quality by fostering clear communication. For more details, refer to the articles located on The Facilitator Web site (**thefacilitator.com/htdocs/article11.html**).

Building a software application is a process that involves many people and requires many decisions. But what happens when the released product is defective—tragically defective?

The most infamous example of this was the computerized radiation therapy machine called the Therac-25 (see Figure 10.3). Between June 1985 and January 1987, six known accidents in the United States and Canada led to massive radiation overdoses by the Therac-25, resulting in the death of three patients and serious injuries to three others. This error has been described as the worst series of radiation accidents in the history of medical accelerators.

The software was responsible for monitoring the machine's status, accepting input about the treatment desired, and setting the machine up for treatment. It turned on the beam in response to an operator command and turned off the beam when treatment was completed, when an operator commanded it, or when a malfunction was detected.

In the first accident, a 61-year-old woman was receiving follow-up radiation after surgery for breast cancer. When the machine turned on, she said that she felt a "tremendous force of heat . . . this red-hot sensation." When the technician came in and the patient said that she had been burned, the technician replied that it was not possible. The patient went home but was soon in so much pain that she went to the local hospital. Hospital staff determined that the patient was experiencing a normal reaction to the radiation therapy and advised her to continue treatments.

Although the therapeutic dose expected was to be about 200 rads, it was later estimated that the patient had received one or two doses of radiation in the 15,000 to 20,000–rad range (doses of 1,000 rads can be fatal). The hospital explained that part of the confusion happened because staff members had never seen a radiation overdose of that magnitude before. Eventually the patient lost her breast, lost the use of her shoulder and arm, and was in constant pain. Other patients had similar incidents, some dying as a result of complications from the error in the dosage.

In the years since these accidents, much analysis has been done to see how the tragedy could have been avoided. One notable item is that remarkably little software documentation was produced by the two manufacturing companies involved during development. A memo by the Food and Drug Administration reviewing the incident said, "Unfortunately, the company response also seems to point out an apparent lack of documentation on software specifications and a software test plan."

In addition, testing was not done in a rigorous manner. A "small amount" of software testing was done on a simulator, but most testing was done at the system level rather than by examining software and hardware separately. It appears that machine and software testing was minimal, with most effort directed at the integrated system test.

Figure 10.3

The Therac-25 incident reminds us of the responsibilities incumbent on programmers, system designers, and system users.

Although the basic mistakes involved poor software engineering practices, many different factors explained the full set of accidents including:

- Simple programming errors
- Inadequate safety engineering
- Poor human–computer interaction design
- Too little focus on safety by the manufacturing organization
- Inadequate reporting structure at the company level and as required by the U.S. government

In events such as this one, who should be held responsible for producing defective software? Is it the corporate management that did not institute a defined software process? Is it the production managers, who forced tight schedules that demanded risky software engineering practices? What about the software engineers who wrote the defective code? The very first article of the code of ethics of the Institute of Electrical and Electronic Engineers (IEEE) states, "[We] accept responsibility in making engineering decisions consistent with the safety, health, and welfare of the public, and to disclose promptly factors that might endanger the public or the environment." What about users of the software? Can they be held responsible for accidents? What if they made changes to the system?

The Association of Computing Machinery (ACM) and the IEEE have established eight principles for ethical software engineering practices:

1. **Public:** Software engineers shall act consistently with the public interest.
2. **Client and Employer:** Software engineers shall act in a manner that is in the best interests of their client and employer consistent with the public interest.
3. **Product:** Software engineers shall ensure that their products and related modifications meet the highest professional standards possible.
4. **Judgment:** Software engineers shall maintain integrity and independence in their professional judgment.
5. **Management:** Software engineering managers and leaders shall subscribe to and promote an ethical approach to the management of software development and maintenance.
6. **Profession:** Software engineers shall advance the integrity and reputation of the profession consistent with the public interest.
7. **Colleagues:** Software engineers shall be fair to and supportive of their colleagues.
8. **Self:** Software engineers shall participate in lifelong learning regarding the practice of their profession and shall promote an ethical approach to the practice of the profession.

Only through constant vigilance on the part of each software programmer, manager, and testing professional will situations such as the Therac-25 be prevented.

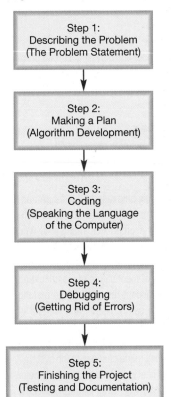

Figure 10.4

The stages followed by each programming project from conception to final deployment are collectively referred to as the program development life cycle.

working prototype. Other developmental models, such as rapid application development (RAD), are being used in the industry to address these issues.

The Life Cycle of a Program

Programming often begins with nothing more than a problem or a request, such as "We can't get our budget reports out on time," or "Can you tell me how many transfer students have applied to our college?" When problems or requests such as these arise, someone realizes that computer programs could solve these problems more efficiently and reliably than the procedures currently in place.

What is programming? As you have just read, once a project has been deemed feasible and a plan is in place, the work of programming begins. **Programming** is the process of translating a task into a series of commands a computer will use to perform that task. It involves identifying which parts of a task a computer can perform, describing those tasks in a highly specific and complete manner, and, finally, translating this description into the language spoken by the computer's central processing unit (CPU).

How do programmers tackle a programming project? Just as an information system has a development life cycle, each programming project follows several stages from conception to final deployment. This process, described below, is sometimes referred to as the **program development life cycle (PDLC)**.

1. **Describing the Problem:** First, programmers must develop a complete description of the problem. The problem statement identifies the task to be automated and describes how the software program will behave.

2. **Making a Plan:** The problem statement is next translated into a set of specific, sequential steps that describe exactly what the computer program must do to complete the work.

   This is known as an **algorithm**. At this stage, the algorithm is written in natural language (that is, whatever

language the programmer speaks, such as English).

3. **Coding:** The algorithm is then translated into programming code, a language that is friendlier to humans than the 1s and 0s that the CPU speaks but is still highly structured. By coding the algorithm, programmers must think in terms of the operations that a CPU can perform.

4. **Debugging:** The code then goes through a process of debugging in which the programmers find and repair any known errors in the code.

5. **Finishing the Project:** The software is tested, both by the programming team and by the people who will use the program. The results of the entire project are documented for the users and the development team. Finally, users are trained so that they can use the program efficiently.

Figure 10.4 illustrates the steps of a program's life cycle.

Now that you have an overview of the process involved in developing a program, let's look at each step in more detail.

Describing the Problem: The Problem Statement

The **problem statement** is the starting point of programming work. It is a clear description of what tasks the computer program must accomplish and how the program will execute these tasks and respond to unusual situations. Programmers develop problem statements so that they can better understand the goals of their programming efforts.

What kind of problems can computer programs solve? Not every problem is well suited to a computerized solution. The strengths of computing machines are that they are fast and work without error. Unlike humans, computers don't introduce mistakes because they're tired or stressed. Thus, as mentioned earlier, tasks that are repetitive, work with electronic information, and follow a series of clear steps are candidates for computerization.

This might sound as if computers only help us with the dullest and most simplistic tasks. However, computer programs also can help solve sophisticated problems. For example, pharmaceutical companies design drugs using complex computer programs that model molecules. Using program simulations, chemists can "create" new drugs in the computer and quickly determine whether they will have the desired pharmacological effects. Based on the program's data, chemists select the most promising choices and begin to test those compounds in the real laboratory. This is not exactly simple stuff.

Still, computers cannot yet act with intuition or be spontaneously creative. They can attack highly challenging problems such as making weather predictions or playing chess, but only in a manner that takes advantage of what computers do best—making fast, reliable computations.

How do programmers create problem statements? Most computer users understand what jobs (or problems) they want to computerize but not the details of the programming process. Therefore, the goal in creating a useful problem statement is to have programmers interact with users to describe three things relevant to creating a useful program: data, information, and method.

1. **Data** is the raw input that users have at the start of the job. It will be fed into the program.

2. **Information** is the result that the users require at the end of the job. The program produces this information from data.

3. **Method**, described precisely, is how the program converts the inputs into the correct outputs.

> **"Users understand the jobs they want done, but not the programming behind them."**

For example, say you want to compute how much money you'll earn working at a parking garage. Your salary is $7.50 per hour for an eight-hour shift, but if you work more than eight hours a day, you will get time and a half, which is $11.25 per hour, for the overtime work. To determine how much money you make in any given day, you could multiply this in your mind, write it on a piece of paper, or use a calculator; alternatively, you could create a simple computer program to do the work for you. In this example, what are the three elements of the problem statement?

1. **Input:** The data you have at the beginning of the problem, which is the number of hours you worked.

2. **Output:** The information you need to have at the end of the problem, which is your total pay for the day.

3. **Processing:** The set of steps that will take you from your input to an output. In this case, the computer program would check if you worked more than eight hours. (That is, it would determine whether you worked any overtime.) If you did not work overtime, then the output would be $7.50 multiplied by the total number of hours you worked ($60.00 for eight hours). If you did work overtime, then the program would calculate your pay as eight hours at $7.50 per hour for the regular part of your shift, plus an additional $11.25 multiplied by the number of overtime hours you worked. This processing thereby transforms your input into your desired output.

How do programmers handle bad inputs? In the problem statement, programmers also must describe what the program should do if the input data is invalid or just gibberish. (Users do make mistakes.) This part of the problem statement is referred to as **error handling**. The problem statement also includes a **testing plan** that lists specific input numbers the program would typically expect the user to enter. It then lists the precise output values that a perfect program would return for those input values. Later, in a testing process, programmers use the input

SOUND BYTE

Programming for End Users

In this Sound Byte, you'll be guided through the creation of a macro in the Microsoft Office 2007 suite. You'll learn how Office enables you to program with macros to customize and extend the capabilities it offers.

Figure 10.5 | COMPLETE PROBLEM STATEMENT FOR PARKING GARAGE EXAMPLE

Problem Statement			
Program Goal	Compute the total pay for a fixed number of hours worked at a parking garage.		
Input	Number of hours worked (a positive number)		
Output	Total pay earned (a positive number)		
Process	Total pay earned is computed as $7.50 per hour for the first 8 hours worked each day. Any hours worked beyond the first 8 are calculated at $11.25 per hour.		
Error Handling	The input (number of hours worked) must be a positive real number. If it is a negative number or other unacceptable character, the program will force the user to re-enter the information.		
Testing plan	Input	Output	Notes
	8	8*7.50	Testing positive input
	3	3*7.50	Testing positive input
	12	8*7.50 + 4*11.25	Testing overtime input
	−6	Error message/ask user to re-enter value	Handling error

and output data values from the testing plan to determine whether the program they created works in the way it should. (We discuss the testing process later in this chapter.)

Does the testing plan cover every possible use of the program? The testing plan cannot list every input that the program could ever encounter. Instead, programmers work with users to identify the categories of inputs that will be encountered, find a typical example of each input category, and specify what kind of output must be generated. In the preceding parking garage example, the error-handling process would describe what the program would do if you happened to enter "-8" (or any other nonsense character) for the number of hours you worked. The error handling would specify whether the program would return a negative value, prompt you to re-enter the input, or yell at you and shut down (well, maybe not exactly). We could expect three categories of inputs in the parking garage example. The user might enter:

- A negative number for hours worked that day
- A positive number equal to or less than eight
- A positive number greater than eight.

The testing plan would describe how the error would be managed or how the output would be generated for each input category.

Is there a standard format for a problem statement? Most companies (and instructors) have their own format for documenting a problem statement. However, all problem statements include the same basic components: the data that is expected to be provided (inputs), the information that is expected to be produced (outputs), the rules for transforming the input into output (processing), an explanation of how the program will respond if users enter data that doesn't make sense (error handling), and a testing plan. Figure 10.5 shows a sample problem statement for our parking garage example.

Making a Plan: Algorithm Development

Once programmers understand exactly what the program must do and have created the final problem statement, they can begin developing a detailed **algorithm**, a set of specific, sequential steps that describe in natural language exactly what the computer program must do to complete its task. Let's look at some ways in which programmers design and test algorithms.

Do algorithms appear only in programming? Although the term *algorithm* may sound like it would fall only under the domain of computing, you design and execute algorithms (or problem-solving procedures) in your daily life. For example, say you are planning your morning. You know you need to (1) get gas for your car, (2) swing past the café and pick up a mocha latté, and (3) stop by the bookstore and buy a textbook before your 9 A.M. accounting lecture. You quickly think over the costs and decide it will take $80 to buy all three. In what order will you accomplish all these tasks? How do you decide? Should you try to minimize the distance you'll travel or the time you'll spend driving? What happens if you forget your credit card?

Figure 10.6 presents an algorithm you could develop to make decisions about how to accomplish these tasks. This algorithm

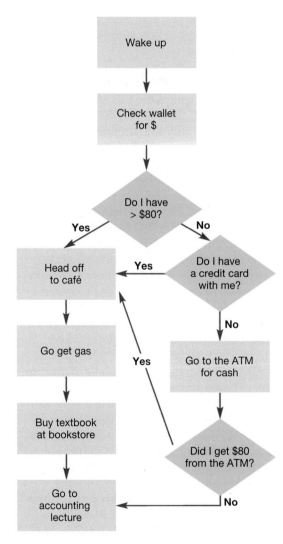

Figure 10.6

An algorithm you might use to plan your morning would include several steps that encapsulate all of the decisions you might need to make and show the specific sequence in which these steps would occur.

lays out a specific plan that encapsulates all of the choices you need to make in the course of completing a particular task and shows the specific sequence in which these tasks will occur. At any point in the morning, you could gather your current data (your inputs)—"I have $20 and my Visa card, but the ATM machine is down"—and the algorithm would tell you unambiguously what your next step should be.

What are the limitations of algorithms? The deterministic nature of an algorithm enables us to describe it completely on a simple piece of paper. An algorithm is a series of steps that is completely known: at each point we know *exactly* what step to take next. However, not all problems can be described as a fixed sequence of predetermined steps; some involve random and unpredictable events. For example, although the program that computes your parking garage take-home pay each day works flawlessly, programs that predict stock prices are often wrong because many random events (inputs), such as a flood in Costa Rica or a shipping delay in California, can change the outcomes (outputs).

How do programmers represent an algorithm? Programmers have several visual tools at their disposal to help them document the decision points and flow of their algorithm.

Flowcharts provide a visual representation of the patterns the algorithm comprises. Figure 10.6 presents an example of a flowchart used to depict the flow of an algorithm. As you can see, specific shape symbols indicate program behaviors and decision types. Diamonds indicate that a yes/no decision will be performed, and rectangles indicate an instruction to follow. Figure 10.7 lists additional flowcharting symbols and explains what they indicate.

Many software packages make it easy for programmers to create and modify flowcharts. Microsoft Visio is one popular flowcharting program.

Pseudocode is a text-based approach to documenting an algorithm. In pseudocode, words describe the actions that the algorithm will take. Pseudocode is organized like an outline, with differing levels of indentation to indicate the flow of actions within the program. There is no standard set of vocabulary for pseudocode. Programmers use a combination of common words in their

Figure 10.7

Standard symbols used in flowcharts.

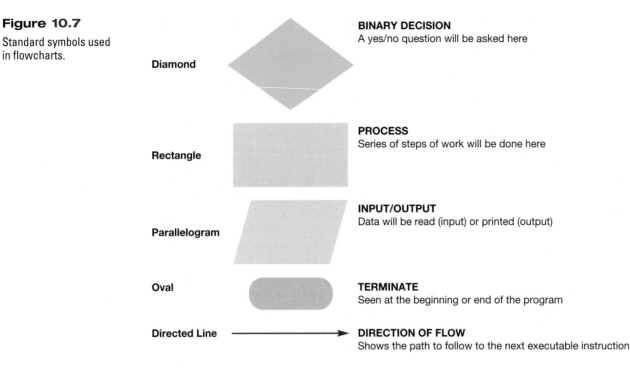

Diamond — **BINARY DECISION**
A yes/no question will be asked here

Rectangle — **PROCESS**
Series of steps of work will be done here

Parallelogram — **INPUT/OUTPUT**
Data will be read (input) or printed (output)

Oval — **TERMINATE**
Seen at the beginning or end of the program

Directed Line — **DIRECTION OF FLOW**
Shows the path to follow to the next executable instruction

natural language and the special words that are commands in the programming language they are using.

Developing an Algorithm: Decision Making and Design

How do programmers develop an algorithm? By now, you understand that when programmers develop an algorithm, they convert the problem statement into a list of steps (or actions) the program will take. For simple problems, this list is straightforward: The program completes this action first, that action second, another action third, and so on. However, only the simplest algorithms execute the same series of actions every time they run.

Problems that are more complex involve choices and, therefore, cannot follow a sequential list of steps to generate the correct output. Instead, the list of steps created for complex problems includes **decision points**, or points at which the program must choose from an array of different actions based on the value of its current inputs. Programmers convert a problem into an algorithm by listing the sequence of actions that must be taken and recognizing the places where decisions must be made.

In our parking garage example, if the number of hours you worked in a given day is eight or less, the program performs one simple calculation: It multiplies the number of hours worked by $7.50. If you worked more than eight hours in a day, then the program takes a different path and performs a different calculation, as shown in Figure 10.8.

What kinds of decision points are there? Two main types of decisions change the flow of an algorithm. One decision point that appears often in algorithms is like a "fork in the road" or a branch. Such decision points are called **binary decisions** because they can be answered in one of only two ways: *yes* (true) or *no* (false). For

Figure 10.8

Decision points force the program to travel down one branch of the algorithm or another.

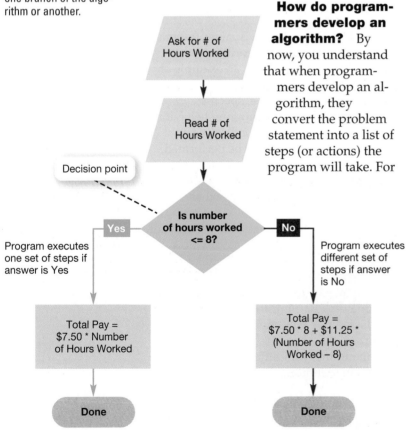

Ask for # of Hours Worked

Read # of Hours Worked

Decision point

Is number of hours worked <= 8?

Yes — Program executes one set of steps if answer is Yes

No — Program executes different set of steps if answer is No

Total Pay = $7.50 * Number of Hours Worked

Total Pay = $7.50 * 8 + $11.25 * (Number of Hours Worked – 8)

Done

Done

example, the answer to the question, "Did you work at most eight hours today?" (Is number of hours worked <= 8 hours?), shown in Figure 10.8, is a binary decision because the answer can be only *yes* or *no*. The result of the decision determines which path the algorithm follows. If the answer is *yes*, the program follows one sequence of steps; if the answer is *no*, it follows a different path.

A second decision point that often appears in algorithms is a repeating loop. In a **loop**, a question is asked, and if the answer is *yes*, a set of actions is performed. Once the set of actions has been performed, the question is asked again, creating a loop. As long as the answer to the question is *yes*, the algorithm continues to loop around and repeat the same set of actions. When the answer to the question is *no*, the algorithm breaks free of the looping and moves on to the first step that follows the loop.

In our parking garage example, the algorithm would require a loop if you wanted to compute the total pay you earned in a full week of work rather than in just a single day. This is because for each day of the week, you would want to perform the same set of steps. Figure 10.9 shows how the idea of looping would be useful in this part of our parking garage program. On Monday, the program would set the Total Pay value to $0.00. It would then perform the following set of steps:

1. Read the number of hours worked that day.

2. Determine whether you qualified for overtime pay.

3. Compute the pay earned that day.

4. Add that day's pay to the total pay for the week.

On Tuesday, the algorithm would loop back, repeating the same sequence of steps it performed on Monday, adding the amount you earned on Tuesday to the Total Pay amount. The algorithm would continue to perform this loop for each day (seven times) until it hits Monday again. At that point the decision "Are we still in the same week?" would become false. The program would stop, calculate the total pay for the entire week of work, and print the weekly paycheck. As you can see, there are three important features to look for in a loop:

1. A beginning point, or **initial value**. In our example, the Total Pay for the week starts at an initial value of $0.00.

2. A set of actions that will be performed. In our example, the algorithm computes the daily pay each time it passes through the loop.

3. A check to see whether the loop is completed, or a **test condition**. In our example, the algorithm should run the loop seven times, no more and no fewer.

Almost every higher-level programming language supports both making binary yes/no decisions and handling repeating loops. **Control structures** is the general term used for keywords in a programming language that allow the programmer to control (redirect) the flow of the program based on a decision.

Figure 10.9

In this example of a loop, we stay in the loop until the test condition is no longer true. We then break free from the loop and move on to the next step in the algorithm, which is outside of the loop.

How do programmers create algorithms for specific tasks? As we've discussed, it's difficult for human beings to force their problem-solving skills into the highly structured, detailed algorithms that computing machines require. Therefore, several different methodologies have been developed to support programmers, including top-down design and object-oriented analysis.

Top-Down Design

What is top-down design? Top-down **design** is a systematic approach in which a problem is broken into a series of high-level tasks. In top-down design, programmers apply the same strategy repeatedly, breaking each task into successively more detailed subtasks. They continue until they have a sequence of steps that are close to the types of commands allowed by the programming language they will use for coding. (Previous coding experience helps programmers know the appropriate level of detail to specify in an algorithm generated by top-down design.)

How is top-down design used in programming? Let's consider our parking garage example again. Initially, top-down design would identify three high-level tasks: Get Input, Process Data, and Output Results (see Figure 10.10a).

Applying top-down design to the first operation, Get Input, we'd produce the more detailed sequence of steps shown in Figure 10.10b: Announce Program, Give Users Instructions, and Read the Input

NumberHoursWorkedToday. When we try to refine each of these steps, we find that they are at the level of commands that most programming languages support (that is, they tell the computer to print and read statements). Therefore, the operation Get Input has been converted to an algorithm.

Next, we move to the second high-level task, Process Data, and break it into subtasks. In this case, we need to determine whether overtime hours were worked and compute the pay accordingly. We continue to apply top-down design on all tasks until we can no longer break tasks into subtasks, as shown in Figure 10.10c.

Object-Oriented Analysis

What is object-oriented analysis? A very different approach to generating an algorithm is object-oriented analysis. With **object-oriented analysis**, programmers first identify all of the categories of inputs that are part of the problem the program is trying to solve. These categories are called **classes**. For example, the classes in our parking garage example might include a TimeCard and an Employee.

Classes are further defined by information (**data**) and actions (**methods** or **behaviors**) associated with the class. For example, data for an Employee would include a Name, Address, and Social Security Number, whereas the methods for the Employee would be GoToWork(), LeaveWork(), or CollectPay(). Think of classes as the things around you in your world—books, accounts, shopping carts. The data of the class

Figure 10.10

In this figure, (a) top-down design is applied to the highest level of task in our parking garage example; (b) the tasks are further refined into subtasks; and (c) subtasks are refined into a sequence of instructions—an algorithm.

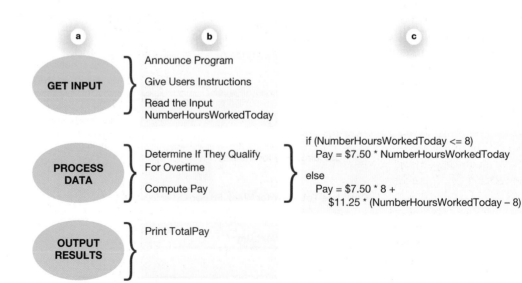

a

GET INPUT

Announce Program

Give Users Instructions

Read the Input NumberHoursWorkedToday

b

PROCESS DATA

Determine If They Qualify For Overtime

Compute Pay

c

```
if (NumberHoursWorkedToday <= 8)
    Pay = $7.50 * NumberHoursWorkedToday
else
    Pay = $7.50 * 8 +
        $11.25 * (NumberHoursWorkedToday – 8)
```

OUTPUT RESULTS

Print TotalPay

describes the class, so classes are often characterized as nouns, whereas methods are often characterized as verbs—the ways that the class acts and communicates with other classes. Figure 10.11 shows the data and methods the Employee class would contain.

In the object-oriented approach, programmers identify and define each class, as well as their data and methods. Programmers then determine how classes interact with each other. For example, when an Employee does GoToWork(), the Employee class must "talk" to the TimeCard class and punch in for the day, setting the StartTime on the TimeCard.

Programmers may need to create several different examples of a class. Each of these examples is an **object**. In Figure 10.11, John Doe, Jane Doe, and Bill McGillicutty are each Employee objects (specific examples of the Employee class). Each object from a given class is described by the same pieces of data and has the same methods; for example, John, Jane, and Bill are all Employees and can use the GoToWork, LeaveWork, and CollectPay methods. However, because John and Jane have different pay grades (PayGrade 5 and PayGrade 10, respectively), and because they all have different Social Security numbers, they are all unique objects.

Why would a developer select the object-oriented approach over top-down design? Object-oriented analysis forces programmers to think in general terms about their problem, which tends to lead to more general and reusable solutions. An important aspect of object-oriented design is that it leads to **reusability**. Because object-oriented design generates a family of classes for each project, programmers can easily reuse existing classes from other projects, enabling them to produce new code quickly.

To take advantage of reuse, programmers must study the relationships between objects. Hierarchies of objects can be built quickly in object-oriented languages using the mechanism of inheritance. **Inheritance** means that a new class can automatically pick up all of the data and methods of an existing class, and then extend and customize those to fit its own specific needs.

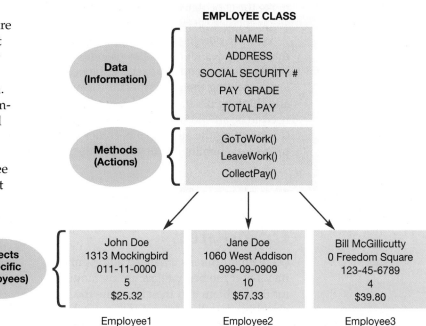

EMPLOYEE CLASS

Figure 10.11

The Employee class includes the complete set of information (data) and actions (methods or behaviors) that describe an Employee.

The original class is called the **base class**, and the new, modified class is called the **derived class**, as illustrated in Figure 10.12. You can compare this with making cookies. For example, you have a basic recipe for sugar cookies (base class: sugar cookies). However, in your family, some people like chocolate-flavored sugar cookies (derived class: chocolate cookies), and others like almond-flavored sugar cookies (derived class: almond cookies). All the cookies share the attributes of the basic sugar cookie. However, instead of creating two entirely new recipes—one for chocolate cookies and one for almond cookies—the two varieties inherit the basic sugar cookie (base class) recipe; the recipe is then customized to

Figure 10.12

In object-oriented programming (OOP), a single base class, for example Shape, helps you quickly create many additional derived classes, such as Polygon and Ellipse.

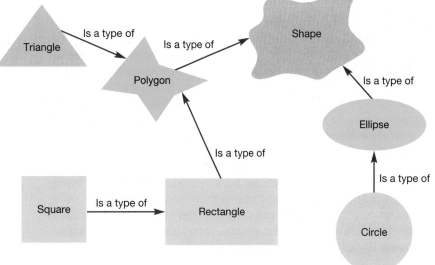

make the chocolate- and almond-flavored sugar cookies (derived classes).

With the object-oriented approach, the majority of design time is spent in identifying the classes required to solve the problem, modeling them as data and methods, and thinking about what relationships they need to be able to have with each other. Constructing the algorithm becomes a process of enabling the objects to interact.

Coding: Speaking the Language of the Computer

Once programmers create an algorithm, they select the best programming language for the problem and then translate the algorithm into that language.

How is a person's idea translated into CPU instructions? Translating an algorithm into a **programming language** is the act of **coding**. Programming languages are (somewhat!) readable by humans, but then are translated into patterns of 1s and 0s to be understood by the CPU.

Although programming languages free programmers from having to think in binary language (the 1s and 0s that computers understand), they still force programmers to translate the ideas of the algorithm into a highly precise format. Programming languages are quite limited, allowing programmers to use only a few specific words while still demanding a consistent structure.

How exactly do programmers move from algorithm to code? Once programmers have an algorithm, in the form of either a flowchart or a series of pseudocode statements, they scan the algorithm and identify the key pieces of information it uses to make decisions. What steps are required for the calculation of new information? What is the exact sequence of the steps? Are there points where decisions have to be made? What kinds of decisions are made? Are there places where the same steps are repeated several times? Once the programmer identifies the required information and the flow of how it will be changed by each step of the algorithm, he or she can begin converting the algorithm into computer code in a specific programming language.

Categories of Programming Languages

What exactly is a programming language? A **programming language** is a kind of "code" for the set of instructions the CPU knows how to perform. Computer programming languages use special words and strict rules so programmers can control the CPU without having to know all of its hardware details.

What kinds of programming languages are there? Programming languages are classified in several major groupings, sometimes referred to as *generations*. With each generation in language development, programmers have been relieved of more of the burden of keeping track of what the hardware requires. The earliest languages—assembly language and machine languages—required the programmer to know a great deal about how the computer was constructed internally and how it stored data. Programming is becoming easier as languages continue to become more closely matched to how humans think about problems.

How have modern programming languages evolved? A first-generation language (1GL) is the actual machine language of a CPU, the sequence of bits (1s and 0s) that the CPU understands. A second-generation language (2GL) is also known as an assembly language. Assembly languages allow programmers to write their programs using a set of short, English-like commands that speak directly to the CPU and give the

---

BITS AND BYTES

My Algorithm Can Beat Your Algorithm!

Programming became a competitive sport with the advent of LEGO MINDSTORMS. The First Lego League conducts a programming competition each year using the LEGO MINDSTORMS series of LEGO kits. These kits include gears, wheels, motors, and a motorized, programmable LEGO "brick" that contains a microprocessor. Sensors feed the robots information such as sounds, images, and temperatures. Teams then use ROBOLAB software to develop programs and send them to the brick's microprocessor. You can try out this software in a small demo at the ROBOLAB site (**robolabonline.com**). The unit can be told to turn the motor on or off, switch the direction of a wheel's rotation, or turn on sensors to measure temperature or light levels. The ROBOLAB software even allows beginning programmers to drag and drop elements such as "if" statements and loops. Synthesizing their understanding of motors and their talent for logical thinking, teams design robots that can travel through mazes, cross bridges, and deliver packages—whatever tasks the LEGO League has come up with for that year's tournament (**usfirst.org/firstlegoleague/community/homepage.html**).

programmer direct control of hardware resources. A **third-generation language (3GL)** uses symbols and commands to help programmers tell the computer what to do. This makes 3GL languages easier for humans to read and remember. Most programming languages today, including BASIC, FORTRAN, COBOL, C/C++, and Java, are considered third generation.

Structured Query Language (SQL) is a database programming language that is an example of a **fourth-generation language (4GL)**. Many other database query languages and report generators are also 4GLs. The following single SQL command would check a huge table of data on the employees and build a new table showing all those employees who worked overtime:

```
SELECT * EMPLOYEES WHERE
"TotalHours" TOTAL MORE THAN 8
```

But programmers must always work from algorithms, correct? Not if they are using a **fifth-generation language (5GL)**. Fifth-generation languages are considered the most "natural" of languages. In a 5GL, a problem is presented as a series of facts or constraints instead of as a specific algorithm. The system of facts can then be queried (asked questions). PROLOG (PROgramming LOGic) is an example of a 5GL. A PROLOG program could be a list of family relationships and rules such as "Mike is Sally's brother. A brother and a sister have the same mother and father." Once a user has amassed a huge collection of facts and rules, she can ask for a list of all Mike's cousins,

for example. PROLOG would find the answers by repeatedly applying the principles of logic, instead of by following a systematic algorithm that the programmer provided. Figure 10.13 shows small code samples of each generation of language.

Do programmers have to use a higher-level programming language to solve a problem with a computer? No, experienced programmers sometimes write a program directly in the CPU's assembly language. However, the main advantage of higher-level programming languages—C or Java, for example—is that they allow programmers to think in terms of the problem they are solving rather than worrying about the internal design and specific instructions available for a given CPU. In addition, higher-level programming languages have the capability to produce a program easily that will run on differently configured CPUs. For example, if programmers wrote directly in the assembly language for an Intel i7 CPU, then they would have to rewrite the program completely if they wanted it to run on a Sun workstation with the UltraSPARC CPU. Thus, higher-level programming languages offer **portability**—the capability to move a completed solution easily from one type of computer to another.

Creating Code: Writing the Program

What happens first when you write a program? All of the inputs a program receives and all of the outputs the program

Figure 10.13 | SAMPLE CODE FOR DIFFERENT LANGUAGE LEVELS AND GENERATIONS

Level	Generation	Example	Sample Code
Low	1 GL	Machine	**Bits** describe the commands to the CPU 1110 0101 1001 1111 0000 1011 1110 0110
	2GL	Assembly	**Words** describe the commands to the CPU ADD Register 3, Register 4, Register 5
High	3GL	FORTRAN, BASIC, C, Java	**Symbols** describe the commands to the CPU TotalPay = Pay + OvertimePay
	4GL	SQL	**More powerful commands** allow complex work to be done in a single sentence SELECT isbn, title, price, price*0.06 AS sales_tax FROM books WHERE price>100.00 ORDER BY title;
Natural	5GL	PROLOG	Programmers can build applications **without specifying an algorithm**. Find all the people who are Mike's cousins as: ?-cousin (Mike, family)

The Building Blocks of Programming Languages: Syntax, Keywords, Data Types, and Operators

Programming languages are evolving constantly. New languages emerge every year, and existing languages change dramatically. Therefore, it would be extremely difficult and time consuming for programmers to learn every programming language. However, all languages have several common elements: rules of syntax, a set of keywords, a group of supported data types, and a set of allowed operators. By learning these four concepts, a programmer will be better equipped to approach any new language.

The transition from a well-designed algorithm to working code requires a clear understanding of the rules (syntax) of the programming language being used. **Syntax** is an agreed-upon set of rules defining how a language must be structured. The English language has a syntax that defines which symbols are words (for example, "poodle" is a word but "oodlep" is not) and what order words and symbols (such as semicolons and commas) must follow.

Likewise, all programming languages have a formal syntax that programmers must follow when creating code **statements**, which are sentences in a code. Syntax errors are violations of the strict, precise set of rules that defines the language. In a programming language, even misplacing a single comma or using a lowercase letter where a capital letter is required will generate a syntax error and make the program unusable.

Keywords are a set of words that have predefined meanings for a particular language. Keywords translate the flow of the algorithm into the structured code of the programming language. For example, when the algorithm indicates a *decision point*—a location where a binary decision must be made—the programmer translates that binary decision into the appropriate keyword or keywords from the language.

To illustrate further, in the programming language C++, the binary decision asking whether you worked enough hours to qualify for overtime pay would use the keywords **if else**. At this point in the code, the program can follow one of two paths: *if* you indicated through your input that you worked fewer than or equal to eight hours, it takes one path; if not (*else*), it follows another. Figure 10.14 shows the binary decision in the algorithm and the lines of C++ code for this decision using the *if else* keywords.

Loops are likewise translated from algorithm to code by using the appropriate keyword from the language. For example, in the programming language Visual Basic, programmers use the keywords **For** and **Next** to implement a loop. After the keyword *For*, an input or output item is given a starting value. Then the statements, or "sentences," in the body of the loop are executed. When the command *Next* is run, the program returns to the For statement and increments the value of the input or output item by 1. It then tests that the value is still inside the range given. If it is, the body of the loop is executed again. This continues until the value of the input or output item is outside the range listed. The loop is then ended, and the statement that follows the loop is run. If we think back to the parking garage example, the following lines of Visual Basic code loop to

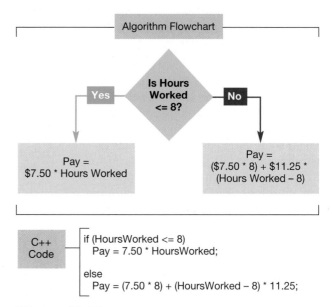

Figure 10.14

The binary decision in the algorithm has been converted into C++ code.

produces need to be stored in the computer's RAM while the program is running. Each input and each output item that the program manipulates, also known as a **variable**, needs to be announced early in the program so that memory space can be set aside. A **variable declaration** tells the operating system that the program needs to allocate storage space in RAM. The following line of code is a variable declaration:

```
int Day;
```

This variable's name is *Day*. The "int" that precedes the Day variable indicates that this variable will always be an integer (a whole number such as 15 or –4).

This statement asks for enough RAM storage space to hold an integer. After the RAM space is found, it is reserved. As long as the program is running, these RAM cells will be saved for the Day variable, and no other program can use that memory until the program ends. From that point on, when the program encounters the symbol Day, it will access the memory it reserved as Day and find the integer stored there.

The following line of C++ code asks that a decimal number (represented by the keyword "float") be stored in RAM:

```
float TotalPay;
```

sum up the total pay for the entire week. In this statement, the starting value of the input item Day is 1, and the program loops until Day equals 7:

```
For Day = 1 to 7
   TotalPay = TotalPay + Pay;
Next Day
```

Often, a quick overview of a language's keywords can reveal the unique focus of that language. For example, the language C++ includes the keywords "public," "private," and "protected," which indicate that the language includes a mechanism for controlling security. Although people who are new to a language might not immediately understand how these keywords are used, examining the keywords of a language you are learning will often tell you what special features the language has and will help you ask important questions about it.

Each time programmers want to store data in their program, they must ask the operating system for storage space at a random access memory (RAM) location. **Data types** describe the *kind* of data that is being stored at the memory location. Each programming language has its own data types (although there is some degree of overlap among languages). For example, C++ includes data types that represent integers, real numbers, characters, and Boolean (true–false) values. These C++ data types show up in code statements as *int* for integer, *float* for real numbers, *char* for characters, and *bool* for Boolean values.

Because it takes more room to store a real number such as 18,743.23 than it does to store the integer 1, programmers use data types in their code to indicate to the operating system how much memory it needs to allocate. Programmers must be familiar with all of the data types available in the language so that they can assign the most appropriate data type for each input and output value, without wasting memory space.

Operators are the coding symbols that represent the fundamental actions of the language. Each programming language has its own set of operators. Many languages include common algebraic operators such as +, −, *, and / to represent the mathematical operations of addition, subtraction, multiplication, and division, respectively. Some languages, however, introduce new symbols as operators. The language A Programmer's Language (APL) was designed to solve multidimensional mathematical problems. APL includes less familiar operators such as rho, sigma, and iota, each representing a complex mathematical operation. Because it contains many specialized operators, APL requires programmers to use a special keyboard (see Figure 10.15).

Programming languages sometimes include other unique operators. The C++ operator >>, for example, is used to tell the computer to read data from the keyboard or from a file. The C++ operator && is used to tell the computer to check whether two statements are both true. "Is your age greater than 20 AND less than 30?" is a question that requires the use of the && operator.

In the following C++ code, several operators are being used. The > operator checks whether the number of hours worked is greater than 0. The && operator checks that the number of hours worked is simultaneously positive AND less than or equal to 8. If that happens, then the = operator sets the output Pay to equal the number of hours paid at $7.50 per hour:

```
if (Hours > 0 && Hours <= 8)
   Pay = Hours * 7.50;
```

Knowing operators such as these, as well as the other common elements described earlier, helps programmers learn new programming languages.

APL keyboard

Figure 10.15

APL requires programmers to use an APL keyboard that includes the many specialized operators in the language.

This line asks the operating system to find enough storage space for one real number.

Can programmers leave notes to themselves inside a program?
Programmers often insert a **comment** (or **remark**) into program code to explain the purpose of a section of code, to indicate the date they wrote the program, or to include other important information about the code so that fellow programmers can more easily understand and update it should the original programmer no longer be available. Comments are written into the code in plain English. The compiler, a

program that translates codes into binary 1s and 0s, just ignores comments. Comments are intended to be read only by human programmers. Languages provide a special symbol or keyword to indicate the beginning of a comment. In C++, the symbol // at the beginning of a line indicates that the rest of the line is a comment. In Visual Basic, a single apostrophe or the keyword "REM," short for "REMark," does the same thing.

What would completed code for a program look like? Figure 10.16 presents a completed C++ program for our parking garage example. We'll discuss later

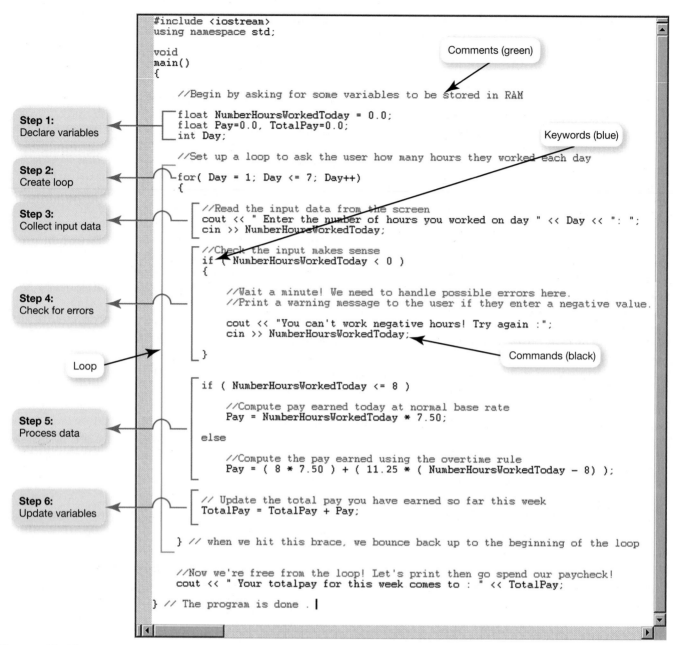

```
#include <iostream>
using namespace std;

void
main()
{
    //Begin by asking for some variables to be stored in RAM

    float NumberHoursWorkedToday = 0.0;
    float Pay=0.0, TotalPay=0.0;
    int Day;

    //Set up a loop to ask the user how many hours they worked each day

    for( Day = 1; Day <= 7; Day++)
    {
        //Read the input data from the screen
        cout << " Enter the number of hours you worked on day " << Day << ": ";
        cin >> NumberHoursWorkedToday;

        //Check the input makes sense
        if ( NumberHoursWorkedToday < 0 )
        {
            //Wait a minute! We need to handle possible errors here.
            //Print a warning message to the user if they enter a negative value.

            cout << "You can't work negative hours! Try again :";
            cin >> NumberHoursWorkedToday;

        }

        if ( NumberHoursWorkedToday <= 8 )

            //Compute pay earned today at normal base rate
            Pay = NumberHoursWorkedToday * 7.50;

        else

            //Compute the pay earned using the overtime rule
            Pay = ( 8 * 7.50 ) + ( 11.25 * ( NumberHoursWorkedToday - 8) );

        // Update the total pay you have earned so far this week
        TotalPay = TotalPay + Pay;

    } // when we hit this brace, we bounce back up to the beginning of the loop

    //Now we're free from the loop! Let's print then go spend our paycheck!
    cout << " Your totalpay for this week comes to : " << TotalPay;

} // The program is done . |
```

Comments (green)

Keywords (blue)

Commands (black)

Step 1:
Declare variables

Step 2:
Create loop

Step 3:
Collect input data

Step 4:
Check for errors

Loop

Step 5:
Process data

Step 6:
Update variables

Figure 10.16

A complete C++ program that solves the parking garage pay problem.

how you would actually enter this program on your system. This program, which is written in a top-down style, does not make use of objects. Each statement in the program is executed sequentially (that is, in order from the first statement to the last) unless the program encounters a keyword that changes the flow. In the figure, the program begins by declaring the variables needed to store the program's inputs and outputs in RAM (step 1). Next, the "for" keyword begins a looping pattern (step 2). All of the steps between the very first bracket ({) and the last one (}) will be repeated seven times to gather the total pay for each day of the week.

The next section (step 3) collects the input data from the user. The program then checks that the user entered a reasonable value (step 4). In this case, a positive number for hours worked must be entered. Next, the program processes the data (step 5). If the user worked eight or fewer hours, he or she is paid at the rate of $7.50, whereas hours exceeding eight are paid at $11.25.

The final statement (step 6) updates the value of the TotalPay variable. The last bracket indicates that the program has reached the end of a loop. The program will repeat the loop to collect and process the information for the next day. When the seventh day of data has been processed, the Day variable will be bumped up to the next value, 8. This causes the program to fail the test (Day <= 7?). At that point, the program exits the loop, prints the results, and quits.

Are there ways in which programmers can make their code more useful for the future? One aspect of converting an algorithm into good code is the programmer's ability to design general code that can adapt easily to new settings. Sections of code that will be used repeatedly, with only slight modification, can be packaged into reusable "containers" or components. Depending on the language, these reusable components are referred to as *functions, procedures, subroutines, modules,* or *packages*.

In our program, we could create a function that implements the overtime pay rule. As it stands in Figure 10.16, the code works only in situations in which the hourly pay is exactly $7.50 and the bonus pay is exactly $11.25. However, if we rewrote this part of the processing rules as a function, we could have code that would work for any base pay rate and any overtime rate. If the base pay rate or overtime rate changed, the function would use whichever values it was given as input to compute the output pay variable. Such a function, as shown in Figure 10.17, may be reused in many settings without changing any of the code.

Compilation

How does a programmer move from code in a programming language to the 1s and 0s the CPU can understand? **Compilation** is the process by which code is converted into machine language—the language the CPU can understand. A **compiler** is a program that understands both the syntax of the programming language and the exact structure of the CPU and its machine language. It can "read" the **source code**, which comprises the instructions programmers have written in the higher-level language, and translate the source code directly into machine language—the binary patterns that will execute commands on the CPU. You can learn more about the details of the binary number system in the "Under the Hood" Technology in Focus section.

Each programming language has its own compiler. It is a program that you purchase and install just like any other software on your system. Separate versions of the compiler are required if you want to compile code that will run on separate processor types. One version of a compiler would create finished programs for a Sun

Figure 10.17

A function is a reusable component that can be used in different settings.

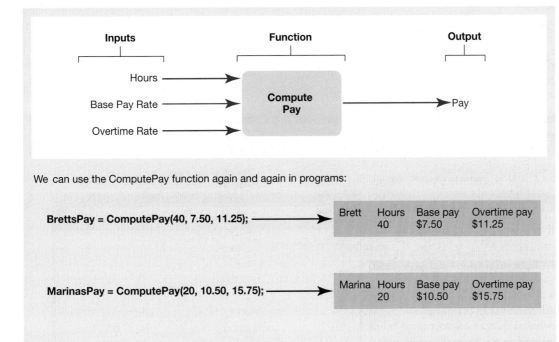

Inputs   Function   Output

Hours →

Base Pay Rate → **Compute Pay** → Pay

Overtime Rate →

We can use the ComputePay function again and again in programs:

BrettsPay = ComputePay(40, 7.50, 11.25); →

Brett	Hours	Base pay	Overtime pay
	40	$7.50	$11.25

MarinasPay = ComputePay(20, 10.50, 15.75); →

Marina	Hours	Base pay	Overtime pay
	20	$10.50	$15.75

UltraSPARC processor, for example, and another version of the compiler would create programs for an Intel i7 CPU.

At this stage, programmers finally have produced an **executable program**, the binary sequence that instructs the CPU to run their code. Executable programs cannot be read by human eyes because they are pure binary codes. They are stored as *.exe or *.com files on Windows systems.

Does every programming language have a compiler? Some programming languages do not have a compiler, but use an interpreter instead. An **interpreter** translates the source code into an intermediate form, line by line. Each line is then executed as it is translated. The compilation process takes longer than the interpretation process because in compilation all of the lines of source code are translated into machine language before any lines are executed. However, the finished compiled

program runs faster than an interpreted program because the interpreter is constantly translating and executing as it goes.

If producing the fastest executable program is important, programmers will choose a language that uses a compiler instead of an interpreter. For development environments in which many changes are still being made to the code, interpreters have an advantage because programmers do not have to wait for the entire program to be recompiled each time they make a change. With interpreters, programmers can immediately see the results of their program changes as they are making them.

Coding Tools: Integrated Development Environments

Are there any tools that make the coding process easier? Modern programming is supported by a collection of

Figure 10.18

The IDE for Microsoft Visual C++ helps the programmer when he or she is entering the code and when logical errors are found.

In this Sound Byte, you'll work in the Microsoft Visual Studio integrated development environment (IDE) with the C++ programming language and examine how the basic control structures of programming languages do their work.

tools that make the writing and testing of software easier. Compiler products feature an **integrated development environment (IDE)**, a developmental tool that helps programmers write, compile, and test their programs. As is the case with compilers, every language has its own specific IDE. Figure 10.18 shows the IDE for Microsoft Visual Studio using C++.

How does an IDE help programmers when they are typing the code? The IDE includes tools that support programmers at every step of the coding process. **Code editing** is the step in which a programmer physically types the code into the computer. An IDE includes an **editor**, a special tool that helps programmers as they enter the code, highlighting keywords and alerting them to typos. Modern IDE editors also automatically indent the code correctly, align sections of code appropriately, and apply color to code comments to remind programmers that these lines will not be executed as code. In addition, IDEs provide help files that document and provide examples of the proper use of keywords and operators.

How does the IDE help programmers after code editing is finished? Editing is complete when the entire program has been keyed into the editor. At that time, the programmer clicks a button in the IDE, and the compilation process begins. A pop-up window shows how the compilation is progressing, which line is currently being compiled, how many syntax errors have been identified, and how many warnings have been generated. A warning is a suggestion from the compiler that the code might not work in the way the programmer intended, although there is no formal syntax error on the line.

As mentioned earlier, a **syntax error** is a violation of the strict, precise set of rules that define the language. Programmers create syntax errors when they misspell keywords (such as typing BEEGIN instead of BEGIN) or use an operator incorrectly (such as typing x = y + + 2 instead of x = y + 2). Once compilation is finished, the IDE presents all of the syntax errors in one list. The programmer can then click any item in the list to see a detailed explanation of the type of error. When the programmer double-clicks an item in the list, the editor jumps to the line of code that contains the error, enabling the programmer to repair syntax errors quickly.

Debugging: Getting Rid of Errors

Once the program has compiled without syntax errors, it has met all of the syntax rules of the language. However, this doesn't mean that the program behaves in a logical way or that it appropriately addresses the task the algorithm described. If programmers made errors in the strategy used in the algorithm or in how they translated the algorithm to code, problems will occur. The process of running the program over and over to find errors and to make sure the program behaves in the way it should is termed **debugging** (see Figure 10.19).

How do programmers know whether there is anything wrong with their program? At this point in the process, the testing plan that was documented as part of the problem statement becomes critically important to programmers. As you'll recall from earlier in this chapter, the testing plan clearly lists input and output values, showing how the users expect the program to behave in each input situation. It is important that the testing plan contain enough specific examples to test every part of the program.

Figure 10.19

Debugging—the process of correcting errors in a program—combines logic with an understanding of the problem to be solved.

In the parking garage problem, we want to make sure the program calculates the correct pay for a day when you worked eight or fewer hours and for a day when you worked more than eight hours. Each of these input values forces the program to make different decisions in its processing path (the sequence of steps that turns inputs into outputs). To be certain the program works as intended, programmers try every possible path.

For example, once we can successfully compile the example code for the parking garage problem, we can begin to use our testing plan. The testing plan indicates that an input of 3 for NumberHours WorkedToday must produce an output of Pay = 3 * \$7.50 = \$22.50. In testing, we run the program and make sure that an input value of 3 yields an output value of \$22.50. To check that the processing path involving overtime is correct, we input a value of 12 hours. That input must produce Pay = 8 * \$7.50 + (12 − 8) * \$11.25 = \$105.00.

A complete testing plan includes sample inputs that exercise all of the error handling required as well as all of the processing paths. Therefore, we would also want to check how the program behaves when NumberHoursWorkedToday is entered as −2.

If the testing plan reveals errors, why does the program compile? The compiler itself is a program. It cannot think through code or decide whether what the programmer wrote is logical. The compiler only can make sure that the specific rules of the language are followed, that all of the keywords are spelled correctly, and that the operators being used are meaningful to that language.

For example, if in the parking garage problem we happened to type the if statement as

```
if (NumberHoursWorkedToday > 88)
//Use the Overtime Pay rule
```

instead of

```
if (NumberHoursWorkedToday > 8)
//Use the Overtime Pay rule,
```

the compiler would not see a problem. It doesn't seem strange to the compiler that you only get overtime after working 88 hours a day. These **logical errors** in the problem are caught only when the program executes. Another kind of error caught when the program executes is a **runtime error**. For example, it is easy for a programmer to accidentally write code for a loop that loops one time too many or one time too few. This can lead to a problem such as dividing a number by zero, a big "no-no" mathematically! That kind of forbidden operation generates a runtime error message.

Are there tools that help programmers find logic errors? Most IDEs include a tool called a **debugger** that helps programmers dissect a program as it runs. The debugger pauses the program while it is executing and allows the programmer to examine the values of all the variables. The programmer can then run the program in slow motion, moving it forward just one line at a time. Working through the program in this way lets the programmer see the exact sequence of steps being executed and the outcome of each calculation. He or she can then isolate the precise place in which a logical error occurs, correct the error, and recompile the program.

Finishing the Project: Testing and Documentation

Once debugging has detected all of the runtime errors in the code, it is time for users to test the program. This process is called *internal testing*. In internal testing, a group within the software company uses the program in every way it can imagine—including how it was intended to be used and in ways only new users may think up. The internal testing group makes sure the program behaves as described in the original testing plan. Any differences in how the program responds are reported back to the programming team, which makes the final revisions and updates to the code.

The next round of testing is external testing. In this testing round, people like the ones that eventually will purchase and use

Many Languages on Display

At the 99 Bottles of Beer site **99-bottles-of-beer.net**, you can find a simple program that displays the lyrics to the song *99 Bottles of Beer on the Wall*. If you have ever sat through round after round of this song on a long school bus trip, you know how repetitive it is. That means the code to write this song can take advantage of looping statements. This site presents the program in more than 1,000 different languages. Take a tour and see how much variety there is in programming!

the software must work with it to determine whether it matches their original vision.

What other testing does the code undergo? Before its final commercial release, software is often provided free or at a reduced cost in a **beta version** to certain test sites or to interested users. By providing users with a beta version of software, programmers can collect information about the remaining errors in the code and make a final round of revisions before officially releasing the program.

What happens if problems are found after beta testing? Users often discover problems in a program after its commercial release. These problems are addressed with the publication of **software updates** or **service packs**. Users can download these software modules to repair errors identified in the program code. For example, the Windows Vista operating system had a revision released as Service Pack 1 that added many bug fixes and security fixes and extended its compatibility so that instead of working with 40,000 devices, it will interact effectively with 80,000 devices.

After testing, is the project finished? Once testing is completed, but before the product is officially released, the work of **documentation** is still ahead. At this point, technical writers create internal documentation for the program that describes the development and technical details, how the code works, and how the user interacts with the program. In addition, the technical publishing department produces all of the necessary user documentation that will be distributed to the program users. User training begins once the software is distributed. Software trainers take the software to the user community and teach others how to use it efficiently.

Programming Languages: Many Languages for Many Projects

In any programming endeavor, programmers want to create a solution that meets several competing objectives. They want the software to run quickly and reliably and to be simple to expand later, when the demands on the system change. They also want it to be completed on time and for the minimum possible cost, and to use the

smallest amount of system resources possible.

Because it will always be difficult to balance these conflicting goals, a wide variety of programming languages has been developed. Earlier in the chapter, you learned about the five main categories (generations) of programming languages. In this section, we discuss the specific programming languages that are members of these different generations. Although programming languages often share many common characteristics, each language has specific traits that allow it to be the best fit for certain types of projects. Sometimes a language builds a loyal following, and that pushes a programmer to apply the same language to every situation.

The ability to understand enough about each language to match it to the appropriate style of problem is an exceptionally powerful skill for programmers.

What languages are popular today? There are far too many languages for one person to become expert at them all, but understanding the range of languages and how they relate to one another is especially useful. One quick way to determine which languages are popular is to examine job postings for programmers. As of this writing, the languages most in demand include C/C++ and Java. In specific industries, certain languages tend to dominate the work. In the banking and insurance industries, for example, the programming language COBOL is still common, although most other industries rarely use it any more. The Web site **Langpop.com** uses a number of different techniques to get a feel for which languages are popular in the software industry at the moment (see Figure 10.20).

How do I know which language to study first? A good introductory

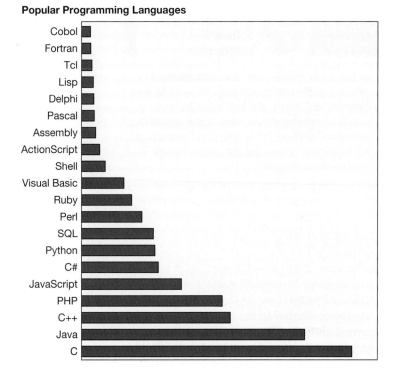

Popular Programming Languages

Cobol
Fortran
Tcl
Lisp
Delphi
Pascal
Assembly
ActionScript
Shell
Visual Basic
Ruby
Perl
SQL
Python
C#
JavaScript
PHP
C++
Java
C

Figure 10.20

When attacking a problem, you can choose from many different programming languages. This chart from **langpop.com** shows how popular certain languages are right now.

programming course will emphasize many skills and techniques that will carry over from one language to another. You should find a course that emphasizes design, algorithm development, debugging techniques, and project management. All of these aspects of programming will help you in any language environment. **Pascal** is the only modern language that was specifically designed as a teaching language, but it is no longer often taught at the college level. Many colleges and universities have opted to have students begin with Java or C++.

How does anyone learn so many languages? Professional programmers can work in a great number of different languages. They become proficient at learning new languages because they have become familiar with the basic components, discussed in this chapter's Dig Deeper feature, that are common to all languages: syntax, keywords, operators, and data types. The Bits and Bytes piece "Many Languages on Display" earlier in this chapter directs you to a site that displays an old song in more than a thousand different languages. Although Figure 10.21 pokes fun at one stereotype about learning to program, the experience has become much more manageable in recent years.

Selecting the Right Language

How do programmers know which language to select for a specific project? A programming team considers several factors before selecting the language it will use for a specific project.

- **Space available:** Not all languages take up the same amount of space. Therefore, the target language should be well matched to the amount of space available for the final program. For example, if the program will be embedded in a chip for use in a cell phone, then it is important for the language to be space efficient.

- **Speed required:** Although poorly written code executes inefficiently in any language, some languages can execute more quickly than others can. Some projects require a focus on speed rather than size. These projects require a language that produces code that executes in the fastest possible time.

- **Organizational resources available:** Another consideration is the resources available in a manager's group or organization. Selecting a language that is easy to use and will be easy to maintain if there is a turnover in programmers is an important consideration. Managers also may factor in the existing pool of talent available for the project. Having to train five programmers to tackle a project in a new language would have significant disadvantages over allowing them to work in a familiar language.

- **Type of target application:** Certain languages are customized to support a specific environment (UNIX or Windows, for instance). Knowing which languages are most commonly used for which environments can be helpful.

Windows Applications

What languages do programmers use if they want to build a Windows application? Software programs that run under the Windows OS are extremely popular. These programs often have a number of common features—scroll bars, title bars, text boxes, buttons, and expanding or collapsing menus, to name a few.

Several languages include customized controls that make it easy for programmers to include these features in their programs.

Can I just point and click to create a Windows application? In languages that support Windows programming, programmers can use the mouse to lay out on the screen where the scroll bars and buttons will be in the application. The code needed to explain this to the computer is then written automatically when the programmer says the layout is complete. This is referred to as **visual programming**, and it helps programmers produce a final application much more quickly. In this section, we'll discuss a few languages that are used to develop Windows applications and that take advantage of visual programming.

Visual Basic

What if programmers want to have a model of their program before it's fully developed? Earlier in the chapter, you read about how information systems are developed through the system development life cycle (SDLC). Although the SDLC has been around for quite some time, it doesn't necessarily work for all

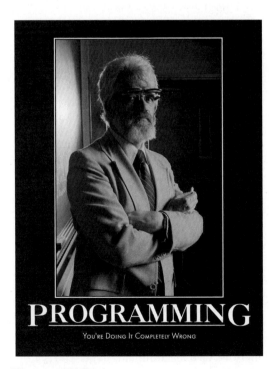

Figure 10.21

This poster mocks the image of a harsh, difficult road to learning programming. Modern tools allow programming to be fun to learn.

ACTIVE HELP-DESK

Selecting the Right Programming Language

In this Active Helpdesk call, you'll play the role of a helpdesk staffer, fielding calls about how programmers select the right programming language for a specific task and what the most popular Windows and Web applications are.

environments and instances. Programmers often like to build a **prototype**, or small model, of their program at the beginning of a large project.

Although an entire project may not be finished for several months, it can be useful to have a simple shell or skeleton of what the final program will look like to help with design. Prototyping is a form of **rapid application development (RAD)**, an alternative to the waterfall approach of systems development described at the beginning of this chapter. Instead of developing detailed system documents before they produce the system, developers create a prototype first, then generate system documents as they use and remodel the product.

Prototypes for Windows applications are often coded in Microsoft **Visual Basic (VB)**, a powerful programming language used to build a wide range of Windows applications. One strength of VB is its simple, quick interface, which is easy for a programmer to learn and use. It has grown from its roots in the language BASIC (short for Beginner's All-purpose Symbolic Instruction Code) to become a sophisticated and full-featured object-oriented language. It is often used in the creation of graphical user interfaces for Windows.

Visual Basic 2008 is the current version of Visual Basic and is designed for building object-oriented applications for Windows, the Web, and mobile devices. Figure 10.22 shows how the interface of Visual Basic makes it easy to drag and drop entire programming components into an application. Visual Basic 2008 provides a multitude of features that are new or an improvement on the previous versions. These changes make development with Visual Basic easier and more powerful than with any earlier version. Visual Basic 2008 and the .NET Framework are both part of Visual Studio 2008, which provides a complete set of developer tools.

Figure 10.22

The Toolbox in Visual Basic 2008 allows the programmer to drag and drop any of these items into a program.

C and C++

What languages do programmers use if the problem requires a lot of "number crunching"? A Windows application that demands raw processing power to execute difficult repetitive numerical calculations is most often a candidate for C/C++. For example, applications that simulate human cells and drug interactions have to solve elaborate mathematical equations many thousands of times each second, and are, therefore, excellent candidates for programming using C/C++. Several companies sell C/C++ compilers equipped with a design environment that makes Windows programming as visual as with VB.

Why was the C language developed? The predecessor of C++, **C**, was originally developed for system programmers. It was defined by Brian Kernighan and Dennis Ritchie of AT&T Bell Laboratories in 1978 as a language that would make accessing the operating system easier. It provides higher-level programming language features (such as *if* statements and *for* loops) but still allows programmers to manipulate the system memory and CPU registers directly. This mix of high- and low-level access makes C highly attractive to "power" programmers. Most modern operating systems (Windows Vista, Windows 7, Mac OS X, and Linux) were written in C.

The **C++** language takes C to the next level. Bjarne Stroustrup, the developer of C++, used all of the same symbols and keywords as C, but he extended the language with additional keywords, better security, and more support for the reuse of existing code through object-oriented design.

Are C and C++ natural choices when I'm looking to learn my first language? Neither C nor C++ was intended as a teaching language. The notation and compactness of these languages make them relatively difficult to master. They are in demand in industry,

How does the Microsoft .NET Framework help programmers? Too often, computer systems cannot exchange information—perhaps because they have different operating systems or use different rules for packaging data. The Microsoft .NET Framework is a software development environment designed to let Web sites "talk" to each other easily. The .NET Framework introduces Web services, which provide a standard way for software to interact. A **Web service** is a program that a Web site uses to make information available to other Web sites. For example, your Web site could use the Google Web service to search for information or to check the spelling of a word. The Google Web service returns the requested information to your program in a standard package that you then decode. Before Web services, programs needed a human being to submit a search to Google and read over the results. Now, the programs themselves can do this.

The power of .NET and Web services will continue to grow as more companies make some or all of their data available this way. The VB.NET programming tool has many supports for the programmer who is interested in using Web services.

```
for (i = 1; i < 20; i++)
{
   System.out.println(i);
}
```

Java code → Compiled once into → byte code

byte code:
. . . . .
. . . . .
FF OE
65 4A
. . . . .
. . . . .

FF OE 65 4A

FF OE 65 4A

FF OE 65 4A

PC running Windows

PDA

however, because C/C++ can produce fast-running code that uses a small amount of memory. Programmers often choose to learn C/C++ because their basic components (operators, data types, and keywords) are common to many other languages.

Java and C#

What language do programmers use for applications that need to collect information from networked computers? Imagine that an insurance company with many locations wants a program that will run each night and will communicate with networked computers in many offices around the country, collecting policy changes and updates from that day's business and updating the company's main records. The team that writes this program would want to use a language that already provides support for network communications.

Java would be a good choice. James Gosling of Sun Microsystems introduced Java in the early 1990s. It quickly became popular because its object-oriented model enables Java programmers to benefit from its large set of existing classes. For example, a Java programmer could begin to use the existing "network connection" class with little attention to the details of how that code itself was implemented. Classes exist for many graphical objects, such as windows and scroll bars, and for network objects such as connections to remote machines. Observing Java's success, Microsoft released a language named **C#** (pronounced "see sharp") that competes with Java.

Can a Java application work on any type of computer? An attractive feature of Java is that it is architecture

neutral. This means that Java code needs to be compiled only once, after which it can run on many CPUs (see Figure 10.23). The Java program does not care which CPU, operating system, or user interface is running on the machine on which it lands. This

Figure 10.23

Java programs can be compiled once and run on many different platforms.

BITS AND BYTES

Really Want to Learn? Work for Free!

The open source software movement is a grassroots collection of developers who believe that software projects can be managed start to finish by groups of individuals instead of companies. Open source software is developed and maintained at no charge by groups of people who are brought together by common interests such as photo editing. When completed, the software product and its source code are distributed free of charge.

The development, testing, and maintenance of the open source code are managed through resources such as SourceForge (**sourceforge.net**), a development Web site that hosts more than 100,000 programs. To support development of open source projects, SourceForge provides services to its more than 1 million users in support of their development of projects. For example, version control tools allow specific versions of a project to be "checked in" or "checked out," as in a library, allowing many people to work on the project at the same time. Communication tools and publicity tools are also provided to help the project succeed in reaching its audience.

Most types of software in the marketplace have an open source equivalent. (See the Technology in Focus section called "Computing Alternatives" on page 252 for more information.) If you are looking to learn about software development by doing it, investigate SourceForge and volunteer for a project!

is possible because the target computer runs a Java Virtual Machine (VM), software that can explain to the Java program how to function on any specific system. A Java VM installed with Microsoft Internet Explorer, for example, allows Internet Explorer to execute any **Java applet** (small Java-based program) it encounters on the Internet. Although Java code does not perform as fast as C++, the advantage of needing to compile only once before it can be distributed to any system is extremely important.

Web Applications: HTML/XHTML and Beyond

What is the most basic language for developing Web applications?

A document that will be presented on the Web must be written using special symbols called *tags*. Tags control how a Web browser will display the text, images, and other content tagged in the **HyperText Markup Language (HTML)** or **eXtensible HyperText Markup Language (XHTML)**. Although knowledge of HTML or XHTML is required to program for the Web, they are not in themselves programming languages. HTML and XHTML are just series of tags that modify the display of text. HTML was the original standard defining these tags. XHTML is a newer standard that corrects some of the inconsistencies found in HTML. To see more detail of HTML/XHTML tags, flip to the "HTML/XHTML" section in Chapter 13 (page 617). Many good HTML and XHTML tutorials are available on the Web at sites such as Learn the Net (**learnthenet.com**), Web Monkey (**webmonkey.com**), and the World Wide Web Consortium (**w3c.org**).

Figure 10.24

Adobe Dreamweaver is a popular tool for creating Web pages.

These sites include lists of the major tags that can be used to create HTML and XHTML documents.

Are there tools that help programmers write in HTML and XHTML?

Several different programs are available to assist in the generation of HTML and XHTML. Adobe Dreamweaver and Microsoft Expression Web present Web page designers with an interface that is similar to a word processing program. Web designers can quickly insert text, images, and hyperlinks, as shown in Figure 10.24. The program automatically inserts the corresponding HTML or XHTML tags. For simple, static (nonchanging) Web pages, no programming is required.

Scripting Languages for the Web

Which programming languages do programmers use to make complex Web pages?

To make their Web pages more visually appealing and interactive, programmers use scripting languages to add more power and flexibility to their HTML code. A **scripting language** is a simple programming language that is limited to performing a set of specialized tasks. Scripts allow decisions to be made and calculations to be performed. Several popular scripting languages work well with HTML, including JavaScript, VBScript, and PHP (Hypertext Preprocessor).

JavaScript is a scripting language that is often used to add interactivity to Web pages. JavaScript is not as fully featured as Java, but its syntax, keywords, data types, and operators are subsets of Java's. In addition, JavaScript has a set of classes that represent the objects often used on Web pages: buttons, check boxes, and drop-down lists.

The JavaScript button class, for example, describes a button with a name and a type—for example, whether it is a regular button or a Submit or Reset button. The language includes behaviors, such as click (), and can respond to user actions. For example, when a user moves his or her mouse over a button and clicks to select it, the button "knows" the user is there and jumps in and performs a special action (such as playing a sound).

Are there other scripting languages besides JavaScript?

Programmers who are more familiar with Visual Basic than Java or C++ often use **VBScript**, a subset of Visual Basic, to introduce dynamic decision making into Web pages. **Dynamic decision making**

STEP 1: User requests information on red bikes.

STEP 2: Server sends request to database computer.

STEP 3: Database computer returns list.

Customer's computer

ABC Bike Company server

ABC Bike Company database

12345
45678
98764
54321
11223
22334

STEP 4: Server's ASP program writes HTML page.

Figure 10.25

An online store is an example of the three-tier client/server type of Internet application.

means that the page can decide how to display itself based on the choices the reader makes. PHP, discussed below, is another scripting language that has become extremely popular. It is a free, open source product that runs very efficiently on multiple platforms, including Windows, Unix, and Linux.

ASP, JSP, and PHP

How are interactive Web pages built?
To build Web sites with interactive capabilities, programmers use **Active Server Pages (ASP)**, **Java Server Pages (JSP)**, or the scripting language **PHP (Hypertext Preprocessor)** to adapt the HTML or XHTML page to the user's selections. The user supplies information that is translated into a request by the main computer at the company that owns the Web site, often using a database query language such as SQL. Scripting code in ASP, JSP, or PHP controls the automatic writing of the custom HTML/XHTML page that is returned to the user's computer.

What does additional programming bring to a Web page? The most advanced Web pages interact with the user, collecting information and then customizing the content displayed based on the user's feedback. For example, as shown in Figure 10.25, the ABC online store's Web page will collect a customer bicycle inquiry for red bikes. It then asks ABC's main server for a list of red bicycles sold by the company. An ASP program running on the server creates a new HTML/XHTML page and delivers that to the user's browser, telling the customer what red bicycles (including details such as model and size) are currently sold by ABC.

Thus, ASP programs can have HTML/XHTML code as their output. They use what the user has told them (via the list boxes, check boxes, and buttons on the page) to make decisions. Based on those results, the ASP program decides what HTML/XHTML to write. A small example of ASP writing its own HTML/XHTML code is shown in Figure 10.26.

Flash and XML

What if a programmer wants to create a Web page that includes sophisticated animation? Many Web sites feature elaborate animations that interact with visitors. These sites include buttons and hyperlinks, along with animation effects. These components can be designed with **Adobe Flash**, a software product for developing Web-based multimedia. Flash includes its own programming language, named **ActionScript**, which is similar to JavaScript in its keywords, operators, and classes.

Microsoft has unveiled a competing product named *SilverLight* that supports the development of rich multimedia and interactive Web applications. Other advances, like the collection of technologies referred to as **AJAX (Asynchronous JavaScript And XML)**, allow the creation of Web applications that can update information on a page without requiring the user to do a page

a ASP code

```
<%Dim I %>

<%

For I = 1 To 5
        ' Output our HTML and text using the value of I as
        ' the FONT TAG's SIZE attribute.
        %>
        <FONT SIZE="<%= I %>">Hello World</FONT><BR>
        <%
Next ' Continue the loop 5 times
%>
```

Uses For loops

Writes five different HTML statements with a different number for font size

b HTML code

```
<FONT SIZE="1">Hello World</FONT><BR>
<FONT SIZE="2">Hello World</FONT><BR>
<FONT SIZE="3">Hello World</FONT><BR>
<FONT SIZE="4">Hello World</FONT><BR>
<FONT SIZE="5">Hello World</FONT><BR>
```

HTML document is program output

c HTML Displayed on User's Screen

Hello World
Hello World
Hello World
Hello World
Hello World

HTML document output in Web browser

Figure 10.26

An ASP program can (a) write HTML/XHTML code as its (b) output. This image illustrates how the HTML/XHTML page would (c) show up in a browser.

refresh or leave the page. By using existing technologies to do more processing in the browser, users have a more responsive experience.

Is HTML/XHTML the only markup language for the Web?   When Web sites communicate with humans, HTML/XHTML work well because the formatting they control is important. People respond immediately to the visual styling of textual information; its layout, color, size, and font design all help to transfer the message of the page to the reader. When computers want to communicate with each other, however, all of these qualities just get in the way. A third markup language, called **eXtensible Markup Language (XML)**, enables designers to define their own data-based tags, making it much easier for a Web site to transfer the key information on its page to another site.

Without XML, a Web site that wanted to look up current stock pricing information at another site would have to retrieve the HTML/XHTML page, sort through the formatting information, and try to recognize which text on the page identified the data needed. With XML, groups can agree on

standard systems of tags that represent important data elements. For example, the XML tags <stock> and </stock> might delimit key stock quote information. Mathematicians have created a standardized set of XML tags named MathML for their work, and biometrics groups are developing an XML standard to describe and exchange data such as DNA and face scans. We discuss HTML/XHTML and XML in more detail in Chapter 13.

Figure 10.27 shows a table of popular programming tools with their features and the typical settings in which they are used.

The Next Great Language

What will be the next great language?   It is never easy to predict which language will become the next "great" language, but software experts predict that as software projects continue to grow in size, the amount of time needed to compile a completed project will also grow. It is not uncommon for a large project to require 30 minutes or more to compile. Interpreted languages, however, have

Figure 10.27 | POPULAR PROGRAMMING TOOLS

Programming Language	Features	Typical Setting
C/C++ and C#	Can create compact code that executes quickly Provides high- and low-level access	Used in industrial applications such as banking and engineering
Flash ActionScript	Is similar in syntax to JavaScript but customized for the Flash animation environment	Used to control Flash animations
Microsoft SilverLight	Is a competitor to Adobe Flash, and supports rich multimedia capabilities	Used to deliver audio and video to Web pages
Java	Is architecture neutral Is object-oriented	Used to create applets that can be delivered over the Web
JavaScript	Is similar in syntax to Java Has classes that represent buttons, drop-down lists, and other Web page components	Creates code that lives on the client machine and supports interaction with Web pages
VBScript	Is similar in syntax to Visual Basic Has classes that represent buttons, drop-down lists, and other Web page components	Creates code that lives on the client machine and adds interaction to Web pages
Visual Basic .NET	Is easy to learn and use Is object-oriented Has a drag-and-drop interface	Used in prototype development Used to design graphical user interfaces
Web Technologies		
ASP, JSP, PHP	Has a set of rules and standards that allow Web sites to create their own HTML code based on user actions	Controls the automated writing of HTML pages
HTML/XHTML	Provide a set of tags that control the display of text on a Web page	Control layout and style of information presented on a Web page
XML	Enables users to define their own tags Facilitates exchange of information between Web sites	Used in the construction of Web services
AJAX	Uses a combination of existing technologies like JavaScript, CSS, and XML	Creates Web sites that can update without the user refreshing the page

virtually no compile time because compilation occurs while the code is being edited. As projects get larger, the capability to be compiled instantaneously will become even more important. Thus, interpreted languages such as Python, Ruby, and Smalltalk could become more important in the coming years.

Will all languages someday converge into one? Certain characteristics of modern programming languages correspond well with how programmers actually think. These traits support good programming practices and are emerging as common features of most modern programming languages. The object-oriented paradigm is one example. Both Visual Basic and COBOL have moved toward supporting objects.

There will always be a variety of programming languages, however.

SOUND BYTE

3D Programming the Easy Way

In this Sound Byte, you'll create a three-dimensional game using the visual drag-and-drop interface provided by Alice, a free software package. This program teaches all the concepts of programming with none of the pain of learning syntax.

Figure 10.28

There will always be a variety of languages, each with its own personality.

Figure 10.28, in which the artist tries to give each language a "personality," illustrates that idea in lighthearted fashion.

Forcing a language to be so general that it can work for any task also forces it to include components that make it slower to compile, produce larger final executables, and require more memory to run. Having a variety of languages and mapping a problem to the best language creates the most efficient software solutions.

So what do I do if I want to learn languages that will be relevant in the future? No particular set of languages is best to learn, and there is no one best sequence in which to learn them. The

Association for Computing Machinery (**acm.org**), encourages educators to teach a core set of mathematical and programming skills and concepts, but school and university departments are free to offer a variety of languages.

When you are selecting which programming languages to study, some geographical and industry-related considerations come into play. For example, in an area in which a large number of pharmaceutical companies exist, there may be a demand for Massachusetts General Hospital Utility Multi-Programming System (MUMPS). This language is often used to build clinical databases, an important task in the pharmaceutical industry. Review the advertisements for programmers in area newspapers and investigate resources such as ComputerJobs (**computerjobs.com**) to identify languages in demand in your area. Also, stay current on the direction of software engineering in general.

Whether or not you pursue a career in programming, having an understanding of software engineering will help you in many IT careers. Software is the set of instructions that allows us to make use of our hardware. Programming skills give you the power to understand, create, and customize a computer system.

Emerging Technologies: Will It Blend? Writing Your First Video Game in Blender

Blender is a free, open source application that supports home video game production by combining many tools into one package. Blender gives you what you need for each stage of beginning 3D video game development, allowing you to create three-dimensional objects with textures and move them around a 3D world with realistic physics.

First, Blender allows you to construct three-dimensional models (see Figure 10.29). Meshes are used to begin any model and can be customized to represent any 3D shape or object. You can add specific textures and shading to make the model more realistic. Blender then allows you to animate the object. That animation can be saved as a movie or connected to specific control keys or movements. You can also play a complete video game within Blender by using the built-in game engine. Finally, Blender incorporates a physics engine that understands basic concepts such as particle collisions and gravity modeling. This is useful, for example, when a game character tosses a plasma grenade toward a target!

The programming rules used to describe object behavior in the game are made simpler by Blender's Logic Bricks. For example, using Logic Bricks you can, in just a few clicks, create a rule that makes one object disappear when it collides with another. You can also use Logic Bricks to map key movements to control objects or cameras in the environment.

Blender is available as a free download (**blender.org**). You will also find an active community to support you as you learn. The Blender Foundation is involved in releasing games to the public that were developed for free using Blender. These open source games include titles such as Yo! Frankie and Apricot. These are available for anyone to learn from and reuse.

Many resources are available for Blender, including free books such as *Blender 3D: Noob to Pro*, on Wiki Books (**en.wikibooks.org/wiki/**

Blender), and a blog of everything Blender at **blendernation.com**. In addition, YouTube has numerous video tutorials on working with Blender, and libraries of Blender routines and objects are freely distributed on the Internet.

If you are interested in video game development, three-dimensional art, or just creating animations, download Blender and realize the power of the open source software movement.

Figure 10.29

Blender allows you to design 3D models, animate them, and apply real physics to create playable video games.

1. What is a system development life cycle, and what are the phases in the cycle?

An information system includes data, people, procedures, hardware, and software. Teams of individuals are required to develop systems. Those teams need to follow an organized process (or set of steps) to ensure that development proceeds in an orderly fashion. This set of steps is usually referred to as the system development life cycle (SDLC). There are six steps in the SDLC: (1) A problem or opportunity is identified. (2) The problem is analyzed, and a program specification document is created to outline the project objectives. (3) A detailed plan for programmers to follow is designed using flowcharts and data-flow diagrams. (4) Using this plan, the program is developed and documented. (5) The program is tested to ensure that it works properly and is installed so that it can be used. (6) Ongoing maintenance and evaluation ensure a working product.

2. What is the life cycle of a program?

Each programming project follows several stages from conception to final deployment. The problem statement identifies the task to be computerized and describes how the software program will behave. An algorithm is developed that specifies the sequence of steps that the program must take to complete the work. The algorithm is then translated into highly structured programming code. The code goes through the processes of debugging, in which the programmers find and repair any errors in the code, testing by the programming team, and further testing by the people who will use the program. The results of the entire project are documented for the users and the development team. Finally, users are trained so that they can use the program efficiently.

3. What role does a problem statement play in programming?

The problem statement is an explicit description of what tasks the computer program must accomplish and how the program will execute these tasks and respond to unusual situations. It describes the input data that users will have at the start of the job, the output that the program will produce, and the exact processing that converts these inputs to outputs. In addition, the problem statement identifies potential errors and plans to address these errors.

4. How do programmers create algorithms?

For simple problems, programmers create an algorithm by converting a problem statement into a list of steps (or actions) the program will take. For more complex problems, programmers must identify where decision points occur in the list of steps. Some decisions are yes/no (binary), whereas others create a repeating action (loop). Algorithms are documented in the form of a flowchart or in pseudocode. Programmers use either top-down or object-oriented analysis to produce the algorithm.

5. How do programmers move from algorithm to code, and in what categories of language might they code?

Computer code uses special words and strict rules to enable programmers to control the CPU without having to know all of its hardware details. Programming languages are classified in several major groupings, sometimes referred to as *generations*, with the first generation being machine language—the binary code of 1s and 0s that the computer understands. Assembly language is the next generation; it uses short, English-like commands that speak directly to the CPU and give the programmer direct control of hardware resources. Each successive generation in language development has relieved programmers of some of the burden of keeping track of what the hardware requires and more closely matches how humans think about problems.

6. How does a programmer move from code in a programming language to the 1s and 0s the CPU can understand?

Compilation is the process by which code is converted into machine language, the language the CPU can understand. A compiler is a program that understands both the syntax of the programming language and the exact structure of the CPU and its machine language. It can translate the instructions written by programmers in the higher-level language into machine language, the binary patterns that will execute commands on the CPU. Each programming language has its own compiler. Separate versions are required to compile code that will run on each different type of processor.

7. How is a program tested?

If programmers make errors in the algorithm or in translating the algorithm to code, problems will occur. Programmers debug the program by running it constantly to find errors and to make sure the program behaves in the way it should. Once debugging has detected all the code errors, users, both within the company and outside the company, test the program in every way they can imagine—both as it was intended to be used and in ways only new users may think up. Before its commercial release, software is often provided at a reduced cost or no cost in a beta version to certain test sites or to interested users for a last round of testing.

8. What steps are involved in completing the program?

Once testing is complete, technical writers create internal documentation for the program and external documentation that will be provided to users of the program. User training, which begins once the software is distributed, teaches the user community how to use the software efficiently.

9. How do programmers select the right programming language for a specific task?

A programming team reviews several considerations before selecting the language. First, certain languages are best used with certain problems. Second, the target language should be well matched to the amount of space available for the final program. Third, some projects require the selection of a language that can produce code that executes in the fastest possible time. Finally, selecting a language with which the programmers are familiar is also helpful.

10. What are the most popular programming applications for Windows and Web applications?

Visual Basic, C/C++, and Java are languages that enable programmers to include Windows control features such as scroll bars, title bars, text boxes, buttons, and expanding and collapsing menus. Programmers use HTML/XHTML for basic Web design. For more complex Web design, scripting programs such as JavaScript and VBScript are popular. Web page animations are done with ASP, JSP, PHP, Flash, and XML.

Word Bank

- algorithm
- beta version
- C/C++
- classes
- compiler
- debugger

- documentation
- HTML/XHTML
- inheritance
- interpreter
- JavaScript
- machine language

- object-oriented
- problem statement
- testing plan
- top-down
- Visual Basic

Instructions: Fill in the blanks using the words from the Word Bank above.

Things are not running smoothly at the Whizgig factory. We need to keep track of how many Whizgigs are made every hour and how many are defective. We begin by calling in the programming team to work with users. Together they begin to build a software solution by creating a(n) (1) _____. All of the input and output information required is identified as well as the (2) _____, which lists specific examples of what outputs the program will produce for certain inputs. The team then begins to design the (3) _____ by listing all the tasks and subtasks required to complete the job. This approach is called (4) _____ design.

An alternative to this design method is the (5) _____ design model, which develops the program based on objects. Objects that have similar attributes and behaviors can be grouped into (6) _____. The benefit of using this type of design approach is that objects and classes can be reused so easily in other programs. If necessary, new classes can be made by first "borrowing" the attributes of an existing class and then adding differentiating attributes. This concept is known as (7) _____.

To select the best language for this problem, the team considers the resources at Whizgig. Although many of the programmers know the visual programming language of (8) _____, the most important factors for this application will be how fast it runs, so the language (9) _____ is selected. Once Whizgig has started to take off, the plan is to expand into a strong Web presence. Then there will be a round of hiring programmers who know (10) _____. For now, the program to track production and quality control has been written in programming language, the (11) _____ translates it to (12) _____, or the binary code that the CPU understands. After that step, the program is ready to be tested.

The (13) _____ helps identify errors in the program code. Then the programmers put together the necessary (14) _____ that explains the program and how to use it. However, because this is a program that is to be used internally, the program does not need to go through a test of the (15) _____ by a group of potential outside users.

**becoming
computer literate**

Your new manager wants to design and deploy an Internet application to collect marketing information about potential customers. She wants to gather data and analyze it in one report, which can be shipped to the marketing department.

Instructions: Write a memo to the manager describing what will have to be considered in the creation of this project. Write the memo using as many of the key terms from the chapter as you can.

ten self-test

Instructions: Answer the multiple-choice and true–false questions below for more practice with key terms and concepts from this chapter.

Multiple Choice

1. In the SDLC, translating from an algorithm to a programming language is considered:
a. coding.
b. debugging.
c. building a testing plan.
d. All of the above.

2. Algorithms document
a. the programming languages to be used in the program.
b. testing operations to be conducted by the program.
c. the sequence of decisions and actions the program will take.
d. the documentation to be included in the program.
e. All of the above.

3. The IDE tool includes
a. a flowcharting tool.
b. an editor and a debugger.
c. a compiler.
d. None of the above.

4. A compiler for a programming language
a. is the same no matter which CPU the program is running on.
b. is the actual machine language of the CPU.
c. translates from a human-friendly programming language to binary 1s and 0s.
d. None of the above.

5. An object, defined by a specific class, is a collection of
a. data and methods.
b. ideas and a testing plan.
c. programming languages.
d. class variables.

6. Syntax errors are mistakes in
a. using the compiler.
b. applying the grammar of the language.
c. the logical thinking and design of the program.
d. Either of the above, depending on the specific language.

7. Why does HTML/XHTML have no compiler?
a. HTML/XHTML is written using English words.
b. Most programming languages do not use compilers.
c. Each is a series of tags that can be understood directly by a browser.
d. Wait! HTML/ XHTML does have to be compiled!

8. Flowcharting is
a. only done by a software package like Visio.
b. a measurement of the efficiency of a program.
c. a term for the stages of the SDLC.
d. a way of documenting an algorithm.

9. Which of the following is used in the design of Web applications?
a. HTML/XHTML
b. JavaScript
c. PHP
d. All of the above
e. None of the above

10. Which of the following languages is used if a problem requires a lot of number crunching?
a. PROLOG   c. HTML/XHTML
b. C/C++   d. Windows Vista

True-False

_____ 1. Algorithms can be represented visually by using Microsoft Silverlight.

_____ 2. Programmers debug a program by delivering it to users to find errors.

_____ 3. Object-oriented programming produces code that is more reusable than that generated by top-down design.

_____ 4. Java is the ideal development language, which is why other programming languages are beginning to lose their importance.

_____ 5. XML allows one Web site to look up and bring back information from another Web site.

making the
transition to...
next semester

chapter

making the
transition to...
next semester

1. The Pipeline of Programming Courses

Research the core programming sequence at the college you are attending.

a. How many courses are in the core sequence?
b. How many languages does the sequence cover?
c. How many sections of each of the classes are offered?
d. What can you infer about the percentage of students that stay in the programming track over time?
e. What does that result mean to the future of your community and country?

2. ACM Recommendations

How will you follow up an introductory programming class at your current school? Examine the recommendations from the Association for Computing Machinery (**acm.org/education/curric_vols/CC2005-March06Final.pdf**) and compare them with the course offerings at your school.

3. A Ruby and a Perl

Perl is an especially useful and convenient language to use for specific types of programming problems. Ruby is a new programming language that has specific advantages for some settings. Research Ruby and Perl on the Web, and identify the key features of these languages. Determine which programming situations call for using Ruby and which would be best suited for Perl.

4. Beta Testing

Companies use beta testing to detect remaining problems in their programs before releasing the final version to the retail market. Go to the Beta News site (**betanews.com**), or to any other site that offers beta versions of your favorite software title. What programs would you be interested in beta testing? Why do you think it might make sense to beta test a software program? What, if any, are the risks involved in beta testing software?

5. Creating a Problem Statement

Create a problem statement for the process of registering for courses next semester. It should describe the inputs, outputs, and decision rules that you would need to follow to register successfully for the correct courses.

6. Code Reusability

This semester you will write a program that plays a game of blackjack with the user. Next semester's course has an instructor who always assigns a more sophisticated version of this problem, for which you will need to develop much more complex logic in the blackjack strategy engine of your game. How could you design your code this semester so that it would be the most reusable and helpful to you next term? Discuss how the importance of reusability would affect your choice of language. How would the object-oriented design model be beneficial here?

1. Programming Is Not Just for Programmers

Think about the range of jobs at the place where you currently work.

a. How many of the employees use computers?
b. How many individuals create macros, scripts, or shortcuts for doing their work in a faster, more automated fashion?
c. How many people actually program in a modern programming language?

2. Algorithm Design

Identify the most commonly performed task at your place of business. Think of a way to document it as an algorithm. Then study it to see if you can find a way to make it even more efficient. A small improvement to the most often performed task means big productivity gains.

3. Choosing the Best Language

Using resources from the Web, determine which programming languages would be best to learn if you were going to program for the following industries:

a. Animated movies
b. Computer games
c. Database management
d. Robotics

4. Testing Software

Your company has a division that designs software to control the automatic transmission in a line of automobiles. How would you develop a testing plan for this software? What conditions would you need to examine to be sure you were minimizing the probability of software failure in the field?

5. Software Development

This chapter presents the traditional software development life cycle (SDLC) in six stages. Review the areas you would examine in the company to see if they are better suited to the traditional SDLC or the joint application development (JAD) model. What qualities in the corporate culture would you look for to see if the company is "agile," in the sense of being able to adapt to changes quickly? What kind of employee qualities and experience would be important in a team that is taking the JAD approach to a project?

6. Accessibility

Web designers and programmers can take specific steps to allow visually impaired users to access Web sites more easily. Examine the information on accessibility at Adobe's Web site (**adobe.com**). What is accessibility in the software context? Explore the details of existing assistive technologies, such as screen readers. What are the legal requirements with which Web sites must comply in order to meet the needs of persons with disabilities? Why is maximizing accessibility important?

Instructions: Albert Einstein used *Gedankenexperiments*, or critical thinking questions, to develop his theory of relativity. Some ideas are best understood by experimenting with them in our own minds. The following critical thinking questions are designed to demand your full attention but require only a comfortable chair—no technology.

1. Using Data and Methods

Think about what classes would be important in modeling a band that is about to go on a national concert tour. What data and methods would each class need? How would the classes be related to each other?

2. Class Hierarchy

A common test for deciding the structure of a class hierarchy is the "is a" versus "has a" test. For example, a motorcycle "has a" sidecar, so Sidecar would be a data field of a Motorcycle object. However, a motorcycle "is a" kind of vehicle, so Motorcycle would be a subclass of the base class Vehicle. Use the "is a" versus "has a" test to decide how a class structure could be created for computer peripherals. Work to separate the unique features into objects and to extract the most common features into higher-level classes.

3. Future Programming Languages

What do you think the computer programming language of the future should be able to do? How simple would it be? Would it use a graphical interface? Would it combine voice-recognition software with the coding process? Do you think computers will ever be able to create their own programs, or will humans always have to play a role in computer programming?

4. Programming Ethics

Some companies make their programmers sign agreements to prevent them from competing with the company later by working for a competitor. Is this ethical conduct on the part of the company? What if the company fires the programmer and she then has trouble finding work? How would this kind of agreement change the employee's work habits and professional development decisions?

5. Language Popularity

At the site Langpop.com, results of many different surveys are combined to decide which programming languages are the most popular today. Where would you go to conduct a survey on which programming languages are popular? What individuals would you survey? How would you expect their answers to differ from one another?

6. Understanding Algorithms

Are there some problems whose solutions cannot be expressed as algorithms? Are there problems that cannot be solved with a fixed algorithm but can be described with an algorithm that incorporates probability and chance?

Working Together for Change

Problem

You and your team have just been selected to write a software program that tells a vending machine how to make proper change from the bills or coins the customer inserts. The program needs to deliver the smallest possible amount of coins for each transaction.

Task

Divide the class into three teams: Algorithm Design, Coding, and Testing. The responsibilities of each team are outlined as follows.

Process

1. The Algorithm Design team must develop two documents. The first document should present the problem as a top-down design sequence of steps. The second document should use object-oriented analysis to identify the key objects in the problem. Each object needs to be represented as data and behaviors. Inheritance relationships between objects should be noted as well. You can use flowcharts to document your results.

   You may also consider using a product such as Alice (**alice.org**) to try to develop the code for a prototype of the system.

2. The Coding team needs to decide which programming language would be most appropriate for the project. This program needs to be fast and take up only a small amount of memory. Use the Web to collect information about the language you select and be sure you have enough information to defend your selection.

   If the Algorithm Design team created prototype code with Alice, be sure to study the choices team members made and how their code would match the language you recommend.

3. The Testing team must create a testing plan for the program. What set of inputs would you test with to be sure the program is completely accurate? Develop a table listing combinations of inputs and correct outputs.

4. As a group, discuss how each team would communicate its results to the other teams. Once one team has completed its work, are the team members finished or do they need to interact with the other teams? How would the tools of a site such as SourceForge (**sourceforge.net**) help your development team across the life of the project?

Conclusion

Any modern programming project requires programming teams to produce an accurate and efficient solution to a problem. The interaction of the team members within the team as well as with the other teams is vital to successful programming.

In addition to the review materials presented here, you'll find additional materials featured with the book's multimedia, including the *Technology in Action* Student Resource CD and the Companion Website (**pearsonhighered.com/techinaction**), which will help reinforce your understanding of the chapter content. These materials include the following:

Active Helpdesk

In Active Helpdesk calls, you'll assume the role of helpdesk operator, taking calls about the concepts you've learned in this chapter. You'll apply what you've learned and receive feedback from a supervisor to review and reinforce those concepts. The Active Helpdesk calls for this chapter are listed below and can be found on your Student Resource CD.

- Understanding Software Programming
- Selecting the Right Programming Language

Sound Bytes

Sound Bytes are dynamic multimedia tutorials that help demystify even the most complex topics. You'll view video clips and animations that illustrate computer concepts and then apply what you've learned in the Sound Byte Labs, which include quizzes and activities specifically tailored to each Sound Byte. The Sound Bytes for this chapter are listed below and can be found on your Student Resource CD.

- Programming for End Users
- Looping Around the IDE
- 3D Programming the Easy Way

Companion Website

The *Technology in Action* Companion Website includes a variety of additional materials to help you review and learn more about the topics in this chapter. The resources available at **pearsonhighered.com/techinaction** include the following:

- **Online Study Guide.** Each chapter features an online true–false and multiple-choice quiz. You can take these quizzes, automatically check the results, and e-mail the results to your instructor.
- **Web Research Projects.** Each chapter features several Web research projects that ask you to search the Web for information on computer-related careers, milestones in computer history, important people and companies, emerging technologies, and the applications and implications of different technologies.

eleven

behind the **scenes:**

databases and information systems

objectives

After reading this chapter, you should be able to answer the following questions:

1. What is a database, and why is it beneficial to use databases? *(pp. 510–511)*

2. What components make up a database? *(pp. 512–515)*

3. What types of databases are there? *(pp. 516–517)*

4. What do database management systems do? *(pp. 517–526)*

5. How do relational databases organize and manipulate data? *(pp. 526–532)*

6. What are data warehouses and data marts, and how are they used? *(pp. 532–536)*

7. What is an information system, and what types of information systems are used in business? *(pp. 536–541)*

8. What is data mining, and how does it work? *(pp. 542–543)*

resources

Active Helpdesk

- Understanding Database Management Systems **(p. 517)**
- Using Databases **(p. 519)**
- Data Warehouses, Data Marts, and Information Systems **(p. 542)**

Sound Bytes

- Creating an Access 2007 Database **(p. 524)**
- Improving an Access 2007 Database **(p. 529)**

Companion Website

The Companion Website includes a variety of additional materials to help you review and learn more about the topics in this chapter. Go to: *pearsonhighered.com/techinaction*

how cool is *this?*

You probably have hundreds of songs that you listen to regularly. Wouldn't it be great if you could receive **music recommendations** based on the common attributes of **music** you already enjoy, instead of random comments from your friends or less reliable data such as buying patterns?

The Music Genome Project provides such recommendations by **analyzing songs** and categorizing them in a database according to almost 400 different attributes, such as "breathy female lead vocalist" or "club rap roots." Pandora Internet Radio (**pandora.com**) currently uses the Music Genome Project to provide music to listeners based on their **music preferences**.

With Pandora, you can create radio stations that play music based on facts you provide, called *seeds*. Seeds can be either **song titles** or the names of musical **artists**. So, if you enjoy music from The Fray or like the song "Sober" (by Pink), you would enter these as seeds for a Pandora station. Pandora then would play music with attributes similar to the seeds you provided. You can't control which songs will play, because they are served up randomly, but they will likely be songs **you will enjoy**, even if you have never heard them before.

Life Without Databases

A **database** is a collection of related data that can be easily stored, sorted, organized, and queried. By creating an organized structure for data, we hope to make data more meaningful and therefore more useful. In other words, we are attempting to turn data into information.

Not every situation in which related data needs to be turned into organized information demands the complexity of a database. For simple tasks, lists are adequate. Often, word processing or spreadsheet software works for creating simple lists. A table you create in Microsoft Word can serve as a list, as can a spreadsheet you create in Microsoft Excel.

Figure 11.1 shows a simple "Books to Buy" list you might create in Excel before beginning college. This list works well because it is simple and suited to just one purpose: to provide you with a list of the books you need to buy for a particular semester. If all the information that needed to be tracked were as simple as the information in Figure 11.1, there would be no need for databases.

When is a list not appropriate? If complex information needs to be organized or more than one person needs access to it, a list is not an efficient solution. For example, when you enrolled in college, you provided information about yourself to a number of people. This information included your name, your address, the classes you wished to take, and the meal plan you selected. Your school also tracks other information about you, such as your residence hall address. Consider the two lists shown in Figure 11.2. Figure 11.2a is a list the registrar's office uses to keep track of students, the classes they are taking, and the meal plan they selected. Figure 11.2b is a list the residence hall manager uses to track where students are housed.

What's the problem with having two lists? First, there is a great deal of duplicated data between the two lists in Figure 11.2. For example, each time Donald Lopez registers for a class, his name and address are entered. He needs to provide the same data to the residence hall manager when he receives his residence hall assignment. This **data redundancy**, though not a problem in the small lists in Figure 11.2, can be problematic when a college or university has 10,000 students. Imagine the time wasted by entering data multiple times, semester after semester. Imagine, too, the increased likelihood that someone will make a mistake.

Second, each time the information in the list changes, multiple lists must be updated. If Li Chan moves, his data will need to be updated in all the lists that contain his address. It would be easy to overlook one or more lists or even one or more rows in the same list. This would lead to a state of **data inconsistency**. It would not be possible to tell easily which data was correct. In addition, notice that Jennifer Evans's last record in Figure 11.2a contains a different street address than that shown in her other records. It's impossible to tell which address is correct, again resulting in data inconsistency.

In addition, correct data can be entered into a list but in an inconsistent format. Look at students Jennifer Evans and Donald Lopez in Figure 11.2a. Both are registered for PSY 110, but two different course names appear: Intro to Psychology and Intro to Psych. Are these the same course? Which name is the correct one? Confusion arises when data is inconsistently entered. Establishing data consistency is difficult to do with a list.

Aside from data redundancy and inconsistency, are there any other problems with using lists instead of databases? What if someone accidentally entered Jennifer Evans's enrollment data twice in the list in Figure 11.2a? Any reports (such as student bills) that are generated based on this list will be inaccurate because of the duplicate data. For example, Jennifer would be sent two separate bills for

Figure 11.1

A simple list created as a spreadsheet in Microsoft Excel or as a table in Microsoft Word is often sufficient to organize simple tasks.

	A	B	C	D
1	Books To Buy			
2				
3	Class	Title	Author	Bought
4	English Comp 1	The Prose Reader: Essays for Thinking, Reading, and Writing	Flachmann	Yes
5	Computer Programming 1	Java: How to Program	Deitel	Yes
6	Western Civilizations 1	The Western Heritage	Kagan, Ozment, Turner	
7	Intro to Psychology	Psychology	Wade	Yes
8	Inorganic Chemistry	Chemistry	McMurry, Fay	
9				

Figure 11.2

(a) A class registration list and (b) a list of residence hall assignments are two lists that a college might create to keep track of student information.

a

	A	B	C	D	E	F	G	H	I	J	K
1	Class Registration List - Fall										
2											
3	SID #	Last Name	First Name	Home Address	City	State	Zip Code	Class Code	Class Name	# Of Credits	Meal Plan #
4	234567891	Chan	Li	123 Main Street	Tuba City	NV	49874-7643	LAN 330	Japanese 1	3	2
5	234567891	Chan	Li	123 Main Street	Tuba City	NV	49874-7643	REL 216	Early Buddhism	3	2
6	234567891	Chan	Li	123 Main Street	Tuba City	NV	49874-7643	ENG 102	English Comp 2	3	2
7	456789123	Coyle	Diane	745 Station Drive	Springfield	MA	18755-5555				
8	123456789	Evans	Jennifer	123 Oak Street	Gotham City	PA	19999-8888	CIS 111	Programming	3	1
9	123456789	Evans	Jennifer	123 Oak Street	Gotham City	PA	19999-8888	ENG 101	English Comp 1	3	1
10	123456789	Evans	Jennifer	123 Oak Street	Gotham City	PA	19999-8888	HIS 103	Western Civ	3	1
11	123456789	Evans	Jennifer	123 Oak Street	Gotham City	PA	19999-8888	CHE 140	Chemistry	4	1
12	123456789	Evans	Jennifer	124 Oak Street	Gotham City	PA	19999-8888	PSY 110	Intro to Psychology	3	1
13	567891234	Lopez	Donald	3421 Lincoln Court	Spalding	ND	87564-2546	HIS 401	16th Century Europe	3	1
14	567891234	Lopez	Donald	3421 Lincoln Court	Spalding	ND	87564-2546	SOC 310	Interpersonal Relationships	3	1
15	567891234	Lopez	Donald	3421 Lincoln Court	Spalding	ND	87564-2546	PSY 110	Intro to Psych	3	1
16	345678912	Wallace	William	654 Front Street	Locust Glen	MI	67744-3584	HIS 204	Scottish History	3	3

b

	A	B	C	D	E	F	G	H	I
1	Residence Hall Assignment List - Fall								
2									
3	SID #	Last Name	First Name	Home Address	City	State	Zip Code	Residence Hall Name	Room Number
4	234567891	Chan	Li	123 Main Street	Tuba City	NV	49874-7643	Wilson Hall	218
5	456789123	Coyle	Diane	745 Station Drive	Springfield	MA	18755-5555	Montgomery Hall	231
6	123456789	Evans	Jennifer	123 Oak Street	Gotham City	PA	19999-8888	Montgomery Hall	312
7	567891234	Lopez	Donald	3421 Lincoln Court	Spalding	ND	87564-2546	Stone House	102
8	345678912	Wallace	William	654 Front Street	Locust Glen	MI	67744-3584	Forsman Quad	124

her classes, resulting in confusion and headaches.

In Figure 11.2a, each student has selected one of the college's meal plans, and this data must be entered into each row. What if someone enters a nonexistent meal plan in one of the rows pertaining to Donald Lopez? This is not only wrong, but also can be confusing to anyone viewing the list. With a list, anything can be entered in a row or column, even if that information is incorrect.

In addition, information can be organized in many ways. Consider the list of residence hall assignments in Figure 11.2b, which is organized alphabetically by last name. This works well for the accounting clerk, who needs to generate bills for student housing. However, for the residence manager who wants to see which residence hall rooms are still vacant, it would be more useful to have the data organized by residence hall and room number. Reorganizing multiple lists in this way can be labor intensive.

A final problem with lists is how to handle incomplete data. In Figure 11.2a, Diane Coyle has enrolled in the college but has not yet selected a meal plan or registered for courses. Her known information has been entered, but it's impossible to tell by looking at her record whether data relating to her course registrations and meal plans is available and just was not entered, or is truly missing.

Can't I just exercise caution and set rules for updating lists? Carefully following the rules when you update a list like the ones shown in Figure 11.2 can address many of the problems mentioned, but there is still room for error. Being careful does not avoid the most pressing problems of lists: (1) the inability of the data to be shared and (2) data redundancy. Even if you could surmount all of these problems, you cannot easily change a list to accommodate the disparate needs of many users.

How can I solve the problems associated with lists? For single topics, a list is sufficient. However, for any complex data that needs to be organized or shared, using a database is the most practical and efficient way to avoid the pitfalls associated with using lists.

Figure 11.3

Using a database lets data be centralized, so that only one copy of relevant data must be maintained. All database users therefore access the same up-to-date information.

Financial Aid Office

Student financial aid records are updated

A teacher enters student grades

Student Registration

A student registers for classes and checks his grades

Student Housing Office

A student is assigned to a residence hall

Student Information Database

Database Building Blocks

Almost any kind of data that needs organization and analysis can be put into a database. For example, Yahoo! maintains an online database (called Yahoo! People Search) that helps users find a person's street address or e-mail address. Publishers such as Condé Nast Publications, which publishes *Wired* magazine, store subscribers' mailing addresses and payment information in a database. In this section, we explore the advantages of using databases as well as the terminology databases use to categorize data.

Advantages of Using Databases

How do databases make our lives easier? Without databases, you could not store and retrieve large quantities of information easily. Consider airline reservation systems. Thousands of people fly across the United States on any given day. Without a database, it would be extremely difficult to keep track of such a large number of airline reservations. In addition, although you can look up information fairly quickly in a list, even extremely large electronic databases can provide the information you request in seconds. Databases provide three main advantages: They enable information sharing, they promote data integrity, and they allow the flexible use of data.

How do databases make information sharing possible? Consider student records at a college. As noted earlier, without databases, financial aid, admissions, and student housing would all need their own student files. The information in these files might not match because each department would maintain its own records. If a change had to be made in a student's address, all three files (the financial aid file, the admissions file, and the student housing file) would have to be changed.

As shown in Figure 11.3, with a database only one file is maintained, which reduces the possibility of errors when data is entered or updated. It also increases efficiency, because there are no files to reconcile with each other. A database therefore provides for data centralization. There is no need for multiple lists. Each department that needs to use student information accesses it from the same set of data.

How do databases promote data integrity? **Data integrity** means that the data contained in the database is accurate and reliable. **Data centralization** goes a long way toward ensuring data integrity. Instead of being in multiple lists that have to be maintained, your name and address information is maintained in only one place. If you move, your address must be changed only once.

How do databases provide flexibility? Another significant advantage of databases is that they are flexibly organized, enabling you to reorganize the information they contain in a variety of ways to suit the needs of the moment. Think back to the earlier example regarding lists. The registrar and housing manager need to see different information. With a list, you can organize information in only one way. If information is in a database, the registrar can easily view just the information she needs (such as the courses the student is taking). Likewise, the housing manager can easily view just the information he needs (such as the residence hall to which the student is assigned).

> **Databases can manage larger amounts of data and process that data more efficiently.**

Data flexibility also makes information dissemination tasks easier. Suppose your school wants to send out a mailing about a new course to all business majors. Having the contact information of students available in a database makes it easy to merge the data, using an application such as Microsoft Word, and create personalized letters and address labels. Obviously, this would be much faster than generating these items manually, and the results should contain fewer errors. Thus, databases can manage larger amounts of data and process that data more efficiently.

Are there any disadvantages associated with databases? Databases are more complex to construct and administer than lists. They also can be time-consuming and expensive to set up. Great care must be exercised in the design of databases to ensure they will function as intended. Although average individuals can design small databases, it is helpful to have an experienced **database administrator** (or **database designer**), an individual trained in the design and building of databases, to assist with the construction of large databases.

Data privacy concerns also arise when using databases. Think about how much information you've provided to your school. The school probably has records of your Social Security number, birth date, address, and credit card information. These are things an identity thief would love to have. For this reason, many colleges and universities no longer use Social Security numbers as student identification (ID) numbers. Instead, they create a unique student ID number when you register, which helps protect your Social Security number from falling into the wrong hands. Despite the increased complexity of databases and the issues surrounding privacy, however, the advantages of databases far outweigh the administrative disadvantages.

Database Terminology

How is data stored in a database? Understanding how databases store information requires knowing the unique terminology developed to describe databases. As shown in Figure 11.4, databases have three main components: fields, records, and tables (or files).

Fields

What is a field? A database stores each category of information in a **field**. Fields are displayed in columns. The city where a student lives can be found in the City field in the class registration list shown in Figure 11.4. Each field is identified by a **field name**, which is a way of describing the field. Class Code is a field name in the class registration list database in Figure 11.4. In a database, fields have other characteristics to describe them, including field data types and field size.

What are data types? When fields are created in the database, the user assigns those fields a **data type** (or **field type**). The data type indicates what type of data can be stored in the field.

Figure 11.4

In a database, a category of information is stored in a field. A group of related fields is called a record, and a group of related records is called a table (or file). This is a table that contains records for all students registered for classes in the current semester.

Common data types are listed and illustrated in Figure 11.5 and described in the remainder of this section.

- A **text field** can hold any combination of alphanumeric data (letters or numbers), but is most often used to hold words. Although text fields can contain numbers (such as telephone numbers), they are stored as text and therefore cannot be used in calculations.
- A **numeric field** stores numbers. Unlike values in text fields, values in numeric fields can be used to perform calculations. For instance, the numbers stored in numeric fields can be used to calculate tuition owed.
- A **computational field** (or **computed field**) is a numeric field that stores the contents of a calculation, which is generated with a formula in the numeric field. This is similar to a formula computation in a spreadsheet cell.
- A **date field** holds data such as birthdays and due dates.
- A **memo field** is like a text field but can hold long pieces of text. For example, a paragraph describing your high school

Figure 11.5 | COMMON DATA TYPES AND ILLUSTRATIVE DATA

Data Type	Used to Store	Examples
Text	Alphabetic or alphanumeric data	Mary CIS110
Numeric	Numbers	256 1.347 $5,600
Computational	Computational formulas	Credit hours x per-credit tuition charges
Date	Dates in standard date notation	4/15/2012
Memo	Long blocks of text	Four score and seven years ago, our fathers brought forth on this continent a new nation, conceived in liberty, and dedicated to the proposition that all men are created equal.
Object	Multimedia files or documents	MP3 file AVI file
Hyperlink	A hyperlink to a Web page	pearsonhighered.com/techinaction

Same name, different primary keys

achievements would be stored in a memo field.

- An **object field** holds items such as pictures, video clips, or documents.
- A **hyperlink field** stores hyperlinks to Web pages.

What is meant by field size? Field size defines the maximum number of characters or numbers that a field can hold. If a numeric field has a size of 5, it can hold a number as high as 99999. As a rule, you should tailor the field size to the length of the data it contains. If you define a field size of 50, space is reserved for 50 characters in that field, whether or not all 50 characters are used. Therefore, if you know that a character field will have a maximum of two characters, defining the field size as 50 wastes space and makes the files unnecessarily large. This can cause decreased database performance, especially in large databases.

Records and Tables

What are records and tables in databases? A group of related fields is called a **record**. For example, a student's name, address, and class registration information comprise a record. A group of related records is called a **table** (or **file**). Tables usually are organized by a common subject. Figure 11.4 shows a table that contains records for all students registered for classes in the current semester.

Primary Keys

Can fields have the same values in the same table? Yes, they can. It is possible that two students may live in the same town or have the same last name. However, to keep records distinct, each record must have one field that has a value unique to that record. This unique field is called a **primary key** or a **key field**. For example, as shown in Figure 11.6, in student records, the primary key is the student ID number (field name SID#). Establishing a primary key and ensuring that it is unique make it impossible to duplicate records.

What makes a good primary key? We already have many numbers that follow us through our lives that make excellent primary keys. In the past, Social Security numbers were often selected as primary keys in databases containing data about individuals. More recently, concerns about identity theft have led many businesses to abandon Social Security numbers as the primary means of identifying individuals. Driver's license numbers are unique within a particular state, as are the license plate numbers on cars. State government agencies often use these numbers to track individuals and their transactions.

Primary keys don't have to be numbers that already represent something. For example, when you place an order with Amazon.com, your transaction gets a unique order number. This number is the Amazon database's primary key. You refer to this number when checking your order status, returning merchandise, and so on. It

Figure 11.6

This table of residence hall assignments uses SID# as the primary key. Unique student ID numbers make ideal primary keys because even students with the same name won't have the same ID number.

is essential to have a unique number for each order because it would be difficult to keep track of it without one.

Database Types

Many different types of electronic databases have been used since the invention of the computer. The three major types of databases currently in use are relational, object oriented, and multidimensional. Of these three, relational databases have the largest market share, but the market share of multidimensional databases is growing at a fast pace.

Relational Databases

What is a relational database? A **relational database** organizes data in table format by logically grouping similar data into a **relation**, (a table that contains related data). As discussed earlier, each record in a database table is assigned a primary key to ensure that the record is unique. In relational databases, tables are logically linked to each other by including their primary keys in other tables with related information.

For example, at your college, a database about students would have a table with student contact information (name, address, and phone number) and another table with class registration information (class number and meeting times). These two tables would be linked by a primary key such as a student ID number. Data types common in relational databases are text, numeric, and date, although relational databases can possess other data types.

Who invented the relational database? E. F. Codd first significantly defined the relational model in 1970. Since then, much research and development have been done on the relational database model, and the model has proven to be extremely reliable for storing and manipulating data.

Object-Oriented Databases

What is an object-oriented database? An **object-oriented database** stores data in objects, rather than in tables. The models on which these databases are formed derive from the object-oriented programming paradigm, discussed in Chapter 10, which was catching on in the programming community in the late 1980s. Objects contain not only data, but also methods for processing or manipulating that data. This allows object-oriented databases to store more types of data than relational databases and to access that data faster.

For example, a "student" object that contains data about the courses a student is taking might also store the instructions for generating a bill for the student based on his or her course load. Because object-oriented databases store the instructions for doing computations in the same place as they store the data, they can usually process requests for information faster than can relational databases (which would only store the student information).

Why would I use an object-oriented database? Whereas relational databases excel in the storage of **structured (analytical) data** (such as "Bill" or "345"), object-oriented databases are more adept at handling unstructured data. **Unstructured data** includes nontraditional data such as audio clips (including MP3 files), video clips, pictures, and extremely large documents. Data of this type is known as a **binary large object (BLOB)** because it is actually encoded in binary form.

BITS AND BYTES

When a Number Isn't Really a Number

You might think that phone numbers should be defined as numeric data types. However, the data type you assign to a phone number depends on what data needs to be stored *with* the phone number. If the phone number will be stored as a 10-digit number with no formatting (such as 3175553456), then a numeric field is appropriate. However, if you want to store the phone number so that it contains formatting to separate the area code, such as (317) 555-3456, then the data type should be a text field because the parentheses and dash are text characters that can't be stored in a numeric field.

Numbers that will be used in a calculation must *always* be defined as numeric data types. Think carefully about how the data in fields will be used before assigning a data type. For instance, the number of credits for a course is often used to compute a student's bill. If you stored this value as text, you couldn't multiply it by the cost per credit hour to generate a bill. However, text fields store data more efficiently than numeric fields; therefore, if size is a consideration, a text field might be more appropriate.

Object-oriented databases are based on complex models for manipulating data. These models are much more complex than relational database models. Because businesses today need to store a greater variety of data, object-oriented databases are becoming more popular. Many relational database systems have been expanded to include object-oriented components. For a business to use its data in an object-oriented database, it needs to undergo a costly conversion process. However, once this initial cost is overcome, the faster access and reusability of the database objects can provide advantages for large businesses.

Object-oriented databases also need to use a query language to access and manage data. Many object-oriented databases use **object query language (OQL)**, which is similar in many respects to SQL (structured query language), a standard language used to construct queries to extract data from databases.

Multidimensional Databases

What is a multidimensional database?
A multidimensional **database** stores data in more than two dimensions. This distinguishes it from a relational database, which stores data in two-dimensional tables. Multidimensional databases organize data in a cube format. Each data cube has a *measure attribute,* which is the main type of data that the cube is tracking. Other elements of the cube are known as *feature attributes,* which all describe the measure attribute in some meaningful way. For example, sales of automobiles (measure attribute) could be categorized by various dimensions such as region, automobile color, automobile model, time period (such as current month), or salesperson—all feature attributes. In addition, the database could be constructed to define different levels within a particular feature attribute (such as state and town within a region).

What are the advantages of multidimensional databases?
The two main advantages of multidimensional databases are that they can easily be customized to provide information to a variety of users (based on their need), and they can process

ACTIVE HELP-DESK

Understanding Database Management Systems

In this Active Helpdesk call, you'll play the role of a helpdesk staffer, fielding calls about database management systems, what they do, and how people can use them.

data much faster than pure relational databases can. The need for processing speed is especially critical when deploying a large database that will be accessed via the Internet. Therefore, large databases such as eBay that are accessed by many users needing to view data in different ways are usually designed as multidimensional databases. Oracle Corporation has slowly morphed its tried-and-true relational database into a multidimensional database in response to customer demand. This was primarily in response to customers who were using an Oracle database for applications deployed on the Web and needed better ways of storing and accessing image, audio, and video files. With multidimensional databases such as the current Oracle Database 11g, businesses do not have to abandon the proven relational database model, because multidimensional databases are based on proven relational database theory.

Database Management Systems: Basic Operations

Databases are created and managed using a **database management system (DBMS)**. A DBMS is specially designed application software (such as Oracle Database or Microsoft Access) that interacts with the user, other applications, and the database to capture and analyze data. The four main operations of a DBMS are

1. Creating databases and entering data.
2. Viewing (or browsing) and sorting data.

3. Querying (extracting) data.

4. Outputting data.

In the next section, we look at each of these operations in detail.

Creating Databases and Entering Data

How do I create a database with a DBMS? To create a database with a DBMS, you must first define the data to be captured. Therefore, you must create a description of the data. This description is contained in the database's files and is referred to as the **data dictionary** or the **database schema**. The data dictionary defines the name, data type, and length of each field in the database. Describing the data helps to categorize and analyze it and sets parameters for entering valid data into the database (such as a 10-digit number in a phone number field).

How do I know what fields are needed in my database? Careful planning is required to identify each distinct piece of data you need to capture. Each field should describe a unique piece of data and should never combine two separate pieces of data.

For example, for student registration at a college, capturing the student's name, street address, city, state, and zip code is important. But should a student's name be placed in one field or two? Because first and last names are separate pieces of data, you would want to create a separate field for each. For instance, suppose you wish to send a form letter to students addressing them by their first name (such as "Dear Susan"). If Susan's first and last names are in the same field in the database, it will be difficult to extract just her first name for the salutation.

What does a data dictionary look like, and how do I create one? In Microsoft Access, the data dictionary is called the Field Properties box. Figure 11.7a shows the Field Properties box for a database table in Access. The first step in creating an entry in the data dictionary is to create a field name. Field names should be unique within a table. In the table in Figure 11.7a, the field name State is used to store the abbreviation for the state where the student lives.

Second, you must define a data type for each field. For the State field, you use a text data type because names are expressed using characters. Third, you should set a maximum field size (in this case, two characters) for the field. Data in the field can be shorter than the maximum but can never exceed it. Sometimes the field name may not be meaningful to the user of the database even though it makes sense to the designer. The Caption value allows you to display a name of your choice on forms and reports.

Finally, you can set a **default value** for a field. A default value is the value the database uses for the field unless the user enters another value. Though not appropriate for first names, because they vary widely, default values are useful for field data that is frequently the same. For example, setting a default value for a State field saves

Figure 11.7

(a) The Field Properties box, shown for the Student Information table in an Access database, represents the database's data dictionary. (b) The Student Information table, ready for data input, results from setting up the data dictionary in Figure 11.7a.

users from having to enter it for each student if most students live in one state.

You need to repeat these steps for each field in the table. When completed, the resulting Student Information table, shown in Figure 11.7b, is ready for data entry.

The attributes (such as data type and field size) shown in Figure 11.7a and 11.7b are **metadata**: data that describes other data. Metadata is an integral part of the data dictionary. You need to build the data dictionary for each table you will use in a database before you enter data into the database. This also has the benefit of forcing you to consider up front the data you need to capture and the metadata that describes it.

What happens if I forget to define a field in the data dictionary or if I want to add another one later? Databases are extremely flexible. You can add additional fields as needed. However, don't forget that you need to populate (enter data into) these new fields with the appropriate data. This could be difficult if you suddenly need to add a Birth Date field to a database that already contains records for 10,000 individuals. If you plan to use the Birth Date field to analyze the data, you need to have a plan for accumulating birth dates to ensure the completeness of the data.

Input Forms

How do I get data into the database? After you create a data dictionary for each table (or file) in the database and establish the fields you want the database to contain, you can begin

creating individual records in the database. There's an old-fashioned way to get data into these records: you can key it directly into the database. However, today, a great deal of data already exists in some type of electronic format (such as word processing documents and spreadsheets). Fortunately, most databases can import data electronically from other application files, which can save an enormous amount of keying.

When importing data, most databases usually apply filters to the data to determine that it is in the correct format as defined by the data dictionary. Nonconforming data is flagged (either on-screen or in a report) so that you can modify the data to fit the database's format.

> **How can I ensure that only valid data is entered into the database?**

How can I make manual entry into a database more convenient? For small databases, or databases in which no electronic information is to be imported, you can create an input form to speed data entry. An **input form** provides a view of the data fields to be filled, with appropriate labels to assist database users in populating the database. Figure 11.8 shows an example of an input form for the Student Information table shown in Figure 11.7.

Figure 11.8

This input form is used for entering data into the Student Information table. Each field has a label that indicates the data to be placed in the field. The data is represented by blank boxes. Notes can be added to the form to guide the users.

Student Info Input Form

SID#: — Blank box for data entry
First Name:
Last Name:
Home Address:
City:
State: — Use 2 Letter State Code
Zip Code: — Use 9 digit US Zip Code
Telephone: — Use 10 digit US Phone Number Only

Note: All fields MUST be filled in. — Notes for users

Record: 7 of 7 — No Filter — Search

Student_Information	
Field Name	**Data Type**
SID #	Number
Social Security Number	Number
FirstName	Text
LastName	Text
Address	Text
City	Text
State	Text
Zip Code	Text
HomePhone	Text
Rate of Pay	Number
Birthdate	Date/Time

Field Properties

General | Lookup

Field Size	Long Integer
Format	
Decimal Places	2
Input Mask	
Caption	
Default Value	0
Validation Rule	>7.25 And <20
Validation Text	
Required	No
Indexed	No

Validation rule restricts entries

Figure 11.9

Here a validation rule is set to restrict rates of pay to a certain range.

Data Validation

How can I ensure that only valid data is entered into the database?
One feature of most DBMSs is the capability to perform data validation. **Validation** is the process of ensuring that data entered into the database is correct (or at least reasonable) and complete. When you registered for college, for example, the admissions clerk most likely asked you for your phone number. A phone number in the United States usually comprises 10 digits formatted in the following fashion: (610) 555-1234. A **validation rule** is set up in the student database to alert the user if a clearly wrong entry, such as "Joh-nSm-ythe" or "2345," is entered in the phone number field instead of a valid 10-digit phone number.

Validation rules are generally defined as part of the data dictionary. Violations of validation rules usually result in an error message being displayed on the screen so that the error can be addressed. Common types of validation checks include range,

completeness, consistency, and alphabetic and numeric checks.

How does a range check work?
A **range check** ensures that the data entered into the database falls within a certain range of numbers. For instance, rates of pay for student jobs usually fall within a certain range. Therefore, in a student pay database, you could set a **field constraint** (a property that must be satisfied for an entry to be accepted into the field) to restrict pay rates to a range you define.

Figure 11.9 shows how you set up a range check in a data dictionary (in the Field Properties box) for an Access database. A validation rule restricts the entries for the Rate of Pay field to amounts between $7.25 (minimum wage) and $20.00 (the maximum rate of pay for students at the college). If users tried to enter a rate of pay less than $7.25 or greater than $20.00, they would be notified of an invalid range error and the input would not be accepted.

What does a completeness check accomplish?
If you have ever bought anything online, you have probably encountered error messages generated by completeness checks. In database systems, fields can be defined as "required," meaning data must be entered into them. A **completeness check**, such as the one shown in Figure 11.10, ensures that all fields defined as "required" have data entered into them. When a user submits this form, the database performs a completeness check and, in this case, notices that the required "Last name" field was left blank. An error message then displays to alert the user of the omission.

What is the function of a consistency check?
A **consistency check** compares the values of data in two or more fields to see if these values are reasonable. For example, your birth date and the date you enrolled in school are often in a college's database. It is not possible for you to have enrolled in college before you were born. Further, most college students are at least 16 years old. Therefore, a consistency check on these fields might ensure that your birth date is at least 16 or more years before the date when you enrolled in college.

How are alphabetic and numeric checks used?
You may want to restrict fields to only alphabetic or numerical data (such as for names and student ID

YAHOO! MAIL

⚠ **Please correct the entries highlighted in yellow. We either had trouble understanding those fields, or need more information.**

• Please specify a **Last Name**. ← Error message

Required fields

Fields marked with an asterisk * are required.

Create Your Yahoo! ID

* First name:	Sui Lin|
* Last name:	
* Gender:	Female
* Yahoo! ID:	suilin3355@yahoo.com
* Password:	[Not Shown for Your Protection]

Figure 11.10

A database completeness check, like this one shown for Yahoo! Mail, ensures that all fields defined as "required" have data in them.

numbers). An **alphabetic check** confirms that only textual characters (such as "Gwen") are entered in a field. A **numeric check** confirms that only numbers are entered in the field. With these checks in place, "St3v3" would not be accepted as a first name or a zip code. Figure 11.11 shows how you can set such checks and customize error messages in Access.

The field properties table for the State field in Access is shown in Figure 11.11. The expression "Like??" tells Access to restrict entries for the State field to two alphabetic characters. Selecting "Yes" for the required attribute means that Access will not allow the field to be left blank. Error messages that display when validation checks fail can be customized by the user.

Viewing and Sorting Data

How can I view the data in a database? Displaying the tables on-screen and **browsing** through the data (viewing records) is an option with most databases. In many instances you'll only want to view the data, not display the entire table. For example, if you want to register for an additional course for the current semester, the admissions clerk would browse the roster database to determine

which courses you are already taking. However, browsing through a large database is time consuming unless the records are in an order that makes your task easy.

How can I reorder records in a database? You can easily **sort** a database into the order that you need. Sorting a database involves organizing it in a new

Figure 11.11

Although several types of validation rules have been activated here, you probably wouldn't find it necessary to use all of them at once.

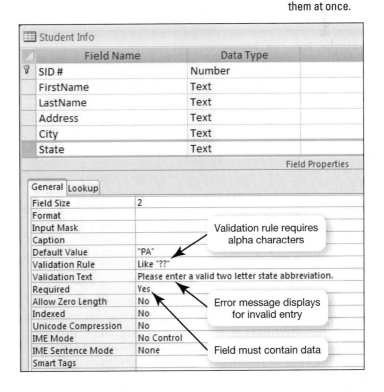

Student Info	
Field Name	**Data Type**
SID #	Number
FirstName	Text
LastName	Text
Address	Text
City	Text
State	Text

Field Properties

General | Lookup

Field Size	2
Format	
Input Mask	
Caption	
Default Value	"PA"
Validation Rule	Like "??"
Validation Text	Please enter a valid two letter state abbreviation.
Required	Yes
Allow Zero Length	No
Indexed	No
Unicode Compression	No
IME Mode	No Control
IME Sentence Mode	None
Smart Tags	

Validation rule requires alpha characters

Error message displays for invalid entry

Field must contain data

To extract records from a database, you use a query language. Almost all relational and object relational databases today use **structured query language**, or **SQL**. Oracle, Microsoft SQL Server, Microsoft Access, IBM DB2, and Sybase are examples of popular databases that use SQL.

When relational databases were first developed in the early 1970s, each DBMS software product contained its own query language. This meant that database administrators had to learn a new language whenever they worked with a different DBMS. The early query languages were mathematically based and often difficult to master. E. F. Codd, who has been called the father of relational databases, proposed a standardized query language when he worked at IBM in the mid-1970s.

The original language was called SEQUEL, short for *structured English query language*. The idea was to make queries easy by using English language–like sentence structure. Database software designers enthusiastically accepted the concept, and a modified version of the original SEQUEL language, named SQL, was developed. Oracle first introduced SQL in a commercial database product in 1979. It has been the unofficial standard language for relational databases since then.

SQL uses relational algebra to extract data from databases. **Relational algebra** is the use of English-like expressions that have variables and operations, much like algebraic equations. Variables include table names, field names, or selection criteria for the data you wish to display. Operations include directions such as *select* (which enables you to pick variable names), *from* (which tells the database which table to use), and *where* (which enables you to specify selection criteria). The two most common queries used to extract data using relational algebra are select queries and join queries.

A **select query** displays a subset of data from a table (or tables) based on the criteria you specify. A typical select query has the following format:

SELECT (Field Name 1, Field Name 2, . . .)
FROM (Table Name)
WHERE (Selection Criteria)

Figure 11.12

When the query on the left is applied to the (a) Student Information table, it restricts the output to (b) only a phone list. The query on the right, which uses a WHERE statement, further restricts the phone list to (c) only students from Massachusetts.

The first line of the query contains variables for the field names you want to display. The FROM statement enables you to specify the table name from which the data will be retrieved. The last line (the WHERE statement) is used only when you wish to specify which records need to be displayed (such as all students with GPAs greater than 3.2). If you wish to display all the rows (records) in the table, then you do not use the WHERE statement. (See Figure 11.12.)

Suppose you want to create a telephone list that includes all students from the Student Information table in Figure 11.13a. The SQL query you would send to the database would look like this:

SELECT (First Name, Last Name, Telephone)

FROM (Student Information Table)

Figure 11.13b shows the output from this query.

What if you want a phone list that only shows students from Massachusetts? In that case, you would add a WHERE statement to the query as follows:

SELECT (First Name, Last Name, Telephone)

FROM (Student Information Table)

WHERE (State = MA)

This query restricts the output to students who live in Massachusetts, as shown in Figure 11.13c. Notice that the State field in the Student Information table can be used by the query (in this case, as a limiting criterion), but the contents of the State field are not required to be displayed in the query results. This explains why the output shown in Figure 11.13c doesn't show the State field.

When you want to extract data that is in two or more tables, you use a **join query**. The query actually links (or joins) the two tables using the common field in both tables and extracts the relevant data from each. The format for a simple join query for two tables is as follows:

SELECT (Field Name 1, Field Name 2)

FROM (Table 1 Name, Table 2 Name)

WHERE (Table 1 Name.Common Field Name = Table 2 Name.Common
   Field Name)

AND (Selection Criteria)

Notice how similar this is to a select query, although the FROM statement must now contain two table names. In a join query, the WHERE statement is split into two parts. In the first part (right after WHERE), the relation between the two tables is defined by identifying the common fields between the tables. The second part of the statement (after AND) is where the selection criteria are defined.

The AND means that both parts of the statement must be true for the query to produce results (i.e., the two related fields must exist and the selection criteria must be valid). Figure 11.13 illustrates using a join query for the Student Information and Roster Master tables to produce a class roster for students.

Figure 11.13

This join query will display a student roster for each student in the Student Information table. Notice that the WHERE statement creates the join by defining the common fields (in this case SID # and Student ID#) in each table.

Figure 11.14

(a) Shown is an unsorted table. Notice that the Last Name column is selected (highlighted) for sorting. Selecting the highlighted sorting option (Ascending) produces the sorted output (b) with the records sorted in ascending alphabetical order by last name.

a

Click to sort highlighted column

Student Info - Microsoft Acc...   Table Tools

Home   Create   External Data   Database Tools   Datasheet

SID #	First Name	Last Name	Address	City	State
123456789	Jennifer	Evans	123 Oak Street	Gotham City	PA
234567891	Li	Chan	123 Main Street	Tuba City	NV
345678912	William	Wallace	654 Front Street	Locust Glen	MI
456789123	Diane	Coyle	745 Station Drive	Springfield	MA
543219876	Austin	Knowland	345 Reston Court	Red Ridge	SD
567891234	Donald	Lopez	3421 Lincoln Court	Spalding	ND
654321987	Susan	Hudson	237 Explorer Circle	Booth Bay	ME
765432198	Michelle	Swanson	1234 North Street	Red Ridge	SD
876543219	Fortuna	Liewiski	141 Central Blvd	Wyandott	ND
987654321	Kevin	Po	1632 Delsey Drive	Blue Ridge	ND

b

SID #	First Name	Last Name	Address
234567891	Li	Chan	123 Main Street
456789123	Diane	Coyle	745 Station Drive
123456789	Jennifer	Evans	123 Oak Street
654321987	Susan	Hudson	237 Explorer Circle
543219876	Austin	Knowland	345 Reston Court
876543219	Fortuna	Liewiski	141 Central Blvd
567891234	Donald	Lopez	3421 Lincoln Court
987654321	Kevin	Po	1632 Delsey Drive
765432198	Michelle	Swanson	1234 North Street
345678912	William	Wallace	654 Front Street

fashion. Figure 11.14a shows an Access data table in which the records were input in no particular order. By highlighting a column (in this case Last Name) and then clicking the Sort Ascending button, the database displays the records in alphabetical order by last name, as shown in Figure 11.14b.

What if I want to find a particular piece of data in a database? Browsing records works for small databases, but if the amount of data you are managing is small, then you probably will just maintain it in a list anyway. To find data in a large database quickly and efficiently, you need to be able to request only the data you are seeking. Therefore, database management systems let you query the data to enable you to find what you're looking for.

SOUND BYTE

Creating an Access 2007 Database

In this Sound Byte, you'll learn how to create an Access database to catalog a collection of CDs and DVDs. The Sound Byte will take you through a systematic process that will result in a fully functional small database.

Extracting or Querying Data

What is a query? A **query** is a question or inquiry. A **database query** is a question you ask the database so that it provides you with the records you wish to view. When you query a database, you instruct it to search for a particular piece of data, such as a student's grade point average (GPA). Queries also enable you to have the database select and display records that match certain criteria, such as all of the students who have GPAs of 3.2 or higher.

Is querying a database as simple as just asking the proper question? All modern DBMSs contain a **query language** that the software uses to retrieve and display records. A query language consists of its own vocabulary and sentence structure, which you use to frame the requests. Query languages are similar to full-blown programming languages but are usually much easier to learn. The most popular query language today is structured query language, or SQL (pronounced "sequel").

Do I have to learn a query language to develop queries for my database? Modern database systems provide wizards to guide you through the process of creating queries. Figure 11.15 shows an example of an Access wizard being used to create a query. Highlighting an available field and then clicking the arrow button adds the field to the selected fields list. Selected fields display in the query. Highlighting a field on the selected fields list and clicking the back arrow removes the field from the list. The wizard speeds up the process of creating queries, and also removes the need to learn a query language.

The Simple Query Wizard can be found on the **Create** tab, in the **Other** group. Click Query Wizard and select Simple Query Wizard. When you use the Simple Query Wizard, you're actually using SQL commands without realizing it. The Simple Query Wizard takes the criteria you specify and creates the appropriate SQL commands behind the scenes.

However, you may want to create your own SQL queries in Access, modify existing queries at the SQL language level, or view the SQL code that the wizard created. To do so, open a query and select SQL View from the View drop-down box on the Ribbon. This displays the SQL code that makes up the query. Figure 11.16 shows the SQL code that the query in Figure 11.15 created.

Figure 11.15

(a) The Simple Query Wizard displays all fields available in your table so that you can select the ones you need. (b) This information is displayed when you run the query defined in (a).

In the next section, we look at the operation of relational databases and explore how relationships are established among tables in these databases.

```
Student Info Query1                                    _  □  X
SELECT [Student Info].FirstName, [Student Info].LastName, [Student Info].Address, [Student Info].City,
[Student Info].State, [Student Info].[Zip Code]
FROM [Student Info];
```

Figure 11.16

The SQL View window shows the SQL code that the wizard created for the query in Figure 11.15. Although it is a relatively simple SELECT statement, it is much easier to create with the wizard.

Outputting Data

How do I get data out of a database?
The most common form of output for any database is a printable electronic report. Businesses routinely summarize the data within their databases and compile summary data reports. For instance, at the end of each semester your school prints a grade report for you that shows the classes you took and the grades you received.

Can I transfer data from a database to another software application?
Database systems also can be used to **export** data to other applications. Exporting data involves putting it into an electronic file in a format that another application can understand. For example, the query shown in the wizard in Figure 11.15 may be used to generate a list of recipients for a form letter. In that case, the query output would be directed to a file that could be easily imported into Microsoft Word so that the data could be used in a mail merge process to generate letters.

Relational Database Operations

As explained earlier, relational databases operate by organizing data into various tables based on logical groupings. For example, all student address and contact information (phone numbers, e-mail addresses, and so on) would be grouped into one table. Because not all of the data in a relational database is stored in the same table, a methodology must be implemented to link data between tables.

In relational databases, a link between tables that defines how the data is related is referred to as a **relationship**. To establish a relationship between two tables, both tables must have a common field (or column). Common fields contain the same data (such as student ID numbers), as shown in Figure 11.17. The fields do not have to have the same field name as long as they contain the same data.

Figure 11.17

(a) The Student Information table and (b) the Roster Master table share the common field of student ID number. This allows a relationship to be established between the two tables.

a

SID #	First Name	Last Name	Home Address	City	State	Zip Code	Telephone
⊞ 234567891	Li	Chan	123 Main Street	Tuba City	NV	49874-7643	(736) 555-8421
⊞ 456789123	Diane	Coyle	745 Station Drive	Springfield	MA	18755-5555	(402) 555-3982
⊞ 123456789	Jennifer	Evans	123 Oak Street	Gotham City	PA	19999-8888	(215) 555-1345
⊞ 567891234	Donald	Lopez	3421 Lincoln Court	Spalding	ND	87564-2546	(612) 555-9312
⊞ 678912345	Harold	Schwartz	756 Fulton Blvd.	West Lake	MA	18745-4433	(402) 555-3294
⊞ 345678912	William	Wallace	654 Front Street	Locust Glen	MI	67744-3584	(413) 555-4021

Common field in each table

b

Registration Code	Class Code	Student ID#
18	CIS 111	123456789
19	ENG 101	123456789
20	HIS 103	123456789
21	CHE 140	123456789
22	PSY 110	123456789
15	LAN 330	234567891
16	REL 216	234567891
17	ENG 102	234567891
28	HIS 204	345678912
29	PEH 125	345678912
30	SOC 220	345678912
23	HIS 401	567891234
24	SOC 310	567891234
25	PSY 110	567891234
26	ENG 102	678912345
27	PSY 110	678912345

In police dramas on TV, detectives often use fingerprints to catch criminals. However, until recently, the process of identifying suspects by their fingerprints was a time-consuming and ineffective way of catching criminals who moved from state to state.

The use of fingerprints as a method of identification dates back to the beginning of the 20th century, when the "Henry" method of fingerprint classification was developed in England. Fingerprints are unique to each individual and do not change during the course of a lifetime. Therefore, they are ideally suited to identify suspects in criminal investigations.

Originally, investigators collected fingerprints by placing ink on a person's fingertips and rolling the person's fingers on a piece of card stock. Fingerprint identification experts then manually compared the new suspect's fingerprints with existing paper files of fingerprints. This was a time-consuming process, and the pool of potential suspects was limited to the fingerprints that the particular law enforcement agency had collected.

Lack of a large pool of fingerprints was less of a problem in the United States during the early 1900s because the population was not particularly mobile. However, in the 1930s, criminals became more mobile. The Federal Bureau of Investigation (FBI) thus undertook the maintenance of a large, centralized, manual database of fingerprint cards and photos of these cards and provided fingerprint identification services to local law enforcement agencies. However, identification was still performed manually, and many local law enforcement agencies had neither the personnel nor the money to submit their fingerprint records to the FBI. Although it still identified many criminals, the system was inefficient.

During the 1960s and 1970s, the FBI began researching methods for using computers to perform fingerprint identification. These early efforts led to the Integrated Automated Fingerprint Identification System (IAFIS). Thanks to the IAFIS, instead of using ink and card stock, new fingerprints are now digitally scanned directly into a computer. In addition, existing fingerprint cards can be scanned and captured in the database. The IAFIS made fingerprint searching and identification much quicker through the use of its computer searching algorithms.

In the late 1990s, the FBI released a software package called Remote Fingerprint Editing Software (RFES). The RFES package (shown in Figure 11.18) enables local law enforcement agencies to capture fingerprints electronically and perform searches in the IAFIS database.

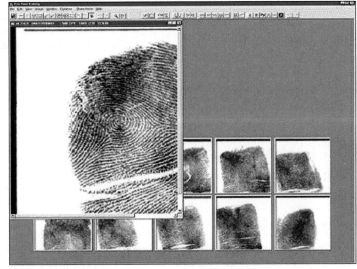

Figure 11.18

Law enforcement agencies can use the FBI's Remote Fingerprint Editing Software to search the IAFIS database, capture fingerprints from new suspects, and scan in information from existing fingerprint cards.

Captured images can be enlarged, printed, or transmitted to other law enforcement agencies as needed. Law enforcement agencies use electronic readers to scan fingerprints lifted from crime scenes into the computer. The software then searches the IAFIS database for prints that match.

As more law enforcement agencies scan old fingerprint cards and post them to the IAFIS, the odds of finding a fingerprint match increase. In fact, criminal investigators are submitting fingerprints from old, unsolved cases to the IAFIS database in attempts to find a match to fingerprints collected in cases where no suspects were found by conventional methods. In Pennsylvania, this approach resulted in the arrest and conviction of a suspect for a murder that had been unsolved for 14 years!

Even more cutting edge on the technology front is the identification of suspects purely by the DNA evidence (such as hair or skin cells from people or their pets) left behind at a crime scene. DNA is a blueprint and instruction manual for how everything in your body is assembled and works. Although much of human DNA does not vary from person to person, 3 million base pairs of DNA do vary. (That's about 0.10 percent of your entire DNA structure.) This is enough to allow identification of a specific individual from a DNA sample.

The FBI maintains a database called the Combined DNA Index System (CODIS) that accumulates DNA profiles based on DNA samples collected from felons by federal, state, and local law enforcement agencies. CODIS enables federal, state, and local crime labs to exchange and compare DNA profiles electronically, which assists in the identification of suspects when no other leads are available.

Aside from convicting offenders, DNA evidence has been used to prove the innocence of people who have been wrongly convicted, usually resulting in their release from prison. A prime example is William Gregory, a Kentucky resident, who was convicted of rape in 1993. He was subsequently released from prison after DNA tests showed that hairs found at the rape scene were not his. Had DNA evidence been available at the time of his arrest, he might never have been incarcerated.

Developing an efficient, nationwide system of fingerprint and DNA identification would not be possible without the use of computerized databases. Databases enable the information to be stored, sorted, and retrieved quickly. Next time you're watching a police drama on television, don't forget that databases are working behind the scenes to identify the criminals. For more information on DNA identification, see **science.howstuffworks.com/genetic-science/dna-evidence.htm**.

Relationships in databases can take three forms: one-to-one, one-to-many, or many-to-many. A **one-to-one relationship** indicates that for each record in a table there is only one corresponding record in a related table. For example, a parking space can be occupied by only one car at a time, so a table that links assigned parking spaces to a table of faculty members would have a one-to-one relationship.

One-to-many relationships occur most frequently in relational databases. A **one-to-many relationship** is characterized by a record in one table (such as the student information table in Figure 11.17). There is only one instance of a student ID in the Student Information table, but there can be many instances of the same student ID in the Master Roster table. Students can register for many classes, but each registration record can relate to only one student.

A **many-to-many relationship** is characterized by records in one table being related to multiple records in a second table and vice versa. For instance, a table of students could be related to a table of student employers. The employers could employ many students, and students could work for more than one employer.

Normalization of Data

How do I decide which tables I need and what data to put in them? You create database tables (or files) for two reasons: to hold unique data about a person or thing and to describe unique events or transactions. In databases, the goal is to reduce data redundancy by recording data only once. This process is called **normalization** of the data. Yet the tables must still work well enough together to enable you to retrieve the data when you need it. Tables should be grouped using logical data that can be identified uniquely.

Let's look at an example. In Figure 11.19, the Class Registration—Fall table contains a great deal of data about individual students and their course registration. However, each table in a relational database should contain a related group of data on a single topic. There are two distinct topics in this list: student contact information and student registration information. Therefore, this list needs to be divided into two tables so that the distinct data (contact data and registration data) can be categorized appropriately. Data about each student is duplicated in this table. Normalizing the data eliminates this duplication.

The Student Information table in Figure 11.20 organizes all of the student contact information found in Figure 11.19, into a separate table. Notice that the information for each student needs to be shown only once, instead of multiple times (as in the list in the figure). The unique primary key for this table is the student's ID number. Student information might be

SID #	Last Name	First Name	Home Address	City	State	Zip Code	Class Code	Class Name	# of Credits
234567891	Chan	Li	123 Main Street	Tuba City	NV	49874-7643	LAN 330	Japanese 1	3
234567891	Chan	Li	123 Main Street	Tuba City	NV	49874-7643	REL 216	Early Buddhism	3
234567891	Chan	Li	123 Main Street	Tuba City	NV	49874-7643	ENG 102	English Comp 2	3
456789123	Coyle	Diane	745 Station Drive	Springfield	MA	18755-5555			
123456789	Evans	Jennifer	123 Oak Street	Gotham City	PA	19999-8888	CIS 111	Programming	3
123456789	Evans	Jennifer	123 Oak Street	Gotham City	PA	19999-8888	ENG 101	English Comp 1	3
123456789	Evans	Jennifer	123 Oak Street	Gotham City	PA	19999-8888	HIS 103	Western Civ	3
123456789	Evans	Jennifer	123 Oak Street	Gotham City	PA	19999-8888	CHE 140	Chemistry	4
123456789	Evans	Jennifer	124 Oak Street	Gotham City	PA	19999-8888	PSY 110	Intro to Psychology	3
567891234	Lopez	Donald	3421 Lincoln Court	Spalding	ND	87564-2546	HIS 401	16th Century Europe	3
567891234	Lopez	Donald	3421 Lincoln Court	Spalding	ND	87564-2546	SOC 310	Interpersonal Relationships	3
567891234	Lopez	Donald	3421 Lincoln Court	Spalding	ND	87564-2546	PSY 110	Intro to Psych	3
678912345	Schwartz	Harold	756 Fulton Blvd.	West Lake	MA	18745-4433	ENG 102	English Comp 2	3

Class Registration - Fall

Figure 11.19

The column headings in blue are related to student contact data, whereas the column headings in red relate to enrollment information. To construct an efficient database, these topics should be contained in separate tables.

SID# ▾	First Name ▾	Last Name ◂	Home Address ▾	City ▾	State ▾	Zip Code ▾	Telephone ▾
234567891	Li	Chan	123 Main Street	Tuba City	NV	49874-7643	(736) 555-8421
456789123	Diane	Coyle	745 Station Drive	Springfield	MA	18755-5555	(402) 555-3982
123456789	Jennifer	Evans	123 Oak Street	Gotham City	PA	19999-8888	(215) 555-1345
567891234	Donald	Lopez	3421 Lincoln Court	Spalding	ND	87564-2546	(612) 555-9312
678912345	Harold	Schwartz	756 Fulton Blvd.	West Lake	MA	18745-4433	(402) 555-3294
345678912	William	Wallace	654 Front Street	Locust Glen	MI	67744-3584	(413) 555-4021

Figure 11.20

Student contact data is grouped in the Student Information table and needs to be entered only once for each student. The primary key for each record is a unique student ID number.

needed in a variety of instances and by a variety of departments, but it needs to reside only in this one database table, which many departments of the school can share.

Next, we could put the registration data found in Figure 11.19 for each student in a separate table, as shown in Figure 11.21. There is no need to repeat student name and address data in this table. Instead, each student can be identified by his or her student ID number. However, there are problems with this table. Each class name and class code has to be repeated for every student taking the course, Also, there is no unique field that can be used as a primary key for this table. Student ID # cannot be used because it will be entered on multiple records when a student enrolls in more than one course. This presents another opportunity to normalize the data further.

If you are unsure which state your property is located in, try the National

Association of Unclaimed Property Administrators (**unclaimed.org**). This site provides the capability to search for money in all 50 states.

What can be done to fix the table in Figure 11.21? In Figure 11.21, we have identified more data that should be grouped logically into another separate table: class code and class name. Therefore, we should create another table for just this information. This enables us to avoid repeating class names and codes.

SOUND BYTE — Improving an Access 2007 Database

In this Sound Byte, you'll learn how to create input forms, queries, and reports to simplify maintenance of your CD and DVD database. You'll follow along step by step, using Microsoft Access wizards to create and modify queries to suit your needs.

Student ID # ◂	Class Code ▾	Class Name ▾	# Of Credits ▾
123456789	PSY 110	Intro to Psychology	3
123456789	CIS 111	Programming	3
123456789	ENG 101	English Comp 1	3
123456789	HIS 103	Western Civ	3
123456789	CHE 140	Chemistry	4
234567891	LAN 330	Japanese 1	3
234567891	ENG 102	English Comp 2	3
234567891	REL 216	Early Buddhism	3
345678912	SOC 220	The Art of Negotiation	2
345678912	HIS 204	Scottish History	3
345678912	PEH 125	Fencing 1	3
567891234	PSY 110	Intro to Psychology	3

Student ID# not unique

Duplicate data

Figure 11.21

Although it contains related data (registration information), this table still contains a great deal of duplicate data and no usable primary key.

Computers in Society: Need Cash? Use Databases to Find Your Property

Did you ever lose a check before cashing it and forget to get it replaced (or figure you couldn't)? Did you ever relocate quickly and forget to get your security deposit back on your apartment? Did your grandmother open a bank account in your name and forget to tell you about it? These are all examples of unclaimed property. Thanks to the Internet and databases, it has never been easier to look for this "found money."

In most states, unclaimed property (bank accounts, security deposits on apartments, uncashed checks, and so on) is required by law to be turned over to the state treasury for safekeeping after a certain period of time. The state treasury is required to hold the property for a period of time (sometimes forever) so that the rightful owner can make a claim.

Until a few years ago, searching for your unclaimed property meant sifting through mountains of paper records at the state capitol.

Today, many states have unclaimed property databases on the Web. Go to the official state Web site for the state where you think you may have unclaimed property and search on the terms "unclaimed property" or "abandoned property." Pennsylvania's site (**patreasury.org/unclaimed/search.html**) features a simple search box where you can enter your name to search for your pot of gold (see Figure 11.22a). Scan the resulting search list (see Figure 11.22b), and if you find an item that might be yours, follow the procedures set by that state to make a claim and prove ownership.

Figure 11.22

(a) Using the state of Pennsylvania's unclaimed property Web site starts with completing a simple search form.
(b) The search results might be just the place to find your missing funds.

Figure 11.23 shows the Course master table. Note that the class code is unique for every course and acts as a primary key in this table.

To solve the other problems with the table in Figure 11.21, we need a way to identify uniquely each student registered for a specific course. This can be solved by creating a course registration number that will be unique and assigned by the database as

records are entered. Figure 11.24 shows the resulting Roster master table. Only three fields are needed: the registration code number (the unique primary key), the class code, and the student's ID number. This approach greatly minimizes duplicate data.

How do I get the data in the tables to work together now that it is split up? The entire premise behind relational

Class Code	Class Name	Credits
⊞ CHE 140	Chemistry	4
⊞ CIS 111	Programming	3
⊞ ENG 101	English Comp 1	3
⊞ ENG 102	English Comp 2	3
⊞ HIS 103	Western Civ	3
⊞ HIS 204	Scottish History	3
⊞ HIS 401	16th Century Europe	3
⊞ LAN 330	Japanese 1	3
⊞ PEH 125	Fencing 1	3
⊞ PSY 110	Intro to Psychology	3
⊞ REL 216	Early Buddhism	3
⊞ SOC 220	The Art of Negotiation	2
⊞ SOC 310	Interpersonal Relationships	3

Figure 11.23

Related information about courses (class code, class name, and the credits for the class) is grouped logically in one table. The unique class code is the primary key.

databases is that relationships are established among the tables to allow the data to be shared. As noted earlier, to establish a relationship between two tables, the tables must have a common field (column). This usually involves the primary keys of a table.

For instance, to track registrations by student in the Roster master table in Figure 11.24, the student ID number is the logical piece of data to use. The student ID number is the primary key in the Student Information table in Figure 11.20; however, in the Roster master table, the student ID number is called a **foreign key**—the primary key of another table that is included for purposes of establishing relationships with that other table. Figure 11.25 shows the relationships that exist among the Course Master, Roster Master, and Student Information tables. Join lines indicate established relationships between tables. Tables must contain fields with common data; this establishes relationships between them. Notice that foreign keys in related tables do not have to have the same field names as the primary keys in the other table; they merely have to contain the same type of data. Relationships among tables can be established whenever you need them.

Because relationships are vital to the operation of the database, it is important to ensure that there are no inconsistencies in the data entered in the common fields of two tables. Each foreign key (Student ID# in the Roster master table in Figure 11.24)

entered into a table must be a valid primary key from the related table (SID# from the Student Information table in Figure 11.20).

For instance, if 392135684 is not a valid student ID number for any student listed in the Student Information table, then it should not be entered into the Roster master table. Each entry in the Roster master table must correspond to a student (linked by his or her SID#) in the Student Information table. If this requirement is not applied to foreign keys, then a relationship cannot be established between tables.

How do I ensure that a foreign key field contains a valid primary key from the related table? To apply this restraint, when defining a relationship in a database, you have the option of enforcing referential integrity for that relationship. **Referential integrity** means that for each value in the foreign key of one table, there is a corresponding value in the primary key of the related table.

For instance, if you attempt to enter a record in the Roster Master table with an SID# of 156784522 and referential integrity is being enforced, the database checks to ensure that a record with SID# 156784522 exists in the Student Information table. If the corresponding record does not exist, then an error message displays. Establishing referential integrity between two tables helps prevent inconsistent data from being entered.

Who manages the data in a database? All of the data that is collected in databases needs to be stored and

Registration Code	Class Code	Student ID#
18	CIS 111	123456789
19	ENG 101	123456789
20	HIS 103	123456789
21	CHE 140	123456789
22	PSY 110	123456789
15	LAN 330	234567891
16	REL 216	234567891
17	ENG 102	234567891
28	HIS 204	345678912
29	PEH 125	345678912
30	SOC 220	345678912
23	HIS 401	567891234

Figure 11.24

The Roster master table shows only pertinent data related to a student's registration.

Figure 11.25

The Relationships screen in Microsoft Access visually represents the relationships established between tables.

Figure 11.26 shows a view of an Oracle 10g database control screen, a tool that is used primarily by DBAs when reviewing the performance of a database. Database administrators can monitor table usage to help determine when table sizes need to be increased.

In the next section, we explore the types of systems where databases are typically used today.

Data Storage

At the simplest level, data is stored in a single database on a database server, and you retrieve the data as needed. This works fine for small databases and simple enterprises where all of the data you are interested in is in a single database. Problems can arise, however, when the data you need is in multiple places. Large storage repositories called *data warehouses* and *data marts* help solve this problem.

managed. Database administrators (DBAs) are the IT professionals responsible for designing, constructing, and maintaining databases. They review and manage data on an ongoing basis to ensure data is flowing smoothly in and out of the database.

Data Warehouses

What is a data warehouse? A data **warehouse** is a large-scale electronic repository of data that contains and organizes all the data related to an organization in one place. Individual

Figure 11.26

The Tablespaces section of Enterprise Manager (in Oracle 10g) makes it easy for DBAs to review data about tables in a glance and make adjustments where appropriate.

ORACLE Enterprise Manager 10g
Database Control

Setup   Preferences   Help   Logout
Database

Database: edrsr11p1_orcl.oracle.com > **Tablespaces**   Logged in As SYSTEM

Tablespaces

Search

Name [   ] (Go)

To run an exact match search or to run a case sensitive search, double quote the search criteria. The wildcard (%) symbol can still be used in a double quoted search string.

Results

(Edit) (View) (Delete) Actions [Add Datafile ▾] (Go)

Select	Name	Type	Extent Management	Segment Management	Status	Size (MB)	Used (MB)	Used (%)	
⦿	EXAMPLE	PERMANENT	LOCAL	AUTO	ONLINE	150.000	80.250	▬▬	53.50
◌	SYSAUX	PERMANENT	LOCAL	AUTO	ONLINE	320.000	306.938	▬▬▬	95.92
◌	SYSTEM	PERMANENT	LOCAL	MANUAL	ONLINE	450.000	446.688	▬▬▬	99.26
◌	TEMP	TEMPORARY	LOCAL	MANUAL	ONLINE	21.000	20.000	▬▬▬	95.24
◌	UNDOTBS1	UNDO	LOCAL	MANUAL	ONLINE	65.000	7.750	▬	11.92
◌	USERS	PERMANENT	LOCAL	AUTO	ONLINE	5.000	2.750	▬	55.00

Maximum table size

Indicates whether tables are online

Percentage of maximum table size

Emerging Technologies: Can Your Business Partner Deliver the Goods? Enhanced Databases Can Help You Decide!

You watch a weather forecast on television to gain information about the weather. The weather forecaster tells you that it will be sunny. When you get out of your car to go to class, rain is pouring down. Yes, you gathered relevant information. Too bad that it was inaccurate information!

Data and information stored in databases can be just as unhelpful as an inaccurate weather forecast if the information is incorrect or distorted. Although a poor weather report is probably nothing more to you than an inconvenience, accurate data in business is mission critical. Businesses rely on information in databases every day just to accomplish even routine tasks.

Developed to respond to business needs, Alibaba.com is one of the world's largest online business-to-business databases. Alibaba.com specializes in matching suppliers with buyers for all types of manufactured goods and raw materials. With the global nature of business, databases such as those maintained by Alibaba.com are essential tools that assist businesspeople in managing their global business. Figure 11.27 shows a search for cotton fabric supplies in mainland China. You could also "google" Chinese fabric manufacturers, and would probably find many leads. The information in the leads available online may be factually correct, but how do you determine how reliable these suppliers are?

There is a wealth of information online, provided by various sources, which you can use to evaluate potential suppliers before you use them. However, it can be difficult for an individual to tell if the data has been altered or falsified. Panjiva.com is a Web site that also has a searchable database of suppliers. However, the founders of Panjiva decided to make their database different. They gather data that indicates reliability of suppliers from sources such as government agencies, independent certification companies, nonprofit organizations, and customers.

Using the reliability information, Panjiva then creates ratings for companies (on a scale of 1 to 100) based on specific business performance criteria such as number of shipments to the U.S. market, their environmental record, and their capability to deliver shipments within promised time frames. Subscribers to Panjiva's database (companies such as The Home Depot) can then feel more comfortable about doing business with suppliers that Panjiva has rated for reliability.

Databases with enhanced information are the wave of the future in the business world. So, before you make that next crucial business decision, ask yourself how much you really know about your prospective business partner. If you don't know enough, then find a database that can make you feel more at ease.

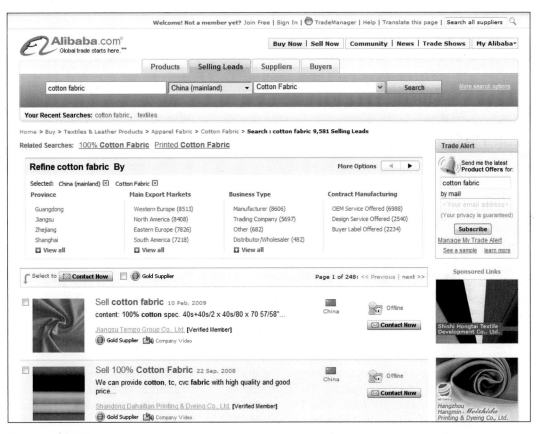

Figure 11.27

Using the database on Alibaba.com, a search for cotton fabric suppliers in China results in 248 pages of links to vendors selling some type of cotton cloth.

databases contain a wealth of information, but each database's information usually pertains to one topic.

For instance, the order database at Amazon.com contains such information about book orders as the buyer's name, address, and payment information, and the book's name. However, the order database does not contain information on inventory levels of books, nor does it list suppliers from which out-of-

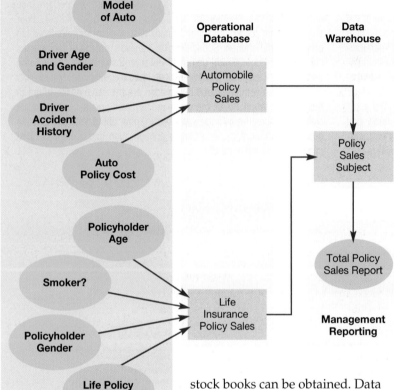

Figure 11.28

Data from individual databases is drawn together under appropriate subject headings in a data warehouse. Managers can then produce comprehensive reports that would be impossible to create from the individual databases.

stock books can be obtained. Data warehouses, therefore, consolidate information from disparate sources to present an enterprise-wide view of business operations.

Is data in a data warehouse organized the same way as in a normal database? Data in the data warehouse is organized by subject. Most databases focus on one specific operational aspect of business operations. For example, insurance companies sell many types of insurance, such as life, automobile, and homeowners' insurance. Different divisions of the insurance company are responsible for each type of insurance and track the policies they sell in different databases (one for automobile insurance policy sales and one for life insurance policy sales, for example), as shown in Figure 11.28.

These databases capture specific information about each type of policy. The Automobile Policy Sales database captures information about driving accident history, car model, and the age and gender of the drivers because this information is pertinent to the pricing of car insurance policies. The Life Insurance Policy Sales database captures information about the age and gender of the policyholder and notes whether he or she smokes, but it does not include details about cars or driving records.

However, data on total policies sold (and the resulting revenue generated) is critical to the management of the insurance company no matter what type of policy is involved. Therefore, an insurance company's data warehouse would have a subject called Policy Sales Subject (see Figure 11.28) that would contain information about *all* policies sold throughout the company. The Policy Sales Subject is a database that contains information from the other databases the company maintains. However, all data in the Policy Sales Subject database is specifically related to policy sales.

From the Policy Sales Subject database, it is easy for managers to produce comprehensive reports such as the Total Policy Sales Report, as shown in Figure 11.28, which can contain information pertaining to all policy sales.

Are data warehouses much larger than conventional databases? Data warehouses, like conventional warehouses, are vast repositories of information. The data contained within them is not operational in nature, but rather archival. Data warehouse data is **time-variant data**, meaning it doesn't all pertain to one period in time.

The warehouse contains current values, such as amounts due from customers, as well as historical data. If you want to examine the buying habits of a certain type of customer, then you need data about both current and prior purchases. Having time-variant data in the warehouse enables you to analyze the past, examine the present in light of historical data, and make projections about the future.

Populating Data Warehouses

How are data warehouses populated with data? Source data for data warehouses can come from three places:

- Internal sources (such as company databases).
- External sources (suppliers, vendors, and so on).
- Customers or visitors to a company's Web site.

Internal data sources are obvious. Sales, billing, inventory, and customer databases all provide a wealth of information. However, internal information is not contained exclusively in databases. Spreadsheets and other ad hoc analysis tools may contain data that needs to be loaded into the warehouse.

External data sources include vendors and suppliers that often provide data regarding product specifications, shipment methods and dates, electronic billing information, and so on. In addition, a virtual wealth of customer (or potential customer) information is available by monitoring the clickstream of the company Web site.

What is a clickstream, and why is it important? Companies can use software on their Web sites to capture information about each click that users make as they navigate through the site. This information is referred to as **clickstream data**. Monitoring the clickstream helps managers assess the effectiveness of a Web site. Using clickstream data capture tools, a company can determine which pages users visit most often, how long users stay on each page, which sites directed users to the company site, and the user demographics. Such data can provide valuable clues to what a company needs to improve on its site to stimulate sales.

Data Staging

Does all source data fit into the warehouse? No two source databases are the same. Although two databases might contain similar information (such as customer names and addresses), the format of the data is most likely different in each database. Therefore, source data must be "staged" before entering the data warehouse. **Data staging** consists of three steps:

1. Extraction of the data from source databases

BITS AND BYTES — Measuring Large Databases

Some databases take up only a few megabytes of space. However, businesses generate extremely large databases. It is widely accepted that the average business doubles the amount of data it accumulates every 12 to 18 months. So, how big are a large corporation's databases? Many large databases are now measured in terabytes. A terabyte is 2^{40} bytes, or more than 1 trillion bytes of data. If the bytes were typed pages of paper, a terabyte of pages would form a stack 51 miles high!

What type of business generates such volumes of data? Wal-Mart tracks information in a data warehouse that holds two years of records—exceeding 600 terabytes in total—relating to all types of inventory and sales transactions in all Wal-Mart stores. Managers use the database to analyze which products are selling well (or poorly) in which regions. This helps them streamline store stock. The database is refreshed every hour so that managers have access to extremely current information.

With data doubling every year, soon we'll be measuring databases in petabytes (that's 1,024 terabytes, or 2^{50} bytes). Now the stack of paper is about 52,000 miles high. Computer scientists are already prepared for even more data: An exabyte is a staggering 1,024 petabytes, or 2^{60} bytes. Large government scientific research projects, such as those conducted at the Stanford Linear Accelerator Center, already have databases containing petabytes of information. So, if databases double in size every year, then it won't be long before there is an exabyte of data stored somewhere near you.

2. Transformation (reformatting) of the data

3. Storage of the data in the warehouse

Many different software programs and procedures may have to be created to extract the data from varied sources and to reformat it for storage in the data warehouse. The nature and complexity of the source data determine the complexity of the data staging process.

Once the data is stored in the data warehouse, how can it be extracted and used? Managers can query the data warehouse in much the same way you would query an Access database. However, because there is more data in the warehouse, much more flexible tools are needed to perform such queries. Online analytical processing (OLAP) software provides standardized tools for viewing and manipulating data in a data warehouse. The key feature of OLAP tools is that they enable flexible views of the data, which the software user can easily change.

Data Marts

Is finding the right data in a huge data warehouse difficult? Looking for the data you need in a data warehouse can be daunting when there are terabytes of data. Therefore, small slices of the data warehouse, each called a **data mart** are often created. Whereas data warehouses have an enterprise-wide depth, the information in data marts pertains to a single department.

For instance, if you work in the sales department, you need accurate sales-related information at your fingertips—and you do not want to wade through customer service data, accounts payable data, and product shipping data to get it. Therefore, a data mart that contains information relevant only to the sales department can be created to make the task of finding this data easier. An overview of the data-warehousing process is illustrated in Figure 11.29. Data staging is vital because different data must be extracted and then reformatted to fit the data structure defined in the data warehouse's DBMS. Data can be extracted using powerful OLAP query tools, or it can be stored in specialized data marts for use by specific employee groups.

Managing Data: Information Systems

Making intelligent decisions about developing new products, creating marketing strategies, and buying raw materials requires timely, accurate information. An **information system** is a software-based solution used to gather and analyze information. A system that delivers up-to-the-minute sales data on books to the computer of Amazon.com's president is one example of an information system. Databases, data warehouses, and data marts are integral parts of information systems because they store the information that makes information systems functional.

All information systems perform similar functions, including acquiring data, processing that data into information, storing the data, and providing the user with a number of output options with which to make the information meaningful and useful (see Figure 11.30). Most information systems fall into one of five

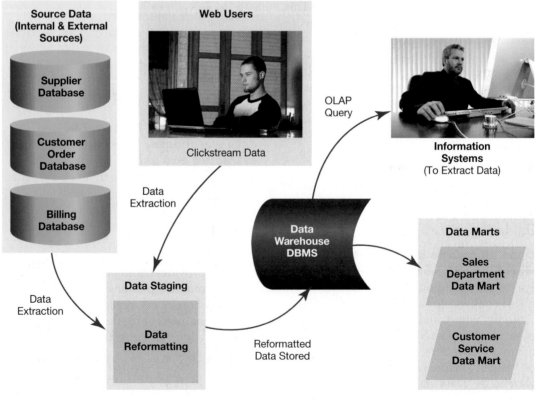

Figure 11.29

An overview of the data warehouse process.

categories: (1) office support systems, (2) transaction processing systems, (3) management information systems, (4) decision support systems, and (5) enterprise resource planning (ERP) systems. Each type of system almost always involves the use of one or more databases.

Office Support Systems

What does an office support system accomplish? An **office support system (OSS)** is designed to improve communications and assist employees in accomplishing their daily tasks. Microsoft Office is an example of an OSS because it assists employees with routine tasks such as maintaining an employee phone list in Excel, designing a sales presentation in PowerPoint, and writing customer letters using Word.

Modern OSSs include software tools with which you are probably familiar, including e-mail, word processing, spreadsheet, database, and presentation programs. Office support systems have their roots in manual, paper-based systems that were developed before computers. After all, maintaining a company phone listing was necessary long before computers were invented. A paper listing of employee phone extensions typed by an administrative assistant is an example of an early OSS. A modern OSS might publish this directory on the company's intranet (its internal network).

Transaction Processing Systems

What is a transaction processing system? A **transaction processing system (TPS)** keeps track of everyday business activities. For example, at your college, transactions that occur frequently include registering students for classes, accepting tuition payments, mailing course listings, and printing course catalogs. Your college has TPSs in place to track these types of activities.

When computers were introduced to the business world, they often were first put to work hosting TPSs. Computers were much faster at processing large chunks of data than previous manual systems had been. Imagine having clerks type up tuition invoices for each student at a 10,000–student

Figure 11.30

All information systems perform similar functions, including acquiring data, processing that data into information, storing the data, and providing the user with a number of output options with which to make the information meaningful and useful.

university. Obviously, a computer can print invoices much quicker from a database.

How do transactions enter a TPS? Transactions can be entered manually or electronically. When you call a company and order a sweater, for example, the call taker enters your data into a TPS. When you purchase gasoline at a pay-at-the-pump terminal, the pump captures your credit card data and transmits it to a TPS, which automatically records a sale (gallons of gasoline and dollar value). Transactions are processed either in batches or in real time. Various departments in an organization then access the TPSs to extract the information they need to process additional transactions, as shown in Figure 11.31.

What is batch processing? **Batch processing** means that transaction data is accumulated until a certain point is reached, and then several transactions are processed all at once. Batch processing is appropriate for activities that are not time sensitive, such as developing a mailing list to mail out the new course catalogs that students have requested. The college could print a mailing label each time someone requests a catalog, but it is more efficient to batch the requests and process them all at once when the catalogs are ready to be addressed.

How does real-time processing work? For most activities, processing and recording transactions in a TPS occur in real time. **Real-time processing** means that the database is queried and updated while the transaction is taking place. For instance, when you register for classes, the registration clerk checks to make sure seats are still available for the classes you want and immediately records your

registration in the class. This **online transaction processing (OLTP)** ensures that the data in the TPS is as current as possible.

Management Information Systems

What is a management information system? A **management information system (MIS)** provides timely and accurate information that enables managers to make critical business decisions. MISs were a direct outgrowth of TPSs. Managers quickly realized that the data contained in TPSs could be an extremely powerful tool only if the information could be organized and output in a useful form. Today's MISs are often built in as a feature of TPSs.

What does an MIS provide that a TPS does not? The original TPSs were usually designed to output detail reports. A **detail report** provides a list of the transactions that occurred during a certain time period. For example, during registration periods at your school, the registrar might receive a detail report that lists the students who registered for classes each day. Figure 11.32a shows an example of a detail report on daily enrollment.

Going beyond the detail reports provided by TPSs, MISs provide summary reports and exception reports. A **summary report** provides a consolidated picture of detailed data. These reports usually include some calculation (totals) or visual displays of information (such as charts and graphs). Figure 11.32b shows an example of a summary report displaying total daily enrollment.

An **exception report** shows conditions that are unusual or that need attention by users of the system. The registrar at your college may get an exception report when all sections of a course are full, indicating that it may be time to schedule additional sections. Figure 11.32c shows an example of such an exception report.

Decision Support Systems

What is a decision support system? A **decision support system (DSS)** is designed to help managers develop solutions for specific problems. A DSS for

Step 1: Consumer places a telephone order for clothing.

Step 2: Clerk takes order.

Details of Order:
Item #
Quantity
Price
Delivery Address

Telephone Order Transaction Processing System

Step 3: Order details entered into TPS.

Step 4: Shipping department extracts information to process order.

Step 5: Billing department extracts information to process customer payment.

Figure 11.31

TPSs help capture and track critical business information needed for successful completion of business transactions such as selling merchandise over the telephone.

Daily Enrollment Report

Class Code	Class Name	Student ID#
CHE 140	Chemistry	123456789
CIS 111	Programming	123456789
ENG 101	English Comp 1	123456789
ENG 102	English Comp 2	234567891
ENG 102	English Comp 2	678912345
HIS 103	Western Civ	123456789
HIS 204	Scottish History	345678912
HIS 401	16th Century Europe	567891234

Enrollment Summary Report

Division Name	Total Credits
Chemistry	4
Computer Information Systems	5
English	9
History	9
Languages	3
Physical Education	3
Psychology	9
Religion	3
Sociology	3
Grand Total Credits	48

Class Sections Fully Enrolled Fall Semester

Class Code	Class Name
CHE 140	Inorganic Chemistry
ENG 101	English Comp 1
SOC 310	Interpersonal Relationships

Figure 11.32

The three types of management information system reports are (a) detail report, (b) summary report, and (c) exception report.

a marketing department might provide statistical information on customer attributes (such as income levels, buying patterns, and so on) that would assist managers in making decisions regarding advertising strategy. A DSS not only uses data from databases and data warehouses, but also enables users to add their own insights and experiences and apply them to the solution.

What does a decision support system look like? Database management systems, while playing an integral part of a DSS, are supplemented by additional software systems in a DSS. In a DSS, the user interface provides the means of interaction between the user and the system. An effective user interface must be easy to learn. The other major components of a DSS are internal and external data sources, model management systems, and knowledge-based systems. As shown in Figure 11.33, all of these systems work together to provide the user of the DSS with a broad base of information on which to base decisions.

Internal and External Data Sources

What are internal and external data sources for decision support systems? Data can be fed into the DSS from a variety of sources. Internal data sources are maintained by the same company that operates the DSS. For example, internal TPSs can provide a wealth of statistical data about customers, ordering patterns, inventory levels, and so on. An **external data source** is any source not owned by the company that owns the DSS, such as customer demographic data purchased from third parties, mailing lists, or statistics compiled by the federal government. Internal and external data sources provide a stream of data that is integrated into the DSS for analysis.

Model Management Systems

What function does a model management system perform? A **model management system** is software that assists in building management models in

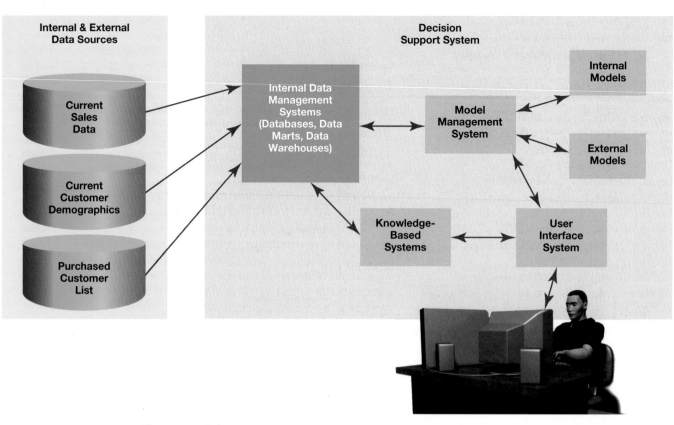

Figure 11.33

Major components of a DSS. Through the user interface, models are analyzed and manipulated to provide information on which management decisions are based.

DSSs. A management model is an analysis tool that, through the use of internal and external data, provides a view of a particular business situation for the purposes of decision making. Models can be built to describe any business situation, such as the classroom space requirements for next semester or a listing of alternative satellite campus locations.

Internal models (such as a spreadsheet that shows current classroom use on a college campus) are developed inside an organization. External models (such as statistics about populations of students at two-year colleges in the United States) are purchased from third parties. Model management systems typically contain financial and statistical analysis tools used to analyze the data provided by models or to create additional models.

Knowledge-Based Systems

What is a knowledge-based system, and how is it used in decision support systems? A knowledge-based

system provides additional intelligence that supplements the user's own intellect and makes the DSS more effective. It can be an **expert system** that tries to replicate the decision-making processes of human experts to solve specific problems. For example, an expert system might be designed to take the place of a physician in a remote location such as a scientific base in Antarctica. A physician expert system would ask the patient about symptoms just as a live physician would, and the system would make a diagnosis based on the algorithms programmed into it.

Another type of knowledge-based system is a **natural language processing (NLP) system**. NLP systems enable users to communicate with computer systems using a natural spoken or written language instead of using a computer programming language. Individuals with disabilities who cannot use a keyboard benefit greatly from NLP systems because they can just speak to the computer and have it understand what they are saying without using specific computer commands. Using an NLP system can simplify the user interface, making it much more efficient and user friendly. The speech-recognition feature of Microsoft Office is a type of NLP system.

All knowledge-based systems fall under the science of artificial intelligence. **Artificial intelligence (AI)** is the branch of computer science that deals with the attempt to create computers that think like humans. To date, no computers have been constructed that can replicate the thinking patterns of a human brain because scientists still do not fully understand how humans store and integrate knowledge and experiences to form human intelligence.

How does a knowledge-based system help in the decision-making process? Databases and the models provided by model management systems tend to be extremely analytical and mathematical in nature. If we relied solely on databases and models to make decisions, then the answers would be derived with a "yes or no" mentality, allowing no room for human thought. Fortunately, human users are involved in these types of systems, providing an opportunity to inject human judgment and experience into the decision-making process.

The knowledge-based system also provides an opportunity to introduce experience into the mix. Knowledge-based systems support the concept of fuzzy logic. Normal logic is highly rigid: If "x" happens, then "y" will happen. **Fuzzy logic** enables the interjection of experiential learning into the equation by considering probabilities. Whereas an algorithm in a database has to be specific, an algorithm in a knowledge-based system could state that if "x" happens, 70 percent of the time "y" will happen.

For instance, managers at Amazon.com would find it extremely helpful if their DSSs informed them that 40 percent of customers who bought a certain book also bought the sequel. This could suggest that designing a discount program for sequels bought with the original book might spur sales. Fuzzy logic enables a system to be more flexible and to consider a wider range of possibilities than would conventional algorithmic thinking.

> **"All knowledge-based systems fall under the science of artificial intelligence."**

Enterprise Resource Planning Systems

What is an enterprise? An enterprise is any business entity, large or small. It could be the pizza shop on the corner or a Fortune 500 manufacturer of sports apparel. All businesses have data and information to manage, and large, complex organizations can benefit from managing that information with a central piece of software.

What does an enterprise resource planning system do? An **enterprise resource planning (ERP) system** is a broad-based software system that integrates multiple data sources and ties together the various processes of an enterprise to enable information to flow more smoothly. ERP systems use a common database to store and integrate information. This enables the information to be used across multiple areas of an enterprise.

For instance, human resource functions (such as the management of hiring, firing, promotions, and benefits) and accounting functions (such as payroll) are often the first processes integrated into an ERP system. Historically, human resource records and accounting records were kept in separate databases, but having the information reside in one database makes the management and paying of employees more streamlined. If manufacturing operations were then integrated into the ERP system, the data that was already in place regarding the employees and payroll could be easily used for determining the cost of running an assembly line (because the workers on the assembly line get paid) or for scheduling workers to run the assembly line. The objective of ERP systems is to accumulate all information relevant to running a business in a central location and make it readily available to whoever needs that information to make decisions.

Almost all Fortune 500 companies have implemented ERP systems, and many medium-sized companies are implementing them also. Although the corner pizza shop probably does not need an ERP system, it would be difficult to coordinate the activities of a multinational corporation without one.

Data Mining

Just because you have captured data in an organized fashion and have stored it in a format that seems to make sense doesn't mean that an analysis of the data will automatically reveal everything you need to know. Trends can sometimes be hard to spot if the data is not organized or analyzed in a particular way. To make data work harder, companies employ data-mining techniques.

Data mining is the process by which great amounts of data are analyzed and investigated. The objective is to spot significant patterns or trends within the data that would otherwise not be obvious. For instance, through mining student enrollment data, a school may discover that 40 percent of new nursing degree students are Latino.

Why do businesses mine their data? The main reason businesses mine data is to understand their customers better. If a company can better understand the types of customers who buy its products and can learn what motivates their customers to do so, it can market effectively by concentrating its efforts on the populations that are most likely to buy.

How do businesses mine their data? Data mining enables managers to sift through data in several ways. Each method produces different information that managers can then base their decisions on. Managers make their data meaningful through the following activities:

- **Classification:** To analyze data, managers need to classify it. Therefore, before mining, managers define data classes that they think will be helpful in spotting trends. They then apply these class definitions to all unclassified data to prepare it for analysis. For example, "good credit risk" and "bad credit risk" are two data classes that managers could establish to determine whether to grant mortgages to applicants. Managers would then identify factors (such as credit history and yearly income) that they could use to classify applicants as good or bad risks.

- **Estimation:** When managers classify data, the record either fits the

ACTIVE HELP-DESK

Data Warehouses, Data Marts, and Information Systems

In this Active Helpdesk call, you'll play the role of a helpdesk staffer, fielding calls about data warehouses, data marts, and information systems.

classification criteria or it doesn't. Estimation enables managers to assign a value to data based on some criterion. For example, assume a bank wants to send out credit card offers to people who are likely to be granted a credit card. The bank may run the customers' data through a program that assigns them a score based on where they live, their household income, and their average bank balance. This provides managers with an estimate of the most likely credit card prospects so that they can include them in the mailing.

- **Affinity grouping (or association rules):** When mining data, managers also can determine which data goes together. In other words, they can apply affinity grouping or association rules to the data. For example, suppose analysis of a sales database indicates that two items are bought together 70 percent of the time. Based on this data, managers might decide that these items should be pictured on the same page in their next mail-order catalog.

- **Clustering:** Clustering involves organizing data into similar subgroups, or clusters. It is different from classification in that there are no predefined classes. The data-mining software makes the decision about what to group, and it is up to managers to determine whether the clusters are meaningful. For example, the data-mining software may identify clusters of customers with similar buying patterns. Further analysis of the clusters may reveal that certain socioeconomic groups have similar buying patterns.

- **Description and visualization:** Often, the purpose of data mining is merely to describe data so that managers can visualize it. Sometimes having a clear picture of what is going on with the data helps people to interpret it in new and different ways. For example, if large amounts of data revealed that left-handed males who live in suburban environments never take automotive technology courses, it would most likely spark a heated discussion about the reasons why. It would certainly provide plenty of opportunities for additional study on the part of psychologists, sociologists, and college administrators!

You may have noticed that products are frequently moved around in supermarkets. This is usually the result of data mining.

With electronic scanning of bar codes, each customer's purchase is recorded in a database. By classifying the data and using cluster analysis, supermarket managers can determine which products people usually purchase with other products. The store then places these products close to each other so that shoppers can find them easily. For instance, if analysis shows that people often buy coffee with breakfast cereal, it makes sense to place these items in the same aisle.

As the human race continues to accumulate data, the development of faster and bigger databases will be a necessity. You can expect to interact with more and more databases every year, even if you don't realize you are doing so.

Ethics: Data, Data Everywhere—But Who Is Viewing It and Why?

As databases have become commonplace, an ever-increasing amount of information about you and your habits has gone into various databases. Every time you purchase something with a credit card, there is a record of that transaction, and both the merchant from whom you purchased the item and the credit card company have information about your buying habits (see Figure 11.34).

Have you used a toll service that allows you to pay your tolls electronically by just driving through a lane without stopping? Toll records are routinely subpoenaed in court cases. Toll records were used in an Illinois court by a husband in a divorce case to prove his wife was rarely home and therefore unfit for custody of their son. All banking transactions are handled by computers (and hence databases) in the United States, and there is a high probability that your employer is electronically transferring your pay to your bank by direct deposit. If you engage in online banking and bill paying, yet another electronic trail of your financial life is being generated in databases.

Do you think you can avoid scrutiny by paying cash? Not if you are a member of a frequent shopper "club" (a popular promotion used by supermarkets and drug stores) and provide the checkout clerk with your personal information in exchange for coupons or a few dollars off your purchases. Remember, you never can be sure of how this data might be used. In October 2004, a firefighter was arrested after his supermarket purchase records revealed he had purchased the same type of fire starters used in an arson case. After three months, the charges were dropped when another person pleaded guilty to committing the arson.

Financial information isn't the only sensitive information that is tracked. The majority of physicians and hospitals in the United States track medical records in electronic databases. Your entire prescription history (and hence hints about your medical history) is in a database at the local pharmacy. Have you applied for insurance lately? Your doctor was probably able to provide (with your permission, of course) your entire medical history to the insurance company with a few clicks of a mouse. All of the data that exists in the world around us should give us pause, and we need to stop and consider the ethical implications of the electronic society we live in.

Figure 11.34

Workmen disassembling a house reveal the contents hidden inside. This is a metaphor for the erosion of our privacy rights. If our personal information is in multiple databases and viewable by many people, is the information still private?

Data Convergence—The Perfect Storm of Privacy Invasion?

Discrete pieces of data, such as that you filled your gas tank last Thursday or bought a copy of *War and Peace* last month, don't mean much in and of themselves. However, with so much data in electronic form, it is getting much easier to combine data from various data sources and build a powerful profile of an individual to which data-mining techniques can be applied. For instance, suppose a marketing company purchased data about your buying habits from your credit card company and the supermarket, pharmacy, and bookstore where you shop. In addition, the marketing company purchased information about you from the company where you bought your lawn mower (it got that from your credit card information). What information did the lawn mower company have about you? The personal information you gave when you filled out your warranty card online (household income, age, whether you rent or own your home, and so on)! By combining all of this information into one database, the marketing company is able to build an extremely detailed picture of who you are.

For example, based on your purchases at the pharmacy, a marketing company might determine that there are both males (shaving gel) and females (cosmetics) living in your home. It also might notice that you have been buying pregnancy test kits once a month for 18 months and conclude you are trying to have a baby (and not having much luck, by the way). By your address and the car you drive (you had charges on your credit card at a Lexus dealer), the company estimated that you have a household income of more than $100,000 per year, making you affluent. It also noticed you shop at many stores that feature outdoor apparel and sports equipment and recently bought a mountain bike, so the company has concluded that you have an active lifestyle. Based on this analysis, you start receiving mail and phone solicitations for canoes, baby clothing, fertility treatments, and plasma TVs. Just because this type of analysis can be done, should we be doing it? Do you want people marketing to you based on sensitive personal information? Where does marketing stop and invasion of privacy begin?

What Can You Do?

Providing information and having it recorded in databases are part of our way of life now. Because refusing to give information out at all is bound to be impractical, you should ask the following questions related to data you are providing:

- **For what purpose is the data being gathered?** When the clerk at the electronics superstore asks for your zip code, ask why she wants it. (It is probably for some marketing purpose).

- **Are the reasons for gathering the data legitimate or important to you?** When you purchase a CD, is asking for your zip code really a legitimate request? However, to validate the warranty on a large-screen TV, you may need to give a clerk your address and zip code. Similarly,

disclosing medical information to key people (such as your pharmacist) may be important to receiving good care and therefore is extremely important to you. If you don't see the advantage, then ask more questions or don't reveal the information.

- **How will the information gathered be protected once it has been obtained?** Ask about data protection policies before you give information. Most Web sites provide access to their data protection policies—readily available through clickable links or pop-up boxes—when they ask for information. If an organization doesn't have a data protection policy, then be wary of giving them sensitive information unless there is a compelling advantage to doing so (such as receiving good medical care). Data protection doesn't just refer to keeping data secure. It also means restricting access to the data to employees of the organization that need to use that data. A shipping clerk might need to see your address, for example, but doesn't need to see your credit card information.

- **Will the information collected be used for purposes other than the purpose for which it was originally collected?** This might be covered in a data protection policy. If it isn't, then ask about it. Will your information be sold to other companies? Will it be used for marketing other products to you?

- **Could the information asked for be used for identity theft?** Identity thieves usually need your Social Security number and your birth date to open credit card accounts in your name. Be especially wary when asked for this information, and make sure there is a legitimate need for this information. Most organizations and businesses are shying away from using Social Security numbers to track customers because of the risk of identity theft.

- **Are organizations that already have your data safeguarding it?** Don't just consider new requests for information. Think about organizations, such as banks, that already have your information and monitor their performance. Have they been in the news lately because of a major data breach (inadvertently exposing information to inappropriate or unauthorized individuals)? You might want to consider switching institutions if yours has a poor record of data security.

Think carefully before providing information and be vigilant about monitoring your data when you can. It may make the difference between invasion of privacy and peace of mind.

1. What is a database, and why is it beneficial to use databases?

Databases are electronic collections of related data that can be organized so that it is more easily accessed and manipulated. Properly designed databases cut down on data redundancy and duplicate data by ensuring relevant data is recorded in only one place. This also helps eliminate data inconsistency, which comes from having different data about the same transaction recorded in two different places. When databases are used, multiple users can share and access information at the same time. Databases are used any time complex information needs to be organized or more than one person needs to access it. In these cases, lists (which are used to keep track of simple information) are no longer efficient.

2. What components make up a database?

The three main components of a database are fields, records, and tables. A category of information in a database is stored in a field. Each field is identified by a field name, which is a way of describing the field. Fields are assigned a data type that indicates what type of data can be stored in the field. Common data types include text, numeric, computational, date, memo, object, and hyperlink. A group of related fields is a record. A group of related records is a table or file. To keep records distinct, each record must have one field that has a value unique to that record. This unique field is a primary key (or a key field).

3. What types of databases are there?

The three major types of databases currently in use are relational, object-oriented, and multidimensional. Relational databases are characterized by two-dimensional tables of data in which a common field is maintained in each of two tables and the information in the tables is linked by this field. Object-oriented databases store data in objects, not in tables. The objects also contain instructions about how the data is to be manipulated or processed. Multidimensional databases represent data in three-dimensional cubes to enable faster retrieval of information from the database.

4. What do database management systems do?

Database management systems (DBMSs) are specially designed applications (such as Oracle or Microsoft Access) that interact with the user, other applications, and the database itself to capture and analyze data. The main operations of a DBMS are creating databases, entering data, viewing (or browsing) data, sorting (or indexing) data, extracting (or querying) data, and outputting data. A query language is used to extract records from a database. Almost all relational databases today use structured query language, or SQL. However, most DBMSs include wizards that enable you to query the database without learning a query language. The most common form of output for any database is a printed report.

5. How do relational databases organize and manipulate data?

Relational databases operate by organizing data into various tables based on logical groupings. Because not all of the data in a relational database is stored in the same table, a methodology must be implemented to link data between tables. In relational databases, the links between tables that define how the data is related are referred to as relationships. To establish a relationship between two tables, both tables must have a common field (or column). Once linked, information can be drawn from multiple tables through the use of queries (for on-screen viewing of data) or report generators (used to produce printed reports).

6. What are data warehouses and data marts, and how are they used?

A data warehouse is a large-scale electronic repository of data that contains and organizes in one place all the relevant data related to an organization. Data warehouses often contain information from multiple databases. Because it can be difficult to find information in a large data warehouse, small slices of the data warehouse called *data marts* are often created. The information in data marts pertains to a single department within the organization, for example. Data warehouses and data marts consolidate information from a wide variety of sources to provide comprehensive pictures of operations or transactions within a business.

7. What is an information system, and what types of information systems are used in business?

Information systems are software-based solutions that are used to gather and analyze information. Information systems fall into one of five categories. An office support system (OSS) is designed to assist employees in accomplishing their day-to-day tasks and improve communications. A transaction processing system (TPS) is a system that is used to keep track of everyday business activities. A management information system (MIS) provides timely and accurate information that enables managers to make critical business decisions. A decision support system (DSS) is a system designed to help managers develop solutions for specific problems. An enterprise resource planning (ERP) system is a large software system that gathers information from all parts of a business and integrates it to make it readily available for decision making.

8. What is data mining, and how does it work?

Data mining is the process by which large amounts of data are analyzed to spot otherwise hidden trends. Through processes such as classification, estimation, affinity grouping, clustering, and description (visualization), data is organized so that it provides meaningful information that can be used by managers to identify business trends.

key terms

buzzwords eleven · eleven

Word Bank

- data dictionary
- data inconsistency
- data mining
- data warehouse
- decision support system
- field
- join query
- memo field
- metadata
- numeric field
- object field
- primary key
- relational algebra
- select query
- structured query language (SQL)
- table
- text field
- transaction processing system (TPS)

Instructions: Fill in the blanks using the words from the Word Bank above.

When constructing a database (1) _____, it is important to ensure each record is identified uniquely. A(n) (2) _____ should be established as a unique field that will be included with each record. In a database, numbers such as 1234 are normally stored in a(n) (3) _____, but they also could be stored in a(n) (4) _____ if calculations do not need to be performed on the number. Extremely lengthy textual data is stored in a(n) (5) _____, whereas video files are appropriately stored in a(n) (6) _____. The (7) _____ fully describes each field in the database and its attributes. Data used to describe other data in this manner is referred to as (8) _____.

Queries are used to prepare data for viewing or printing. A(n) (9) _____ usually displays requested information from only one table. For displaying related information that is stored in multiple tables, a(n) (10) _____ must be used. The most popular query language in use today is (11) _____. Queries generated by this language make use of English-language statements driven by the mathematical principles of (12) _____.

When individual databases are not sufficient to maintain all the data that needs to be tracked, a(n) (13) _____ should be created. Databases are often key components of (14) _____, which record routine business activities. A(n) (15) _____ utilizes databases and other related systems to assist management with building business models and making critical decisions.

becoming computer literate

Everyone loves the handbags that your best friend, Linh, makes, and she has decided to start selling them to the general public. Linh has a few existing customers already (mostly family and friends), but she plans to put her work in a few art shows, make some deals with area stores to feature it, and sell it online at Etsy.com. Keeping track of all this information is going to be important, but she is not computer literate.

Linh has approached you to be her database consultant and to design a database for her new business. Write a proposal that outlines what you intend to do for your friend. What kind of database will you create? What kind of information will your friend need in the database to run her business? How should that information be organized? Can the database be created and stored online so that Linh can access it from her phone? As her business grows, how do you imagine the database will grow with the business?

549

Instructions: Answer the multiple-choice and true–false questions below for more practice with key terms and concepts from this chapter.

Multiple Choice

1. Having the exact same information about a person on two different lists is an example of
   a. data redundancy.
   b. data inconsistency.
   c. data disparity.
   d. data duplication errors.

2. Which of the following is NOT an advantage of using a database versus lists?
   a. Information assurance can be guaranteed by using a database.
   b. Data entry errors can be minimized with databases.
   c. Data integrity can be ensured with a database.
   d. Data redundancy can be reduced by using databases.

3. A group of related records in a relational database is called a(n)
   a. primary key.
   b. SQL grid.
   c. master key.
   d. table.

4. In databases, tables are related using
   a. locks.
   b. database logic.
   c. keys.
   d. multivariate relations.

5. A field that has a unique value for each record in a database is called the
   a. key field.
   b. logical key.
   c. primary key.
   d. master field.

6. A foreign key contained in a related table is a
   a. linked key.
   b. subordinate key.
   c. secondary key.
   d. primary key.

7. Which is one of the four main operations of a DBMS?
   a. Consolidating data
   b. Dissecting data
   c. Sorting data
   d. Structuring data

8. Ensuring that a field must be filled in with data is an example of a(n)
   a. existence check.
   b. completeness check.
   c. range check.
   d. consistency check.

9. A system designed to hold large amounts of information about an enterprise is known as (a)n
   a. decision support system.
   b. office support system.
   c. data warehouse.
   d. management information system.

10. An electronic system used to emulate human decision making is an example of a
   a. transaction processing system.
   b. decision support system.
   c. management information system.
   d. knowledge-based system.

True-False

_____ 1. A query is designed to make extracting relevant data from a database easier.

_____ 2. Range checks ensure that only reasonable data values are entered into a database.

_____ 3. Reducing incorrect or incomplete data by recording data in only one place is called data normalization.

_____ 4. A data mart is a smaller slice of a data warehouse.

_____ 5. One of the main reasons businesses use data mining is to spot customer trends.

1. Researching the Alumni Database

Many schools try to maintain contact with former students to keep them informed of new programs and courses being offered at the institution. Visit your school's alumni office and determine the following:

a. Is a separate database maintained for the purposes of communicating with alumni?
b. What type of database software is used?
c. What data is captured in this database?
d. How often is the data contained in the database verified with the alumni?

2. Developing an Alumni Database

If the alumni office doesn't maintain a separate database for the purposes of communicating with graduates, use the previous questions as a guideline for developing an alumni database design for your school.

3. Creating a Database

Imagine that you own 400 DVDs and want to track them in a database. Determine the following:

a. What fields do you need in your database for categorizing and tracking your DVDs? What would be a good primary key to use for this "DVD" table?
b. What fields do you need for capturing information about your friends to whom you have loaned DVDs? What would be the primary key of this "borrower" table?
c. What common field would you include in both tables to relate the "DVD" table to the "borrower" table? Justify your answer.

4. Database Conversion

You've just volunteered to assist the director of a club at your school with a membership drive. The first order of business is to convert the existing paper membership records into an Access database. Consider the following issues:

a. What fields do you need in your "membership" table for tracking valid members?
b. How would you distinguish active members in the "membership" table from members who have not attended meetings in more than a year? Would it be more efficient to put the inactive members into a separate table? Justify your answer.
c. After the Access database is constructed, what software would you suggest be used to generate appeal letters for the club's fund-raising campaign to benefit a homeless shelter? How would you suggest the results of the fund-raising campaign be stored in the member database? Explain your answer sufficiently to convince the director of your decision.

1. Data Warehousing

You are a summer intern in the information technology group of an athletic apparel manufacturer. At the weekly staff meeting, the chief information officer (CIO) indicates that the president is requesting information about sales of all lines of goods for the past 10 years. Unfortunately, data more than three years old is not maintained in the current sales database and has been archived to tape. A volunteer is needed (and everyone looks to you) to extract the data from the backup tapes and prepare the needed reports.

As you are spending your 16th evening extracting the data, the CIO mentions that manufacturing, shipping, and accounts receivable may need their own reports that include different data but span the same time period as your current assignment. The CIO assures you that most of the information is available on tape, and if it isn't, it can be located in the mountains of paper stored in the old warehouse. You know that this tedious work could be avoided by the introduction of a data warehousing system!

a. Prepare a data-warehousing plan for the CIO. Describe briefly the benefits of data warehousing and provide an overview of the process.
b. For sales, manufacturing, shipping, and accounts receivable data, suggest the types of information that should be captured in the data warehouse.
c. What types of data marts would you suggest setting up for this company?

2. Creating a Data Access Policy

You have an internship in the information technology department at the regional office of Mammoth Insurance Company, which sells automobile, life, and medical insurance. Colossal Insurance Company, one of your firm's competitors, was recently raked over the coals in the news media because a few employees were looking up medical records of insurance customers for the purpose of developing a mailing list for people with certain illnesses. The employees were then using the list to market a new mail-order prescription drug Web site (owned by the employees, not Colossal) directly to Colossal's customers. Many customers were upset by the solicitations, which they viewed as an invasion of their privacy. The Colossal employees contended that no one ever told them they couldn't use the company records for this purpose.

The CIO of Mammoth wants to ensure that such a controversy doesn't happen to her company. She has asked your supervisor (who in turn drafted you to help) to prepare a data access policy for Mammoth. Prepare a draft of the policy and consider the following:

a. Who should have access to the medical information of insurance company customers? The insurance underwriters (the people who approve or disapprove policies) need the information. Does anyone else?
b. Should marketing personnel be granted access to medical and driving records for the purposes of marketing Mammoth's products? If so, who should approve the access? Should customers be informed before conducting marketing campaigns using their "sensitive" information? Who should be responsible for notifying customers?
c. Describe the types of uses of customer information that would be deemed inappropriate by the company. What should the penalties be for violating the policy?

Instructions: Albert Einstein used *Gedankenexperiments,* or critical thinking questions, to develop his theory of relativity. Some ideas are best understood by experimenting with them in our own minds. The following critical thinking questions are designed to demand your full attention but require only a comfortable chair—no technology.

1. Database Ethics

Internet databases abound with personal information about you. You probably provided some of this information, but it may have been sold to other companies. Other information about you may have been obtained without your knowledge while you surfed Web sites. Consider the following:

a. Is it ethical for a company to sell personal information (such as household income) that you voluntarily provide? What should a company be able to do (or not able to do) with the personal information you provide to it?

b. Is gathering information about people's surfing and buying habits by tracking their clicks through a Web site an invasion of privacy? Why or why not?

c. Should Web sites be legally required to inform users that they are tracking surfing habits? Why or why not?

2. IRS Databases

The Internal Revenue Service (IRS) maintains large databases about taxpayers that include a wealth of information on personal income and can be easily sorted by geographic location. This information would be of great value to marketing professionals for targeting marketing programs to consumers. Currently, the IRS is prohibited from selling this information to third parties. However, the IRS and other government agencies face increasing pressure to find ways to increase revenue or decrease expenses.

a. Do you favor a change in the laws that would permit the IRS to sell names and addresses with household income information to third parties? Why or why not?

b. Would it be acceptable for the IRS to sell income information to marketing firms if it did not include personal information (such as names and addresses), but only included income statistics for certain geographic areas? How is this better (or worse) than selling personal information?

c. How would you feel about the IRS marketing financial products (such as tax software) directly to consumers? Would this be a conflict of interest with the IRS's main mission, which is the collection of tax revenue and enforcement of tax compliance?

3. Information About You

There are many databases such as **411.com** on the Web, and some of them probably contain your personal information. Using Google (or other search engines), perform a Web search on your name. Because many people have the same name, you may need to use some other identifying attributes (such as your address, employer, high school attended, and so on) to ensure that the search returns results about you. Consider the following:

a. What information did you find about yourself? What was the most surprising piece of information you located?

b. Did you find enough information about yourself to enable a criminal to steal your identity? What pieces of information about you that an identity thief would need to steal your identity aren't available on the Web?

c. Repeat this same exercise but instead use the name of one of your friends. What obligation do you have to your friend to inform him or her of any potentially sensitive information you located?

Student Data Tracking

Problem

Many schools use student data information systems that were installed more than 10 years ago. When preparing to transition to a newer system, additional information is often identified that was not recorded in the old system (such as e-mail addresses) but needs to be captured in the new system. In addition, in preparing to transfer legacy data to a new system, the data often needs to be "groomed." Grooming data means verifying data accuracy, ensuring data consistency, and correcting problems.

Task

Your class has volunteered to assist the IT department with the transition to a new student information system. Customers (students) often provide unique perspectives, and they should be consulted whenever possible during the design and implementation of new systems. The school administration feels your input into the design process will enhance the usability of the new system.

Process

Divide the class into small groups.

1. Your group should examine your school's current student information system from a user perspective. Identify the data that is being captured from students when they enroll in or register for courses. Compile a list of suggestions for data that does not need to be captured but currently is being captured, and for additional data that should be gathered but is not currently gathered. Determine the extent to which student services can be accessed over the Internet and suggest services that require Internet accessibility but are not currently offered.

2. Investigate whether your school has a written data access policy and obtain a copy if possible. If your school does not have an access policy, have members of your group draft a policy that addresses the types of data that various groups of employees (faculty, administrators, business office workers, and so on) should be able to access.

3. Present your group's findings to the class. Compare your suggestions to those of other groups. Be sure to address the needs of all groups of students (such as residents, commuters, and online students).

4. Prepare a list of recommendations for improvements to the current student information system for the director of student affairs. Clearly indicate how the proposed changes will benefit both students and the school employees who are interacting with the system.

Conclusion

Colleges and universities are competing for students more fiercely than ever before. Those institutions that listen to their students and find innovative ways to serve their needs will have a distinct advantage in attracting and retaining students. Listening to customers is a basic principle of business that educational institutions should not overlook.

In addition to the review materials presented here, you'll find additional materials featured with the book's multimedia, including the *Technology in Action* Student Resource CD and the Companion Website (**pearsonhighered.com/techinaction**), which will help reinforce your understanding of the chapter content. These materials include the following:

Active Helpdesk

In Active Helpdesk calls, you'll assume the role of helpdesk operator, taking calls about the concepts you've learned in this chapter. You'll apply what you've learned and receive feedback from a supervisor to review and reinforce those concepts. The Active Helpdesk calls for this chapter are listed below and can be found on your Student Resource CD:

- Understanding Database Management Systems
- Using Databases
- Data Warehouses, Data Marts, and Information Systems

Sound Bytes

Sound Bytes are dynamic multimedia tutorials that help demystify even the most complex topics. You'll view video clips and animations that illustrate computer concepts and then apply what you've learned by reviewing it with the Sound Byte Labs, which include quizzes and activities specifically tailored to each Sound Byte. The Sound Bytes for this chapter are listed below and can be found on your Student Resource CD:

- Creating an Access 2007 Database
- Improving an Access 2007 Database

Companion Website

The *Technology in Action* Companion Website includes a variety of additional materials to help you review and learn more about the topics in this chapter. The resources available at **pearsonhighered.com/techinaction** include:

- **Online Study Guide.** Each chapter features an online true–false and multiple-choice quiz. You can take these quizzes, automatically check the results, and e-mail the results to your instructor.
- **Web Research Projects.** Each chapter features several Web research projects that ask you to search the Web for information on computer-related careers, milestones in computer history, important people and companies, emerging technologies, and the applications and implications of different technologies.

twelve
behind the scenes:

networking and security in
the business world

resources

Active Helpdesk

- Using Servers **(p. 566)**
- Selecting a Network Topology and Cable **(p. 571)**
- Selecting Network Navigation Devices **(p. 583)**

Sound Bytes

- Network Topology and Navigation Devices **(p. 568)**
- What's My IP Address? (And Other Interesting Facts about Networks) **(p. 580)**
- A Day in the Life of a Network Technician **(p. 584)**

Companion Website

The Companion Website includes a variety of additional materials to help you review and learn more about the topics in this chapter. Go to: *pearsonhighered.com/techinaction*

how cool is *this?* Planning a meeting

with classmates to work on a **group project** can be **difficult**. E-mail is not an efficient planning tool because it is difficult to coordinate numerous messages. Even using threaded message postings on Facebook can be cumbersome. A simple free tool that solves this problem is Doodle (**doodle.com**).

With **Doodle**, you can quickly set up a grid with possible meeting dates and times. You then provide the URL of the meeting poll to the other members of the group. As members come to the meeting site, they enter their names and indicate their availability for various meeting times (**yes, no, or maybe**) as indicated by the colors green, red, and yellow. Doodle then provides a visual summary of all input from the group so you can easily select a meeting time that works for the majority of the participants.

So stop **tearing your hair out** about getting your group together and use Doodle to simplify your planning!

Networking Advantages

As you learned in Chapter 7, a **network** is a group of two or more computers (or nodes) that are configured to share information and resources such as printers, files, and databases. Essentially, a network enables computers and other devices to communicate with each other. But why do we network computers? As discussed in Chapter 7, home networks enable users to share peripherals, transfer files simply, and share Internet connections. Businesses, such as your college or an insurance company, also gain advantages from deploying networks.

What advantages do businesses gain from networks? Large business networks provide advantages similar to those of home networks, and therefore have advantages over individual stand-alone computers:

- **Networks increase productivity.** Computers are powerful stand-alone resources. However, to increase productivity, people need to be able to share data and peripherals with co-workers and communicate with them efficiently. Without a network, only one person at a time can access information because it resides on a single computer. Information sharing is therefore the largest benefit gained by installing a network.

- **Networks enable expensive resources to be shared.** Networks enable people to share peripherals such as printers, eliminating the need for duplicate devices. You probably have a printer hooked up to your home computer. Think about how often it sits idle. Compound that by having 20 students in a lab, each with his or her own printer. Having 20 printers sitting idle 90 percent of the time is a tremendous waste of money. Installing a network that enables one printer (working most of the time) to serve all 20 students saves money.

- **Networks facilitate knowledge sharing.** The databases you learned about in Chapter 11 become especially powerful when deployed on a network. Networked databases can serve the needs of many people at one time and increase the availability of data. Your college's databases are much more useful when all college employees can look up student records at the same time.

- **Networks enable software sharing.** Installing a new version of software on everyone's desktop in a college with 500 employees can be time consuming. However, if the computers are networked, all employees can access the same copy of a program from the server. Although the college must still purchase a software license for each employee, with a network they avoid having to install the program on every computer. This also saves space on individual computers, because the software doesn't reside on every computer.

- **Networks facilitate Internet connectivity.** Most college students need to connect to the Internet to complete classwork. Providing each computer on a network with its own dedicated connection to the Internet is costly. Through a network, large groups of computers can share one Internet connection, reducing Internet connectivity expenses.

- **Networks enable enhanced communication.** E-mail and instant messaging are extremely powerful applications when deployed on a network (especially one that is connected to the Internet). College students can easily exchange information with each other and their

BITS AND BYTES

Print Documents Anywhere . . . Even Without a Printer!

E-mailing documents to someone so they can print them isn't always feasible. With legal documents, you often want to ensure that no one can change the document, which you can't be certain of if you e-mail a Microsoft Word file. What if you need to send a file created with software (such as Microsoft Publisher) that your friend doesn't own? How can your friend print out the newsletter you created for him? PrinterShare (**printeranywhere.com**), a free software program, provides a solution.

When you install PrinterShare on a computer, it enables you to configure any printers connected to that computer for printer sharing. When your friend installs the PrinterShare software on his computer (which is connected to a printer), you can then direct any documents that could be printed from a program on your computer to the printer connected to your friend's computer. Even though you are in Seattle, you can print the Microsoft Publisher newsletter on your friend's printer in Tacoma as long as both computers are connected to the Internet. Your friend does not need to have Publisher installed on his computer. Check it out for yourself—it could save you some aggravation in the future.

professors, and can share valuable data by transferring files to other users.

Are there disadvantages to using networks? Because business (or college) networks are often complex, additional personnel are usually required to maintain them. These people, called **network administrators**, have training in computer and peripheral maintenance and repair, networking design, and the installation of networking software.

Another disadvantage is that operating a network requires special equipment and software. However, most companies feel that the cost savings of peripheral sharing and the ability to give employees simultaneous access to information outweigh the costs associated with network administrators and equipment.

Aside from the smallest networks, such as peer-to-peer networks, which are typically used in homes and small businesses, the majority of computer networks are based on the client/server model of computing.

Client/Server Networks

As you've learned, a server is a computer that both stores and shares resources on a network, whereas a **client** is a computer that requests those resources. A **client/server network** (also called a **server-based network**) contains servers as well as client computers. The inclusion of servers is what differentiates a client/server network from a typical peer-to-peer (P2P) network. (As you'll recall, each node connected to a P2P network can communicate directly with every other node on the network, instead of having a separate device exercise control over the network.) Figure 12.1 illustrates the client/server relationship.

The main advantage of a client/server relationship is that it makes data flow more efficiently than in peer-to-peer networks. Servers can respond to requests from a large number of clients at the same time. In addition, servers can be configured to perform specific tasks (such as handling e-mail or database requests) efficiently.

Say you are hungry and go to a fast-food restaurant. In your role as the customer ordering food, you are the client making a request. The cook, in the role of the server, responds to the request and prepares the meal. Certainly, you could go to the restaurant and cook your own meal, but this hardly would be efficient. You would be floundering around in the kitchen with other customers as they try to cook their own meals. If the manager assigns specialized tasks to a fast food cook (the server), many customers (clients) can be served efficiently at the same time. This is how servers work: one server can provide services efficiently to a large number of clients at one time.

Step 1: Client computer requests service from server computer.

What are the names of the customers who bought more than 500 television sets this month?

Query submitted from client

Answer provided by server

Mega-Discount Appliances
Wall-To-Wall Televisions, Inc.
Televisions-R-Us

Computer A (client)

Computer B (server)

Step 2: Server computer provides requested service to client computer.

Figure 12.1

Basic client/server interaction.

Does my home network have a server? As you'll recall from Chapter 7, peer-to-peer networks, which are typically set up in homes or very small businesses, do not require servers. In these networks, computers act as both clients and servers when appropriate.

When shouldn't a peer-to-peer network be used? P2P networks become difficult to administer when they are expanded beyond 10 users. Each individual computer may require updating if there are changes to the network, which is not efficient because administration of the network is decentralized. In addition, security can't be implemented centrally on a P2P network but instead must be handled by each individual user. As noted earlier, client/server networks contain at least one server that provides shared resources and services (including security) to the client computers that request them.

In addition, client/server networks move data more efficiently than P2P networks, making them appropriate for large numbers of users. For example, Figure 12.2 shows a small client/server arrangement. The server in this figure provides printing and Internet connection services for all the client computers connected to the network.

Besides having a centralized server, what makes a client/server network different from a peer-to-peer network? The main difference is that client/server networks

have increased scalability. With a **scalable network**, more users can be added easily without affecting the performance of the other network nodes (computers or peripherals). Because servers handle the bulk of tasks performed on the network (printing, Internet access, and so on), it is easy to accommodate more users by installing additional servers to help with the increased workload. Installing additional servers on a network is relatively simple and can usually be done without disrupting services for existing users.

In addition, peer-to-peer networks are **decentralized**. This means that users are responsible for creating their own data backups and for providing security for their computers. In client/server networks, all clients connect to a server that performs tasks for them. Therefore, client/server networks are said to be **centralized**. Many tasks that individual users must handle on a P2P network can be handled centrally at the server.

For instance, data files are normally stored on the server. Therefore, backups for all users on a college's network can be performed by merely backing up all the files on the server. Security, too, can be exercised over the server instead of on each user's computer; this way, the server, not the individual user, coordinates file security.

Figure 12.2

This small client/server network enables users to share a printer and an Internet connection.

Classifications of Client/Server Networks: LANs, WANs, and MANs

Networks are generally classified according to their size and the distance between the physical parts of the network. The three main classifications are local area networks, wide area networks, and metropolitan area networks.

A **local area network (LAN)** is a (generally small) group of computers and peripherals linked together over a relatively small geographic area. The computer lab at your school or the network serving the floor of the office building where you work is probably a LAN.

A LAN is not sufficient for meeting the computing needs of large companies that operates at diverse geographic locations, **Wide area networks (WANs)** comprise large numbers of users or separate LANs that are miles apart. For example, a large college campus might have a WAN that spans all of its lecture halls, residence halls, and administrative offices.

Corporations often use WANs to connect two or more geographically distant branches. For example, ABC Shoe Company has manufacturing plants and administrative offices all over the globe. The LAN at each ABC Shoe Company office is connected to other ABC Shoe Company LANs, forming a global ABC Shoe Company WAN. Figure 12.3 shows an example of what part of the ABC Shoe Company WAN might look like.

Sometimes government organizations or civic groups establish WANs to link users in a specific geographic area (such as within a city or county). A WAN of this special type of WANs is known as a **metropolitan area network (MAN)**. Many MANs are implemented as wireless networks that provide Internet access within large portions of cities. San Diego's Traffic Management Center (TMC) uses a MAN to analyze traffic patterns. You can check out the traffic maps they generate at **dot.ca.gov/sdtraffic**.

What sort of network connects devices such as PDAs and smartphones? A **personal area network (PAN)** is a network used to connect wireless devices (such as Bluetooth-enabled devices) that are in close proximity to each other.

BITS AND BYTES

Too Much Data? Here Comes the SAN

Databases can become so large that conventional database servers can't handle the information flowing in and out of them. A storage area network (SAN) is specifically designed to store and distribute large amounts of data to client computers or servers. SANs are made up of several network attached storage (NAS) devices, specialized devices attached to a network whose sole function is to store and disseminate data. Picture a computer that contains nothing but hard drives and you have a pretty good idea of what a NAS device looks like. NAS devices are the filing cabinets of the new millennium. They exist merely to store the huge amounts of data that network users generate.

(Bluetooth technology uses radio waves to transmit data over short distances.) PANs are wireless and work within the personal operating space of an individual, which is generally defined to be within 30 feet (or 10 meters) of one's body. Today, PANs free you from having wires running to and from the devices you're using. One day, though, PANs may use your body to transmit and receive signals.

What other sort of networks do businesses use? An **intranet** is a private network set up by an entity (such as a business, charity, or government organization) that is used exclusively by a select group of individuals (employees, customers, suppliers, volunteers, supporters, etc.). It can facilitate information sharing, database access, group scheduling, videoconferencing, and other employee collaborations. Intranets are deployed using Transmission Control Protocol/Internet Protocol (TCP/IP) networks (discussed in Chapter 13) and generally include links to the Internet. An intranet is not accessible by unauthorized individuals; a firewall (software or hardware used to prevent unauthorized entry) protects it from unauthorized access through the Internet.

One of the first main uses of intranets was to run groupware (software that enables users to share and collaborate on documents). One example, Lotus Notes, facilitates information sharing and solving problems through brainstorming. Most groupware programs also support messaging and group calendaring. Now, many organizations supplant groupware applications by deploying Web 2.0 tools such as blogs, wikis, and social networks on an intranet.

Microwaves

Microwaves

High-speed
Communications
Line

Satellite

High-speed
Communications
Line

Microwave Tower

Microwave Tower

Modem

Modem

Client Computer

Client Computer

Server

Server

Client Computer

Printer

Printer

Client Computer

LAN at
ABC Shoe Company
Beaverton, Oregon

LAN at
ABC Shoe Company
Hilversum, Netherlands

Figure 12.3

A WAN comprises several LANs in different geographic locations connected by telecommunications media. Satellite communication is often used to transmit data over long distances.

An area of an intranet that only certain corporations or individuals can access is called an **extranet**. The owner of an extranet decides who will be permitted to access it. For example, a company's customers and suppliers may be permitted to access information on the company's extranet. Extranets are useful for enabling electronic data interchange (EDI). EDI allows the exchange of large amounts of business data (such as orders for merchandise) in a standardized electronic format. Other uses of extranets include providing access to catalogs and inventory databases and sharing information among partners or industry trade groups.

What security tools do intranets and extranets use? Because of security concerns, intranets and extranets often use virtual private networks to keep information secure. A **virtual private network (VPN)**

uses the public Internet communications infrastructure to build a secure, private network among various locations. Although wide area networks (WANs) can be set up using private leased communications lines, these lines are expensive and tend to increase in price as the distance between points increases. VPNs use special security technologies and protocols that enhance security, enabling data to traverse the Internet as securely as if it were on a private leased line. Installing and configuring a VPN requires special hardware such as VPN-optimized routers and firewalls. In addition, VPN software must be installed on users' PCs.

The main technology for achieving a VPN is, in fact, called *tunneling*. In tunneling, data packets are placed inside other data packets. The format of these external data packets is encrypted and is understood only by the sending and receiving hardware, which is known as a *tunnel interface*. The hardware is optimized to seek efficient routes of transmission through the Internet. This provides a high level of security and makes information much more difficult to intercept and decrypt.

Imagine you have to deliver a message to a branch office. You could have one of your employees drive to the other office and deliver the message. But suppose he has to go through a bad neighborhood or has never been to the office before? The messenger could be waylaid by a carjacker or could become hopelessly lost. Using a VPN (as shown in Figure 12.4) is the equivalent of hiring a limousine and an armed guard to drive your employee through a private tunnel directly to the destination. Of course, a VPN avoids the enormous cost associated with this method!

Constructing Client/ Server Networks

In Chapter 7, we discussed the main components of peer-to-peer networks. Client/server networks have many of the same components that P2P networks do, as well as some components specific to client/ server networks:

- **Server:** Unlike peer-to-peer networks, client/server networks contain at least one computer that functions solely as a server.
- **Network topology:** Because client/server networks are more complex than peer-to-peer networks, the layout and

structure of the network, which is called the **network topology**, must be carefully planned.

- **Transmission media:** Data needs a way to flow between clients and servers on networks. Therefore, an appropriate type of transmission media (cable or wireless communications technology) based on the network topology is needed. Client/server networks use a wider variety of cable types than do simpler P2P networks.
- **Network operating system (NOS) software:** All client/server networks require network operating system (NOS) software, which is specialized software that is installed on servers and client computers and enables the network to function. Most modern operating systems (such as Windows 7, Windows Vista, and OS X) include the software computers need to function as clients on a network.
- **Network adapter:** As is the case with peer-to-peer networks, network adapters (or network interface cards) must be attached to or installed on each device on the network. These adapters enable a computer (or peripheral) to communicate with the network using common data communication language or protocol.

Figure 12.4

Local area networks (LANs) in different cities can communicate securely over the Internet using VPN technology.

- **Network navigation device:** Because of the complexity of a client/server network, specialized network navigation devices (such as routers, switches, and bridges) are needed to move data signals around the network.

Figure 12.5 shows the components of a simple client/server network. In the following sections, we will explore each component in more detail.

Servers

Servers are the workhorses of the client/server network. They interface with many different network users and assist them with a variety of tasks. The number and types of servers on a client/server network depend on the network's size and workload. Small networks (such as the one pictured in Figure 12.2) would have just one server to handle all server functions, such as file storage, delivery of applications to the clients, printing, and so on.

When more users are added to a network, dedicated servers are also added to reduce the load on the main server. A **dedicated server** is a server used to fulfill one specific function (such as handling e-mail). Once dedicated servers are deployed, the main server becomes merely an authentication server or a file server.

What are authentication and file servers? An **authentication server** is a server that keeps track of who is logging on to the network and which services on the network are available to each user. Authentication servers also act as overseers for the network. They manage and coordinate the services provided by any other dedicated servers located on the network. A **file server** is a server that stores and manages files for network users. On the network at your workplace or school, you may be provided with space on a file server to store files you create.

What functions do dedicated servers handle? Any task that is repetitive or demands a lot of time from the server's processor (CPU) is a good candidate to relegate to a dedicated server. Common types of dedicated servers are print servers, application servers, database servers, e-mail servers, communications servers, and Web servers. Servers are connected to a client/server network so that all client

Figure 12.5

The basic components of a typical client/server network.

Network interface card (NIC)
Installed in each client

Network interface card (NIC)
Installed in server

Client Computer #3

Cable (transmission media)

Client Computer #2

Switch (Network navigation device)

Server

Client Computer #1

Network operating software
Often included in operating system software for client computers

Network operating software
Installed on server

Client Computer #1

Client Computer #2

Client Computer #3

Print server

Laser printer 1

Laser printer 2

Database server

Switch

Authentication/
file server

Web server

Communication
server

INTERNET

Application
server

E-mail server

Figure 12.6

This is a typical large-scale client/server network with several dedicated servers installed.

computers that need to use their services can access them, as shown in Figure 12.6.

Print Servers

How does a print server function?
Printing is a function that takes a large quantity of central processing unit (CPU) time and that most people do quite often. Setting up a **print server** to manage all client-requested printing jobs for all printers on the network helps client computers to complete more productive work by relieving them of printing duties. When you tell your computer to print a document, it passes off the task to the print server. This frees the CPU on your computer to do other jobs.

When the print server receives a job (a printing request) from a client computer, it puts the job into a print queue on the print server. A **print queue** is a software holding area for printing jobs. Normally, each printer on a network has its own uniquely named print queue. Jobs receive a number when they enter the queue and go to the printer in the order in which they were received. Print queues thus function like the "take a

number" machines at a supermarket deli. Thus, print servers organize print jobs into an orderly sequence to make printing more efficient on a shared printer. Another useful aspect of print servers is that network administrators can set them to prioritize print jobs. Different users and types of print jobs can be assigned different priorities so higher-priority jobs will be printed first. For instance, in a company in which documents are printed on demand for clients, you would want these print jobs to take precedence over routine employee correspondence.

Application Servers

What function does an application server perform?
In many networks, all users run the same application software (such as Microsoft Office) on their computers. In a network of thousands of personal computers, installing application software on each individual computer is time consuming. An **application server** acts as a repository for application software.

When a client computer connects to the network and requests an application, the application server delivers the software to the client computer. Because the software does not reside on the client computer itself, this eases the task of installation and upgrading. The application needs to be installed or upgraded only on the application server, not on each network client.

Database Servers

What does a database server do? As its name implies, a **database server** provides client computers with access to information stored in a database. Often, many people need to access a database at the same time. For example, multiple college advisors can serve students at the same time because the advisors all have access to the student information database. This is made possible because the database resides on a database server that each advisor's computer can access through the network. If the database were on a stand-alone computer instead of a network, only one advisor could use it at a time, making the process of serving students terribly inefficient.

E-mail Servers

When is an e-mail server necessary? The volume of e-mail on a large network could quickly overwhelm a server that was attempting to handle other functions as well. The sole function of an **e-mail server** is to process and deliver incoming and outgoing e-mail. On a network with an e-mail server, when you send an e-mail from your computer, it goes to the e-mail server, which then handles the routing and delivery of your message. The e-mail server functions much like a postal carrier, who picks up your mail and sees that it finds its way to the correct destination.

Communications Servers

What types of communications does a communications server handle? A **communications server** handles all communications between the network and other networks, including managing Internet connectivity. All requests for information from the Internet and all messages being sent through the Internet pass through the communications server. Because Internet traffic is substantial at most organizations, the communications server has a heavy workload.

The communications server often is the only device on the network connected to the Internet. E-mail servers, Web servers, and other devices needing to communicate with the Internet usually route all their traffic through the communications server. Providing a single point of contact with the outside world makes it easier to secure the network from hackers.

Web Servers

What function does a Web server perform? A **Web server** is used to host a Web site so it will be available through the Internet. Web servers run specialized software such as Apache (open source server software) and Microsoft Internet Information Services (IIS) that enable them to host Web pages. Not every large network has a Web server. Many colleges and businesses use an Internet service provider (ISP) to host their Web sites instead.

Network Topologies

Just as buildings have different floor plans depending on their uses, networks have different blueprints denoting their layout. *Network topology* refers to the physical or logical arrangement of computers, transmission media (cable), and other network components. *Physical topology* refers to the layout of the "real" components of the network, whereas *logical topology* refers to the virtual connections among network nodes. Logical topologies usually are determined by network protocols instead of the physical layout of the network or the paths electrical signals follow on the network.

Because networks have different uses, not all networks have the same topology. For example, assume that your class has to send a message to the class next door. You decide to arrange your class in a straight line from your classroom to the other classroom. Each student will whisper the message to the next student in the line until the message is eventually passed to a student in the other classroom. The arrangement of the students in a straight line is the topology. The passing of the message from student to student using the English language is the protocol.

In this section, we will explore the most common network topologies (bus, ring, and star) and discuss when each topology is used. As you'll see, the type of network topology used is important because it can affect a network's performance and scalability. Knowing how the basic topologies work, and the strengths and weaknesses of each one, will help you understand why particular network topologies were chosen on the networks you use.

Bus Topology

What does a bus topology look like?

In a **bus** (or **linear bus**) **topology**, all computers are connected in sequence on a single cable, as shown in Figure 12.7. This topology was deployed most often in peer-to-peer networks (not client/server networks). It has largely become legacy technology due to the decreased cost of Ethernet networks

(which use a star topology). Each computer on the bus network can communicate directly with every other computer on the network. A limitation of bus networks is that data collisions can occur easily if two computers transmit data at the same, because a bus network is essentially composed of one main communication medium (a single cable).

Think of a data collision as having a group of three people (e.g., Emily, Reesa, and Luis) sitting in a room having a conversation. For the conversation to be effective, only one person can speak at a time; otherwise, they would not be able to hear and understand each other. Therefore, if Emily is speaking, Reesa and Luis must wait until she finishes before presenting their ideas, and so on.

Because two signals transmitted at the same time on a bus network may cause a data collision, an **access method** has to be established to control which computer is allowed to use the transmission media at a certain time. Computers on a bus network behave like a group of people having a conversation. The computers "listen" to the network data traffic on the media. When no other computer is transmitting data (that is, when the "conversation" stops), the

Figure 12.7

A linear bus topology.

A cable break here cuts off Computer #1 and Computer #2 from peripherals

Computer #1

Computer #4

Computer #3

Terminator

Terminator

Computer #2

Laser printer

Scanner

SOUND BYTE

Network Topology and Navigation Devices

In this Sound Byte, you'll learn about common network topologies, the types of networks they are used with, and various network navigation devices.

computer knows it is allowed to transmit data on the media. This means of taking turns "talking" prevents **data collisions**, which happen when two computers send data at the same time and the sets of data collide somewhere in the media. When data collides, it is often lost or irreparably damaged.

How does data get from point to point on a bus network? When it is safe to send data (that is, when no other computers are transmitting data), the sending computer broadcasts the data onto the media. The data is broadcast throughout the network to all devices connected to the network. The data is broken into small segments, each called a **packet**. Each packet contains the address of the computer or peripheral device to which it is being sent. Each computer or device connected to the network listens for data that contains its address. When it "hears" data addressed to it, it takes the data off the media and processes it.

For example, say your computer needs to print something on the printer attached to the network. Your computer "listens" to the network to ensure no other nodes are transmitting. It then sends the print job out onto the network. When the printer "hears" a job addressed to it (here, the print job your computer just sent), it pulls the data off the network and executes the job.

The devices (nodes) attached to a bus network do nothing to move data along the network. This makes a bus network a **passive topology**. The data travels the entire length of the medium and is received by all network devices. The ends of the cable in a bus network are capped off by terminators (as shown in Figure 12.7). A **terminator** is a device that absorbs a signal so that it is not reflected back onto parts of the network that have already received it.

> **"What are the advantages and disadvantages of bus networks?"**

What are the advantages and disadvantages of bus networks?

Its simplicity and low cost were the major reasons bus network topology was deployed most often in P2P networks. The major disadvantage is that if there is a break in the cable, the bus network is effectively disrupted, because some computers are cut off from others on the network. Only one computer can communicate at a time, so adding a large number of nodes to a bus network limits performance and causes delays in sending data. Because Ethernet networks don't suffer from these limitations, you rarely see bus topologies today.

Ring Topology

What does a ring topology look like? Not surprisingly, given its name, the computers and peripherals in a **ring** (or **loop**) **topology** are laid out in a configuration resembling a circle, as shown in Figure 12.8. Data flows around the circle from device to device in one direction only. Because data is passed using a special data packet called a **token**, this type of topology is commonly called a *token-ring topology*. The original token-ring networks could achieve a **data transfer rate** (bandwidth) of either 4 Mbps or 16 Mbps, but more recent token technologies can deliver speeds as high as 100 Mbps.

How does a token move data around a ring? A token is passed from computer to computer around the ring until it is grabbed by a computer that needs to transmit data. The computer "holds onto" the token until it has finished transmitting data. Only one computer on the ring can "hold" the token at a time, and usually only one token exists on each ring.

If a node (a computer or device) has data to send, such as a document that needs to go to the printer, it waits for the token to be passed to it. The node then takes the token out of circulation and sends the data to its destination. When the receiving node receives a complete transmission of the data (in this example, when the document is received by the printer), it transmits an

Step 1: Token travels around ring until a computer needs to transmit data.

Step 2: Computer #2 needs to print and grabs token.

Computer #1

Computer #4

Token Ring

Step 4: Cable break stops movement of token and data transmission.

Computer #2

Computer #3

Step 3: Computer #2 completes transmission and releases token.

Printer

Scanner

Figure 12.8
A ring topology.

acknowledgment to the sending node. The sending node then generates a new token and starts it going around the ring again. This is called the **token method** and is the access method ring networks use to avoid data collisions.

A ring topology is an **active topology** because each node on the network is responsible for retransmitting the token or the data to the next node on the ring. Large ring networks have the capability to use multiple tokens to help move more data faster.

Is a ring topology better than a bus topology? A ring topology provides a fairer allocation of network resources than

does a bus topology. By using a token, a ring network enables all nodes on the network to have an equal chance to send data. One "chatty" node cannot monopolize the network bandwidth as easily as in a bus topology because it must pass the token on after sending a batch of data. In addition, a ring topology's performance will remain acceptable even with large numbers of users.

One disadvantage of a ring network is that if one computer fails, it can bring the entire network to a halt because that computer is unavailable to retransmit tokens and data. Another disadvantage is that problems in the ring can be hard for network administrators to find. It's easier to expand a ring topology than a bus topology, but adding a node to a ring does cause the ring to cease to function while the node is installed.

Star Topology

What is the layout for a star topology?

A **star topology** is the most widely deployed client/server network layout in homes and businesses today because it offers the most flexibility for a low price. In a star topology, the nodes connect to a central communications device called a *switch* in a pattern resembling a star, as shown in Figure 12.9. The switch receives a signal from the sending node and retransmits it to all other nodes on the network. Each network node examines the data and picks up only the transmissions addressed to it. Because the switch retransmits data

signals, a star topology is an active topology. (We discuss switches in more detail later in this chapter.) The only drawback is that if the switch fails, the network no longer functions. However, it is relatively easy to replace a switch.

Many star networks use the Ethernet protocol. Networks using the Ethernet protocol are by far the most common type of network in use today.

Although many students think that Ethernet is a type of network topology, it is actually a communications protocol. A topology is a physical design of a network, whereas a **protocol** is a set of rules for exchanging communication. Therefore, an Ethernet network could be set up using a bus, a ring, or a star topology. The original Ethernet networks achieved maximum data transfer rates of 10 Mbps. However, newer equipment for the home delivers 1-gigabit transfer rates at affordable prices. For

Figure 12.9

In a star topology, network nodes are connected through a central switch to form a star shape.

A cable break here means Computer #1 cannot communicate with the network. However, all other computers and devices can still communicate with each other.

businesses that need even more speed, the 10-gigabit standard supports a transfer rate of up to 10 Gbps, but the equipment supporting this standard is still relatively expensive and therefore small businesses do not use it unless very high bandwidth is required.

How do computers on a star network avoid data collisions?

Because most star networks are Ethernet networks, they use the method used on all Ethernet networks to avoid data collisions: **CSMA/CD** (short for *carrier sense multiple access with collision detection*). With CSMA/CD, a node connected to the network uses carrier sense (that is, it "listens") to verify that no other nodes are currently transmitting data signals. If the node doesn't hear any other signals, it assumes that it is safe to transmit data. All devices on the network have the same right (that is, they have multiple access) to transmit data when they deem it safe. It is therefore possible for two devices to begin transmitting data signals at the same time. If this happens, the two signals collide.

What happens when the signals collide?

As shown in Figure 12.10, when two nodes (Computer #1 and Computer #4) begin transmitting data signals at the same time, signals collide, and a node on the network (Computer #3) detects the collision (Step 1). That node (Computer #3) then sends a special signal called a **jam signal**

Figure 12.10

Avoiding data collisions on an Ethernet network.

Computer #1   Computer #2   Computer #3   Computer #4

Signal #1   Collision Detected   Signal #4

Collision!

Signal #1   Signal #4

Step 1: When two nodes transmit simultaneous data signals, a data collision occurs and is detected.

Computer #1   Computer #2   Computer #3   Computer #4

Jam Signal   Jam Signal   Jam Signal Sent   Jam Signal

Jam Signal   Jam Signal   Jam Signal

Step 2: The detecting node sends a jam signal.

Computer #1   Computer #2   Computer #3   Computer #4

Retransmit Signal #1   Retransmit Signal #4

Step 3: The two nodes that sent simultaneous data signals retransmit their signals after a random amount of time.

14 nanoseconds later   18 nanoseconds later

to all network nodes, alerting them that a collision has occurred (Step 2). The original nodes (Computer #1 and Computer #4) then stop transmitting and wait a random amount of time before retransmitting their data signals (Step 3). The wait times need to be random; otherwise, both nodes would start retransmitting at the same time and another collision would occur.

What are the advantages and disadvantages of a star topology? The main reason a star topology generally is considered to be superior to a ring topology is that if one computer on a star topology fails, it doesn't affect the rest of the network. This is extremely important in a large network in which having one disabled computer affect the operations of several hundred other computers would be unacceptable.

Another advantage is that it is easy to add nodes to star networks. Furthermore, performance remains acceptable even with large numbers of users. In addition, centralizing communications through a switch makes troubleshooting and repairs on star networks easier for network technicians. Technicians can usually pinpoint a communications problem just by examining the switch, as opposed to searching for a particular length of cable that broke in a ring network.

The disadvantage of star networks used to be cost. Because of the complexity of the layout of star networks, they require more cable and used to be more expensive than bus or ring networks. Because the price of cable has fallen, this has ceased to be a barrier in most cases.

Comparing Topologies

Which topology is the best one? Figure 12.11 lists the advantages and disadvantages of bus, ring, and star topologies. Star topologies are the most common, mainly because large networks are constantly adding new users. The ability to add new users simply—by installing a new switch—without affecting users already on the network is the deciding factor. The networks you'll encounter at school and in the workplace will almost certainly be laid out in a star topology. Bus topologies have become all but extinct now that most home networks utilize a star topology. Ring topologies are still popular in certain businesses where fair allocation of network access is a major requirement of the network.

Can topologies be combined within a single network? Because each topology has its own unique advantages, topologies are often combined to construct business networks. Combining multiple topologies into one network is known as constructing a **hybrid topology**. For instance, fair allocation of resources may be critical for reservation clerks at an airline (thereby requiring a ring network), but the airline's purchasing department may require a star topology. One disadvantage of hybrid topologies is that hardware changes must

Figure 12.11 | ADVANTAGES AND DISADVANTAGES OF BUS, RING, AND STAR TOPOLOGIES

Topology	Advantages	Disadvantages
Bus	It uses a minimal amount of cable. Installation is easy, reliable, and inexpensive.	Breaks in the cable can disable the network. Large numbers of users will greatly decrease performance because of high volumes of data traffic.
Ring	Allocates access to the network fairly. Performance remains acceptable even with large numbers of users.	Adding or removing nodes disables the network. Failure of one computer can bring down the entire network. Problems in data transmission can sometimes be difficult to find.
Star	Failure of one computer does not affect other computers on the network. Centralized design simplifies troubleshooting and repairs. High scalability: adding computers or groups of computers as needed is easy. Performance remains acceptable even with large numbers of users.	Requires more cable (and possibly higher installation costs) than a bus or ring topology. The switch is a single point of failure. If it fails, all computers connected to that switch are affected.

usually be made to switch a node from one topology to another.

Transmission Media

A variety of building materials are available for constructing a house; the ones chosen will depend on the needs of the builder. Similarly, when building a network, network engineers can use different types of media. **Transmission media**, whether for cable or wireless communications technology, comprise the routes data takes to flow between devices on the network. Without transmission media, network devices would be unable to communicate.

Wired Transmission Media

What types of cable are commonly used for networks? In Chapter 7, you learned that most home networks use either twisted-pair cable (phone wire or Ethernet) or electrical wires as transmission media. For business networks, the three main cable types that are used today are twisted pair, coaxial, and fiber optic.

What are the important factors in choosing a cable type? Although each cable type is different, the same criteria always need to be considered when choosing a cable type:

- **Maximum run length:** Each type of cable has a maximum run length over which signals sent across it can be "heard" by devices connected to it. Therefore, when designing a network, network engineers must accurately measure the distances between devices to ensure that they select an appropriate cable.
- **Bandwidth:** As you learned in earlier chapters, **bandwidth** is the amount of data that can be transmitted across a transmission medium in a certain amount of time. Each cable is different and is rated by the maximum bandwidth it can support. Bandwidth is measured in bits per second, which represents how many bits of data can be transmitted along the cable each second.
- **Bend radius (flexibility):** When installing cable, it is often necessary to bend the cable around corners, surfaces, and so on. The bend radius of the cable

defines how many degrees a cable can be bent in a one-foot segment before it is damaged. If many corners need to be navigated when installing a network, network engineers use cabling with a high bend radius.

- **Cable cost:** The cost per foot of different types and grades of cable varies widely. Cable selection may have to be made based on cost if adequate funds are not available for the optimal type of cabling.
- **Installation costs:** Certain types of cable (such as twisted pair) are easy and inexpensive to install. Fiber-optic cable requires special training and equipment to install, which increases the installation costs.
- **Susceptibility to interference:** Signals traveling down a cable are subject to two types of interference. Electromagnetic interference (EMI), caused when the cable is exposed to strong electromagnetic fields, can distort or degrade signals on the cable. Fluorescent lights and machinery with motors or transformers are the most common sources of EMI emissions. Cable signals also can be disrupted by radio frequency interference (RFI), which is usually caused by broadcast sources

BITS AND BYTES — Vi-Fi—Wi-Fi for Those on the Move!

With the proliferation of portable computing devices, demand for connectivity is increasing exponentially. To meet the demand, technologies such as Wi-Fi are now deployed even in moving vehicles. Numerous cities in the United States, including San Francisco, California; Cincinnati, Ohio; and Austin, Texas offer Wi-Fi connectivity on city buses. Initiatives like Aspirnaut, in Kentucky, provide rural children with school bus rides in excess of one hour with free Wi-Fi access and computing devices to use while riding the bus. However, Wi-Fi connectivity is tricky to achieve while on the move because you can connect to only one wireless access point at a time, and the access points have limited range. As you drive along and get out of range, you need to change to other access points. As you switch from one access point to another, connectivity speeds drop dramatically or connectivity is lost altogether.

A joint initiative among the University of Massachusetts, the University of Washington, and Microsoft may be close to solving the problem. They have developed a new technology called Vehicle Wi-Fi (Vi-Fi), which allows a device to connect to more than one access point at the same time. The software your device runs determines which access point has the best signal strength and sends data packets through it. By connecting with multiple access points at once, it makes switching from point to point less likely to sever your Internet connection. Perhaps you'll be able to take advantage of Vi-Fi in the next new car you buy, and your passengers can surf effortlessly while you whiz along at 55 miles per hour!

(television and radio signals) located near the network. Cable types are rated as to how well they resist interference.

- **Signal transmission methods:** Both coaxial cable and twisted-pair cable send electrical impulses down conductive material to transmit data signals. Fiber-optic cable transmits data signals as pulses of light.

In the sections that follow, we will discuss the characteristics of each of the three major types of cable. We will also discuss the use of wireless media as an alternative to cable.

Twisted-Pair Cable

What does twisted-pair cable look like? Twisted-pair cable should be familiar to you because the telephone cable (or wire) in your home is one type of twisted-pair cable. **Twisted-pair cable** consists of pairs of copper wires twisted around each other and covered by a protective sheath (jacket). The twists are important because they cause the magnetic fields that form around the copper wires to intermingle, which makes them less susceptible to outside interference. The twists also reduce the amount of crosstalk interference (the tendency of signals on one wire to interfere with signals on a wire next to it).

If the twisted-pair cable contains a layer of foil shielding to reduce interference, it is known as **shielded twisted-pair (STP) cable**. If it does not contain a layer of foil shielding, it is known as **unshielded twisted-pair (UTP) cable**. This type is more susceptible to interference. Figure 12.12

shows illustrations of both types of twisted-pair cable. Because of its lower price, UTP is more widely used, unless significant sources of interference must be overcome (such as in a production environment where machines create magnetic fields).

What types of UTP cable are available? There are different standard categories of UTP cable from which to choose. The two most common types of UTP cable in use today are Category 5E (Cat 5E) and Category 6 (Cat 6). Cat 6 cable can handle a bandwidth of 1 gigabit per second (Gbps), whereas Cat 5E can handle a bandwidth of just 200 megabits per second (Mbps).

Unless severe budget constraints are in place, network engineers usually install the highest-bandwidth cable possible because reinstalling cable later (which often requires tearing up walls and ceilings) can be very expensive. Therefore, since the fall of 2002, when the standard for Cat 6 cable was approved, new cable runs in businesses have been made with Cat 6 cable. Home networks that use twisted-pair cable generally use Cat 5E cable because it's less expensive. (Most homes don't need gigabit networks.)

Coaxial Cable

What does coaxial cable look like? **Coaxial cable** should be familiar to you if you have cable television, because most cable television installers use coaxial cable. Coaxial cable (as shown in Figure 12.13) consists of four main components:

1. The core (usually copper) is in the very center and is used for transmitting the signal.

2. A solid layer of nonconductive insulating material (usually a hard, thick plastic) surrounds the core.

3. A layer of braided metal shielding covers the insulation to reduce interference with signals traveling in the core.

4. An external jacket of lightweight plastic covers the internal cable components to protect them from damage.

Figure 12.12

Anatomy of (a) unshielded twisted pair (UTP) cable and (b) shielded twisted pair (STP) cable.

Twisted pairs of copper wires

Protective sheath

Protective sheath

Foil shielding

Twisted pairs of copper wires

Although coaxial cable used to be the most widely used cable in business networks, advances in twisted-pair cable shielding and transmission speeds, as well as twisted pair's lower cost, have reduced the popularity of coaxial cable.

Fiber-Optic Cable

What does fiber-optic cable look like? As shown in Figure 12.14, the core of **fiber-optic cable** is composed of a glass (or plastic) fiber (or a bundle of fibers) where the data is transmitted. A protective layer of glass or plastic cladding is wrapped around the core to protect it. Finally, for additional protection, an outer jacket (sheath) is added, often made of a durable material such as Kevlar (the substance used to make bulletproof vests). Data transmissions can pass through fiber-optic cable in only one direction. Therefore, at least two cores are located in most fiber-optic cables to enable transmission of data in both directions.

How does fiber-optic cable differ from twisted-pair and coaxial cable? As we noted earlier, the main difference between fiber-optic cable and other types of cable is the method of signal transmission. Twisted-pair and coaxial cable use copper wire to conduct electrical impulses. In a fiber-optic cable, electrical data signals from network devices (client computers, peripherals, and so on) are converted to light pulses before they are transmitted. Because EMI and RFI do not affect light waves, fiber-optic cable is virtually immune to interference.

Wireless Media Options

What wireless media options are there? Although the word *wireless* implies "no wires," in businesses, **wireless media** are usually add-ons that extend or improve access to a wired network. In the corporate environment, wireless access is often provided to give employees a wider working area. For instance, if conference rooms offer wireless access, employees can bring their notebooks (laptops) to meetings and gain access to the network during the meeting. However, when they go back to their offices, they may connect to the network through a wired connection. Accordingly, corporate networks are often a combination of wired and wireless media.

Are there standards defined for wireless communication? As you learned in earlier chapters, wireless devices must use the same communications standard to communicate with each other. Wireless networks in the United States are currently based on the **802.11 standard**, also known as **Wi-Fi**, established by the Institute of Electrical and Electronics Engineers (IEEE). Wireless devices attached to networks using the 802.11 standard communicate with each other using radio waves.

The 802.11 standard is actually divided into a number of separate standards. The 802.11g standard was the most common standard in use until recently. With a maximum **throughput** (bandwidth) of 54 Mbps and a low cost, 802.11g devices were quickly adopted by consumers and businesses. However, the new 802.11n standard supports throughput up to 600 Mbps (although current devices achieve bandwidths of approximately 300 Mbps) and greatly increases the range of wireless signals. This makes it an ideal choice for providing wireless coverage over an entire office or large house, or in environments where large data files (such as video) are being transmitted wirelessly.

Figure 12.13

Coaxial cable consists of four main components: the core, an insulated covering, a braided metal shielding, and a plastic jacket.

Figure 12.14

Fiber-optic cable is made up of a glass or plastic fiber (or a bundle of fibers), a glass or plastic cladding, and a protective sheath.

The OSI Model: Defining Protocol Standards

The Institute of Electrical and Electronics Engineers (IEEE) has taken the lead in establishing recognized worldwide networking protocols, including a standard of communications called the Open Systems Interconnection (OSI) reference model. The OSI model, which has been adopted as a standard throughout the computing world, provides the protocol guidelines for all modern networks. All modern network operating system (NOS) protocols are designed to interact in accordance with the standards set out in the OSI model.

The OSI model divides communications tasks into seven distinct processes called layers. Each layer of an OSI network has a specific function and knows how to communicate with the layers above and below it. Figure 12.15 shows the layers of the OSI model and their functions.

This layering approach makes communications more efficient because specialized pieces of the NOS perform specific tasks. The layering approach is akin to assembly-line manufacturing. Producing thousands of cars per day would be difficult if one person had to build a car on his or her own. However, by splitting up the work of assembling a car into specialized tasks (such as installing the engine or bolting on the bumpers) and assigning them to people who perform exceptionally well at certain tasks, greater efficiency is achieved. This is how the OSI layers work. By handling specialized tasks and communicating only with the layers above and below them, OSI layers make communications more efficient.

Let's look at how each OSI layer functions by following an e-mail you create and send to your friend:

- **Application layer:** Handles all interaction between the application software and the network. It translates the data from the application into a format that the presentation layer can understand. For example, when you send an e-mail, the application layer takes the e-mail message you created in Microsoft Outlook, translates it into a format your network can understand, and passes it to the presentation layer.
- **Presentation layer:** Reformats the data so that the session layer can understand it. It also handles data encryption (changing the data into a format that makes it harder to intercept and read the message) and compression, if required. In our e-mail example, the presentation layer notices that you selected an encryption option for the e-mail message and encrypts the data before sending it to the session layer.

- **Session layer:** Sets up a virtual (not physical) connection between the sending and receiving devices. It then manages the communication between the two. In our e-mail example, the session layer would set up the parameters for the communications session between your computer and the Internet service provider (ISP) where your friend has her e-mail account. The session layer then tracks the transmission of the e-mail until it is satisfied that all the data in the e-mail was received at your friend's ISP.
- **Transport layer:** Breaks up the data into packets and sequences them appropriately. It also handles acknowledgment of packets (that is, it determines whether the packets were received at their destination) and decides whether packets need to be sent again. In our e-mail example, the transport layer breaks up your e-mail message into packets and sends them to the network layer, making sure that all the packets reach their destination.
- **Network layer:** Determines where to send the packets on the network and identifies the best way to route them there. In our e-mail example, the network layer examines the address on the packets (the address of your friend's ISP) and determines how to route the packets so they get to your ISP and can ultimately get to the receiving computer.
- **Data link layer:** Responsible for assembling the data packets into frames (a type of data packet that holds more data), addressing the frames, and delivering them to the physical layer so they can be sent on their way. It is the equivalent of a postal worker who reads the address on a piece of mail and makes sure it is sent to the proper recipient. In our e-mail example, the data link layer assembles the e-mail data packets into frames, which are addressed with appropriate routing information that it receives from the network layer.
- **Physical layer:** Takes care of delivering the data. It converts the data into a signal and transmits it over the network so that it can reach its intended address. In our e-mail example, the physical layer sends the data over the Internet to its ultimate destination (your friend's ISP).

By following standardized protocols set forth by the OSI model, NOS software can communicate happily with the computers and peripherals attached to the network as well as with other networks.

Figure 12.15 | LAYERS OF THE OSI MODEL AND THEIR FUNCTIONS

Application layer	Handles all interfaces between the application software and the network Translates user information into a format the presentation layer can understand
Presentation layer	Reformats data so that the session layer can understand it. Compresses and encrypts data
Session layer	Sets up a virtual (not physical) connection between the sending and receiving devices. Manages communications sessions
Transport layer	Creates packets and handles packet acknowledgment
Network layer	Determines where to send the packets on the network
Data link layer	Assembles the data into frames, addresses them, and sends them to the physical layer for delivery
Physical layer	Transmits (delivers) data on the network so it can reach its intended address

Comparing Transmission Media

So who decides which medium is best for client/server networks?

Network engineers specialize in the design and deployment of networks and are responsible for selecting network topology and media types. Their decision as to which transmission medium a network will use is based on the topology selected, the length of the cable runs needed, the amount of interference present, and the need for wireless connectivity. Coaxial cable has been made largely obsolete by advances in twisted-pair cabling throughput and decreases in its cost.

Figure 12.16 compares the attributes of the major cable types. Most large networks have a mix of media. For example, fiber-optic cable may be appropriate for the portion of the network that traverses the factory floor, where interference from magnetic fields is significant. However, unshielded twisted-pair cable may work fine in the general office area. Wireless media may be required in conference rooms and other areas where employees are likely to connect their notebooks or where it is impractical or expensive to run cable.

Network Operating Systems

Merely using media to connect computers and peripherals does not create a client/server network. Special software known as a **network operating system (NOS)** needs to be installed on each client computer and server connected to the network to provide the services necessary for them to communicate. Many modern operating systems, such as Windows 7, Windows Vista, and Mac OS X, include NOS client software as part of the basic installation. However, if your operating system does not include NOS client software, it must be installed on each client. The NOS provides a set of common rules (a protocol) that controls communication among devices on the network. The major NOSs on the market today include Windows Server 2008, Linux, UNIX, and Novell SUSE Linux Enterprise.

Do peer-to-peer networks need special NOS software?

The software that P2P networks require is built into the Windows and Macintosh operating systems. Therefore, if you have a simple P2P network, there is no need to purchase specialized NOS software. When a peer-to-peer network won't suffice (such as in a network with more than 10 computers), you can't use the networking software included in Windows and Mac OS X. Instead, you will need to purchase additional NOS software.

How does NOS software differ from operating system software?

Operating system (OS) software is designed to facilitate communication between the software and hardware components of your computer. NOS software is specifically designed to provide server services, network communications, management of network peripherals, and storage. To provide network communications, the client computer must run a small part of the NOS in addition to the OS. Windows 7 is an OS and is installed on home computers. As noted above, because it also has some NOS functionality, client computers (in a client/server network) that have Windows 7 installed as the OS do not need an additional NOS. Windows Server 2008 is a NOS that is deployed on servers in a client/server network.

How does the NOS control network communications?

Each NOS has its own proprietary communications language, file management structure, and device management structure. The NOS also sets and controls the protocols (rules) for all devices wishing to communicate on the network. Many different proprietary networking protocols exist, such as Novell Internetwork Packet Exchange (IPX), Microsoft NetBIOS Extended User Interface (NetBEUI), and the

Figure 12.16 │ CHARACTERISTICS OF MAJOR CABLE TYPES

Cable Characteristics	Twisted Pair (Cat 6)	Fiber-Optic
Maximum run length	328 feet (100 m)	Up to 62 miles (100 km)
Bandwidth	1,000 Mbps	100 Mbps to 2 Gbps
Bend radius (flexibility)	No limit	30 degrees/foot
Cable cost	Extremely low	High
Installation cost	Extremely low	Most expensive because of installation training required
Susceptibility to interference	High	None (not susceptible to EMI or RFI)

Apple File Protocol (AFP). These protocols were developed for a specific vendor's operating system. For example, IPX was developed for networks running the Novell NOS. Proprietary protocols such as these do not work with another vendor's NOS.

However, because the Internet uses an open protocol (called TCP/IP) for communications, many corporate networks use TCP/IP as their standard networking protocol regardless of the manufacturer of their NOS. All modern NOSs support TCP/IP. (We discuss TCP/IP in more detail in Chapter 13.)

Can a network use two different NOSs? Many large corporate networks use several different NOSs at the same time. This is because different NOSs provide different features, some of which are more useful in certain situations than others are. For instance, although the employees of a corporation may be using a Microsoft Windows environment for their desktops and e-mail, the file servers and Web servers may be running a Linux NOS.

Because NOSs use different internal software languages to communicate, one NOS can't communicate directly with another. However, if both NOSs are using the same protocol (such as TCP/IP), they can pass information between the networks and it can be interpreted by the receiving network.

Figure 12.17

A NIC is responsible for breaking down data into packets, preparing packets for transmission, receiving incoming data packets, and reconstructing them.

Network Adapters

As we noted in Chapter 7, client computers and peripherals need an interface to connect with and communicate on the network. **Network adapters** are devices that perform specific tasks to enable computers to communicate on a network. Most network adapters are installed *inside* computers and peripherals as expansion cards. These adapters are referred to as network interface cards (NICs).

Although you could use network adapters that plug into universal serial bus (USB) ports on a client/server network, most network adapters are NICs. That's because they are less susceptible to damage than external adapters are.

What do network adapters do? Network adapters such as NICs perform three critical functions:

1. **They generate high-powered signals to enable network transmissions.** Digital signals generated inside the computer are fairly low powered and would not travel well on network media (cable or wireless technology) without network adapters. Network adapters convert the signals from inside the computer to higher-powered signals that have no trouble traversing the network media.

2. **They are responsible for breaking the data into packets and preparing the packets for transmission across the network.** They also are responsible for receiving incoming data packets and, in accordance with networking protocols (rules), reconstructing them, as shown in Figure 12.17.

3. **They act as gatekeepers for information flowing to and from the client computer.** Much like a security guard

Step 1: You request information from network database.

Step 2: NIC breaks request into packages and sends packets to server.

Request packet #1

Server

Request packet #2

Response packet #1

Request packet #3

Response packet #2

Network interface card

Your computer (client)

Step 4: NIC reassembles response packets and displays information on your screen.

Step 3: Server executes request, assembles response into package, and sends packets to client.

in a gated community, a network adapter is responsible for permitting or denying access to the client computer (the community) and controlling the flow of data (visitors).

You should note that there will not always be the same number of response packets as there are request packets. The number of packets depends on the volume of the data being sent. A simple response may have less data than a complex one.

Are there different types of network adapters? Although there are different types of network adapters, almost without exception, Ethernet (either wired or wireless) is the standard communications protocol used on most current networks. Therefore, the adapter cards that ship with computers today are Ethernet compliant. The majority of Ethernet adapters provide connection ports that accept RJ-45 (Ethernet) connector plugs for connection to twisted-pair cable. However, adapters that provide other types of connectors for direct connections to other types of network media (such as fiber-optic cables) are available.

Do wireless networks require network adapters? Most corporate networks are not entirely wireless, but they do provide wireless connectivity to some computers and to portable devices such as smartphones. A computer that connects to the network using wireless access needs to have a special network adapter card, called a **wireless network interface card (wireless NIC)**, installed in the system unit. Unlike wired NICs, wireless NICs don't connect to the network with cables. Instead, the network must be fitted with devices called wireless access points. A **wireless access point (WAP)** gives wireless devices a sending and receiving connection point to the network.

Figure 12.18 shows an example of a typical corporate network with a wireless access point. The access point is connected to the wired network through a conventional cable. As we discussed in Chapter 7, when a notebook (or other device with a wireless NIC) is powered on near a wireless access point, it establishes a connection with the access point using radio waves. Many devices can communicate with the network through a single wireless access point.

Do network adapters require software? Because the network adapter is responsible for communications between the client computer and the network, it needs to speak the same language as the network's special operating system software. Therefore, special communications software called a **device driver** is installed on all client computers in the client/server network. Device drivers enable the network adapter to communicate with the server's operating system and with the operating system of the computer in which the adapter is installed.

Figure 12.18

This small corporate network has an added wireless access point.

Desktop computer

Cat 6 cable

Server

Notebook computer with wireless NIC

Switch

Smartphone with wireless NIC

Radio waves

Wireless access point

What are my options if I'm not located in range of a wireless network? You can bring your own wireless network with you! Most cellular telephone companies, such as AT&T and Sprint, offer broadband PC adapters for your notebook that will keep you connected (for a fee, of course). A PC adapter plugs into a USB port on your notebook and enables it to send and receive data using your cellular provider's wireless network. Broadband download speeds now can reach a respectable 3.5 Mbps, making this a viable option if you need to ensure you have connectivity everywhere you go—or virtually everywhere. Check with the cellular provider to ensure they have coverage in most places you will travel through.

Network Navigation Devices

Earlier in this chapter, you learned that to flow through the network, data is broken into small segments called packets. Data packets are like postal letters. They don't get to their destinations without some help. In this section, we explore the various conventions and devices that help speed data packets on their way through the network.

Mac Addresses

How do data packets know where to go on the network? Each network adapter has a physical address similar to a serial number on an appliance. This is called a **media access control (MAC) address**, and it is made up of six two-position characters such as 01:40:87:44:79:A5. (Don't confuse this MAC with the Apple computers of the same name.) The first three sets of characters (in this case, 01:40:87) specify the manufacturer of the network adapter,

SOUND BYTE

What's My IP Address? (And Other Interesting Facts about Networks)

In this Sound Byte, you'll learn how to determine your IP address, which is commonly required to set up online gaming. You'll also explore several Web sites that can reveal interesting information about your connection to the Internet.

whereas the second set of characters (in this case, 44:79:A5) makes up a unique address. Because all MAC addresses must be unique, there is an IEEE committee responsible for allocating blocks of numbers to network adapter manufacturers.

Are MAC addresses the same as IP addresses? MAC addresses and Internet Protocol (IP) addresses are not the same thing. A MAC address is used for identification purposes *internally* on a network, which is similar to giving people different names to differentiate them. An IP address is the address *external* entities use to communicate with your network and is similar to your home street address. Think of it this way: The postal carrier delivers a package (data packet) to your dorm building based on its street address (IP address). The dorm's mail clerk delivers the package to your room because it has your name on it (MAC address) and not that of your neighbor. Both pieces of information are necessary to ensure that the package (or data) reaches its destination.

How does a data packet get a MAC address? Data packets are not necessarily sent alone. Sometimes groups of data packets are sent together in a group called a frame. A **frame** is a container that can hold multiple data packets. This is similar to placing several letters going to the same postal address in a big envelope. While the data packets are being assembled into frames, the NOS software assigns the appropriate MAC address to the frame. The NOS keeps track of all devices and their addresses on the network. Much like a letter that is entrusted to the postal service, the frame is delivered to the MAC address that the NOS assigned to the frame.

What delivers the frames to the correct device on the network? In a small bus network, frames just bounce along the wire until the correct client computer notices the frame is addressed to it and pulls the signal off the wire. This is inefficient in a larger network. Therefore, many types of devices have been developed to deliver data to its destination efficiently. These devices are designed to amplify signals, route signals, and exchange data with other networks.

Are MAC addresses useful for anything besides identifying a particular network device? On networks with wireless capabilities, MAC addresses can be used to enhance network security. Most wireless routers and access points can be

Computer #1

Message for Computer #3

Broadcast of message for Computer #3

Hub

Server

Broadcast of message for Computer #3

Broadcast of message for Computer #3

Computer #2

Broadcast of message for Computer #3

Computer #4

Computer #3

Figure 12.19

A hub broadcasts messages to all devices attached to it, regardless of the intended recipient.

used to filter MAC addresses and eliminate addresses of unauthorized devices. Because each MAC address is unique, you can input a list of authorized MAC addresses into the router. If someone who is using an unauthorized network adapter (one with an unauthorized MAC address) attempts to connect to the network, he or she will be unable to make a connection. Although it would be impractical for a large organization, in which employees constantly are being hired and leaving, MAC address filtering is a useful security tool on home networks and small business networks.

Repeaters and Hubs

What types of devices amplify signals on a single network?   A **repeater** is a relatively simple device whose sole function is to amplify a signal and retransmit it. Repeaters are used to extend cable runs beyond the maximum run length (the distance beyond which a signal would degrade and be unreadable). Repeaters do not transmit signals to specific devices; they just forward the signals along the media.

Which devices transmit signals to all nodes on networks?   As you learned in Chapter 7, a **hub** is a device that

also transmits signals. In addition, hubs have multiple ports to which devices are connected. As shown in Figure 12.19, a hub receives the signal from a device, reconstructs it, and transmits it to all other ports on the hub. Hubs are not usually used in modern networks because transmitting data to all nodes on a network is inefficient.

Switches and Bridges

Which devices are used to route signals through a single network?

Switches and bridges are used to send data on a specific route through the network. A **switch** can be viewed as a "smart" hub. It makes decisions, based on the MAC address of the data, as to where the data is to be sent. Therefore, only the intended recipient of the data receives the signal. This distinguishes it from a hub, which sends out data to all devices connected to it. This improves network efficiency by helping ensure that each device receives only the data intended for it.

Do I need a switch on my home network?   Switches are technically unnecessary on small networks (such as home networks) because there is not a large

Figure 12.20

Like a hub, a switch rebroadcasts messages— but only to the devices to which the messages are addressed. Because the cost of switches has fallen significantly, you are more likely to encounter switches than hubs.

Message for Computer #3

Switch

Computer #1

Server

Broadcast of message for Computer #3

Computer #2

Computer #4

Computer #3

amount of data traffic. Therefore, there is no need for increased efficiency. However, because switches are so inexpensive today, most home networks have switches built into their routers. Figure 12.20 shows a switch being used to rebroadcast a message.

When a corporate network grows in size, performance can decline, because many devices compete for transmission time on the network media. To solve this problem, a network can be broken into multiple segments known as collision domains. A **bridge** is a device that is used to send data between these different collision domains. A bridge sends data between collision domains depending on where the recipient device is located, as indicated in Figure 12.21. Signals received by the bridge from collision domain A are forwarded to collision domain B only if the destination computer is located in that domain. Most home networks contain only one segment, and therefore do not require bridges.

Routers

What device does a network use to move data to another network?

Whereas repeaters, hubs, switches, and

bridges perform their functions within a single network, a **router** is designed to send information between two networks. To accomplish this, the router must look at higher-level network addresses (such as IP addresses), not MAC addresses. When the router notices data with an address that does not belong to a device on the network from which it originated, it sends the data to another network to which it is attached (or out onto the Internet).

Network Security for Client/Server Networks

A major advantage that client/server networks have over peer-to-peer networks is that they offer a higher level of security. With client/server networks, users can be required to use a user ID and a password to gain access to the network. The security can be centrally administered by network administrators, freeing individual users of the responsibility of maintaining their own data security (as they must do on a peer-to-peer network).

In the next section, we will explore the challenges network administrators face in keeping a client/server network secure. We

Bridge

Collision Domain A

Signal to Computer #2 not passed on to Collision Domain B

Signal to Computer #4 must be passed to Collision Domain B

Collision Domain B

Signal to Computer #4

Switch

Signal to Computer #2

Signal to Computer #4

Signal to Computer #4

Switch

Signal to Computer #4

Computer #1

Computer #2

Computer #3

Computer #4

use a college network as our example, but note that the same principles apply to all client/server networks.

What sources of security threats do all network administrators need to watch for? Threats can be classified into three main groups: human errors and mistakes, malicious human activity, and natural events and disasters.

- **Human errors and mistakes:** Everyone makes mistakes. For example, the clerk processing your tuition payment could accidentally delete your records. A member of the computer support staff could mistakenly install an old database on top of the current one. Even physical accidents fall into this category; for example, someone could lose control of a car and drive it through the wall of the main server room.

- **Malicious human activity:** Malicious actions can be perpetrated by current employees, former employees, or third parties. For example, a disgruntled employee could introduce a virus to the network. A hacker could break into the student database server to steal credit card records. A former employee who feels he or she was unjustly fired could deliberately destroy data.

- **Natural events and disasters:** Some events—such as broken water pipes or fire, or disasters such as hurricanes, floods, earthquakes, and other acts of nature—are beyond human control. All can lead to the inadvertent destruction of data.

Who and what do a college network need to be secure against? A college network, like any network, is vulnerable to unauthorized users and manipulation or misuse of the data contained on it. The person who sat next to you last semester in English class—and failed—may be interested in changing his or her grade to an *A*. Hackers may be interested in the financial and personal information (such as Social Security numbers and credit card numbers) stored in college financial office

Figure 12.21

Bridges are devices used to send data between different network collision domains.

ACTIVE HELP-DESK

Selecting Network Navigation Devices

In this Active Helpdesk call, you'll play the role of a Helpdesk staffer, fielding calls about how network adapters enable computers to participate in a client/server network and what devices assist in moving data around a client/server network.

Bought anything at Wal-Mart or Best Buy lately? If so, there is a good chance that you brought home a **radio frequency identification tag (RFID tag)** with your purchase. Originally, RFID tags were used to keep track of cattle, but now they've moved into the retail sector to keep track of products. What are RFID tags, how did they end up in retail stores, and why should you care about them?

RFID tags can look like stickers or labels, or like the thin plastic wristbands you get when you check into a hospital. The tags are attached to batches of merchandise (usually cases or pallets), and all tags contain a microchip that holds a unique sequence of numbers used to identify the product to which it is attached. The tags also contain a tiny antenna that broadcasts information about the merchandise, such as its date of manufacture or price. Think of RFID tags as the next generation of UPC codes.

Two types of tags are in use: active and passive. Active tags are equipped with a battery and constantly transmit information. Passive tags don't have their own power source but instead get their energy from tag readers. Passive tags are more common because they are cheaper. Tag readers are devices that scan the information on the tags as the tags are passed by the reader. They do this through antennas that generate magnetic fields, which the passive tags sense. In response, the passive tags transmit their product code to the tag reader. The reader then sends the digital information to a computer network, and most likely into a database.

So how do RFID tags help retailers? For large retailers, inventory can be daunting to manage. Retailers such as Wal-Mart have tens of thousands of suppliers sending hundreds of thousands of products to their warehouses and stores. The use of RFID tagging allows the recording of inventory receipts and shipments to stores to be largely automated, resulting in fewer mistakes, fewer instances of merchandise being lost and forgotten in the warehouse, and tighter control over stock

levels. This helps retailers and their suppliers ensure that the correct inventory levels are maintained at all times, resulting in fewer shortages of merchandise and, ultimately, increased sales because the product is on the shelf when you go to buy it. Retailers also can use the product serial number information, which can be embedded in tags, to speed repair or return service. This process is shown in Figure 12.22.

Someday, RFID could be a huge benefit for consumers. Imagine if all products in your local grocery store had RFID tags. When you entered the store and grabbed a shopping cart, you could swipe your credit card through a reader on the cart. After you finished shopping, you could just walk out the door, at which time an RFID reader would take an inventory of the contents of your cart and charge your credit card for what you purchased. No more waiting in checkout lines! This streamlining of payment could result in lower costs for consumers. After you got home, if your refrigerator was equipped with RFID equipment, it could scan your purchases and keep track of your groceries, including expiration dates. Your refrigerator might contact your smartphone (via the Internet) and let you know that your milk was out of date so you could buy more on the way home. Now that's a smart fridge!

All this convenience could come with a price. There is concern that people might gather information about consumers' buying habits without their knowledge, similar to the concerns people have about spyware on computers today, because the RFID tags would be operational outside of the retail store. For example, someone could sit in the parking lot with a tag reader and detect exactly what you had purchased as you pushed your shopping cart by his or her car. If this person were from a competing retailer, this information could be especially valuable to that company. Alternatively, this person could be from a government enforcement agency trying to determine whether underage consumers were

---

databases on the network. Thus, one of the network administrator's key functions is to keep network data secure.

Authentication

How does a college ensure that only authorized users access its network? **Authentication** is the process whereby users prove they have authorization

SOUND BYTE

A Day in the Life of a Network Technician

In this Sound Byte, you'll learn firsthand about the exciting, fast-paced job of a computer technician. Interviews with actual network technicians and tours of networking facilities will provide you with a deeper appreciation for the complexities of the job.

to use a computer network. The type of authentication most people are familiar with consists of providing a user ID and password. However, authentication can also be achieved through the use of biometric devices (discussed later in this chapter) and through possessed objects. A **possessed object** is any object that a user carries to identify himself and that grants him access to a computer system or computer facility. Examples include identification badges, magnetic key cards, and smart keys (similar to flash drives).

How do most colleges handle authentication on their networks? As mentioned earlier, to gain access to a typical college client/server network, you have to go through authentication by entering a user ID and a password. By correctly inputting your ID and password, you prove who you are to the network and

| Truck | Warehouse | Sales Floor | Customer |

Pallets of merchandise being unloaded at the dock

42000 06200

42000 06200

42000 06200

Data being scanned as boxes go into the warehouse

Data being scanned as boxes go into the retail space

Data being scanned as customers take boxes out to their cars

Figure 12.22

As merchandise equipped with RFID tags enters the warehouse, the tags are scanned, and the inventory database is updated. When merchandise is moved to the sales floor, scanning updates the inventory database again for the new stock location. One last scan occurs when customers purchase items, which triggers the stock ordering system to place another order with a supplier if inventory is too low.

purchasing alcoholic beverages. Some pundits have speculated that if the tags had a long enough range, thieves could drive by houses and scan for desirable items to steal, such as large-screen TVs. However, this is unlikely given the state of current RFID technology.

Many consumers resent any potential invasion of their privacy. Therefore, retailers will need to educate consumers about RFID tags and their benefits. Retailers also will need to ensure that consumers have the option to deactivate or remove tags to protect their privacy.

show that you have authorized access. (This is because the ID was generated by the network administrator when you became a student.)

Can hackers use my account to log on to the network? If a hacker knows your user ID and password, he or she can log on and impersonate you. Sometimes network user IDs are easy to figure out because they have a certain pattern (such as your last name and the first initial of your first name). Because of this potential vulnerability, network administrators often configure accounts so that they will disable themselves after a set number of logon attempts using invalid passwords have been made. This prevents a hacker from using a **brute force attack** to attempt to crack the password. Brute force attacks are delivered by specialized hacking software that tries many combinations of letters, numbers,

words, or pieces of a user ID in an attempt to discover the associated password. If a network account isn't set to disable itself after a small number of incorrect passwords is tried, the attack may eventually succeed.

Access Privileges

How can I gain access to everything on the college network? The simple answer is that you can't! When your account was set up, certain access privileges were granted to indicate which systems you were allowed to use. For example, your access privileges probably include the ability to access the Internet. You also might have access privileges to view your transcript and grades online, depending on the sophistication of your college network. However, you definitely were not granted access to the grade reporting system, because this would

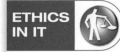

Ethics: Network Technicians' Access to Networks—Who Is Watching the Watchers?

According to **Salary.com**, the majority of employers report monitoring their employees in some fashion. The monitoring of phone calls, e-mail, and Web usage by employers is legal in almost all jurisdictions in the United States. Employers that suspect employees are goofing off can install spyware to monitor employee computer keystrokes and keep track of Web sites visited, down to the individual computer level. Naturally, network administrators are often involved in employee monitoring. Consider the case of Vernon Blake, the network administrator at the Alabama Department of Transportation. His boss was constantly playing computer games at work. This was common knowledge, yet no action was taken. Vernon installed software on his boss's computer and captured screen images that verified the boss was playing solitaire about 70 percent of the time. When Blake reported the results to management, the boss was reprimanded and Blake was fired! The company cited Blake's lack of authority or permission to install the monitoring software.

In addition, businesses are constantly receiving sensitive information from their customers such as Social Security numbers, birth dates, and credit card numbers—all valuable information for identify thieves. The job of protecting this data ultimately falls on the network administrators who are in charge of network and data security. Another example involves the American Institute of Certified Public Accountants (AICPA), a professional organization of CPAs. The AICPA maintains membership lists that include names, addresses, birth dates, and Social Security numbers.

The AICPA has clearly defined written policies that forbid sending equipment containing member information (such as a computer or hard drive) to external vendors for repair. Nevertheless, an IT staff member violated this policy and sent a hard drive containing membership information on 330,000 members to an external vendor. The hard drive was lost in transit while being returned to the AICPA. The AICPA quickly notified members of the security breach and offered them a free year of credit monitoring service to head off any problems—most likely at considerable expense to the AICPA. Although the AICPA has not indicated the disciplinary action it took against the staff members involved, it would seem likely that the penalties were severe.

So who is in charge of monitoring network administrators so that they don't abuse their access to sensitive information or fail to exercise proper safeguards over sensitive data? Savvy companies put written policies in place for employees regarding computer usage. These policies need to include guidelines for network administrators who have higher levels of access than normal employees do. Procedures for safeguarding data and guidelines for investigating employee misuse of computers must be clearly explained, and management needs to periodically review the activities of the network administrators to ensure compliance with polices. Although all employees need to follow approved company procedures regarding computer usage, it is especially important to ensure that employees with high levels of access and critical security responsibilities are adhering to company guidelines.

---

enable you to change your grades. Likewise, you did not receive access to the financial systems; otherwise, you might be able to change your account, indicating that your bill was paid when it had not been.

How does restricting access privileges protect a network?

Because network access accounts are centrally administered on the authentication server, it is easy for the network administrator to set up accounts for new students and grant them access only to the systems and software they need. The centralized nature of the creation of access accounts and the ability to restrict access to certain areas of the client/server network make it more secure than a peer-to-peer network. If you shouldn't go somewhere (such as into the files that record student grades), you can't get there on your school network!

Aside from improper access, how else do data theft and destruction occur?

Data storage devices are becoming smaller even as their capacities are increasing. One problem that devices such as flash drives pose is theft of data or intellectual property. Because these devices are so portable and have such large memory capacity, it is easy for a disgruntled employee to walk out the front door with stacks of valuable documents tucked in his or her pants pocket. Industrial espionage has never been easier—and no spy cameras are needed!

Flash drives can also introduce viruses or other malicious programs to a network, either intentionally or unintentionally. Just Secure Network Technologies, a security consulting firm, decided to test a client's security procedures by leaving 20 flash drives at random locations around the client's office. By the end of the day, employees had picked up 15 of the flash drives and plugged them into computers on the company network. The flash drives contained a simple program to display images as well as a Trojan horse program. While the employees were viewing the images, the Trojan horse program enabled the consultants to access the company network (if they wanted to do so) and steal or compromise data. It isn't hard to imagine hackers leaving flash drives around your company that could act as "skeleton keys" to your company's network.

How should network administrators protect their networks from portable storage devices? First, educate employees to the dangers posed by portable media devices and other untrusted media. Second, create policies regulating the use of media in the workplace. Third, install security measures such as personal firewalls or antivirus software on all computers in the company. The firewalls should be able to prevent malicious programs from running, even if they are introduced to a computer via a flash drive. Last, lock down and monitor the use of USB devices. Although Microsoft networking software allows network administrators to shut off access to the USB ports on computers, this prevents employees from using flash drives and other USB devices for legitimate purposes.

Other software products, such as DeviceLock and Safend, can be deployed on a network to provide options such as detailed security policies. Such products can also monitor USB device connections and track which users have connected devices to the network (including devices other than flash drives).

Don't forget to inform the employees that their use of these devices is being monitored. That alone will be enough to scare many employees from connecting untrusted devices to the network.

Physical Protection Measures

Can any physical measures be taken to protect a network? Restricting physical access to servers and other sensitive equipment is critical to protecting the network. Where are the servers that power your college network? They are most likely behind locked doors to which only authorized personnel have access. Do you see any routers or hubs lying about in computer labs? Of course you don't. These devices are securely tucked away in ceilings, walls, or closets, safe from anyone who might tamper with them in an attempt to sabotage the network or breach its security.

> "A biometric authentication device uses some unique characteristic of human biology to identify authorized users."

As shown in Figure 12.23, access to sensitive areas must be controlled. Many different devices can be used to control access. An **access card reader** is a relatively cheap device that reads information from a magnetic strip on the back of a credit card–like access card (such as your student ID card). The card reader, which can control the lock on a door, is programmed to admit only authorized personnel to the area. Card readers are easily programmed by adding authorized ID card numbers, Social Security numbers, and so on.

Biometric authentication devices are becoming more popular, although they are still prohibitively costly for many organizations, especially colleges. A **biometric authentication device** uses some unique characteristic of human biology to identify authorized users. Some devices read fingerprints or palm prints when you place your hand on a scanning pad. Other devices shine a beam of laser light into your eye and read the unique patterns of your retina to identify you. Facial recognition systems store unique characteristics of an individual's face for later comparison and identification. All of these devices are programmable. When an authorized individual uses a device for the first time, his or her fingerprints, face patterns, or retinal patterns are scanned and stored in a database.

Financial institutions and retail stores are considering using such devices to attempt to eliminate the growing fraud problems of identity theft and counterfeiting of credit and debit cards. If fingerprint authorization were required at the supermarket to make a purchase, a thief who stole your wallet and attempted to use your credit card would be unsuccessful.

The biometric devices currently on the market don't always function as intended. Facial recognition and retinal scanning systems can sometimes be fooled by pictures or videos of an authorized user. Researchers have fooled biometric fingerprint readers by using fingers made out of modeling clay, using the fingers of cadavers, or having unauthorized persons breathe on the sensor, which makes the previous user's fingerprint visible. (Fingers leave an oily residue behind

Biometric Authentication Device

IT Manager's Office

Biometric Authentication Device

Wiring Closet

Server Room

Biometric Authentication Device

General IT Office Area

Access Card Reader

Figure 12.23

Access card readers can be used to limit access to semi-sensitive areas such as the IT office. Higher-security areas, such as the server room, may deserve the additional protection that biometric authentication devices offer.

when they touch a surface.) Research institutions, such as Clarkson University in New York, are designing next-generation fingerprint readers that are much more difficult to fool. These will use specially designed algorithms that will detect moisture patterns on a person's fingers. Another approach may involve readers that detect an electrical current when a finger touches the reader, which is possible because the human body conducts electrical current. Future retinal readers may check whether a person blinks (or his or her pupils contract) when a bright light shines on him or her. Suffice it to say, these devices have a way to go before they are foolproof.

Firewalls

Is the college Internet connection vulnerable to hackers? Just like a home network, a college network that is connected to the Internet can create an attractive nuisance. A college network will most likely have a high-bandwidth connection to the Internet that will attract hackers. For this reason, a well-defended college network, just like a well-defended home network, includes a firewall. Firewalls can be composed of software or hardware, and many sophisticated firewalls include both. Routers are often equipped to act as hardware firewalls.

Does the firewall on my college's network work the same way as a personal firewall installed on a home network does? Although the firewall at your school may contain a few extra security options, making it even harder to breach than a personal firewall, the school's firewall works on the same basic principles as a

Emerging Technologies: Wi-Fi Phones Keep Doctors and Nurses Connected

Have you ever noticed signs inside a hospital forbidding you to make cell phone calls? Cell phone signals can interfere with sensitive electronic equipment such as heart monitors and IV monitors, rendering them ineffective. Unfortunately, this means doctors and nurses can't communicate quickly by using cell phones in the hospital either. However, using a Wi-Fi network, they can.

A number of U.S. hospitals, such as Mission Community Hospital in Panorama City, California, are providing their nurses and doctors with SpectraLink's NetLink Wi-Fi–enabled smartphones. These devices enable communication over the hospital's wireless network (instead of by conventional cell phone signals). These phones cause no interference with medical equipment, and unlike conventional cell phones, they offer a special feature that allows users to broadcast a message to multiple phones throughout the hospital. This is especially useful for emergency situations (such as a "code blue" cardiac arrest alert) when various personnel must gather quickly to deal with a crisis.

How does this all work? Unlike traditional cell phone calls that flow through a telephone company's switching or microwave system, Wi-Fi–enabled smartphones route calls through the Internet, either to landlines or out to other cell phones (Figure 12.24). This prevents the smartphones from generating the interference associated with traditional cell phone calls. In addition, the NetLink system can be integrated with conventional phone systems.

Any business or college with a physical campus could benefit from the connectivity achieved by such a network. Because concerns about responding to emergencies have grown since 9/11, its ability to let a user alert an entire organization at once by pushing a button and talking makes this type of network communications highly attractive.

In a hospital, appropriate security measures need to be implemented on the wireless network to protect sensitive medical data. There is a need to prevent hackers from cruising around the hospital, connecting to wireless networks, and then scanning them for medical and billing information. In addition to the expense of beefing up wireless security, the NetLink system requires all participants in the network to have a Wi-Fi–enabled smartphone. Time will tell whether more organizations decide that it is worth the cost of equipping key personnel (such as security guards) with smartphones when the time comes to replace their existing phones.

Figure 12.24

Keeping connected, especially in emergencies, is safe and easy when doctors and nurses can use special Wi-Fi–enabled smartphones to communicate.

home network. At a minimum, most firewalls work as packet screeners. **Packet screening** involves examining incoming data packets to ensure that they originated from or are authorized by valid users on the internal network. The router is the device that performs the packet screening. Unauthorized or suspect packets are discarded by the firewall before they reach the network.

Packet screening also can be configured for outgoing data to ensure that requests for information to the Internet are from legitimate users. This helps detect Trojan horse programs that may have been installed by hackers. As you learned in Chapter 9, Trojan horses masquerade as harmless programs but have a more sinister purpose. They often try to disguise where they are sending data from by using bogus IP addresses on the packets the programs send instead of using an authorized IP address belonging to the network.

If packet screening is working, packets going into and out of the network are checked to ensure they are either from or addressed to a legitimate IP address on the network. If the addresses are not valid addresses on the network, the firewall discards them.

What other security measures does the firewall on a client/server network use? To increase security even further, most large networks add a **bastion host**, which is a heavily secured server located on a special perimeter network between the company's secure internal network and the firewall. A bastion host gets its name from the fortified towers (called bastions), located along the outer walls of medieval castles, which were specifically designed to defend the castles against attackers.

To external computers, the bastion host gives the appearance of being the internal network server. Hackers can waste a lot of time and energy attacking the bastion host. However, even if a hacker breaches the bastion host server, the internal network is not vulnerable because the bastion host is

INTERNET

Firewall

Packets to/from the Internet

Accepted packets from authorized users

Perimeter Network

Rejected packets from unauthorized users

Authorized requests for Internet services

Secure Internal Network

Valid Internet services

External screening router
External screening routers examine all incoming and outgoing packets to/from the Internet. Only packets to/from authorized internal users are permitted into the perimeter network. Packets from unauthorized users are rejected.

Bastion host & proxy server
The bastion host/proxy server acts as the single point of contact for all incoming and outgoing Internet traffic. Even if this server is breached, because it is not located on the internal network, the computers on the internal network are still secure.

Internal screening router
Internal screening routers can be set to only allow certain types of Internet services (such as e-mail and Web browsing) and to reject all other requests.

Computer #1

Computer #2

Figure 12.25
A typical college network firewall layout.

not on the internal network. Moreover, during the time the hackers spend trying to penetrate the bastion host, network administrators can detect and thwart their attacks.

Bastion hosts are often configured as proxy servers. A **proxy server** acts as a go-between, connecting computers on the internal network with those on the external network (the Internet). All requests from the internal network for Internet services are directed through the proxy server. Similarly, all incoming requests from the Internet must pass through the proxy server. It is much easier for network administrators to maintain adequate security on one server than it is to ensure that security is maintained on hundreds or thousands of computers in a college network. Figure 12.25 shows a network secured by a firewall, a bastion host, and a screening router.

Now that you know a bit more about business network computing, you should be able to comfortably navigate the network at your college or your place of employment and understand why certain security measures have been taken to protect network data.

summary

1. What are the advantages of a business network?

A network enables employees to communicate with each other more easily, even over large distances. Networks also enable expensive resources, such as printers, to be shared, avoiding the cost of providing these resources to individual employees. Software can be deployed from a network server, thereby reducing the costs of installation on each user's computer. Finally, networks enable employees to share an Internet connection, avoiding the cost of providing each employee with a dedicated Internet connection.

2. How does a client/server network differ from a peer-to-peer network?

A client/server network requires at least one server to be attached to the network. The server coordinates functions such as data transmission and printing. In a peer-to-peer network, each node connected to the network can communicate directly with every other node on the network. In a client/server network, a separate device exercises control over the network. Data flows more efficiently in client/server networks than in peer-to-peer networks. In addition, client/server networks have increased scalability, meaning users can be added to the network easily.

3. What are the different classifications of client/server networks?

Local area networks (LANs) are small groups of computers (as few as two) and peripherals linked together over a small geographic area. A group of computers on the floor of the office building where you work is most likely a LAN. Wide area networks (WANs) comprise large numbers of users (or of separate LANs) that are miles apart and linked together. Corporations often use WANs to connect two or more branches (such as an office in California and one in Ohio). Sometimes government organizations or civic groups establish WANs to link users in a specific geographic area (such as within a city or county). These special WANs are known as metropolitan area networks (MANs).

4. What components are needed to construct a client/server network?

Client/server networks have many of the same components of peer-to-peer networks as well as some components specific to client/server networks, including servers, a network topology, transmission media, network operating system (NOS) software, network adapters, and network navigation devices.

5. What do the various types of servers do?

Dedicated servers are used on large networks to increase efficiency. Authentication servers control access to the network and ensure that only authorized users can log on. File servers provide storage and management of user files. Print servers manage and control all printing jobs initiated on a network. Application servers provide access to application software (such as Microsoft Office). Database servers store database files and provide access to users who need the information in the databases. E-mail servers control all incoming and outgoing e-mail traffic. Communications servers are used to control the flow of information from the internal network to outside networks (such as the Internet). Web servers are used to host a Web site.

6. What are the various network topologies (layouts), and why is network topology important in planning a network?

In a bus topology, all nodes are connected to a single linear cable. Ring topologies are made up of nodes arranged roughly in a circle. The data flows from node to node in a specific order. In a star topology, nodes are connected to a central communication device (a switch) and branch out like points of a star. A hybrid topology blends two or more topologies in one network. Each topology has its own advantages and disadvantages. Topology selection depends on two main factors: (1) the network budget, and (2) the specific needs of network users (such as speed or fair allocation of resources).

7. What types of transmission media are used in client/server networks?

In addition to wireless media, three main cable types are used: twisted-pair cable, coaxial cable, and fiber-optic cable. Twisted-pair cable consists of four pairs of wires twisted around each other to reduce interference. Coaxial cable is the same type of cable used by your cable TV company to run a signal into your house. Fiber-optic cable uses bundles of glass or plastic fiber to send signals using light waves. It provides the largest bandwidth but is expensive and difficult to install. Wireless media uses radio waves to send data between nodes on a network.

8. What software needs to run on computers attached to a client/server network, and how does this software control network communications?

Network operating system (NOS) software needs to be installed on each computer and server connected to a client/server network to provide the services necessary for the devices to communicate. The NOS provides a set of common rules (called a *protocol*) that controls communication between devices on the network.

9. How do network adapters enable computers to participate in a client/server network?

Without a network adapter, a computer could not communicate on a network. A network adapter provides three critical functions. First, it takes low-power data signals generated by the computer and converts them into higher-powered signals that can traverse network media easily.

Second, it breaks the data generated by the computer into packets and packages them for transmission across the network media. Last, it acts as a gatekeeper to control the flow of data to and from the computer.

10. What devices assist in moving data around a client/server network?

Repeaters are used to amplify signals on a network ensuring that signals are received even at the end of a long cable run. Hubs receive and retransmit signals to all devices attached to them. Switches are "smart" hubs in that they can read the addresses of data packets and retransmit a signal to its destination instead of to every device connected to the switch. Routers are used to route data between two different networks (such as between a corporate network and the Internet).

11. What measures are employed to keep large networks secure?

Access to most networks requires authentication procedures (such as having users enter a user ID and password) to ensure that only authorized users access the network. The system administrator defines access privileges for users so that they can access only specific files. Network equipment is physically secured behind locked doors, which are often protected by biometric authentication devices. Biometric devices, such as fingerprint and palm readers, use unique physical characteristics of individuals for identification purposes. Firewalls are employed to keep hackers from attacking networks through Internet connections. Packet screeners review traffic going to and from the network to ascertain whether it was generated by a legitimate user.

key terms

Word Bank

- application server
- bastion host
- bridges
- bus
- database server
- fiber-optic

- LAN
- network administrator
- packet screener
- packets
- repeaters
- routers

- scalable
- star
- switches
- twisted-pair
- WAN
- wireless access points

Instructions: Fill in the blanks using the words from the Word Bank above.

As a(n) (1) _____, Susan's first task was to configure her college's new network. Because the college had campuses in three different towns, she knew it would be necessary to configure the network as a(n) (2) _____. However, to handle all of the wireless devices the students carried, (3) _____ would need to be installed throughout the building. Software would need to be shared among 500 employees, so a robust (4) _____ would be a necessity. Because the college was experiencing rapid growth, the network would have to be highly (5) _____, which would require the selection of a(n) (6) _____ topology instead of a(n) (7) _____ topology, which would only work for a very small network.

The transfer of large files by the digital media department would mean that using (8) _____ cabling would be an absolutely necessity in the fine arts building, whereas (9) _____ cabling would be sufficient for other areas of the campus. Because the college had experienced hacking on its old network, Susan insisted that a(n) (10) _____ be installed to bolster the network defenses further by filtering unauthorized transmissions of data. Combined with a(n) (11) _____ installed as part of the perimeter network, she felt they would be adequately protected from wily hackers.

(12) _____ would be necessary to shift data (13) _____ between collision domains on the network. For the farthest reaches of the science building, (14) _____ would need to be installed to amplify the network data signals. If a star topology was to be used, many (15) _____ would need to be deployed to handle all 500 network users.

becoming computer literate

Ginormous State University is constructing a new building to house its Fine Arts and Digital Media programs. The digital media students and faculty work primarily on the first floor of the building at fixed workstations but need to transfer extremely large media files among various workspaces. The rest of the Fine Arts faculty can teach on any of the three floors in the building and need to access the network from wherever they may be teaching. Students will also need connectivity to the campus network and the Internet from any point in the building.

Instructions: Draft a memo (with supporting diagrams, if necessary) that details how to deploy network connectivity in the 25 classrooms, 12 faculty offices, and the common areas of the building. Justify the network topology you select, explain your choice of transmission media, and indicate the device(s) needed to connect the computers to the existing campus network.

Instructions: Answer the multiple-choice and true–false questions below for more practice with key terms and concepts from this chapter.

Multiple Choice

1. Which of the following is NOT an advantage of installing a network in a college?
   a. Increased productivity
   b. Centralization of network security protection
   c. Increased costs for NOS software
   d. Sharing of peripherals

2. Why aren't peer-to-peer networks usually installed in large businesses?
   a. Peripherals can't be shared on peer-to-peer networks.
   b. They require dedicated servers.
   c. They are less scalable than client/server networks.
   d. More cabling is needed on peer-to-peer networks.

3. When networks are deployed throughout a town to provide connectivity for the entire population, the networks would be classified as a
   a. WAN.   c. PAN.
   b. MAN.   d. LAN.

4. Which of the following is necessary in every client/server network?
   a. Bridge
   b. Database server
   c. Transmission media
   d. E-mail server

5. To provide for sharing of software, which server would a corporate network include?
   a. Database
   b. Authentication
   c. Communications
   d. Application

6. Which type of network topology is most popular today?
   a. Star   c. Ring
   b. Ethernet   d. Bus

7. Twisted-pair cable most likely would be used in a corporate network when
   a. cost is more important than speed.
   b. electrical or magnetic interference is present.
   c. especially long cable runs are required.
   d. speed is more important than cost.

8. NOS software is
   a. not absolutely essential for running a client/server network.
   b. needed only on the servers in a client/server network.
   c. needed on all computers in a client/server network.
   d. needed only when configuring a network in a bus topology.

9. Network adapters are
   a. necessary to connect computers to all types of networks.
   b. only needed for connecting computers wirelessly to networks.
   c. used only in peer-to-peer networks.
   d. necessary only in networks using the star topology.

10. Providing adequate security on a corporate network involves all of these issues, except
   a. NOS software freeze out.
   b. authentication.
   c. configuring a firewall.
   d. restricting access to servers.

True–False

_____ 1. Switches are used to route data between two or more network collision domains.

_____ 2. Two different types of network operating software cannot be deployed on the same network.

_____ 3. Fiber-optic cable is never susceptible to magnetic interference.

_____ 4. Client/server networks are more scalable than peer-to-peer networks.

_____ 5. An authentication server is used to share application software on a client/server network.

making the
transition to...
next semester

twelve chapter

making the
transition to...
next semester

1. Internet Usage Policy

Schools face many potential liability issues when they connect students to the Internet. Your school most likely has a written policy (perhaps posted on the school's Web site) on appropriate usage of the network and the Internet by students. Other issues that network usage policies typically address include guidelines on student file storage, antivirus protection, and backups. Obtain a copy of your school's policy (or speak with the appropriate IT personnel) and answer the following questions:

a. What types of sites are students not permitted to access?
b. Are restrictions in effect for using peer-to-peer file-sharing sites? What are those restrictions?
c. How much storage space (if any) is provided for student files?
d. How often (if ever) are student files backed up? Are these incremental backups, in which only new files or files that have changed are backed up, or full backups, in which all files are backed up?
e. Are files deleted after each semester?
f. Are students prohibited from commenting about the school and professors on blogs, wikis, or other Web sites? If so, how do you feel about that?

2. Wireless Connections at School

Wireless networks are growing in popularity now that more and more students are bringing notebook computers and other portable devices onto campus. Investigate the following:

a. Does your school offer wireless connectivity to students? If so, which areas of the campus are currently covered by wireless access? If the entire campus is not covered, are there plans to increase coverage?
b. What technologies are being deployed for connectivity (802.11g or 802.11n)? If 802.11g is currently deployed, is there a plan to upgrade to a faster standard in the future?
c. Is access to the wireless network restricted? (For example, is authentication required to log on?) If not, is the school considering implementing access restrictions to prevent poaching of bandwidth by neighbors and unauthorized visitors?

3. Internet Security Measures at School

Visit your IT services department and investigate which security measures currently are in place for the following:

a. **Firewall protection of the Internet connection.** What hardware and software are installed? Have there been any recent hacking attempts? If so, were they successful?
b. **Antivirus protection.** Is antivirus software installed on all computers deployed on campus? If so, what package is being used, and how often is it updated? What measures (if any) are in place to prevent users who bring their own computers (such as notebooks) onto campus and connect to the network wirelessly from infecting the network with a virus? Are products (other than antivirus software) installed to detect and prevent the installation of other malware, such as adware and spyware?

1. Security Issues at Work

You have been interning in the IT department of an insurance company, and you have applied for a full-time job at the company. One morning, you come to work and are told to clean out your desk. Your internship has ended, effective immediately, and you will not be considered for a full-time position. Your boss explains that the human resources director was checking your references when she located your profile on Facebook.com. She noted that you had made derogatory comments about certain company personnel and that you described your current work assignments as boring. Although this is not covered by the computer usage policy at your workplace, company management feels you are disgruntled.

a. Using the Internet, research employment laws in your state. Can you be fired for what you wrote on your Facebook page? Do you have any legal recourse against the company?

b. Would the company be more justified in firing you if you had been warned (in the company's computer usage policy) that the types of activities for which you were fired were not permitted? Would the company be in a better legal position had it included these infractions in its written policies?

2. Client/Server Networks

The owner of the company for which you work announces that the company will be hiring another 50 workers over the next six months. Currently, your peer-to-peer network is adequately handling the needs of the 10 employees who now work at the company. However, you know that adding 50 more employees to the network would overload it.

a. Write a memo explaining why a switch to a client/server network would be appropriate. Be sure to explain which topology you think would be best to install.

b. In the memo, estimate the costs of constructing a 60-person client/server network, including the costs of one server, cabling, workstations for the 50 new employees, and switches. Use resources such as dell.com and compaq.com to design the network and price its components.

3. Antivirus Solutions at Work

Recently, the company you work for had its network brought to a halt by an employee who inadvertently infected the server after opening an e-mail attachment containing a worm. Your boss has assigned you the task of locating a cost-effective antivirus solution that will protect the corporate network. Complete the following tasks:

a. Compare the costs of installing antivirus products from two major software providers, McAfee (**mcafee.com**) and Norton (**symantec.com**), on each of the 20 computers and the one server in your corporate network.

b. Would your company consider using a free antivirus program such as avast! or AVG? What are the risks associated with relying on a free product?

c. Write a draft memo to employees explaining the types of e-mail messages and attachments they should avoid opening and passing on to others. Make sure to include warnings about phishing, attachments containing viruses, and hoaxes.

Instructions: Albert Einstein used *Gedankenexperiments* (critical thinking questions) to develop his theory of relativity. Some ideas are best understood by experimenting with them in our own minds. The following critical thinking questions are designed to demand your full attention but require only a comfortable chair—no technology.

1. Internet Risks at School

Most people agree that Internet access is essential for students if they are to research projects and papers adequately. However, granting that access may invite people to engage in dangerous or unacceptable behaviors.

a. Do you think your school should restrict access to certain Internet sites (such as peer-to-peer file sharing services) to prevent students from violating laws by illegally sharing copyrighted material?

b. Plagiarism is thought to be spreading because of the easy exchange of information on the Internet. What should the penalty be for a student who plagiarizes material from a Web site? Why? Should a student who plagiarizes have his or her Internet access privileges revoked? Why or why not?

c. Should schools prohibit students from writing negative comments about faculty and administrators on their blogs and Facebook pages? Why or why not?

2. Ethical Hackers?

Some hackers argue that hacking should not be a crime because they are performing a service to the companies whose systems they are hacking by pointing out weaknesses in network security.

a. Should hackers be punished for gaining unapproved access to computer systems?

b. Are there any instances in which hacking is a "necessary evil" and law enforcement officials should just look the other way?

c. Is it unethical for software companies not to tell users about known security risks in their software?

3. Acceptable-Use Internet Policies

Most schools have drafted acceptable-use policies for computers and Internet access to inform students and employees of the approved uses of college computing assets. Consider these areas of a potential college policy:

a. Should employees be allowed to use their computers and Internet access for personal tasks (such as checking non–college-related e-mail, shopping online, or playing games)? If so, how much time per day is reasonable for employees to spend on personal tasks? Should employees be permitted to use their computers for personal tasks only during personal time (such as breaks and lunch hours)?

b. Should student computer and Internet usage be monitored to ensure compliance with the personal use policies? Should the college inform students that they are being monitored? What should the penalties be for violating these policies? Should your grades ever be affected by what activities you perform during the day, as monitored by the college via computers, cameras, tracking devices, etc.?

c. Many colleges block access to Web sites that enable students to participate in potentially illegal activities such as downloading music, gambling, or viewing pornography. Should colleges have the right to block students' access to these Web sites when they are on campus? Why or why not?

4. Network Layout Designs

Assume you are designing the network layout for a local coffee shop. In which areas of the store would you provide wireless network access? Would you charge customers for access or provide it free of charge? Should customers and employees access the same network, or should a separate one be established for business activities? Would you provide all employees with Internet access? If not, whom would you exclude?

Wireless Network Access on Campus

Problem

As wireless devices become more prevalent, increased demands for wireless access will be placed on networks. Although many schools already deploy adequate wireless access, there is room for improvement of coverage in numerous areas.

Task

The network manager at your school has requested that you assist in developing a plan for deploying or expanding wireless coverage for the campus. Your group has been selected to assist with the research. Before presenting your findings to the network manager, your group needs to fine-tune its recommendations.

Process

Divide the class into small teams.

1. Explore the areas of your campus where students congregate to socialize or engage in research. Determine if these areas are covered by wireless Internet access and the speed (802.11g or 802.11n) at which connections are offered. This may require interviewing your school's network manager or testing for connectivity with a notebook or other portable device, such as a hot spot detector. For areas of the school that are already covered by wireless technology (such as the library), test the signal strength of the connection by attempting to connect to the Internet in various locations.

2. Present your findings to your class. Lead a discussion with the other students and solicit feedback as to their experiences with wireless connectivity on the campus. In which other areas of the campus do you feel wireless technology should be deployed? What other technologies should be deployed that would benefit student learning?

3. Prepare a report for the network manager that includes your suggestions for improvements and upgrades to the wireless network on your campus. If possible, address options for wireless connectivity when students are off campus for field trips, seminars, and so on.

Conclusion

Being tied down to a wired computer terminal just doesn't cut it in the 21st century. Although wireless technology can be difficult and expensive to deploy in some instances (such as in old campus buildings), today's students will continue to demand the portable connections that they need to function effectively. Someday we'll probably wonder why we even bothered with wired connections at all!

In addition to the review materials presented here, you'll find additional materials featured with the book's multimedia, including the *Technology in Action* Student Resource CD and the Companion Website (**pearsonhighered.com/techinaction**), which will help reinforce your understanding of the chapter content. These materials include the following:

Active Helpdesk

In Active Helpdesk calls, you'll assume the role of helpdesk operator, taking calls about the concepts you've learned in this chapter. You'll apply what you've learned and receive feedback from a supervisor to review and reinforce those concepts. The Active Helpdesk calls for this chapter are listed below and can be found on your Student Resource CD:

- Using Servers
- Selecting a Network Topology and Cable
- Selecting Network Navigation Devices

Sound Bytes

Sound Bytes are dynamic multimedia tutorials that help demystify even the most complex topics. You'll view video clips and animations that illustrate computer concepts and then apply what you've learned by reviewing with the Sound Byte Labs, which include quizzes and activities specifically tailored to each Sound Byte. The Sound Bytes for this chapter are listed below and can be found on your Student Resource CD:

- Network Topology and Navigation Devices
- What's My IP Address? (And Other Interesting Facts about Networks)
- A Day in the Life of a Network Technician

Companion Website

The *Technology in Action* Companion Website includes a variety of additional materials to help you review and learn more about the topics in this chapter. The resources available at **pearsonhighered.com/techinaction** include:

- **Online Study Guide.** Each chapter features online true–false and multiple-choice quizzes. You can take these quizzes, automatically check the results, and e-mail the results to your instructor.
- **Web Research Projects.** Each chapter features several Web research projects that ask you to search the Web for information on computer-related careers, milestones in computer history, important people and companies, emerging technologies, and the applications and implications of different technologies.

objectives

After reading this chapter, you should be able to answer the following questions:

1. Who owns, manages, and pays for the Internet? *(p. 604)*

2. How do the Internet's networking components interact? *(pp. 604–607)*

3. What data transmissions and protocols does the Internet use? *(pp. 607–608)*

4. Why are IP addresses and domain names important for Internet communications? *(pp. 609–615)*

5. What are FTP and Telnet, and how do you use them? *(pp. 615–616)*

6. What are HTML/XHTML and XML used for? *(pp. 616–622)*

7. How do e-mail, instant messaging, and Voice over Internet Protocol work, and how is information using these technologies kept secure? *(pp. 622–629)*

8. How do businesses use the Internet to reduce computing costs? *(pp. 629–631)*

resources

Active Helpdesk

- Understanding IP Addresses, Domain Names, and Protocols **(p. 611)**
- Keeping E-Mail Secure **(p. 625)**

Sound Bytes

- Creating Web Pages with HTML **(p. 618)**

Companion Website

The Companion Website includes a variety of additional materials to help you review and learn more about the topics in this chapter. Go to: *pearsonhighered.com/techinaction*

how cool is *this?* Do you have several

e-mail accounts that need checking, such as your school e-mail account, which has
directives from your instructor, and your personal e-mail account, which receives
messages from friends and family? Do you have accounts on multiple social networking sites, such as Facebook and MySpace? Are half of your friends
using AOL Instant Messenger while the other half uses Yahoo! Instant Messenger?
Keeping up with your **online social life** can be challenging.

Digsby is a free tool that consolidates all of your online communications into a
single application. You just enter all the login information for your social networking,
e-mail, and IM accounts into the Digsby setup screen. Then, whenever you run
Digsby, it logs into all your accounts and checks for updates. You can easily see
all of your friends who are online, regardless of the IM service they use. You can also
easily view the status of your

Facebook page and
see all activity at a glance.
Clicking on any activity
shown, such as a new e-mail
received, takes you to a browser
window for the relevant application so
you can take appropriate action.

Digsby makes managing your digital
life **a snap** no matter how many
different applications you need to
use!

The Management of the Internet

The Internet is the largest network that you use. To keep a massive network like the Internet functioning at peak efficiency, it must be governed and regulated. However, no single entity is in charge of the Internet. In addition, new uses are created every day by a variety of individuals and companies.

Who owns the Internet? Even though the U.S. government funded the development of the technologies that spawned the Internet, no one really owns it. The particular local networks that constitute the Internet are all owned by different entities, including individuals, universities, government agencies, and private companies. Government entities such as the National Science Foundation (NSF) and the National Aeronautics and Space Administration (NASA), as well as many large, privately held companies, own pieces of the communications infrastructure (the high-speed data lines that transport data between networks) that makes the Internet work.

Does anyone manage the Internet? Because the individual networks that participate in the Internet are owned by several different entities, the Internet would cease to function without some sort of organization. Therefore, several nonprofit organizations and user groups, each with a specialized purpose, are responsible for its management. Figure 13.1 shows the major organizations that play a role in the governance and development of the Internet.

Many of the functions handled by these nonprofit groups were previously handled by U.S. government contractors because the Internet developed out of a defense project. However, because the Internet now serves the global community, not just the United States, assigning responsibilities to organizations with global membership is helping to speed the Internet's internationalization. Through close collaboration among the organizations listed in Figure 13.1 (and a few others), the Internet's vast collection of users and networks is managed.

Who pays for the Internet? You do! The U.S. government pays for a large portion of the Internet's infrastructure and funds research and development for new technologies. The primary source of these funds is your tax dollars. Originally, U.S. taxpayers footed the entire bill for the Internet, but as the Internet grew and organizations were formed to manage it, businesses, universities, and other countries began paying for Internet infrastructure and development.

Internet Networking

The Internet's response to our requests for information seems almost magical at times. By simply entering a URL in your browser

---

Figure 13.1 | MAJOR ORGANIZATIONS IN INTERNET GOVERNANCE AND DEVELOPMENT

Organization	Purpose	Web Address
Internet Society (ISOC)	Professional membership society comprising more than 100 organizations and more than 20,000 individual members in more than 180 countries. Provides leadership for the orderly growth and development of the Internet.	**isoc.org**
Internet Engineering Task Force (IETF)	A subgroup of ISOC made up of individuals and organizations that research new technologies for the Internet that will improve its capabilities or keep the infrastructure functioning smoothly.	**ietf.org**
Internet Architecture Board (IAB)	Technical advisory group to the ISOC and a committee of the IETF. Provides direction for the maintenance and development of the protocols that are used on the Internet.	**iab.org**
Internet Corporation for Assigned Names and Numbers (ICANN)	Organization responsible for management of the Internet's domain name system (DNS) and the allocation of IP addresses.	**icann.org**
World Wide Web Consortium (W3C)	Consortium of more than 400 member organizations that sets standards and develops protocols for the Web.	**w3.org**

or going to Yahoo! or Google and entering a search topic, you can summon up information that is stored on servers around the world. However, there is no magic involved, just a series of communication transactions that enable the Internet to function as a global network. In this section, we explore the various networks that make up the Internet, explain how to connect to them, and examine the workings of Internet data communications.

Connecting to the Internet

How are computers connected to the Internet?

A "network of networks," the Internet is similar to the highway system in the United States. The top level of the highway system consists of interstate highways such as I-95, which runs up and down the East Coast; I-80, which runs from the Northeast to the West Coast; and I-5, which runs north and south along the West Coast. These are the fastest and largest roadways. Regional highways connect to the interstate highways, and local roads connect to the regional highways.

As shown in Figure 13.2, the main paths of the Internet, along which data travels the fastest, are known collectively as the **Internet backbone**. Analogous to the interstate highway system, the Internet backbone is a collection of large national and international networks, most of which are owned by commercial, educational, or government organizations (such as NASA). These backbone providers, which are required to connect to other backbone providers, have the fastest high-speed connections. At the time this was written, the large companies that provided backbone connectivity included Verizon Business, AT&T, Sprint Nextel, and Qwest.

How do the ISPs that form the Internet backbone communicate?

Backbone ISPs initially connected with T lines. A **T line** carried digital data over twisted-pair wires. T-1 lines, which were the first to be used, transmit data at a throughput rate of 1.544 Mbps. T-3 lines, which were developed later, transmit data at 45 Mbps. Today, a backbone is typically a high-speed fiber-optic line, designated as an **optical carrier (OC) line**. OC lines come in a variety of speeds, as shown in Figure 13.3. Although

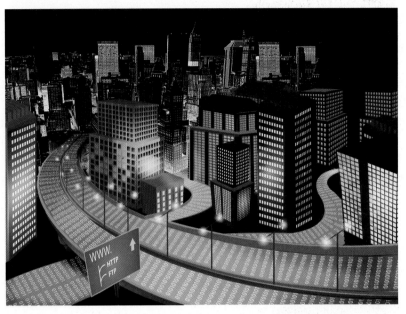

Figure 13.2

When you connect to the Internet at home, work, or school, you most likely are connecting through intermediate or local Internet service providers. Just as regional and local highways connect to the interstate highways, local and regional Internet service providers connect to the Internet backbone.

most large ISPs connect to the Internet with OC-192 lines, AT&T has begun to use OC-768 connections in its Internet backbone network.

The bandwidth of the connections between ISPs and end users depends on the amount of data traffic required. Whereas your home might connect to the Internet with DSL, cable, or even fiber-optic lines, the volume of Internet traffic at your college probably requires it to use at least T-3 lines or even an OC line to move data to the school's ISP. Large companies usually must connect to their ISPs using high-throughput OC lines.

How are the ISPs connected to each other?

The points of connection between ISPs were once known as *network access points (NAPs)*. Network access points were designed to move large amounts of

Figure 13.3	SPEED AND CONFIGURATION OF OC LINES
OC-1	.052 Gbps
OC-3	.155 Gbps
OC-12	.622 Gbps
OC-24	1.244 Gbps
OC-48	2.488 Gbps
OC-96	4.976 Gbps
OC-192	9.953 Gbps
OC-768	39.813 Gbps

Point of presence (POP)

Your teacher's home computer

Dial-up or cable/DSL connection

Dial-up or cable/DSL connection

Your neighbor's computer

Dial-up or cable/DSL connection

Your computer

Modems

Your ISP

Figure 13.4

Home users connect to their ISPs through a single point of presence that can handle many simultaneous connections.

data quickly between networks. They allowed the early Internet, which began as a government-funded academic experiment, to grow into the modern Internet of many commercial companies working together— the Internet that we all know and use today. Now, private sector companies make up the Internet system, and the data exchange mechanism is known as an **Internet exchange point (IXP)**. A typical IXP is made up of one or more network switches to which ISPs connect. As you'll recall from Chapter 7, **switches** are devices that send data on a specific route through a network. By connecting directly to each other through IXPs, networks can reduce their costs and improve the speed and efficiency with which data is exchanged.

How do individuals connect to an ISP? Whether they dial up through a conventional modem or connect through high-speed access (such as cable or DSL), individual Internet users enter an ISP through a **point of presence (POP)**, which is a bank of modems (shown in Figure 13.4) through which many users can connect to an ISP simultaneously. ISPs maintain multiple POPs throughout the geographic area they serve.

The Network Model of the Internet

What type of network model does the Internet use? The majority of Internet communications follows the **client/ server model** of network communications, which we defined in earlier chapters as one in which client computers request

services and other computers, known as servers, provide those services to the clients. In the case of the Internet, the clients are devices such as computers, PDAs, and smartphones that use browsers (or other interfaces) to request services such as Web pages. Various types of servers from which clients can request services are deployed (installed) on the networks that make up the Internet:

- **Web server:** Computer that runs specialized operating systems, enabling it to host (provide Web space for) Web pages and other information and provide requested Web pages to clients.

- **Commerce server:** Computer that hosts software that enables users to purchase goods and services over the Web. These servers generally use special security protocols to protect sensitive information (such as credit card numbers) from being intercepted.

- **File server:** Computer that is deployed to provide remote storage space or to act as a storehouse for files that users can download. Google Docs, Snapfish, and Delicious offer online storage services for productivity documents, pictures, and Web pages, respectively.

Do all Internet connections take place in a client/server mode? Certain services on the Internet operate in a peer-to-peer (P2P) mode, as depicted in Figure 13.5. For example, BitTorrent (**bittorrent.com**) is a popular file sharing service through which Internet users can exchange files. BitTorrent and other file sharing services require the user's computer to act as both a client and a server. When requesting files from another user, the computer behaves like a client. It switches

STEP 1: Request for file.

STEP 2: File identified on User A computer.

BitTorrent server

STEP 3: Client request for file.

STEP 4: User A (server mode) supplies file.

Your computer

User A

STEP 5: User B (client) requests file.

STEP 6: Your computer (in server mode) provides file.

User B

Figure 13.5
File sharing services in action.

to server mode when it provides a file stored on its hard drive to another computer. The following steps are illustrated in Figure 13.5:

1. Your computer, acting as a client, runs the BitTorrent software (which you downloaded from BitTorrent's Web site). Using this software, you request access to a particular music file. Your computer transmits this request to BitTorrent's server.

2. The BitTorrent server makes your computer aware of other users (Users A and B) running BitTorrent software.

3. Your computer determines that User A has the music file you wish to access. Acting as a client, your computer requests the file from User A.

4. User A's computer, acting as a server, sends the requested file to your computer.

5. Having been alerted to your presence by the BitTorrent server, User B's computer determines you have a file it wants. Acting as a client, it requests the file from your computer.

6. Your computer receives the request from User B. It then switches roles from client to server and serves the requested file up to User B.

Data Transmission and Protocols

Just like any other network, the Internet follows standard protocols to send information between computers. A **computer protocol** is a set of rules for exchanging electronic information. If the Internet is the information superhighway, then protocols are the rules of the road.

Why were Internet protocols developed? To accomplish the early goals of the Internet, protocols needed to be written and agreed upon by users. Each protocol had to be an **open system**, meaning its design would be made public for access by any interested party. This was in direct opposition to the **proprietary system** (private system) model that was the norm at the time.

As we mentioned in earlier chapters, when common communication protocols (rules) are followed, networks can communicate even if they have different topologies, transmission media, or operating systems. The idea of an open system protocol is that anyone can use it on his or her computer system and be able to communicate with any other computer using the same protocol. The three biggest Internet tasks—communicating, seeking information, and shopping—all are executed the same way on any system that is following accepted Internet protocols.

Were there problems developing an open system Internet protocol?

Agreeing on common standards was relatively easy. The tough part was developing a new method of communication because the current technology—circuit switching—was inefficient for computer communication. Circuit switching has been used since the early days of the telephone for establishing communication. In **circuit switching**, a dedicated connection is formed between two points (such as two people on telephones), and the connection remains active for the duration of the transmission. This method of communication is extremely important when communications must be received in the order in which they are sent (again, like telephone conversations).

When applied to computers, however, circuit switching is inefficient. Computers process communication in bursts. As a computer processor performs the operations necessary to complete a task, it transmits data in a group (or burst). The processor then begins working on its next task and ceases to communicate with output devices or other networks until it is ready to transmit data in the next burst. Circuit switching is inefficient for computers because the circuit either would have to remain open (and therefore unavailable to any other system) with long periods of inactivity or would have to be reestablished for each burst.

> **"Computers process communication in bursts."**

Packet Switching

If they can't use circuit switching, what do computers use to communicate?

Packet switching is the communications methodology that makes computer communication efficient. Packet switching doesn't require a dedicated communications circuit to be maintained. With packet switching, data is broken into smaller chunks (each one called a **packet** or a **data packet**) that are sent over various routes at the same time. When the packets reach their destination, they are reassembled by the receiving computer. This technology resulted from one of the original goals of creating the Internet: if Internet nodes are disabled or destroyed (such as through an act of warfare or terrorism), the data can travel an alternate route to its destination.

What information does a packet contain?

Packet contents vary depending on the protocol being followed. At a minimum, all packets must contain (1) an address to which the packet is being sent; (2) the address from where the packet originates; (3) reassembling instructions, if the original data was split between packets; and (4) the data that is being transmitted.

Sending a packet is like sending a letter. Assume you are sending a large amount of information in written format from your home in Philadelphia to your aunt in San Diego. The information is too large to fit in one small envelope, so you mail three different envelopes to your aunt. Each envelope includes your aunt's address, a return address (your address), and the information being sent inside it. The pages of the letters in each envelope are numbered so that your aunt will know in which order to read them.

Each envelope may not find its way to San Diego by the same route. However, even if the letters are routed through different post offices, they will all eventually arrive in your aunt's mailbox. Your aunt will then reassemble the message (put the pages of the letters in order) and read it. The process of sending a message through the Internet works in much the same way. This process is illustrated in Figure 13.6, which traces an e-mail message sent from a computer in Philadelphia to a computer in San Diego.

Why do packets take different routes, and how do they decide which route to use?

The routers that connect ISPs with each other monitor traffic and decide on the most efficient route for packets to take to their destination. The router works in the same way as a police officer does during a traffic jam. When routes are clogged with traffic, police officers are deployed in areas of congestion, directing drivers to alternate routes to their destinations.

TCP/IP

What protocol does the Internet use for transmitting data?

Although many protocols are available on the Internet, the main suite of protocols used is **TCP/IP**. The

Your computer
in Philadelphia

E-mail to your aunt
broken into packets
by your computer

Packet 1

Packet 2

Packet 3

Your ISP in PA

ISP in
MN

ISP in
NC

ISP
in
NJ

ISP in
OR

ISP in
FL

E-mail to your aunt
reconstructed by
her computer

Packet 1

Packet 2

Packet 3

Your aunt's
computer
in San Diego

Your aunt's
ISP in CA

ISP in
TX

INTERNET

Figure 13.6

Each packet can follow
its own route to its final
destination. Sequential
numbering of packets
ensures they are
reassembled in the
correct order at their
destination.

suite is named after the original two protocols that were developed for the Internet: the **Transmission Control Protocol (TCP)** and the **Internet Protocol (IP)**. Although most people think that the TCP/IP suite consists of only two protocols, it actually comprises many interrelated protocols, the most important of which are listed in Figure 13.7.

Which particular protocol actually sends the information? The Internet Protocol (IP) is responsible for sending the information from one computer to another. The IP is like a postal worker who takes a letter (a packet of information) that was mailed (created by the sending computer) and sends it on to another post office, which in turn routes it to the addressee (the receiving computer). The postal worker never knows whether the recipient actually receives the letter. The only thing the postal worker knows is that the letter was handed off to an appropriate post office that will assist in completing the delivery of the letter.

IP Addresses and Domain Names

Each computer, server, or device (such as a router) connected to the Internet is required to have a unique identification number. However, because humans are better at remembering and working with words than with numbers, the numeric IP addresses were given more "human," word-based addresses.

IP Addresses

What is an IP address? You will recall from Chapter 3 that an **IP address** is a unique identification number that defines each computer, service, or other device that connects to the Internet. IP addresses fulfill the same function as street addresses. For example, to send a letter to John Doe's house in Walla Walla, Washington, you have to know his address. John might live at 123 Main Street, which is not a unique address (many towns have a Main Street); but 123 Main Street, Walla Walla, WA 99362 *is* unique.

Figure 13.7 | TCP/IP PROTOCOL SUITE—MAIN PROTOCOLS

Internet Protocol (IP)	Sends data between computers on the Internet.
Transmission Control Protocol (TCP)	Prepares data for transmission and provides for error checking and resending of lost data.
User Datagram Protocol (UDP)	Prepares data for transmission; lacks resending capabilities.
File Transfer Protocol (FTP)	Enables files to be downloaded to a computer or uploaded to other computers.
Telnet	Enables user to log in to a remote computer and work on it as if sitting in front of it.
HyperText Transfer Protocol (HTTP) and Secure HTTP (S-HTTP)	Transfers HyperText Markup Language (HTML) data from servers to browsers. S-HTTP is an encrypted protocol for secure transmissions.
Simple Mail Transfer Protocol (SMTP)	Used for transmission of e-mail messages across the Internet.

What's Your IP Address?

Curious as to what your IP address is? You could go through the operating system to find out. Click the Start button and type CMD in the Search box. Then, at the command prompt, type *ipconfig* and press Enter. Windows will provide you with information about your IP address. Alternatively, just go to a Web site such as What Is My IP (**whatismyip.com**) or IP Chicken (**ipchicken.com**). Figure 13.8 displays the output from What Is My IP, which shows the IP address your PC is currently using.

Figure 13.8

Some Web sites, such as WhatIsMyIP.com, determine your IP address for you.

The numeric zip code is the unique postal identification for a specific geographic area. Zip codes are regulated by the U.S. Postal Service. Similarly, IP addresses must be registered with the **Internet Corporation for Assigned Names and Numbers (ICANN)** to ensure they are unique and have not been assigned to other users. The ICANN is responsible for allocating IP addresses to network administrators, just as the U.S. Postal Service is responsible for assigning zip codes to geographic areas.

What does an IP address look like? A typical IP address is expressed as follows:

197.169.73.63

An IP address expressed this way is called a **dotted decimal number** (also known as a **dotted quad**). However, recall that computers work with binary numbers. The same IP address in binary form is as follows:

11000000.10101000.00100000.00111111

Each of the four numbers in a dotted decimal number is referred to as an **octet**. This is because each number would have eight positions when shown in binary form. Because 32 positions are available for IP address values (four octets with eight positions each), IP addresses are considered 32-bit numbers. A position is filled either by a 1 or a 0, resulting in 256 (2^8) possible values for each octet. Values start at 0 (not 1); therefore, each octet can have a value from 0 to 255. The entire 32-bit address can represent 4,294,967,296 values (or 2^{32}), which are quite a few Internet addresses!

Will we ever run out of IP addresses? When the original IP addressing scheme, **Internet Protocol version 4 (IPv4)**, was created in the early 1980s, no one foresaw the explosive growth of the Internet in the 1990s. Four billion values for an address field seemed like enough to last forever. However, as the Internet grew, it quickly became apparent that we were going to run out of IP addresses.

Because the unique IP addressing system described earlier offers only a fixed number of IP addresses, a different addressing scheme known as **classless interdomain routing (CIDR)**, pronounced "cider," was developed. CIDR, or supernetting, allows a single IP address to represent several unique IP addresses by adding a **network prefix** (a slash and a number) to the end of the last octet. The network prefix identifies how many of the possible 32 bits in a traditional

IP address are to be used as the unique identifier, leaving the remaining bits to identify the specific host. For example, in the IP address 206.13.01.48/25, "/25" is the network prefix. It indicates that the first 25 bits are used as the unique network identifier; the remaining 7 bits identify the specific host site.

Are there other Internet addressing systems? Internet Protocol version 6 (IPv6) is an IP addressing scheme developed by the Internet Engineering Task Force, or IETF, to make IP addresses longer, thereby providing more available IP addresses. IPv6 uses eight groups of 16-bit numbers, referred to as **hexadecimal notation** (*hex* for short), which you learned about in the Technology in Focus piece titled "Under the Hood." An IPv6 address would have the following format:

0000:0000:0000:0000:0000:0000:0000:0000

Hex addressing provides a much larger field size, which will enable a much larger number of IP addresses (approximately 340 followed by 36 zeros). This should provide a virtually unlimited supply of IP addresses and will allow many different kinds of non-PC devices such as cell phones and home appliances to join the Internet more easily in the future. Many companies and government agencies are starting to replace their networking equipment with equipment that can handle the IPv6 protocol.

How does my computer get an IP address? You learned in Chapter 7 that IP addresses are assigned either statically or dynamically. **Static addressing** means that the IP address for a computer never changes and is most likely assigned manually by a network administrator. **Dynamic addressing**, in which your computer is assigned an address from an available pool of IP addresses, is more common. A connection to an ISP could use either method. If your ISP uses static addressing, then you were assigned an IP address when you applied for your service and had to configure your computer manually to use that address. More often, though, an ISP assigns a computer a temporary (dynamic) IP address, as shown in Figure 13.9.

How exactly are dynamic addresses assigned? Dynamic addressing is normally handled by the **dynamic host configuration protocol (DHCP)**, which belongs to the TCP/IP protocol suite. DHCP takes a pool of IP addresses and shares them with hosts on the network on an as-needed basis. ISPs don't need to maintain a pool of IP addresses for all of their subscribers because not everyone is logged on to the Internet at one time. Thus, when a user logs on to an ISP's server, the DHCP server assigns that user an IP address for the duration of the session. Similarly, when you log on to your computer at work in the morning, DHCP assigns an IP address to your computer. These temporary

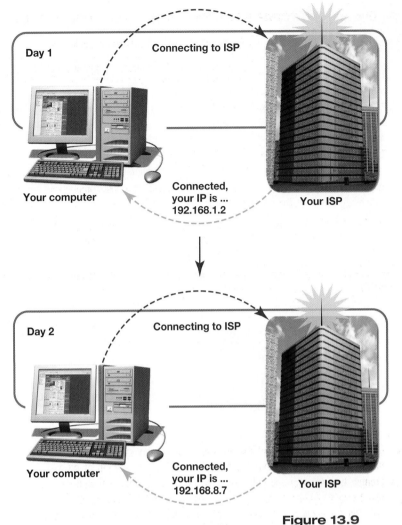

Figure 13.9

Dynamic IP addressing changes your IP address every time you connect to the Internet.

ACTIVE HELP-DESK

Understanding IP Addresses, Domain Names, and Protocols

In this Active Helpdesk call, you'll play the role of a helpdesk staffer, fielding calls about which data transmissions and protocols the Internet uses, and why IP addresses and domain names are important for Internet communications.

Making the Connection: Connection-Oriented Versus Connectionless Protocols

The Internet Protocol is responsible only for *sending* packets on their way. The packets are created by either the TCP or the **User Datagram Protocol (UDP)**. You don't decide whether to use TCP or UDP. The choice of protocol is made for you by the developers of the computer programs you are using or by the other protocols (such as those listed in Figure 13.7) that interact with your data packet.

As explained earlier, data transmission between computers is highly efficient, if connections do not need to be established (as in circuit switching). However, there are benefits to maintaining a connection, such as reduced data loss. The difference between TCP and UDP is that

TCP is a connection-oriented protocol, whereas UDP is a connectionless protocol.

A **connection-oriented protocol** requires two computers to exchange control packets, thereby setting up the parameters of the data exchange session, before sending packets that contain data. This process is referred to as **handshaking**. TCP uses a process called a **three-way handshake** to establish a connection, as shown in Figure 13.10a. Perhaps you need to report sales figures to your home office. You phone the sales manager and tell him or her that you are ready to report your figures. The sales manager then prepares to receive the

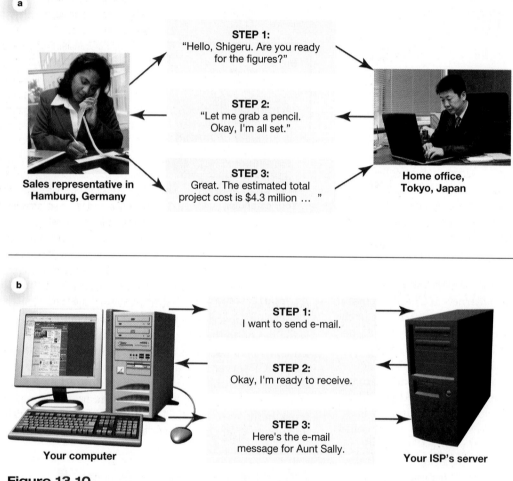

Figure 13.10

(a) Colleagues in Hamburg and Tokyo establish communication using a three-way handshake. (b) Here, two computers establish communication the same way.

IP addresses may or may not be the same from session to session.

What are the benefits of dynamic addressing? Although having a static address would seem to be convenient, dynamic addressing provides a more secure environment by keeping hackers out of computer systems. Imagine how hard it would be for burglars to find your home if you changed your address every day!

information by getting a pencil and a piece of paper. By confirming that he or she is ready and by your beginning to report the figures, a three-way (three-step) handshaking process is completed.

Your computer does the same thing when it sends an e-mail through your ISP, as shown in Figure 13.10b. It establishes a connection to the ISP and announces it has e-mail to send. The ISP server responds that it is ready to receive the e-mail. Your computer then acknowledges the ready state of the server and begins to transmit the e-mail.

A **connectionless protocol** does not require any type of connection to be established or maintained between two computers that are exchanging information. Just like a letter that is mailed, the data packets are sent without notifying the receiving computer or receiving any acknowledgment that the data was received. UDP is the Internet's connectionless protocol.

Besides establishing a connection, TCP provides for reliable data transfer. Reliable data transfer means that the application that uses TCP can rely on this protocol to deliver all the data packets to the receiver free from errors and in the correct order. TCP achieves reliable data transfer by using acknowledgments and providing for the retransmission of data, as shown in Figure 13.11.

Assume that two systems, X and Y, have established a connection. When Y receives a data packet that it can read from X, it sends back a **positive acknowledgment (ACK)**. If X does not receive an ACK in an appropriate period of time, it resends the packet. If the packet is unreadable (damaged in transit), then Y sends a **negative acknowledgment (NAK)** to X, indicating the packet was not received in understandable form. X then retransmits that packet. Acknowledgments assure that the receiver has received a complete set of data packets. If a packet is unable to get through after being resent several times, the user is generally presented with an error message indicating the communications were unsuccessful.

You may wonder why you wouldn't always want to use a protocol that provides for reliable data transfer. On the Internet, speed is often more important than accuracy. For certain applications (such as e-mail), it's critically important that your message be delivered completely and accurately. For streaming multimedia, it's not always important to have every frame delivered accurately because most streaming media formats provide for correction of errors caused by data loss. It is, however, extremely important for streaming media to be delivered at a high rate of speed. Otherwise, playback quality can be affected. Therefore, a protocol such as TCP, which uses handshakes and acknowledgments, would probably not be appropriate for transmitting a movie trailer over the Internet.

Sending computer

Receiving computer

Packet 1

Packet 1 received and readable. ACK sent.

ACK for packet 1 received. Need to send next packet.

ACK 1

Packet 2

Packet 2 received and unreadable. NAK sent.

NAK for packet 2 received. Must resend packet 2.

NAK 2

Packet 2 resend

Packet 2 received and readable. ACK sent.

ACK 2 lost in transit

ACK for packet 2 never received. Must resend packet 2.

Packet 2 resend

Packet 2 already received. Resend ACK for packet 2.

Figure 13.11

Packet acknowledgment in action.

Domain Names

I've been on the Internet, so why have I never seen IP addresses?

Computers are fantastic at relating to IP addresses and other numbers. However, humans remember names better than they remember strings of numbers. (Would you rather call your friend 1236231 or Sanjay?) When the Web was being formed, a naming system was necessary so people could work with names instead of numbers. Hence, domain names were born.

As you learned in Chapter 3, a **domain name** is simply a name that takes the place of an IP address, making it easier for people to remember. You've most likely visited Yahoo! (**yahoo.com**). Yahoo.com is a domain name. The server where Yahoo!'s main Web site is deployed has an IP address (such as 123.45.67.89), but it's much easier for you to remember to tell your browser to go to Yahoo.com than it is to recall the nine-digit IP address.

How are domains organized?

Domains are organized by level. As you'll recall from Chapter 3, the portion of the domain name after the dot is the top-level domain (TLD). In the .com domain are popular sites such as Amazon (**amazon. com**), Google (**google.com**), and Microsoft (**microsoft.com**). The TLDs are standardized pools (such as .com and .org) that have been established by ICANN. (Refer back to Figure 3.22 in Chapter 3 for a list of the TLDs that are currently approved and in use.) Within each top-level domain are many second-level domains. A **second-level domain** needs to be unique within its own top-level domain but not necessarily unique to all top-level domains. For example, Mycoolsite.com and Mycoolsite.org could be registered as separate domain names.

Who controls domain name registration?

ICANN assigns companies or organizations to manage domain name registration. Because names can't be duplicated within a top-level domain, one company is assigned to oversee each TLD and maintain a listing of all registered domains. VeriSign is the current ICANN-accredited domain name registrar for the .com and .net domains. VeriSign provides a database that lists all the registered .net and .com domains and their contact information. However, for simplicity you can look up any .com or .net domain at the Network Solutions Web site (**networksolutions.com**) to see if it is registered and who owns it. Country-specific domains such as .nz for New Zealand and .sg for Singapore are controlled by groups in those countries. You can find a complete list of country-code top-level domains on the Internet Assigned Numbers Authority Web site (**iana.org**).

DNS Servers

How does my computer know the IP address of another computer?

Say you want to get to Yahoo.com. To do so, you type the company URL—**yahoo.com**—into your browser's address box. However, the URL is not important to your computer; only the IP address of the computer hosting the Yahoo! site is. When you enter the URL in your browser, your computer must convert the URL to an IP address. To do this, your computer consults a database that is maintained on a **DNS (Domain Name System) server** that functions like a phone book for the Internet.

Your ISP's Web server has a default DNS server (one that is convenient to contact) that it goes to when it needs to translate a URL to an IP address (illustrated in Figure 13.12). It uses the following steps:

1. Your browser requests information from ABC.com.

2. Your ISP doesn't know the address of ABC.com, so it requests the address from its default DNS server.

3. The default DNS server doesn't know the IP address of ABC.com either, so it queries the root server of the .com domain.

How to Register a Domain Name

Would you like to create a Web site with your own domain name, for example me.com? The process of creating your own Web site is straightforward, but finding a name that you like and that is available may be difficult.

The first thing you need to do is to create a list of domain names that are acceptable to you. If you are creating the Web site for business purposes, then you might want to keep search strategies in mind. With your list of acceptable domain names in hand, go to Whois.net (**whois.net**) to determine if your preferred name has already been taken. If the search results indicate that there is no match, then the name is available. If the name is already taken, try making small variations to that name.

After you find a name you like that's available, find an official Internet registrar (InterNIC has a link to the Accredited Registrar Directory). Registrars offer a variety of services for a range of prices, so compare prices among the registrars that offer the services you want. Once you provide the registrar with their required information, you've got yourself a Web site.

STEP 1: Request from ABC.com.

STEP 2: Request IP address from DNS server.

STEP 3: Request IP address from root server.

Your computer

Your ISP's Web server

Your ISP's default DNS server

Root server for .com domain

STEP 7: Computer routes request to correct IP address.

STEP 6: Web server stores IP address and passes it along.

STEP 5: DNS server stores IP address and passes it along.

STEP 4: Root server provides IP address.

Figure 13.12
DNS servers in action.

4. The root server provides the default DNS server with the appropriate IP address of ABC.com.

5. The default DNS server stores the correct IP address for ABC.com for future reference and returns it to your ISP's Web server.

6. Your ISP's Web server also stores the correct IP address for ABC.com for future reference and returns it to your computer.

7. Your computer then routes its request to ABC.com and stores the IP address in cache for later use.

Your ISP or network administrator defines the default DNS server. If the default DNS server does not have an entry for the domain name you requested, then it queries another DNS server.

If all else fails, your ISP's Web server will contact one of the 13 root DNS servers maintained throughout the Internet. Each **root DNS server** knows the location of all the DNS servers that contain the master listings for an entire top-level domain. Your default DNS server receives the information from the master DNS server (say, for the .com domain). It then stores that information in its cache for future use and communicates the appropriate IP address to your computer.

Other Protocols: FTP and Telnet

The TCP/IP protocol suite contains numerous protocols, although some of them are used infrequently. Two of the more commonly used protocols on the Internet are the File Transfer Protocol and Telnet.

File Transfer Protocol

How does FTP work? The **File Transfer Protocol (FTP)** enables users to share files that reside on local computers with remote computers. If you're attempting to download files to your local computer using FTP, the FTP client application (most likely a Web browser) first establishes a TCP session with the remote computer. FTP provides for authentication and password protection, so you may be required to log in to an FTP site with a username and password.

Can you upload files with FTP? Most FTP sites allow you to upload files. To do so, you either need a browser that handles FTP transfers (current versions of Internet Explorer and Firefox do), or you need to obtain an FTP client application. Many FTP client programs are available as freeware or shareware. Searching on the term "FTP" on Download.com (**download. com**) will produce a list of programs from which to choose. FileZilla (**filezilla-project. org**) is an open source FTP program that is available free of charge.

Telnet

What is Telnet? Telnet is both a protocol for connecting to a remote computer and a TCP/IP service that runs on a remote computer to make it accessible to other computers. At colleges, students sometimes use Telnet to connect to mainframe computers or servers from their personal computers. The

What Is an Internet Cache?

Your **Internet cache** is a section of your hard drive that stores information, such as IP addresses and frequently accessed Web pages, that you may need again. However, caching of domain name addresses also takes place in DNS servers. This helps speed up Internet access time because a DNS server doesn't have to query master DNS servers for TLDs constantly. However, caches have limited storage space, so entries are held in the cache only for a fixed period of time and then are deleted. The time component associated with cache retention is known as the time to live (TTL). Without caches, surfing the Internet would take a lot longer.

Beware—you can't always tell whether your browser is loading the current version of a page from the Web or a copy from your Internet cache. If a Web site contains time-sensitive information (such as a snow day alert on a college Web site), clicking the browser's refresh button will ensure that the most current copy of the page loads into your browser.

Telnet client application, which runs on your personal computer, connects to the Telnet server application, which runs on a remote computer. Telnet enables you to take control of a remote computer (the server) with your computer (the client) and manipulate files and data on the server as if the server were your own computer.

How do you use Telnet? To establish a Telnet session, you need to know the domain name or IP address of the computer to be connected to using Telnet. In addition, logon information (ID and password) is generally required. With Windows, you also need to turn on the Telnet feature. To do so, click the Start button in the taskbar, select Control Panel, and then select Programs. In the Programs and Features group, select the option to turn Windows features on or off. In the list of features, click Telnet Client and then click OK. After Telnet has been configured in Windows, click the Start button and enter "telnet" in the quick search box. You should see the window shown in

Figure 13.13. Typing ?/ at the command prompt displays the available Telnet commands. To connect to a remote computer, type "open" and the host name (or IP address) of the remote computer and follow the logon instructions. (These vary from system to system.)

HTTP, HTML, and Other Web Jargon

Although most people think that the Internet and the Web are the same thing, the World Wide Web (WWW or the Web) is actually a grouping of protocols and software that resides on the Internet. The Web provides an engaging interface for exchanging graphics, video, animations, and other multimedia over the Internet. One other aspect that distinguishes the Web from the Internet is the Web's use of special languages such as HTML (HyperText Markup Language) and protocols such as HTTP (HyperText Transfer Protocol), which allow different computers to talk to each other.

HTTP and SSL

Which Internet protocol does a browser use to send requests? The **HyperText Transfer Protocol (HTTP)** was created especially for the transfer of hypertext documents across the Internet. **Hypertext** documents are documents in which text is linked to other documents or media (such as video clips, pictures, and so on). Clicking a specific piece of text (called a *hyperlink*) that has been linked elsewhere takes you to the linked file.

When the browser sends a request, does it do anything to make the information secure? As you read in Chapter 3, some Web sites require extra layers of security to ensure that banking or purchasing transactions can be done safely and without personal and financial information being mishandled. Commerce servers use security protocols to protect sensitive information from interception by hackers.

Figure 13.13

This Telnet command window shows available commands.

```
C:\Windows\system32\telnet.exe
Welcome to Microsoft Telnet Client

Escape Character is 'CTRL+]'

Microsoft Telnet> ?/

Commands may be abbreviated. Supported commands are:

c       - close          close current connection
d       - display        display operating parameters
o       - open hostname [port]   connect to hostname (default port 23).
q       - quit           exit telnet
set     - set            set options (type 'set ?' for a list)
sen     - send           send strings to server
st      - status         print status information
u       - unset          unset options (type 'unset ?' for a list)
?/h     - help           print help information
Microsoft Telnet> _
```

HyperText Transfer Protocol Secure (HTTPS) is actually a combination of the HTTP protocol and a network security protocol (usually SSL or TLS). HTTPS ensures data is sent securely over the Web. **Transport Layer Security (TLS)** and the **Secure Sockets Layer (SSL)** are two protocols that provide data integrity and security for transmissions over the Internet. Online shopping sites frequently use HTTPS to safeguard credit card information. Online banking sites and other Web sites that require user authentication beyond just a simple user ID and password also use HTTPS.

HTML/XHTML

How are Web pages formatted? Web pages are text documents that are formatted using HTML or XHTML. Style sheets (described in more detail later in this chapter) provide developers an easier way to update and revise Web pages. Although XHTML is the development environment of choice for Web developers today, many people still refer to Web site formatting as "HTML tagging."

HTML and XHTML are not programming languages; rather, they are sets of rules for marking up blocks of text so that a browser knows how to display them. Blocks of text in HTML/XHTML documents are surrounded by pairs of **HTML tags** (such as <b> and </b>, which indicate bolding). HTML tags surround and define HTML content. Each pair of tags and the text between them are collectively referred to as an **element**. The elements are interpreted by the browser, and appropriate effects are applied to the text. The following is an element from an HTML/XHTML document:

```
<i>This should be
italicized.</i>
```

The browser would display this element as:

This should be italicized.

The first tag, <i>, tells the browser that the text following it should be italicized. The ending </i> tag indicates that the browser should cease applying italics to the text. Note that multiple tags can be combined in a single element such as the following:

```
<b><i>This should be bolded
and italicized.</i></b>
```

The browser would display this element as

This should be bolded and italicized.

Obviously, the <b> tag indicates bolding. Tags for creating hyperlinks appear as follows:

```
<a href="http://www.
pearsonhighered.com">Pearson
Higher Education</a>
```

The code `<a href="http://www.pearsonhighered.com">` defines the link's destination. The <a> tag is the anchor tag and creates a link to another resource on the Web (denoted by the `href` attribute), such as an HTML page, an image, or a sound. In this case, the link is to the pearsonhighered. com Web page. The text between the open and close of the anchor tag (Pearson Higher Education) is the link label. The link label is the text (or image) that is displayed on the Web page as clickable text for the hyperlink.

Can you see the HTML/XHTML coding of a Web page? HTML/XHTML documents are merely text documents with tags applied to them. If you want to look at the HTML/XHTML coding behind your favorite Web page, just right-click anywhere on the page, select View Source from the shortcut menu, and the HTML/XHTML code for that page will be displayed, as shown in Figure 13.14. Alternatively, you can select View Source from

Figure 13.14

Viewing the source code of a Web site.

your browser menu. For more information on how to build Web pages, see the Sound Byte "Creating Web Pages with HTML."

XML

How is XML different from HTML/ XHTML? As you learned in Chapter 10, the extensible markup language (XML) describes the content in terms of what data is being described rather than how it is to be displayed. Instead of being locked into standard tags and formats for data, users can build their own markup languages to accommodate particular data formats and needs.

For example, three pieces of typical information that need to be captured for an e-commerce transaction are a credit card number, a price, and a zip code. In HTML/ XHTML, the paragraph tags (`<p>` and `</p>`) are used to define text and numeric elements. Almost any text or graphic can fall between these tags and be treated as a paragraph. Therefore, in our example, the HTML/ XHTML code would appear as follows:

```
<p>1234567890123456</p>
(credit card number)
<p>12.95</p> (price)
<p>19422</p> (zip code)
```

The browser will interpret the data contained within the `<p>` and `</p>` tags as separate paragraphs. However, the paragraph tags tell us nothing about the data contained within them. Without the labels (which are not part of the HTML/ XHTML code), we may not realize what data was contained within. In addition, tags don't provide any methodology for data validation. Credit card numbers are usually 16 numbers long, but any length of data may be inserted between `<p>` and `</p>` tags. How would we know if the credit card number was a valid length? The answer lies in creating tags that are specific to the task at hand and that actually describe the data

contained within them. Here's how our data might look in XML:

```
<credit_card_number>
1234567890123456
</credit_card_number>
<price>12.95</price>
<zip_code>19422</zip_code>
```

We have created the tags we need for data capture. Our XML specification provides a tag called "credit card number" that is used exclusively for credit card data.

How has XML influenced other Web page developments? XML has spawned quite a few custom packages for specific communities. For example, Mathematical Markup Language (MathML) is an XML-based markup language that is used to describe mathematical symbols and formulas so that they can be presented in a familiar way in Web documents. Wireless Markup Language (WML) uses XML to output Web resources on mobile devices; MusicXML is used to create and publish musical scores online; and GraphML is an XML-based format for creating graphs. These are just a few of the many examples that illustrate the goal of XML—information exchange standards that can be easily constructed and customized to serve a growing variety of online applications.

The Common Gateway Interface

Can you use HTML/XHTML to make a Web page interactive? Because HTML/XHTML was originally designed to link text documents, HTML/ XHTML by itself can't do all the amazing things we expect modern Web pages to do. As we mentioned earlier, HTML and XHTML are not programming languages; rather, they are sets of tags that determine how text is displayed and where elements are placed. Fortunately, the limitations of HTML/XHTML were recognized early, and the common gateway interface (CGI) was developed.

Most browser requests merely result in a file such as the eBay home page (**eBay.com**) being displayed in your browser. Displaying a file is fine if you're just going to be reading text. However, to make a Web site interactive, you may need to run a program to perform a certain action (such as gathering a name and address and adding them to a database). The **common gateway interface (CGI)** provides a methodology by which your browser can request that a program file be executed (run) instead of just being delivered to the browser. This enables functionality beyond the simple display of information.

CGI files can be created in almost any programming language, and the programs created are often referred to as **CGI scripts**. Common languages that are used to create CGI scripts are PERL, C, and C++. Because programming languages are extremely powerful, almost any task can be accomplished by writing a CGI script. You have probably encountered CGI scripts on Web pages without realizing it. Have you ever left an entry in a guest book on a Web page? Have you used a search engine to create a customized results page based on keywords you entered? Have you filled out a form in which you asked to be added to a mailing list? All of these tasks are commonly done using CGI scripts.

How are CGI programs executed?
On most Web servers, a directory called **cgi-bin** is created by the network administrator who configures the Web server. All CGI scripts are placed into this directory. The Web server knows that all files in this directory are not just to be read and sent, but also need to be run. Because this type of program runs on the Web server rather than inside your browser, it is referred to as a **server-side program**.

For instance, a button on a Web site may say "Click Here to Join Mailing List" (see step 1 in Figure 13.15). Clicking the button

may call a script file (perhaps called "mailinglist.pl") from the cgi-bin directory on the Web server hosting the site (step 2). This file generates a form that is sent to your browser. The form includes fields for a name and e-mail address and a button that says "Submit" (step 3). After the user fills in the fields and clicks the Submit button, the mailinglist.pl program sends the information back to the server. The server then records the information in a database (step 4).

Dynamic HTML

Can Web pages be made more interactive without accessing Web servers?   Dynamic HTML (DHTML) is a combination of technologies—HTML/XHTML, cascading style sheets, and JavaScript—that is used to create lively and interactive Web sites. Recall that the Web is based on a client/server network. Once a Web server processes a Web page and sends the page to the computer that requested it (the client), the receiving computer cannot get any new data from the server unless a new request is made. If interactivity is required on a Web page, this exchange of data between the client and server can make the interactivity inefficient and slow. DHTML technologies allow a Web page to change after it has been loaded. Change generally occurs in response to such user actions as

Figure 13.15

Information flow when a CGI program is run.

STEP 1: You want to join XYZ's mailing list. You push a button on their Web site labeled "Click Here to Join Mailing List."

STEP 2: Pushing the button tells the XYZ.com server to execute a CGI program (called mailinglist.pl) located in the cgi-bin directory on the server.

STEP 3: The server executes the CGI program mailinglist.pl, which generates a form that is sent to your browser.

Your computer

XYZ.com server

STEP 4: You enter your mailing list information and click the "Submit" button on the mailing list form. This sends your information back to the server. The server saves your information into its database.

clicking a mouse or mousing over objects on a page. DHTML brings special effects to otherwise static Web pages without requiring users to download and install plug-ins or other special software.

AJAX is the acronym for a newer group of technologies that facilitates the creation of Web applications. These technologies can update information on the page without requiring the user to do a page refresh or leave the page. AJAX does not actually require the use of JavaScript or XML (even though they are in the name) but can use a variety of Web programming techniques and languages. JavaScript and XML are frequently used by AJAX web developers.

What is JavaScript? JavaScript is the most commonly used scripting language for creating DHTML effects. It was developed through the joint efforts of Netscape and Sun Microsystems, two software development companies. JavaScript is often confused with the Java programming language because of the similarity in their names. However, though they share some common elements, the two languages function quite differently.

Pure HTML/XHTML documents don't respond to user input. With JavaScript, though, HTML/XHTML documents can be made responsive to mouse clicks and typing. For example, JavaScript is often used to validate the information you input in a Web form (for example, to make sure you filled in all required fields).

When JavaScript code is embedded in an HTML/XHMTL document, it is downloaded to the browser with the HTML/ XHTML page. All actions dictated by the embedded JavaScript commands are executed on the client computer (the one with the browser). Without JavaScript and other scripting languages, Web pages would be lifeless.

How can you easily change the formatting of HTML/XHTML elements? In addition to the HTML/XHTML formatting tags described earlier,

some tags describe areas of a Web page. This helps with layout. For example, the tag <h1> declares an area as a header. Similarly, <p> says, "This is a paragraph," and <table> says, "This is a table." In addition to tags defining certain areas as headers, paragraphs, or tables, Web developers needed additional tags to indicate how each header, paragraph, or table would be formatted and displayed. Although this system worked for a while, as more and more tags and attributes were created it became increasingly difficult to manage the differences between content and presentation layout.

To solve this problem, cascading style sheets were created. A **cascading style sheet (CSS)** is a list of statements (also known as *rules*) that defines in one single location how to display HTML/XHTML elements. Style rules enable a Web developer to define a style for each HTML/XHTML element and apply it to multiple elements on as many Web pages as needed. Thus, when a global change is necessary, the developer only needs to change the style on the style sheet; all the elements in the Web document are then updated automatically (see Figure 13.16).

For example, a Web page has an <H1> heading tag, and all <H1> tags in the Web page are formatted with a white background and an orange border. Before CSS, if you wanted to change the border color from orange to yellow, you had to change the background color of every <H1> tag. With CSS, the change from orange to yellow only needs to happen once on the style sheets; all the <H1> tags then update to yellow without individual changes.

Where does the cascading come in? In Web documents, there are different layers of styles: external, embedded, and inline. Therefore, it's possible that different rules can be created for the same type of element. In other words, in an external style sheet, there might be a rule that defines the background color for all paragraphs as blue. Somewhere else, in an embedded style

Figure 13.16

Cascading style sheets place formatting for specific document elements together in one place to simplify Web page development and revision. Just as all the pages of this book have a similar look and feel, one cascading style sheet can control the formatting of many Web pages.

sheet, a rule for background color for paragraphs might be white; and in an inline style sheet, the background color might be light pink. Eventually, all these style sheets must be merged to form one style sheet for the document. This creates conflicts among rules. Therefore, rules are assigned weights so that when the rules are collected and merged, the rule or style with a higher weight overrides the rule or style with a lower weight. This hierarchy of competing styles creates a "cascade" of styles ranked according to their assigned weights.

How are the individual components of a Web page organized? Just as cascading style sheets organize and combine the attributes of objects on a Web page, DHTML uses the **document object model (DOM)** to organize the objects and page elements. The document object model defines every item on a Web page—including graphics, tables, and headers—as an object. Then with DOM, similar to CSS, Web developers can easily change the look and feel of these objects.

Client-Side Applications

Aside from CGI scripts, are there other ways to make a Web site interactive? Sometimes running programs on the server is not optimal. Server-side program execution can require many communication sessions between the client and the server to achieve the goal. Often it is more efficient to run programs on

your computer (the client). Therefore, client-side programs were created. A **client-side program** is a computer program that runs on the client computer and requires no interaction with a Web server. Client-side programs are fast and efficient because they run on your desktop and don't depend on signals going back and forth to the Web server. Two main types of client-side methods exist. The first involves embedding programming language code directly within the HTML or XHTML code of a Web page using an **HTML/XHTML embedded scripting language**. The most popular embedded language is JavaScript, which is used extensively in dynamic HTML files.

The second type of client-side program is an **applet**, a small application that resides on a server. When requested, a compiled version of the program is downloaded to the client computer and run there. The Java language is the most common language used to create applets for use in browsers. The applets can be requested from the server when a Web page is loaded; they will run once they're downloaded to the client computer.

Although the user can experience some delay in functionality while waiting for the Java applet to download to the client, once the applet arrives, it can execute all its functions without further communication with the server. Games are often sent to your browser as applets. As an example, in Figure 13.17 your browser makes contact with a game on the game site ArcadePod.

Figure 13.17

Deployment of a Java applet on a computer.

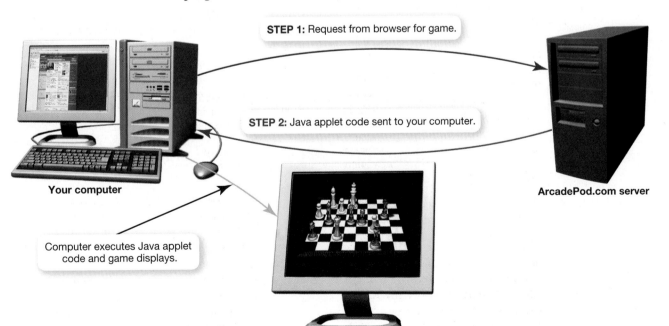

STEP 1: Request from browser for game.

STEP 2: Java applet code sent to your computer.

Your computer

Computer executes Java applet code and game displays.

ArcadePod.com server

com (**arcadepod.com**) and makes your request to play a game (step 1). The Web server returns the Java applet (step 2) that contains all the code to run the game on your computer. Your computer executes the applet code, and the game runs on your computer.

Communications over the Internet

A new communications revolution was started when Internet use began to explode in the mid-1990s. The volume of Internet e-mail is growing exponentially every month. Unfortunately, it is estimated that 90 percent of it is spam. Instant messaging is a major method of communication, and the popularity of Voice over Internet Protocol is also on the rise. In the following sections, we explore all of these communications media in

more detail and show you how to keep your information exchanges efficient and secure.

E-Mail

Who invented e-mail? In 1971, Ray Tomlinson, a computer engineer who worked on the development of the ARPANET (the precursor to the Internet) for the U.S. government, created e-mail. E-mail grew from a simple program that Tomlinson wrote to enable computer users to leave text messages for each other on a single machine. The logical extension of this was sending text messages between machines on the Internet. Tomlinson created the convention of using the @ sign to distinguish between the mailbox name and the destination computer. E-mail became the most popular application on ARPANET; by 1973, it accounted for 75 percent of all data traffic.

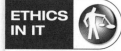

ETHICS IN IT Ethics: Politics Web 2.0 Style

The Internet and Web 2.0 technologies were leveraged for political campaigning in the recent 2008 presidential election more than in any other campaign in recent history. Twenty-first century politicians have realized the best way to reach the voting public is through the Internet.

Hillary Clinton, for example, announced her campaign with a YouTube video. Pictures of candidates on the campaign trail appeared on Flickr. President Obama waged a highly successful media campaign using a blog, YouTube, and social networking sites such as Facebook and MySpace. By the end of the campaign, his social networking accounts were connected to millions of individuals, and the campaign's YouTube channel had generated more than 110 million views. President Obama's administration continues to use Web 2.0 tools to communicate with the public and solicit feedback and opinions. The Internet has become the new "town meeting" location.

The insurgence of Web 2.0 technologies allowed Internet users to create and modify Internet content through videos, blogs, and podcasts—and it also changed how the voting public responded to political campaigns. Voter-generated content such as the "Vote Different" YouTube video ad that appeared in the beginning of the 2008 presidential campaign is a good example of the use of 2.0 technologies. That YouTube video is a remake of the classic 1984 Mac ad, features voice-over comments made by Hillary Clinton in her candidacy announcement video, and ends with an Obama 2008 endorsement. The Obama campaign did not create the ad, and neither the Clinton nor Obama campaigns knew who did until a citizen—Phil de Vellis—admitted he had created the ad to illustrate how voters can voice and broadcast their personal opinions for all to hear and see. As de Vellis said, "This shows that the future of American politics rests in the hands of ordinary citizens." Unfortunately, this could lead to ordinary citizens distorting the truth because no one is responsible for vetting the content of videos placed on YouTube.

Tech President, a blog site created specifically for the 2008 presidential campaign, tracked how the candidates used the Web and how voter content affected the campaign by showing the current number of MySpace friends and YouTube views each candidate had. With the 2008 election over, Tech President has expanded its scope to explore how elections at state and local levels are making use of Web 2.0 technologies.

Being able to express personal opinions and reach a majority of American voters is a benefit of the Internet. However, the medium also poses some issues that we should think about. As with any publicly generated content, how much online campaign information can we trust to be true and valid? Internet content has always had problems when determining authenticity, currency, relevance, and bias. When the main distribution channel for political information is neither reviewed nor validated, should we anticipate that bias might be interjected?

Anyone can upload video, image, or text content to the Web, but there is no governing authority that checks for content validity. At least with public information generated by 20th-century media, including TV, radio, and print (newspapers and magazines), there were some standards of authentication because information had to go through some form of editorial review. Although we needed to be prepared to look for the other side of a story or determine the role of personal opinion or editorial bias, the factual content in traditional media could reasonably be determined. Although some sites do police themselves, there is no official review board or evaluation authority through which Internet content must pass. On the other hand, can we be our own editorial board, as we are with wiki pages? Is there enough knowledge and participation to ensure we will act to review and censor our own public content? Because this is just the beginning of politics Web 2.0 style, only time will tell. What do you think?

How does e-mail travel the Internet? Just like other kinds of data that flow along the Internet, e-mail has its own protocol. The **Simple Mail Transfer Protocol (SMTP)** is responsible for sending e-mail along the Internet to its destination. As in most other Internet applications, e-mail is a client/server application. To send an e-mail message, you will need some form of e-mail software to compose the document as well as to include an attachment such as a spreadsheet or photograph. Popular client-based e-mail software (software that needs to be installed on your computer) includes Microsoft Outlook and Thunderbird, as well as Web-based e-mail software such as the increasingly popular Yahoo!, Hotmail, and Gmail.

As you read in Chapter 3, client-based software is installed on your computer, and all of its functions are supported and run from your computer. Web-based software is launched from a Web site; the programs and features are stored on the Web and are accessible anywhere you have access to an Internet connection. No matter which type of

Are Old Web Pages Really Gone Forever?

Have you ever tried to find a site you've visited on the Web, only to find it no longer exists? Have you ever discovered that information you wanted to access has been removed from a site? Is the information lost forever? Groups such as the Internet Archive (**archive.org**) are trying to prevent the loss of information on the Internet as a result of Web site updates or the discontinuance of a site. Since 1996, the Internet Archive has been collecting information from the Web and preserving it. Visit the Internet Archive site, and use the "Wayback Machine" to visit archived versions of Web sites from times past. Want to see how Yahoo! has changed since 1996? Just type the URL into the Wayback Machine engine and you'll see links to snapshots of Yahoo! at various points in time. So next time you try to access a site that is no longer there, check the Wayback Machine—all may not be lost.

client software you use, on the way to its destination your mail will pass through **e-mail servers**—specialized computers whose sole function is to store, process, and send e-mail.

Where are e-mail servers located? If your ISP provides you with an e-mail account, it runs an e-mail server that uses SMTP. For example, as shown in Figure 13.18, say you are sending an e-mail

Figure 13.18

A sample route an e-mail takes on the Internet.

STEP 1: You send an e-mail message to your friend Cheyenne.

STEP 2: Your ISP's Web server forwards the message to its e-mail server.

STEP 3: Your ISP's e-mail server consults the DNS server for Cheyenne's domain address.

Your ISP's Web server

Your ISP's e-mail server (SMTP)

DNS server

STEP 4: The DNS server provides the domain IP address.

STEP 5: The e-mail server forwards your e-mail through the Internet to Cheyenne's ISP's Web server.

Your computer

STEP 6: Cheyenne's ISP's Web server forwards the e-mail for storage on the e-mail server.

STEP 7: The next time Cheyenne checks her e-mail, she gets your e-mail.

Cheyenne's ISP's Web server (cheapISP.com)

Cheyenne's ISP's e-mail server (SMTP)

Cheyenne's computer

message to your friend Cheyenne. Cheyenne uses Juno.com as her ISP. Therefore, your e-mail to her is addressed to Cheyenne@juno.com.

When you send the e-mail message, your ISP's Web server receives it and passes it to your ISP's e-mail server. The e-mail server reads the domain name (**juno.com**) and communicates with a DNS server to determine the location of juno.com. Once the address is located, the e-mail message is forwarded to juno.com through the Internet and arrives at a mail server maintained by Cheyenne's ISP. The e-mail is then stored on Cheyenne's ISP's e-mail server. The next time Cheyenne logs on to her ISP and checks her mail, she will receive your message.

If e-mail was designed for text messages, why are we able to send files as attachments? SMTP was designed to handle text messages. When the need arose to send files by e-mail (in the early 1970s), a program had to be created to convert binary files to text. The text that represented the file was appended to the end of the e-mail message. When the e-mail arrived at its destination, the recipient had to run another program to translate the text back into a binary file. Uuencode and uudecode were the two most popular programs used for encoding and decoding binary files.

This was fine in the early days of the Internet when most users were computer scientists. However, when the Internet started to become popular (in the early 1990s), it became apparent that a simpler methodology was needed for sending and receiving files. The **multipurpose Internet mail extensions (MIME)** specification was introduced in 1991 to simplify attachments to e-mail messages. All e-mail client software now uses this protocol to attach files.

E-mail is still sent as text, but the e-mail client using the MIME protocol now handles the encoding and decoding for the users. For instance, in Yahoo! mail, on the Attach Files screen you merely browse to the file you want to attach (located somewhere on your hard drive), select the file, and click the Attach Files button. The Yahoo! e-mail client transparently encodes and decodes the file for transmission and receipt.

E-Mail Security: Encryption and Specialized Software

If e-mail is sent in regular text, can other people read my mail? E-mail is highly susceptible to being read by unintended parties because it's sent in plain text. Additionally, copies of your e-mail messages may exist (temporarily or permanently) on numerous servers as the messages make their way through the Internet. To protect your sensitive e-mail messages, encryption practices are used.

How do you encrypt e-mail? **Encryption** refers to the process of coding your e-mail so that only the person with the key to the code (the intended recipient) can decode (or decipher) and read the message. Secret codes for messages can be traced almost to the dawn of written language. The military and government espionage agencies are big users of codes and ciphers. The trick is making the coding system easy enough to use that everyone who needs to communicate with you can do so.

There are two basic types of encryption: private key and public key. In **private-key encryption**, only the two parties involved in sending the message have the code. This could be a simple shift code where letters of the alphabet are shifted to a new position (see Figure 13.19). For example, in a two-position right-shift code, the letter *a* becomes *c*, *b* becomes *d*, and so on. Alternatively, it could be a more complex

A = C	N = P
B = D	O = Q
C = E	P = R
D = F	Q = S
E = G	R = T
F = H	S = U
G = I	T = V
H = J	U = W
I = K	V = X
J = L	W = Y
K = M	X = Z
L = N	Y = A
M = O	Z = B

The word **C O M P U T E R** using the two-position code at the left now becomes:

E Q O R W V G T

This is difficult to interpret without the code key at the left.

Figure 13.19

Writing the word "COMPUTER" using a two-position right-shift encryption code.

substitution code ($a = h$, $b = r$, $c = g$, etc.). The main problem with private-key encryption is key security. If someone steals a copy of the code or is savvy about decoding, the code is broken.

In **public-key encryption**, two keys, known as a **key pair**, are created. You use one key for coding and the other for decoding. The key for coding is generally distributed as a **public key**. You can place this key on your Web site, for instance. Anyone wishing to send you a message can then download your public key and code the message using your public key.

When you receive the message, you use your **private key** to decode it. You are the only one who ever possesses the private key, and therefore it is highly secure. The keys are generated in such a way that they can work only with each other. The private key is generated first. The public key is then generated using a complex mathematical formula, often using values from the private key. The computations are so complex that they are considered unbreakable. Both keys are necessary to decode a message. If one key is lost, the other key cannot be used by itself.

What type of encryption is used on the Internet? Public-key encryption is the most commonly used encryption on the Internet. Tried-and-true public-key packages such as **Pretty Good Privacy (PGP)** are available for download at sites such as Download.com (**download.com**), and you can usually use them free of charge (although there are now commercial versions of PGP). After obtaining the PGP software, you can generate key pairs to provide a private key for you and a public key for the rest of the world.

What does a key look like? A key is a binary number. Keys vary in length, depending on how secure they need to be. A 10-bit key has 10 positions and might look like this:

```
1001101011
```

Longer keys are more secure because they have more values that are possible. A 10-bit key provides 1,024 different possible values, whereas a 40-bit key allows for 1,099,511,627,776 possible values. The key and the message are run through a complex algorithm in the encryption program (such as PGP) that converts the message into unrecognizable

BITS AND BYTES

Random Numbers: The Lifeblood of Encryption

E-mail encryption, SSL encryption, and just about anything we do to achieve privacy on the Internet requires random numbers. Encryption is accomplished using random number sequences, which are sequences of numbers in which no patterns can be recognized. Even for an e-commerce transaction (say, buying a book from Amazon.com) that uses SSL encryption to encode your credit card number, as many as 368 bits of random data might be needed. Only 128 bits are needed for the encryption key, but other random data is needed to create authentication codes and to prevent replay attacks. Replay attacks occur when hackers attempt to copy packets traveling across the Internet and extract data (such as encryption codes) from them. The hackers then can replay (reuse) the data to gain access to networks or transactions.

So where do all these random numbers come from? Generating true random sequences is more difficult than it sounds. However, in 1996, Landon Noll and two colleagues came up with a system called *LavaRnd* that used Lava Lite lamps (**lavalite.com**) to generate random numbers. The lamps have since been replaced with another random source: a webcam with the lens cap still on. The webcam emits "thermal noise," which is then digitized and run through a mathematical algorithm that generates the number set and strips out any sections that are predictable. This service is open source, unpatented, and license free, so anyone can set up a server and generate much-needed random numbers. For more information, check out the LavaRnd site (**lavarnd.org**).

code. Each key turns the message into a different code.

Is a private key really secure? Because of the complexity of the algorithms used to generate key pairs, it is impossible to deduce the private key from the public key. However, that doesn't mean your coded message can't be cracked. As you learned in Chapter 12, a brute force attack occurs when hackers try every possible key combination to decode a message. This type of attack can enable hackers to deduce the key and decode the message.

What is considered a safe key? In the early 1990s, 40-bit keys were thought to be totally resistant to brute force attacks and were the norm for encryption. However, in 1995, a French programmer used a unique algorithm of his own and 120 workstations simultaneously to attempt to break a 40-bit key. He succeeded in just eight days.

ACTIVE HELP-DESK

Keeping E-Mail Secure

In this Active Helpdesk call, you'll play the role of a helpdesk staffer, fielding calls about how e-mail works and how messages are kept secure.

The Internet and the ways we use it are constantly evolving. In the 1990s, most home users connected to the Internet with a dial-up modem. Today, DSL, cable, and fiber optics provide faster connections. Now fiber-optic technology, once available only for corporate and urban America, is beginning to reach homes in suburban and rural areas. This technology not only enables the transmission of data at close to the speed of light but also provides an uninterrupted data pathway that makes the delivery of communications more reliable.

Perhaps You Would Prefer to Use Your Wall Outlet?

There is more on the horizon than just increased fiber-optic reach. Many companies are exploring a technology that sends data, voice, and video signals over normal electrical power lines. That's right: Someday you may be able to connect to the Internet through your normal wall outlet. Called *broadband over power line* (BPL), this technology is currently deployed in Europe and Australia but has been slower to roll out in the United States. Duke Power, Ambient Corporation, Amperion, and Current Technologies are among the U.S. providers offering limited deployment in some communities. Although the current connectivity speeds of BPL are not quite as fast as cable or DSL broadband alternatives, the prospect is that with a power-line Internet connection, you could one day transfer *exobits* of data—that's 1 with 18 zeros after it—per second through power lines. Now that's *fast*.

How About WiMAX?

Because of the rise in portable computing devices, people want Internet access wherever they go. An up-and-coming wireless alternative to standard Wi-Fi connections is WiMAX (short for worldwide interoperability for microwave access). Instead of the 300 feet of connectivity that Wi-Fi offers, WiMAX has a range of as far as 31 miles, and its transmission speed will run up to 72 Mbps, making it much faster than current cable or DSL connections. The WiMAX Forum, a nonprofit group consisting mainly of WiMAX

Figure 13.20

Airships such as the Sanswire Stratellite will help break down barriers to high-speed wireless access.

providers and component suppliers, reports there are more than 400 WiMax networks deployed in 130 countries, although the technology has been catching on slowly in the United States. Assuming that the technology proves reliable, your next provider of Internet services may well be a company that offers WiMax wireless connectivity.

Or Blimps?

Most people are unaware that the satellites currently used to provide wireless Internet access are deployed at high altitudes that actually pose barriers to high-speed data communications. One solution currently being developed is the deployment of communications platforms at lower

Since then, 128-bit keys have become the standard. Even using supercomputers, no one has yet cracked a 128-bit key. It is believed that even with the most powerful computers in use today, it would take hundreds of billions of years to crack a 128-bit key.

How do businesses protect e-mail? Encryption doesn't solve the other problems associated with e-mail. Messages leave a trail as they travel over the Internet, and copies of messages can exist on servers for long periods of time. In addition, immediate reading of sensitive documents is often essential, but encryption software doesn't provide a means for confirming that your messages have been delivered. To combat these issues, companies including Securus Systems Ltd. (**safemessage.com**) have developed secure data transmission software that works outside of the conventional SMTP mail servers. Let's look at Securus Systems' product, SafeMessage.

How is SafeMessage software used? Parties who wish to send or receive secure messages install the SafeMessage software. When messages are to be sent, a secure point-to-point connection is established between the sender's and the recipient's e-mail boxes. Instead of SMTP, proprietary protocols with encryption are used to send the messages. Additional options are provided such as delivery confirmation, message shredding (destruction of messages on command), and the ability to have messages erase themselves after a set period of time. Although this type of software is not free, it is catching on in those sections of the business

Figure 13.21

Google Maps provides a list of hot spots where you can go to connect to the Internet.

the Internet wirelessly. Often there is no charge to connect. If you're looking for a hot spot, portable wireless network detectors, such as the Wi-Fi Finder from Kensington, make it easy to detect wireless networks wherever you are. If you know in advance where you'll be, you can use Wi-Fi Free Spot (**wififreespot.com**). Another option is offered by Google Maps. Type "free Wi-Fi hotspots" and your location in the search bar. Google Maps will produce a map with locations highlighted and exact addresses in the margin (see Figure 13.21). Of course, just because you can locate a coffee shop with a hot spot doesn't always mean you can get a table!

Want a Safer Internet?

More research is needed to anticipate and defend against future cyberterror attacks. To this end, the National Science Foundation (NSF) and the Department of Homeland Security (DHS) have funded the development of the DETERlab (cyber-**DE**fense **T**echnology **E**xperimental **R**esearch **lab**oratory). The DETERlab is composed of two computing clusters, one at the University of California at Berkeley, and one at the University of Southern California Information Sciences Institute. This computer network is used for research and development of new cybersecurity technologies. The network can be configured to simulate the real Internet. All types of cyberattacks (from worms to denial-of-service attacks) can be launched on the network's infrastructure. The DETERlab allows researchers to learn how to better detect and deter cyberattacks without posing a danger to the actual Internet during testing.

Look for these and other Internet-related technologies coming soon to computers near you.

altitudes using airships (blimps). The company GlobeTel Communications has developed the Sanswire Stratellite (see Figure 13.20), a 245-foot-long unmanned airship that is designed to sail 13 miles above the Earth's surface. One such airship could provide communications coverage for an area as large as the state of Texas—that's 268,581 square miles! In addition to providing wireless Internet access, this technology could serve as an alternative to satellites for cellular telephony.

Looking for a Free Hot Spot?

With mobile computing devices now commonplace, many businesses offer connectivity in the form of **hot spots**—places where users can connect to

community where fear of industrial espionage is high.

Instant Messaging

What do you need to run instant messaging?
As we said in Chapter 3, instant messaging is the act of communicating over the Internet with one or more people in real time. It differs from e-mail in that conversations are able to happen at the same time rather than lagging by minutes or hours. Instant messaging requires the use of a client program that connects to an instant messaging service. AOL Instant Messenger (AIM), ICQ, Yahoo! Messenger, and Windows Live Messenger are the top four instant messaging services in use today. No matter which one you choose, you need to

have the appropriate client software installed on your computer.

How does instant messaging work?
The client software running on your computer makes a connection with the chat server using your Internet connection, as shown in Figure 13.22. Once contact is established, you can log in to the server with your name and password. (You can sign up for a free account the first time you connect.) The client software provides the server with connection information (such as the IP address) for your computer. The server then consults the list of contacts ("Buddies" or friends) that you have previously established in your account and checks to see if any of your contacts are online (step 1). If any are, the server sends a message back to your client providing the necessary connection information (the IP addresses) for your

Figure 13.22

How an instant messaging
program works.

STEP 1: Contact chat server to see who is online.

STEP 2: IP addresses of your Buddies sent to your computer.

Your computer running instant messaging client software for chatting

Chat server

INTERNET

STEP 3: Chat with your Buddy commences via his IP address.

Your Buddy's computer running the same instant messaging client software for chatting

friends who are online (step 2). You can now click your friends' names to establish a chat session with them (step 3).

Because both your computer and your friend's computer have the connection information (the IP addresses) for each other, the server isn't involved in the chat session. Chatting takes place directly between the two computers over the Internet.

Is sending an instant message secure? Most instant messaging services do not use a high level of encryption for their messages—if they bother to use encryption at all. In addition to viruses, worms, and hacking threats, instant messaging systems are vulnerable to eavesdropping, in which someone using a packet sniffer "listens in" on IM conversations. Although several measures are under way to increase the security of this method of real-time communication, major vulnerabilities still exist. Therefore, it is not a good idea to send sensitive information using instant messaging because it is susceptible to interception and possible misuse by hackers.

Voice over Internet Protocol (VoIP)

What is Voice over Internet Protocol? Voice over Internet Protocol (VoIP) turns a standard Internet connection into a way to make free long-distance phone calls. If you have friends and relatives that live a long-distance phone call away from you, then you need to know more about VoIP.

What's so good about VoIP? From a user's perspective, the true advantage is that the service is cheaper than conventional phone service or, in some instances, is free. Even some cell phones are VoIP-enabled. T-Mobile's HotSpot@Home service allows customers to make cell phone calls over a VoIP network as long as the device can connect to a Wi-Fi signal. When a Wi-Fi signal is not detected, the cell phone makes the call through your usual cellular network.

How does VoIP work? From a user's perspective, there is little difference between VoIP and traditional phone service (see Figure 13.23), although the technology behind the wires and devices is a bit different. As explained in Chapter 3, VoIP is a method of taking analog voice signals that normally travel telephone wires and turning them into digital data that can be transmitted over the Internet. Like e-mail, VoIP uses packet switching as the method of transferring data. Unlike circuit switching (the method used with traditional phone calls), when a VoIP call is made, the transmission lines are only used when the two computers are communicating, thus allowing the computers to accept and process other information. Because digital

Figure 13.23 | CONVENTIONAL AND VoIP CALLING COMPARED

Conventional Telephone Call	VoIP Telephone Call
1. Pick up the phone and wait for a dial tone to signal that you are connected to the local office of your telephone carrier.	1. Pick up the phone, which sends a signal to the computer or telephone adapter. The computer sends a dial tone, indicating that you have a connection to the Internet.
2. Dial the number of your friend's phone.	2. Dial the number of your friend's phone. The tones are converted into digital data.
3. The call is routed through the switch at your local carrier, passing through several switches along the way.	3. As long as the phone number is in a valid format, your VoIP company will translate the phone number into an IP address and then connects to the receiving device.
4. The phone at the other end rings, and your friend answers the call.	4. The signal "asks" the receiving device to ring, and your friend answers the call.
5. When the call is answered, a circuit is opened.	5. When your friend picks up the phone, each computer knows to expect packets of data from the other computer.
6. As you talk, the circuit remains open. No other data can be transmitted over the phone line during this time. A busy signal occurs if someone else tries to call.	6. As you talk, the packets of data are sent over the same Internet infrastructure as e-mail or a Web page. The digital data is translated into analog audio signals so that you and your friend can understand each other.
7. When you hang up, the circuit is closed, enabling another call to come in.	7. When you hang up, the session is terminated.

data is far more efficient than analog data with respect to size, transmission speed, and compression capabilities, VoIP's long-term advantage is that it will be able to handle more phone calls at the same time. Although today's traditional phone calls have increased efficiency and reduced costs since they were first invented, there is considerable room for improvement compared to how digital data (such as e-mail) is transmitted.

How are VoIP security issues being handled? Because VoIP technology is similar to that of e-mail, VoIP is vulnerable to some of the same threats. However, the use of encryption methodologies, updated antivirus software, firewalls, and antispam tools helps cut down on VoIP's security vulnerabilities.

Using the Internet to Deliver Computer Services

Businesses are taking advantage of the Internet in some fairly obvious ways, such as the explosion in e-commerce over the last decade. In addition, businesses are using the Internet in ways that are transparent (invisible) to the end user and that result in considerable cost savings and increases in business efficiencies.

Cloud Computing

What is cloud computing? The Internet is often represented in diagrams as a picture of a cloud. **Cloud computing** refers to using the Internet to deliver business services online that were previously delivered locally by company-owned IT departments. You have probably used cloud computing services yourself because many Web 2.0 applications (such as blogs, wikis, and social networks) and Web-based e-mail (such as Yahoo! or Gmail) are provided to you via cloud computing.

Why would a company need cloud computing? Amazon.com needs the computing power of many computers (servers) to manage the millions of products they offer and handle the tens of thousands of orders they receive and deliver each day. Amazon has made a significant investment in computer hardware, software, and human programming talent to build a comprehensive e-commerce system to acquire, sell, and deliver products. If you were going to start a business that required a sophisticated inventory system such as the one Amazon uses to manage their stock, you would need a rather large pile of cash to purchase the equipment, software, and labor needed to develop your own product tracking system.

Certain companies, like Amazon, that have already made the investment in their systems have now started to offer other companies services via cloud computing. Under the Amazon Elastic Compute Cloud (Amazon EC2), Amazon offers other companies (for a fee, of course) the capability to use their proven systems and technology to host computer applications that those other companies require. This means that companies can have Amazon set up and maintain servers for them that can be accessed via the Internet. The companies pay Amazon only for the storage and processing capacity that they use.

Imagine that you wanted to start a company to sell shoes online. Instead of hiring an entire IT department and investing tens of thousands of dollars in software and hardware, you could lease server space from Amazon's computing services. Your computing systems would then be deployed on hardware and software maintained by Amazon, and your computer services would be delivered in the "cloud" (via the Internet). It would be much more cost effective for your company to use Amazon's proven systems and technology because

Amazon can add servers to its network to meet your computing needs for a fraction of the cost of building your own system. You still would need experienced IT talent to customize the delivery of services for your employees and customers and to connect your employees' computers to Amazon's servers. However, you would need significantly fewer people than you would need to build and maintain your own complex system.

What types of businesses can benefit the most from cloud computing? Businesses that need to process large amounts of data every once in a while can significantly reduce costs by using cloud computing. Instead of investing in large amounts of equipment and software that they will use only infrequently, a company can rent as much computing power as it needs at specific times. Businesses that tend to be busy during certain months or seasons of the year are also good candidates. For example, a company that makes fireworks might want to acquire more computing power during the months that lead up to the Fourth of July to handle a large increase in orders pertaining to that holiday. The fireworks company could then scale back their processing capacity on July 5. Furthermore, a start-up business that might not have the capability to raise large amounts of capital can often save significant amounts of money by paying for just the computing power it needs, instead

Figure 13.24

Jamglue uses Amazon.com's cloud computing services to process music mixes for its users.

of installing a large data processing center early on.

One example of a company that relies on cloud computing is Jamglue (**jamglue.com**). Jamglue is a Web site that allows users to upload music or sound tracks and then mix them with other tracks that have been uploaded or mixed by other users (see Figure 13.24). Processing the mixes requires a lot of computing power, and Jamglue uses Amazon EC2 services to process user data.

Is it safe to rely on other companies to process sensitive data? Security is one of the main concerns related to using cloud computing services. Running your own IT department requires careful consideration of how to protect and safeguard data. When you turn over processing to a third party, it's important to carefully investigate the security and backup capabilities of the cloud computing service provider to determine if their procedures meet your requirement for data security.

Security measures for all forms of communication technologies are constantly being evaluated. It is important for all users of Internet technologies to understand that threats to our security and privacy are real but are controllable with the proper precautions.

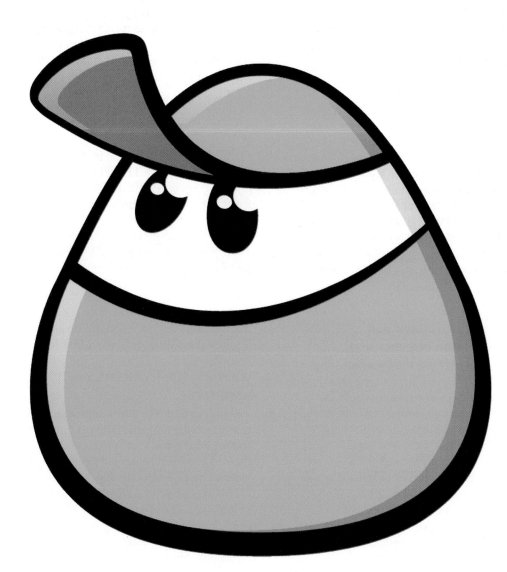

summary

1. Who owns, manages, and pays for the Internet?

Management of the Internet is carried out by several nonprofit organizations and user groups such as the Internet Society (ISOC), the Internet Engineering Task Force (IETF), the Internet Architecture Board (IAB), the Internet Corporation for Assigned Names and Numbers (ICANN), and the World Wide Web Consortium (W3C). Each group has different responsibilities and tasks. Currently, the U.S. government (and subsequently the U.S. taxpayer) funds a majority of the Internet's costs.

2. How do the Internet's networking components interact?

Individual computers or networks connect to the Internet using Internet service providers (ISPs). These providers vary in size and work like the physical highway system. The largest paths, along which data travels the most efficiently and quickly, make up the Internet backbone. Homes and all but the largest businesses connect to the Internet through these regional or local connections, which then connect to the Internet through the entities that make up the Internet backbone. The largest businesses, educational centers, and some government agencies such as NASA make up the Internet backbone.

3. What data transmissions and protocols does the Internet use?

Data is transmitted along the Internet using packet switching. Data is broken up into discrete units known as packets, which can take independent routes to the destination before being reassembled. Although many protocols are available on the Internet, the main suite of protocols used to move information over the Internet is TCP/IP. The suite is named after the original two protocols that were developed for the Internet: the Transmission Control Protocol (TCP) and the Internet Protocol (IP). Whereas TCP is responsible for preparing data for transmission, IP actually sends data between computers on the Internet.

4. Why are IP addresses and domain names important for Internet communications?

An IP address is a unique number assigned to all computers connected to the Internet. The IP address is necessary so that packets of data can be sent to a particular location (computer) on the Internet. A domain name is merely a name that stands for a certain IP address and makes it easier for people to remember it. For example, MyWebPage.com is a domain name and is much easier to remember than the IP address 124.53.111.14. DNS servers act as the phone books of the Internet. They enable your computer to find out the IP address of a domain by looking up its corresponding domain name (which you typed into your browser).

5. What are FTP and Telnet, and how do you use them?

The File Transfer Protocol (FTP) enables users to share files that reside on local computers with remote computers. Current versions of browsers enable you to connect to FTP sites on the Internet to facilitate downloading or uploading files to and from FTP sites. Telnet is both a protocol for connecting to a remote computer and a TCP/IP service that runs on a remote computer to make it accessible to other computers. Telnet enables you to take control of a remote computer (the server) with your computer (the client) and manipulate files and data on the server as if you were sitting in front of that server.

6. What are HTML/XHTML and XML used for?

The HyperText Markup Language (HTML) is a set of rules for marking up blocks of text so that a browser knows how to display them. Most Web pages are generated with at least some HTML code. Blocks of text in HTML documents are surrounded by a pair of tags (such as <b> and </b> to indicate bolding). These tags and the text between them are referred to as elements. By examining the elements, your browser determines how to display them on your computer screen. Because HTML was not designed for information exchange, eXtensible Markup Language (XML) was created. Instead of locking users into standard tags and formats for data, XML enables users to create their own markup languages to accommodate particular data formats and needs. XML is used extensively in e-commerce for exchanging data between corporations.

7. **How do e-mail, instant messaging, and Voice over Internet Protocol work, and how is information using these technologies kept secure?**

Simple Mail Transfer Protocol (SMTP) is the protocol responsible for sending e-mail over the Internet. As is true of most other Internet applications, e-mail is a client/server application. E-mail passes through e-mail servers whose functions are to store, process, and send e-mail to its ultimate destination. ISPs and portals such as Yahoo! maintain e-mail servers to provide e-mail functionality to their customers. Your ISP's e-mail server uses DNS servers to locate the IP addresses for the recipients of the e-mail you send. Encryption software, such as Pretty Good Privacy (PGP), is used to code messages so that they can be decoded only by the authorized recipients.

8. **How do businesses use the Internet to reduce computing costs?**

Many businesses are taking advantage of cloud computing to reduce costs. Cloud computing refers to business services provided online by other companies and delivered to a customer through the Internet. These services were formerly delivered locally by company-owned IT departments. A company might use Amazon.com's cloud computing servers, for example, to store their data instead of purchasing and installing their own servers. Cloud computing initiatives, while cost effective, generate data security concerns because a third party is managing sensitive data.

key terms

Word Bank

- AJAX
- applet
- circuit switching
- DNS server
- FTP
- HTML tags
- HTTP
- ICANN
- Internet backbone
- IP address
- OC line
- packet switching
- PGP
- point of presence
- public-key encryption
- SMTP
- SSL
- TCP/IP

Instructions: Fill in the blanks using the words from the Word Bank above.

As a network administrator, Patricia knows that she can count on the organization (1) _____ to ensure that she has an appropriate range of IP addresses for her work site. Her high-speed connection to her company's ISP was vital to providing the connectivity her employees need to get their jobs done. Recently, the company moved up from a DSL connection to a(n) (2) _____ because of the high volume of Internet traffic it was generating. Patricia hopes the government will continue to fund projects to continue research to improve the Internet (3) _____, the main highway to the Internet, and other vital technologies.

But Patricia has indulged in enough daydreaming. It is time to ensure that the Internet connection to the bank of modems, or (4) _____, provided by the ISP her company is using is fully functional before the majority of the employees arrive for work. Because Patricia's company sends a tremendous amount of e-mail, old-fashioned (5) _____ technology would never have sufficed for sending messages. Fortunately, the Internet employs (6) _____ to enable messages to be sent over widely varying routes. Of course, she knows that the main suite of protocols that controls Internet data traffic is called (7) _____.

After ensuring that all is functional, Patricia begins to assist the Web development team with Web page creation. To provide robust interaction with company databases, (8) _____ is being used to code Web pages for the corporate Web site instead of HTML, which requires developers to use a standard set of (9) _____. Unsure of her instructions, she e-mails the director of Web development for clarification, knowing that the (10) _____ protocol will ensure that the e-mail is delivered to the director at the company's office in the United Kingdom. Requiring secure communications, she encrypts the e-mail using a(n) (11) _____ algorithm, knowing that the director can retrieve Patricia's key from her personal Web site.

After reading the director's response to her e-mail, she quickly writes a Java (12) _____ to produce an interactive form to collect customer information. Using the (13) _____ protocol, Patricia posts her Web page to the corporate site. Of course, users will view the Web page using the (14) _____ protocol. Because the Web page contains potentially sensitive information, Patricia makes sure to use the (15) _____ protocol to provide added security for the data.

becoming
computer literate

While attending college, you are working at Shoe Station, a small retailer of children's and women's footwear. The owner has charged your supervisor with establishing a Web presence for the company by developing a company Web site and establishing online communications with international suppliers. Your supervisor has asked you to help draft a memo to the CEO that sets forth the technologies the company should deploy to create an Internet presence.

Instructions: Draft a memo for your boss that details the benefits of connecting the company to the Internet. Make sure to suggest which types of Internet connections will be appropriate and which type of ISP will be needed. Use as many of the keywords from the chapter as you can, and ensure that the report will be understandable by managers who may be unfamiliar with computers or the Internet.

Instructions: Answer the multiple-choice and true–false questions below for more practice with key terms and concepts from this chapter.

Multiple Choice

1. So that all computers on the Internet can communicate with each other, they must use common rules called *protocols*. Which is a common protocol used on the Internet?
 a. HTML
 b. XML
 c. TCP
 d. DNS

2. Data is sent over the Internet in small chunks called
 a. pockets.
 b. data envelopes.
 c. packets.
 d. switches.

3. A URL is used by humans to represent the numeric
 a. public key.
 b. dynamic address.
 c. routing address.
 d. IP address.

4. IP addresses that are assigned from an available pool of IP addresses are
 a. called *static*.
 b. less secure.
 c. called *dynamic*.
 d. permanent.

5. Which is the Internet protocol that ensures secure transmission of data on a Web page?
 a. XML
 b. HTTPS
 c. Telnet
 d. FTP

6. SMTP is the Internet protocol that
 a. uploads files to another computer.
 b. makes VoIP connections possible.
 c. controls the delivery of e-mail messages.
 d. provides for encryption of e-mail.

7. Points of presence are the
 a. way individuals connect to the Internet.
 b. points of connection between ISPs.
 c. connection points between Internet tiers.
 d. routes taken by e-mail pieces as they are sent over the Internet.

8. Internet e-mail is
 a. never encrypted.
 b. encrypted only if the SMTP protocol is used.
 c. encrypted only when special encryption software is used.
 d. prohibited by the Department of Homeland Security.

9. FTP is the protocol used to
 a. create a secure connection between client and server.
 b. load Web pages into a browser.
 c. encrypt e-mail messages.
 d. upload files to the Internet.

10. Which is NOT a key component of cloud computing?
 a. Delivery of computing services via the Internet
 b. Decreased computing start-up costs
 c. Increase in IT employee head count
 d. Ease of adding increased computing capacity

True–False

_____ 1. The costs associated with running the Internet are paid through fees levied by government agencies on e-commerce transactions.

_____ 2. VoIP uses circuit switching technology that is similar to e-mail.

_____ 3. A computer needs either the URL or the IP address to locate a Web page accurately.

_____ 4. The main suite of protocols used on the Internet is SMTP/FTP.

_____ 5. E-mail messages are generally not secure because the SMTP protocol does not provide for encryption.

1. Creating a Web Site: Issues 1

Your American history instructor has asked your group to design a Web site about the battle of Gettysburg. The site will include textual and graphic information on the battle as well as an interactive quiz. Users will be encouraged to post college term papers on the site as a resource for other students. The following issues need to be addressed:

a. In which domain should you register the site? Why do you think this is appropriate?

b. Choose an easy-to-remember domain name. Is this name already registered? Be sure to check in the appropriate top-level domain and provide proof that the name isn't already registered.

c. How would you ensure that people are able to find the site once it's on the Web?

d. What Internet protocols will users need to access the site?

e. What browsers or plug-ins may be required to access the site?

2. Creating a Web Site: Issues 2

As president of your school's Phi Beta Lambda (PBL) club, you would like to build a mailing list for your quarterly newsletter. You also would like to ensure that the newsletter is available on the college's Web site. When you visit the college Web developer, she asks you the following questions:

a. What data will you require all online subscribers to provide?

b. What optional data would you like subscribers to provide?

c. Will an e-mail address be provided to potential subscribers if they wish to make inquiries? If so, who will be reviewing and responding to these e-mails? How quickly will you promise to answer these e-mails?

3. Creating a Web Site: Issues 3

You have been asked to create a Web page to promote a campus club to which you belong. Investigate the following and explain which ISP you will recommend and why:

a. Most schools will provide Web pages for sanctioned clubs on their Web server. Does your school place any content restrictions on club Web sites? How much storage space is provided for club Web pages? Can club Web pages gather data from prospective members (such as contact information) for storage in a database?

b. Assume your club is unsanctioned and your school will not provide space for a Web page. Using Web sites such as The List (**thelist.com**) and Find An ISP (**findanisp.com**), find three ISPs that could potentially host the Web site and prepare a chart comparing the following for each ISP:
- Cost per month for hosting
- Amount of disk storage space
- Number and type of e-mail accounts
- Throughput allowed per month
- Level of technical support

4. Searching for Employment on the Web

With tuition costs rising, you feel it would be appropriate to find a part-time job next semester. Visit some popular employment sites such as Monster (**monster.com**) and Career Builder (**careerbuilder.com**) or your school's online career center Web site and complete the following tasks:

a. Search for a part-time job or internship opportunity in your field of study. Provide a listing of opportunities you think would be appropriate for you and briefly describe why they would be appropriate.

b. Search for full-time jobs for which you might apply when you graduate.
- What are the average starting salaries?
- Do the starting salaries vary by geographic location, or are they reasonably similar?
- What are the educational and previous experience requirements for the job?
- What gaps in your background, if any, would you need to fill to pursue this job?

1. Web Site Security Issues

Your employer, a distributor of specialty stereo equipment, offers high-speed Internet access at the office where you work. Thirty-five workstations are connected to the Internet and are used by employees to send e-mail and conduct research. Recently, company trade secrets were printed in the local press. They have been traced to an employee e-mail. The company president has enlisted your help in determining preventive measures to avoid such security breaches in the future. Draft a memo that includes the following:

a. An employee e-mail policy that requires the use of encryption technologies
b. Benefits and drawbacks of programs that monitor employee e-mails
c. Policies on instant messaging in the workplace, including whether or not instant messaging should be banned

2. Posting a Résumé Online

The director of your college placement office has suggested that you prepare a résumé that can be posted on the new alumni employment site that the university is developing. It must be in HTML format and should include your picture (although this is not required if you feel uncomfortable posting your picture). Answer the following questions:

a. What software would you use to develop the résumé?
b. Would straight HTML be sufficient, or would you need to use JavaScript to display the picture?
c. Find at least three Web sites (in addition to your college's site) where you could post your résumé for employers to view.

3. "Googling"

At your company, someone was just fired because sensitive information related to a company product was associated with the person's name on the Internet. Discretion being the better part of valor, you decide to do a search for your name on the Web using a search engine such as Google (**google.com**) just to see what is out there. Prepare a report on what you found. Your report should answer the following questions:

a. Did you find any accurate information about yourself (such as your home page URL or résumé)? Did you find any erroneous information that you need to correct?
b. Did you find Web sites or information about other people with the same name as you? Could any of that information be damaging to your reputation if someone thought the other person was you? If so, provide examples.
c. Is there information that you found about yourself or others that you think should never be available on the Internet? Provide examples and an explanation of why you feel certain information should not be available.
d. Is there any information on social networking sites, such as MySpace (**myspace. com**) or Facebook (**facebook.com**), that could be damaging to you if an employer or school administrator were to see it?

Instructions: Albert Einstein used *Gedankenexperiments* (critical thinking questions) to develop his theory of relativity. Some ideas are best understood by experimenting with them in our own minds. The following critical thinking questions are designed to demand your full attention but require only a comfortable chair—no technology.

1. Domain Names

Domain names often spark fierce controversy between competing companies. Legal wrangling over the rights to attractive names such as Buynow.com and Lowprices.com can generate large fees for attorneys. Meanwhile, some famous individuals such as Julia Roberts have had to fight for the right to own domains based on their own names.

a. Should everyone be entitled to a Web site in a certain domain (say, .com) that contains their own name? How would you handle disputes by people who have the exact same name (say, two people named John Smith)?

b. Cybersquatting is registering a domain name (say, Coke.net) just for the purpose of selling it to the organization that may benefit from it the most (in this case, the Coca-Cola Company). Is cybersquatting ethical? Why or why not? Is cybersquatting legal in the United States?

c. Aside from the domains currently approved (such as .com and .org), what domain names do you think would have commercial appeal? For which types of Web sites would these domains be used?

2. Illegal File Sharing Among Students

The College Opportunity and Affordability Act, passed by Congress in 2008, almost included a provision requiring colleges to monitor and punish students who were illegally swapping or downloading copyrighted material such as music or movies.

a. As a condition to receiving federal funding, should colleges be required to prevent students from illegally downloading or sharing material? Why or why not?

b. What measures has your school taken to prevent the illegal downloading of media? Are these measures effective? What other actions would you recommend your school take?

3. Encryption

Encryption programs built on 128-bit encryption algorithms are currently considered unbreakable.

a. Because of their secure nature, the U.S. government places restrictions on exports of these encryption products. The government is also considering a requirement that all encryption products should have a "backdoor" code that would enable government agencies (such as the CIA and FBI) to read encrypted messages. Do you think this should be implemented? Why or why not?

b. Assuming you figure out how to break 128-bit encryption, should you post that information on the Internet for anyone to use? Why or why not?

Creating a Business Web Presence

Problem

In today's fast-paced business environment, establishing a Web presence for a new business is critical. Having a Web site that is designed around the needs of customers is essential if a business is to compete in the 21st century. In this Team Time, you'll research Web hosting options and providers for a start-up company.

Task

Your group has just received a request from a friend who is starting a new apparel company called Trendz. It will sell clothing designed by young, urban artists and will target active young adults who are skateboarders and snowboarders. Your friend wants to sell the clothing over the Internet and needs your group's advice as to where to deploy a Web site and what features to offer.

Process

Break the class into small teams of three or four students. Each team should prepare a report as follows:

1. Determine an appropriate domain name for the Trendz Web site. Make sure that the Web address you propose is available by using a Whois service such as **whois.net**.
2. Select a company that can cost effectively register the domain name you have chosen and host the Web site. Investigate companies such as Network Solutions, 1and1.com, GoDaddy, Tucows, and Yahoo!. You might also want to consider free hosting solutions from Google or Microsoft Office Live.
3. Investigate options such as PayPal, Google Checkout, Authorize.net, or CyberSource and determine a provider for collecting payments from customers. Make sure to consider fixed monthly fees charged as well as per transaction fees.
4. Determine what shopping cart software will be necessary to manage customer orders. Volusion, Fortune 3, and Early Impact are examples of companies that offer possible solutions.
5. Develop a PowerPoint presentation to summarize your findings and present your proposed solution to the class.

Conclusion

E-commerce Web sites are relatively easy to deploy using the vast array of tools available on the Internet today. Substantial growth of new small businesses is expected in the United States over the next several decades. Therefore, you may soon be in a position where you will need to set up an e-commerce solution for friends, family, or an employer.

In addition to the review materials presented here, you'll find additional materials featured with the book's multimedia, including the *Technology in Action* Student Resource CD and the Companion Website (**pearsonhighered.com/techinaction**), which will help reinforce your understanding of the chapter content. These materials include the following:

Active Helpdesk

In Active Helpdesk calls, you'll assume the role of helpdesk operator, taking calls about the concepts you've learned in this chapter. You'll apply what you've learned and receive feedback from a supervisor to review and reinforce those concepts. The Active Helpdesk calls for this chapter are listed below and can be found on your Student Resource CD:

- Understanding IP Addresses, Domain Names, and Protocols
- Keeping E-Mail Secure

Sound Bytes

Sound Bytes are dynamic multimedia tutorials that help demystify even the most complex topics. You'll view video clips and animations that illustrate computer concepts and then apply what you've learned by reviewing with the Sound Byte Labs, which include quizzes and activities specifically tailored to each Sound Byte. The Sound Byte for this chapter is listed below and can be found on your Student Resource CD:

- Creating Web Pages with HTML

Companion Website

The *Technology in Action* Companion Website includes a variety of additional materials to help you review and learn more about the topics in this chapter. The resources available at **pearsonhighered.com/techinaction** include:

- **Online Study Guide**. Each chapter features an online true–false and multiple-choice quiz. You can take these quizzes, automatically check the results, and e-mail the results to your instructor.
- **Web Research Projects**. Each chapter features several Web research projects that ask you to search the Web for information on computer-related careers, milestones in computer history, important people and companies, emerging technologies, and the applications and implications of different technologies.

Glossary

3D sound card An expansion card that enables a computer to produce sounds that are omnidirectional or three dimensional.

802.11 standard A wireless standard established in 1997 by the Institute of Electrical and Electronics Engineers; also known as WiFi (short for Wireless Fidelity), it enables wireless network devices to work seamlessly with other networks and devices.

A

access card reader A device that reads information from a magnetic strip on the back of a credit card–like access card (such as a student ID card); card readers are easily programmed by adding authorized ID card numbers, Social Security numbers, and so on.

access method A program or hardware mechanism that controls which computer is allowed to use the transmission media in a network at a certain time.

access time The time it takes a storage device to locate its stored data.

accounting software An application program that helps business owners manage their finances more efficiently by providing tools for tracking accounting transactions such as sales, accounts receivable, inventory purchases, and accounts payable.

ActionScript A programming language included in Flash; similar to JavaScript in its keywords, operators, and classes.

Active Server Pages (ASP) A scripting environment in which users combine HyperText Markup Language (HTML), scripts, and reusable Microsoft ActiveX server components to create dynamically generated Web pages.

active topology A network topology in which each node on the network is responsible for retransmitting the token, or the data, to other nodes.

adapter card See *expansion card*.

Adobe Flash A software product for developing Web-based multimedia.

adware A program that downloads on your computer when you install a freeware program, game, or utility. Generally, adware enables sponsored advertisements

to appear in a section of your browser window or as a pop-up ad box.

affective computing A type of computing that relates to emotion or deliberately tries to influence emotion.

aggregator A software program that goes out and grabs the latest update of Web material (usually podcasts) according to your specifications.

AI See *artificial intelligence*.

aircard A device that enables users to have wireless Internet access with mobile devices such as PDAs and notebooks.

AJAX A collection of technologies that allows the creation of Web applications that can update information on a page without requiring the user to do a page refresh or leave the page.

algorithm A set of specific, sequential steps that describe in natural language exactly what a computer program must do to complete its task.

all-in-one computer A desktop system unit that houses the computer's processor, memory, and monitor in a single unit.

all-in-one printer See *multifunction printer*.

alphabetic check Confirms that only textual characters are entered in a database field.

ALU See *arithmetic logic unit*.

American Standard Code for Information Interchange (ASCII) A format for representing each letter or character as an 8-bit (or 1-byte) binary code.

analog Waves that illustrate the loudness of a sound or the brightness of the colors in an image at a given moment in time.

analog-to-digital converter chip Converts analog signals into digital signals.

analytical data See *structured data*.

antivirus software Software that is specifically designed to detect viruses and protect a computer and files from harm.

applet A small program designed to be run from within another application. Java applets are often run on your computer by your browser through the Java Virtual Machine (an application built into current browsers).

application programming interface (API) A block of code in the operating system that software applications need to interact with.

application server A server that acts as a repository for application software.

application software The set of programs on a computer that helps a user carry out tasks such as word processing, sending e-mail, balancing a budget, creating presentations, editing photos, taking an online course, and playing games.

arithmetic logic unit (ALU) The part of the central processing unit (CPU) that is designed to perform mathematical operations such as addition, subtraction, multiplication, and division, and comparison operations, such as greater than, less than, and equal to.

arrow keys See *cursor control keys*.

artificial intelligence (AI) The science that attempts to produce computers that display the same type of reasoning and intelligence that humans do.

ASCII See *American Standard Code for Information Interchange*.

ASP See *Active Server Pages*.

assembly language A language that enables programmers to write their programs using a set of short, English-like commands that speak directly to the central processing unit (CPU) and give the programmer very direct control of hardware resources.

Asynchronous JavaScript and XML See *AJAX*.

audio editing software Programs that perform basic editing tasks on audio files such as cutting dead air space from the beginning or end of a song or cutting a portion from the middle.

authentication The process of identifying a computer user, based on a login or username and password. The computer system determines whether the computer user is authorized and what level of access is to be granted on the network.

authentication server A server that keeps track of who is logging on to the network and which services on the network are available to each user.

B

B2B See *business-to-business*.

B2C See *business-to-consumer*.

backdoor program A program that enables a hacker to take complete control of a computer without the legitimate user's knowledge or permission.

Backup and Restore utility A Windows utility (found in the Control Panel) that allows the user to create a duplicate copy of all the data on a hard drive (or just the folders and files the user specifies) and copy it to another storage device, such as a DVD or external hard drive.

backup utility A software application that creates a duplicate copy of selected data on the hard drive and copies it to another storage device.

bandwidth (data transfer rate) The maximum speed at which data can be transmitted between two nodes on a network; usually measured in megabits per second (Mbps). See also *data transfer rate*.

base 2 number system See *binary number system*.

base 10 number system (decimal notation) A number system that uses 10 digits, 0 through 9, to represent any value.

base class The original object class from which other classes derive.

base transceiver station A large communications tower with antennas, amplifiers, and receivers/transmitters.

basic input/output system (BIOS) A program that manages the data between a computer's operating system and all the input and output devices attached to the computer; also responsible for loading the operating system (OS) from its permanent location on the hard drive to random access memory (RAM).

bastion host A heavily secured server located on a special perimeter network between a company's secure internal network and its firewall.

batch processing The process of accumulating transaction data until a certain point is reached, then processing those transactions all at once.

BD-ROM disc BD-ROM is defined as BluRay Disc Read Only Memory. BD-ROM is an optical disc storage media format for high-definition video and data storage.

behavior See *method*.

benchmark A measurement used in comparing software and hardware performance. Benchmarks are created using software applications that are specifically designed to push the limits of computer performance.

binary decision A decision point that can be answered in one of only two ways: *yes* (true) or *no* (false).

binary digit (bit) A digit that corresponds to the on and off states of a computer's switches. A bit contains a value of either 0 or 1.

binary language The language computers use to process data into information, consisting of only the values 0 and 1.

binary large object (BLOB) In databases, a type of object that holds extremely large chunks of data in binary form; this data is usually video clips, pictures, or audio clips.

binary number system The number system used by computers to represent all data. Because it includes only two digits (0 and 1), the binary number system is also referred to as the *base 2 number system*.

biometric authentication device A device that uses some unique characteristic of human biology to identify authorized users.

bit See *binary digit*.

bit depth The number of bits a video card uses to store data about each pixel on the monitor.

black-hat hacker A hacker who uses his knowledge to destroy information or for illegal gain.

BLOB See *binary large object*.

blog See *Web log*.

Blu-ray disc A method of optical storage for digital data, developed for storing high-definition media. It has the largest storage capacity of all optical storage options.

Bluetooth technology A type of wireless technology that uses radio waves to transmit data over short distances (approximately 30 feet for Bluetooth 1 and 60 feet for Bluetooth 2). Often used to connect peripherals such as printers and keyboards to computers or headsets to cell phones.

bomb software Software that destroys data on a computing device if someone continually tries to access information by guessing the password.

bookmark A feature in some browsers that places a marker of a Web site's Uniform Resource Locator (URL) in an easily retrievable list. (Bookmarks are called Favorites in Microsoft Internet Explorer.)

Boolean operator A word used to refine logical searches. For Internet searches, the words AND, NOT, and OR describe the relationships between keywords in the search.

boot process The process for loading the operating system (OS) into random access memory (RAM) when the computer is turned on.

boot-sector virus A virus that replicates itself into the master boot record of a flash drive or hard drive.

botnet A large group of software applications (called *robots* or *bots*) that runs without user intervention on a large number of computers.

breadcrumb list A list that shows the hierarchy of previously viewed Web pages within the Web site that you are currently visiting. Shown at the top of some Web pages, it aids Web site navigation.

bridge A network device that is used to send data between two different local area networks (LANs) or two segments of the same LAN.

brightness A measure of the greatest amount of light showing when a monitor is displaying pure white; measured as candelas per square meter (cd/m²) or *nits*.

broadband A high-speed Internet connection such as cable, satellite, or digital subscriber line (DSL).

browser See *Web browser*.

browsing (1) The process of viewing database records. (2) The process of "surfing" the Web.

brute force attack An attack delivered by specialized hacking software that tries many combinations of letters, numbers, and pieces of a user ID in an attempt to discover a user password.

bus (linear bus) topology A system of networking connections in which all devices are connected to a central cable called the *bus* (or backbone).

business-to-business (B2B) E-commerce transactions between businesses.

business-to-consumer (B2C) E-commerce transactions between businesses and consumers.

byte Eight binary digits (bits).

C

C The predecessor language of C++; developed originally for system programmers by Brian Kernighan and Dennis Ritchie of AT&T Bell Laboratories in 1978. It provides higher-level programming language features (such as if statements and for loops) but still allows programmers to manipulate the system memory and central processing unit (CPU) registers directly.

C# A programming language released by Microsoft to compete with Java. Pronounced *see sharp*.

C++ The successor language to C. Developed by Bjarne Stroustrup, C++ uses all of the same symbols and keywords as C but extends the language with additional keywords, better security, and more support for the reuse of existing code through object-oriented design.

C2C See *consumer-to-consumer*.

cable A type of broadband Internet connection that uses a television's cable service provider to connect to the Internet.

cache memory Small blocks of memory, located directly on and next to the central processing unit (CPU) chip, that act as holding places for recently or frequently used instructions or data that the CPU accesses the most. When these instructions or data are stored in cache memory, the CPU can more quickly retrieve them than if it had to access the instructions or data from random access memory (RAM).

CAD See *computer-aided design*.

cascading style sheets (CSS) A list of statements (also known as rules) that define in one single location how HTML/XHTML elements are to be displayed.

Cat 6 cable A UTP cable type that provides more than 1 GB of throughput.

cathode ray tube (CRT) A picture tube device found in old-style "boxy" monitors.

CD See *compact disc*.

cellular phone (cell phone) A telephone that operates over a wireless network. Cell phones can also offer Internet access, text messaging, personal information management (PIM) features, and more.

central processing unit (CPU or processor) The part of the system unit of a computer that is responsible for data processing (the "brains" of the computer); it is the largest and most important chip in the computer. The CPU controls all the functions performed by the computer's other components and processes all the commands issued to it by software instructions.

centralized A type of network design in which users are not responsible for creating their own data backups or providing security for their computers; instead, those tasks are handled by a centralized server, software, and a system administrator.

CGI See *Common Gateway Interface*.

CGI script A computer program that conforms to the Common Gateway Interface (CGI) specification, which provides a method for sending data between end users (browser users) and Web servers.

cgi-bin A directory where Common Gateway Interface (CGI) scripts are normally placed.

chat room An area on the Web where people come together to communicate online. The conversations are in real time and are visible to everyone in the chat room.

chip See *integrated circuit*.

CIDR See *classless inter-domain routing*.

circuit switching A method of communication in which a dedicated connection is formed between two points (such as two people on telephones) and the connection remains active for the duration of the transmission.

class A collection of descriptive variables and active functions that together define a set of common properties. Actual examples of the class are known as *objects*.

clickstream data Information captured about each click that users make as they navigate a Web site.

client A computer that requests information from a server in a client/server network (such as your computer when you are connected to the Internet).

client/server model A way of describing typical network functions. Client computers (such as your desktop PC) request services, and servers provide ("serve up") those services to the clients.

client/server network A network, consisting of client and server computers, in which the clients make requests of the server and the server returns the response.

client-side program A computer program that runs on the client computer and requires no interaction with a Web server.

clock cycle The "ticks," or base time unit, of the system clock; one cycle equals one "tick."

clock speed The steady and constant pace at which a computer goes through machine cycles, measured in hertz (Hz).

cloud computing The process of using the Internet to deliver business, entertainment, or other services that were previously delivered by conventional means.

coaxial cable A single copper wire surrounded by layers of plastic insulation and sheathing; used mainly in cable television and cable Internet service.

codec A rule, implemented in either software or hardware, which squeezes a given amount of audio and video information into less space.

code editing The step in which programmers actually type code into the computer.

coding The process of translating an algorithm into a programming language.

cold boot The process of starting a computer from a powered-down or off state.

collaboration tool A product that allows you to connect easily with other individuals, often in remote locations, for the purposes of communicating or working together on a project.

command-driven interface Interface between user and computer in which the user enters commands to communicate with the computer system.

comment (remark) A plain English notation inserted into program code for documentation. The comment is not ever seen by the compiler.

commerce server A computer that hosts software that enables consumers to purchase goods and services over the Web. These servers generally use special security protocols to protect sensitive information (such as credit card numbers) from being intercepted.

Common Gateway Interface (CGI) Provides a methodology by which a browser can request that a program file be executed (or run) instead of just being delivered to the browser.

communications server A server that handles all communications between the network and other networks, including managing Internet connectivity.

compact disc (CD) A method of optical storage for digital data; originally developed for storing digital audio.

compilation The process by which code is converted into machine language, or the language the central processing unit (CPU) can understand.

compiler The program that understands both the syntax of the programming language and the exact structure of the central processing unit (CPU) and its machine language. It can "read" the source code and translate the source code directly into machine language.

completeness check A process that ensures that all database fields defined as "required" have data entered into them.

computational field (computed field) A numeric field in a database that is filled as the result of a computation.

computed field See *computational field.*

computer A data-processing device that gathers, processes, outputs, and stores data and information.

computer forensics The application of computer systems and techniques to gather potential legal evidence; a law enforcement specialty used to fight high-tech crime.

computer literate Being familiar enough with computers that you understand their capabilities and limitations and know how to use them.

computer protocol A set of rules for accomplishing electronic information

exchange. If the Internet is the information superhighway, then protocols are the driving rules.

computer-aided design (CAD) A 3D modeling program used to create automated designs, technical drawings, and model visualizations.

connectionless protocol A protocol that a host computer can use to send data over the network without establishing a direct connection with any specific recipient computer.

connection-oriented protocol A protocol that requires two computers to exchange control packets, which set up the parameters of the data exchange session, before sending packets that contain data.

connectivity port A port that enables the computer (or other device) to be connected to other devices or systems such as networks, modems, and the Internet.

consistency check The process of comparing the value of data in a database field against established parameters to determine whether the value is reasonable.

consumer-to-consumer (C2C) E-commerce transactions between consumers through online sites such as eBay.com.

contrast ratio A measure of the difference in light intensity between the brightest white and the darkest black colors that a monitor can produce. If the contrast ratio is too low, colors tend to fade when the brightness is adjusted to a high or low setting.

control structure The general term used for keywords in a programming language that allow the programmer to control, or redirect, the flow of the program based on a decision.

control unit A component that controls the switches inside the central processing unit (CPU).

cookie A small text file that some Web sites automatically store on a client computer's hard drive when a user visits the site.

copyleft A simplified licensing scheme that enables copyright holders to grant certain rights to a work while retaining other rights.

core A complete processing section from a CPU, embedded into one physical chip.

course management software A program that provides traditional classroom tools,

such as calendars and grade books, over the Internet, as well as areas for students to exchange ideas and information in chat rooms, discussion forums, and e-mail.

CPU See *central processing unit.*

CPU usage The percentage of time a central processing unit (CPU) is working.

CRM software See *customer relationship management (CRM) software.*

CSMA/CD A method of data collision detection in which a node connected to the network listens (that is, has carrier sense) to determine that no other nodes are currently transmitting data signals; short for Carrier Sense Multiple Access with Collision Detection.

CSS See *cascading style sheets.*

custom installation The process of installing only those features of a software program that a user wants on the hard drive.

customer relationship management (CRM) software A business program used for storing sales and client contact information in one central database.

cybercrime Any criminal action perpetrated primarily through the use of a computer.

cybercriminal An individual who uses computers, networks, and the Internet to perpetrate crime.

cyberloafing Doing anything with a computer that is unrelated to a job (such as playing video games), while one is supposed to be working. Also called *cyberslacking.*

D

data Numbers, words, pictures, or sounds that represent facts, figures, or ideas.

data centralization Having all data in one central location (usually a database). Data centralization helps ensure data integrity by requiring data to be updated only in one place if the data changes.

data collision When two computers send data at the same time and the sets of data collide somewhere in the media.

data dictionary (database schema) A file that defines the name, data type, and length of each field in the database.

data file File that contains stored data.

data inconsistency Any difference in data in lists caused when data exists in multiple lists and not all lists are updated when a piece of data changes.

data integrity The process of ensuring that data contained in a database is accurate and reliable.

data line surge suppressor A device that protects lines carrying data (such as phone or cable modem lines) from power surges.

data mart Small slices of a data warehouse.

data mining The process by which great amounts of data are analyzed and investigated to spot significant patterns or trends within the data that would otherwise not be obvious.

data packet See *packet*.

data plan A connectivity plan or text messaging plan in which data charges are separate from cell phone calling charges and are provided at rates different from those for voice calls.

data redundancy When the same data exists in more than one place in a database.

data staging A three-step process: extracting data from source databases, transforming (reformatting) the data, and storing the data in a data warehouse.

data transfer rate (bandwidth) The maximum speed at which data can be transmitted between two nodes on a network; usually measured in megabits per second (Mbps).

data type (field type) An attribute of a data field that determines what type of data can be stored in the database field or memory location.

data warehouse A large-scale electronic repository of data that contains and organizes in one place all the data related to an organization.

database A collection of related data that can be easily stored, sorted, organized, and queried.

database administrator (database designer) An individual trained in the design, construction, and maintenance of databases.

database designer See *database administrator*.

database management system (DBMS) A type of specially designed application software (such as Oracle or Microsoft Access) that interacts with the user, other applications, and the database to capture and analyze data.

database query An inquiry the user poses to a database to extract a meaningful subset of data.

database schema See *data dictionary*.

database server A server that provides client computers with access to information stored in a database.

database software An electronic filing system best used for larger and more complicated groups of data that require more than one table and the ability to group, sort, and retrieve data and generate reports.

date field A field in a database that holds date data such as birthdays, due dates, and so on.

DBMS See *database management system*.

DDoS attack See *distributed denial of service (DDoS) attack*.

debugger A tool that helps programmers step through a program as it runs to locate errors.

debugging The process of repeatedly running a program to find errors and to make sure the program behaves in the way it should.

decentralized A type of network in which users are responsible for creating their own data backups and for providing security for their computers.

decimal notation See *base 10 number system*.

decision point A point at which a computer program must choose from a set of different actions based on the value of its current inputs.

decision support system (DSS) A system designed to help managers develop solutions for specific problems.

decode To translate the program's instructions into commands the CPU can understand.

dedicated server A server used to fulfill one specific function (such as handling e-mail).

default value The value a database will use for a field unless the user enters another value.

denial of service (DoS) attack An attack that occurs when legitimate users are denied access to a computer system because a hacker is repeatedly making requests of that computer system that tie up its resources and deny legitimate users access.

derivative work Intellectual property that is based on an original work but is modified in some way.

derived class A class created based on a previously existing class (i.e., a base class). Derived classes inherit all of the member variables and methods of the base class from which they are derived.

desktop As its name implies, the computer's desktop puts at your fingertips all of the elements necessary for a productive work session and that are typically found on or near the top of a traditional desk, such as files and folders.

desktop computer A computer that is intended for use at a single location. A desktop computer consists of a case that houses the main components of the computer, plus peripheral devices.

desktop publishing (DTP) software Programs for incorporating and arranging graphics and text to produce creative documents.

detail report A report generated with data from a database that shows the individual transactions that occurred during a certain time period.

device driver Software that facilitates the communication between a device and the operating system.

Device Manager A feature in the Windows operating system that lets individuals view and change the properties of all hardware devices attached to the computer.

DHCP See *Dynamic Host Configuration Protocol*.

DHTML See *Dynamic HyperText Markup Language*.

dial-up connection A connection to the Internet using a standard telephone line.

dial-up modem A device that converts (modulates) the digital signals the computer understands to analog signals that can travel over phone lines. The computer on the other end also must have a modem to translate (demodulate) the received analog signal back to a digital signal that the receiving computer can understand.

digital divide The discrepancy between those who have access to the opportunities and knowledge computers and the Internet offer and those who do not.

digital home A home that has a computer(s) and other digital devices that are all connected to a home network.

digital media receiver (DMR) A specialized entertainment device that is specifically designed to retrieve digital media (music, movies, or pictures) from computers or storage devices on a network and display them on televisions or home theater systems. Also called a *media extender* or a *media adapter*.

digital signal processor A specialized chip that processes digital information and transmits signals very quickly.

digital subscriber line (DSL) A type of connection that uses telephone lines to connect to the Internet and that allows both phone and data transmissions to share the same line.

digital video disc (DVD) A method of optical storage for digital data that has greater storage capacity than compact discs.

digital video editing software A program for editing digital video.

digital video interface (DVI) Video interface technology that newer LCD monitors, as well as other multimedia devices such as televisions, DVD players, and projectors, use to connect to a PC.

directory A hierarchical structure that include files, folders, and drives used to create a more organized and efficient computer.

Disk Cleanup A Windows utility that removes unnecessary files from the hard drive.

disk defragmenter A utility that regroups related pieces of files on the hard drive, enabling faster retrieval of the data.

distributed denial of service (DDoS) attack An automated attack that is launched from more than one zombie computer at the same time.

DMR See *digital media receiver*.

DNS server See *Domain Name System (DNS) server*.

Document Object Model (DOM) A means to organize objects and page elements in a Web page. DOM defines every item on a Web page, such as graphics, tables, and headers, as an object.

documentation A description of the development and technical details of a computer program, including how the code works and how the user interacts with the program.

DOM See *Document Object Model*.

domain name A part of a Uniform Resource Locator (URL). Domain names consist of two parts: the site's host and a suffix that indicates the type of organization. (Example: popsci.com)

Domain Name System (DNS) server A server that contains location information for domains on the Internet and functions like a phone book for the Internet.

DoS attack See *denial of service (DoS) attack*.

dotted decimal number (dotted quad) One of the numbers in an Internet Protocol (IP) address.

DRAM See *dynamic RAM*.

drawing software (illustration software) Programs for creating or editing two-dimensional line-based drawings.

drive bay A special shelf inside a computer that is designed to hold storage devices.

DSL See *digital subscriber line (DSL)*.

DSL/cable router A router that is specifically designed to connect to digital subscriber line (DSL) or cable modems.

DSS See *decision support system*.

DTP software See *desktop publishing software*.

dual-processor design A design that has two separate central processing unit (CPU) chips installed on the same system.

DVD drive A drive that enables the computer to read (play) digital video discs (DVDs) and compact discs (CDs).

DVD-RAM One of three competing technologies for rewritable DVDs.

DVD-ROM DVD format in which data can only be read and not written.

DVD-R/RW One of two recognized DVD formats that enable you to read, record (R), and rewrite (RW) data on the disc.

DVD+R/RW One of two recognized DVD formats that enables you to both read, record (R), and rewrite (RW) data on the disc.

DVI See *digital video interface*.

dynamic addressing The process of assigning Internet Protocol (IP) addresses when users log on using their Internet service provider (ISP). The computer is assigned an address from an available pool of IP addresses.

dynamic decision making A mechanism that allows a Web page to decide how to display itself, based on the choices the reader makes as he or she looks at the page.

Dynamic Host Configuration Protocol (DHCP) The protocol that handles dynamic addressing. Part of the Transmission Control Protocol/Internet Protocol (TCP/IP) protocol suite, DHCP takes a pool of IP addresses and shares them with hosts on the network on an as-needed basis.

Dynamic HyperText Markup Language (DHTML or dynamic HTML) A combination of Web development technologies including HTML, cascading style sheets, and a scripting language that are used to add interactivity to a Web site after the Web site has been loaded onto the client computer.

dynamic RAM (DRAM) The most basic type of random access memory (RAM); used in older systems or in systems for which cost is an important factor. DRAM offers access times on the order of 60 nanoseconds.

E

e-commerce (electric commerce) The process of conducting business online for purposes ranging from fund-raising to advertising to selling products.

e-mail (electronic mail) Internet-based communication in which senders and recipients correspond.

e-mail client A software program that runs on a computer and is used to send and receive e-mail through the ISP's server.

e-mail server A server that processes and delivers incoming and outgoing e-mail.

e-mail virus A virus transmitted by e-mail that often uses the address book in the victim's e-mail system to distribute itself.

editor A tool that helps programmers as they enter code, highlighting keywords and alerting the programmers to typos.

EISA bus See *Extended Industry Standard Architecture (EISA) bus.*

electrical switch A device inside the computer that can be flipped between two states: 1 or 0, signifying *on* or *off.*

electronic commerce See *e-commerce.*

electronic mail See *e-mail.*

element The tags and the text between the tags in HyperText Markup Language (HTML).

embedded computer A specially designed computer chip that resides inside another device, such as a car. These self-contained computer devices have their own programming and typically neither receive input from users nor interact with other systems.

encryption The process of encoding data (ciphering) so that only the person with a corresponding decryption key (the intended recipient) can decode (or decipher) and read the message.

encryption virus A malicious program that searches for common data files and compresses them into a file using a complex encryption key, thereby rendering the files unusable.

Enterprise Resource Planning (ERP) system A large-scale software system that accumulates data from all parts of an organization for the purpose of providing key information as needed to efficiently manage all key business operations.

entertainment software Programs designed to provide users with entertainment. Computer games make up the vast majority of entertainment software.

Entertainment Software Rating Board (ESRB) A self-regulatory body established in 1994 by the Entertainment Software Association that rates computer and video games according to the age appropriateness of content.

ergonomics How a user sets up his or her computer and other equipment to minimize risk of injury or discomfort.

ERP system See *Enterprise Resource Planning (ERP) system.*

error handling In programming, the instructions that a program runs if the input data is incorrect or another error is encountered.

Error-Checking A Windows utility that checks for lost files and fragments as well as physical errors on a hard drive.

eSATA A fast data transfer point where a user can easily add peripheral devices. Short for *external SATA.*

ESRB See *Entertainment Software Rating Board.*

Ethernet network A network that uses the Ethernet protocol as the means (or standard) by which the nodes on the network communicate.

Ethernet port A port that is slightly larger than a standard phone jack and transfers data at speeds of up to 10,000 Mbps; used to connect a computer to a DSL or cable modem or a network.

event The result of an action, such as a keystroke, mouse click, or signal to the printer, in the respective device (keyboard, mouse, or printer) to which the operating system responds.

exception report A report that shows conditions that are unusual or that need attention by users of a system.

executable program The binary sequence (code) that instructs the central processing unit (CPU) to perform certain calculations.

expansion bus An electrical pathway that expands the capabilities of a computer by enabling a range of different expansion cards, such as video cards and sound cards, to communicate with the motherboard.

expansion card (adapter card) A circuit board with specific functions that augment the computer's basic functions and provide connections to other devices; examples include the sound card and the video card.

expansion hub A device that connects to one port, such as a universal serial bus (USB) port, to provide additional new ports; similar to a multiplug extension cord for electrical appliances.

expert system A system designed to replicate the decision-making processes of human experts to solve specific problems.

export The process of putting data into an electronic file in a format that another application can understand.

Express Card An electronic card that, when plugged into a notebook computer, provides functionality such as wireless network connections, USB ports, or FireWire ports.

Extensible HyperText Markup Language (XHTML) A standard established by the World Wide Web Consortium (W3C) that combines elements from both Extensible Markup Language (XML) and HyperText Markup Language (HTML). XHTML has much more stringent rules than HTML does regarding tagging.

Extensible Markup Language (XML) A language that enables designers to define their own tags, making it much easier to transfer data between Web sites and Web servers.

extension (file type) In a file name, the three letters that follow the user-supplied file name after the dot (.); the extension identifies what kind of family of files the file belongs to, or which application should be used to read the file.

external data source Any source not owned by the company that owns a decision support system, such as customer demographic data purchased from third parties.

external hard drive An internal hard drive that is enclosed in a protective case to make it portable; the drive is connected to the computer with a data transfer cable and is often used to back up data.

external SATA See *eSata.*

extranet The portion of a company's intranet that is used to share business information with business partners such as vendors, suppliers, and customers.

F

FAQ See *frequently asked questions.*

FAT See *file allocation table.*

Favorites A feature in Microsoft Internet Explorer that places a marker of a Web site's Uniform Resource Locator (URL) in an easily retrievable list in the browser's toolbar. (Called Bookmarks in some browsers.)

fiber-optic cable A cable that transmits data at close to the speed of light along glass or plastic fibers.

Fiber-Optic Service (FiOS) Internet access that is enabled by transmitting data at the speed of light through glass or plastic fibers.

field A field where a category of information in a database is stored. Fields are displayed in columns.

field constraint Any property that must be satisfied for an entry to be accepted into the database field.

field name An identifying name assigned to each field in a database.

field size The maximum number of characters (or numbers) that a field in a database can contain.

field type See *data type*.

fifth-generation language (5GL) A computer language that uses natural language processing or expert systems to make the programming experience better matched to human thinking processes.

file A collection of related pieces of information stored together for easy reference; in database terminology, a file or *table* is a group of related records.

file allocation table (FAT) An index of all sector numbers that the hard drive stores in a table to keep track of which sectors hold which files.

file compression utility A program that takes out redundancies in a file to reduce the file size.

file management The process by which humans or computer software provide organizational structure to a computer's contents.

file name The first part of the label applied to a file; it is generally the name a user assigns to the file when saving it.

file path The exact location of a file, starting with the drive in which the file is located, and including all folders, subfolders (if any), the file name, and the extension. (Example: C:\Users\username\Documents\Illustrations\EBronte.jpg)

file server A computer deployed to provide remote storage space or to act as a repository for files that users can access.

File Transfer Protocol (FTP) A protocol used to upload and download files from one computer to another over the Internet.

financial planning software Programs for managing finances, such as Intuit's Quicken and Microsoft Money, which include electronic checkbook registers and automatic bill payment tools.

FiOS See *Fiber-Optic Service*.

firewall A software program or hardware device designed to prevent unauthorized access to computers or networks.

FireWire (previously called IEEE 1394) An interface based on a standard developed by the Institute of Electrical and Electronics Engineers (IEEE) with transfer rates of 400 and 800 megabits per second (Mbps). Today, it is most commonly used to connect digital video devices such as digital cameras to the computer.

FireWire 400 (IEEE 1394) An interface port that transfers data at 400 Mbps.

FireWire 800 One of the fastest ports available, moving data at 800 Mbps.

firmware System software that controls hardware devices.

first-generation language (1GL) The actual machine language of a central processing unit (CPU); the sequence of bits—1s and 0s—that the CPU understands.

Flash A software product from Adobe for developing Web-based multimedia.

flash drive A drive that plugs into a universal serial bus (USB) port on a computer and stores data digitally. Also called *USB drive, jump drive,* or *thumb drive*.

flash memory Portable, nonvolatile memory.

flash memory card A form of portable storage; this removable memory card is often used in digital cameras, portable media players, and personal digital assistants (PDAs).

flat-panel monitor A type of monitor that is lighter and more energy-efficient than a CRT monitor; often used with portable computers such as notebooks.

flowchart A visual representation of the patterns an algorithm comprises.

folder A collection of files stored on a computer.

For Keyword in Visual Basic used with the Next keyword to implement a loop.

foreign key The primary key of another database table that is included for purposes of establishing relationships with another table.

fourth-generation language (4GL) A sophisticated level of programming language such as a report generator or database query language.

frame A container designed to hold multiple data packets.

freeware Any copyrighted software that can be used for free.

frequently asked questions (FAQ) A list of answers to the most common questions.

front side bus (FSB) See *local bus*.

FTP See *File Transfer Protocol*.

full backup A type of file backup that will back up all files on a device.

full installation The process of installing all the files and programs from the distribution CD to the computer's hard drive.

fuzzy logic A type of logic that allows the interjection of experiential learning into an equation by considering probabilities.

G

gadget A mini-application that runs on the desktop, offering easy access to a frequently used tool such as weather or a calendar item.

gateway See *wireless router*.

GHz See *gigahertz*.

gigabyte (GB) About a billion bytes.

gigahertz (GHz) One billion hertz.

Global Positioning System (GPS) A system of 21 satellites (plus 3 working spares), built and operated by the U.S. military, that constantly orbit the earth. They provide information to GPS-capable devices to pinpoint locations on the earth.

graphical user interface (GUI) Unlike the command- and menu-driven interfaces used in earlier software, GUIs display graphics and use the point-and-click technology of the mouse and cursor, making them much more user-friendly.

graphics processing unit (GPU) A specialized logic chip that is dedicated to quickly displaying and calculating visual data such as shadows, textures, and luminosity.

H

hacker Anyone who unlawfully breaks into a computer system (whether an individual computer or a network).

HAN See *home area network*.

handshaking The process of two computers exchanging control packets that set up the parameters of a data exchange.

hard drive A device that holds all permanently stored programs and data; can be located inside the system unit or attached to the system unit via a USB port.

hardware Any part of the computer you can physically touch.

head crash Impact of read/write head against magnetic platter of the hard drive; often results in data loss.

hexadecimal notation A number system that uses 16 digits to represent numbers; also called a *base 16 number system*.

Hibernate mode A power-saving mode that puts the computer in a state of deep sleep. Pushing the power button awakens the computer from hibernation, at which time the computer reloads everything to the desktop exactly as it was before it went into hibernation.

hoax An e-mail message or Web site that contains information that is untrue, and is published with the purpose of deceiving others.

home area network (HAN) A network located in a home that is used to connect all of its digital devices.

home page The main or opening page of a Web site.

host The portion of a domain name that identifies who maintains a given Web site. For example, *berkeley.edu* is the domain name for the University of California at Berkeley, which maintains that site.

hot spot A place where users can connect to the Internet wirelessly.

HTML See *HyperText Markup Language*.

HTML tag The bracketed information that surrounds elements of a Web page in order to convey information about them and define how their content is to be displayed.

HTML/XHTML embedded scripting language A client-side method of embedding programming language code directly within the HTML/XHTML code of a Web page.

HTTP See *HyperText Transfer Protocol*.

hub A simple amplification device that receives data packets and retransmits them to all nodes on the same network (not between different networks).

hybrid topology A topology comprised of several topologies and combined into one network.

hyperlink A type of specially coded text that, when clicked, enables a user to jump from one location, or Web page, to another within a Web site or to another Web site altogether.

hyperlink field A field in a database that stores hyperlinks to Web pages.

hypertext Text that is linked to other documents or media (such as video clips or pictures).

HyperText Markup Language (HTML) A set of rules for marking up blocks of text so that a Web browser knows how to display them. It uses a series of tags that defines the display of text on a Web page.

HyperText Transfer Protocol (HTTP) The protocol that allows files to be transferred from a Web server so that you can see them on your computer by using a browser.

hyperthreading A technology that permits quicker processing of information by enabling a new set of instructions to start executing before the previous set has finished.

I

ICANN See *Internet Corporation for Assigned Names and Numbers*.

icon A picture on a computer display that represents an object such as a software application or a file or folder.

IDE See *integrated development environment*.

identity theft The process by which someone uses personal information about someone else (such as the victim's name, address, and Social Security number) to assume the victim's identity for the purpose of defrauding others.

IE See *Internet Explorer*.

IEEE 1394 See *FireWire 400*.

if else In the programming language C++, keywords for a binary decision within an algorithm.

illustration software See *drawing software*.

IM See *instant messaging*.

image backup A copy of an entire computer system, created for restoration purposes.

image editing software (photo editing software) Programs for editing photographs and other images.

impact printer A printer that has tiny hammer-like keys that strike the paper through an inked ribbon, thus making a mark on the paper. The most common impact printer is the dot-matrix printer.

incremental backup A type of backup that only backs up files that have changed since the last time those files were backed up.

index See *sort*.

information Data that has been organized or presented in a meaningful fashion.

information assurance As defined by the NSA, "the set of measures intended to protect and defend information and information systems by ensuring their availability, integrity, authentication, confidentiality, and non-repudiation."

information system A system that includes data, people, procedures, hardware, and software and that is used to gather and analyze information.

information technology (IT) The set of techniques used in processing and retrieving information.

inheritance The ability of a new class of objects to pick up all of the data and methods of an existing class automatically and then extend and customize those to fit its own specific needs.

initial value A beginning point in a loop.

inkjet printer A nonimpact printer that sprays tiny drops of ink onto paper.

inoculation A process used by antivirus software; compares old and current qualities of files to detect viral activity.

input device A hardware device used to enter, or input, data (text, images, and sounds) and instructions (user responses and commands) into a computer. Some input devices are keyboards and mice.

input form A form that provides a view of the data fields to be filled in a database, with appropriate labels to assist database users in populating the database.

instant messaging (IM) A program that enables users to communicate online in real time with others who are also online.

instruction set The collection of commands a specific central processing unit (CPU) can run.

integrated circuit (chip) A tiny region of semiconductor material such as silicon that supports a huge number of transistors.

integrated development environment (IDE) A development tool that helps programmers write, compile, and test their programs.

integrated help Documentation for a software product that is built directly into the software.

integrated software application A single software program that incorporates the most commonly used tools of many productivity software programs.

internal hard drive A hard drive that is installed inside the system unit.

Internet A network of networks that is the largest network in the world, connecting millions of computers from more than one hundred countries.

Internet backbone The main pathway of high-speed communications lines over which all Internet traffic flows.

Internet cache A section of your hard drive that stores information that you may need again for surfing (such as IP addresses and frequently accessed Web pages).

Internet Corporation for Assigned Names and Numbers (ICANN) The organization responsible for allocating IP addresses to network administrators to ensure they are unique and have not been assigned to other users.

Internet exchange point A device that allows different Internet service providers to exchange information between networks.

Internet Explorer (IE) A popular graphical browser from Microsoft Corporation for displaying different Web sites, or locations, on the Web; it can display pictures (graphics) in addition to text, as well as other forms of multimedia such as sound and video.

Internet Protocol (IP) A protocol for sending data between computers on the Internet.

Internet Protocol address (IP address) The means by which all computers connected to the Internet identify each other. It consists of a unique set of four numbers separated by dots such as 123.45.178.91.

Internet Protocol version 4 (IPv4) The original IP addressing scheme.

Internet Protocol version 6 (IPv6) A proposed IP addressing scheme that makes IP addresses longer, thereby providing more available IP addresses. It uses eight groups of 16-bit numbers.

Internet service provider (ISP) A company that connects individuals, groups, and other companies to the Internet.

Internet tablet A very light, portable computing device without a keyboard.

interpreter A software program that translates source code into an intermediate form line by line. Each line is then executed as it is translated.

interrupt A signal that tells the operating system that it is in need of immediate attention.

interrupt handler A special numerical code that prioritizes requests from various devices. These requests then are placed in the interrupt table in the computer's primary memory.

intranet A private corporate network that is used exclusively by company employees to facilitate information sharing, database access, group scheduling, videoconferencing, and other employee and customer collaborations.

IP address See *Internet Protocol address*.

ISP See *Internet service provider*.

IT See *information technology*.

J

jam signal A special signal sent to all network nodes, alerting them that a data collision has occurred.

Java A platform-independent programming language that Sun Microsystems introduced in the early 1990s. It quickly became popular because its object-oriented model enables Java programmers to benefit from its set of existing classes.

Java applet A small Java-based program.

Java Server Pages (JSP) An extension of the Java servlet technology with dynamic scripting capability.

JavaScript A scripting language often used to add interactivity to Web pages. JavaScript is not as fully featured as Java, but its syntax, keywords, data types, and operators are a subset of Java's.

join query A database query that links (or joins) two database tables using a common field in both tables and extracts the relevant data from each.

JSP See *Java Server Pages*.

jump drive See *flash drive*.

K

KB See *kilobyte*.

kernel (supervisor program) The essential component of the operating system that is responsible for managing the processor and all other components of the computer system. Because it stays in random access memory (RAM) the entire time the computer is powered on, the kernel is called *memory resident*.

kernel memory The memory that the computer's operating system uses.

key field See *primary field*.

key pair A public and a private key used for coding and decoding encrypted messages.

keyboard A hardware device used to enter typed data and commands into a computer.

keystroke logger A type of spyware program that monitors keystrokes with the intent of stealing passwords, login IDs, or credit card information.

keyword (1) A specific word a user wishes to query (or look for) in an Internet search. (2) A specific word that has a predefined meaning in a particular programming language.

kilobyte (KB) A unit of computer storage equal to approximately one thousand bytes.

knowledge-based system A support system that provides additional intelligence that supplements the user's own intellect and makes a decision support system (DSS) more effective.

L

LAN See *local area network*.

laptop computer See *notebook computer*.

large-scale networking (LSN) A program created by the U.S. government, the objective of which is to fund the research and development of cutting-edge networking technologies. Major goals of the program are the development of enhanced wireless technologies and increased network throughput.

laser printer A nonimpact printer known for quick and quiet production and high-quality printouts.

Last Known Good Configuration A Windows feature that starts the computer by using the registry information that was saved during the last shutdown.

latency The process that occurs after the read/write head of the hard drive locates the correct track, and then waits for the correct sector to spin to the read/write head.

LCD See *liquid crystal display*.

LCD monitor See *flat-panel monitor*.

legacy technology Comprises computing devices, software, or peripherals that use techniques, parts, and methods from an earlier time that are no longer popular.

Level 1 cache A block of memory that is built onto the central processing unit (CPU) chip for the storage of data or commands that have just been used.

Level 2 cache A block of memory that is located either on the central processing unit (CPU) chip or on a separate chip near the CPU. It takes somewhat longer to access than the CPU registers. Level 2 cache contains more storage area than Level 1 cache.

Level 3 cache On computers with Level 3 cache, the central processing unit (CPU) checks this area for instructions and data after it looks in Level 1 and Level 2 cache, but before it looks in random access memory (RAM); often designed to hold between 2 megabytes (MB) and 4 MB of data.

library In Windows 7, a folder that is used to display files from different locations as if they were all saved in a single folder, regardless of where they are actually stored in the file hierarchy.

linear bus topology See *bus (linear bus) topology*.

Linux An open source operating system based on UNIX. Because of the stable nature of this operating system, it is often used on Web servers.

liquid crystal display (LCD) The technology used in flat-panel computer monitors.

listserv An electronic mailing list of e-mail addresses of people who are interested in a certain topic or area of interest.

live bookmark A bookmark that delivers updates to you as soon as they become available, using Really Simple Syndication (RSS).

local area network (LAN) A network in which the nodes are located within a small geographic area.

logic bomb A computer virus that runs when a certain set of conditions is met, such as when specific dates are keyed off the computer's internal clock.

logical error A mistake in the design and planning of the algorithm itself rather than in the use of syntax in the coding.

logical port A virtual communications gateway or path that enables a computer to organize requests for information (such as Web page downloads and e-mail routing) from other networks or computers.

logical port blocking A condition in which a firewall is configured to ignore all incoming packets that request access to a certain port so that no unwanted requests will get through to the computer.

loop An algorithm that performs a repeating set of actions. A logical yes/no expression is evaluated. As long as the expression evaluates to TRUE (yes), the algorithm will perform the same set of actions and continue to loop around. When the answer to

the question is FALSE (no), the algorithm breaks free of the looping structure and moves on to the next step.

loop topology See *ring (loop) topology*.

LSN See *large-scale networking*.

M

MAC address See *media access control (MAC) address*.

Mac OS Snow Leopard Apple Inc.'s operating system. In 1984, Mac OS became the first operating system to incorporate the user-friendly point-and-click technology, based on the UNIX operating system, in a commercially affordable computer.

machine cycle (processing cycle) The time it takes the central processing unit (CPU) to fetch and execute a single machine-level instruction.

machine language A set of instructions executed directly by the central processing unit (CPU).

macro A small program that groups a series of commands to run as a single command.

macro virus A virus that is distributed by hiding it inside a macro.

mainframe A large, expensive computer that supports hundreds or thousands of users simultaneously and executes many different programs at the same time.

malware Software that is intended to render a system temporarily or permanently useless or to penetrate a computer system completely for purposes of information gathering. Examples include spyware, viruses, worms, and Trojan horses.

MAN See *metropolitan area network*.

management information system (MIS) A system that provides timely and accurate information that enables managers to make critical business decisions.

many-to-many relationship A database relationship in which one record in a database table (A) can have many related records in another table (B), and any record in table B can have many related records in table A.

mapping program Software that provides street maps and written directions to locations.

master boot record (MBR) A small program that runs whenever a computer boots up.

MB See *megabyte*.

MBR See *master boot record*.

media access control (MAC) address A physical address, similar to a serial number on an appliance, that is assigned to each network adapter; it is made up of six 2-digit characters such as 01:40:87:44:79:A5.

megabyte (MB) A unit of computer storage equal to approximately 1 million bytes.

megahertz (MHz) A measure of processing speed equal to 1 million hertz.

memo field A text field in a database that is used to hold long pieces of text.

memory bound A system that is limited in how fast it can send data to the central processing unit (CPU) because there is not enough random access memory (RAM) installed.

memory card See *memory module*.

memory module (memory card) A small circuit board that holds a series of random access memory (RAM) chips.

menu A list of commands that displays on the screen.

menu-driven interface A user interface in which the user chooses a command from menus displayed on the screen.

meta search engine A search engine that searches other search engines rather than individual Web sites.

metadata Data that describes other data.

method (behavior) An action associated with a class of objects.

metropolitan area network (MAN) A wide area network (WAN) that links users in a specific geographic area (such as within a city or county).

MHz See *megahertz*.

microbrowser Software that makes it possible to access the Internet from a PDA/smartphone.

microphone (mic) A device that allows you to capture sound waves, such as those created by your voice, and transfer them to digital format on your computer.

microprocessor A chip that contains a central processing unit (CPU).

Microsoft Disk Operating System (MS-DOS) A single-user, single-task operating system created by Microsoft. MS-DOS was the first widely installed operating system in personal computers.

Microsoft Windows A proprietary operating system (OS) developed by Microsoft based on a visual interface. Windows is the most popular OS for desktop computers.

MIME See *multipurpose Internet mail extensions*.

MIS See *management information system*.

MMS See *multimedia message service*.

mobile switching center A central location that receives cell phone requests for service from a base station.

model management system A type of software that assists in building management models in decision support systems (DSSs).

modem card An expansion card that provides the computer with a connection to the Internet via conventional phone lines.

modem port A port that uses a traditional telephone signal to connect a computer to the Internet.

monitor (display screen) A common output device that displays text, graphics, and video as soft copies (copies that can be seen only on screen).

Moore's Law A prediction, named after Gordon Moore, the cofounder of Intel; states that the number of transistors on a CPU chip will double every two years.

motherboard A special circuit board in the system unit that contains the central processing unit (CPU), the memory (RAM) chips, and the slots available for expansion cards; all of the other boards (video cards, sound cards, and so on) connect to it to receive power and to communicate.

mouse A hardware device used to enter user responses and commands into a computer.

multi-core technology When a chip uses two or more processors on the same chip to enable the execution of two sets of instructions at the same time.

multidimensional database A database that stores data in multiple dimensions and is organized in a cube format.

multimedia Anything that involves one or more forms of media plus text.

multimedia message service (MMS) An extension of short message service (SMS) that enables messages that include text, sound, images, and video clips to be sent from a cell phone or PDA to other phones or e-mail addresses.

multimedia software Programs that include image, video, and audio editing software, animation software, and other specialty software required to produce computer games, animations, and movies.

multipartite virus Literally meaning "multipart" virus; a type of computer virus that attempts to infect both the boot sector and executable files at the same time.

multiplayer online game An online game in which play occurs among hundreds or thousands of other players over the Internet in a persistent or ever-on game environment. In some games, players can interact with other players through trading, chatting, or playing cooperative or combative mini-games.

multipurpose Internet mail extensions (MIME) A specification that was introduced in 1991 to simplify attachments to e-mail messages. All e-mail client software now uses this protocol for attaching files.

multitasking The capability of the operating system to allow a user to perform more than one task at a time.

multiuser operating system (network operating system) An operating system (OS) that enables more than one user to access the computer system at one time by efficiently juggling all the requests from multiple users.

N

NAK See *negative acknowledgment*.

nanoscience The study of molecules and nanostructures whose size ranges from 1 to 100 nanometers (one billionth of a meter).

nanotechnology The science of using nanostructures to build devices on an extremely small scale.

NAT See *network address translation*.

natural language processing (NLP) system A system that enables users to communicate with computer systems using a natural spoken or written language as opposed to using computer programming languages.

negative acknowledgment (NAK) What computer Y sends to computer X if a packet is unreadable, indicating the packet was not received in understandable form.

netbook A computing device that runs a full-featured operating system but weighs two pounds or less.

netiquette The general rules of etiquette for Internet chat rooms and other online communication.

network A group of two or more computers (or nodes) that are configured to share information and resources such as printers, files, and databases.

network adapter A device that enables the computer (or peripheral) to communicate with the network using a common data communication language, or protocol.

network address translation (NAT) A process that firewalls use to assign internal Internet Protocol (IP) addresses on a network.

network administrator Someone who has training in computer and peripheral maintenance and repair, network design, and the installation of network software; installs new equipment, configures computers for users, repairs equipment, and assigns network access to users.

network architecture The design of a computer network; includes both physical and logical design.

network attached storage (NAS) device A specialized device attached to a network whose sole function is to store and disseminate data.

network interface card (NIC) An expansion card that enables a computer to connect other computers or to a cable modem to facilitate a high-speed Internet connection.

network navigation device A device on a network such as a router, hub, and switch that moves data signals around the network.

network operating system (NOS) Software that handles requests for information,

Internet access, and the use of peripherals for the rest of the network nodes.

network prefix The part of a network address under the CIDR IP addressing scheme. It consists of a slash and a number added to the end of the last octet in an IP address.

network topology The layout and structure of the network.

network-ready device A device (such as a printer or external hard drive) that can be attached directly to a network instead of needing to attach to a computer on the network.

newsgroup A method of communication, similar to a discussion group or forum, in which people create threads, or conversations. In a thread, a newsgroup member will post messages and read and reply to messages from other members of the newsgroup.

Next In the Visual Basic programming language, the keyword used to implement a loop.

NIC See *network interface card*.

NLP See *natural language processing system*.

node A device connected to a network such as a computer, a peripheral (such as a printer), or a communications device (such as a modem).

nonimpact printer A printer that sprays ink or uses laser beams to make marks on the paper. The most common nonimpact printers are inkjet and laser printers.

nonvolatile storage Permanent storage, as in read-only memory (ROM).

normalization The process of recording data only once in a database to reduce data redundancy.

NOS See *network operating system*.

notebook computer (laptop computer) A powerful mobile computing solution that offers a large display and all of the computing power of a full desktop system.

number system A set of rules for representing integer numbers with symbols.

numeric check A data validation routine that confirms that only numbers are entered in a database field.

numeric field A field in a database that stores numbers.

O

object A variable in a program that is an example of a class. Each object in a specific class is constructed from similar data and methods.

object field A field in a database that holds objects such as pictures, video clips, or entire documents.

object-oriented analysis An approach to software design that differs from the traditional "top-down" design. In object-oriented (OO) analysis, programmers first identify all of the classes (collections of data and methods) that are required to describe completely the problem the program is trying to solve.

object-oriented database A database that stores data in objects, not in tables.

object query language (OQL) A query language that is used to extract information from an object-oriented database.

OC (optical carrier) line A transmission channel consisting of high-speed fiber optic lines.

octet Eight bits. For example, each of the four numbers in the dotted decimal notation of an Internet Protocol (IP) address is represented by an octet.

office support system (OSS) A system (such as Microsoft Office) designed to assist employees in accomplishing their day-to-day tasks and to improve communications.

offshore To have work performed in a country other than the home country of the business.

OLTP See *online transaction processing*.

omnidirectional microphone A microphone that picks up sounds from all directions at once; best for recording more than one voice.

one-to-many relationship A database relationship in which one record in a data table can have many related records in another data table.

one-to-one relationship A database relationship in which one record in a data table has only one related record in another data table.

online mapping service An alternative to more traditional mapping software programs; easily accessible with any Internet connection and updated more frequently than offline services. Examples include MapQuest, Yahoo! Maps, Google Maps, and Google Earth.

online transaction processing (OLTP) The immediate processing of user requests or transactions.

open source software Program code made publicly available for free; it can be copied, distributed, or changed without the stringent copyright protections of proprietary software products.

open system A system whose designs are public, enabling access by any interested party.

operating system (OS) The system software that controls the way in which a computer system functions, including the management of hardware, peripherals, and software.

operator Any of the coding symbols that represent the fundamental actions of a computer language.

optical carrier line See *OC (optical carrier) line.*

optical drive A hardware device that uses lasers or light to read from, and maybe even write to, CDs, DVDs, or Blu-ray discs.

optical media Portable storage devices, such as CDs, DVDs, and Blu-ray discs, that use a laser to read and write data.

optical mouse A mouse that uses an internal sensor or laser to control the mouse's movement. The sensor sends signals to the computer, telling it where to move the pointer on the screen.

OQL See *object query language.*

OS See *operating system.*

output device A device that sends processed data and information out of a computer in the form of text, pictures (graphics), sounds (audio), or video.

P

P2P network See *peer-to-peer network.*

P2P sharing See *peer-to-peer sharing.*

packet (data packet) A small segment of data that is bundled for sending over transmission media. Each packet contains the address of the computer or peripheral device to which it is being sent.

packet filtering A feature found in firewalls that filters out unwanted data packets sent to specific logical ports.

packet screening A process that involves examining incoming data packets to ensure they originated from, or are authorized by, valid users on the internal network.

packet sniffer A program that looks at (sniffs) each data packet as it travels on the Internet.

packet switching A communications methodology in which data is broken into small chunks (called packets) and sent over various routes at the same time. When the packets reach their destination, they are reassembled by the receiving computer.

page file The file the operating system builds on the hard drive to enable processing to continue when it is using virtual memory.

paging The process of swapping data or instructions that have been placed in the swap file for later use back into active random access memory (RAM). The contents of the hard drive's swap file then become less active data or instructions.

PAN See *personal area network.*

parallel port A port that sends data between devices in groups of bits at speeds of 92 kilobits per second (Kbps). This legacy technology was commonly used to connect printers to computers.

parallel processing A network computer environment in which each computer works on a portion of the same problem simultaneously.

Pascal The only modern computer language that was specifically designed as a teaching language; it is seldom taught now at the college level.

passive topology When data merely travels the entire length of the communications medium and is received by all network devices.

passive-matrix display A screen that uses computer monitor technology in which electrical current passes through a liquid

crystal solution and charges groups of pixels, either in a row or a column, causing the screen to brighten with each pass of electrical current and subsequently to fade.

path The information following the slash or colon in a Uniform Resource Locator (URL). Also called a *subdirectory.*

path separator The backslash mark (\) used by Microsoft Windows and DOS in file names. Mac files use a colon (:), and UNIX and Linux use the forward slash (/) as the path separator.

patient simulator A computer-controlled mannequin that simulates human body functions and reactions. Patient simulators are used in training doctors, nurses, and emergency services personnel by simulating dangerous situations that would put live patients at risk.

PC card (or PCMCIA, short for Personal Computer Memory Card International Association) A credit card–sized card that enables users to add fax modems, network connections, wireless adapters, USB 2.0 and FireWire ports, and other capabilities; primarily used with notebook computers.

PCMCIA See *PC card.*

PDA See *personal digital assistant.*

PDLC See *program development life cycle.*

peer-to-peer (P2P) network A network in which each node connected to the network can communicate directly with every other node on the network.

peer-to-peer (P2P) sharing The process of users transferring files between computers.

peripheral device A device such as a monitor, printer, or keyboard that connects to the system unit through ports.

personal area network (PAN) A network used to connect wireless devices (such as Bluetooth-enabled devices) in close proximity to each other.

Personal Computer Memory Card International Association See *PC card.*

personal digital assistant (PDA) A small device that enables a user to carry digital information. Often called *palm computers* or *handhelds*, PDAs are about the size of a hand and usually weigh less than 5 ounces.

personal firewall A firewall specifically designed for home networks.

personal information manager (PIM) software Programs such as Microsoft Outlook or Lotus Organizer that strive to replace the various management tools found on a traditional desk such as a calendar, address book, notepad, and to-do lists.

PGP See *Pretty Good Privacy*.

pharming Planting malicious code on a computer that alters the browser's ability to find Web addresses and directs users to bogus Web sites.

phishing The process of sending e-mail messages to lure Internet users into revealing personal information such as credit card or Social Security numbers or other sensitive information that could lead to identity theft.

photo editing software See *image editing software*.

PHP (Hypertext Preprocessor) A scripting language used to produce dynamic Web pages.

physical memory The amount of random access memory (RAM) that is installed in a computer.

piggybacking The process of connecting to a wireless network without the permission of the owner of the network.

PIM software See *personal information manager (PIM) software*.

pipelining A technique that enables the central processing unit (CPU) to work on more than one instruction (or stage of processing) at a time, thereby boosting CPU performance.

pixel A single point that creates the images on a computer monitor. Pixels are illuminated by an electron beam that passes rapidly back and forth across the back of the screen so that the pixels appear to glow continuously.

platform The combination of a computer's operating system and processor. The two most common platform types are the PC and the Apple Macintosh.

platter A thin, round, metallic storage plate stacked onto the hard drive spindle.

player See *plug-in*.

plotter A large printer that uses a computer-controlled pen to produce oversize pictures that require precise continuous lines to be drawn, such as maps and architectural plans.

Plug and Play (PnP) The technology that enables the operating system, once it is booted up, to recognize automatically any new peripherals and configure them to work with the system.

plug-in (player) A small software program that "plugs in" to a Web browser to enable a specific function—for example, to view and hear certain multimedia files on the Web.

PMP See *portable media player*.

PnP See *Plug and Play*.

podcast A clip of audio or video content that is broadcast over the Internet using compressed audio or video files in formats such as MP3.

point of presence (POP) A bank of modems through which many users can connect to an Internet service provider (ISP) simultaneously.

polymorphic virus A virus that changes its virus signature (the binary pattern that makes the virus identifiable) every time it infects a new file. This makes it more difficult for antivirus programs to detect the virus.

POP See *point of presence*.

pop-up window A small box that opens up automatically on a computer screen, often displaying unwanted advertisements or other promotional information.

port An interface through which external devices are connected to the computer.

portability The capability to move a completed solution easily from one type of computer to another.

portable media player (PMP) A small portable device (such as an iPod) that enables you to carry your MP3s or other media files around with you.

positive acknowledgment (ACK) What computer Y sends when it receives a data packet that it can read from computer X.

possessed object Any object that a user carries to identify him- or herself and that grants the user access to a computer system or computer facility.

power supply A power supply regulates the wall voltage to the voltages required by computer chips; it is housed inside the system unit.

power-line network A network that uses the electrical wiring in a building to connect the nodes in the network.

power-on self-test (POST) The first job the basic input/output system (BIOS) performs, ensuring that essential peripheral devices are attached and operational. This process consists of a test on the video card and video memory, a BIOS identification process (during which the BIOS version, manufacturer, and data are displayed on the monitor), and a memory test to ensure memory chips are working properly.

preemptive multitasking When the operating system processes the task assigned a higher priority before processing a task that has been assigned a lower priority.

presentation software An application program for creating dynamic slide shows such as Microsoft PowerPoint or Apple Keynote.

pretexting The act of creating an invented scenario (the pretext) to convince someone to divulge information.

Pretty Good Privacy (PGP) A popular public-key encryption package.

primary key (key field) The unique field that each database record in a table must have.

print queue A software holding area for printing jobs.

print server A server that manages all client-requested printing jobs for all printers on the network.

printer A common output device that creates tangible or hard copies of text and graphics.

private key One-half of a pair of binary files that is needed to decrypt an encrypted message. The private key is kept only by the individual who created the key pair and is never distributed to anyone else. The private key is used to decrypt messages created with the corresponding public key.

private system See *proprietary system*.

private-key encryption A procedure in which only the two parties involved in sending a message have the code. This could be a simple shift code where letters of the alphabet are shifted to a new position.

problem statement A clear description of which tasks the computer program must accomplish and how the program will execute these tasks and respond to unusual situations. It is the starting point of programming work.

processing Manipulating or organizing data into information.

processing cycle See *machine cycle*.

processor See *central processing unit*.

processor speed The number of operations (or cycles) the processor completes each second, measured in hertz (Hz).

productivity software Programs that enable a user to perform various tasks generally required in home, school, and business. Examples include word processing, spreadsheet, presentation, personal information management (PIM), and database programs.

program A series of instructions to be followed by a computer to accomplish a task.

program development life cycle (PDLC) A number of stages, from conception to final deployment, which a programming project follows.

program file A file that is used in the running of software programs and does not store data.

programming The process of translating a task into a series of commands a computer will use to perform that task.

programming language A kind of "code" for the set of instructions the central processing unit (CPU) knows how to perform.

project management software An application program, such as Microsoft Project, that helps project managers generate charts and tables used to manage aspects of a project.

proprietary (private) system A system whose design is not made available for public access.

protocol (1) A set of rules for exchanging data and communication. (2) The first part of the Uniform Resource Locator (URL) indicating the set of rules used to retrieve the specified document. The protocol is generally followed by a colon; two forward slashes; *www* (indicating World Wide Web); and then the domain name.

prototype A small model of a computer program, often built at the beginning of a large project.

proprietary software Custom software application that is owned and controlled by the company that created it.

proxy server Acts as a go-between for computers on the internal network and the external network (the Internet).

pseudocode A text-based approach to documenting an algorithm.

public domain The status of software (or other created works) that are not protected by copyright.

public key One-half of a pair of binary files that is needed to decrypt an encrypted message. After creating the keys, the user distributes the public key to anyone he wishes to send him encrypted messages. A message encrypted with a public key can be unencrypted only using the corresponding private key.

public-key encryption A procedure in which the key for coding is generally distributed as a public key that may be placed on a Web site. Anyone wishing to send a message codes it using the public key. The recipient decodes the message with a private key.

Q

quarantining The placement (by antivirus software) of a computer virus in a secure area on the hard drive so that it won't spread infection to other files.

query The process of requesting information from a database.

query language A language used to retrieve and display records. A query language consists of its own vocabulary and sentence structure, used to frame the requests.

QWERTY keyboard A keyboard that gets its name from the first six letters on the top-left row of alphabetic keys on the keyboard.

R

RAD See *rapid application development*.

radio frequency identification tag (RFID tag) A tag that looks like a sticker or label, is attached to a batch of merchandise, and contains a microchip that holds a unique sequence of numbers used to identify the product to which it is attached.

random access memory (RAM) The computer's temporary storage space or short-term memory. It is located in a set of chips on the system unit's motherboard, and its capacity is measured in megabytes or gigabytes.

range check A type of data validation used in databases to ensure that a value entered falls within a specified range (such as requiring a person's age to fall in a range of between 1 and 120).

rapid application development (RAD) A method of system development in which developers create a prototype first, generating system documents as they use and remodel the product.

read/write head The mechanism that retrieves (reads) and records (writes) the magnetic data to and from a data disk. They move from the outer edge of the spinning platters to the center, up to 50 times per second.

read-only memory (ROM) A set of memory chips, located on the motherboard, which stores data and instructions that cannot be changed or erased; it holds all the instructions the computer needs to start up.

real-time operating system (RTOS) A program with a specific purpose that must guarantee certain response times for particular computing tasks, or else the machine's application is useless. Real-time operating systems are found in many types of robotic equipment.

real-time processing The process of updating a database (or information system) immediately as changes are made.

Really Simple Syndication (RSS) technology An XML-based format that allows frequent updates of content on the World Wide Web.

record A collection of related fields in a database.

Recycle Bin A folder on a Windows desktop in which deleted files from the hard drive are held until permanently purged from the system.

referential integrity For each value in the foreign key of one table, there is a corresponding value in the primary key of the related table.

register A special memory storage area built into the central processing unit (CPU).

registry A portion of the hard drive containing all the different configurations (settings) used by the Windows operating system (OS) as well as by other applications.

relation A database table that contains related data.

relational algebra The use of English-like expressions that have variables and operations, much like algebraic equations.

relational database A database that organizes data in table format by logically grouping similar data into relations (or tables) that contain related data.

relationship In relational databases, the link between tables that defines how the data are related.

remark See *comment*.

repeater A device that is installed on a long cable run to amplify a signal.

resolution The clearness or sharpness of an image, which is controlled by the number of pixels displayed on the screen.

response time The measurement (in milliseconds) of the time it takes for a pixel to change color; the lower the response time, the smoother moving images will appear on the monitor.

restore point The snapshot of the entire system's settings that Windows creates every time the computer is started, or when a new application or driver is installed.

reusability The ability to reuse existing classes of objects from other projects, enabling programmers to produce new code quickly.

RFID tag See *radio frequency identification tag*.

ribbon A group of icons collected for easy access.

ring topology A network layout in which computers and peripherals are laid out in a logical circle and data is passed using a special data packet called a *token*.

ROM See *read-only memory*.

root directory The top level of the filing structure in a computer system. In Windows computers, the root directory of the hard drive is represented as C:\.

root DNS server A group of servers maintained throughout the Internet to which ISP Web servers connect to locate the master listings for an entire top-level domain.

router A device that routes packets of data between two or more networks.

RSS See *Really Simple Syndication (RSS) technology*.

RTOS See *real-time operating system*.

runtime error An error in the problem logic that is only caught when the program executes.

S

SaaS See *Software as a Service*.

Safe mode A special diagnostic mode designed for troubleshooting errors that occur during the boot process.

sampling rate The number of times per second a signal is measured and converted to a digital value. Sampling rates are measured in kilobits per second.

satellite Internet A way to connect to the Internet using a small satellite dish, which is placed outside the home and is connected to a computer with coaxial cable. The satellite company then sends the data to a satellite orbiting the Earth. The satellite, in turn, sends the data back to the satellite dish and to the computer.

scalable network A type of network that enables the easy addition of users without affecting the performance of the other network nodes (computers or peripherals).

screen saver An animated image that appears on a computer monitor when no user activity has been sensed for a certain time.

script A list of commands (mini-programs or macros) that can be executed on a computer without user interaction.

script kiddy An amateur hacker who lacks sophisticated computer skills. These individuals are typically teenagers, who don't create programs used to hack into computer systems but instead use tools created by skilled hackers that enable unskilled novices to wreak the same havoc as professional hackers.

scripting language A simple programming language that is limited to performing a specific set of specialized tasks.

scrollbar On the desktop, the bar that appears at the side or bottom of the window and controls which part of the information is displayed on the screen.

SDLC See *system development life cycle*.

search engine A set of programs that searches the Web for specific words (or keywords) you wish to query (or look for) and then returns a list of the Web sites on which those keywords are found.

second-generation language (2GL) Also known as an assembly language. Second-generation languages deal directly with system hardware but provide acronyms that are easier for human programmers to work with.

second-level domain A domain that falls within top-level domains of the Internet. Each second-level domain needs to be unique within that particular domain but not necessarily unique to all top-level domains.

sector A section of a hard drive platter, wedge-shaped from the center of the platter to the edge.

Secure Sockets Layer (SSL) A protocol that provides for the encryption of data transmitted using the Internet. The current versions of all major Web browsers support SSL.

seek time The time it takes for the hard drive's read/write heads to move over the surface of the disk, between tracks, to the correct track.

select query A query that displays a subset of data from a table based on the criteria the user specifies.

semiconductor Any material that can be controlled to either conduct electricity or act as an insulator (not allowing electricity to pass through).

Serial Advanced Technology Attachment (Serial ATA) A type of hard drive that uses much thinner cables, and can transfer data more quickly, than IDE drives.

serial port A port that enables the transfer of data, one bit at a time, over a single wire at speeds of up to 56 kilobits per second (Kbps); this legacy technology was used to connect external modems to the computer.

server A computer that provides resources to other computers on a network.

server-side program A program that is run on a Web server as opposed to inside a Web browser.

service set identifier (SSID) A network name that wireless routers use to identify themselves.

service packs See *software updates*.

shareware Software that enables users to "test" the software by running it for a limited time free of charge.

shielded twisted pair (STP) cable Twisted pair cable that contains a layer of foil shielding to reduce interference.

short message service (SMS) Technology that enables short text messages (up to 160 characters) to be sent over mobile networks.

Sidebar In Windows Vista, the pane on the right side of the desktop that organizes gadgets for easy access.

sign bit In the binary (base 2) system, the representation of a negative number; usually the left-most bit.

simple mail transfer protocol (SMTP) A protocol for sending e-mail along the Internet to its destination.

simulation software Software, often used for training purposes, which allows the user to experience or control an event as if it is reality.

single-user, multitask operating system An operating system that allows only one person to work on a computer at a time, but that can perform a variety of tasks simultaneously.

single-user, single-task operating system An operating system that allows only one user to work on a computer at a time to perform just one task at a time.

sleep mode A low-power mode for electronic devices such as computers that saves electric power consumption and saves your computer settings where you left off. When the computer is "woken up," you can resume working more quickly than when cold booting the computer.

smartphone A device that combines the functionality of a cell phone, a PMP, and a PDA into one unit.

SMS See *short message service*.

SMTP See *simple mail transfer protocol*.

social bookmark (tag) A keyword or term that Internet users assign to a Web resource such as a Web page, digital image, or video.

social engineering Any technique that uses social skills to generate human interaction for the purpose of enticing individuals to reveal sensitive information.

social networking site A system of personal networks where individuals are invited or allowed to join and that are supported by electronic tools such as e-mail, instant messaging, and file transfer. Members create personal profiles, exchange information, and find others with similar interests.

software The set of computer programs or instructions that tells the computer what to do and enables it to perform different tasks.

Software as a Service (SaaS) Software that is delivered on demand over the Internet.

software license An agreement between the user and the software developer that must be accepted before installing the software on a computer.

software piracy Violating a software license agreement by copying an application onto more computers than the license agreement permits.

software suite A collection of software programs that have been bundled together as a package.

software update (service pack) A downloadable software module that repairs errors identified in commercial program code.

solid state drive (SSD) A drive that uses the same kind of memory that flash drives use, but can reach data in only a tenth of the time a flash drive requires.

sort (index) The process of organizing a database into a particular order.

sound card An expansion card that attaches to the motherboard inside the system unit and that enables the computer to produce sounds by providing a connection for the speakers and microphone.

source code The instructions programmers write in a higher-level language.

spam Unwanted or junk e-mail.

spam filter An option you can select in your e-mail account that places known or suspected spam messages into a folder other than your inbox.

speaker An output device for sound.

speech-recognition software (voice-recognition software) Software that translates spoken words into typed text.

spider A program that constantly collects information on the Web, following links in Web sites and reading Web pages. Spiders get their name because they crawl over the Web using multiple "legs" to visit many sites simultaneously.

spooler A program that helps coordinate all print jobs being sent to the printer at the same time.

spreadsheet software An application program such as Microsoft Excel or Lotus 1-2-3 that enables a user to do calculations and numerical analyses easily.

spyware An unwanted piggyback program that downloads with the software you want to install from the Internet and then runs in the background of your system.

SQL See *structured query language*.

SRAM See *static RAM*.

SSD See *solid state drive*.

SSID See *service set identifier*.

SSL See *Secure Sockets Layer*.

star topology An active topology (meaning that data is retransmitted) in which the nodes connect to a central communications device called a *switch*. The switch receives a signal from the sending node and retransmits it to the node that should receive it.

statement A sentence in programming code.

static addressing A means of assigning an Internet Protocol (IP) address that never changes and is most likely assigned manually by a network administrator.

static RAM (SRAM) A type of random access memory that is faster than DRAM. In SRAM, more transistors are used to store a single bit, but no capacitor is needed.

stealth virus A virus that temporarily erases its code from the files where it resides and hides in the active memory of the computer.

streaming audio Technology that enables audio files to be fed to a browser continuously. This lets users avoid having to download an entire file before listening.

streaming video Technology that enables video files to be fed to a browser continuously. This lets users avoid having to download the entire file before viewing.

structured (analytical) data Data that can be identified and classified as discrete bits of information (such as a name or phone number). Unstructured data includes non-traditional data such as audio clips (including MP3 files), video clips, and pictures that must be viewed in their entirety rather than in discrete segments.

structured query language (SQL) The most popular database query language today.

stylus A pen-shaped device used to tap or write on touch-sensitive screens.

subdirectory See *path*.

subject directory A structured outline of Web sites organized by topics and subtopics.

summary report A report that summarizes data in some fashion (such as a total of the day's concession sales at an amusement park). Also known as a *summary data report*.

super video See S-*video*.

supercomputer A specially designed computer that can perform complex calculations extremely rapidly; used in situations in which complex models requiring intensive mathematical calculations are needed (such as weather forecasting or atomic energy research).

surge protector A device that protects computers and other electronic devices from power surges.

surround sound A type of audio processing that makes the listener experience sound as if it were coming from all directions.

surround-sound speakers Speaker systems set up in such a way that they surround an entire area (and the people in it) with sound.

S-video (super video) A type of technology used to transmit video signals; used on newer LCD monitors, as well as other multimedia devices such as televisions, DVD players, and projectors.

swap file (page file) A temporary storage area on the hard drive where the operating system "swaps out" or moves the data or instructions from random access memory (RAM) that have not recently been used. This process takes place when more RAM space is needed.

switch A device for transmitting data on a network. A switch makes decisions, based on the media access control (MAC) address of the data, as to where the data is to be sent.

synchronizing The process of updating data so that the files on different systems are the same.

syntax An agreed-upon set of rules defining how a programming language must be structured.

syntax error An error that violates the strict, precise set of rules that defines a programming language.

system clock The computer's internal clock.

system development life cycle (SDLC) An organized process (or set of steps) for developing an information processing system.

system evaluation The process of looking at a computer's subsystems, what they do, and how they perform to determine whether the computer system has the right hardware components to do what the user ultimately wants it to do.

system file Any of the main files of an operating system.

system requirements The set of minimum storage, memory capacity, and processing standards recommended by the software manufacturer to ensure proper operation of a software application.

System Restore A utility in Windows that restores system settings to a specific previous date when everything was working properly.

system software The set of programs that enables a computer's hardware devices and application software to work together; it includes the operating system and utility programs.

system unit The metal or plastic case that holds all the physical parts of the computer together, including the computer's processor (its brains), its memory, and the

many circuit boards that help the computer function.

T

T line A high-speed fiber-optic communications line that is designed to provide much higher throughput than conventional voice (telephone) and data (DSL or cable) lines.

table In database terminology, a group of related records. Also called a *file*.

Tablet PC A notebook computer designed specifically to work with handwriting recognition technology.

tag A keyword or label that you use to categorize your favorite Web sites.

Task Manager utility A Windows utility that shows programs currently running and permits you to exit nonresponsive programs when you click End Task.

Task Scheduler utility A Windows utility that enables you to schedule tasks to run automatically at predetermined times with no interaction necessary on your part.

tax preparation software An application program, such as Intuit's TurboTax or H&R Block's TaxCut, for preparing state and federal taxes. Each program offers a complete set of tax forms and instructions as well as expert advice on how to complete each form.

TCP/IP The main suite of protocols used on the Internet.

telephony The use of equipment to provide voice communications over a distance.

template A form included in many productivity applications that provides the basic structure for a particular kind of document, spreadsheet, or presentation.

terabyte 1,099,511,627,776 bytes or 2^{40} bytes.

terminator A device that absorbs a signal so that it is not reflected back onto parts of the network that have already received it.

test condition A check to see whether a loop is completed.

testing plan In the problem statement, a plan that lists specific input numbers that the program would typically expect the user to enter. It then lists the precise output values that a perfect program would return for those input values.

text field A database field that can hold any combination of alphanumeric data (letters or numbers) and is most often used to hold text.

thermal printer A printer that works either by melting wax-based ink onto ordinary paper (in a process called *thermal wax transfer printing*) or by burning dots onto specially coated paper (in a process called *direct thermal printing*).

third-generation language (3GL, or high-level language) A computer language that uses symbols and commands to help programmers tell the computer what to do.

thrashing A condition of excessive paging in which the operating system becomes sluggish.

three-way handshake A process used by the Transmission Control Protocol (TCP) to establish a connection.

throughput The actual speed of data transfer that is achieved. It is usually less than the data transfer rate and is measured in megabits per second (Mbps).

thumb drive See *flash drive*.

time bomb A virus that is triggered by the passage of time or on a certain date.

time-variant data Data that doesn't all pertain to one period in time—for example, data in a data warehouse.

TLD See *top-level domain*.

token A special data packet used to pass data in a token-ring network.

token method The access method that ring networks use to avoid data collisions.

token-ring topology See *ring topology*.

toolbar A group of icons collected for easy access.

top-down design A systematic approach in which a programming problem is broken down into a series of high-level tasks.

top-level domain (TLD) The suffix, often of three letters, in the domain name (such as .com or .edu) that indicates the kind of organization the host is.

touch screen A type of monitor (or display in a notebook or PDA) that accepts input from a user touching the screen.

touchpad A small, touch-sensitive screen at the base of a notebook keyboard. To use the touchpad, you simply move your finger across the pad to direct the cursor.

TPS See *transaction processing system*.

track A concentric circle that serves as a storage area on a hard drive platter.

trackball mouse A mouse with a rollerball on top instead of on the bottom. Because you move the trackball with your fingers, it doesn't require much wrist motion, so it's considered healthier for your wrists than a traditional mouse.

trackpoint device A small, joystick-like nub that enables you to move the cursor with the tip of your finger.

transaction processing system (TPS) A system used to keep track of everyday business activities (such as sales of products).

transceiver In a wireless network, a device that translates the electronic data that needs to be sent along the network into radio waves and then broadcasts these radio waves to other network nodes.

transistor An electrical switch that is built out of layers of a special type of material called a *semiconductor*.

Transmission Control Protocol (TCP) A protocol that prepares data for transmission and provides for error checking and resending lost data.

transmission media The radio waves or cable that transport data on a network.

Transport Layer Security (TLS) A protocol that provides data integrity and security for transmissions over the Internet.

Trojan horse A computer program that appears to be something useful or desirable (such as a game or a screen saver), but at the same time does something malicious in the background without the user's knowledge.

twisted pair cable Cables made of copper wires that are twisted around each other and are surrounded by a plastic jacket (such as traditional home phone wire).

U

ubiquitous computing The condition in which computing is so woven into the

fabric of everyday life that it becomes indistinguishable from it.

UDP See *User Datagram Protocol*.

Unicode An encoding scheme that uses 16 bits instead of the 8 bits used in ASCII. Unicode can represent more than 65,000 unique character symbols, enabling it to represent the alphabets of all modern languages and all historic languages and notational systems.

Uniform Resource Locator (URL) A Web site's unique address; an example is microsoft.com.

uninterruptible power supply (UPS) A device designed to power a computer from large batteries for a brief period during a loss of electrical power.

universal serial bus (USB) port A port that can connect a wide variety of peripheral devices to the computer, including keyboards, printers, mice, smartphones, PDAs, flash drives, and digital cameras.

UNIX An operating system originally conceived in 1969 by Ken Thompson and Dennis Ritchie of AT&T's Bell Labs. In 1974, the UNIX code was rewritten in the standard programming language C. Today there are various commercial versions of UNIX.

unshielded twisted pair (UTP) cable The most popular transmission media option for Ethernet networks. UTP cable is composed of four pairs of wires that are twisted around each other to reduce electrical interference.

unstructured data Nontraditional database data such as audio clips (including MP3 files), video clips, pictures, and extremely large documents. Data of this type is known as a *binary large object* (BLOB) because it is actually encoded in binary form.

UPS See *uninterruptible power supply*.

urban legend A hoax that becomes so well known that it is accepted by society as true even though it is false. Also known as an *urban myth*.

URL See *Uniform Resource Locator*.

USB 2.0 port An external bus that supports a data throughput of 480 Mbps; these buses are backward compatible with buses using the original universal serial bus (USB) standard.

USB drive See *flash drive*.

USB port See *universal serial bus (USB) port*.

User Datagram Protocol (UDP) A protocol that prepares data for transmission but that has no resending capabilities.

user interface Part of the operating system that enables individuals to interact with the computer.

utility program A small program that performs many of the general housekeeping tasks for the computer, such as system maintenance and file compression.

UTP cable See *unshielded twisted pair (UTP) cable.*

V

vacuum tube Used in early computers, a vacuum tube acts as a computer switch by allowing or blocking the flow of electrical current.

validation The process of ensuring that data entered into a database is correct (or at least reasonable) and complete.

validation rule A rule that is set up in a database to alert the user to possible wrong entries.

variable A name or symbol that stands for a value.

variable declaration A line of programming code that alerts the operating system that the program needs to allocate storage space in random access memory (RAM) for the variable.

VB See *Visual Basic.*

VBScript A subset of Visual Basic; also used to introduce interactivity to Web pages.

vertical market software Software that is developed for and customized to a specific industry's needs (such as a wood inventory system for a sawmill) as opposed to software that is useful across a range of industries (such as word processing software).

VGA See *video graphics array.*

video adapter See *video card.*

video blog See *video log.*

video card (video adapter) An expansion card that is installed inside a system unit to translate binary data (the 1s and 0s the computer uses) into the images viewed on the monitor.

video graphics array (VGA) port A port to which a CRT monitor connects.

video log (vlog or **video blog)** A personal online journal that uses video as the primary content in addition to text, images, and audio.

video memory RAM that is included as part of a video card.

virtual memory The space on the hard drive where the operating system stores data if there isn't enough random access memory (RAM) to hold all of the programs you're currently trying to run.

virtual private network (VPN) A network that uses public communication pathways (usually the Internet) to provide branch offices or employees who are not at the office with secure access to the company network. VPNs maintain privacy by using secure data communication protocols.

virtual reality program Software that turns an artificial environment into a realistic experience.

virus A computer program that attaches itself to another computer program (known as the host program) and attempts to spread itself to other computers when files are exchanged.

virus signature A portion of the virus code that is unique to a particular computer virus and makes it identifiable by antivirus software.

Visual Basic (VB) A programming language used to build a wide range of Windows applications quickly.

visual programming A technique for automatically writing code when the programmer says the layout is complete. It helps programmers produce a final application much more quickly.

vlog See *video log.*

Voice over Internet Protocol (VoIP) The transmission of phone calls over the same data lines and networks that make up the Internet. Also called *Internet telephony.*

voice-recognition software See *speech-recognition software.*

VoIP See *Voice over Internet Protocol.*

volatile storage Temporary storage, such as in random access memory (RAM). When the power is off, the data in volatile storage is cleared out.

VPN See *virtual private network.*

W

WAN See *wide area network.*

WAP See *wireless access point; Wireless Application Protocol.*

warm boot The process of restarting the system while it's powered on.

Web See *World Wide Web.*

Web 2.0 Tools and Web-based services that emphasize online collaboration and sharing among users.

Web browser (browser) Software installed on a computer system that allows individuals to locate, view, and navigate the Web.

Web page authoring software Programs you can use to design interactive Web pages without knowing any HyperText Markup Language (HTML) code.

Web server A computer running a specialized operating system that enables it to host Web pages (and other information) and provide requested Web pages to clients.

Web service A program used by a Web site to make information available to other Web sites.

Web site A location on the Web.

Web-based application software A program that is hosted on a Web site and does not require installation on the computer.

webcam A small camera that sits on top of a computer monitor (connected to the computer by a cable) or is built into a notebook computer and is usually used to transfer live video.

webcast The broadcast of audio or video content over the Internet. Unlike a podcast, a webcast is not updated automatically.

Weblog A personal log, or collection of journal entries, that is posted on the Web; also called a *blog.*

white-hat hacker A hacker who breaks into systems just for the challenge of it (and who doesn't wish to steal or wreak havoc on the systems). Such hackers tout themselves as experts who are performing a needed service for society by helping companies realize the vulnerabilities that exist in their systems.

whole-house surge protector A surge protector that is installed on (or near) the breaker panel of a home and protects all electronic devices in the home from power surges.

wide area network (WAN) A network made up of local area networks (LANs) connected over long distances.

widget A mini-application developed for the Macintosh platform.

WiFi (Wireless Fidelity) The 802.11 standard for wireless data transmissions established by the Institute of Electrical and Electronics Engineers (IEEE).

wiki A type of Web site that allows anyone visiting the site to change its content by adding, removing, or editing the content.

wildcard A symbol used in an Internet search when the user is unsure of a keyword's spelling or when a word can be spelled in different ways or can contain different endings. The asterisk (*) is used to replace a series of letters and the percent sign (%) to replace a single letter in a word.

window In a graphical user interface, a rectangular box that contains programs displayed on the screen.

Windows 7 Microsoft operating system that builds upon the security and user interface upgrades that the Windows Vista release provided, and gives users with touch-screen monitors the ability to use touch commands to scroll, resize windows, pan, and zoom.

Windows Explorer The main tool for finding, viewing, and managing the contents of your computer by showing the location and contents of every drive, folder, and file.

wired Ethernet network A popular type of home network that connects computers with physically wired media.

wireless access point (WAP) A device similar to a switch in an Ethernet network. It takes the place of a wireless network adapter and helps relay data between network nodes.

Wireless Application Protocol (WAP) The standard that dictates how handheld devices will access information on the Internet.

wireless Ethernet network A network based on the 802.11 standard. (The 802.11 standard is also known as *WiFi*.)

wireless Internet service provider (wireless ISP) An ISP that provides service to wireless devices such as PDA/smartphones.

Wireless Markup Language (WML) A format for writing content viewed on a cellular phone or personal digital assistant (PDA) that is text-based and contains no graphics.

wireless media Communications media that do not use cables but instead rely on radio waves to communicate.

wireless network A network that uses radio waves instead of wires or cable as its transmission medium.

wireless network adapter A device that is required for each node on a wireless network for the node to be able to communicate with other nodes on the network.

wireless network interface card (wireless NIC) A card installed in a system that connects with wireless access points on the network.

wireless router (gateway) A device that combines the capabilities of a wired router with the ability to receive wireless signals.

wizard A step-by-step guide that walks you through the necessary steps to complete a complicated task.

WML See *Wireless Markup Language*.

word size The number of bits a computer can work with at a time.

word processing software Programs used to create and edit written documents such as papers, letters, and résumés.

World Wide Web (WWW or Web) The part of the Internet used the most. What distinguishes the Web from the rest of the Internet are (1) its use of common communication protocols (such as Transmission Control Protocol/Internet Protocol, or TCP/IP) and special languages (such as the HyperText Markup Language, or HTML) that enable different computers to talk to each other and display information in compatible formats; and (2) its use of special links (called hyperlinks) that enable users to jump from one place to another in the Web.

worm A program that attempts to travel between systems through network connections to spread infections. Worms can run independently of host file execution and are active in spreading themselves.

WWW See *World Wide Web*.

X

XHTML See *Extensible HyperText Markup Language*.

XML See *Extensible Markup Language*.

Z

zombie A computer that is controlled by a hacker who uses it to launch attacks on other computer systems.

Index

Credits

Cover photo	David Wall\Alamy Images

Chapter 1

Chapter opener	Shutterstock
Figure 1.1	Courtesy of Dell Inc.
Figure 1.1b1	sweetym\iStockphoto
Figure 1.1b2	Logitech Inc.
Figure 1.1b3	Logitech Inc.
Figure 1.2	www.CartoonStock.com
Figure 1.3h	Hewlett-Packard Company
Figure 1.3a	TIMURA\Shutterstock
Figure 1.3b	PRNewsFoto/D-Link Systems\AP Wide World Photos
Figure 1.3c	Handout/MCT\Newscom
Figure 1.3d	Apple/Splash News\Newscom
Figure 1.3e	Belkin International, Inc.
Figure 1.3e.1	ExpressCard - PCMCIA
Figure 1.3g	Sony Electronics Inc.
Figure 1.4a	Editorial Image; LLC\Alamy Images
Figure 1.4b	United Parcel Service
Figure 1.4c	Mary Kate Denny\PhotoEdit Inc.
Figure 1.6	Peter Schaaf
Figure 1.7	Camille Utterback, "Untitled 5", from the "External Measures" series. Photo by Peter Harris, © 2007
Figure 1.8	Konami Corporation of America
Figure 1.10	Moeskau Photography
Figure 1.11a	Polhemus/Fast Scan
Figure 1.11b	© Digital Art/CORBIS All Rights Reserved
Figure 1.12	Paul Ekman Group, LLC.
Figure 1.15	Ninth Judicial Circuit Court of Florida
Figure 1.16	© Schlegelmilch/CORBIS All Rights Reserved
Figure 1.18	Photo courtesy of METI © METI
Figure 1.19	Computational Bioengineering Laboratory
Figure 1.20	© 2008 Intuitive Surgical, Inc.
Figure 1.21	Courtesy of Dr. Peter Fromherz/Max Planck Insitute of Biochemistry
Figure 1.22	Reuters/Eriko Sugita\Landov Media
Figure 1.23	Courtesy of Ilia Iankov Roussev, Ph.D.
Figure 1.24	Media from the Discovery Channel's Pompeii: The Last Day, courtesy of Crew Creative, Ltd.
Figure 1.25	Interactive Sports Technologies
Figure 1.26	Mazur Group
Figure 1.27	AP Wide World Photos
Figure 1.28	SparkFun Electronics
Figure 1.29	Gerald Herbert\AP Wide World Photos
Figure 1.30	Getty Images/Digital Vision

TECHNOLOGY IN FOCUS: The History of the PC

Chapter opener 1	SuperStock\Jupiter Images
Chapter opener 2	Smithsonian Institution/Museum of American History
Figure 1	Heinz Nixdorf Musuemsforum\AP Wide World Photos
Figure 2a	Getty Images
Figure 2b	© Roger Ressmeyer/CORBIS All Rights Reserved
Figure 3	SSPL\The Image Works
Figure 4	Roger Ressmeyer\CORBIS - NY
Figure 6	Jerry Mason/SPL\Photo Researchers, Inc.
Figure 7	Photo Courtesy of The Computer History Museum
Figure 8	Photo Courtesy of The Computer History Museum
Figure 9	Roberto Brosan\Time Inc. Magazine
Figure 10	© Doug Wilson/CORBIS All Rights Reserved
Figure 11	Daniel Bricklin
Figure 13	Photo Courtesy of The Computer History Museum

seventh EDITION
7

Chapter 9

TECHNOLOGY IN FOCUS:
Careers in IT

Chapter 10

Chapter 11

Figure 11.34 Clay Bennett\The Christian Science Publishing Society

Chapter 12

Chapter opener Norebbo\Shutterstock

Figure 12.24a JHDT Stock Images LLC\Shutterstock

Figure 12.24b Dash\Shutterstock

Chapter 13

Chapter opener dotSyntax, LLC

Figure 13.10a Rob Marmion\Shutterstock

Figure 13.10b Tan Kian Khoon\Shutterstock

Figure 13.22a Thomas Peter Voss\Shutterstock

Figure 13.22b Nagy Melinda\Shutterstock

SINGLE PC LICENSE AGREEMENT AND LIMITED WARRANTY

READ THIS LICENSE CAREFULLY BEFORE OPENING THIS PACKAGE. BY OPENING THIS PACKAGE, YOU ARE AGREEING TO THE TERMS AND CONDITIONS OF THIS LICENSE. IF YOU DO NOT AGREE, DO NOT OPEN THE PACKAGE. PROMPTLY RETURN THE UNOPENED PACKAGE AND ALL ACCOMPANYING ITEMS TO THE PLACE YOU OBTAINED THEM. *THESE TERMS APPLY TO ALL LICENSED SOFTWARE ON THE DISK EXCEPT THAT THE TERMS FOR USE OF ANY SHAREWARE OR FREEWARE ON THE DISKETTES ARE AS SET FORTH IN THE ELECTRONIC LICENSE LOCATED ON THE DISK:*

1. GRANT OF LICENSE and OWNERSHIP: The enclosed computer programs ("Software") are licensed, not sold, to you by Prentice-Hall, Inc. ("We" or the "Company") and in consideration of your purchase or adoption of the accompanying Company textbooks and/or other materials, and your agreement to these terms. We reserve any rights not granted to you. You own only the disk(s) but we and/or our licensors own the Software itself. This license allows you to use and display your copy of the Software on a single computer (i.e., with a single CPU) at a single location for academic use only, so long as you comply with the terms of this Agreement. You may make one copy for back up, or transfer your copy to another CPU, provided that the Software is usable on only one computer.

2. RESTRICTIONS: You may not transfer or distribute the Software or documentation to anyone else. Except for backup, you may not copy the documentation or the Software. You may not network the Software or otherwise use it on more than one computer or computer terminal at the same time. You may not reverse engineer, disassemble, decompile, modify, adapt, translate, or create derivative works based on the Software or the Documentation. You may be held legally responsible for any copying or copyright infringement which is caused by your failure to abide by the terms of these restrictions.

3. TERMINATION: This license is effective until terminated. This license will terminate automatically without notice from the Company if you fail to comply with any provisions or limitations of this license. Upon termination, you shall destroy the Documentation and all copies of the Software. All provisions of this Agreement as to limitation and disclaimer of warranties, limitation of liability, remedies or damages, and our ownership rights shall survive termination.

4. DISCLAIMER OF WARRANTY: THE COMPANY AND ITS LICENSORS MAKE NO WARRANTIES ABOUT THE SOFTWARE, WHICH IS PROVIDED "AS-IS." IF THE DISK IS DEFECTIVE IN MATERIALS OR WORKMANSHIP, YOUR ONLY REMEDY IS TO RETURN IT TO THE COMPANY WITHIN 30 DAYS FOR REPLACEMENT UNLESS THE COMPANY DETERMINES IN GOOD FAITH THAT THE DISK HAS BEEN MISUSED OR IMPROPERLY INSTALLED, REPAIRED, ALTERED OR DAMAGED. THE COMPANY DIS-CLAIMS ALL WARRANTIES, EXPRESS OR IMPLIED, INCLUDING WITHOUT LIMITATION, THE IMPLIED WARRANTIES OF MERCHANTABILITY AND FITNESS FOR A PARTICULAR PURPOSE. THE COMPANY DOES NOT WARRANT, GUARANTEE OR MAKE ANY REPRESENTATION REGARDING THE ACCURACY, RELIABILITY, CURRENTNESS, USE, OR RESULTS OF USE, OF THE SOFTWARE.

5. LIMITATION OF REMEDIES AND DAMAGES: IN NO EVENT, SHALL THE COMPANY OR ITS EMPLOYEES, AGENTS, LICENSORS OR CONTRACTORS BE LIABLE FOR ANY INCIDENTAL, INDIRECT, SPECIAL OR CONSEQUENTIAL DAMAGES ARISING OUT OF OR IN CONNECTION WITH THIS LICENSE OR THE SOFTWARE, INCLUDING, WITHOUT LIMITATION, LOSS OF USE, LOSS OF DATA, LOSS OF INCOME OR PROFIT, OR OTHER LOSSES SUSTAINED AS A RESULT OF INJURY TO ANY PERSON, OR LOSS OF OR DAMAGE TO PROPERTY, OR CLAIMS OF THIRD PARTIES, EVEN IF THE COMPANY OR AN AUTHORIZED REPRESENTATIVE OF THE COMPANY HAS BEEN ADVISED OF THE POSSIBILITY OF SUCH DAMAGES. SOME JURISDICTIONS DO NOT ALLOW THE LIMITATION OF DAMAGES IN CERTAIN CIRCUMSTANCES, SO THE ABOVE LIMITATIONS MAY NOT ALWAYS APPLY.

6. GENERAL: THIS AGREEMENT SHALL BE CONSTRUED IN ACCORDANCE WITH THE LAWS OF THE UNITED STATES OF AMERICA AND THE STATE OF NEW YORK, APPLICABLE TO CONTRACTS MADE IN NEW YORK, AND SHALL BENEFIT THE COMPANY, ITS AFFILIATES AND ASSIGNEES. This Agreement is the complete and exclusive statement of the agreement between you and the Company and supersedes all proposals, prior agreements, oral or written, and any other communications between you and the company or any of its representatives relating to the subject matter. If you are a U.S. Government user, this Software is licensed with "restricted rights" as set forth in subparagraphs (a)-(d) of the Commercial Computer-Restricted Rights clause at FAR 52.227-19 or in subparagraphs (c)(1)(ii) of the Rights in Technical Data and Computer Software clause at DFARS 252.227-7013, and similar clauses, as applicable.

Should you have any questions concerning this agreement or if you wish to contact the Company for any reason, please contact in writing: Multimedia Production, Higher Education Division, Prentice-Hall, Inc., 1 Lake Street, Upper Saddle River NJ 07458.

Please see the Read Me file in the root directory of this CD or visit www.pearsonhighered.com/skills for detailed system requirements.

PLAYING ACTIVE HELPDESKS IN WINDOWS VISTA AND WINDOWS 7:
In order to play the Active Helpdesks in Windows Vista and Windows 7, you will need to disable Protected Mode in Internet Explorer. To do so, please follow these instructions:

1. **Open Internet Explorer**
2. **Click Tools**
3. **Select Internet Options**
4. **Select the Security Tab**
5. **Uncheck the "Enable Protected Mode" box**
6. **Restart Internet Explorer**